THE CONOLLY ARCHIVE

PATRICK WALSH
and
A.P.W. MALCOMSON

IRISH MANUSCRIPTS COMMISSION
2010

In memory of Lena Boylan,
to whom all students of Castletown
and the Conolly family are forever indebted

Published by
Irish Manuscripts Commission
45 Merrion Square
Dublin 2
Ireland
www.irishmanuscripts.ie

ISBN 978-1-906865-09-2

Typeset by Carole Lynch in Adobe Garamond
Printed by ColourBooks, Dublin on Munken Pure
Index prepared by Patrick Walsh

CONTENTS

INTRODUCTION

The Conolly archive, which is now dispersed among a number of mainly institutional locations in Ireland, comprises circa 15,000 letters and papers, dating from 1570 to 1953. It derives from the Conolly family of Castletown, Co. Kildare, and mainly relates to William Conolly (1662–1729), Speaker of the Irish House of Commons, 1715–29, William Conolly junior (1706–54), Thomas Conolly (1738–1803), and to the Conolly estates in counties Kildare, Dublin, Londonderry, Donegal, Fermanagh, Meath, Westmeath, Roscommon and Wexford.

The archive is important in Irish national terms because of the prominence of William and Thomas Conolly in eighteenth-century Irish politics. In particular, it is useful in documenting the rise of the Conolly family from obscure origins to its apogee in the mid eighteenth-century, and also its fall through indebtedness, childlessness and bad luck later in the century. While the Conolly estates were scattered across ten Irish counties, the most significant portions were in counties Donegal, Londonderry and Kildare, and these are particularly well documented. The papers appertaining to Donegal and Londonderry also provide excellent insights into the politics of these two counties, in which the Conolly family were long prominent (and in county Londonderry dominant). The day to day management of the Castletown demesne, particularly during the lifetime of Thomas Conolly and his wife, Lady Louisa (1743–1821), and the alterations effected by her on the house, one of Ireland's greatest country houses, are covered in great detail. Unfortunately the Conolly archive contains little information on the construction of Castletown in the 1720s, which means that many of the details surrounding it remain, much to the frustration of successive architectural historians, shrouded in mystery. The Conolly archive does, however, provide much of the context for its construction through the extensive surviving papers, political, personal and financial, of its builder William Conolly.

The Conolly archive was located at Castletown until the 6th Lord Carew, who had inherited it from his maternal uncle Major E.M. Conolly, sold the house in 1965. Prior to this sale all or some of the papers were the subject of a 'National Library Report on Special Collections' (No. 314), which provided a brief outline of their content. In 1966, Lord Carew divided the papers and most generously donated them to three major repositories as follows:

1. The eighteenth-century political and personal correspondence (but including much estate correspondence, and also Castletown account books), 1683–1900, to Trinity College, Dublin (MSS 3939–84A).
2. The eighteenth century estate papers (deeds, leases, rentals, accounts, etc) for the Conolly estates in the now Northern Ireland (specifically, in Co. Londonderry) to the Public Record Office of Northern Ireland, Belfast (D/2094).
3. The same in respect of the estates (principally the Ballyshannon estate, Co. Donegal) in the now Republic of Ireland, to the National Archives, Dublin, which also received the wills and testamentary papers deriving from the Conolly and related families (M.6917).

These three categories overlap at almost all points due to shortcomings in the original 'sort' made in 1966. However, the more serious shortcoming of this well-intentioned plan (apart from the doubtful principle of making a division in the first place) was that it was incomplete; circa 3,000 papers and volumes (including some more Castletown account books) were not included, having been overlooked and left behind in the house. There they were found at various times following the Hon. Desmond Guinness's purchase of Castletown in 1967, and have been given the name 'Castletown Papers' in order to distinguish them from the rest. The first *c.* 1,000 of them to come to light were microfilmed in the early 1970s by the National Library on its own behalf and that of the Public Record Office of Northern Ireland.[1] The present list incorporates the listing and calendaring done by PRONI at that time, but covers the entire *c.* 3,000 documents. The Castletown Papers are now the property of the Castletown Foundation, and are currently deposited in the Irish Architectural Archive in Dublin.

In addition, some 150 letters and papers, 1760–1822, deriving from Thomas Conolly and his executors and trustees, have found their way into a cache of Fitzgerald, Dukes of Leinster, papers sold by the Hon. Desmond Guinness to the National Library in 1997 (Acc. 5493). They may have got mixed up with these Leinster papers as a result of an early nineteenth-century muddle. But the likelihood is that the muddle occurred only in recent years. The Conolly material has now been separated out, and bears reference MS 41,341.

Finally the National Library acquired two volumes of letters in 1998, including letters from Thomas and Lady Louisa Conolly about the 1798 rebellion.[2] These volumes, now bearing references MS 34,922 and MS 40,242, previously formed part of the collection of the late Mr B.Y. McPeake, who had purchased them from the Bunbury family. It seems likely that these letters arrived in the Bunbury collection through the agency of Lady Louisa Conolly's niece, Emily Napier, who married Sir Henry Edward Bunbury in 1830. Material pertaining to the Conolly family has been extracted from this collection and calendared below.

As well as these six major collections there are several smaller collections of papers which have been detached from the main Conolly archive at various times. These smaller collections either in public repositories (particularly the National Library of Ireland and PRONI) or in private collections are detailed in an appendix at the end of this volume. This introduction continues with a brief historical introduction to the Conolly family, before embarking on a detailed introduction to the six major collections of Conolly papers listed in the volume.

HISTORY OF THE CONOLLY FAMILY

WILLIAM CONOLLY (1662–1729)

William Conolly was born in Ballyshannon, county Donegal in 1662. His father Patrick has been variously described as a publican, blacksmith or miller but this seems improbable.[3] Both Conollys were sufficiently prominent to be attainted by James II's parliament in 1689, while William was a practicing attorney in Dublin in the 1680s. The Williamite revolution was to prove a watershed in William Conolly's career, providing opportunities for enrichment and advancement. In 1691, he became legal agent to Derry Corporation, acting on their behalf in a number of important cases during the following decade. He also became involved in the long-running legal battle between the Irish Society and the See of Derry. In 1692, he was appointed agent to Capt. James Hamilton, later sixth Earl of Abercorn, acting as his deputy in the Alnage Office, as well as managing his property holdings in Dublin, a position he continued to hold until 1700. In 1694, Conolly married Katherine Conyngham, a daughter of Sir Albert Conyngham, a prominent county Donegal landowner and hero of the Williamite war. This marriage brought Conolly into contact with many of the leading political interests in the northwest, many of whom were making names for themselves in the post-war administration in Dublin.[4]

Importantly, Katherine also brought with her a dowry of £2,300 which Conolly invested in land. He had already acquired an estate at Rodanstown, county Meath in 1691, but this was just the beginning of his acquisitions. In 1697, he acquired the manor of Limavady in county Londonderry from the Phillips family, who had owned it since the Ulster plantation. From 1695 onwards, he acted as Irish agent to the first Earl of Albemarle, one of William III's Dutch favourites, who had been granted extensive forfeited Jacobite estates in Ireland. Conolly's role as agent to Albemarle brought him into controversy when a 1699 parliamentary report claiming he and an associate 'took vast quantities of lands and in great measure governed the cants (few daring to bid against them)'. Conolly himself admitted to having taken money for himself from purchasers of Albemarle's grants. He also purchased 9,000 acres spread across counties Dublin, Meath, Roscommon, Westmeath, and Wexford, for £3,000. These purchases were called into doubt when the English parliament resumed all grants to the King's favourites in 1700. The real potential losers by the Act of Resumption were not the grantees but the mostly Irish protestant purchasers who purchased the confiscated estates from them.[5] The greatest of these was Conolly and he emerged as the leader of the partly successful agitation against the act, increasing his profile on both sides of the Irish Sea. The forfeited estates were resumed but the purchasers were allowed to buy back their original purchases at a special rate from the Trustees of Forfeited Estates. Conolly duly reacquired his original purchases in 1703. During this period he also purchased two small estates in Wales from his brother-in-law Henry Conyngham for £5000.

Conolly continued subsequently to acquire further estates in Ireland, making his most famous acquisition in 1709 when he purchased the Castletown estate in county Kildare. The estate had an interesting recent history. It had been in the possession of the Dongan family since 1588. The Dongans were an Irish Catholic family, who were rewarded for their adherence to the Stuart cause throughout the seventeenth century with the Earldom of Limerick in 1685.[6] Following the Jacobite defeats at the Boyne and Limerick (where the Dongan heir was killed), their estates were forfeited and granted to General Ginkel, Earl of Athlone by King William. This grant was contested by Colonel Thomas Dongan who had served as Governor General of New York, and who had succeeded to the Limerick title. Following protracted legal and political manoeuvres he was restored to his estates in 1703. The dispute however was extremely costly and Dongan was forced to sell his estates in 1709. Conolly purchased the 1,730 acre Castletown estate in September 1709 for £15,000. Of this £6,000 was used to pay off mortgages and encumbrances on the estate including compensation owed to those purchasers who had bought parts of it from Ginkel before it was restored to Thomas Dongan. A contemporary rent roll, specially drawn up for intending purchasers, states the rental as £975 per annum. Amongst the tenants attracted to the estate were political allies of Speaker Conolly such as Arthur Price, Bishop of Clonfert and later Archbishop of Cashel, as well as Thomas Marlay, the Attorney General, whose holding was previously leased to Esther Van Homrigh better known as Swift's Vanessa. Conolly subsequently expanded his county Kildare holdings. In 1725 he purchased the neighbouring estate of Killadoon from the Plunkett family (it later became home to the Clements family, earls of Leitrim) and in 1728 the adjoining manor of Leixlip, Co. Kildare.

Conolly also to purchased further lands in his native northwest, where his political base was located, acquiring the manor of Castlefinn, county Donegal in 1711, and his home town of Ballyshannon, in the same county, in 1718. This latter purchase came with the manors of Ballyshannon and Newporton, Co Fermanagh, which he acquired from the Folliott family for £52,000. He also held leases of lands in the Barony of Tirhugh Co. Donegal from Trinity College, having acquired his first lease of College lands in 1690. In Co. Londonderry, Conolly held long-term leases of the Grocers' and Vintners' Proportions from the Irish Society. Meanwhile, in 1723, he acquired the manor of Rathfarnham, including the eponymous castle from the indebted Philip, Duke of Wharton, who had inherited it from his grandfather Adam Loftus, for £62,000. By the end of his life, Conolly was widely regarded, and with reason, as the wealthiest commoner in Ireland, with an estimated annual income of over £17,000. His wealth was so great that Jonathan Swift observed satirically in the *Drapier's Letters* that it would take 250 horses to transport his rent and two cellars at Castletown to store it, if it was paid in Wood's halfpence.

Conolly's political career

Conolly first entered the Irish House of Commons in 1692 for the borough of Donegal, and was re-elected for the same seat in 1695. From 1703 until his death he represented county Londonderry. In parliament he was an industrious MP who served on a great number of committees, and played an active part in the Whig-Tory conflict that dominated Irish politics until 1714. In April 1709, he was appointed a Commissioner of the Revenue, but was dismissed from office along with many Whigs in September 1710. Following the death of the Tory Queen Anne and the accession of George I in 1714, Conolly was restored to the Revenue Board, of which he became *de facto* First Commissioner; and in the following year, 1715, he was unanimously elected Speaker of the House of Commons.

This elevation owed much to his political skills, and to his growing electoral empire in the northwest, which gave him control of up to eight seats in the Commons. In 1717 he was also named one of the three lords justices chosen to administer the government of the country in the absence of the lord lieutenant. The nomination of an Irishman of such humble origin was greatly resented in some quarters, but Conolly served as one of the lords justices on nine further occasions and continued to remain 'at the head of his country's interest'. He steadfastly opposed the appointment of Englishmen to posts in the Irish administration and recommended to successive lords lieutenant those of Irish birth who were qualified.

Conolly achieved pre-eminence as a parliamentary manager through holding these three important offices, which had never before been held simultaneously by one man. The Speakership enabled him to influence the proceedings of the Commons, and it made his goodwill vitally necessary to the government. If the occupant of the Chair favoured the interests of the ministry he could make things go smoothly; if not, there was certain to be trouble. The office of lord justice was coveted for the prestige it conferred: it carried no patronage of its own (although the Lords Justices were consulted by the English government before the appointment of new judges and bishops), but Conolly's nomination served to show that he retained the trust of the ministry. The 'First' Commissionership of the Revenue was in a way the most important post of the three as it provided Conolly with a source of patronage which he was able to use much as he liked. Just how valuable this patronage was as an engine of political power can be deduced from the fact that the Revenue Service was the fastest-growing department of state in Ireland, with several hundred officers in its employ (the majority of whom were appointed by the Revenue Commissioners themselves) and an expenditure on salaries alone of almost £50,000 a year. The concentration of these offices in Conolly's hands owed something to his ability and something to chance. Conolly, as one of the foremost men in parliament, was able to overawe his colleagues on the Revenue Board; added to which, he was of a hard-working disposition, while the other Commissioners were for the most part absentees. Additionally, the wholesale dismissal of Tory officers from the Revenue service after Queen Anne's death gave the new Whig Commissioners more vacancies to fill than would otherwise have been the case, and temporarily increased the amount of patronage at their disposal.

However, the political dominance of Conolly derived, not only from his personality and ability and from the unique combination of crucial offices which he held, but also from an important changes in the political system in Ireland that took place immediately after the Hanoverian succession. In Anne's reign the conflict of Whigs and Tories had tended to swamp all other considerations governing political behaviour. Ties of kinship or patronage, for example, might count for little against the pull of party. With the disintegration of the two-party system these other factors became more important, and principle no longer exerted the most powerful influence on men's conduct. One of the most important effects produced by this change on the government's method of parliamentary management was to decrease the number of managers or 'undertakers' involved. The Whig and Tory parties had each been directed by a caucus of politicians, and negotiations with the lord lieutenant were conducted by the leadership as a whole: the replacement of the Whig and Tory parties by smaller factions narrowed the circle of political leadership and meant that now there were two or three principal managers at the most to see that the government's business was transacted, and usually one of them was pre-eminent. The existence of this presiding individual was the most notable characteristic of the 'undertaker system' of the mid-eighteenth-century, and it had appeared before the end of George I's reign.[7]

Conolly established his position as the leading government manager in the Commons as early as 1715, but he had to wait until 1725 before he became the principal and unrivalled 'undertaker', following the enforced resignation of his rival, Alan Brodrick Lord Midleton, a Whig politician who had been raised to the office of Lord Chancellor of Ireland in 1714. Conolly did not enjoy his pre-eminence for long, as ill-health obliged him to retire from public life in September 1729, two weeks before his death.

Conolly's ascent to a position of wealth and power was symbolised by the construction of his Palladian house at Castletown in the 1720s. The architectural history of the house is the subject of much debate between architectural historians, and unfortunately little new information is to be found in the Conolly archive. The two major figures involved were the Florentine

Alessandro Galilei and the young Irishman Edward Lovett Pearce, who later designed the new Irish houses of parliament, a commission he gained through Conolly's patronage. Castletown's significance lies not only in its architectural innovations, which exerted huge influences on Irish country house building throughout the eighteenth century, but also in its size and purpose.[8] It was built to impress, and as a venue for political entertainment. Conolly already had an impressive townhouse on Capel Street (acquired *c.* 1707), but he wanted a comparable country house as well. Castletown fitted the bill, and even before his new house was finished he used it to provide the Duke of Grafton with a refuge following the lord lieutenant's bungled handling of the Wood's halfpence crisis. Although Castletown was unfinished at the time of his death, Conolly's desire to be associated with it was so strong that he made clear his wish to be buried in Celbridge, rather than in Dublin or ancestral Ballyshannon.

Conolly's will and inheritance

Conolly died at his house in Capel Street, Dublin, on 30 October 1729. He had no children, but he was a generous benefactor to his own and his wife's relatives. In his will, made on 18 October 1729, he left to his wife all his estates in Wales, his mansion house in Dublin, his mansion house and manor of Castletown and all his manors, lands and tenements in counties Kildare, Meath, Westmeath and Roscommon. After the death of his wife, they were to pass to his nephew, William, to whom he bequeathed direct his estates in Donegal, Dublin, Fermanagh, Wexford and Waterford. To his wife's nephews, Williams and Henry Conyngham, he left his Limavady estate (which, as a result of their childlessness, reverted eventually in 1781 to his great-nephew, Thomas Conolly).

Katherine Conolly was 67 years of age when her husband died. She survived him by 23 years, living at Castletown or in the great house in Capel Street. Mrs Conolly had always shared her husband's political interests and after his death people continued to flock to Capel Street to enlist her support, while she also oversaw the emergence of Castletown as a social hub rivalling Dublin Castle (especially during the 1730s). Mrs Delany described Katherine Conolly as 'a plain and vulgar woman in her manner, but [who] had very valuable qualities'.[9] She died in 1752 at Castletown.

WILLIAM CONOLLY JUNIOR (1706–54)

William Conolly junior was the son of Speaker Conolly's only brother, Patrick (d. 1713), on whom the Speaker had settled £2,000 in 1705.[10] In 1721 Conolly obtained a sinecure employment, the Cursitorship of Chancery, for his nephew, who was still a student at Greenwich Academy.[11] Conolly junior's education at Greenwich, and his subsequent grand tours which took him to Italy and Hanover, were probably funded by his uncle, as preparation for his inheritance of the Conolly fortune.[12] In 1727 Conolly was elected M.P. for Ballyshannon and continued to represent that borough until his death in 1754. In 1733 he made a grand English marriage, to Lady Anne Wentworth, eldest daughter of Thomas Wentworth, first Earl of Strafford. In the following year, Conolly was returned to the British parliament for a vacancy at Aldeburgh, where Lord Strafford had influence. Voting consistently with the government, he called himself 'an incorrigible Whig'. He decided not to stand for Aldeburgh in 1747, when he was returned for Petersfield (where Speaker Conolly had owned property in the mid-1720s). His support for Sir Robert Walpole's government led to rumours that he would be created an English peer in 1735 and 1739 with the title Lord Aldeburgh.[13] Later it was suggested he would be raised in the peerage of Ireland as Baron Castletown, but this too came to nothing.[14] Mrs Conolly shared Castletown and her Capel Street house with the newly-weds, until Leixlip Castle, which he purchased in 1731, was ready for their reception.

Late in 1744 the Conollys moved to London, where they remained until 1748, returning to Leixlip at intervals or to Conolly's English country house, Stretton Hall, Staffordshire (purchased in 1733). After Mrs Conolly's death, they and their seven children moved into Castletown. Two years later, in 1754, William Conolly himself died. Sadly very little of his papers survive in the family archive. He was succeeded at Castletown by his only son, Thomas, who was then under age. Lady Anne moved to Stretton Hall with her family, and Castletown was for the time being deserted.

THOMAS CONOLLY (1738–1803)[15]

On 30 December 1758, when he was 20 years of age, Thomas Conolly married Lady Louisa Lennox, third daughter of the 2nd Duke of Richmond. Lady Louisa's older sister, Lady Emily, had married James twentieth Earl of Kildare in 1747, and was living at Carton, while her eldest sister, Caroline, eloped with and married Henry Fox, later first Lord Holland. The Lennox daughters were remarkable for their beauty and intelligence, although a younger sister, Lady Sarah, considered by all her family to have the greatest share of beauty, had not an equal amount of common sense. Lady Louisa and Lady Sarah lived at Carton with their sister Emily, Lady Kildare, from 1751. Under the influence of her husband, Lord Kildare, later first Duke of Leinster, they developed a real affection and sympathy for the country of their adoption. Following seven months in England, during which time Lady Louisa was presented at Court and made her debut in London society, the Conollys settled down at Castletown in October 1759.

THOMAS CONOLLY'S INHERITANCE

Conolly's Irish estates were valued at £15,275 per annum in 1758. They covered a wide area ranging through counties Donegal, Derry, Leitrim, Fermanagh, Roscommon, Westmeath, Meath, King's County, Kildare and Dublin, but were heavily encumbered, being subject to his father's debts and his sisters' portions – in all amounting to £124,000. By 1773, this load was reduced to about £43,000 by the sale of leases and lands not entailed. However, Thomas Conolly added £42,000 of his own debts, so that the total was now £85,000. This expenditure was incurred in buying up new property, as well as houses in Dublin and London. £25,000 had been spent on improvements and alterations to the house and demesne at Castletown, work in which Lady Louisa played a prominent part.[16] The total rental had also increased at this stage to £21,000 per annum.

Some idea of the far-from-satisfactory economic state of Conolly's inheritance may be obtained from the particular instance of his county Londonderry property. He was a more considerable landowner in Londonderry than in any other county, and for the unusually long (though not quite record) period of forty years – 1761–1800 – he represented it in parliament, '... faithfully ... [discharging] the duties of that station with credit and advantage to his constituents, and with a dignified spirit becoming a man at the head of the landed interest of Ireland. ...'[17] The 'landed interest' in Londonderry itself, on the strength of which he (and Speaker Conolly) sat for that county in parliament, was threefold: the Phillips family's manor of Limavady, purchased in 1697; the Grocers Proportion at Muff, alias Eglinton, leased in 1713 and renewed in 1760; and the Vintners Proportion at Bellaghy, leased in *c.* 1718, and purchased at the end of Speaker Conolly's life, in 1729.

In 1697, the year of its sale by William Phillips to Speaker Conolly, the Limavady estate had the highest valuation in the county – £900 a year (a figure greatly in excess of the then rental). The rental stood at £591 at the time of Speaker Conolly's death in 1729, and £1,529 in *c.* 1800; by 1782, the acreage had dwindled to £1,795 (Irish). The explanation of the low rental and contracting acreage can be accounted for by the practice of perpetuity-leasing – a process which must have begun under the Phillipses and been continued by Speaker Conolly. On the Speaker's death, Limavady – as has been seen – passed to his wife's nephew, Colonel Henry Conyngham, later Earl Conyngham. Conyngham seems to have been only tenant-for-life under the terms of Speaker Conolly's will, because on his death, childless, in 1781, Limavady reverted to Thomas Conolly. The Conyngham interregnum militated against efficient management, as the tenants cannot have been unaware that Conyngham and Conolly were on bad terms, the more so after they publicly came to blows in 1765 over the parliamentary borough of Newtownlimavady, which was on the estate. On the positive side, the Conyngham interregnum at least arrested the process of perpetuity-leasing.

The Grocers Proportion, the lease of which was acquired by Speaker Conolly in 1713, almost marched at its eastern extremity with the Limavady estate, and lay between it and Derry City, bounded on the north by Lough Foyle and on the south by the Berntullet River. In *c.* 1760, the 'Manor of Muff' was surveyed at 8,799 Irish acres – a figure confirmed by a survey made for the Grocers in 1820, sixteen years after the Conolly interest had been sold. In 1820, 5,053 acres out of the then computation of 8,877 were described as arable and pasture. The rental was £476 in 1729, *c.* £1,000 in 1759 (both subject to a head rent of £200 to the Grocers), and £4,650 in 1820.

The third major component of the Conolly estate, the Vintners Proportion, resembled the Limavady estate in that it was freehold and was acquired outright (subject only to a chief rent of £200 a year). It was centred on the town of Bellaghy, and was bounded on the north by the Mercers Proportion, on the south by Lough Beg, on the west by the barony of Keenaght, and on the east by Co. Antrim. The lessees prior to Speaker Conolly were the 2nd and 3rd Viscounts Massereene, to whom the Vintners had granted a 61-year lease in 1673, subsequently extended by about ten years. Conolly seems to have bought the Massereene lease, possibly in 1718, prior to buying the Proportion in fee farm in 1729 for £15,000 plus the chief rent. The rental of the Proportion which was a mere £317 in 1701 (although the 1697 valuation had been £600), rose to £594 in 1718, to £714 in 1729, to £1,843-plus in 1734, £2,688 in 1775 and £3,117 in 1791. Since the estate in 1775 comprised 28,628 acres, perpetuity-leasing explains the discrepancy between this and the contemporary rental of £2,688. There were seven 'freeholders' (which in this context means perpetuity-tenants) on the estate in 1718. In 1734, William Conolly junior granted away most of it in almost 80 perpetuities – no doubt because £10,000 of the purchase price of £15,000 became payable in that year. Ruinous in the short term, this ploy seems not even to have succeeded in the short, because in 1737 he had to raise £10,500 on a mortgage of the estate. Even this did not stop the process of perpetuity-leasing; 65 more perpetuities were granted between 1740 and the death of Thomas Conolly in 1803.

Thomas Conolly's economic and political position in Co. Londonderry was therefore compromised by three factors: his Grocers estate was held on a terminable lease; his Limavady estate was in other ownership until 1781; and a high proportion of both the Vintners and Limavady estates was let in perpetuity. Yet another complication was Conolly's already-mentioned debts; from the early 1790s it appears to have been fairly widely known that he contemplated selling Limavady. The Bellaghy agent, John Spotswood, complained in 1797 that the creditors were pressing him for payment and even threatening law. Simultaneously, his Dublin bankers, Latouche & Co., pressed Conolly to reduce his borrowings from them (currently standing at £47,667) which he had not done for years past. To meet this crisis he attempted to raise money off the estate quickly by encouraging the tenants to make substantial down payments, or entry fines, in return for perpetuity leases at fixed rents fined down to earlier levels. Following his death in April 1803, it was discovered that he had '... anticipated by drafts all his income, and Lady Louisa will have at least £10,000 of interest to pay with the half year's rent of this [the Ballyshannon] estate, £4,000 ...'[18].

Conolly's debts were compounded by his lack of a direct heir, a situation that was apparent from as early as 1762, when Lady Louisa suffered a miscarriage which seems to have precluded any future chances of her bearing a child. Under the terms of his father's will and a private act of parliament in 1766, one-third of his estates were to descend to his six sisters and their issue, in the event of Conolly's failure to produce a son. As it became increasingly clear that the Conollys would remain childless, Conolly's borrowing power was considerably curtailed despite his apparent wealth. His childlessness also, in Malcomson's words, 'encouraged Conolly's existing fecklessness – he remarked fatuously in 1773. "I have no occasion to save money, having no children, and I flatter myself that the money I have spent annually was rationally employed by living, not extravagantly, but like a gentleman.'[19] The subtraction of his sisters' one-third share of the estates reduced the capacity of his executors to pay off his extensive debts following his death in 1803. This led to fears that Castletown House itself would have to be sold, and converted into a barracks, an eventuality which was rejected by the Board of Works and their architect Francis Johnston in 1808.

Finally, Conolly's financial situation was complicated by his expectations of gaining a substantial inheritance from his uncle, the second Earl of Strafford, through his mother, Lady Anne Wentworth. The complexities of Conolly's pursuit of the Strafford inheritance are covered in great detail in Malcomson's 'The fall of the house of Conolly', which is based on papers in the Conolly Archive. Conolly's relationship with his mother and his sisters was embittered by disputes and a lawsuit over their respective shares in the Strafford inheritance. He was unreconciled to his mother when she died in March 1797, and the lawsuit which he lost, ran on until 1801.

Thomas Conolly the politician

The defects of character implicit in his handling of his difficult but still dazzling inheritance, had early been apparent to contemporaries. Lady Caroline Fox (later Lady Holland), the most discerning of his sisters-in-law, found him on first acquaintance 'free and easy and good-humoured' and, what pleased her more, in love with his wife, but later complained that he was 'immensely silly' and 'a tiresome boy'. According to Lady Kildare, writing on 11 November 1762, Conolly 'talked a vast deal of nonsense about politics in order to make me think him mighty cunning, and that he knew *the way of the world* as well as anybody.'[20]

Conolly's political *debut* was made in England, as M.P. for Malmesbury (where Henry Fox had influence between 1759 and 1768), and then for the Duke of Richmond's borough of Chichester. He spoke occasionally in the British parliament, mostly on Irish affairs, but made little impression in English politics – owing, it was later remarked, to 'the radical defect ... of having a *wrong* head'.[21] In Ireland he was, inevitably, much more important, although there he seems for some time to have been overshadowed by his Irish mentor, the first Duke of Leinster. In 1775, a government list of the members of the Irish Parliament said of Conolly: 'He is so capricious and unsteady, that there is very little dependence to be had on him, and it would be better for government that he was a declared opponent of its measures.'[22]

To some extent Conolly's political vagaries can be explained by the fact that he was an independent country gentleman, who considered it a merit rather than the reverse to be influenced by the course of events and by parliamentary debate. Moreover, he was an English-type Whig, seeking always to maintain what he considered a correct balance between crown and people. Another factor was his situation as member for an open, county constituency. Londonderry was more precocious in its political awareness and activity than most counties, and in terms of effective landownership Conolly was a less influential landowner than many county MPs. He therefore could not afford to neglect his popular standing in the constituency. His own family and personal connections were also important in determining his political course. They probably were a principal factor in his decision (and that of the Duke of Leinster) to oppose the absentee tax of 1773, and they were at the very least a complicating factor in the important period 1777–80, when his brother-in-law, the second Earl of Buckinghamshire, was Lord Lieutenant. The letters calendared in this volume for these years show that Conolly played an important role in Buckinghamshire's administration despite his own expressed declarations of independence. In 1778 he was instrumental in the Catholic relief bills introduced in both Westminster and Dublin. At Westminster, in May 1778, he seconded a bill to repeal the protestant purchasers clauses from legislation enacted in William III's reign, which had been lobbied for by his granduncle Speaker Conolly. Back in Dublin later that summer he helped ensure that Buckinghamshire's government had a majority to pass Gardiner's relief acts. For this initiative he was commended by Edmund Burke, in a previously unpublished letter contained in this collection.[23] Conolly's political activities, as documented in this collection, suggest that he had more sense and savvy than he has been credited with by some historians, perhaps unduly influenced by his wife's sister's correspondence and prejudices.

What follows is a brief resumé of Conolly's political stance on some of the major issues of the day. His attitude to the Volunteers was ambivalent. It was he who proposed in the Irish House of Commons in 1779 the celebrated vote of thanks to the Volunteers, Leinster following suit in the Lords; but, basically, while recognizing their military necessity, Conolly saw no justification for their involvement in politics. Later, during the debates on the Dublin Police Act of 1785, he was at pains to pay tribute to the way in which the Volunteers had accepted the authority and direction of parliament by their peaceful withdrawal from public affairs. He was unenthusiastic about the modification of Poynings' Law and the repeal of the Perpetual Mutiny Act – in effect, about the constitution of 1782. In November of that year, he likened the British indulgence of the Irish demands to the spoiling attitude of a nurse towards neglected children. In September 1783, he was described by a friend as 'croaking [i.e. pessimistic] as usual' about the second Volunteer Convention at Dungannon, to which he was elected a delegate and at which plans were laid for the National Volunteer Convention to be held in Dublin in November for the purpose of concerting a plan of parliamentary reform. He did not attend the National Convention, although exhorted privately by the administration to do so and do what he could to exert a moderating influence. When the resolutions of the Convention about parliamentary reform were laid before the House of Commons by Flood, Conolly was loud in denouncing this attempt of an armed body to overawe parliament, and was the proposer of the motion to 'preserve our present happy constitution inviolate at the risk of our lives and fortunes'.[24] When the Commercial Propositions were first laid before the Irish parliament early in 1785, Conolly supported them. However, like many other Irish MPs, he saw much to object to in the Propositions as revised and returned by the British parliament in the summer.

In one respect Conolly's political thinking was entirely consistent: he steadfastly opposed the practice of successive lords lieutenant maintaining power by corruption. Nevertheless, he held aloof from the new and ostensibly reforming administration of the Marquess of Buckingham (1787–1790), and in 1789, was in the forefront of the opposition during the Regency crisis. He spoke in favour of Grattan's motion in February that the Irish parliament should vote an immediate address to the Prince inviting him to an unrestricted Regency of Ireland; and when the lord lieutenant refused to transmit this address, Conolly was one of the MPs selected for the deputation to wait personally on the Prince. He was a founder-member of the Whig Club, which was set up in the aftermath of the Regency crisis, and in the limited 'internal' and 'economical' reforms advocated by that body, reached what was probably his *ne plus ultra.*

However, the fast-moving events of the early 1790s did not allow him to stop there. For Conolly, as for many Irish MPs, the session of 1793 was disruptive of past political conduct and decisive of future. At the start, he gave notice that he would bring forward what he had hitherto opposed, a measure of parliamentary reform. This was a reaction to, indeed a retaliation against, the Catholic relief bill prefigured in the speech from the throne. Conolly had strongly supported Luke Gardiner's Catholic Relief Acts of 1778 and 1782; but his support for political concessions to Catholics was grudging and constrained. In the same session, he declared strongly in favour of the Convention Bill, but said he would not desert his friends, particularly Leinster and Lord Edward Fitzgerald, to vote with the administration. He voted for the militia bill, accepted the colonelcy of the Londonderry Militia, and declined that of the Derry City Militia in favour of Lady Louisa's brother-in-law, Colonel George Napier (Lady Sarah Lennox's second husband). In 1794–95, he supported the short-lived administration of Lord Fitzwilliam, and subsequently spoke against Fitzwilliam's recall in the debate on the subject in the House of Commons. He also opposed the coercive measures of the administration of Fitzwilliam's successor, Lord Camden, and in 1797 resigned his commission in the Kildare Militia (not in the Londonderry) in protest against the disarming of Ulster. Between February and July of that year he was involved in an abortive approach to the Prince of Wales which had as its object the appointment of the Prince as Lord Lieutenant of Ireland.

The Union and Thomas Conolly's demise

By the late 1790s Conolly was becoming increasingly disillusioned with Irish politics. The Duke of Richmond found him favourable to the idea of a Union when they discussed the subject in 1797. In 1796, Conolly sold Ballyshannon and Limavady, the parliamentary boroughs which he controlled, to two of his numerous connections by marriage, Lords Belmore and Londonderry (for £12,000 each); and when he eventually retired as M.P. for Londonderry, in 1800, he effectively transferred his seat for that constituency, too, to Lord Londonderry's family. This was indicative of the increasing influence over him which Londonderry's son and heir, Lord Castlereagh, had gained. Castlereagh, who as Chief Secretary, 1799–1801, and was responsible for carrying the Union, had married Conolly's niece, Lady Emily Hobart, in 1794.

The rebellion of 1798 cast a gloom over Castletown, for the Conollys had relatives on both sides. Renewing his pledge of 1796 to Lord Camden that he would uphold the monarchy with his life and fortune, Conolly wrote to the new viceroy, Lord Cornwallis, in June 1798, begging leave to offer his unconditional service, and ardently supported '... the consolidation of the strength of both islands in one legislative Union. If this can be done, in spite of the private interest of one set of men and the nonsensical noisy clamour of the other, I shall die content. ...'[25] The Union extinguished Conolly's political career. His health was not good; and the general depression to which he succumbed following the troubles of 1798 was greatly aggravated by the lawsuit with his sisters and, from March 1797, with the executor of his mother's will. Generous, affectionate, and kind-hearted, Conolly felt keenly the bitterness of all those events. The Conollys wanted to settle in Sussex or Devonshire, but were dissuaded by the existence of an income tax in England, although they did spend much of 1801–02 in England, including a sojourn at the Strafford seat Wentworth Castle, Yorkshire, in which Conolly had acquired a life-interest and where he intended to spend a part of every year thereafter. He also continued to pursue his claims to other parts of the Strafford estates. These aspirations were cut short by his death, which occurred at Castletown on 27 April 1803. It is difficult to resist the conclusion that, though more 'right-headed' than is commonly supposed, and though greatly hampered by legal difficulties arising out of previous family settlements, he was deficient in both the ability and stability requisite for the position of landownership and leadership he had inherited.

THE CONOLLY FAMILY AFTER 1803

Under Thomas Conolly's will, Lady Louisa continued to live at Castletown, and enjoyed a life interest in the remaining Conolly estates. Following her death in 1821 the bulk of the estates passed to Edward Michael Pakenham, Conolly's grandnephew, who under the terms of Conolly's will took the name and arms of Conolly. Edward Michael Conolly did not 'draw one farthing' from the Conolly estates until 1821, and the estates he inherited were reduced to roughly one-third of Thomas Conolly's original inheritance. None of the county Londonderry estates came his way, and he found himself a landowner in only two counties, Kildare and Donegal.

Instead Edward Michael Conolly and his son Thomas (1823–76) concentrated their political ambitions on county Donegal which they represented at Westminster from 1830 to 1876. Their dramatically reduced incomes, compared to that of their eighteenth-century forebears, meant that little improvement was made to Castletown in this period, except for a short burst of expansion in the 1850s during the stewardship of the flamboyant and adventurous Thomas Conolly. His thirst for adventure found expression in his sojourns at the court of Napoleon III in Paris, and his travels in Virginia during the American Civil War. The latter trip is detailed in his published diaries.[26] His remaining diaries are in private possession. Otherwise few of his papers survive. Following his death in 1876 at the age of 53, a minority ensued before his eldest son, also Thomas, reached his majority in 1891, during which time, the management of the estate devolved on his widow, Sarah Eliza Conolly (nee Shaw). Major Thomas Conolly was killed during the Boer war in 1901, and Castletown passed to his younger brother Major Edward Conolly, who died in 1956. Their nephew Lord Carew, whose mother was a Conolly, was the heir, and he sold Castletown, the last remaining Conolly estate in 1965. Castletown, having initially been purchased by a property developer, was saved for posterity in 1967 by Desmond Guinness, and was opened to the public, under the auspices of the Irish Georgian Society, in the same year. In 1979 control of the house and its collections passed to the Castletown Foundation, before the house was transferred to state ownership in 1994.

THE CONOLLY ARCHIVE: A GUIDE TO THE PAPERS

The purpose of this volume is to reunite the dispersed Conolly Archive by providing a detailed calendar incorporating all of the surviving collections. Each collection is listed separately according to its original arrangement in each recipient institution with the exception of the 'Castletown Papers' and the Thomas Conolly papers, in the National Library, which have been calendared as part of this project. The calendars which follow do however supersede existing lists both in accuracy and detail. The contents of the individual collections are detailed below.

I. THE CASTLETOWN PAPERS (I.A.A. 97/84)

The Castletown Papers comprise *c.* 3,000 letters and papers, 1570–1945, mainly relating to or deriving from William (Speaker) Conolly (1662–1729). This part of the Conolly archive is varied in content, reflecting William Conolly's varied activities as an attorney and estate agent, a landowner in counties Kildare, Dublin, Meath, Westmeath, Roscommon, Wexford, Londonderry, Fermanagh and Donegal, and as an important political figure.

Included are a series of rough figures for the Alnage duties (on the sealing of woollen goods) of Ireland, 1690–95; letters and papers about Derry City and County, with particular reference to the Irish Society, the Foyle fishery, etc. 1687–1701; a large number of title deeds, legal papers bearing on title, and rentals of the Conolly estates of Rathfarnham, county Dublin, Castletown and Leixlip, Co. Kildare, and of other properties in Dublin City and County, Meath, Westmeath, etc, 1570–1945; title deeds, leases, legal case papers, rentals, accounts and agents' correspondence about the Conolly estates in counties Londonderry, Fermanagh and Donegal (and the Conyngham estate in Donegal), with some references to the political affairs of those counties, 1609–1849; correspondence and accounts relating to the Conyngham estate at Slane, county Meath, and Minster, Isle of Thanet, Kent, 1696–1728; personal accounts of members of the Conolly family, 1697–1801; vouchers, accounts and account books for household, garden, demesne and farm expenditure at Castletown, 1761–1803; and correspondence between William Conolly, as Speaker of the House of Commons or a lord justice, with lords lieutenant, chief secretaries, etc, 1719–29.

II. THE CONOLLY PAPERS IN TRINITY COLLEGE DUBLIN (MS 3939–3984A)
This section of the Conolly archive comprises *c.* 2,000 documents and volumes, 1683–1900. They include: political, personal and estate correspondence of several generations of the Conolly family, including details of local politics in Co. Londonderry and in the boroughs of Limavady, county Londonderry, and Ballyshannon, county Donegal, 1709–1900; personal and Castletown household, demesne and farm account books, 1758–1893; and rent accounts for property in counties Kildare, Meath, Dublin and Roscommon, 1781–92, together with a survey of property in Drumhome, county Donegal, 1770. There is also a copy out-letter book of a Dutch merchant in Dublin, 1683–5. Included is much of Thomas Conolly's correspondence with Lord Buckinghamshire, during the latter's time as Lord Lieutenant of Ireland (1776–80), as well as letters to other prominent figures including Bishop Richard Woodward of Cloyne, Walter Hussey Burgh, and Lord Castlereagh. There is also an interesting run of letters pertaining to attempts made by a Major Apollos Morris to negotiate a peace between General Sir William Howe (Conolly's brother-in-law) and George Washington, during the early stages of the American War.

III. THE CONOLLY PAPERS IN THE PUBLIC RECORD OFFICE OF NORTHERN IRELAND (D/2094)
This section of the Conolly archive comprises *c.* 100 documents and volumes – title deeds, leases, rentals and legal papers, 1612–1802 – relating mainly to the Limavady estate, which had originally been granted to Sir Thomas Phillips. In addition to a good series of eighteenth-century Limavady rentals and abstracts of leases, there are also: title deeds to the manor of Castlefinn, county Donegal, 1707–28, with a rental of 1721–4; rental and survey of Ballyshannon, county Donegal, including Newporton, county Fermanagh, 1718, with rent accounts, 1729; rent account for Thomas Conolly's Newporton estate, 1774; rentals and rent rolls, with gaps, for the Vintners' Company lands at Bellaghy, 1729 and 1775–93; rental for the manor of Grocers, 1729; instructions from the Earl-Bishop of Derry about work on churches at Tamlaght and Maghera, county Londonderry, 1775; an examination by Thomas Conolly's agent, of signatories to a petition from Tamlaght Finlagan parish, county Londonderry, published in the *Freeman's Journal*, 18–21 June 1774, protesting against the act which excluded Dissenters from voting at parish vestries; a map of Aghaderrard, county Leitrim, by William Starrat, 1731; Patrick Roe's map of Limavady mill, *c.* 1781; and a map of Carrowclare, county Londonderry, *c.* 1800.

IV. THE CONOLLY PAPERS IN THE NATIONAL ARCHIVES OF IRELAND (M 6917)

There are 661 documents in this collection, covering the period 1633–1868, mostly referring to Conolly estates in the modern Republic of Ireland, although there are some papers relating to the Conolly estates in county Londonderry. The majority of the papers in this collection relate the Conolly estates in county Donegal, particularly the Ballyshannon estate and the Trinity College estates in the barony of Tirhugh. These papers include rentals, estate correspondence, receipts and accounts, marriage settlements and leases, mostly dating from the period 1775–1840. There are also a number of documents relating to William Conolly's purchases from the Trustees of Forfeited Estates in 1703. Amongst the most important documents in the collection is the marriage settlement of Thomas and Louisa Conolly (1758). Also included are the marriage settlements of later owners of Castletown, Edward Michael Conolly and his son Thomas. There is no personal correspondence or accounts in this collection.

V. THE CONOLLY PAPERS IN THE NATIONAL LIBRARY OF IRELAND (Mainly MS 41,341)

In addition to items of uncertain provenance (MSS 5751, 15550, 17302 and 22005), these comprise a small but important bundle of *c.* 150 letters and papers, 1760–1822, from the Castletown Papers proper. This includes: agent's letters to Thomas Conolly from his chief agent and man of business, Michael Clarke, 1765; letters to him from his protégé, Richard Woodward, Dean of Clogher and subsequently Bishop of Cloyne, 1760–94; an original cache of correspondence documenting Thomas Conolly's relations, personal and financial, with his mother and her brother, the 2nd Earl of Strafford, 1766–93; and bundles of general, annual correspondence of Thomas Conolly on political, financial and personal topics for the years, 1778, 1779, 1781 and 1782. These include correspondence with Edmund Burke, Lord Rockingham, Lord Buckinghamshire and Lord Temple amongst others.

VI. THE CONOLLY/NAPIER PAPERS IN THE NATIONAL LIBRARY OF IRELAND (Mss 34,922, 40,242)

This collection contains two volumes of correspondence mostly about the 1798 rebellion and its aftermath. Included are a number of long letters and descriptions by Lady Louisa Conolly of the effects of the rebellion in Celbridge. Also included is correspondence with John FitzGibbon, Lord Clare, about comments he made in a speech in the Irish House of Commons regarding the rebellious activities of the Castletown servants.[27] These letters were previously part of the Bunbury family archive, but are almost wholly related to the Conollys in content, and seem to have been detached from the Conolly archive by Emily Napier (later Bunbury) in the early nineteenth century.

APPENDIX: OTHER MISCELLANEOUS COLLECTIONS OF CONOLLY PAPERS.

The following section includes papers formerly belonging to the Conolly archive, which have been detached from it over time.

Other Conolly papers in PRONI

D/1062/1: This collection comprises 16 boxes of a Ballycastle, county Antrim solicitor's archive relating to the Vintners/Conolly/Earl of Strafford estate at Bellaghy, county Londonderry. [This Earl of Strafford was Thomas Conolly's nephew, John Byng (1772–1860), 1st Earl of a new creation. At Conolly's death in 1803, the Bellaghy estate passed under the terms of his father's will into the joint ownership of the issue of Conolly's sisters, one of whom was Lord Strafford's mother.] The material comprises title deeds, leases, maps, accounts and correspondence relating to the estate, *c.* 1700–*c.* 1940. The leases begin in *c.* 1730 and there is a composite volume of 29 maps and surveys, 1743–c.1837, together with a separate map of Bellaghy town, *c.* 1750.

D/663: This collection comprises *c.* 40 documents and volumes relating to the corporation and parliamentary borough of Limavady, including a complete run of four Limavady corporation minute books, 1659–1808.

In addition to these papers of Conolly provenance, the following small groups of papers, one in family possession in Co. Westmeath and two in PRONI, relate to the estate and other affairs of Thomas Conolly and have been sorted and listed by PRONI.

The papers in Co. Westmeath are at Tullynally Castle, Castlepollard (PRONI: Register of Irish Archives, Pakenham papers, G/2/20), and include a bundle of political letters to Thomas Conolly, 1796–1800, one of them a long letter from Henry Grattan. These concern the case against coercive measures for Ireland, wrangles over the colonelcy of the Co. Londonderry Militia, and the Union. They are present at Tullynally because Conolly was succeeded in the major part of his estates by his great-nephew by marriage, Edward Michael Pakenham (who assumed the name of Conolly), son of Admiral the Hon. Sir Thomas Pakenham and the Admiral's wife, Louisa Staples, daughter of Conolly's sister, Harriet.

The first cache of papers in PRONI are part of the Staples archive, D/1567/F/1/11 and 2/11 and 17. These comprise letters and papers, 1817–20, of Richard Staples relating to the Vintners Proportion at Bellaghy, the joint property of the issue of Thomas Conolly's sisters, one of whom, Harriet, was the first wife of Richard Staples' father, John. In view of this family connection, Staples appears to have had some involvement with the administration of the estate prior to 1819, in which year he was appointed agent for it. The correspondents include his half-sister, Louisa Pakenham (wife of Admiral the Hon. Sir Thomas Pakenham and mother of Edward Michael Pakenham/Conolly), Lord Castlereagh (later 2nd Marquess of Londonderry, whose wife was one of the co-heiresses to Bellaghy), George Hutchinson (the Dublin attorney or man of business for the Conolly estate), John A. Smyth of Londonderry, etc, etc. There are also letters, 1819–22, to Richard Staples's brother, the Rev. J.M. Staples, about Richard's death (which took place in 1820, not 1819, as stated in Burke's *Peerage*), about the condition of the agent's house at Bellaghy, about arrears of rent on the Bellaghy estate, etc.

The second cache of papers in PRONI (T/3110) comprises letters, legal case papers, rentals, etc (13 documents), 1817–42, relating to the Vintners Proportion at Bellaghy, an interest in which had passed in 1803 to Thomas Conolly's sister, Caroline, Countess of Buckinghamshire, and thence to her daughter, Lady Emily-Anne Hobart, wife of Lord Castlereagh. On Lady Castlereagh's death in 1829, her interest in the estate passed to the family of her eldest half-sister, Lady Harriet Hobart, Marchioness of Lothian (d.1805), whose husband's seat was at Blickling in Norfolk. For this reason, the originals of this material are now in the Norfolk and Norwich Record Office, Norwich.

NOTES TO THE INTRODUCTION

1 The NLI microfilm reference number is p.6951; PRONI's, MIC/244; and PRONI's print-outs are T/2825.
2 See NLI Special List 91. Photocopies of these letters are available in PRONI at T/3048/B.
3 This account of William Conolly's career is based on Patrick Walsh, 'The career of William Conolly, 1689–1729' (PhD thesis, Trinity College Dublin, 2007); Lena Boylan, 'The Conollys of Castletown', *Quarterly Bulletin of the Irish Georgian Society,* XI, no 4 (1968); and Edith Johnston-Liik, *History of the Irish parliament,* (6 vols, Belfast, 2002), iii, 474–79.
4 For this point see T.C. Barnard, 'A tale of three sisters: Katherine Conolly of Castletown' in T.C. Barnard (ed.), *Irish protestant ascents and descents, 1641–1770* (Dublin, 2004), p. 270.
5 See J.G. Simms, *The Williamite Confiscation in Ireland 1690–1703* (London, 1956), pp 126–27.
6 On the Dongans see, T.P. Dungan, *John Dongan of Dublin, an Elizabethan gentleman and his family* (Baltimore, 1996), and F. Van Wyck, *Ancestry of Governor Dongan* (Boston, 1935).
7 For the best study of Irish politics in this period and the rise of the undertakers see D.W. Hayton, *Ruling Ireland, 1685–1742: Politics, politicians and parties* (Woodbridge, 2004).
8 On Castletown see, Patrick Walsh, *Castletown* (Dublin, 2007).
9 Lady Llanover, *The autobiography and correspondence of Mrs Delany,* (3 vols, London, 1861), iii, 282.
10 For Conolly junior see Johnston-Liik, *History of the Irish Parliament* (6 vols, Belfast, 2002), iii, 479–80
11 *Daily Post (London),* 27 Mar. 1721.
12 For his Grand Tour see John Ingamells, *A dictionary of British and Irish travellers in Italy, 1701–1800* (London, 1997), p. 234; *Daily Post (London),* 21 June 1728.
13 *London Evening Post,* 14 Oct. 1735; *Daily Gazetteer,* 17 Oct. 1735; *The Craftsman,* 18 Oct. 1735; *London Daily Post and Daily Advertiser,* 8 Oct. 1739.
14 *London Evening Post,* 28 Jan. 1744; *London Daily Post,* 30 Jan. 1744.
15 This account of Thomas Conolly's career is based on Anthony Malcomson, 'The fall of the house of Conolly' in Eoin Magennis & Allan Blackstock (eds.) *Politics and political culture in Britain and Ireland, 1750–1850: essays in tribute to Peter Jupp* (Belfast, 2007), pp 107–156; Johnston-Liik, *History of the Irish parliament,* iii, 467–73. For Lady Louisa Conolly see Stella Tillyard, *Aristocrats: Caroline, Emily, Louisa and Sarah Lennox, 1740–1832* (London, 1994).
16 On Lady Louisa's contribution to Castletown see David Griffin, 'Castletown, Co. Kildare: the contribution of James first Duke of Leinster,' *Irish architectural and decorative studies,* 1 (1998), pp 120–146; Christopher Moore, 'Lady Louisa Conolly, mistress of Castletown, 1759–1821' in Jane Fenlon, Nicola Figgis and Christopher Marshall (eds.), *New perspectives in art history in honour of Anne Crookshank* (Dublin 1987); Finola O'Kane, *Landscape design in eighteenth century Ireland, mixing foreign trees with the natives* (Cork 2004).
17 John Robert Scott, *Parliamentary representation: being a political and critical review of all the counties, cities, and boroughs of the kingdom of Ireland ...* (Dublin, 1790), p. 59
18 Admiral Thomas Pakenham to Richard Lord Dunlo, 3 June 1803 (T.C.D., Conolly Papers Ms 3981/1457).
19 Malcomson, 'The fall of the house of Conolly', p. 114.
20 Tillyard, *Aristocrats,* p. 109; Lady Kildare to James Lord Kildare, 11 Nov. 1762 in Brian Fitzgerald, *Correspondence of Emily, Duchess of Leinster* (3 Vols. Dublin, 1949–57), i,134
21 Second Earl Camden to Lord Castlereagh, 22 Mar. 1796, quoted in Malcomson, 'The fall of the house of Conolly', p. 109.
22 William Hunt (ed.), *The Irish parliament in 1775* (London, 1907), p. 21.
23 Edmund Burke to Conolly, 27 Aug. 1778 (NLI, Conolly Papers, Ms 41,341/5/10). See Patrick Walsh, 'A new Edmund Burke letter from 1778', *Eighteenth-Century Ireland,* 23 (2009), pp 160–4.

24 *The parliamentary register: or, history of the proceedings and debates of the House of Commons of Ireland,* (17 vols. Dublin, 1784–1801), ii, 264.
25 Conolly to Lord Cornwallis, 25 June 1798 (I.A.A., Castletown Papers, 97/84/A/10/6).
26 Nelson D. Lankford, (ed.), *An Irishman in Dixie: Thomas Conolly's diary of the fall of the confederacy* (South Carolina, 1988).
27 There is also a bundle of letters originating from Lady Louisa Conolly, about Lord Edward's attainder and the families' efforts to get his forfeited estates restored to his children, in the Leinster Papers in the National Library (NLI Ms 41,552/50). The principal correspondent is Lord Clare. These letters were given by Lady Louisa to the 2nd Duke of Leinster and therefore do not belong in the Conolly archive.

ACKNOWLEDGEMENTS

This project commenced in 2005 when one of the present editors, Dr Malcomson, proposed to the IMC and the Castletown Foundation that he continue and conclude his c. 1970 calendar of the Castletown Papers then and currently on loan to the Irish Architectural Archive. Patrick Walsh, who was at that time working on his doctoral thesis in Trinity College Dublin on Speaker William Conolly, was invited to collaborate in the project, in his case with special reference to sections B and E of the IAA material. It was then decided to expand the scope of the project into a compilation and publication of a union calendar of the entire Conolly archive under the aegis of the Irish Manuscripts Commission. This necessitated the calendaring of new Conolly material discovered by Dr Malcomson in the National Library, and the expansion of the existing lists in the National Archives, PRONI and Trinity College Dublin by Dr Walsh. This work has been carried out over the last three years, with the bulk of it being carried out by Dr Walsh while he was a research fellow in the Centre for Historic Irish Houses and Landed Estates at NUI Maynooth between January and July 2008.

The historical introduction is based on the introduction to the original *c.* 1970 PRONI list of the Castletown Papers, written by Dr Malcomson, but has been updated by Dr Walsh, utilising both authors' recent researches. The arrangement of the IAA material follows the original PRONI classification scheme, which has been modified where necessary to accommodate additional material. The arrangement of most of the other collections has of necessity respected existing inconsistencies and idiosyncrasies.

Several individuals and institutions have contributed indispensably to the compilation of this union calendar. Firstly it is a duty and a pleasure to acknowledge the contribution of the late Mrs Lena Boylan of Celbridge, who pioneered archival research at Castletown, and in whose hands the Castletown Papers were kept until 1997 when they transferred to the Irish Architectural Archive. In acknowledgement of her contribution, this volume is dedicated to her memory. Desmond Guinness and successive members of the Castletown Foundation, the owners of the Castletown Papers, especially their current director Christopher Moore, also deserve great thanks for their efforts in preserving the archive and indeed in preserving Castletown itself. The staff at the relevant archives, we have worked in, especially David Griffin, Colum O'Riordan, and all their staff in the IAA, as well as the various archivists in the NAI, NLI, PRONI and TCD Manuscripts Department, have co-operated most helpfully. At the Irish Manuscripts Commission, James McGuire, the chairman, James Kelly and the indispensable Cathy Hayes have all made working on this project a pleasurable experience.

Patrick Walsh would like to acknowledge the support of David Dickson in Trinity College Dublin, Charles Ivar McGrath in University College Dublin, as well as Terence Dooley and Vincent Comerford at the Centre for the Study of Historic Irish Houses and Landed Estates, NUI Maynooth, where he did much of the work on this project, during a period spent as a research fellow in 2008. Anthony Malcomson would like to acknowledge the support of his former colleagues in PRONI and of the late T.D. Scott.

Finally special acknowledgement must be made to the Conolly Carew family, now represented by Patrick Conolly Carew, 7th Baron Carew, for their generosity and public spirit in placing most of the Conolly archive in the relevant record repositories and thus making this volume possible.

PATRICK WALSH
A.P.W. MALCOMSON

GENEALOGY OF THE CONOLLY FAMILY

GENEALOGY OF THE WENTWORTH/CONOLLY FAMILY

William Wentworth

Thomas Wentworth, 1st Earl Strafford (1672–1711) = Anne Johnson (*c.* 1684–1754

Peter Wentworth

Anne (1714–97)
= William **Conolly** (1706–54)

William 2nd Earl of Strafford (1722–91)
= Lady Anne Campbell (1715–81)
d.s.p (Succeeded by his cousin
Frederick Thomas William Wentworth 3rd Earl
of Strafford (1732–99) grandson of Peter Wentworth

Lucy (d.1771)
= Sir George Howard (1718–96)

Henrietta (d.1786)
= Henry Vernon (b.1718)

Anne
=Gen. Richard Vyse (1746–1825)

Henry (1748–1814)
= (1) Penelope Graham
= (2) Margaret Acton

Thomas Six sisters incl. Anne
= George Byng

Richard William Howard Vyse (1784–1853)

George Byng (1764–1847)

John Byng created 1st Earl of Strafford
the Third Creation in 1847 (1772–1860)

Henry Charles Edward Vernon
(1779–1860)

Frederick Wlliam Thomas
Vernon Wentworth (1795–1885)
He took the name Wentworth and
inherited Wentworth Castle.

PART I

THE CASTLETOWN PAPERS

THE CASTLETOWN PAPERS

(Currently deposited by the Trustees of the Castletown Foundation in the Irish Architectural Archive, 45 Merrion Square, Dublin 2 where the list which follows was compiled.)

Reference	**Description**
A/1–12	Personal and political letters and papers of members of the Conolly and Conyngham families, 1696–1801
B/1–10	Legal papers, accounts, etc, mainly relating to William Conolly's early career as an attorney and agent, 1614–1724
C/1–50	Deeds, letters and papers relating to the Conolly and Conyngham estates in Cos. Donegal and Londonderry
D/1–26	Deeds, leases, accounts, etc, relating to the Conolly estate of Rathfarnham and to Conolly lands elsewhere in Co. Dublin and in Dublin City, 1607–1782
E/1–24	Deeds, leases, case papers, etc, about the Conolly estates in Co. Kildare, mainly Castletown and Leixlip, 1570–1862
F/1–6	Deeds, leases, etc, about Conolly estates elsewhere in Ireland and in England, including the Conyngham estate at Slane, Co. Meath (1696–1728), 1650–1827
G/1–18	Deeds, vouchers and other papers relating to settlements, mortgages, debts, wills and general matters of Conolly family finance.
H/1–16	Rentals of the Co. Kildare estates, outsize rentals of all the estates, and outsize maps, 1684–1945
J/1–11	Castletown household and demesne account books, and accounts for personal and domestic expenditure, 1697–1938

A/	DATE	DESCRIPTION
A/1–12	c.1696–1801: 1833: 1890	**PERSONAL AND POLITICAL LETTERS AND PAPERS OF MEMBERS OF THE CONOLLY AND CONYNGHAM FAMILIES, AS FOLLOWS:**
A/1/1	2 May, 9 William III	Patent appointing William Conolly Collector of the Revenue for Londonderry and Coleraine.
A/2/ 1–2	[c.1714?]: 17 Jan., 4 George I [1718]	Badly damaged and/or seriously incomplete patents appointing William Conolly a Commissioner of the Revenue and a Lord Justice.
A/3/ 1–54	1708–29	Political letters and papers of William Conolly, as Speaker of the House of Commons, a Lord Justice, First Commissioner of the Revenue, and Governor of and M.P. for Co. Londonderry, including correspondence with Lords Lieutenant, Secretaries, etc.
A/3/1	26 May 1708	Account of expenses for entertainment at a court held at 'Navin' (£3 17s. 7d.), mostly for drink.
A/3/2 A–B	[1713?]	Memoranda by one Trotter about an election in some unspecified constituency. William Conolly is to get the following Co. Donegal people to attend the election: Mr Folliott, Mr Gilbert Eccles, Mr Cotnam, Dr Maddin and Mr Saunders. He is to ask Charles Eccles to do the same, and is to speak to Robert Spence and get him to send Alexander and James Hogg to the election. Conolly is also to find out from '... Mr Saunders whether tenants for the lessor's life have votes, and whether a verbal grant without writing can make a freehold, the grantee being in possession; [also] that he [Saunders] may be here at the election to resolve doubts of this kind in Sir John's behalf. ...'
A/3/4	14 Feb. 1718 [/19]	Richard Conyngham to Mrs Conolly referring to the number of bankruptcies among merchants, and asking her to use her influence with 'Lord Conolly' to get Lt William Napier's pension paid promptly, as Napier has assigned this money to Conyngham.
A/3/5	14 Feb. 1718 [/19]	Colonel John Corry, Castle Coole, [Co. Fermanagh.], to his Excellency, Lord Justice Conolly, Dublin. Complaining that the quitrent of part of his estate in Co. Longford, which was at one time reduced, has now been re-set at a figure which is beyond all reason, and asking Conolly to use his influence on Corry's behalf. [Missing]

A/3/6	16 Feb. 1718 [/19]	'Arrears due by the several common brewers summoned to appear before his Majesty's Chief Commissioners of Excise ...'.
A/3/7	8 Mar. [1718?]	Bruen Worthington to Conolly, Dublin. '... J. Corry['s?] and [?] my cause this day without a division [sense?].'
A/3/8	16 Mar. 1718	Margaret Smith to her 'brother', William Conolly, Dublin asking for a pass for the bearer, who is going to London.
A/3/9 A–B	[pre-June 1719]	Two lists of members of the House of Commons 'in employment', the first endorsed by William Conolly: 'The copy of this given L[or]d. L[ieutenan]t. before the parliament met'. 1. Humphrey May. 2. Thomas Upton. 3. George Macartney. 4. John Chichester. 5. Mervin Pratt. 6. T. Clements. 7. Charles Delafaye Absent. 8. Samuel Bindon. 9. St. John Brodrick. 10. Edward Southwell. 11. Henry Hawley Esq. 12. Martin Bladen Absent. 13. Anthony Jephson. 14. William Brodrick. 15. William Southwell. 16. William Boyle. 17. John Rogerson. 18. Rich. Molesworth. 19. Dan Reading. 20. Sir Ralph Gore. 21. Gust. Hamilton. 22. James [To]pham. 23. Owen Wynne. 24. David [Bi]ndon. 25. Thom. [?]licout [Medlicott]. 26. Robt. Clements. 27. Arthur Hill. 28. Sir Gust. Hume. 29. John Pratt. 30. Rich. Allen. 31. Rob. Johnson. 32. Maurice Cuff[e]. 33. John Pepper. 34. Stephen Dean. 35. John Usher. 36. Rich. St. George. 37. George Gore. 38. John Parnell. 39. Henry Edgeworth. 40. Will. Conolly. 41. Fred Hamilton. 42. Sir Marcus Beresford. 43. Isaac Manley. 44. Thomas Marley. 45. Michael Tisdall. 46. Thom. Blith. 47. Thom. Trotter. 48. Ld. Fred. Howard Absent. 49. William Purefoy. 50. Will. Molyneux. 51. James Forth. 52. Dudley Cosby. 53. Ephraim Dawson. 54. Rob. Pigott. 55. Samuel Freeman. 56. John Weaver. 57. Henry Sandford. 58. William Ormsby. 59. Matt. Penefether. 60. Charles Stewart Absent. 61. Rich. Stewart. 62. Edward May. 63. Will. Maynard. 64. Ben. Parry. 65. Thom Merideth. 66. Pat. Fox. 67. Edw. Jones. 68. Will. Berry. 69. Hen. Ponsonby. 70. George Ram. 71. Sam. Whitshed. 72. Edward Webster. The second is endorsed by Conolly: 'This list for private use. W.C.' Wm Brown[low]. Sil. Cross. John Eyre. James Caulfield [sic]. Brent. Spencer. Thom. Burdet. John Beauchamp. St. Ledger Gilbert. Brin. Butler. David Bindon. Edward Southwell. Francis Bernard. M. Coghill. S[amue]l Dopping. Hen. Singleton. Edw. Singleton. [piece missing] [For?]ward. [piece missing]ford. [piece missing]in. [piece missing]don. [Emmanue?]l Moore. H[ans] Hamilton. Acheson Moore in France. John Cole. Fred. Trench.

A/3/9A–B *contd.*

Ag. Vesey. Wm. Vesey. Sir Maur. Crosby [sic]. Thom. Crosby. Wm. Crosby. James Barry. Thom. Burgh. Theob. Burgh. Sir Stand. Hartstonge. Sir Robt. Maude. James Agar. Jeffrey Paul. Francis Flood. Edw. Worth. George King. Hen. Edgworth. Rob. Edgworth. Rich. Tisdall. Step. Ludlow. John Bingham. Henry Bingham. John Bliih [Bligh]. Thomas Taylor. Thomas Taylor. Rich. Gorges. Wm. St. Lawrence. Francis Lucass [sic]. Charles Plunket. Thomas Lestrange. Henry King. Rob. Carew. Thom. Bellew. Will Smith. James Stopford. Nic. Loftus. Edward Jones. Cadw. Edwards. [—] Meredeth [Thomas or Arthur?]. [Dr Edward Worth Thrice Noble. [Richard or William Molesworth?]. [—]t. [—]ier. [Michael? Cu]ffe. George Haughton. Phil. Doyne. Rich. Sanders. Rich. Edwards. Char. Boyle, Ld. Bles[inton].
[Only the endorsements are in Conolly's handwriting: the lists themselves are in someone else's.]

A/3/10 8 Mar. 1719 [/20?]

Leo. Wilberfoss, Strabane, to Conolly, Dublin apparently about remitting taxes collected to Conolly. 'I received a letter from the board to pay to John Wootton Esq., collector of Londonderry, the balance of cash in my hands, which was as by the last weekly abstract £1506. 5s. 0d. I have this day paid him £1400. I would have paid him more, but had not time to collect where it was owing to me. ...'

A/3/11 25 June 1720

Rough draft of a letter from [William Conolly, at this time a Lord Justice along with the Lord Chancellor Alan Brodrick 1st Viscount Midleton, acting under the newly appointed Lord Lieutenant, Charles Fitzroy, 2nd Duke of Grafton]. Congratulating him on his appointment and discussing the Hon. Capt. Hamilton's desire for a job in Grafton's household. Conolly explains that many people have been applying to him for such jobs, remembering the countenance which Grafton had shown him during Grafton's previous time in the government of Ireland [as a Lord Justice in 1715–17], but Conolly has refused to trouble him on anyone's behalf. Capt. Hamilton, however, is a son of Lord Boyne, and the family is influential in parliament; so he cannot be so lightly refused. Another aspirant for the same job is Major Whitshed, a nephew of the Lord Chief Justice of the King's Bench.

A/3/12 2 July 1720

Rough draft of a letter from Conolly, Dublin [to the newly appointed Lord Lieutenant, the Duke of Grafton].
Offering advice about the person to be appointed Lord Chief Justice of the Common Pleas in succession to John Forster. 'I have the honour of your Grace's of the 25th, and return my humble thanks for the good opinion which your Grace has of me, and it shall be my utmost study never to forfeit the same. And since your Grace has commanded me to write with freedom and [word

A/3/12 *contd.*

illegible], I shall upon allowance [?]. ...' He begins by dealing with Grafton's queries, apparently about the income which the Lord Lieutenant receives from Phoenix Park. He then goes on to discuss the question of a new Lord Chief Justice of the Common Pleas, Forster being gravely ill [in fact he died that day]. The two contenders are Judges Macartney and Gore. Macartney is an honest, well-principled man, who was displaced during Queen Anne's reign and re-instated at the accession of George I. He is the senior judge, but is old and rather deaf. Gore was Attorney General when Grafton was last in the government of Ireland [as a Lord Justice in 1715–17], and it is usual for the Attorney General to be given one of the Chief Justiceships. Gore has many influential friends and relations who press his pretensions strongly. The difficulty will be jumping him over Macartney. [Missing]

A/3/13 5 July 1720

Rough draft of a letter from Conolly, Dublin, to Grafton about the succession to the Lord Chief Justiceship of the Common Pleas. A new factor has entered the situation, as the Lord Chief Justice of the King's Bench [William Whitshed] has informed Conolly that he is anxious to go to the Common Pleas, even though this means demotion. In Conolly's view, it would be impossible to ignore Whitshed's pretensions. If he goes to the Common Pleas, this will put an end to the competition between Macartney and Gore, as the former would not be in the running for the King's Bench. (This draft is endorsed by Conolly: 'The letter of the 5th was not sent'.)

A/3/14 [c.5 July 1720]

Rough note by Conolly on the whole series of promotions which would take place if Whitshed succeeded as Chief Justice of the Common Pleas; in Conolly's scheme of things Gore is to become Chief Justice of the King's Bench.

A/3/15A–B 29 Aug. 1720

Rough draft of a letter from Conolly, Dublin, to Grafton about the promotions and about the jurisdictional and constitutional disputes between the British and Irish parliaments.

He is glad that Grafton accepts the plan to fill up the vacancies, but sorry that he '... lies under the difficulties you mention. To answer that the House of Lords would be in better temper before the King's servants there would make any concessions or give up their employments, etc – this, I think, is very hard, though really my humble opinion is that the House of Lords will be in better temper, for as to the point of jurisdiction, that is over and determined and cannot be returned or repeated, and sure no wise or thinking man will or can stir further in it, especially when they consider they may risk future parliaments and do the nation more mischief than they can ever do them good. So that I cannot but say matters will cool and I hope go easy under your Grace's administration. But I beg leave to ask if it is not more likely so to

A/3/15A–B *contd.*

do when the king's servants find their friends and acquaintance put into employments. And, further, why should this resentment reach the House of Commons, who never concerned themselves in the Lords' jurisdiction or had anything to do in that matter, but many of them to my knowledge using all their endeavours not to have the Lords commit my L[or]d C[hief] B[aron] and the rest of the Barons, and your Grace will observe that the persons that are here desired to be put into the vacant employments are not Lords but Commoners, and if the Lords have been wrong, must the whole nation suffer for that?

I am a very unfit undertaker but I dare say there is not any that your Grace will use your good offices for, to put into the vacancies, that will put themselves into any hands that will lead them out of the way, but on the contrary in your Grace's and use their utmost endeavours and interest to make all things go easy in both Houses of Parliament, or I assure your Grace I had never mentioned them, and particularly Mr Justice Gore from whom I had all the assurances imaginable before I wrote in his favour ... and discoursed him fully as to the jurisdiction. ...' Whoever told Grafton that Gore and Conolly did not agree in politics last session, told the truth; but it was in the House of Commons about the toleration for Dissenters and not about the jurisdiction. Attached (15B) is a letter from Professor J.L. McCracken to Mrs Lena Boylan, 11 March 1975, in which he draws attention to the significance of Conolly's self description as an 'undertaker'.

A/3/16 24 Sep. 1720

Rough draft of a letter from Conolly, Dublin, to Grafton about the Common Pleas and about the election of Grafton's Secretary, Horatio Walpole, for T.C.D. Conolly '... cannot doubt whoever your Grace has recommended to fill up the vacancies here will succeed, and think they will be entirely in your Grace's interest and merit the favours your Grace confers upon them. ...'

He has spoken to Mr Synge, who has an interest in the College, but no vote himself. '... I have fully discoursed the provost and showed him his Royal Highness's [the Prince of Wales, Chancellor of T.C.D.] letter to your Grace but would not let him make use of it, not knowing how the Prince would be pleased without his giving leave to do so. But I believe there will be no occasion, for the provost is a very honest gentleman and to be depended upon, and is very hearty, and if your Grace thinks fit to write him a line in behalf of Mr Walpole, and to thank those that are for having him elected, it will be of use. And your Grace judges right that the Archbishop of Dublin [William King]may take it ill if he is not wrote [?] to, so that your Grace's desiring [?] his interest with his friends in the College will make the matter easier, and though I believe it will do without it, yet it will be of use. ...' He has written fully to Walpole on the subject.

A/3/17 18 Oct. 1720 Rough draft of a letter from Conolly, Dublin, to Grafton expressing strong objections to Grafton's plan for a reshuffle of the highest judicial offices in Ireland, including the Lord Chancellorship.

'I must own I never was more surprised than when I had the honour of your Grace's of the 7th from Evesham [?], with the copy of Mr Secretary Cragg's letter to your Grace, and your answer to him, relating to the dispositions [?] of the law employments, and especially making Lord Chief Baron, Chancellor, that which with great [word illegible] will give universal dislike and dissatisfaction – I mean that my Lord Chief Baron should be Lord Chancellor, after what passed in the House of Lords here. As to Sir R[ichard] Levinge's being Lord Chief Justice of the Common Pleas, that will not be agreeable in this country.

I see [?] it's too late to give my humble advice that, if possible, my Lord Chief Baron may not be Lord Chancellor, for I dread the consequences of it to his Majesty's affairs and the ease of your Grace's administration ... I fear it will not be in the power of your Grace's friends to answer your expectation or be [word illegible] to your service [?] as they are inclined. I have a great value for my Lord Chief Baron Gilbert, and I think for his own sake and the quiet of this kingdom it is [sense hard to follow] here ought most to avoid to be Chancellor. As Sir R. Levinge, all I shall say further about him is that he has little or no interest in the parliament here, and consequently cannot be so useful as some people there imagine. As to Mr Serjeant Reynolds, being a stranger to him I know not what to say. But again [words illegible] my great surprise and concern at these steps as what I am apprehensive may prove very detrimental to his Majesty's interests and administrations [?] in this kingdom. Your Grace's commands and the confidence you are pleased to repose [?] in me shall remain entirely secret [?].

There are many letters to [words illegible] giving an account of all the dispositions [?] mentioned in Mr Secretary Cragg's letter to your Grace, but I hope [hear?] nothing of the hint your Grace gives about [words illegible].

The bad effect of the South Sea has reached this kingdom to a great degree, insomuch that numbers are ruined by it. There has been a run upon all the banks here, who have all hitherto stood it, but our Mr Swift also appears again [?]. We have no manner [?] of trade and the kingdom is quite [?] drained [?] of money, so that [illegible comments on the state of the country]. Our revenue has fallen of late greatly, and where all this will end I cannot tell.' [The patchiness of this transcript is due to the difficulty of deciphering Conolly's handwriting, particularly in a rough draft.]

A/3/18	3 Dec. 1720	Rough draft letter from Conolly, Dublin, to Grafton about the proposed re–shuffle of the judicial offices. He acknowledges Grafton's two letters, and says that he will not repeat his previous sentiments, particularly with regard to the suitability of Whitshed for the Chancellorship. It is clear that '... there are a considerable number of people who profess friendship and are sorry for him [Midleton] that would be easy under that affliction and drop him without concern, if it were not for his successor, which I still wish could be anyways prevented; but I must not dwell more on that subject. ...' He refers to the depressed state of the trade of the country, '... which of course must make a great demand next session of parliament here. ...', and thanks Grafton for his favours to Conolly. He concludes with a reference to the mismanagement of the collector of Dublin, who has been replaced by a Mr Arkwright, not upon grounds of favouritism, but purely as a measure which the Revenue Commissioners consider necessary for the sake of the revenue.
A/3/19	16 Dec. 1720	Rough draft of a letter from Conolly, Dublin, to Grafton about the Lord Chancellorship and other, lesser employments. He gathers from Grafton's letter that the arrangement outlined by Grafton for the Lord Chancellorship is not finally settled. He refers to vacant bishoprics, but assumes that Grafton's hands are so full of parliamentary affairs that he has not time to think of such things. He regrets that, for once, he is unable to comply with Grafton's request in the matter of Mr Topham's employment, and concludes by observing that the whole of the revenue of Ireland is '... scarce sufficient to pay the subsistence of the army'.
A/3/20	24 Dec. 1720	Rough draft of a letter from Conolly to [Horatio] Walpole [Secretary to Grafton] thanking Grafton for appointing Conolly's nephew, William, to an office [the Cursitorship of Chancery]. Conolly points out that it is not worth more than £200 pr annum, and expresses the hope that it will be granted for 2 lives, as in the previous patent.
A/3/21	9[?] Jan. 1720 [/21]	Rough draft of a letter from Conolly, Dublin, to Grafton about a near-dispute between Conolly and Midleton over the conflicting claims of two rival banks. After lengthy meetings and some dispute they have at last agreed on a report, which they have transmitted to Grafton. The report favours the first bank, but Midleton wanted it to favour the first bank much more strongly. This was the bank which both of them subscribed to '... before my Lord H., etc, set up Sir R. G. ... Mr St. George and Mr [name illegible] are going to London to solicit in behalf of the first bank. ...' Conolly does not know which he ought to recommend Grafton to favour, as both are full of parliament men and men of fortune. [Missing]

A/3/22	2 Feb. 1720 [/21]	H[oratio] Walpole, [Secretary to the Lord Lieutenant], Dover Street, [London], to [Conolly], about a bye-election for Coleraine, Co. Londonderry. 'Last Saturday I transmitted to your Excellency a letter I received that morning from Sir William Withers [Governor of the Irish Society] acquainting me that the Society had agreed to recommend Mr Burton to be elected at Coleraine, and I have since expected to have received from their secretary a duplicate of their letter to the corporation for that purpose, when I was told last Tuesday that Sir William Withers died on Monday, which I indeed did not then believe. But it proves too true. Who his successor will be, or whether the Society will continue in the same mind relating to the election of Coleraine, I can't tell. However, I will inform myself about it. In the meantime, any particular directions from your Excellency will be punctually obeyed. ...'
A/3/23	4 Feb. 1720 [/21]	Walpole, Dover Street, to Conolly about the Coleraine bye-election. 'When I did myself the honour to write to your Excellency last, I was apprehensive that Sir W. Withers's death would have occasion some alteration in the Coleraine affair, because the secretary who brought me Sir William's last letter, which I sent you, appeared somewhat cool and very inquisitive about Mr Burton. But what I said to him to desire him to bring himself and me the duplicate of the Society's recommendatory letter to the corporation, had the desired effect, and he was accordingly with me yesterday and delivered to me the enclosed [not found], which I think is so worded as cannot fail of success.'
A/3/24	7 Feb. 1720 [/21]	Rough draft of a letter from Conolly, Dublin, to Walpole about the Coleraine bye-election. Mr Burton is extremely obliged to Walpole for his trouble on Burton's behalf. However, it appears that, now that Withers is dead, the corporation of Coleraine are trying to wriggle out of the engagement entered into by him. It would be a help if Walpole would send Burton the original of Withers's letter. Conolly concludes by recommending to Walpole a clergyman called Mr Ashe. [This letter is particularly difficult to decipher.]
A/3/25	7 Feb. 1720 [/21]	Rough draft of a letter from Conolly, Dublin, to Grafton concerning, amongst other things, the promotion of Judge Gore. He thanks Grafton for his continued favours, but expresses regret that some letter concerning the Lord Chief Baron and Barons of the Exchequer had not been worded in such a way as to obviate 'clamour and observations'. If Lord Chief Baron [Gilbert] is removed to the English bench, Conolly hopes that Grafton will bear in mind the pretensions of Gore to succeed him.

A/3/26	11 Mar. 1720 [/21]	Walpole, Dover Street, to Conolly about the Coleraine bye-election. 'The many mails that lately arrived together brought me the honour of your Excellency's letters of 11 and 25 past, and I am very sorry to find by the last of them that the secretary's letter had no better effect upon the corporation of Coleraine. I shall consider of the best means to relieve [retrive ?] that matter if possible, though I must own to you, I did not like the secretary's way of talking when Sir William Withers first sent him to me, and as I have not heard anything from him relating to the corporation's answer to the Society's letter, I very much suspect his being a friend to the other interest. However, no endeavours of mine shall be wanting to settle this matter right if possible. I believe the constant hurry and attendance in parliament made me forget to answer your Excellency's letter of the 7th past, and to let you know that my Lord Lieutenant readily consented to put Mr St. George [Ashe] down in the list of his chaplains. ... PS. You will receive from my Lord Lieutenant a very extraordinary letter. You will from by [sic] the character and conversation of the person that wrote, be able to judge of the kind of the intelligence.' [On the side is a rough draft of Conolly's reply, dated Dublin, 21 March 1720[/21]. This is so heavily abbreviated that it is virtually indecipherable.]
A/3/27	4 Apr. 1721	Walpole, Dover Street, to Conolly announcing his resignation as Secretary to the Lord Lieutenant and the probability that he will be succeeded by [Edward] Hopkins.
A/3/ 28A–B	1720–21: 1725–6	Accounts of the custom revenue of Londonderry for these two periods.
A/3/29	11 May 1721	Rough draft of a letter from Conolly, Dublin, to Grafton about the proposal to replace Lord Chancellor Midleton. 'This morning I had the honour of your Grace's of the 6th, acquainting me with the conference your Grace had lately with two of the chief ministers and their proposal of continuing Lord Chancellor, grounded upon difficulties of finding a successor and the disturbances the threat [?] might give to the measures in parliament, which your Grace conceives may be their motive; in which your Grace is pleased to desire my thoughts. I hope your Grace will pardon me if [I] judge wrong, for I think their proposal determines the matter and of course continues this Lord Chancellor, since a proper successor cannot be found; for the time of doing that had been when it was first spoke of (after the Lord Chief Baron was set [word illegible]), so that by this time whoever was made Chancellor [would have] had time to make

A/3/29 *contd.*

himself acquainted in the people and affairs of the kingdom, [words erased or illegible] to have given your Grace assistance in the King's affairs, and the removing the present lord been quite forgotten. But any successor [?] now, the parliament being so near, I fear would not answer expectations. I make bold to acquaint your Grace that for some time past it has been taken for granted here the present Chancellor would continue, his relation [Thomas Brodrick] and friends in England having [?] sued [?] for, and truly by my observation of his son's [?] conduct, I find he [words illegible] safe.

As to that part relating to the disturbances [?] he might give to matters in parliament, I will not take upon me to say how far they might reach. But I cannot but think with plain war [?] that if he was to be continued his son ... [the passage which follows is particularly difficult to read: it seems to relate to getting a promise of support from Midleton's son, St. John Brodrick, and to the question of whether 'his Lordship' – probably Lord Carteret – can answer for Midleton's own good behaviour.] 'Your Grace knows the son so well that I need not trouble you with my opinion of him [?]. I am very sensible, by the present situation of affairs and the prejudices your Grace has to struggle with, that your Grace is laid under difficulties and cannot do all that is to be wished for at present. ...'

Conolly fears that Midleton's continuance in office will be interpreted as meaning '... that his interest and merit is so great that he could not be removed, nor could the King's affairs be carried on without him. But that and more must be borne. And as to my own particular, I shall never put that [words illegible] in balance with the King's affairs and the ease and quiet [?] of your Grace's administration, but I assure your Grace I have nothing at heart but that. ...

Upon the whole, I think, if my Lord Chancellor is to be continued, since you do not undertake for him, it is better that the proposal is made to your Grace by the ministers, than by you to them; for 'tis not possible to judge how he'll behave. But if matters were to be conducted ... [this passage, too, is very hard to read: the sense seems to be that if Thomas Brodrick and perhaps Carteret will undertake for Midleton's and St. John Brodrick's good behaviour] it were better than pressing them into the service. But as to this, your Grace is much a better judge, and I hope you'll pardon the freedom I have taken. ...

Brodrick talks now [?] of going over in a few days about his election that is contested.'

A/3/30 8 July 1721

Copy letter [in Mrs Conolly's clearer hand] from Conolly, Dublin, to Grafton about the terms on which Midleton is to retain his office.

A/3/30 *contd.*		'I have the honour of your Grace's of the 29 last, acquainting me with the promises that are made in behalf of our great man. I will not take up your Grace's time on that or about poor Capt. [?] Ram's [?] commission, since I hope to see your Grace soon here, and that you are so good to respite that matter till your Grace's arrival. As to what your Grace is pleased to mention about the bank, and that the government men will be soon over and that I may have an eye to our friends getting in, I can give no particular answer till I see what methods is [sic] resolved upon. When the charter arrives here I then will trouble your Grace with a letter. In the meantime, I return my hearty thanks for your Grace's friendship about my naming anybody. I am apprehensive that as matters stand circumstanced in this kingdom, through the great scarcity of money and want of trade, it will be with the utmost difficulty that many who are subscribers and others who desire to come in, will be able to raise the first payment, if it be considerable. A little time will show this. What remains at present is to assure your Grace that nobody can be more sensible of all the obligations conferred upon. ...'
A/3/31	20 Aug. [1721]	Grafton, Coventry, to Conolly about the election of Grafton's new secretary, Hopkins, for T.C.D. 'I have just time to trouble you for a minute. As Hopkins is my secretary, I hope you will be so good to take the proper measures, that he may have the same honour as was intended Mr Walpole of serving for the University. The Prince has done him the honour to write in his behalf, so that it will not be expected I should write to everybody I did before, whilst I am in the hurry of a journey, and hope to be with you so soon. I pardon parliament for not answering a letter you writ to me some time since, but as I have not writ to anybody upon that subject, in relation to the judge's place, I thought it better to be able to say so when I got over.'
A/3/32	21 Mar. 1723 [/4]	Francis Alen, Frankfort, post-marked Maynooth, to Conolly, Dublin. He believes that, following the death of Lord Newtown[butler], '... there will probably be a vacancy among the clerks in your Secretary's office: if you are not already engaged, I wish you would give me leave to place my son there a while, not so much for the profit (which I suppose is but £50 per annum), as that I would have him bred to business.'
A/3/33 A–B	11 Oct. 1723: 1724[/5]	Two letters from Lieutenant Ben. Cushin, Strabane, to Conolly, Dublin, asking him to submit the enclosed [not found] application to the Lord Lieutenant (1723), and soliciting a vacant lieutenancy in a grenadier company (1725).

A/3/34 28 Apr. 1726 Rough draft of a letter [this time in Conolly's handwriting] from Conolly, Dublin, to Thomas Clutterbuck, Secretary to the Lord Lieutenant, [Lord Carteret].
Fulsome expressions of gratitude and sincere friendship, with a reference to [Thomas] Tickell's marriage to Miss Eustace. '... I am glad my Lord Lieutenant was so graciously received [by the King]. ...'

A/3/35 30 June 1726 Clutterbuck, London, to Conolly asking him to obtain a revenue job worth £150 a year for a Mr Philips, in whom both Sir Robert Walpole and Lord Carteret interest themselves.

A/3/36 8 July 1726 List of field officers, captains, lieutenants and ensigns [in the Co. Derry militia], signed by Thomas Ash.

A/3/37 18 July 1726 Copy of a letter [in Mrs Conolly's hand] from Conolly, Custom House, Dublin, to Clutterbuck about the application on behalf of Philips.
'I have the honour of your letter of 30th of last month, which I communicated to my breathren of this board, who all agree with me in the most respectful regard for all recommendations from his Excellency [Carteret] and Mr Chancellor of the Exchequer. But I am sorry to acquaint you that we find a compliance in this case of Mr Philips to be impracticable; for excepting the few that follow, all the places in our disposal fall very short in value of his pretension, and all that comes near it require a long and thorough experience in the execution, and cannot safely be given to persons unacquainted with the laws and practice of the revenue; which you will readily believe, when I have told you that the only employment of the value desired are the clerk of the quit rents, the three surveyors-general, the collectors of this port and of the port of Cork, the collector of the inland excise of this city, and the two examiners of the customs. I shall only add that by our rules, no person can be appointed an officer in any of the upper stations who has not first served in some inferior post of the same branch.'

A/3/38 [mid-Aug. 1726] Draft of a letter [in Conolly's own handwriting] from Conolly, Dublin, to [Grafton] condoling with him on the death of his wife.

A/3/39 3 Sep. 1726 Rough draft of a letter [partly in his own handwriting] from Conolly to Clutterbuck about Philip's case [see A/3/35]. Philips has agreed to acquire experience in a lower rank of the revenue service, and the board will then advance him as he deserves. '... As Mr Philips has cheerfully accepted our offer, we hope his Excellency and Mr Chancellor [of the Exchequer] will be pleased with this instance of our respect for their command.'

A/3/40 c.5 Sep. 1726 'Abstract of receipts and payments in the Treasury Office, Dublin, from 29th August inst. to 5th September 1726.'

A/3/41 c.12 Sep. 1726 The same, from 5 to 12 September.

A/3/42 12 Dec. 1726 Clutterbuck, London, to Conolly about the death of Lord Chancellor [Richard] West and the appointment of a successor. 'I am sure this will find you extremely concerned for the loss of our friend, my Lord Chancellor, who is very much lamented here, and we who have been in Ireland know, with a great deal of reason.

My Lord Lieutenant [Carteret], as soon as the news came, determined to recommend my Lord Chief Justice [Thomas] Wyndham, in which he met with a general concurrence from all the ministry, and is this morning gone to wait upon the King, so that I take it for granted he will be the man. Though I am glad of this upon many accounts, yet upon none more than because I am persuaded, from the manner in which he always expressed himself of you, that it will not be an unacceptable thing to those whom I can't forbear wishing may be always pleased. ...'

A/3/43 22 Dec. 1726 Rough draft of a letter [in his handwriting] from Conolly, Dublin, to Clutterbuck expressing pleasure at the promotion of Wyndham. The Chief Baron has refused the vacant Chief Justiceship, and the Chief Justice of the King's Bench, [Whitshed], has applied to be removed to the Common Pleas. If this application is acceded to, Judge Gore would be a proper person to succeed to the King's Bench, and the Lords Justices have written over to that effect.

A/3/44 2 Jan. 1726[/7] Rough draft of a letter from Conolly, Dublin, to Clutterbuck announcing the death of the Archbishop of Cashel [William Palliser] and strongly recommending the Bishop of Elphin [Theophilus Bolton] as his successor. The Lord Lieutenant needs no reminding of the Bishop's eminent qualifications for the position, and it would be of great advantage to the King's affairs if he were in a see which brought him nearer to Dublin.

A/3/45 4 Jan. 1726[/7] State of [Capt. John] Pratt's [the defaulting Deputy Vice-Treasurer, dismissed in June 1725] debt to the public, endorsed by Conolly: 'from Mr Clements'.

Pratt owed £52,083 19s. 18½d, and his real and personal estates, debentures and securities will produce £43,320. In addition, his Co. Cavan and Co. Meath estates have so far realised £3,685 6s. 10½d, of which £800 14s 7½ worth was bought by Mr Clements (who paid 11 years' purchase). This leaves land worth £298 7s. per annum net still to be sold.

A/3/46	17–18 Feb. 1726[/7]	Rough drafts of a letter from Conolly, Dublin, to Clutterbuck urging the Bishop of Elphin's pretensions to the Archbishopric of Cashel [now vacant for the second time in just over a month], and giving his ideas for the string of consequential episcopal appointments. These include a recommendation that Dean Gore, now chaplain to the House of Commons, should succeed to Clonfert or some other bishopric.
A/3/47	17 May 1727	Copy of a letter [in his own handwriting] from Conolly, Dublin, to Grafton [?] about some requests concerning Lady Tyrconnell.
A/3/48	27 July 1727	[Theophilus] Clements, MP, Dublin [this must be a mistake for London], to Conolly about the dismissal of William Brodrick. 'Since I wrote your Excellency this morning, I have been with my Lord Lieutenant, who has commanded me to let you know that all commissions in his gift shall be forthwith renewed, except the second sergeant's, and that if they [sic] Lords Justices will write to him, to represent Mr William Brodrick to have been many years out of the kingdom, and that it is proper that post should be filled up, and recommend Mr Dixon, he will give it to him, for he only wants a handle to turn him out. I believe he intends this as a step to make Dixon a judge. All the posts in his Majesty's gift will be renewed. He tells me that my pension is safe ... Mr Herbert does not leave this in a month. The letter goes tonight.'
A/3/49	29 July 1727	Theophilus Clements, London, to Conolly about the appointment of a new Revenue Commission, upon the accession of King George II. 'What I wrote to your Excellency last post about Mr Medlicott was declared yesterday. I was only concerned that I should have been the author, in case it had not been made public; for I wrote it without any reserve, imagining the letter would have been sent over last post. Mr Herbert, Lord Pembroke's second son, who was Groom of the Bedchamber to his late Majesty, whose wife is daughter to the Speaker, Smith, and one of the dressers to her Majesty, is his successor, and is preparing to go immediately to Dublin. I was yesterday evening to take my leave of Mr Edgcumbe. Lord Falmouth's letter and his were signed a Tuesday, before their Majesties went to Winglington [?]. He goes this day to Cornwall, where he makes no doubt of success in his elections. His colleague and he will have a good understanding in that affair. My Lord Lieutenant yesterday desired me to let you know that Mr Southwell had promised him that Sir Robert Maude, who he hears is in distress at Irishtown, shall be elected at Downpatrick in the place of Mr Medlicott, and would have you acquaint Sir Robert with it, and my Lord Burlington has promised him that Sir John Osborne shall be elected at Lismore.

A/3/49 *contd.*		I have many compliments to you from Mr Edgcumbe, who is very much your humble servant. ...'
A/3/50	c.16 Oct. 1727	Abstract of receipts and payments in the Treasury, 7–16 October 1727.
A/3/51	28 May 1728	Alexander Montgomery, Dublin, to [Conolly] informing him that General [Abraham] Creighton is about to die, and asking to succeed him.
A/3/52	1 June 1728	Rough copy of a letter from Conolly to Lord Carteret recommending Colonel 'Dollway' as Creighton's successor.
A/3/53	8 Oct. 1728	Sarah Gage, Garvagh, to Isaac Manley, Post-Master General, Dublin.

'We are informed that application has been made to you to change the post-mistress of Coleraine. It may not therefore be amiss to inform you who and what the person is that is endeavouring this change, and the vileness of the motives inducing him to effect it. As in most parts of this kingdom so in Coleraine here has been some struggling and divisions about who should represent the corporation. My Lord Tyrone and the Jacksons were the two contending parties. Now Coleraine belonging to the Society of London, my Lord Tyrone employs one Richardson (who had lately been in the service of my Lord Louth and is now concerned for one Mr Edwards, the Hollow Blade gentleman) to solicit the Society in my Lord's favour. This Richardson, in conjunction with Mr Edwards having lately taken the fishery of Coleraine from the Society and also undermined the widow Gorge in the Merchant Tailors' proportion, was thereby well acquainted with the way to an application of Society, and prevailed on them to write to this their corporation in favour of himself, to their great surprise, notwithstanding the major part of the corporation thought fit to reject him. However he has lodged his petition.

Now Mr Conolly, your Speaker, having some of the proportion lands and a very great desire to have more that very shortly will fall out of lease, he is paying great court to Mr Richardson to negotiate his affairs in England, he himself being a little too big to cringe to a company of mechanics or their clerks, to which there's an absolute necessity. And in return for this Mr Richardson promises himself Mr Conolly's favour. Now in order to pave his way to carry his election, he is endeavouring to punish those who have or will give him opposition and to encourage those who seem to favour his pretensions. And first he wrote to the Society some false informations against Alderman Charles Church, a gentleman that has been agent to the Society many years, in hopes to succeed him in that business, but was disappointed. Now Alderman Church

A/3/53 *contd.*		being a charter justice of the peace this Richardson procures some false affidavits against the alderman in hope to have him disfranchised. What those affidavits were and their success the judges of the last assizes can best inform you. Another of Mr Richardson's cruelties is this; here is one Mr Every, a clergyman, who has £30 a year from the Society for being a schoolmaster. Now because this man was not in his interest, he wrote to the Society and falsely represented him as very unfit to be schoolmaster, and this poor man has a numerous family of children. Another of Mr Richardson's cruelties is this. Here are two young ladies, relations of my own, whose father is dead, and all their support is by the little profits arising by a lease of some lands which they hold under the Bishop of Derry. I understand you are well acquainted with his Lordship and may prevent Richardson's cruelty to them, he having a design to undermine them in the renewal with his Lordship because they have not nor cannot say anything in his favour. ...' The present post-mistress, Mrs Jordan, bears a good character, and if she is replaced by a creature of Richardson's many gentlemen of the county will feel that their letters are not safe. [Missing]
A/3/54	24 Jan. 1728/9 [?]	Lord Tyrone, Curraghmore, [Co. Waterford], to [Conolly] about a Coleraine job. 'I was honoured with your Lordship's of the 31st of last month, and I should not have been so long in returning your Lordship my most humble thanks for your great favours, but that I have been much out of order with the gout in both my feet and right hand, and it is with some difficulty I am now writing. My Lord, I am sensible of your Lordship's friendship to me by providing for Lyon [Lynam?] but I can't tell whether it will be agreeable to my friends at Coleraine to have him removed so far as Waterford, but Colonel McCausland being in town will inform your Lordship. ...'
A/4	c.1718–24	c.65 letters and petitions to William Conolly as Lord Justice and First Commissioner of the Revenue making patronage request, particularly for jobs in the Revenue, and thanking him for requests granted.
A/5/1	30 Dec. 1690	Letter to William Conolly's father-in-law, Sir Albert Conyngham, Mount Charles, [Co. Donegal], from Colonel Frederick Hamilton, Dublin, about the affairs of Conyngham's regiment and about Conyngham's hopes of being appointed Lt-General of the Ordnance.
A/6	1706–19	c.100 letters and papers of William Conolly, as executor to his brother-in-law, Major-General Henry Conyngham [who had

A/6 *contd.*		been killed in battle in Spain in January 1706] about reimbursement due to Conyngham's estate on account of 'off-reckonings' – i.e. expenditure by Conyngham out of his personal resources on regimental clothing and accoutrements.
A/7	1697–1714	c.12 letters, with related papers, to William and Katherine Conolly from her sister and brother-in-law, Mary and Richard Jones of Dollanstown, Co. Meath. Relations between the Conollys and Joneses were generally strained, and there is, for example, a pained letter from Mary Jones to her sister, [1708?], about the political reasons for Conolly's decision not to return Richard Jones again for the borough of Killybegs.
A/8	c. 1721–5	c.15 letters to Katherine Conolly from her widowed sister, Mrs Jane Bonnell – mostly very brief, but mentioning Lord Sunderland and some political matters.
A/9	1735; 1744–7	c.25 letters to Lady Anne Conolly, wife of William Conolly's nephew and principal heir, William Conolly junior, from the widowed Katherine Conolly, writing from Castletown and Dublin, 1744–7, together with 3 other items of Lady Anne's correspondence, one of them a letter from her to her 'brother' [Lord Strafford] describing a punch-up at a ball in Dublin Castle, [1735].
A/10/ 1–6	1760–1801: N.D.	c.75 personal and political letters to Thomas Conolly of Castletown, son and successor of William Conolly junior (d.1754) and Lady Anne Conolly, arranged as follows:
A/10/1	1760–65	Folder of personal and political letters to Thomas Conolly, including:
	8 Sep. 1761	Apollos Morris, London, to Conolly. About the arrival of the Queen at Harwich. 'Her person is, even after her fatigue, [so] pleasing that they call her a good prize.'
	19 Sep. 1761	Robert Clements, St James's Coffee House, [London], to Conolly giving an account of the royal wedding. Her Majesty is not handsome. She has some resemblance to Lady Headfort.
	26 Sep. 1761	Apollos Morris, London, to Conolly reporting that a Spanish war much talked of.
	29 Sep. 1761	Apollos Morris, London, to Conolly reporting news from the War Office about increased recruiting. Those now recruiting have so raised the prices [i.e. the bounty paid to each recruit] that the old corps may give up.

A/10/1 *contd.*	29 Sep. 1761	Robert Clements, Dublin, to Conolly commenting on the coronation. Mr Conolly's chaise at Mr Wright's now ready.
	1 Oct. 1761	Benjamin Harenc, Greenwich, to Conolly. The general English conversation is about the coronation, which is tiresome. War with Spain expected.
	8 Oct. 1761	Apollos Morris to Conolly on Pitt's resignation over the measures in regard to Spain and Portugal.
	6 Dec. [1761]	Lady Anne Conolly, Wrotham Park [near Barnet, Middlesex, seat of George Byng senior the husband of her daughter Anne], to Conolly ('My dearest son'). Mentioning among other things the possibility of a peerage for him. '... Have you laid aside all thoughts of nobility? This is the time to ask it. I agree with you in wishing Mr Byng had some preferment in Ireland. I otherwise fear his being sent next summer to some part of the East or West Indies. ... Many prudential reasons have determined my late stay in the country, for as this place is very expensive to me, the only way to lighten that is living a good deal at it. I hope Mr Clark[e] will send my daughters' money soon, and if you are so good to let me have £500 by Christmas (having then many bills to pay), I shall not want to hurry you for the rest, but will leave it to you to send when convenient. ... I am obliged to you for sending me the particulars of poor Miss Knox's tragical fate. ... What a dreadful example of the dismal effects of ungoverned passion. ...'
	20 Feb. 1762	Benjamin Harenc, London, to Conolly on 'the public and almost universal report' of Lady Louisa's pregnancy.
	18 Mar. 1762	Harenc to Conolly, who has been made a Privy Councillor. 'I will give you up for my patron as to military preferments.'
	25 Jan. 1763	[J. Calcraft?], Munster, to Conolly. The troops ordered to march through Holland. Lord Granby dangerously ill. Writer in charge of a division of cavalry.
	1 Feb. 1763	Benjamin Harenc [London] to Conolly. Bay Boulton, his horse, is the admiration of Hyde Park.
	3 Feb. 1763	Lady A[nne] Conolly, London, to 'Dear Son. I last night received a draft from Mr Crane for £84 01s. 9d., which he says is the balance of his accounts to the 5th of last month. I have sent him a receipt for it, and enclose you an abstract of what I have received on my November half year, and should be glad you sent me the rest as soon as it suits your convenience. ...'

A/10/1 *contd.*	11 Feb. 1763	Harenc, London, to Conolly about horses and hounds.
	15 Sep. 1763	Henry Vernon [of Hilton Park, Wolverhampton, Staffordshire, husband of Conolly's aunt, Lady Henrietta Wentworth], Savile Row, [London] to Conolly. Endorsed by Conolly 'About Water Eaton estate [Oxfordshire]'. '… The estimate Mr Crane made of our estate at Water Eaton …' was 35 years' purchase of a rental of £1,449 16s. 0d. per annum, plus timber valued at £1,000, making £51,743. '… I represented to him that, though people might talk of 35 years' purchase for estates, I did not expect to find bidders upon such terms. However, I sent his valuation to the Duke of Marlborough by his agent, Mr Butcher, and informed him that we agreed to abate £3,000 of our steward's valuation. I received a letter from him whilst I was at Hilton to say the Duke of Marlborough was obliged to us for a sight of the valuation, but could not think of becoming a purchaser upon those terms. If he would have treated, I had your authority and had left room for abatement. But we ought not, I think, to drop the estate too fast, and had better try somebody else first, or old Crane will be very angry indeed if we hold his advice so cheap, though if you please we will take upon ourselves to have some opinion of our own. …'
	29 Nov. 1763	Thomas Knox to Conolly informing him of George Lo[w]ther's proposal to address the King for £1,500 for Arthur Mervyn's mills. Racing. Bagenal and friends to match Ferdinand against Apollo.
	15 Mar. [1764?]	George Byng [senior, of Wrotham Park, Middlesex, husband of Conolly's sister, Anne], Bond Street, to 'My dear Conolly'. Reporting that Mr Waple has marked his 'friendship and affection' for the Byngs by leaving, out of a fortune of £33,000, £20,000 to Byng and the rest to his brother, '… as my mother has so much more than she can spend …'. Byng goes on to thank Conolly warmly for his two attempts to induce the government to promote Byng in the army, even though these have met with no success. '… I suppose I have been represented as one declaiming at the present measures. This I confess freely to you I have done. That is a fault (if there is any) of my education. Bred up in contrary principles to the reigning ones now, I am sure you would not wish me to become a weathercock, for if one acts in one shape against principle, I am afraid the rest of one's actions will be guided by chance. I know very well the latitude you give to mankind, and therefore can more freely talk to you upon this subject. I know that you think that man honest that acts up to what he thinks, though perhaps his opinion may not altogether draw with yours. I hope, therefore, my dear Conolly, that if you should hear that my

A/10/1 *contd.* name is erased from the list of soldiers, you will not think that I have been too impatient, but that I bore [for] a proper time all the insults of power ...'

2 Nov. 1764 Lady Anne Conolly, Stretton [Hall, Staffordshire (fifteen miles from Wolverhampton)] to 'My dear son'.
'... I deferred answering your letter till I had settled all your accounts here with Mr Crane, of which I enclose you an abstract, and have added by way of memoranda some things for you to consider of and answer at your leisure. ... I have planted a good many trees in the ground before the house and am now busy at the sunk fence, and shall be happy if the little improvements I make meets [sic] with your approbation. ...'

23 Nov. 1764 George Grenville, Downing Street, to Conolly requesting him to attend parliament [at Westminster].

A/10/2 1771–6 Folder of personal and political letters to Thomas Conolly, including:

3 June 1771 Draft of a hostile letter from Conolly, Castletown, to Lord [—]. Disagreement over racing.

5 Oct. 1773 [Simon Harcourt, 1st Earl] Harcourt [Lord Lieutenant of Ireland], Dublin Castle, to Conolly requesting him to move the address to his Majesty.

6 Oct. 1773 Conolly's reply to Lord Harcourt. Such motions are usually made by younger Map's.

3 Feb. 1774 Lord Harcourt, Dublin Castle, to Conolly explaining that he has appointed Mr Moore to the surveyorship of Derry, for which Conolly had recommended Mr O'Neill.

3 Feb. 1774 Conolly's reply to Lord Harcourt.

26 Mar. 1774 J. Henry, Dublin, to Conolly about the clause in the Fishery Bill which the writer believes is aimed directly at Conolly. The clause grants full permission to every person worth £1,000 capital or £40 p.a. rental income in any county to fish the banks of any river in that county. He annexes a House of Lords division list on the clause.

4 May 1774 Lord Harcourt, Dublin Castle, to Conolly replying to Conolly's request (draft attached) for a bishopric for Dean Woodward. 'The Archbishop of Cashel is not dead, nor is the see of Tuam likely to be soon vacant, for the Archbishop is said to enjoy as good a state

A/10/2 *contd.*

of health as usually falls to the share of persons so far advanced in years as he is. I am uncertain how far it may be in the power of the Crown to separate the bishopric of Ardagh from the see of Tuam, but I have no doubt of the inexpediency of such a measure because I don't apprehend the present income of it to be more than barely sufficient to support the archpiscopal [sic] dignity.

My principal object ever must be to pay the greatest regard and attention to those who contribute most to the support of government, and I wish I had wherewithal not only to satisfy them, but to gratify the wishes of my friends. But if that should not be the case, I trust they will be candid enough to impute it, not to want of inclination on my part, but for [sic] want of proper opportunities of doing it.

I know that Dean Woodward is your friend, and that he is a man of spirit, and as such I am sorry he has met with any disappointments, but I should be much more concerned if any of those disappointments could be laid at my door. ...'

16 July 1775 — Lady Anne Conolly, Twickenham, to 'My dear son.
I was happy to receive your kind letter of the 2nd and ... assure you that I love you too well to put a wrong construction on any seeming omission you are guilty of, neither would it be for my ease to believe your want of attention was owing to want of affection. I hope your tour to the North will be as little disagreeable as possible, considering the business that carries you there. ... I gave you in my last an account of what I had received from Mr Cole, having but just heard from him. As he pleads his bad health as an excuse for his delays, I have advised him not to involve himself in more business than he can go through with ease and punctuality. ...'
She encloses a receipt for rents received from some English property [Stretton Hall and/or Water Eaton?], which amount, when translated into Irish money to, £750.

6 Sep. 1775 — T[homas] Townshend, Cleveland Court, [London], to Conolly. About the debate in the Irish House of Commons over the proposal to send 4,000 troops out of Ireland and replace them with 4,000 foreign troops, if required. Those latter are to be Scottish or Dutch. So Great Britain is to pay the troops being sent to America from Ireland.

A/10/3 1783–4 — Folder of personal and political letters to Thomas Conolly, including:

18 Feb. 1783 — George Byng senior, Berkeley Square, to Conolly, Castletown about the formation of the Fox-North coalition. He requests Conolly 'not to show his letter to anybody but Lady Louisa and [General John] Burgoyne.'

A/10/3 *contd.*	2 Apr. 1783	Robert Hobart, St James's Square, to Conolly, Merrion Street about recent ministerial appointments in England.
	6 Sep. 1783	H. Carncross [identified by Mrs Boylan as Major Hugh Carncross of Roselawn, Celbridge], Strasbourg, to [Conolly] about the educational progress and the general activities of [George] Byng [junior, Conolly's nephew, whom Carncross is evidently accompanying as tutor on the grand tour].
	29 Sep. 1783	[Robert Henley, 2nd Earl of] Northington [Lord Lieutenant of Ireland], Phoenix Lodge, to Conolly. Details of his engagements which prevent him meeting Conolly on a certain day.
	8 Oct. 1783	Printed pro forma letter addressed from Union Lodge, Loughbrickland, Co. Down, sent to Conolly by James Dawson, Secretary to the Ulster Volunteer Committee. The plan of Parliamentary Reform as submitted to the Delegates of the Volunteer Army of Ulster on 8 Sep. 1783.
	12 Oct. 1783	H. Carncross, Strasbourg, to Conolly about George Byng junior and their travels together.
	18 Oct. 1783	George Byng to Conolly, Merrion Street. The Bishop of Derry and the Volunteers are going too far.
	16 Dec. 1783	Lesley Alexander, Limavady, to Conolly urging him to support a bill for banning the exportation of linen yarn. 'The linen committee of Dublin sent by the last post to this town [a] copy of a petition they have laid before parliament showing the expediency of preventing the exportation of linen yarn from this kingdom. All people concerned in the trade here coincide in the same opinion, and this day have sent their petition hoping you will be pleased to prefer and support the same. I hope you will see the salutary purpose of it, for from the present high price of yarn occasioned by factors buying up such quantities for the English market that the weavers and manufacturers of linen cannot earn 6d. per day, which from the present price of bread is not able to maintain them; and therefore it will absolutely oblige the people in the province of Ulster to emigrate to America for the mere purpose of providing a maintenance for themselves and families. ... Scarce any event would add more to your honour, interest or fame, for if the inhabitants of this land will not acknowledge this favour done them, the face of nature herself – nay the hills and dales – will echo the name of Mr Conolly with approbation and applause. I have heard you say you wish to hear the notable occurrences of this country, and therefore have made free to write this letter.'

A/10/3 *contd.* [Dec. 1783] Lord Northington to Conolly enclosing a copy of a resolution passed in the British House of Commons. Pitt v. Fox. The latter's speech very fine.

[Dec. 1783] Lord Northington to Conolly informing him of Lord Temple's resignation of the seals of the Home Department, which he had received only the previous Friday. Various offices mentioned. 'I long to be with you at Castletown and get a quiet night's sleep unbroke in upon by messengers, and a good day's exercise, with the society of the long room in the evening.'

21 Dec. 1783 [John Hobart, 2nd Earl of] Buckingham[shire*, lord lieutenant of Ireland, 1776–80, and husband of Conolly's sister, Caroline] to Conolly.
Lord Temple's successful operations in the Closet. How he accepted the seals two days after he had been informed that he might be impeached. The insane attempts at influence of the Bishop of Derry [Frederick Hervey] and his followers.

25 Jan. 1784 William Peacock to Conolly.
Meeting of the county of Anglesey concerning a road across the river Menai. A stone bridge to be built across the river, estimated to cost £26,500.

25 Jan. 1784 Luke Gardiner to Sir Michael [Cromie] reporting the outcome of a negotiation he has had with Mr Vernon in London, and advising '... Mr Conolly to lose no time in settling the business with Lord Northington.' [This seems to refer to Richard Vernon, younger brother of Conolly's uncle-by-marriage, Henry Vernon, and Clerk of the Quit Rents in Ireland. The proposal appears to be that Richard Vernon should resign the office in favour of Cromie (whose name has not so far been mentioned to him), and that Cromie through Conolly's influence should then obtain a re-grant of the office for Cromie's life.] Vernon '... is entirely sensible of the advantage this transaction will be of to him, and determined to do everything Mr Conolly could wish ..., [but] hinted that he supposed Mr Conolly would be answerable to him for the payment of the full salary without deductions.' [This must mean that Vernon, as an absentee from Ireland, was paying absentee tax, which Cromie, as a resident, would not. Since Cromie had been born *c.* 1744 and Vernon in 1726, there was every probability that a life-grant to Cromie would easily see Vernon out and in the meantime would increase Vernon's net income from the office. The Northington administration was presumably not going to be admitted to the details of the arrangement, and was too well

* Though earl of Buckinghamshire, Hobart always signed himself 'Buckingham', even after the Lord Temple mentioned in this letter was created marquess of Buckingham in 1784.

A/10/3 *contd.*		disposed towards Conolly to ask awkward questions. Nothing in any case came of the negotiation, presumably because the Fox-North coalition in Great Britain fell from power and Northington was replaced as lord lieutenant.]
	24 Feb. 1784	Lord Buckinghamshire to Conolly on Pitt's proceedings in the House of Commons. '... The Duke of Rutland is possibly by this time with you. The Earl Temple laboured at his head for several days preceding his departure, and all the milliners in London are now labouring to accomplish her Grace's. Some time since you will be able to inform me whether his Excellency shines most in the Cabinet or the Vice-Queen in the ballroom. From appearances it may be presumed that Beresford will be first Minister, and as the grateful Robinson deserting Lord North is principal whipper-in to the present ministry, his Grace's credit will have the full support *at home* of that secret influence which damned me. You will see him at his hours of dissipation, as I am told he says he means to hunt with Tom Conolly. ...'
	28 Feb. 1784	Sir John Coghill to Conolly reports on the condition of the English fleet in America and on the dispute between Lord Macartney and General 'Stewart', who was cast into a dungeon. [This refers to Macartney's action, as Governor of Madras, in placing the commander of the forces there, General John Stuart, under arrest and sending him back to England.]
	6 June 1784	George Ash [agent for Conolly's Limavady estate], Ash Brook, [Co. Londonderry] to Conolly expressing satisfaction that Conolly no longer seems to think that Ash had mismanaged his affairs. [See the Conolly Papers TCD, No. 850]. '... Were you here, I make no doubt but the tenants would comply with the terms you have mentioned. ... I will go to Newtown tomorrow and do everything I can. I will try what can be done as to the setting of your house. Lord B[ristol's] political fever is returned. ... [I] wish much that some person of consequence such as you, Lord Tyrone and Mr Beresford, would come to the country [sic] and countenance us, as it certainly would be a means to quiet the minds of the people. ...'
	7 June 1784	Lord Buckinghamshire to Conolly. 'If your Lord Lieutenant [The Duke of Rutland] is generally intoxicated, his subjects are not always sober.'
A/10/4	1791–4	Folder of personal and political letters to Thomas Conolly, including:
	17 Sep. 1791	Lady Anne Conolly, London, to Conolly, Merrion Street about her inheritance from her brother, Lord Strafford.

A/10/4
contd.

'... I came here last night in order to have the house in St James's Square given up to me today, the inventory being swore to and given up to Mr Boodle, to whom I have given security for the payment of the money out of the dividend I am to receive at Michaelmas. I am going to the house to look over what I have paid for, and shall make my housekeeper see 'tis in order for your reception, and hope you won't think of going to any other place, but will give me the pleasure of seeing you take possession of it ... .

In regard to the partition of the estates that comes [sic] to me, and the value of them, if you settle it to your satisfaction and in the way that is most to your advantage, that will be answerable to my wishes, who desire to make you easy as far as in my power, and to convey my share of them to you by any deed that is requisite. As to your *farther schemes*, I wish they may succeed, but fear there is little chance of it. ...'

23 Jan. 1793 — William Cruise [the lawyer who advised him on his English estate affairs (see F/5–6)], Lincoln's Inn, to Conolly about proposals for reforming parliament in Ireland.

29–30 Mar. 1793 — Draft letter from Conolly to [his brother-in-law, Charles Lennox, 3rd] Duke of Richmond [a member of Pitt's cabinet]. Acquainting him with the ills of Ireland [original in TNA, HO 100/43, ff 169–73:
'... [From] the comparative expenses of government in Lord Townshend's time and at the present day, you will see the enormous increase of every expense, mostly incurred by corruption (in the last war, the greatest part of our army being sent by our Parliament for America, saved us so much expense), and this corruption has not procured either a quiet, peaceable or respectable government, but just the reverse. It has been a government working everything by force and coercion, always leading to and giving excuse for further expense, *vide* police, etc.; and now I will venture to say that, at the beginning of a war, by the improvidence in time of peace, she is almost destitute of resources to defend ourselves [sic] or to assist Great Britain, her excess of expenditure over income last year being by our Chancellor of Exchequer's own calculation £153,000. When a private man outruns the constable, it is on [sic] no consequence to the state, but when a nation does so, its government loses its energy, and everything goes to confusion. Its parliament may vote money, but people won't lend what extravagant government cannot secure. In 1779 we were unable to pay about 4,000 men, till assisted by Great Britain, who lent us £50,000 and gave us £50,000 more. What way shall we now be able to pay 36,000 including militia?

A/10/4
contd.

Don't imagine I wish to recommend one set of men for government in preference to those now in office. I will venture to assert that none of those with whom I am politically connected would undertake any situation of personal responsibility in the present situation of affairs. But *I* would wish to have our present constitution, though extravagantly worked, go on, in spite of what levellers, republicans and Frenchmen with to put in the place of it.

You must first get national confidence and credit to get money, and you must leave off extravagance and corruption to get that confidence. The latter has not answered the purpose for which it was intended of a strong and respectable government, and the first has very nearly annihilated all government, for the want of means to go on on the present extended system. Do you think that the government of France would have been convulsed and annihilated, if she had had the means of carrying on her extravagant, corrupt system? You must alter your system here, or we are undone; and I do not believe that our ruin will forward your prosperity.

You must give us a Place Bill and Pension Bill, similar to your own, or at least as much so as the relative situation of the two kingdoms will admit. We shall not differ about trifles. A Responsibility Bill ... may be got the better of by an *Irish Board of Treasury*. An official place of £1,500 per annum might be created – a Privy Seal, for example – without any further expense, taken out of the £11 a year now paid to *innumerable useless Privy Counsellors*, and the Board of Treasury will be paid for out of the salaries of our *English-Irish useless Vice-Treasurers.*

But all our new-created boards and places for undue influence must cease, unless our worthy Chancellor of the Exchequer can show where he is to get the money, without altering the frugal mode of living of the industrious part of the community, luxuries being almost as much taxed here as in Great Britain. The common answer to all attacks upon corruption is that government must be supported. But I will venture to assert, from my own experience in Parliament, that opposition to government has increased here, in proportion to its extravagance, by the adhesion of those Patriots who might wish for a similar distribution of loaves and fishes, and of some from more disinterested motives, and from the people out of doors, from the weight of taxes, and from the expectation of many to be provided for once their political champions should come into power. This keeps us in a continual ferment, and I would rather pay soldiers than members of Parliament to keep the peace of the country. Upon that principle I have encouraged and supported government in the establishment of a militia, which will in time, *without saying it*, get the better of Volunteering, and will preserve us hereafter from Oakboys, Steelboys, Whiteboys, Rightboys, Peep-of-Day Boys and Defenders – all which I have seen in my time, to the distress of our national credit, and to the

A/10/4 *contd.*

loss of [?character] and to the attempt to annihilate government itself. But money must be found to pay for it, and you cannot continue to pay Parliament, as now paid, and to pay the militia likewise. A Parliament so paid, can never command respect: a militia may defend our lives and properties.

The opposition here have given no peevish impediment to government this session, unless you say that offering a plan of reform is such. That was called for from the throne, for when you admit all the sans culottes 40 shilling Catholic freeholders into the constitution and leave the same undefined power of purchase in the minister, you create a necessity and of course an excuse for so much additional corruption to pay the additional expense of the candidate – all ultimately paid for by the people. Therefore, amongst a people over-taxed, where is the money to be found? You must reform corruption. A Place Bill, a Pension Bill, a Qualification bill and an Election Bill, will go a great way towards it, and I think I could venture to assert that your government *then* can meet with but little or no opposition here, either in or out of doors, and if we are to go to blows with our fellow-creatures, let us start in the right.

At the time we voted our army here 36,000 men, militia included, our ministry declared their intention of assimilating our constitution to that of Great Britain. Give us therefore the bills in question, and you will have the gratitude, thanks and support of this kingdom, and every exertion will be made to bear all the necessary expense in question. If not, and if the present system is to be pursued, take all the consequences upon yourselves, and remember that the opposition of Ireland will ultimately be the ruin of Great Britain. ...'

4 July 1793 — J. Williamson to Conolly reporting the death of Mr E. Shepherd, a young gentleman of the 32nd Regiment [and son of the Rev. Shepherd of Celbridge.]

4 Feb. 1794 — Sir Laurence Parsons 5th Bt. to Conolly.
He is strongly of the opinion that the French will descend upon Ireland. Only 10,698 troops are available for its defence.

19 Mar. 1794 — George Byng junior, St James's Square, to Conolly, his uncle, Drogheda, where Conolly's militia regiment was stationed.
'I must return you *many, many* thanks for your kind letter ... . There is no mark of attention or affection that can be thrown away upon me. I must be very sensible of them, and love so deeply rooted cannot easily be eradicated. I could enlarge much upon this subject, were I to express half what I felt upon it, but to proceed to business: I must inform you that the furniture, wine, kitchen utensils, etc, are packed up and I hope will arrive safe ... . I had the

A/10/4 *contd.*

coals gauged upon my first entering the house. It was supposed by the coal merchant to contain about 40 pounds' worth, which I will of course allow you when I next draw for my interest. I had flattered myself that you would have returned shortly to England and I meant in that case to have replaced them. The wine you have given me, as coming from you, must be particularly grateful: even to an indifferent person, it must be reckoned good. ...

I explained very fully your sentiments to Fox with respect to the affairs of Ireland. He laments with me that good and moderate men are unable from the circumstances of the times and from want of support to take any decided part. The part you will take will no doubt be honourable to yourself and conducive to the dearest and best interests of your country. Your presence at this time among your militia cannot fail to be of use. ...

Your mother continues well. I am in favour. It must be always pleasing to me to be beloved by my family, and I know that I shall never deserve to forfeit their affection or good opinion. ...'

13 June 1794 — [John Fane, 10th Earl of] Westmoreland [the Lord Lieutenant] to Conolly communicating Lord Howe's victory of the 1st of June over the French fleet; together with a draft of Conolly's reply, written from Castletown.

5 Oct. 1794 — John Forbes [MP for Drogheda], London, to Conolly, Dublin, giving him the good news that Lord Fitzwilliam is to be lord lieutenant and [Thomas] Grenville his secretary.

A/10/5 1797 — Folder of personal and political letters to Thomas Conolly, including:

5 Jan. 1797 — N. Frost, Cove, to Major Carncross, M.P. [for Limavady, Conolly's borough, which Conolly sold shortly after returning Carncross in 1795], College Green, Dublin about activities of the fleet at Cork.

[pre-13 Jan.] 1797 — Draft of a letter from Conolly to the Prince of Wales about the state of Ireland.

14 Jan. 1797 — Frost, Cove, to Major Carncross.
'Utterly impossible' for the French to escape. General Hoche's coach is aboard this transport. Some of his horses had to be thrown over in the gale of wind. 'Though most of the French are old soldiers, they are all young men. The name of the transport ship taken is "La Ville L'Orient".'

17 Jan. 1797 — [John Bligh, 4th Earl of] Darnley to [Lady Louisa] about a letter from Ireland [obviously Conolly's] which Darnley was alleged to have had charge of for delivery to the Prince of Wales.

A/10/5 *contd.* 4 Feb. 1797 Dr Will. Nesbitt, Drogheda, to Conolly.
Nesbitt's grandfather was an officer in King William's army and his father a clergyman of the Established Church, and 'I was bred up with a total abhorrence of Popery'. But 'being early in life a curate in the shire town of Westmeath (a very Popish county), had the happiness to live for many years in the greatest intimacy with the principal gentlemen of that religion.' They were loyal to a degree and wanted only to have the Gavel Act repealed. He cites the case of Sir Patrick Bellew. 'Lord Temple, accompanied by his Popish wife and her bigoted father, Lord Nugent'. 'The Viceregal coach was seen regularly at the mass house – the Presbyterians always Republican and alive to anarchy and confusion and in their hearts abhor the RCs.'

9 Feb. 1797 Sir Michael Cromie 1st Bt., London, to Conolly.
He has presented Conolly's dispatches to the Prince of Wales who was most impressed by Conolly's sentiments. [For the main run of Cromie's letters of this period (which contain some incidental political comment), see F/5–6.

The 'dispatches' comprised a letter to the Prince of Wales from the Duke of Leinster, Lord Charlemont, Conolly and W.B. Ponsonby, together presumably with enclosures. It is printed in A. Aspinall (ed.), *The correspondence of George, Prince of Wales, 1770–1812*, vol. 3, (London, 1965), pp. 320–21, where it is described as a letter from 'Thomas Conolly and others'. A copy exists, probably in Lady Louisa's handwriting, among the Leinster Papers (NLI, MS 41,552/46). It is dated 'June', and it is clear from other evidence that another 'embassy' and/or letter went to the Prince, *c* 13 June 1797.]

16 Feb. 1797 General R[ichard] Vyse [husband of Georgiana, the daughter of Sir George Howard and Conolly's aunt, Lady Lucy Wentworth], Lambeth, to Conolly, Merrion Square [sic], Dublin announcing the death of Conolly's mother, Lady Anne. He begins: '… I know how little you like being troubled with letters …'.

28 Feb. 1797 Mrs A[nne] Byng, Berkeley Square, to Conolly, Merrion Street, Dublin about their mother's death.
'Your very kind and friendly letters of the 22nd and 23rd are just arrived, and I can't express the satisfaction I feel in finding your sentiments so well agree with mine. Litigation must be always horrible, and with the brother I have so long and so dearly loved would appear indeed in its most hideous form. … Sir M. Cromie of course sent you an account of my poor mother's will, but perhaps did not mention all particulars. The service of plate is yours, and *your* picture and the Pains of Castletown in the drawing room in Grosvenor Square are Lady Louisa's. You know *our*

A/10/5 *contd.*

legacies, and £800 each to all her granddaughters, £400 [to] Caroline Vernon, £200 [to] Jane Vernon. … Lady B[uckinghamshire] means to sell the house in Grosvenor Square. Lady Howe wishes much to live at Twickenham, if she can afford it (but Sir W. prefers Hampshire). If Staples dies before Lady H., Twickenham will be in her power. But what you so kindly wish in regard to what Staples gets, is not fixed as you mention. It is a much less sum than was expected, for the executors say that, when all the legacies and debts are paid, there will be £24,000 remaining, and his legacy is no more than £9,000, as he has no house in present. My dear mother had promised to buy me the house I rent on Mount Ephraim, and she talked of it every time I saw her this winter, and said, when Lord Thurlow paid her what was due, I should have it. But it was not in the will. … I never saw anybody look so ill in my life [as Staples]. I saw him but once. His brother *is* always with him and will probably get him to make a will in his favour. … Lady Howe assures me over and over she never said anything aggravating to my mother in regard to you, and she begged I would tell you how much it was her wish to live in friendship with you and Lady L. …'

2 Mar. 1797

[Sir Ralph Gore, 6th Bt, one and only Earl of] Ross, Belleisle, [Co. Fermanagh], to 'My dear Mr Conolly', Merrion Street. 'Though I fear that I had entirely lost the affection and regard your mother at one time professed to have for me, yet I own I was much affected at the account of her death which I received from you, and am really sorry to find that she persevered to the last in accusing you of having imposed upon her. God forgive them that were the cause of this. I shall very shortly be in town and shall at any time be ready to declare what I did before in London relative to my conversations with Lady Anne Conolly. …' Conolly has endorsed this: 'Ready to give testimony as to the deed of appointment'.

25 Mar. 1797

Anne Byng [Mrs George Byng senior, Conolly's sister] , Berkeley Square, to Conolly, Merrion Street.
'… My poor mother's executors won't pay the legacies she left till the year is near come round again, as the stocks are so low they say Staples would be quite ruined were they to pay them now … . He went to Bath the week after my mother's death, where he remains, and leaves all business to Sir W. Howe, Mr Hoare and Mr Boodle. He writes word he is much better in health. Lady Buckingham[shire] is trying to sell the house in Grosvenor Square. … My house on Mount Ephraim [Tunbridge Wells, Kent] is to be sold (with another belonging to the same lady and the gardens and a field of six acres) for about £2,500. I think of buying them and selling off the smaller house, and I must pay interest till I can

A/10/5 *contd.*

receive my £6,000 to pay the principal. My poor mother … said she would go as far as £3,000, but as she did not put this in her will, I have no claim … . General Vyse is going to command in the Isle of Wight and has been so kind to name John [Byng, her second son] his aide-de-camp. … George [Byng, her eldest son] desires his kindest love (with my girls) to you and dear Lady Louisa. He will have the house in St James's Square to furnish by degrees from top to bottom (all the furniture now in it being left to Lady Howe and directed to be sent to Twickenham …). The Chancellor will decide *how* Lord Strafford's money is to go hereafter. It was always said nothing would be fixed till it became George's. …'

3 Apr. 1797 — Henry Vernon [junior (son of Henry senior)], 'Chritchell' [Dorset], to Conolly [his cousin].
He reports that he has been on hunting parties with the Prince of Wales, and comments on lawsuits over the Strafford inheritance. '… A few days past I called on Lord Strafford, who resides at a miserable place seven miles from here [Henbury]. I asked his Lordship if he had received any letter lately from you. He told me he had, to explain that by the death of your mother you now became unavoidably a party in a suit instituted by the Duke of Leeds against him. His Lordship told me that he knew the Duke of Leeds would take possession of the property, if his suit proceeded and we had not put in our claim. Lord Strafford is in perfect health, and William Churchill, who resides at Henbury, close to Lord Strafford's house, when the Prince is not here, tells me that he introduces his wife's nephews, the Mr Bullers, as heirs to his different estates. They are much with him, and Churchill seems to think he will, notwithstanding anything he may have said to the contrary, make them his heirs. Lord S. is living, as Churchill states, on a scanty pittance, not spending in the course of a year above £1,000. …'

8 June 1797 — George Cotter, Fermoy [Co. Cork], to Conolly ('My dear Colonel'). He has heard that Conolly and Lady Louisa were attacked by one of their servants and offers one of his own, an honest loyal fellow. '… My dear Colonel, as I am sure you must find it impossible to get your rents from the North, and as the employment I now hold affords me a subsistence, I shall not draw for the quarterly payment of my annuity in future, until times grow better and it may suit your convenience. …'

16 June 1797 — Two letters: Henry Vernon to Conolly about the mutiny at the Nore; and a note from Lady Louisa that Lord Bridport's fleet is in sight.

A/10/5 *contd.*	30 June 1797	Sir Michael Cromie to Conolly. Political: Ogilvie, Fox, Pitt and Lord Malmesbury's peace mission to France. Also some references to Conolly's English estate business [F/5/4].
	12 Sep. 1797	Benjamin Harenc to Conolly. He has heard that Conolly's servants had turned 'Revolutionaries'. He refers to Conolly's 'bill' in the lawsuit between Conolly and his sisters.
	3 Dec. 1797	Sir L[aurence] Parsons, Parsonstown [King's County], to Conolly. More talk of invasion. '… The situation of this country is very delicate. Any concession now to the people would have the appearance of fear, and an appearance of fear on the part of the government now might be attended with the most fatal consequences. The people should be persuaded as much as possible that any attempted invasion must be unsuccessful, that our superiority at sea, our army here ready to be seconded by the great armaments of England, must frustrate the invaders. A high tone should be held. Let the people think they are safe and they are safe. I like your surmise that the King's procession to St Paul's is for the purpose of opening the English purse-strings. It is a good mountebank trick, and I hope will be successful.'
	29 Dec. 1797	William Glascock [Conolly's Dublin attorney], York Street, to Conolly. About the lawsuit with his sisters. Glascock stresses the importance of proving that Conolly's voluntary undertaking to charge his Irish estates with £30,000 was '… in consequence of a supposition, founded in misrepresentation, that your mother had not then of her own property £30,000 to leave between your three sisters to whom she had intended that bequest at her death … . I only lament now that your delicate respect to Lady Anne prevented your filing your bill in her lifetime …'.
A/10/6	1798–1801; n.d.	Folder of personal and political letters to Thomas Conolly, including:
	6 Jan. 1798	[Francis Rawdon–Hastings, 2nd Earl of] Moira, Donington Park, [Leicestershire], to Conolly referring to an address from the freeholders of Co. Londonderry which he fully understood was contrary to the sentiments of Conolly as one of their representatives. He proceeds to discuss the issue in a very highfalutin and affected style. He goes on to explain '... a letter of mine in the papers respecting the political negotiation which took place in June last.' He concludes: '... The people here are now opening their eyes on [sic] their situation, and the gloom which is general in consequence of the opinion they form of their circumstances must strike every observer. We have come so near to the point at which the calamities of France commenced that it is

A/10/6 *contd.* impossible to speculate on probable events without the most serious alarm. ...'

26 Apr. 1798 Sir L[aurence] Parsons to Conolly. Refers to Conolly's retirement from military life. This saves him from taking part in the 'severe proceedings against our poor and ignorant people at which I know your humanity would recoil.'

25 June 1798 Conolly's draft of a letter to [Charles Cornwallis, 1st] Marquess Cornwallis [Lord Lieutenant]. Offering his unconditional support after over forty years' service in parliament.'... I shall not presume to give you advice, but I can give you much information not tinctured with party prejudice or disappointed ambition for I never asked for, nor will I have, even from my best friend, any favour than a conviction that whatever part I have ever politically taken, for I have differed with both sides, was founded upon a firm belief of the rectitude and expediency of the measure at the time. I shall take care to be in Dublin for the meeting of Parliament on Wednesday and shall at any time obey any commands you may have for me ...'.

25 June 1798 Cornwallis's reply, written from Dublin Castle.

28 June 1798 Mrs Byng, Mount Ephraim [Tunbridge Wells], to Conolly (her brother), Castletown. She is concerned for him and Lady Louisa in this unhappy rebellion. Refers to the departure of Emily, Duchess of Leinster, for Ireland in distress (at Lord Edward's death), and expresses her feelings for the Fitzgeralds in their tragedy.
'... Do not, my dear brother, misstate our unlucky lawsuit so much as to say your sisters drove you to it, as you know how much we wished to have had it amicably settled, and that I wrote on this subject to Lady Louisa, who when I saw her seemed to wish to have had friends on both sides settle the business. But I never got an answer or a hope of your consenting to this. I am still most willing to compromise, and believe my sisters would eagerly do so. but I fear you have advisers that won't agree to this. You *were* so convinced my mother meant us to have the £10,000 each that you would have given it from your Irish estate if she could have settled it so. The *mistake* that happened between you and her (which you give a very harsh name to) was all that *I* subscribed my belief to, and you cannot wonder that I believed there was a mistake when *she* wrote a solemn assurance of it and signed with her name at a time she knew her death was fast approaching. ...'

3 July 1798 Draft of a letter from Conolly, Castletown, to Lord Cornwallis. Explains that he interpreted the proclamation in a different manner from Cornwallis's intention.

A/10/5 *contd.* 4 July 1798 Cornwallis, Dublin Castle, to Conolly. Conolly is to adopt such measures as are most likely to get the deluded people to submit.

26 July 1798 [William Robert Fitzgerald, 2nd] Duke of Leinster [Lady Louisa's nephew], Goodwood [the Duke of Richmond's seat near Chichester, West Sussex], to Conolly reflecting on the recent death of Leinster's wife and responding to Conolly's plea that Leinster return to Ireland.

'As the Duke of Richmond, when he came up to town about dear Edward's situation (in which he showed so much good nature) gave me a pressing invitation here, and there having been a great coolness between us, I thought I could not take a better opportunity of renewing that friendship and love I always entertained for him, though we have some years differed in politics ...

As to your letter of [the] 19th, it needed no preface. I have long known and received marks of your friendship, and though we have now and then differed, yet I am conscious it was only from seeing things in a different light – that we mean the same thing. As to my returning to Ireland ...', he is deterred by '... the melancholy situation of pecuniary affairs, the distress this unfortunate business in the county of Kildare has brought upon my party and of course myself; that, instead of adding comfort or consolation, I must deprive myself almost of the common necessaries of life and scarce live as a common gentleman ought to, much less in that splendour [I] formerly did ...', and be deprived of the means of supporting the poor at a time of their greatest need.

... As to public concerns, I defy mortal man to say that I ever encouraged or approved of the conduct of the lower order of the people in the county I am so much interested in. But I have been well used to be calumniated and I do not expect anything better in this world. I have little reason to complain of my past life. ... I have distressed myself very much in my circumstances certainly, but on that score I cannot accuse myself of having squandered or thrown away my money. What I did spend went amongst those from whom I got it. I think that, if I even had a wish to see disturbance in Ireland, it was not in the county of Kildare I should have begun it. I have long seen the storm brewing. I did what I could to avert it, and would say a great deal more on that subject but I fear to trust too much to paper.

As to my returning home, which you think might do away or confute those idle reports, and that my presence would have any weight with the common people, I fear the contrary, and I tell you why. This time twelve months I exerted myself as much as possible and my steward well knows did invite them to come in and take the oath of allegiance, and near 1,000 of them came in the course of the week. The names I have enrolled at Carton. Yet many of

A/10/5
contd.

these people were punished, and others joined the insurgents through fear of punishment. What can I expect from these people to whom I promised protection?

The accusation against me by certain persons who have chose to supersede me in the county of Kildare was that I did not exert myself at the time of [sic] O'Connor's rescue was attempted. I was not in the county at the time, but as soon as I came home I attended the meeting of the magistrates. I wrote to Lord Camden and Mr Pelham, certainly to the latter, my opinion of the state of the county and where troops were necessary to be posted. I received an answer that General Craig should call on me at Carton on his way to Kilcock and settle the different dispositions with me. I waited at home all the next day and for some days after, till I heard that General Craig had been at Kilcock, and from that letter of Mr Pelham to this hour, I never heard a word more. Certain it is, my having sold my seats in parliament offended many people who expected to have negotiated a seat for their votes in the county, and also seeing, by the immense body of catholic tenants, that I did not want the assistance of the gentlemen as much as formerly.

Secondly, I confess [that] last summer, when the yeomanry were searching for arms and taking up people promiscuously, I did disapprove of it, as I always said ... take any man that you have evidence against that can be depended upon, but if we go and take up innocent as well as guilty, we shall only irritate them and drive those who are peaceably inclined into despair. The consequence was, we did not search or go about. At the same time, I told them that, if any one person would make resistance, we should then really get at the offenders, and the consequence was that we did take two of the banditti who under pretence of being *United Irishmen* were a gang of thieves, and they were punished by the law. If the proclamation and good intentions of Lord Cornwallis has [sic] the effect which I trust in God it will have, and my coming over to urge that should succeed, it may then be said that I was encouraging them, for they would not come in until I desired. ...

I never did sanction the United Irishmen even in the beginning. I am sure no one has more reason to curse them than I have, for few people have lost more and has [sic] less chance of being reimbursed. I always warned dear Edward of what would happen and put him on his guard against trusting many people with whom he was living. I certainly, on the other hand, did disapprove of the measures of government, particularly ... [those] aimed so much [at], and [which] succeeded so well in, alarming the protestants that all this was a popish plot and that they were all to be murdered. If they were in possession of the facts which have come out upon the trials, why did [they] not bring them home as

A/10/5 *contd.*

they are now doing to individuals, and not commit a whole body of people the majority at least so [sic – too] bigoted to the religious tenets ever to have thought of calling in the French, whose first object has been to destroy all religion? Why did they disband my [?only two] yeomanry corps worth talking of because it [sic] was my tenantry and composed of catholics? Who did they take their information from but an avowed Orange party in Athy? Was not [?the] protestant yeomen in the Maynooth corps the cause of the disunion in that corps?

I shall never change my opinion that, had Lord Fitzwilliam's system been carried through, all this would not happen [ie. have happened], or had the catholics even after Bantry Bay business been taken up, this would not have happened, or at least to the extent that it has now ... when the hot-headed ones of that persuasion were worked upon. However, if you think my return will be use, I have no objection to your giving out that you expect me soon, and which must be the case in order to settle my affairs. ...

[N.B. The above is a free rendering of an original which is full of misspellings, erasures, non-sequiturs and incomplete sentences.]

28 Nov. 1798 James Scott, Willsborough [Londonderry?], to Conolly reporting on an affray between an Orange Lodge and some Roman Catholics. Some heads broken.

20 Dec. 1798 Benjamin Harenc, Foots Cray, [Kent], to Conolly, Castletown welcoming a renewal of their correspondence following the disruption of their friendship by political differences.

'... Your Whig Club I thought naturally drew to it the very persons likely to form wicked designs. ... Our Whig Club has in like manner, or at least some of its leading members, declared for the rebellion in Ireland, not directly but to my understanding tantamount. I conclude you have left them, and so have most prudent and well intentioned people ours. We have been very long indeed in habits of differing on political sentiments. I think we were of the same mind in Wilkes's matters, and I fear never since that time. Your last letter, which indeed I value much, promises our being in unison again. I am always hurt to be otherwise. The Bishop [Richard Woodward] and I (who to use a common and most respectable friend of ours' expression) was worse than you, were obliged to restrain our conversations on subjects of this nature, and we banished the questions on politics. ... I rejoice to find you disposed kindly towards a Union. I remember you have been at times for it, but I have known some strong expressions from you against. ...

I know not what to think of your having totally dropped the subject of your unhappy suit with Sir William Howe. But, if it is a

A/10/5 *contd.*		subject you wish to drive from your mind, do not let the earnest interest I take in what concerns you lead you to bring it forward. ...'
	25 Dec. 1798	General Wilford, Naas, to Conolly. Arranging to meet at the obelisk near Castletown when he has completed his visit to Rathcoffey and Maynooth.
	28 Jan. 1799	Benjamin Harenc to Conolly. Lord Castlereagh gives up the promotion of the plan of Union, and speaks of the two days of this question as most frightful.
	9 June 1801	The [Hon.] Richard Trench [later Lord Dunlo and then 2nd Earl of Clancarty], London, to Conolly about the Wakefield property inherited from the 1st and 2nd Earls of Strafford [his uncle-by-marriage]. He congratulates Conolly on the purchase of Rockfield, Celbridge, and mentions some family matters. '... The Wakefield business, if the return shall be made by the commissioners, and that it shall be found that you have no other claim than to one-third of the copyholds, will I should conceive be immediately settled, except so far as relates to the partition, which as I before informed you cannot during Vyse's minority be otherwise ultimately arranged than by act of parliament. But if it should appear that you have fair claim to the whole of the copyholds, then the final arrangements must necessarily depend upon whether Vernon and the guardians of Vyse shall or shall not give opposition to your peaceable entry. ...'
A/11	1793–4: 1797: 1799	c.20 letters and accounts of Thomas Conolly about the Co. Londonderry Militia [of which he was Colonel], and about yeomanry corps in [the neighbourhood of Bellaghy], Co. Londonderry, and Ardara, Co. Donegal.
A/12/ 1–3	3 Aug., 16 George III [1776]: 1883: 1890	Patent creating Thomas Conolly's friend, political follower and man of business, Michael Cromie, a baronet of Ireland, together with a DL's commission and a militia commission for members of the Conolly family.

B/	DATE	DESCRIPTION
B/1–10	**1614–1724**	**ACCOUNTS, LEGAL PAPERS, ETC, RELATING TO WILLIAM CONOLLY'S CAREER AS AN ATTORNEY AND LAND AGENT AND TO PROPERTY IN DUBLIN CITY, LONDONDERRY CITY AND COUNTY AND ELSEWHERE; INCLUDED AMONG THE PEOPLE OR BODIES FOR WHOM HE ACTED ARE THE IRISH SOCIETY, THE ALNAGER OF IRELAND, THE KEEPER OF IRISH LIGHTHOUSES, ETC.**
B/1/ 1–63	1685–1703	Bonds, bills, letters rough notes and legal case papers relating mainly to the north-west circuit and all apparently to William Conolly's practice as an attorney.
B/1/1	1 Feb. 1685/6	Letter from Conor O'Clery writing from Co. Donegal to William Conolly and James Hamill attorney, Dublin, about a debt owed to O'Clery by a John Hamilton.
B/1/2	27 Sep. 1687	John Cowan, St Johnston, [Co.Donegal], to Conolly, attorney in Dublin, Dear Will, I doubt not but Mr James [Lorkey?] has given you an account concerning Captain Hamilton ....had he been as well informed of you as now it should be very readily employed you...I trust in God that your faithfulness will procure more business for you than any one man can manage...' [See B/5–6]
B/1/3	4 Jan. 1687/8	Thomas [ ], Moignhall, to Conolly, 'one of the attorneys of his Majesties Court of Common Pleas at his lodgings upon Cork Hill in Dublin', 'Your last I received the 10th....but there was one thing in my letter to which you neglected to answer that was the [ ] of the fees. By reason I will send you them speedily by next post ...' *This letter is very faded and therefore difficult to read.*
B/1/4–39	1688–1700	Thirty-six documents including cases notes, memos and bonds relating to Conolly's practice as an attorney on the northwest circuit. Names mentioned include William Jackson, Abraham Creighton, Samuel Norman and Jane Countess of Donegall, James Brownlow, Edward Edwards, Con. MacOwen O'Neal, Shan O'Neale, Con MacShane Oneal, Owen Macdavitt etc. *Some documents are quite badly damaged.*
B/1/ 40–42	1695–1700	Three legal documents relating to Conolly's work as legal agent to the 2nd Duke of Ormonde in the 1690s. Includes accounts relating to the preparing of a bill, possibly a private act of parliament. Individuals mentioned include Lord Longford, Thomas Medlycott and Ormond.

B/1/ 43–52	1695	Case papers relating to land in Kings County. Conolly connection is unclear.
B/1/ 53–60	1701–03	Eight documents including a letter dated 8 August 1703 from a James Magrath to an unknown recipient which relates to lands in Co. Clare, Conolly acting as attorney for one of the parties, James Lesly/Leslie?
B/1/ 61–63	N.D.	3 blank printed bonds.
B/2/ 1–16	1681–1694	Legal case papers concerning a Chancery suit between Mrs Margaret Hamilton (nee Cooper of Markree, Co. Sligo) and William Hamilton, a minor, over lands in the parish of Devenish, barony of Magheraboy, Co. Fermanagh, which had belonged to the late Gustavus Hamilton (d.1681), and in 1681 had a rental of £230 a year. [See also PRONI Conolly Papers D2094/10].
B/3/1–9	c.1687–c.1694	Rough lists of cases in which William Conolly was engaged as an attorney, with heavily abbreviated notes on their outcome and some details of the fees he received.
B/3/1	1687	Roughly bound volume listing cases. There are over 200 cases listed, divided into the three different courts, Chancery, Exchequer, Kings Bench etc. No fees mentioned
B/3/2	1691	Roughly bound volume listing cases. There are 85 cases divided into the three different courts, Chancery, Exchequer, Kings Bench etc. No fees mentioned.
B/3/3	1691–2	Roughly bound volume listing cases and payments received. There are about 150 cases listed. The average fee is 4*s* 9*d*. Also listed at back of the volume is the rent of The Four Sheafs (a property in Ballyshannon), which amounted to £50 9*d* in 1692.
B/3/ 4–9	1691–4	Six further miscellaneous lists of cases and accounts with legal clients. Names mentioned include Richard Hennessy and Capt. Thomas Newburgh.
B/4/1	1687	Chancery bill filed by Laurence Deane and Francis French, two Galway merchants, relating to a cargo, which has gone astray.
B/5/ 1–33	1663–99	Series of accounts for the produce of the alnage duties (on the sealing of woollen goods); deriving from William Conolly's role in this period (1692–1700) as agent for the Alnager of Ireland, Capt. James Hamilton. Also included are accounts relating to Hamilton's responsibilities as Keeper of the Irish Lighthouses. Hamilton had

		inherited both these offices from his father-in-law Sir Robert Reading in 1684. The material is arranged as followed:
B/5/ 1–7	1663–88	Seven documents including, bonds, receipts and accounts relating to Sir Robert Reading as Kings Alnager in Ireland. Reading was succeeded by his son in law Captain James Hamilton in this position in 1684.
B/5/8	1691–3	Alnage account book 1691–3. Document is 48 pages long and contains a day by day account; William Conolly first mentioned in April 1691 when £34 was paid to Mr Burton by order of Mr Conolly. On August 4 1691 William Conolly paid £15 *6s* 10*d*.
B/5/9	1693–4	Alnage account book for 1693–4
B/5/ 10–26	1693–7	Series of accounts relating to alnage. Includes Conolly's accounts with Capt. Hamilton as well as correspondence with Dan Condy of the Alnage Office in Dublin. Also included are the alnage returns for Dublin and Cork in 1693.
B/5/ 27–33	1692–9	Series of accounts relating to Hamilton's role as Keeper of the Irish Lighthouses. These include references to repairs to Howth Lighthouse, as well the importation of coal for the same lighthouse. Hamilton earned £500 per annum as Keeper, of which £15 was paid to Conolly to act as his deputy.
B/6/ 1–22	1692–1700	Series of accounts furnished by William Conolly, apparently as agent for Hamilton's Dublin property in York Street and elsewhere. The material is arranged as follows:
B/6/1	4. Nov. 1692	Indenture of lease from Capt. James Hamilton to Charles Lord Shelburne for a house in St Stephens Green. House lately in possession of Sir Robert Reading.
B/6/ 2–4	1697–1700	Three rent rolls for Hamilton property on York Street. Total annual rent was £214 *5s* in 1700
B/6/ 5–22	1692–1700	Series of accounts including references to building repairs, lists of arrears as well as Conolly's accounts with Hamilton.
B/7	1694–1883	Box of miscellaneous deeds and papers relating to land and house property in Co. Dublin and Dublin City, including Dolphin's Barn, Carbery House (Skinners Row), and premises in the Liberties (the material includes a printed rental of the estate of the Earl of Meath, 1883). Among the individuals mentioned are Capt. James Hamilton, Sir Robert Reading [Hamilton's father-in-law] and the Duke of Ormond.

B/8/ 1–18	1685–1724	Letters and legal case papers concerning disputes over the Foyle and Bann fisheries, mainly the former, although the documents of 1707 and 1724 relate solely to the latter; the principal disputants are: the Irish Society, London, on whose behalf Conolly acted; the Society's tenant of the Foyle [and Bann?] fishery (up to 1699), the 3rd Viscount Massereene; the Bishop of Derry William King; Dr Squire (rector of the parish of Coleraine); and Sir Alexander Cairnes, 1st Bt.
B/8/1	1685	Brief for case between Francis Nevil, lessee of Ezekiel [Hopkins] Bishop of Derry, and the Irish Society to be heard in the Court of Common Pleas, Thursday 19 November 1685. Fishings at Ballynase on the River Bann. 2 copies.
B/8/2–3		Two copies of the statement of John Downing, Sheriff of Londonderry, about the attempt to install Richard Anderson as the tenant of the fishing weir at Ballynase Co. Londonderry which was resisted by the Bishop of Derry.
B/8/4	27 May 1696	Letter from the 3rd Viscount Massereene, Antrim, to Sir Robert Clayton, Irish Chamber, Guildhall, London, about the destruction of the Irish Society's woods. 'My father was always very careful to preserve the Society's woods as well as his own, and at my coming over from England hither last year, I heard him with great concern complain of the destruction of your woods. After his Lordship's death, I observed vast quantities of timber, boards, staves and bark brought from the county of Derry to this county, more than in several years before. Thereupon, I acquainted some friends of Mr Conyngham, the ranger, that I would complain to the Society of the destruction committed, but his friends desired I might forbear complaining, assuring me the occasion should be prevented. But finding the mischief to increase, and that there would not in a short time be timber left to supply the fishings and to serve the tenants to repair their burnt houses, I gave Mr Conyngham an account thereof hoping thereby to reform the abuse. But instead of a reformation the destruction increases, and he took my admonition very unkindly, resenting it as if he had thereby been affronted [?]. Since which time he has refused to give me shingles to cover [?] part of the house at Bellaghy, which was burnt by the Irish last war, notwithstanding my father had a warrant for the same, and is so unkind to my tenants in Bellaghy (and Moneymore proportion, assigned to me for debt) that he makes them pay such unreasonable rates for timber to build their ruined houses with, that the planting and improving [text defective] Derry is thereby discouraged and prevented and [text defective] that some tanners of the county of Derry were refused [text defective] last [?] year

B/8/4 *contd.*

some tanners of this county have t'other day bought old bark of Mr Conyngham, and there is bark and timber coming over daily now, and the tanners beyond are refused bark.

As for your letter of 4th instant, I suppose it's grounded upon information from Mr Conyngham, out of prejudice to me and to Mr Rowley, against whom he bears an implacable hatred. It's [?] true, when Mr Rowley was the Society's servant, I granted to him a deputation to be deputy master of the game, and no sooner than my Lord Deputy directed me in December to supersede him from his command of a troop of dragoons, but I took away the commission which I granted him, and employed other gentlemen. So that Mr Conyngham has misinformed you in that matter, as he has done about the money for the staves. He was entrusted by my father to manage the proportion of Moneymore and to receive the rents. By his accounts (which admit of many exceptions, though sworn in Chancery) he owed me £200 and odd pounds, and I directed him to [word illegible] these out [of] what was due for staves, which he consented to do. What has altered his mind since, I know not, unless it be that he has not the management of the proportion, which I have made appear he has mismanaged. And if he give you no better account of the proceeds [?] of the woods than he does me of the rent, it will be but a sorry one. I find Mr Brown hath not already paid the Society's rents. They shall be cleared by Midsummer. ....'

B/8/5 18 May 1699

Massereene, Antrim, to [the Irish Society] about his lease of the Foyle fishery.

'[First two words missing] the favour of yours of the 19th April, and have ordered Mr Browne [to seal] the contract he made with you on my account for your fishings, for one year to commence from Lady Day last and to end at Lady Day next, at the rent of £850 to be paid at London by two equal payments, the one moiety at Michaelmas, the other at Lady Day following, without any manner of deduction or abatement whatsoever, with which agreement I am fully satisfied and you shall be sure to have punctual performance from me. However, [I] think it proper to acquaint you that the commissioners for putting an act of parliament in force, passed here last session, entitled an act for raising the sum of £120,000 on all lands, tenements and hereditaments in this kingdom, have taxed all the fishings, which I cannot hear was ever done before. But as the article is drawn, I do not see how it can be avoided. In the article there is three clauses in these words: "And be it further enacted by the authority aforesaid that the several tenants of all houses, lands, tenements, hereditaments, tithes and impropriations in this kingdom rated howards the said tax, shall pay such sum or sums as are or shall be so rated or charged thereof and may deduct [?] so much out of the

B/8/5 *contd.*

rent reserved and payable by them to their landlords as the proportion of the said tax payable by their several landlords, mediate and immediate, shall amount unto; and that the said tenants paying the said landlords [the] proportion of the said tax shall be a full discharge to the said tenants for so much of their rent, notwithstanding any contract or covenant to the contrary. And for ascertaining the proportion of the said tax between the said landlords and tenants, be it further enacted that the chief landlord or proprietor of the said several lands, tenements, hereditaments, tithes and impropriations shall be charged with and pay one full half or moiety of the said tax or rate charged on the said respective lands, tenements, hereditaments, tithes and impropriations, and that the several tenants, mediate and immediate, according to their respective interest, do and shall pay the other half or moiety thereof; and that in the distribution or apportioning the said half or moiety of the said tax among the said tenants, mediate and immediate, each mediate tenant be accounted [?] and pay as a landlord, with regard to his tenant or tenants." Therefore, I resolve to pay the whole of the said tax, but hope you will think it reasonable at the end of my year to allow me your part out of my rent. As soon as I received yours, I sent a servant to Mr John Harvy [?], who was then in your woods, to acquaint him that I would accept your bill, which was done accordingly, and shall be punctually paid by me, though I am very much a [word illegible] by Mr Cunningham to be charged with this or any arrears; for I have seen his account, and he has thought fit not to mention any payment made to him by my order in the year 1697. And there was several sums for which he gave me acquittances, which [can] be produced. So that I hope you will not take it ill if I take such due methods as the law directs to recover what was paid him by my [words missing] ...'.
[Letter incomplete.]

B/8/6 26 Jun. 1699

Massereene, Coleraine, to the Irish Society, Guildhall, London, about the arrears of rent he owes them.
'I had the favour of ours of the 15th by last post, and am extremely obliged to you for laying the state of the arrear so plainly before me, for I was not privy to the many transactions you mention, neither did Mr Brown acquaint me, more than in general. I am very much concerned that there is now any arrear. I am sure I gave positive orders to him constantly to pay you. I beg the favour of you that you will please to let me know as soon as possible what is due since I became tenant, for I am resolved not to give you any reason for complaint of non-payment for the future, and the present arrear shall be transmitted to you as soon as I again hear from you.

B/8/6 *contd.*

I find Mr Brown has not followed my directions in signing the last agreement, but I will make it good. I cannot send an account of my payments to Mr Cuningham till I go home, which will be in a few days, my papers of that kind being all there.

I have been lately through a great part of this county, and had occasion to discourse with some now employed in the management of your woods. I hear you have not ordered any fall this year. By the strictest enquiry I can make, I find it will be impossible for staves and heading for next season to be provided out of the lying timber, therefore hope, for those uses, you will give such directions as will be necessary soon, else the wood will be so green and moist that fish cannot be put in them next season. I fear I shall have damage this season by the staves being not sooner made, for I have not yet received half my quantity.

The affidavits you mention I received from Mr Cairnes or Mr Conolly as soon as they came to Dublin, and as I was obliged, immediately I acquainted the government therewith, who by that night's post did send orders for the officers to come to Dublin, and in a few days after their Excellencies ordered me to deliver the affidavits to their Secretary, Mr May, to whom I have writ this post to let him know your desire. But you may be assured that the Lord Justices did extremely resent the carriage of Col. Lucy in that affair, and confined him all the time I was in Dublin, and I am creditably informed he is still under suspension and has not since this matter received any pay.'

B/8/7 5 Aug. 1699

Massereene, Antrim, to [Clayton] about the misconduct of Mr Brown.

'By the several letters which I have lately received from the Society, it is plain to me that Mr Brown has not acted as I directed him in relation to payments to them, therefore thought it most proper to send you a bill on him, which I suppose he will accept and pay. If he does refuse it, be pleased to send it back to me without protesting [it]. There is much more due to me on a balance of a true account. The reason of the delays of the payment to the Society was occasioned by his not sending me his accounts for three years, which I often desired; and now I have them, they are wrong, which I shall plainly show. But I suppose he will not venture not to accept my bill. I beg your pardon for this trouble, which I would not have given you but that I thought he would have a greater obligation on him to be punctual in an answer to you, on the Society's account, than to any other. I hope neither you nor the Society will think that, if this bill be not accepted by Mr Brown, that it is any sham[e] of mine; for if he does not pay it, I will immediately send you bills on others for the money.'

B/8/8 19 Aug. 1699 Massereene, Antrim, to [the Irish Society, Guildhall, London] about sending the money he owes them.

'I had the favour of yours of 29th July by last post acknowledging the receipt of the bills I sent you for £700, and that they were all accepted but that of £50 on Mr Blackwell, which I doubt not will be accepted, and also these enclosed for £200, which I have endorsed. I have sent for more bills for you, being resolved to follow my former intentions; for I will never depend on any person again for payment of your rent.

I writ to you of the 26th of July and 5th of August, the answers to which I am impatient to receive, because of the provision for staves for next season. Those several persons, I am informed, are endeavouring, or are resolved soon, to take your fishings, which have been so long in my father's and my hands. I doubt not of the truth of this, but hope you will please to let me have the preference, for I am sure none shall be more punctual in paying the rent and serving you on all occasions.'

B/8/9 26 Aug, 1699 Massereene, Antrim, to [the Irish Society, Guildhall, London] about sending the money he owes them.

I had the favour of yours of the 7th. I received, since mine, of the 19th in which I sent you two bills each for £100...I had a letter from Mr Brown of the 10th of this month about buying fish that does not name this business, for he knows I can make it appear everything above mentioned is true. I am informed since my last that Mr Brown, joins with some of the others to endeavour to undermine me in taking the fisheries, but I doubt not of your justice...'

B/8/10 23 Sep. 1699 Massereene, Antrim, to the Irish Society, Guildhall, London, about Mr Lennox's interference with his fishing rights, and about the termination of Massereene's lease of the fishery.

'I received yours of the 13th by last post, and am obliged to you for assuring me that you will not countenance nor encourage any of your tenants in fishing or doing anything else contrary to law. But I am assured that Mr Lennox does give out that he will fish in such a manner as is illegal. However, since I have such an assurance from you, if I be forced to prosecute those who may be guilt of such unlawful actions, I hope you will not take it ill.

I have ordered my servants to deliver up possession of your fishhouse at Cranagh and the other houses there, and also ordered them that they should not hinder Mr Lennox or those he employs to take possession of all the water in the river Bann as far as the flux and re-flux of the sea; which I suppose is as far as you claim there; and I have also ordered possession to be given of all I fished about Derry and Lough Foyle, and the fish-houses at Gerbbon. But the fish-houses at Culmore I built at my own charge, and is

B/8/10 *contd.*		[sic] not on your land. However, I am willing to sell them to you for the accommodating your fishings, if you please to pay me what they cost and the interest of my money since. I am making all the haste I can to know exactly what charges my servants were at, which I cannot refuse to allow to them, and myself in defending your title in several places against the Bishop, that I may charge it to your account, which I doubt not you will allow, it being so reasonable; and I am satisfied the money I advanced for the provisions [?] for next year shall be charged as you desire ...'.
B/8/11	24 Oct. 1699	Letter from Lord Massereene to John Mogridge (Clerk, Londonderry Corporation) about the Bishop's case.
B/8/ 12–16	1700	Five further case papers relating to Massereene's dispute with the Irish Society over the fisheries on the river Bann near Coleraine. The fisheries had been held on a lease by Massereene until 1699, then farmed by a group led by Alderman James Lenox commencing 25 March 1700. Massereene disputed the new lease.
B/8/17	20 Aug. 1707	Indenture of lease between the Irish Society of one part and Alexander Cairnes of the other part for salmon fishing on River Bann and Lough Foyle. All fisheries in Counties Londonderry, Antrim, Tyrone and Donegal formerly held by the Bishop of Derry. Yearly rent of £1,600 with entry fine of half year rent of £800 up front.
B/8/18	1724	Exchequer case papers between Rev. Dr Squire of Coleraine and Alexander Cairnes over Bann fisheries.
B/9/1– c.44	1614–99	Legal case papers concerning the celebrated lawsuit between the Irish Society and the Bishop of Derry, William King, over 1,500 acres on 'the island of Derry', with multiple copies/versions of the Bishop's appeal to the Irish House of Lords and of papers setting forth the arguments against admitting an appeal to that body, arranged as follows:
B/9/1	Nov. 1692	12 page document about the case between the Bishop and the Corporation over the 1500 acres in Derry. Recites history. Endorsed as 'State of the Society's case,' November 1692.
B/9/ 2–3	27 Jun. 1694	State of the case concerning lands held by the City of Londonderry at present as lessees to the Bishop thereof which lies near the city and is reckoned to be 1,500 acres. Signed John Meade. 2 copies
B/9/ 4–6	1695–6	Three legal case papers relating to case lodged in the Court of Chancery by Bishop King, including two copies of a chancery bill submitted in 1695.

B/9/ 11–15	1697	Five copies of the Bishop's appeal to the Irish House of Lords against the judgement in the High Court of Chancery.
B/9/16	16 Aug. 1697	Order from the House of Lords to the Irish Society to submit answer to Bishop's appeal.
B/9/ 17–22	1697	Six versions/copies of 'The reasons humbly offered why the Lords and Commons assembled ought not receive the Bishop's petition.'
B/9/23	1697?	17 page document containing the answers of the Irish Society to the petition and appeal of the Bishop of Derry.
B/9/ 24–41	1614–99	Series of miscellaneous legal documents and fragments of documents, including case papers, receipts relating to the case between the Bishop of Derry and the Irish Society.
B/10/ 1–4	1692: 1695	Miscellaneous legal case papers concerning Derry City/leading citizens of Derry, as follows:
B/10/1	27 Mar. 1691/2	Examination of a witness in McRabb v O'Dogherty – a case over 'a small, reddish-coloured cow ... taken away by the enemy at the siege of Londonderry'.
B/10/2	20 May 1695	Chancery bill filed by John Forward of Co. Donegal claiming reimbursement of his expenses in looking after horses belonging to Lord Massereene and Colonel Skeffington during the siege of Derry.
B/10/3	28 May 1695	Answer of Alderman William Smith of Londonderry to the complaint of Kilner Brazier Esq.; the answer discusses in great detail a sum of money which Brazier is alleged to owe Smith, and mentions incidentally a certain Dean Manby of Derry, who was deprived of his deanery on turning Roman Catholic.
B/10/4	15 Oct. 1695	Details of the composition of a court of enquiry held at Derry, which found nothing on the annexed [missing] writs.

C/	**DATE**	**DESCRIPTION**
C/1–50	**1609–1851**	**LETTERS AND PAPERS OF THE CONOLLY AND CONYNGHAM FAMILIES RELATING TO THEIR ESTATES IN COS. DONEGAL AND LONDONDERRY, AS FOLLOWS:**
C/1	19 Oct., 18 James I [1620]	'Mystery' Co. Donegal commission of the peace for one Thomas Bruce.

C/2/ 1–8	1672–85	'Mystery' bundle of deeds and case papers relating to the Brassey or Bracey family of Dromore, barony of Tirhugh, Co. Donegal, and church lands in the barony held under the bishops of Raphoe, the Murrays of Broughton, Wigtownshire. [It is not clear whether this relates to William Conolly's practice as an attorney, to a lease, which he later acquired, or to a lease, which the Conynghams later acquired.]
C3/1	N.D.	Paper establishing the relativities of Plantation, Cunningham and statute acres [of particular relevance to Co. Donegal, where the Cunningham acre was prevalent.]
C/4–19	1684–1802	Papers about the Conolly estates in Co. Londonderry, principally the Limavady estate and the Vintners' Proportion, as follows:
C/4/1	1684–93	70-page account book of James Buoy, [apparently the Philips agent for the Limavady estate, prior to its purchase by William Conolly in 1697], recording among other things tenants' names and payments.
C/5/ 1–5	1691-3: 1764	Limavady title deed and leases of the Philips era, with a copy memorial of a deed of 1764 relating to one of the leases.
C/6/ 1–15	1711-46: 1794	Box of *c.* 15 deeds and case papers about William Conolly's settlement of the Limavady estate in 1706 on his wife's nephews, Williams and Henry Conyngham in succession and on their issue male, and the other charges he placed upon it by his will of 1729. [From the timing, it would seem that he did this because their father, General Henry Conyngham, had just been killed.] Under the settlement of 1706, Limavady was to pass to Williams Conyngham in the event of the failure of William Conolly to produce an heir, male or female. The estate was settled on Williams Conyngham for his life and for the lives of any male heirs. If he failed to produce a male heir it was to pass to his brother, Henry Conyngham, and **his** male heirs. If he failed to produce an heir, Limavady was to revert to the right heir of William Conolly. [The estate accordingly reverted to William Conolly's great-nephew, Thomas Conolly, in 1781 because both Williams and Henry Conyngham (later Baron, Viscount and Earl Conyngham) had failed to produce a male heir.] Under the terms of the settlement, William Conolly was allowed to put a charge of up to £15,000 sterling on the estate, which he duly did in his will (the deed of mortgage of 1711 present in the box seems not to have been executed). In a settlement made in September 1725 he charged the estate with £15,000 in legacies to members of the Burton and Conyngham families. This settlement was subsequently revoked in his will, and its revocation of the 1725

C/6/1–15 *contd.*		settlement led to lawsuits involving the Burtons, Conynghams and William Conolly junior in the 1730s. The leasing powers granted by Conolly to the Conynghams also gave rise to disputes between William Conolly's nephew and principal heir, William Conolly junior, and Henry Conyngham of Slane, Co. Meath, successor to his short-lived elder brother, Williams Conyngham. These disputes were settled by agreements of 1740 and 1746. However, the mortgage for £15,000 remained a charge on the estate after 1781.
C/7/ 1–10	1700: N.C.: 1718: 1726: 1755: 1758: 1766: 1773	Limavady leases granted by William Conolly, together with later renewals and assignments deriving from them.
C/8/ 1–11	1740	The same granted by Henry Conyngham of Slane, Co. Meath.
C/9/ 1013	1742: 1744–5: 1749: 1754: 1760: 1766: 1772: 1779–80	The same. During this period, Henry Conyngham was created successively Baron, Viscount and Earl Conyngham.
C/10/ 1–8	1781–2: 1784: 1787–8: 1794	Limavady leases granted by Thomas Conolly, great-nephew of William Conolly and successor to the Limavady estate on the death of Lord Conyngham in 1781; some of these leases are replacements for Conyngham leases which Conolly 'broke' on inheriting the estate. Also present are some related papers.
C/11/ 1–20	1718: 1721: 1724–9	c.20 rentals, accounts, etc, between William Conolly and Robert McCausland of Limavady, his agent [see also C/26–7], for 'the manor of Newtownlimavady', the adjoining church lands of Drumachose, and the separate and distinct Grocers' Proportion, including information on tenants who had thrown up their Limavady farms to go to New England, 1718, and an account of October 1727 for the May rent of the whole then Londonderry estate: Limavady (£604), church lands (£132), Grocers (£365, and Vintners (£353).] Also present is an account of 23 September 1727, of expenses on the Co. Londonderry general election held on 26 September 1727. The total comes to £129, paid equally by the two successful candidates, William Conolly and Hercules Langford Rowley. The account is signed by their respective agents, Robert McCausland and Dominick Heyland.
C/12/	1712: 1728: N.D.	c.10 miscellaneous Limavady estate papers of William Conolly: a letter about the freehold of Balteagh, 1712; charges and countercharges of the officers of Colonel Stanhope's regiment, on the one hand, and sundry inhabitants of Limavady, on the other,

C/12/ *contd.*		about the inadequacy of the regiment's accommodation in the town back in 1724, with some incidental comment on the state of the local markets, March-June 1728; and memorial from the tenants of 'Bellymore', N.D.
C/13/ 1–4	Post-1729: 1734	Legal case papers about the Limavady estate, principally the extent of Henry Conyngham's leasing power under the settlement of the estate made by William Conolly in 1706.
C/14/ 1–5	1765: 1794	Letters to Thomas Conolly about elections in and political control of the parliamentary borough of Newtownlimavady, particularly about the fear that Lord Conyngham will take advantage of his life-interest in the estate to deprive Conolly of the future possession of the borough, as follows:
C/14/1	9 Nov. 1765	Conolly McCausland, Fruit Hill, [Limavady], to [Conolly]. '... Mr Staples has now acquainted you with the proceedings at the election here, and [I] hope you and your friends are of opinion there is pretty good foundation for a petition. I have been making the strictest enquiry since he left us into the corporation proceedings for some years past, but can get no information of any importance. But if the petition goes on you will have the provost of Newtown on his oath before the House, and the corporation books, of which he has had the sole custody these fourteen years as provost and recorder. On inspecting them you may easily discover what members attended each common council at the election of every burgess, and this will afford more authentic evidence than any we can furnish you with from hence. I think they won't dare to make any [e]rasures or alterations in the books. If any such are made, the provost must be privy to it and he will be on his oath. The only material information you require is to find what numbers of members attended each common council at every election for burgess. ...'
C/14/2	12 Nov. 1765	W. Burton to Conolly. Lord Conyngham has already told Conolly by their common friend, Mr Malone, that he has no desire that two families which have hitherto been so closely allied should enter into a contest over the borough. It is Lord Conyngham's intention that, provided Conolly does not interfere in the borough during Lord Conyngham's lifetime, it should not be alienated '... and that the present burgesses and those hereafter to be elected (who shall be gentlemen) shall understand that the borough is to be always annexed to the estate.'
C/14/3	17 Dec. 1765	W. King to Rev. B. King, Dublin. He has with much difficulty got to see the acts of council in the corporation books. '... those of the old burgesses being five in number, I do think that Harry

C/14/3 *contd.*		Hamilton, William Conyngham and Andrew Hamilton, who were all elected in Robert Campbell's time and sworn the day the provost was made and sworn, on 24 September 1754, five days ere Michaelmas day, all good ones; so that our corporation I imagine consist [sic] at present of eight good burgesses, and by this time I hope Mr Conolly knows how many of them he can depend on future elections. ...'
C/14/4	26 May 1794	Conolly McCausland Junior, Fruit Hill, to [Conolly] agreeing with pleasure to continue as provost of Newtown until such times as Conolly gets someone elected a burgess to succeed him. His brother Gage cannot take on the agency or the vacant burgesship because of pressure of business, but suggests Gage's brother-in-law, Mr Stirling, for whom he will supply security.
C/14/5	23 Aug. 1794	McCausland to Conolly. He has sounded Mr Campbell about being elected a burgess. Mr Campbell is very grateful, but declines on the ground that he has already declined to serve as a burgess of Coleraine, and cannot therefore serve for Newtown without giving offence to Lord Waterford.
C/15/ 1–35	1771: 1781–4	c.35 surrender of leases, schedule of leases, rentals, surveys of the whole manor (1771) and of individual farms, calculations and comments, all concerning the re-letting of much of the Limavady estate on Thomas Conolly's succession to it, the breaking of leases granted by Lord Conyngham and his agent, Thomas Smith, which exceeded Conyngham's leasing power, etc.
C/16/ 1–2	1802	Account of sales of land in the Limavady estate to pay off the mortgage for £15,000 [see C/6] on which interest of £7,500 had accrued, and rental of Thomas Conolly's 'remaining estate' at Limavady.
C/17/1	1736[/7?]	Security for Abraham Hamilton of Bellaghy's faithful discharge of his trust as agent for the Vintners' Proportion estate of William Conolly junior, [father of Thomas Conolly].
C/18/ 1–100	1777–1802	c.100 receipts and letters to John Spotswood of Bellaghy, the then agent for the Vintners' Proportion estate, and to Edward Bulkeley, the Conolly man of business in Dublin, from Thomas Conolly, Latouches' Bank in Dublin, and sundry tradesmen, workmen, etc; included in the section are receipts for the half-year's rent of £300 to the Grocers' Company for the Grocers' Proportion, and a letter from Conolly to Spotswood asking that Conolly's Co. Londonderry friends with votes in the forthcoming election for county treasurer should support Andrew Ferguson, 21 May 1787; receipt from Peter McDonagh to Conolly for £17 5s for registering

C/18/1–100 *contd.*		207 freeholders, preparing the necessary affidavits, and reading the oaths to 16 Roman Catholics, 14 July 1796; receipt from Lawrence Lafort to Conolly for £424, being two years' rent for the Vintners' Proportion, 10 July 1798; and account, 10 January 1801, of the expenses of the 1800 by-election for Co. Londonderry – £201, of which Lord Londonderry paid half.
C/19/ 1–13	1778: 1781–2: 1786: 1795–1801: 1818	Rentals of the Vintners' Proportion: the May half-year's rent in 1782 was £1,661.
C/20/ 1–25	1718–19: 1726–9: N.D.	*c.* 25 letters, a case paper and accounts of William Conolly about his Co. Fermanagh estate, the manor of Newporton, of which the half year's rental in 1726 was £264; almost all the letters and accounts come from James Crawford of 'Enniskilling', the agent, but there is also a tenants' memorial of 1724 to Conolly, with a copy of Conolly's reply [in Mrs Conolly's handwriting. For other Fermanagh references, see C/21–2.]
C/21	1609–1849	Papers about the Conolly estates in Co. Donegal, principally at Ballyshannon and Castlefin, as follows:
C/21/ 1–55	1609: 1614: 1618: N.D.: 1636: 1649: 1674: 1688: 1692–4: *c.* 1702–3: 1723–4: 1727–9: 1749–50: 1760: 1773–7: 1790: 1849: 1851	Box of *c.* 55 case papers, title deeds, leases, correspondence and receipts concerning the Belleek fishery, in dispute between [the 2nd and 3rd] Lords Folliott of Ballyshannon, and Sir James and John Caldwell, successive baronets of Castle Caldwell, Co. Fermanagh, whose estate of Rathmore, barony of Lurg, Co. Fermanagh, seems to have bordered the fishery; William Conolly took over the dispute along with the Ballyshannon estate, and the letters and papers of 1723–4 and 1727–9 relate to his part in it. The final item is a fee farm grant of the fishery, 1851.
C/22	1620: [1622?]: 1634: 1639: 1654–5: 1674: 1692–5: 1697: 1702–3: 1707: 1718–20: 1724	Box of *c.* 35 title deeds (including wills of the 1st and 2nd Lords Folliott, [1622?] and 1695), case papers, leases, etc, relating to the manors of Ballyshannon, Co. Donegal, and Newporton, Co. Fermanagh, with the accompanying 'College lands' of Tirhugh, Co. Donegal, leased from TCD, all of which were sold by the grandchildren and devisees of the 3rd Lord Folliott (d.1716) to William Conolly in 1718. The purchase price was £48,000 plus an annuity of £500 per annum to the late Lord Folliott's widow [who lived until 1743]. According to a subsequent valuation of 1727 [C/26], Ballyshannon contained 18,908 [Irish] acres and Newporton 4,212, valued respectively at £2,364 and £582 a year; at the same time the 'College lands' were reckoned at 1,719 acres and valued at £582

C/23/1	1680–87	Rent book for the manor of Ballyshannon, kept by Thomas Atkinson, [apparently the Folliott agent, as well as the lessee of the fishery and William Conolly's brother-in-law]; the half year's rent in 1687 was £493.
C/24/ 1–7	1686: 1692–4: 1706: 1709	Rentals of William Conolly's College manor of Tirhugh (which was in Conolly's possession in 1686); the rental was £417 in 1686 and £447 in 1706; the lands include Rossnowlagh.
C/25	1703–7: 1712–17: 1719	c.25 letters and accounts to William Conolly from his cousins, Thady and Terence Coane (respectively father and son), who write from Ballyshannon and appear to be acting as Conolly's agents there prior to the great enlargement of his estate as a result of the purchase from the Folliotts. The material is arranged as follows:
C/25/ 1–13	1703–7: 1712–14	Accounts and fairly routine correspondence, as above.
C/25/ 14	4 Nov. 1714	Thady Coane, Ballyshannon, to his cousin William Conolly, Dublin, about routine estate affairs, but beginning: '... Yours I have received, and first and foremost I pray God give you long days and defend you from your enemies. What should become of me: Godfrey would have me in gaol, and then my family would be ruined. So I need not add any more on this subject. ...'
C/25/ 15	29 Nov. 1714	Terence Coane, Ballyshannon, to William Conolly, Dublin, about the previous year's rent and about the activities of a Mr Glasgow. '... If some speedy remedy be'nt taken with some sparks in Dartry, no honest man can safely do any business there. I was lately assaulted by two of Mr Glasgow's sons and several others in the middle of my farm, without any provocation and with no other design but to take away my life, and was it not for Capt. Donlavey that was in company [with me] I'm sure they would. The circumstances of it is [sic] too tedious to trouble you with, having already told it to Sir Ralph Gore. I have sent Mr Glasgow's letter to my father to Mr Clarke, by which you may judge how much they are in the wrong, and there's no other way to suppress them but to get Mr Glasgow out of the [commission of the] peace. He has these four years past given me what trouble he could in several respects. ...'
C/25/ 16–21	Dec. 1714–1716	Further correspondence and accounts with the Coanes, including renewed lamentations about the Glasgows and Sir Ralph Gore's lack of success in dealing with them.

C/25/ 22	28 Oct. 1717	Jonathan Hooper to Thady Coane informing him that on the expiry of his lease from Lord Folliott, the land will be re-let to the highest bidder.
C/25/ 23	20 Jan. 1718/19	Thady Coane, Ballyshannon, to [Conolly]: brief news of the estate.
C/26	1718: 1722: 1724–7	*c.* 12 rentals and a valuation of the manor of Ballyshannon, including the College lands of Tirhugh and Bundrews, signed by Thomas Dickson or Robert McCausland or by both; in 1722 there were 26 tenants on the College lands of Tirhugh, with either no lease or leases for 12 years starting in May 1718, and in 1726 all 26 Tirhugh tenants had leases for 12 years with 11 years remaining; in the same year, 1726, there were 94 tenants in the manor of Ballyshannon, 60 with 3-life leases, the rest with leases for years, usually 31.
C/27	1718–29: 1731: 1737	*c.* 100 letters and accounts to William Conolly from Robert McCausland of Limavady, who acted as Ballyshannon agent as well, including copies of some letters from Conolly to McCausland; the very first letter refers to emigration from Ballyshannon to South Carolina and New England; Ballyshannon estate affairs are the principal topic of correspondence, but inevitably there are some references to Limavady as well.
C/28	1722–7: 1731	*c.* 25 letters and accounts to William Conolly from his 'brother [-in-law]', Capt. Thomas Dickson, also concerning the Ballyshannon estate; with memoranda by Conolly on Dickson's accounts. Dickson's 1722 account shows that the May rent for the manor of Ballyshannon was £1,031 and of the College lands of Tirhugh £235. Included in the section is a list of the burgesses of the parliamentary borough of Ballyshannon, 15 May 1722, as follows: Thomas Dickson (provost), Lord Justice Conolly, Capt. Wynne, Sir Henry Caldwell, Mr Baugh, Major Folliott, William Dickson, Thomas Atkinson, Michael Hewetson, Mr Jennings, Mr Gardner, Mr Jones and Samuel Atkinson; endorsed by Conolly. 'January 1st 1725. Write to choose my nephew, Mr Bayly[?], having promised[?] to W.C[?].' Also included in the section is a letter from Thomas Dickson, Ballyshannon, to Conolly, Dublin, 12 March 1727/8, suggesting a more expeditious method of paying the officers and men of the company of foot stationed at Ballyshannon; '... This is like to be a hard year with the poor for bread. Grain is extravagant dear and scarce.'
C/29/ 1–10	1718–31	Original bundle of correspondence and accounts between William Conolly and the 3rd Lord Folliott's widow, and daughters, concerning their leases under Conolly of Ballymacward, the site of

C/29/1–10 *contd.*		the Folliott mansion, Rossnowlagh and other College lands; included is a letter from Lucy Folliott, Ballymacward, to Conolly 28 August 1724, asking for a lease for lives renewable of her farm at Timnor[?], and stating that she has heard that he has recently made several' such leases in the neighbourhood, with a copy of Conolly's reply, 5 September 1724, asking time to consider, and adding that he has never granted or renewed a lease of any consequence if the existing one had still time to run, as hers has
C/30/ 1–12	1721–36	Receipts to William Conolly and his nephew and namesake from the Provost or Bursar of TCD in respect of the half-yearly head rent for the College lands of Rossnowlagh and Cowlowdown.
C/31/ 1–4	1724–5: 1729: 1736	Accounts and a lease concerning the barrack at Ballyshannon.
C/32/ 1–3	1724: 1748: 1760	Three Conolly leases of Ballyshannon farms.
C/33	1694: 1713: 1717–18: 1720: 1722–4: 1728–9	*c.* 10 miscellaneous letters and papers of William Conolly concerning Ballyshannon, some of them from or about Revs. John and James Forbes of Kildony, successive incumbents of Kilbarron; the isolated item of 1694 is a Chancery bill filed by Rev. John Forbes alleging that William and Phelim Conolly and other members of the Conolly family have withheld from Forbes a debt owed him by the late Terence Conolly of Co. Donegal.
C/34/ 1–2	1761: 1766	Two letters concerning [Rossnowlagh?]
C/35	1773–89	*c.* 350 receipts and letters to Henry Major, Thomas Conolly's Ballyshannon agent, about Co. Donegal electioneering, repairs to the barrack and market house at Ballyshannon, the expenses of Conolly's nursery there (c.1785), and legal costs arising out of an affray between the locals and a party of troops sent to enforce the revenue laws. Included in the section is an account from Henry Major for expenses in registering freeholders at Lifford assizes, [October?] 1775; the expense of registering 32 freeholders in January and April comes to £13 12 6; 4 more registered later in the year; the main item is expenses incurred on the way to Lifford. In June 1776, Major spent £73 10s on freeholders' expenses at the election. Also included is a letter from Thomas Conolly, Castletown, to [Henry Major], 4 July 1776, announcing that he will be at Ballyshannon in the autumn to thank his tenants for their attachment to him at the last election; and another letter, of 18 March 1786, reporting that [John] Beresford [Chief Commissioner of the Revenue], claims to have advised the gauger

C/35 *contd.*		of Ballyshannon to stand trial for his part in the affray between the army and the inhabitants, and promising that, if the government makes any improper attempt to screen the gauger or the army, Conolly will raise the matter in the House of Commons.
C/36	1774: 1777: 1782–6: 1789–90: 1800: 1831: 1848	*c.* 15 rentals of the Ballyshannon estate (£4,270 a year in 1800, including the College lands of Tirhugh), 1774, 1782–6, 1800, 1831 and 1848, together with accounts of cash spent on the Conolly estates in Donegal and Leitrim, 1777, 1785 and 1789–90.
C/37/ 1–12	1780: 1789: 1805: 1823–31	Leases from TCD to the Conollys of the College lands of Tirhugh (Cowlowdown and Rossnowlagh).
C/38	1693–1700: N.D.	Original and copy of the will of Major John Kingsmill, owner of the manor of Castlefin, Co. Donegal (then producing £700 a year in rent), with *c.* 12 related papers about his legacies to his sons-in-law, James Tazwell (to whom he left the estate), Dr Edmund Evans, Henry Phillips, and James Hodder (to whom he left sums of money charged upon it).
C/39	1700–1713	*c.* 25 conveyances and other deeds among the heirs of John Kingsmill and others, such as James Young of Castlefin, Dillon Pollard of Castlepollard, Co. Westmeath, Viscount Mountjoy, etc, with interests in the estate, and from all or some of them to William Conolly and Oliver McCausland of Rash, Co. Tyrone, who purchased it jointly, *c.* 1707–8.
C/40	1704: 1707	*c.* 15 bonds and affidavits in connection with the conveyance of Castlefin.
C/41	1704–11	*c.* 90 letters and other papers of William Conolly in connection with his [outright?] purchase of Castlefin [in 1711?], with incidental mention of other matters. A letter from Alexander Montgomery, for example, urges Conolly as his cousin and best benefactor, to use his 'extraordinary good interest with Lord Pembroke and the Secretary', to get Montgomery a regiment, because Montgomery finds he cannot live off his country affairs, 29 March 1708. The principal correspondent is Oliver McCausland, whose letters contain occasional political and general comment. On 8 January 1709/10, for example, he writes from Dublin: 'I had a letter this morning that our Speaker [Alan Brodrick] succeeds the Lord Chief Justice Pyne, and the Recorder to be Attorney General. He is making interest to succeed him in the Speaker's place. Pray let me hear your opinion in this, that I may give such answer as may not disoblige. … I doubt not but a word from you to Baron Echlin would excuse me from my accounts until Easter term. I have not £5 to discount for in the

C/41 *contd.*		Exchequer, and if I can get over it until Easter Term it may save me a double journey. … Pray take no notice of my saying anything to you of the Recorder's putting in for Speaker lest it might be taken ill by one of the g[entlemen] that writ to me of it.
C/42	N.D.: 1706–7: 1709	*c.* 10 case papers in suits over the various interests in the Castlefin estate, principally in Tazewell v Evans.
C/43	1704–7	*c.* 15 drafts of many of the conveyances and other deeds in C/39.
C/44/ 1–2	1707: N.D.	Rental of Castlefin (now only £490 a year), and survey by [William] Starrat of Cloghard; this latter was a part of the manor containing 2,057 Irish acres, which is described as 'sometimes rockey'.
C/45/ 1–2	1713: 1723	Fee farm grant, 1713, and letter, 1723, relating to Castlefin.
C/46	1748: 1787–9	Memorial of a lease, 1748, and 4 receipts, 1787–9, all concerning Castlefin.
C/ 47–50	1678–1729	Letters and papers of William Conolly about the Mount Charles and Killybegs estate of Mrs Conolly's brother, General Henry Conyngham, in the barony of Boylagh and Banagh, of which Conolly took overall charge after Conyngham's death in 1706, including references to parliamentary elections for the boroughs of Ballyshannon, Donegal and Killybegs. The papers are arranged as follows:
C/47/ 1–c.50	1678–1704	Bonds, correspondence, accounts, etc, about the borrowings of Sir Albert Conyngham, General Henry Conyngham's father, and General Conyngham's successful efforts to pay them off. The papers contain a number of references to the unproductivity of the Conyngham estates (owing to the Williamite War). Included is the following letter dated, 11 Dec. 1688: Samuel Jackson, Dublin, to Sir Albert Conyngham, Mount Charles House, Strabane. '... We have been in great consternation here about a letter which I presume you must have heard of, wherein it was said that on the 7th instant the Protestants was [sic] to be cut off; which alarm hath caused I believe 2000 [?] people to go for England. But, God be thanked, now people begin to come into their right wits again. For my part, I never believed anything of that report, and I do not doubt but in a little time all things in England will come to a good accommodation. ...'

C/48/ 1–150	1687–1729	*c.* 150 letters and papers of William Conolly and his wife, Katherine (General Henry Conyngham's sister), about the Conyngham estate in Boylagh and Banagh, including:
	10 Sep. 1702	William Cairnes, Dublin, to Colonel Henry Conyngham, Mount Charles, Strabane, offering very detailed advice on the best way to sell cattle. He recommends the home market in preference to the foreign, and strongly urges that the cattle should be sold on the hoof, as slaughtering them '... must be the last shift ...'. Endorsed, '... advice about disposing of Brigadier Conyngham's bullocks.'
	6 Aug. 1710	Thomas Knox, [Mount Charles], to William Conolly, Dublin, reporting that this corporation Ballyshannon have made a satisfactory reply to some request of Conolly's. The corporation of Killybegs, having received letters from Conolly and 'My Lady' [Shelburne, widow of General Henry Conyngham?] recommending Conolly's brother vice Mr Hamilton, have agreed to elect him. There was no danger of their electing anyone without Conolly's concurrence.
	24 Jan. 1711 [/12]	Thomas Knox's account of money paid by him to William Conolly out of the baronies of Boylagh and Banagh since October 1710; the total sum comes to £2,461; included is £11 paid on 30 January 1710/11 'to Provost Blaine at Counsellor Pearson's [Conolly's 'brother'?] election', and £3 paid on 9 February 1710/11 to 'said Provost [to] treat at your own election [as] Provost'.
	28 Jan. 1711/12	Thomas Knox, M[ount] Ch[arles] to [William Conolly] enclosing [the next item] a revised account which comes to £2,563, and discussing the accounting procedure between them.
	28 January 1711[/12]	Revised account of money paid William Conolly by Thomas Knox out of the barony of Boylagh and Banagh.
	9 Mar. 1712/13	Daniel Miles, Wicklow, to William Conolly, Capel Street, Dublin, asking him to give Miles's father a lease of a bog in the parish of Killaghtee, [barony of Banagh], Co. Donegal.
	16 Nov. 1713	Thomas Knox [a different person to the previous Thomas Knox, who is 'Colonel Knox'; possibly the two Knoxes were cousins], Lougheashe, to William Conolly, Capel Street, Dublin, about elections in the boroughs of Donegal and Ballyshannon. 'On Thursday last we had our election at Donegal, where Sir Arthur Gore and Mr Macartney were unanimously elected by all except Mr Spence, who named Mr Jones, pretending to have a letter from him. However, he signed the indenture, which I gave to

		the sub-sheriff, who was with us next day, with whom I prevailed to go to Ballyshannon to deliver them all with the writ to Sir Ralph Gore, who would take care to have them timely returned. I am concerned that Ballyshannon election did not succeed in favour of Mr Geering. I hope you will take care that our representatives be mindful of us, as to the votes [?] and otherwise. Underneath the charge that was expended at Killybegs election. Colonel Knox took care to manage that at Donegal.' The charge for the Killybegs election amounts to £13 2s 0d., which he has received from Colonel Knox on Conolly's account.
	[?22] Nov. 1713	[Colonel] Thomas Knox, Mount Charles, to William Conolly, Dublin, about the election accounts. £13 2s. 3d. has been spent on the Killybegs election, for which Knox has the provost's voucher. £16 4s. 6d. has been spent on the Donegal election, '... whereof I paid for George Macartney, Esq., £8 2s. 3d. ...' and half a guinea to the sheriff. Knox has Mr Ingram's voucher, '... who paid the like sum of £8 2s. 3d. for Sir Arthur, and Sir Ralph paid half a guinea to the sheriff for Sir Arthur, which perhaps you will forget.'
	[1690s onwards?]	Petition of Widow Hendry to Conolly asking to be reinstated in the lands of Drumrush, from which she was extruded by Conolly's agent, Colonel Knox, when her husband died.
	1722: 1729	Letters and accounts between Conolly and James Hamilton, [the new agent at Mount Charles?].
C/49	1708–37	*c.* 10 letters, leases, a case paper, etc, about the churchlands of Glencolmcille, barony of Boylagh and Banagh, let by the bishops of Raphoe to General Henry Conyngham whose heirs, at some time between 1709 and 1737, were succeeded in the lease by William Conolly senior or junior.
C/50/ 1–11	1805–15	Leases from and to the Conollys of the Glencolmcille church lands.

D/	DATE	DESCRIPTION
D/1–26	1607–1782	**DEEDS, LEASES, ACCOUNTS, CORRESPONDENCE, SURVEYS, RENTALS, CASE PAPERS, ETC, ABOUT THE LORDSHIP OR MANOR OF RATHFARNHAM, CO. DUBLIN, PURCHASED BY WILLIAM CONOLLY IN 1723, AND ABOUT HIS OTHER PROPERTIES IN CO. DUBLIN AND DUBLIN CITY. RATHFARNHAM WAS FROM *C.* 1615 THE PROPERTY OF THE**

D/1–26 *contd.*		**LOFTUS FAMILY, FROM WHOM IT PASSED BY MARRIAGE TO THE DUKE OF WHARTON, WHO SOLD IT TO WILLIAM CONOLLY FOR £62,000 IN 1723. AT THAT TIME THE ESTATE CONSISTED OF 3,682 ACRES OF ARABLE, MEADOW AND PASTURE AND 2,442 OF MOUNTAIN, AND THE RENTAL STOOD AT £2171 A YEAR; IN 1723 IT WAS CALCULATED THAT THE ESTATE WAS CAPABLE OF AN INCREASE OF RENT OF £1,228 A YEAR, AND BY 1782 IT WAS PRODUCING £4,084 A YEAR. THE MATERIAL IS ARRANGED AS FOLLOWS:**
D/1	*c.* 1723	Schedules of deeds and leases, 1616–*c.* 1724, relating to Rathfarnham. Most of the documents described are present in the arrangement, which follows.
D/2	1616: 1680: 1682: 1695: 1698	Title deeds to Kilnamanagh, part of the Rathfarnham estate, sold in 1616 by William Talbot of Carton, Co. Kildare, and others, to William Parsons of Dublin and others, and re-sold by Sir Richard Parsons, [3rd Bt, created Viscount Rosse in 1681], to Sir Adam Loftus of Rathfarnham, 1680–82. The documents of 1695 and 1698 relate to accounts still unsettled between the 1st Viscount Rosse and the representative of Sir Adam Loftus, who was then the 5th Lord Wharton.
D/3	20 Mar. 16 James 1 [1619]: 18 James 1 [1620–21]: 4 Mar. 1625	Copy constat of Sir Adam Loftus's patent of Rathfarnham, 1619, fine of Newtown, Woodtown, etc, parts of the Rathfarnham estate, [1620–21], and settlement on the marriage of Sir Arthur Loftus of Rathfarnham and Lady Dorothy Boyle [daughter of the 'Great' Earl of Cork], 1625.
D/4	1665–1724	Deeds of mortgage, and related papers, relating to Schollarstown, part of the Rathfarnham estate. At the time of William Conolly's purchase in 1723, Schollarstown seems still to have been liable to a mortgage for £1,000 originally granted by Sir Adam Loftus's son and namesake, Lord Lisburne, to Charles Monck of Charleville, Enniskerry, Co. Wicklow. Conolly subsequently discharged this mortgage, which probably means that the Rathfarnham estate cost him a further £1,000 on top of the £62,000.
D/5	1668–82	Grant of administration to the goods of Sir Adam Loftus [father of Lord Lisburne], and fines and recoveries of the Rathfarnham estate.
D/6	1670–1703	Bonds, accounts, affidavits, a letter, etc, all relating to the financial affairs of Lord Lisburne [who was raised the peerage in 1685, was killed in battle in 1690, and whose daughter and heiress, Lucy, married Thomas, 5th Lord, and later 1st Marquess of, Wharton in 1692] and to the Rathfarnham estate, including a rental of the latter, 1686.

D/7	1684: 1695: 1712: 1736	Maps and surveys of all or parts of the Rathfarnham estate, including a map of Butterfield and Ballyroan, parish of Rathfarnham, 1684, a reference to a survey [missing] of the whole Rathfarnham estate, 1695, and a survey and rental of the whole estate, 1712.
D/8	1696–1723	Series of leases of churchlands which were an adjunct to the Rathfarnham estate, Ballycullen and Ballycreagh. The first lease, of 1696, is from Narcissus Marsh, Archbishop of Dublin, to Robert King [Lord Wharton's agent].
D/9	1697–1729	Original bundle of letters and papers about the corn, paper and hemp mills of Rathfarnham and the watercourse driving them, including a letter of 6 May 1727 to William Conolly from the disgraced Deputy Vice-Treasurer for Ireland, Capt. John Pratt, who seems to have been the tenant of the hemp mill.
D/10	1706–23: 1738	Deeds, etc, entered into by Lord Wharton and his son and successor, the Duke of Wharton, which affected the title to the Rathfarnham estate prior to the sale to William Conolly, including the will of Lucy, Marchioness of Wharton, 1715.
D/11	1720–24	Searches for judgements against Lord Lisburne and the Whartons, with related correspondence. These legal searches were all preparatory to William Conolly's purchase of the estate.
D/12	1721–7	Rentals of all or parts of the Rathfarnham estate, with related accounts.
D/13	1722–6	Valuations of all or parts of the Rathfarnham estate, mostly in connection with the sale to William Conolly.
D/14	1723–4	Correspondence of Charles Campbell of Dublin, man of business and property speculator (*d.* 1725), who seems to have been William Conolly's Irish agent in the negotiations over the Rathfarnham purchase. Conolly is one of the correspondents, and others are Thomas Gibson of London, who may have been the Wharton man of business, and John Jacob of Lothbury, London, to whom the Duke of Wharton had mortgaged Rathfarnham for £60,000 in 1720. It seems to have been part of the conditions of purchase that Conolly should repay £30,000 of this sum direct to Jacob.
D/15	1723–6	Other letters, accounts and papers relating to Jacob and the instalments of the payments to be made to him.
D/16	1723–4	Drafts and copies of the deeds which collectively effected William Conolly's purchase of Rathfarnham.

D/17 1723–6 Characteristically illegible memoranda by William Conolly about the details of the purchase, arrangements for letting parts of the estate, etc.

D/18 1723–6 Correspondence between William Conolly and Francis Annesley of London, who seems to have been his English agent in the Rathfarnham negotiation and in other estate and business affairs, including some papers which Conolly has noted were copied to Annesley, and some instructions from Conolly to Annesley. The material includes:

16 Sep. 1725 Francis Annesley to [Conolly] about estate and patronage matters. 'I received the favour of yours about my son [Francis Annesley junior], and am very sensible of the favours and civilities he has received from you in Dublin, and must always own the obligations I lie under to you on that account, as well as for many others. He has conquered all his difficulties and is now inducted into the rectory of Winwick.

A friend of mine hears from the tenants near Petersfield, Hampshire, that you intend to sell your estate there. I told him I knew you long in a purchasing condition, and that I knew nothing of it. He desired to be the purchaser if you parted with it. I promised to write to you to know. If you have such resolution, send over the rental of it and the price, and I believe I shall from him get you the value of it.

Mr Bailie of the county of Down will be by this post recommended to you from hence for the collection of Donaghadee. I hope he will have your countenance therein.

I shall in a few days be prepared to give you a full account of the affair of your late purchase [Rathfarnham].

I wish you a peaceable session and a happy conclusion. I see no rub to it, now Wood's brass is melted down.'

22 Sep. 1725 Copy of a letter from Conolly, Dublin, to Annesley in reply to the foregoing.

'... As to what you mention about Mr Bailey, the letter you mention in your last is not yet arrived, but I hope it will soon. All I need say is that the board have ordered your nephew to town and your desire in his behalf will succeed, though the letter you mention will be of advantage to him in this as well as in other matters. Therefore let it come.

I heartily wish you and your son joy. You may always depend upon any services I can do to you or any of your family.

As to the small estate I have near Petersfield, if I part with it, you may be assured it will be at as good a rate as I can. I have no reason to sell, but that I have been ill-used by a parson [person?] in England I employed there. When I have determined with myself

D/18 *contd.*		what to do, you shall hear from me. I am glad to find by yours I shall hear from you in a few days about my late purchase. It's full time it was settled, for there remains due in all of the purchase money about £10,000. Matters in the House goes [sic] hitherto very well, smooth and easy. I am just sent for to the chair, and can add no more. ...'
	18 Jan. 1725 [/6]	Annesley to Conolly about the Rathfarnham purchase and about the possible sale of Conolly's Petersfield estate. Individuals mentioned in the letter include [Thomas] Gibson and [John] Jacob, Lord Bingley and Mr Caldwell.
	5 Feb. 1725 [/6]	Copy of a letter from Conolly, Dublin, to Annesley in answer to the foregoing. '... The 1st instant I paid Mr James Hamilton £5,000 sterling. The remaining £5,000 I believe you and they [Gibson and Jacob] will think little enough to keep in my hands till everything is adjusted and my bond and all papers etc are delivered up. ...'
D/19	1727–8	Inventories of, and proposals to buy, ash and other trees on the Rathfarnham estate.
D/20	1723–6	Miscellaneous accounts, letters and receipts to William Conolly relating to Rathfarnham.
D/21	1752: 1766	Deeds whereby Simon Luttrell of Luttrellstown, Co. Dublin, leases and then sells the lands of Killakee, part of or adjoining the Rathfarnham estate, to William Conolly junior and Thomas Conolly. Luttrell's attorney in these transactions was [Adam] Williams of Dublin].
D/22	1759–67: 1782	Rathfarnham rentals and accounts.
D/23	*c.* 1765	List of determinable leases in the Rathfarnham estate, numbering only twelve [ie. The rest of it had been granted away in perpetuity or fee farm].
D/24	1679–*c.* 1760	Box of Rathfarnham leases, etc, including leases of Ballybowden the Cherry Tree Inn and grounds, Crevagh, Timon, Tybrodane, Woodtown, Killiney, etc, Co. Dublin, and deeds of conveyance naming Theobald Wolfe, Robert Clibborn and William Conolly junior.
D/25	*c.* 1697–1766	Box of Rathfarnham leases, etc, including leases of Butterfield and Ballyroan, Great Newtown Court [Stagony], Little Newtown, Kilgobbin, Schollarstown, etc.

D/26	1590: 1607 –1782	Box of Co. Dublin deeds and leases (mainly 17th century) relating to Abbotstown, Dunsink and Scribblestown, all or parts of which had previously belonged to Sir George Wentworth (1657), William Earl of Strafford (1659), the Earl of Sussex (1694) and then to Richard Barrett of Clones, Co. Monaghan, whose will, dated 11 December 1696, is present in the bundle. [Although the Conolly and Strafford families intermarried in 1733, the Wentworth presence in this section must be pure coincidence.] A rentroll present in the box shows that, by 1782, these lands were producing £453 a year and, along with the Conolly estate in Co. Westmeath, which was producing £590, were mortgaged to David Latouche & Sons for £18,969 (18 years' purchase). This debt remained unsatisfied, and the Co. Dublin lands (and presumably the Westmeath) were sold in 1782.

E/	**DATE**	**DESCRIPTION**
E/1–24	**1570–1953**	**DEEDS, LEASES, CASE PAPERS, ETC, ABOUT THE CO. KILDARE ESTATES OF THE CONOLLY FAMILY, PRINCIPALLY CASTLETOWN (CELBRIDGE) AND NEXT-DOOR LEIXLIP (WHICH OVERSPILLS INTO CO. DUBLIN), IN THE BARONY OF SALT, BUT ALSO INCLUDING THE DETACHED ESTATE OF SHERLOCKSTOWN IN THE BARONY OF NAAS.**
E/1–13	1570–1953	Deeds, leases case papers etc, about the Castletown estate in Celbridge (purchased by William Conolly in 1709) and related properties including references to Killadoon, Oakley Park, Celbridge Abbey, Stacumney and St Wolstans, arranged as follows:
E/1/ 1–16	1570–*c.* 1969	Box containing early deeds relating to lands at Castletown, Celbridge, including a grant from Queen Elizabeth 1 to John Dongan, ancestor of Thomas Dongan, Earl of Limerick, the owner of Castletown when William Conolly bought the estate. The deeds are mainly in Latin and in some cases full seals are attached. Also present is a typescript copy of a talk given by the late Mrs Lena Boylan *c.* 1969 on the early history of the estate.
E/1/1	1509	Exemplification of a fine relating to Kildrought.
E/1/2	4 Nov. 1570	Bargain and sale of lands in Kildrought from Sir Maurice Fitzgerald of Lackagh to Gerald Sutton Gent.
E/1/3	1582	Grant from Queen Elizabeth of lands at Castletown to Edward Byrne for 30 years.

E/1/4	1583	Grant from Queen Elizabeth of Castletown to Edward Byrne.
E/1/5	28 Mar. 1588	Deed of defeasance between John Dongan and Dudley Loftus of Rathfarnham relating to lands in Celbridge. Sum of £500 mentioned.
E/1/6	1589	Grant from Fitzgerald to John Dongan?
E/1/7		Document from reign of Elizabeth I concerning grant of Castletown to Sir John Dongan. (In separate folder, seal attached).
E/1/8	1589	An Exemplification of a fine concerning Castletown from 1589 [3 seals attached].
E/1/9	*c.* 1590s	An unidentifiable document possibly from 1590s relating to Castletown ([in Latin].
E/1/10	1590	An exemplification of a fine for Kildrought (1590) [in Latin].
E/1/11		A damaged indenture, date unclear, mentions an Ormsby.
E/1/12	1612	Lease from 1612 of Aylmer's farm in Kildrought to Edward Dowdall of Rathmore Co. Meath. [Attached is transcript by Lena Boylan].
E/1/13	1614	Castletown document from 1614 with seals attached.
E/1/14	1637	Document of 1637 in Latin concerning William and John Dongan.
E/1/15	*c.* 1695	Document from the 1690s annotated Conolly and Allen (in Latin) possibly relates to Conolly lease of St Wolstans from Revenue Commissioners *c.* 1695
E/1/16	*c.* 1969	Typescript copy of a paper by Lena Boylan on the early history of Castletown, specifically the connection of the Fitzgerald family to the Castletown lands. The paper appears to be a draft for an article intended for publication in the *Journal of the Kildare Archaeological Society.*
E/2/ 1–32	1588–1700	Box containing seventeenth century deeds and settlements relating to the lands at Castletown. All related to the Dongan family who owned the lands of Castletown and Kildrought/Celbridge from 1589 to 1709. Included are various settlements of the estate. Included are references to Sir Walter Dongan and his son Sir William Dongan.

E/2/ 1–14	1588–1700	Folder of deeds and typed transcripts relating to the title to lands in Kildrought. Many in Latin.
E/2/15	1610	Conveyance from Thomas Allen of Allenscourt, Co. Kildare, and John Davies of Kill, Gent., to Walter Dongan of Posseckstown, the lands of Kildrought etc.
E/2/16	1615	Settlement of Castletown by Walter Dongan.
E/2/17	1618	Deed involving Walter Dongan and Christopher Walshe concerning lands in Mooretown, Co. Kildare.
E/2/18	1625	Mortgage of lands at Donore, Garret Fitzgerald to Sir William Talbot of Carton; Sir Walter Dongan of Castletown and Gerald Keating.
E/2/19	1637	Mortgage of houses in Fishamble, Street Dublin, Sir John Dongan to John Walsh of Kilgobbin, Co. Dublin.
E/2/20	1638	Dongan lease to Christopher Walshe of lands at Mooretown, Co. Kildare.
E/2/21	1656?	Copy of the Deputy Surveyor General's certificate of the return of the parish of Kildrought as it is found in the civil survey.
E/2/ 22–23	1656	Two copies of the inquisition taken of the parish of Kildrought 1656.
E/2/24	1661	Release of Walshe lands to William Viscount Dongan.
E/2/25	1664	Right Hon. William Viscount Dongan's appointment of trustees to manage his estates. Trustees: Sir Henry Talbot, Thomas Dongan and Garrett Cavanagh.
E/2/26	2 May 1681	Lease of Mooretown by William Viscount Dongan to William Porter.
E/2/27	1681	Porter mortgage on Mooretown.
E/2/28	1682	Conveyance of three tenements and garden in Kildrought for £80 from Sir Robert Colvill, Co. Antrim, to William Viscount Dongan of Clane.
E/2/29	1682	Counterpart of above lease.
E/2/30	1684	Peter Nottingham, Dublin, to William Viscount Dongan. Lease of four houses in Kildrought for £100.

E/2/31	1684	Counterpart of above.
E/2/32	15 May 1694	Indenture tripartite between Mariana Chambers als Villa Lobos, Widow of Sir Richard Chambers of London; Nicholas Lord Viscount Kingsland; and Thomas Dongan. Conveyance of rent charge out of Dongan lands. She was the mother of Maria Euphemia, wife of William Viscount Dongan.
E/3/ 1–53	1700–10	Box containing documents relating to the recovery of the Castletown estate by Thomas Dongan, Earl of Limerick from the Trustees of the Forfeited Estates in 1701–3 and the subsequent sale to William Conolly in 1709. Included are details of mortgages held on the estate, including references to Robert Rochfort; General Ginkel, 1st Earl of Athlone; Nehemiah Donnellan and Lord Trimlestown. The material is arranged as follows:
E/3/1	26 Jan. 1700	Claim to Trustees of the Forfeited Estates, Chichester House, for a mortgage debt held by a Richard Spence on William Dongan's lands at Mooretown.
E/3/2	1700	Henry Goodwin and his wife's assignment of two mortgages for £300 on Lord Dongan's estate.
E/3/3	3 Mar. 1701	Articles of agreement between Thomas Dongan, Earl of Limerick and Elizabeth Cooke and John Knight.
E/3/4	1701	Articles of agreement between Elizabeth Cooke and Thomas Dongan, Earl of Limerick.
E/3/5	10 Sep. 1702	Conveyance from the Trustees of the Forfeited Estates (Chichester House) to Thomas Dongan, Earl of Limerick. Restoration of estates to Thomas Dongan Earl of Limerick.
E/3/6–8	1701–3	Folder containing three documents relating to Thomas Dongan, Earl of Limerick's claim to the Castletown estate from the Trustees of the Forfeited Estates, 1701–3
E/3/9	1 Jan. 1704	Lease for a year of Castletown to Thomas Dongan, Earl of Limerick from Colonel Oliver Long.
E/3/10	2 Jan. 1704	Conveyance of 502 acres at Castletown to Colonel Oliver Long from Thomas Dongan, Earl of Limerick and trustees for £1,500 being the amount owed to Nehemiah Donnellan who purchased the land from the Earl of Athlone.
E/3/11	2 Jan. 1704	Counterpart of above conveyance to Colonel Oliver Long.

E/3/12	2 Jan. 1704	Colonel Oliver Long's re-demise of Castletown to Thomas Dongan, Earl of Limerick at annual rent of £120. Sum of £1,500 to be paid by 2 January 1709.
E/3/13	2 Jan. 1704	Counterpart of Colonel Long's re-demise of Castletown to Thomas Dongan, Earl of Limerick for 5 years at £120 per annum and the principal of £1,500 payable 2 January 1709.
E/3/14	11 July 1706	Bargain and sale between Thomas Dongan, Earl of Limerick, John Lord Viscount Netterville, John Lord Baron of Trimlestown, Anderson Saunders of the City of Dublin and John Hussey of Leixlip of the one part and the honourable Robert Rochfort Esq., Her Majesty's Attorney General of the other part. Lands in Kildrought, 360 acres. Consideration one shilling.
E/3/15	12 July 1706	Indenture between Thomas Dongan, Earl of Limerick, John Lord Viscount Netterville, John Lord Baron of Trimlestown, Anderson Saunders of the City of Dublin and John Hussey of Leixlip of one part and the honourable Robert Rochfort Esq., Her Majesty's Attorney General of the other part. Lands in Kildrought, 360 acres. Consideration of £300. Term of one year.
E/3/16	12 July 1706	Counterpart of conveyance of townlands of Kildrought to Robert Rochfort.
E/3/17	24 July 1706	Counterpart of deed of defeasance between Robert Rochfort and Thomas Dongan, Earl of Limerick. Related to lease of 360 acres in Kildrought leased to Rochfort. Rochfort lent £300 plus 10% for each of the trustees conditional on the redemption of the £300 plus a years rent paid by the Earl of Limerick by 24 July 1709.
E/3/18	19 Sep. 1709	Thomas Dongan, Earl of Limerick's deed remitting the lands of Castletown etc. to John Dongan upon trust that he should convey the same to William Conolly.
E/3/19	1709?	Exemplification of recovery suffered by John Dongan gent. Of the Manor of Castletown, from reign of Queen Anne. [in Latin and seal attached].
E/3/20	1709?.	Exemplification of recovery suffered by Thomas Earl of Limerick of the Manor of Castletown, from reign of Queen Anne. [in Latin].
E/3/21	21 Sep. 1709	Conveyance of Castletown estate from Thomas Dongan, Earl of Limerick to William Conolly. Consideration of £15,000 paid as follows: £1,500 to Theobald Butler, counsellor at law in discharge of his bond to the Earl of Limerick; £1,624 principal and interest

E/3/21 *contd.*		to Nehemiah Donnellan in settlement of 2/3 of his purchase of the said lands from the Earl of Athlone; £2,000 principal and interest to Mrs Elizabeth Cooke due to her from the Earl of Limerick charged on the estate; £3,000 to the Earl of Rochester in respect of the proper debt of the said Earl; £6,000 to the Earl of Limerick. Deed witnessed by John Finey and Hugh Conolly.
E/3/22	2 Jan. 1709/10	Conveyance of 502 acres at Castletown from Thomas Dongan, Earl of Limerick to Bruen Worthington on behalf of William Conolly for £2,048 8s.
E/3/23	16 May 1710	Settlement of debt of £2,000 between Thomas Dongan, Earl of Limerick and Mrs Elizabeth Cooke of the Parish of St James, Westminster. Debt dated back to 1701.
E/3/ 24–50	1709–10	1709–10: 'The Papers of the Earl of Limerick.' This folder contains 27 documents relating to mortgages on Limerick estates and purchase by Conolly of Castletown estate. Includes bonds made by Conolly with Limerick, Hugh Leeson of Dublin and Lawrence Hyde, the 1st Earl of Rochester. Money to be paid in instalments over three years to each person owed part of the purchase price.
E/3/51	c.1709	Folder entitled Celbridge Church containing correspondence about tithes in Celbridge, including references to Arthur Price, Rector of Celbridge, later Bishop of Clonfert and Archbishop of Cashel.
E/3/52	1704–6	Undated letter from Limerick to Conolly at his lodgings in Dame Street, 'You promised to bring Sir Toby Butler along with you yesterday to the Commons and I am of the opinion that advice would be necessary how to manage this affair. I have had a letter received last night, no name of it but right honourable. Whether I ought to take notice of it or not I can't tell, by reason, it is not directed to me but I know it is from Arthur Price for the small tithes of Castletown. I send you the former letter and pray send it me back. I would be glad to see you and Sir Toby Butler here today. I am your most humble servant. Limerick.
E/3/53	13 June 1706?	Letter from Limerick, [Dublin] to Conolly at his lodgings in Dame Street. 'Major Delamar told me of a note written to you from England. I have been offering to sell lands since I got the estate. But the purchasers from Lord Athlone hindered several people from giving

E/3/53 *contd.*		me money even to pay themselves upon security. Colonel Long was so kind, notwithstanding all the endeavours used against me as to lend me, as much money as paid my Lord Chief Baron {Robert Rochfort] and Burgh upon the same security, but I am forced to give my Lord Chief Baron a lease of Castletown for seven years at his own rate, now I hope to bring the rest of the purchasers to accept of the respective lands they purchased as security till I got them their money. I believe you are not of an opinion that it's fit for a man to be laying out all he can scrape out of the rotten estate in interest and continual lawsuits, if possibly he could get purchasers. I have not got £200 pounds out of the estate since I got it and half of that Mrs Betty Cook had. As soon as I get purchasers, which I am labouring to find, she shall be the first creditor I'll pay, she being more troublesome to me than the rest. Sir, I would be very loath to tell you a lie. I only set out the true state of my case, which is well known in Chancery and in the Exchequer. Believe me Sir nobody can have more esteem and value for you than. Your Humble servant Limerick.
E/4/ 1–12	1695–1728	Box mainly containing material relating to the Van Homrigh family. Bartholomew Van Homrigh was the Earl of Athlone's agent and he acquired some lands at Celbridge Abbey, which were later acquired by the Conollys. [Hester Van Homrigh, daughter of Bartholomew, Lord Mayor of Dublin, was Swift's 'Vanessa'.] The material is arranged as follows:
E/4/1	25 Mar. 1696	Grant by the Earl of Athlone to Bartholomew Van Homrigh of the town and lands of Kildrought containing 254 acres. Rent of £40 per annum for ever. [Photostat copy]
E/4/2	17 Jan. 1695	Lease of 18 acres in Kildrought from Dublin Corporation to the Earl of Athlone. Term of 99 years.
E/4/3	3 June 1701	2 copies in of Bartholomew Van Homrigh's will, dated 3 June 1701. 3 pages.
E/4/4	9 Oct. 1703	Indenture to Bartholomew Van Homrigh of dwelling house, outhouses and 65 acres in the liberties of Kildrought. Rent of £24 8s.
E/4/5	15 Oct. 1703	Conveyance between the Lord Mayor of Dublin, Sheriffs, Commoners and citizens of Dublin; and Thomas Dongan, Earl of Limerick. 18 acres belonging to Corporation in Kildrought to be exchanged for property owned by Limerick in the City near Kilmainham.

E/4/6	1712	Manuscript copy of an Act for vesting the estates of Bartholomew Van Homrigh, deceased. Manuscripts on a vellum roll, approximately 12 feet long.
E/4/7	1712	Printed copy of previous document, Act for vesting the estates of Bartholomew Van Homrigh.
E/4/8	3 Mar. 1713	Copy of the will of Bartholomew Van Homrigh the younger.
E/4/9	18 Sep. 1723	Draft of deed tripartite regarding disposal of Van Homrigh estate.
E/4/10	N.D.	Title of Bartholomew Partinton who, in accordance with the wishes expressed in the will of Bartholomew Van Homrigh, the younger, took the name Van Homrigh, thereby becoming entitled to the estate and inheritance of the said Bartholomew Van Homrigh the younger.
E/4/11		Contemporary copy on paper.
E/4/12	*c.* 1960s	Undated letter from a P.W. Hill to [Lena Boylan?] and photo of Jonathan Swift's cradle.
E/5/ 1–14	1728–1807	Box containing documents relating to the Charity School in Celbridge. William Conolly established the charity school under the terms of his will, made in October 1729. It was run by a board of trustees appointed in his will and was endowed with £250 per annum forever from the proceeds of the Conolly estate at Rathfarnham Castle. The school was established on 50 acres at Ballymakealy in Celbridge. These lands had been acquired from the trustees of the estate of the late Bartholomew Van Homrigh between 1728 and 1733.
E/6/ 1–22	1729–87	Box containing documents relating to Oakley Park, Celbridge. Oakley Park was built by Speaker Conolly's protégé, Rev. Arthur Price, then Rector of Celbridge and later Archbishop of Cashel. It was later the home of Thomas Conolly's sister-in-law, Lady Sarah Lennox/Bunbury/Napier. Included in this box are papers related to the title of the lands in reference to a loan taken out by Thomas Conolly from Latouche's bank in 1787.
E/7/ 1–87	1720–1953	Documents, mainly of a legal nature, relating to premises at Kildrought, Celbridge, particularly Kildrought House built circa. 1723 by Robert Baillie, upholsterer, of Dublin. It was later used as a school known as Bagnell's Academy where the sons of Lady Sarah Napier were amongst the students. It also served as a fever hospital in the early 19th century. Also present are three bundles

E/7/1–87 *contd.*		of legal documents relating to a later dispute between Adam Williams of Williamstown, [Carbury], Co. Kildare, and Colonel Edward Michael Conolly of Castletown over the ownership of the lease of Kildrought House. The dispute was settled in Conolly's favour in 1836.
E/8/ 1–28	1709–1785	Leases mainly relating to property and houses in Celbridge village, part of the Castletown estate. Individuals mentioned include Thomas Dongan, Arthur Baillie and George Finey, William Conolly's Celbridge agent.
E/9/ 1–27	1762–1853	Documents including leases and legal papers relating to lands at Skeaghgutta, Oldtown and the Bog of Celbridge. Includes references to a legal case involving Thomas Conolly MP (1823–76). The material is arranged as follows:
E/9/1–5	1743–1821	Folder entitled Celbridge Bog: Five documents including maps relating to Celbridge Bog, part of Castletown estate.
E/9/ 6–13	1762–1844	Eight leases relating to part of Celbridge Bog. Leases made by Thomas Conolly; Admiral Pakenham and Richard, Earl of Clancarty; and Edward Conolly.
E/9/ 14–17	1788–96	Four leases of property at Oldtown Celbridge made by Thomas Conolly.
E/9/ 18–25	1800–53	Three leases and Five legal papers relating to lands in Celbridge known as Skeaghgutta held by members of the Cotter family from 1800. Includes papers relating to legal dispute in 1857 involving Thomas Conolly (1823–76).
E/9/ 26–27	1838	Two printed notices to quit made by Edward Michael Conolly 1838; lands in Celbridge.
E/10/ 1–50	1711–1803	Leases and other documents relating to the Conolly estate in Celbridge. Individuals mentioned include Bishop Arthur Price, Rev. Oliver Nelson, George Finey and Rev. George Marlay.
E/11/ 1–54		Deeds and leases and letters relating to townland of Killadoon (Celbridge). William Conolly purchased the Killadoon estate in 1725 from Matthew Plunkett, titular 9th Baron Louth. It was leased to the Clements family (later Earls of Leitrim) from 1765, who built the country house there *c.* 1767–71. Includes references to George Finey, Michael Clarke, Robert Clements [later 1st Earl of Leitrim] and Nathaniel Clements [Robert's father].

E/12/ 1–38	1603–1752	Documents relating to lands at Possextown and Killmacredock (part of Castletown estate). Also includes documents relating to Stacumney, Co. Kildare, purchased in 1728 from John Whyte with the Leixlip estate. Stacumney is, however, geographically closer to Celbridge and has been included here. Individuals mentioned include Joseph Marriott and William Cromie, successive tenants of the lands at Stacumney. The material is arranged as follows:
E/12/ 1–13	1603–1709	Bundle of 13 documents including leases and mortgages relating to lands at Possextown and Killmacredock Co. Kildare. Includes references to members of the Dongan family as well as the Earl of Athlone and Bartholomew Van Homrigh. The lands at Possextown were part of the Dongan estate and later part of the Conolly estate.
E/12/ 14–21	1756–1831	Eight documents including leases of land at Possextown and Barberstown, Co. Kildare. Names mentioned include members of the Wilson and Kelly families.
E/12/ 22–26	1770–81	Five accounts relating to Possextown, of which Thomas Conolly was a tenant. But he seems to have purchased the property in 1775. Persons mentioned include Ms Charlotte Drury, William Coane and Garrett Wilson.
E/12/ 27–37	1715–64	Eleven documents including leases relating to Stacumney, Co. Kildare. Purchased by William Conolly from John Whyte in 1728. Leased to Joseph Marriott from 1715 to 1743. Later leased by Thomas Conolly to William Cromie, 1764.
E/12/38	1734–52	Document reciting leases of Newtown and Stacumney near Leixlip.
E/13/ 1–8	1706–73	Box containing deeds mainly relating to St Wolstans, Celbridge, and Parsonstown, Leixlip. The land at Parsonstown was purchased to complete the Castletown estate, while the land at St Wolstans was purchased to improve Lady Louisa's river walk in the Castletown Demesne. Individuals mentioned include Rev. Thomas Barnard and James Glascock.
E/14–23	1600–1858.	Deeds, leases and other legal papers relating to the Conolly estate in Leixlip (purchased by William Conolly in 1728). Also includes papers relating to Leixlip Castle (purchased in 1731 by William Conolly junior).
E/14/ 1–41	1600–1740	Leases and other documents relating to the Manor of Leixlip, Co. Kildare purchased by William Conolly in 1728. Most of the material in this box dates from before 1728 and relates to the

E/14/1–41 *contd.*		affairs of the Whyte family, who were the previous owners of the Leixlip estate. Individuals mentioned include John Whyte, who sold the estate to Conolly, and Richard Talbot, Earl of Tyrconnel.
E/15/ 1–24	1707–1731	Early eighteenth-century leases and other legal documents relating to the Manor of Leixlip before its purchase by William Conolly. Includes references to Newtown, Leixlip. The material is arranged as follows:
E/15/ 1–11	1707–13	Eleven documents including leases relating to Leixlip estate prior to Conolly purchase. Individuals mentioned include John White, Francis Allen, John Kearns, Philip Fernley and Viscount Loftus.
E/15/ 12–20	1716–31	Bundle of nine documents relating to Leixlip estate. Mostly relate to members of Kearns family who held 110 acres at Newtown Leixlip from John White who sold the estate to Conolly. Includes assignment of John White's mortgage from Mr Robert Kearns and others to Mr Geo. Finey in trust for William Conolly, 18 July 1728.
E/15/ 21–24	1721–8	Bundle of four documents relating to the holdings of members of the Johnston family of the Leixlip estate.
E16/ 1–26	1728–1853	Documents, mainly of a legal nature, relating to the Manor of Leixlip purchased in 1728 and to Leixlip Castle purchased in 1731. Also included are leases of Leixlip Castle. Successive tenants of the Castle include, Anne Countess Dowager of Massereene, Major General Robert Sandford and the Hon. George Cavendish.
E16/1	22 June 1728	Articles of agreement between William Conolly and John Whyte made 22 June 1728 for sale of Leixlip estate. There is mention also of Tipperary lands of Whyte which were conveyed to John Usher of Dublin in April 1720. The total purchase price paid by William Conolly was £11,883. Also included is a list of 27 leases on the Leixlip estate.
E16/2	29 June 1728	Assignment of mortgage from John Whyte and John Usher to George Finey in trust for William Conolly. Indenture quadripartite between John Whyte, John Usher, Brabazon Newcomen and William Conolly. Reference made to mortgages on Tipperary estate of Whyte including a debt of £4,100 owed to Newcomen and Usher; these debts led to the sale of Leixlip etc to Conolly. This is a 4 page long debenture and the primary focus is on Whyte's debts with Usher and particularly Newcomen. £6494.16.9 of purchase money of Leixlip paid by George Finey on behalf of Conolly to Newcomen.

E16/ 3–7	June 1728	Four further documents relating to debts owed by John Whyte and encumbrances on Leixlip estate.
E16/8	June 1728	Bond between William Conolly and John Whyte.
E16/9	June 1728	List of current leases on Leixlip estate at time of Conolly's purchase.
E16/10	14 Mar. 1729/30	Lease from John Whyte to the Rt. Hon. William Conolly [junior] of the mansion house of Leixlip for 9 years from 25 March 1730. Fine of £600. Peppercorn rent.
E16/ 11–14	1730–31	Four miscellaneous accounts relating to John Whyte of Leixlip.
E16/15	7 Aug. 1731	Deed of conveyance from John Whyte of the castle and some lands in Leixlip to the Right Hon. William Conolly. Purchase price of £1,770.
E16/16	7 Aug. 1731	Counterpart of same.
E16/17	Aug. 1731	Account of purchase of Leixlip. Details payment of £1,770.
E16/18	22 Jan. 1731	Deed of surrender from Mrs Katherine Conolly of the Manor of Leixlip to the Rt. Hon. William Conolly. Grant and release of her interest in the Manor of Leixlip for ever, for payment of £1,000.
E16/19	1731	List of arrears due to William Conolly out of the Manor of Leixlip to Michaelmas 1731.
E16/ 20–22	1733–41	Envelope containing three receipts from the Leixlip estate.
E16/ 23–25	1771: 1782: 1803	Leases of Leixlip Castle by Thomas Conolly to respectively Lady Massereene, Major General Robert Sandford and George Cavendish.
E16/26	29 July 1853	Conveyance of Leixlip Castle from the Commissioners for sale of Encumbered estates in Ireland to Daniel Simmonds in trust for Thomas Conolly, MP. Purchased for £650.
E/17/ 1–20	1732–1866	Documents, mainly leases, relating to Leixlip tenements and the paper, tuck and corn mills in Leixlip.
E/18/ 1–25	1732–1852	Bundles, mainly containing leases, relating to lands and urban premises at Leixlip. Includes references to Colonel John Ligonier and James, Earl of Kildare. The material is arranged as follows:

E/18/ 1–4	1732–1848	Folder entitled leases of 'the island near Leixlip. Four leases included. Amongst tenants are Colonel John Ligonier, Alice Starrat, James Glascock and Rev. James Thomas Conolly Saunders.
E/18/5	22 Mar. 1748	Lease from William Conolly to Jane Key, of a house in Leixlip for 31 years.
E/18/6	5 Apr. 1749	Lease from Katherine Conolly and William Conolly to James Earl of Kildare of Coolmacthomas in Counties Kildare and Meath, for 3 lives renewable. Rent of £41 15s. Map attached.
E/18/7	5 Apr. 1749	Counterpart of the same.
E/18/8	N.D.	Undated document referring to exchange of lands at Coolmacthomas between William Conolly and the Earl of Kildare.
E/18/ 9–13	1760–1852	Bundle of 5 leases relating to lands at Cumminmore, Leixlip, Co. Kildare. Tenants include John Williams, Thomas Williams and Daniel Simmonds.
E/18/ 14–16	1762–83	Three leases of 3 houses in Leixlip. Tenants include John Flanagan and John Tierney.
E/18/ 17–21	1764–1800	Five leases of property in Leixlip granted by Thomas Conolly to John Keegan.
E/18/22	1782–96	Leases and renewals of lands at Leixlip including Hamilton's farm. Thomas Conolly to Cuthbert Fetherston.
E/18/ 23–25	1852	Three letters regarding lands in Leixlip in envelope addressed to Roland Cooper, 7 Henrietta Street.
E/19/ 1–43	1736–1836	Documents, mainly leases, referring to lands and houses in Leixlip Co. Kildare. Includes leases granted by both William Conolly junior and Thomas Conolly, one of them a 1765 lease of the Salmon Leap Inn. This material is arranged as follows:
E/19/1	13 Oct. 1736	Lease from William Conolly to Hugh Wilson, carpenter, lease of a house and gardens in Leixlip. Lease of three lives.
E/19/2	13 Oct. 1736	Counterpart of same.
E/19/ 3–5	1744–77	Lease from William Conolly to John Barton, brewer, of part of Leixlip estate known as Levy's. Lease of 3 lives renewable. Also two deeds for insertion of lives dated 1767 and 1777.

E/19/6 –17	1744–94	Twelve leases of parts of Leixlip estate. Mostly houses and gardens in Leixlip, including a 1765 lease of the Salmon Leap Inn, Leixlip.
E/19/ 18–22	1751–1836	Bundle of five documents including leases relating to the holding of the McGowan family in Leixlip.
E/19/ 23–29	1759–1858	Bundle of seven documents including leases relating to the Barnhall portion of the Leixlip estate. Tenants include members of the Cooper and Coley families.
E/19/30	26 Aug. 1772	Renewal from Thomas Conolly to Wilfred Studholme, of lease of part of Leixlip estate called Glinn's tenement.
E/19/31	1777	Lease from Thomas Conolly to Thomas Coony of part of Collinstown, Leixlip, called Kilcorragh or Coony's farm for 31 years.
E/19/32	1797	Draft surrender of the same lease.
E/19/ 33–37	1786	Five documents relating to the case of Michael Bryan regarding title to tenement leased by William Casey from Thomas Conolly in Leixlip.
E/19/38	16 Sep. 1794	Lease from Thomas Conolly to William Douglas of part of the Manor of Leixlip. Rent of £43.5.0.
E/19/39		Counterpart of same.
E/19/40	1801	Lease from Thomas Conolly to John Downing Nesbitt of old quarry, Leixlip, for 3 lives renewable.
E/19/41	Jan. 1801	Lease from Thomas Conolly to Peter Tyrell of a house and garden in Leixlip, for 31 years or 3 lives. Rent of £9.2.0.
E/19/42		Counterpart of same.
E/19/43	N.D.	Damaged lease of Swords Lane, Leixlip [undated].
E/20/1 –*c.* 21	1738–1843	Legal documents relating to lands and houses in Leixlip, including 7 documents referring to the donation of a plot of ground for a new Roman Catholic chapel at Leixlip by Edward Michael Conolly in 1834. Also includes references to the Luttrell family.
E/21/ 1–29	1743–1848	Further leases of property in Leixlip. Included are references to Robert Earl of Kildare, whose estates adjoined the Manor of Leixlip. Also includes drafts of unexecuted deeds of exchange drawn up in 1742 between William Conolly and Robert Earl of Kildare, relating to the site of Conolly's Folly.

E/22/ 1–27	1744–1841	Bundles of legal documents, mainly leases, relating to lands at Leixlip. Includes patent granted unto Thomas Conolly in 1780 to hold fairs in the town. Also included are notices to quit issued by Edward Michael Conolly dating from 1841. The material is arranged as follows:
E/22/ 1–7	1744–94	Seven deeds of lease and renewal relating to a portion of the Leixlip estate called Levy's holding or the Shingle house.
E/22/ 8–10	1748–88	Three leases of houses in Leixlip. Tenants include Daniel O'Neill, Mary Closkie and Bartholomew Keegan.
E/22/11	1764	Lease from Thomas Conolly to Anne Swords of part of Leixlip estate.
E/22/ 12–17	1764–84	Six leases from Thomas Conolly of houses in Leixlip. Tenants include Samuel Yeates, William Bruce, Paul Delabatouche and Peter Berill.
E/22/18	1767	Copy fine of a house and garden in Leixlip. Parties are Matthew Clarke and wife, and Thomas Conolly.
E/22/19	1780	Patent granted unto the Right Honourable Thomas Conolly to hold fairs in Leixlip. Complete with seal attached.
E/22/ 20–27	1835–41	Eight notices to quit parts of Leixlip estate signed by Edward Michael Conolly.
E/23/ 1–34	1748–1851	Further leases of parts of the Leixlip estate, including 17 leases relating to Collinstown, Leixlip. Includes leases made by Admiral Thomas Pakenham, Richard Earl of Clancarty and the Duke of Leinster acting as Trustees of Thomas Conolly (1738–1803).
E/23/ 1–6	1748–94	Bundle of six leases of parts of the Leixlip estate.
E/23/ 7–16	1784–1851	Bundle of ten documents including leases of part of Leixlip to members of the Ferguson and Herbert families.
E/23/ 17–33	1758–1853	Seventeen leases relating to lands at Collinstown, Leixlip. Includes leases made by Admiral Thomas Pakenham, Richard Earl of Clancarty and the 2nd Duke of Leinster.
E/23/ 34–36	1806–33	Three deeds relating to the holding of the White family of Woodlands, Luttrellstown, Co. Dublin, in Leixlip.

E/24/ 1–22	*c.* 1704–1839	Documents mainly legal in nature, relating to the Sherlockstown estate, Barony of Naas, Co. Kildare, including references to William Sherlock and Francis Sherlock, and to lands at Sherlockstown. Also includes rentals and copy of will. These lands, though not near Castletown, were originally part of the Dongan estate.

F/	**DATE**	**DESCRIPTION**
F/1–6	**1650–1827**	**DEEDS, LEASES AND OTHER PAPERS ABOUT THE ESTATES OF THE CONOLLY (AND CONYNGHAM) FAMILIES ELSEWHERE IN IRELAND AND IN ENGLAND, AS FOLLOWS:**
F/1	1667–1728	Box of deeds, leases, case papers, etc (*c.* 25), relating to estates in Counties. Cork, Kilkenny, Tipperary, Wexford and Wicklow, including a deed referring to land in Wexford granted by Queen Elizabeth (1576), a deed of mortgage referring to the Tipperary estate of John Whyte of Leixlip, Co. Kildare, a Chancery bill relating to an estate near Fethard, Co. Wexford, filed by Sir Laurence Esmonde, Bt (1693), and other legal documents relating to land in Wexford.
F/2	1650: 1702–83	Box of deeds, leases, maps, correspondence, etc (*c.* 30), relating to the Conolly estate in the barony and county of Roscommon.
F/ 3	1656–1760	Box of deeds, leases, etc (*c.* 35), relating to lands in Cos. Cavan, Meath and Westmeath, mainly to Rodanstown (William Conolly's first country seat), Batterstown and Dollanstown, Co. Meath.
F/4	1696–1728	Box of correspondence, rentals, accounts, etc (*c.* 300), relating to the Slane estate of General Henry Conyngham, managed by William Conolly on behalf of Conyngham's heirs after Conyngham's death in 1706, arranged as follows:
	1699	Damaged and incomplete perpetuity lease granted by William Earl of Rochford [a Dutch favourite of King William III, who may have been granted the Slane estate until it was 'resumed' and sold by the Trustees of the Forfeited Estates to Conyngham in 1703].
	1696–1708	Folder of personal accounts, receipts, etc, of Conyngham and his wife, Lady Shelburne.
	1705–14	The same: Lady Shelburne.

F/4 *contd.*	1710	Folder of inventories, etc, for Slane Castle, following the death of Lady Shelburne, including Katherine Conolly's 'recollection' of the jewellery and trinkets in Lady Shelburne's possession.
	1701	Folder containing 2 documents relating to the Williams/ Conyngham estate at Minster, Isle of Thanet, Kent.
	1711–17	Two folders full of (severely damaged) Minster estate papers. The agent for that estate was James Medlycott.
	1706–12	Two folders of accounts for building work on Slane Castle.
	c. 1706–*c.* 1710	Folder of petitions to William Conolly from tenants on the Slane estate.
	1710–21	Folder of tenants' petitions, agent's letters (William Billings), accounts, etc, relating to the Slane estate.
	1710–28	Folder of letters and receipts from the bankers, Hugh Henry and Sir Alexander Cairnes, all relating to a mortgage on the Slane estate.
	1710–21	Folder of Slane estate rentrolls.
F/5–6	1793–1827	Two boxes containing case papers and correspondence (c.300 documents), all relating to the Toddington estate, Bedfordshire, two-thirds of which Thomas Conolly inherited after the death of his mother's brother, the 2nd Earl of Strafford, in 1791, and following a partition effected in 1795 among the three co-heirs to Lord Strafford's landed property. There were complications over the partition and over the sums of money with which Conolly's share was charged, and the correspondence relates to these and to the selling of the estate to clear Conolly's vast debts. After *c.* 1805, the only part of the estate, which remained unsold was Conolly's interest in the advowson of the rectory of Toddington. This, too, was eventually sold in 1827. The contents of the boxes have been arranged as follows:
F/5/1	1793–4	Letters to Thomas Conolly from Brook Bridges, Red Lion Square, London, and others about the partition which resulted in Conolly's receiving two-thirds of the Toddington estate, including:
	8 July 1793	William Cruise, Lincoln's Inn, to Conolly. 'Mr Bridges and Mr Green called on me this morning on behalf of Colonel Vyse and Mr Levison Vernon [co-heirs with Conolly to the reversion of the Johnson estates of the late Lord Strafford]

F/5/1 *contd.*

respecting the intended partition of the estates. Mr Bridges showed me a letter of yours of the 26th of last month in which you object to the agreement for a partition because your share is to be in Bedfordshire, where the lands have been lately considerably raised, where all repairs are to be made by the landlord, and where the Land Tax is at 4 shillings in the pound, and also because nothing is mentioned about the borough of Aldborough [*sic* – Aldeburgh].

When the idea of this partition was first mentioned to me, I thought you would be much pleased with it, as I always understood that you looked upon the Bedfordshire estate as the best of the three. Your choice could only lie between the Bedfordshire and the Suffolk, as it was always made a previous condition that Colonel Vyse's son should have Boughton. Now I am certain that two-thirds of the Bedfordshire estate would form an infinitely better property than any share of the Suffolk, and I understand that this is the opinion of the surveyors, who wonder at Mr Levison Vernon's taste in preferring barren land to the best soil in the kingdom. As to your objection respecting the Bedfordshire estate being lately raised and the repairs being thrown on the landlord, the answer is a very simple one. The estate will be valued to you at a much lower price on account of those circumstances. And as to the Land Tax, it is always considered as a favourable point that it should be high, for being deducted from the rent, the valuation of the estate is so much the lower, and if any alteration should ever take place in the assessments of the Land Tax, it must inevitably operate in favour of those estates where it is high, and against those where it is low. As to the borough of Aldborough, since I saw Mr Douglas's opinion, I have not considered it to be of any real value. It would certainly cost the lord of the manor of Aldborough ten years' labour and probably £10,000 to get the borough, which would then be an open one. Now, I confess that I do not consider that as a valuable property. ...

If the valuation of your share of the Bedfordshire shall not amount to one-third of the sum at which all the estates shall be valued, then the deficiency is to be made up to you either in money or in parts of the detached property. ...'

F/5/2 1794–5

Letters to Thomas Conolly, Ireland, from Sir Michael Cromie, 1st Bt, Howland Street, [London], and Toddington. [Cromie sat until 1797 in the Irish parliament for Conolly's borough of Ballyshannon; but he had banking interests in England and was employed by Conolly as agent for Conolly's newly acquired and growing inheritance from the Earls of Strafford.] Included is the following memorandum:

F/5/2 *contd.* June 1795 'Sir M. Cromie's statement of Mr Conolly's case respecting his mother.'

'Upon the death of the late Earl of Strafford [in 1791], Lady Anne Conolly [his sister and one of his three co-heiresses] became entitled in fee to a third of his real estates under the original settlements, and to an estate for life in his monied property by the will of the said Earl. That funded property exceeding the expectation of all his family, Lady Anne Conolly by a voluntary deed made over the real estates to trustees in trust for her son, Mr Conolly, in fee, reserving to herself a power of charging said estates with £40,000 as a further provision for her three daughters and for the late Miss [Mary Anne] Fitzgerald [who died 31 March 1794], the then representative of her fourth daughter. At that time, Lady Anne Conolly was taught to imagine that the property thus assigned to Mr Conolly was well worth £100,000. And her Ladyship further declared that, if she lived a sufficient time to save £40,000 for her daughters, etc, she would exonerate Mr Conolly's estate in the whole or in part from the said charge. The dividends received by Lady Anne since that time amount to £47,908 in the year 1795, beside the interest of other money from the executors to a great amount still due.

An act of parliament having passed in the session of 1795 for the partition of the said real estates, it appeared before the judges upon the solemn *oaths* of the three commissioners appointed to divide and value the same, that Mr Conolly's share fell very short of Lady Anne's and his expectation, amounting only to £72,463 18s. 1½d., and the expenses of passing said act cost Mr Conolly above £2,000 ...'. When these facts were made known to Lady Anne, she voluntarily and after due deliberation signed a deed whereby she made over to Conolly the entire £72,463 at which his share of the estates was valued, and subsequently declared to Conolly's brother-in-law, Lord Ross, that this had been her voluntary act. Lady Howe, one of Conolly's sisters (whose husband, Sir William Howe, was one of Lady Anne's trustees, the other being Sir George Howard) took strong exception to this arrangement; and it later transpired '... that Lady Anne's money business was so shamefully managed that she did not possess a sufficient sum at present to provide for the several legacies mentioned in her will and £10,000 for each of his [Conolly's] sisters ...'. On learning this, Conolly offered to charge the £30,000 intended for his sisters [Miss Fitzgerald having died in the interim] on the part of his Irish estates which was currently security for Lady Anne's jointure [which presumably meant that the £30,000 could not be raised off it until she died and the jointure ceased to be payable]. '... So that all this fomentation of discord between a mother and her only son is for no other cause but that those ladies are to receive £10,000 apiece off an Irish instead of an English

F/5/2 *contd.*

estate, and that their brother, who has been depressed his whole life by the intolerable load of his father's debts, *not his own*, should now be in some measure relieved from that weight by opening his credit a little in England. ...'

A note at the end of the document states: 'The above was drawn in June 1795, prior to the discovery of the original settlement in 1733, which shows that the act which Lady Conolly now wishes to avoid [ie. her voluntary conveyance of the £72,463 to Conolly] is nothing more than a proper compliance with her original covenants prior to her marriage.'

F/5/3 Mar.–Dec. 1796

Letters to Conolly from Cromie, Howland Street, and Toddington.

Cromie, Howland Street, to Conolly, Dublin.

'... With you I seek merit, not fame. I employ all my thoughts for your service, and still flatter myself that from the beginning of this business to this moment I deserve your approbation, the withholding of which is the highest mortification to a heart so sincerely devoted to you for more than thirty years. ...

I hope Lord O'Neill will become a purchaser of a lot of your Bedfordshire estate to the amount of £400 per annum. He wrote to me to look out for such a purchase for him. I have stated to him the beauties of Toddington, the hills and valleys, the woods and water, the luxuriance of the soil and the beautiful shape of the grounds in the neighbourhood of the Duke of Bedford and Lord Upper Ossory, its vicinity to London, etc. I also added my full conviction of your wish to accommodate him in the exact quantity he wanted. He has the money ready. ...'

18 June 1796

Cromie, Howland Street, to Conolly, Castletown.

'... There is to be no Imperial loan. The bankers have absolutely refused to advance one guinea, alleging that the export of three millions in specie would ruin the kingdom, and the Emperor must have it all in gold. Mr Pitt is in a sad hobble. He promised the Emperor for a certainty he should have a loan to that amount, which he cannot now fulfil, and it is apprehended here that the Emperor will march his army directly and take possession of Hanover. A Spanish war is suspected. I know the clerks in Lord Grenville's office sat up the whole of last night writing dispatches. ...

Lord Valentia is to sail for Hamburg this night to fight Mr Gawler, the brother of the gentleman who intrigued with Lady Valentia and gave testimony upon the trial against Lord Valentia. Such is the resentment they bear to each other that one of them must fall. ...'

F/5/3 *contd.*	7 July 1796	Cromie, Toddington, to [Conolly]. '... I have no doubt but you could easily on a future day settle amicably with young Staples [William Conolly Staples, Conolly's nephew and heir, who died young in 1798] so far as his influence could reach. ... I humbly conceive Lady Anne's release to you in 1795 completely repeals the act of parliament as to the power of charging your estate with £40,000, and complies with her original covenant before marriage. If nothing is done during her Ladyship's life, I foresee many difficulties you will have to encounter after, and much loss. Let me entreat you once more to consider whether it would not be advisable to have a bill filed against you and the trustees ..., that you may thereby establish the facts relative to Lady Anne's deed of appointment in 1795, which must invalidate any other appointment she has made of the said £40,000 subsequent thereto ... . [Otherwise, Cromie fears] that the trustees, even *without your consent*, can sell your estates here to raise that £40,000 whenever they please.'
	8 Sep. 1796	Cromie, Howland Street, to Conolly. '... I was always sure that Lady Anne never would settle amicably with you. It is neither the interest nor the principle of Mr [Edward] Boodle [her attorney or man of business], and he influences all her determinations and relies upon the operation of that unfortunate act of parliament. ...'
	29 Nov. 1796	Cromie, London, to Conolly, Dublin. '... As you are about to enlarge your confidence in me, I thought it right to give you the best security in my power for the faithful discharge thereof. For which purpose, the day before I sailed from Ireland I deposited in your house in Merrion Street an oak chest containing the title deeds of my Westmeath estate and all the leases, with the like of my Stacumnie freeholds, and every other paper of value and consequence to me. ... My patent as a baronet [A/12/1] I gave to Hare to lock up for me. ...'
	8 Dec. 1796	Cromie, London, to Conolly, Dublin. '... Mr Thompson leaves town tomorrow for Ireland. It is well worth your consideration to deal with him who has ready money, and to get yourself out of the power of all those vultures that would suck up your very vitals. ... Lord Massereene's estate is his object. If you give him a better bargain, he will of course deal with you. Where you pay 6 per cent, recollect that with the compound interest you double the principal in less than twelve years. ...'
F/5/4	Jan.–Dec. 1797	Letters to Conolly from Cromie, London and Toddington.

F/5/4 *contd.*	28 Jan. 1797	Cromie, London, to Conolly, Dublin. '... How the Latouches can treat you with such disrespect astonishes me, who am persuaded they have from time to time in the course of your dealings with them made £50,000 of you. ... If you would be so good [as] to recommend me to the Prince of Wales, who is now much displeased at the manner his debts are paid and his household conducted, I am almost sure he would take me into his service. ... He desired I would leave my address at Carlton House. Doyle's place as secretary is not filled up. I would work without emolument till his R.H.'s affairs are settled. Anything you are so kind [as] to say or promise for me, I will most strictly perform. The Prince told me with his own lips in my ear *he wants* to go to Ireland to settle all those discontents there. Ministry entertain the idea of sending the Duke of Portland and this matter is now in agitation.'
	20 Feb. 1797	Cromie to Conolly, Dublin. 'I could not sleep all night thinking of this will [Lady Anne's, she having just died] and the scene of hostility that I saw yesterday prepared against you ..., [including] an office copy of the deed of 1795 with the following words written by Lady Anne on the back: "*This is a copy of the deed I was deceived into signing.*" The will disposes of the £40,000, the five codicils confirm it. The second codicil strikes you off as an executor, and pray observe William Staples, who is residuary legatee to the whole remnant of her property, is to have also £10,000 of that £40,000. The reversionary interest left to you in all the forms of legal expression, I do not consider worth *sixpence*, but contrived by Mr Boodle to blind our senses. Under these impressions, I have determined to hold a consultation this night at 7 o'clock with the Attorney and Solicitor General, Mr Plummer and Cruise to consider whether it may not be prudent to enter a *caveat* against the will. You may then compromise the matter if you please. But I fear, the executors being in power to act under the will, may bring ejectments and caution the tenants of Toddington [not] to pay their rents to you, and as the whole of the expenses of the suit will fall upon the residuary legatee, Sir William [Howe] and Mr Hoare may go on with impunity and deceive the young man, who is now *interested* in the cause to the amount of £10,000. I will open Staples's eyes today, as I am this moment going off to him ...'.
	1 Mar. 1797	Cromie, London, to Conolly, Dublin. '... The moment Sir William Howe conveys the *legal* estate [in small, detached portions of the Strafford estates] to you, I will put that farm and the farm at Sandwich up to auction, and I trust, as people begin to be alarmed about the Funds, that lands will bring

F/5/4
contd.

a good price in small lots. Mr Christie [who held a mortgage for £10,000 on the Toddington estate] is mad about his interest. I told him you sold that property in Lambeth for the purpose of paying him (as you found great difficulty getting your rents in the north of Ireland owing to the invasion and also to the amazing quantity of linen unsold in Ireland in consequence of the war) ..., that we would do everything in our power at these times to get the money for him. ...'

7 Mar. 1797 Cromie, London, to Conolly, Dublin.
'... Mr Pitt has floundered so in all his business of finance of late as to have lost what was his greatest support, the opinion of the monied people in the City. He might have had 30 millions at the commencement of the voluntary loan. He said 18 was quite *sufficient*. Yet, before the expiration of one month, he wanted 10 more. On Saturday last, without consulting the Bank Director, he issued a proclamation to receive stamped dollars at 4s. 6d. The Bank was astonished and sent to inform him that a dollar was intrinsically worth 4s. 7d. and a fraction, and that if issued at 4s. 6d. they would soon be melted down. Yesterday a *new* proclamation came forth to say dollars were to be taken at 4s. 9d. Several of the great army agents were with him today, [and said] that they had exhausted all their credit and their own stock, and knew not what to do. He replied that they could only be furnished with *mere subsistence* for some little time.

I saw General Vyse this morning. He says, if Lady Anne's soundness of mind could possibly be called in question, he has many letters received from her just at that time [ie. of executing the deed of 1795] to prove her clearness of understanding, etc. Vernon is come to town. If we wanted any witness in addition to Lord Ross, he could be a material one, from the messages he carried from me to her Ladyship last year upon this business. ...'

15 Mar. 1797 Cromie, London, to Conolly, Castletown, recounting a discussion he has just had with Conolly's nephew, George Byng.
'... In the first instance, he wishes you not to feel the smallest inconvenience about the payment of interest to him till you are perfectly at your ease; that you will empower me to settle that account as it now stands, you having no receipt from him for £1,500 paid on account of principal and interest. ... Whether he is to have only a life estate in Lord Strafford's property or a power over the money, is yet very doubtful, or whether under the extraordinary wills of his Lordship and Lady Anne he can ever make a compromise with the parties in remainder, is also a question. ... I believe Lady Buckingham[shire] coincides in the same sentiment ...'.

F/5/4 *contd.*	13 Apr. 1797	Cromie, London, to Conolly, Dublin. '... I think your proposal to Mr Byng, like yourself, generous and affectionate. ...'
	14 Aug. 1797	Cromie, London, to Conolly, Dublin. '... Mr Kipling on the part of the executors of Lord Buckingham[shire] wrote twice to me upon the subject of interest due upon the £8,000 at his death. ...'
	3 Nov. 1797	Cromie, New Road, London, to Conolly, Dublin. '... I observe Lady B[uckingha]ms[hire's] and Mrs Byng's answers are drawn by one and the same lawyer, who has exerted his ingenuity to flitter away the force of Lord Ross's evidence [about the late Lady Anne's kind intentions towards Conolly]. ... When you consented to the act of parliament and the charge of £40,000, you were ignorant of your birthright [under the marriage settlement of 1733]. When you became acquainted with that circumstance and found Lady Anne had *not lived* long enough to save £10,000 apiece for your sisters, you most generously offered to secure that sum for them, on a proviso never fulfilled. Lady Anne has since *lived* to save *more* than £10,000 apiece, yet Sir William and Co. would now insist that you should give up your birthright to aggrandize them.'
F/5/5	[1797?]	Lengthy legal case paper, post-dating the death of Conolly's mother, Lady Anne Conolly [sister of the late Lord Strafford] in March 1797, and relating to the legal obligation on Conolly, if any, to pay £10,000 to each of his three sisters or their representatives. Case of Thomas Conolly proving that his mother was unjustified in charging his share of the late Lord Strafford's estates with £40,000 divided equally among his sisters, Lady Howe, Mrs Byng and the Countess of Buckinghamshire and his nephew, William Conolly Staples. Among many other things, the case '... charges that said Lady Anne Conolly did at different times ... inform several persons that she had given her son ... the sum of £72,400 ... as some compensation for the disappointment he experienced under the will of his late uncle, William Earl of Strafford, who had promised to leave plaintiff £100,000 by his will, but had neglected so to do ..., and also as some return or acknowledgement on the part of the said Lady Anne Conolly to plaintiff for having declined to enter a caveat against the said will and to dispute the same, which he so declined doing at the particular request of his said mother, Lady Anne Conolly, who took very large property under the said will and in consequence of the said Earl's death, to the amount of £12,000 a year and upwards. ...'

F/5/6 May–Oct. 1798 Letters to Conolly from Cromie, London.

3 May 1798 Cromie, New Road, London, to Conolly.
'If I had not received yours of the 28th ult. shortly after I read of your resignation [as colonel of the Co. Londonderry Militia] in the paper with a paragraph annexed, it would have alarmed me much. What you mention as to Sir George Hill carries with it cause for consideration, which I am sure you will give to it.
I saw his Royal Highness yesterday. He commanded me to return you his best thanks for your constant attention to him, to assure you he highly approves of your letters and sentiments and hopes you will not be niggard of your pen, but let him hear often from you. ...'

F/5/7 Jan.–Dec. 1799 Letters to Conolly from Cromie, London and Toddington, including letters about the passing of the Act of Union

16 Feb. 1799 Cromie, Toddington, to Conolly, Castletown, about the defeat of the Union proposal in the Irish House of Commons.
'... Had it passed, you may rely upon it that I *know one* great firm in the City of London which would have established a house in Ireland with a capital of £300,000, and many, many families of small incomes from £400 to £800, £900 or £1,000 would have gone over to your kingdom to escape this hated tax on income, besides numbers of great merchants neither approving of that tax or [sic] liking to have their circumstances laid open to inspectors. And here let me request you will immediately send me over a list of those persons to whom you pay interest, annuities or rents in England, that it may be my care to rescue your estates in this kingdom from that tax, which I *can do* with those materials, as the law now stands. ...'

27 Feb. 1799 Cromie, New Road, London, to Conolly, Castletown.
'... I have read your arguments in favour of the Union with great satisfaction and am sure they must have due weight in Ireland ... . I rose early this morning to transcribe the manuscript, and took it at two o'clock to the press of *The Times*, a paper much in the interest of government and always perused by His Majesty and the Prince. ... I could not engage the immediate insertion for less than three guineas ... . I have little doubt but some of the evening papers will adopt it of their own accord.
Your description of the distracted situation of our ill-fated country is truly alarming, and I am comforted to find that Lady Louisa and you have determined to make this kingdom your sanctuary, though the cursed income tax will fall heavy upon your great income. I will watch all advertisements in Sussex and Devonshire ... and give you intimation. ...

F/5/7 *contd.*

The ingratitude of Mr Barrington and the madness of his now associates is [sic] not only base and astonishing, but an indelible stain to [sic] the Irish character. ... [Ireland's] independence has been her ruin. Your sagacity not only foresaw it but foretold it. ...'

9 May 1799 Cromie, London, to Conolly, Castletown.
'... Mr Pitt is likely to experience much disappointment from his income tax. All the returns are almost made. The supposed produce was 10 millions, but the real one will not be more than £6,500,000. The deficit in the calculation is found among the commercial people. ...'

13 Aug. 1799 Cromie, Toddington, to Conolly, Castletown.
'... When I saw Mrs Byng at Tunbridge she mentioned that the three pictures belonging to Lady Louisa were in her house and not hung up, as she had no room for them, and feared they might be injured. One is your portrait, the others two views of Castletown. I shall be happy to take charge of them and to keep them in the best preservation till Lady Louisa pleases to order them over. ...'

14 Sep. 1799 Cromie, London, to Conolly, Castletown.
'The late Lord's [Strafford, a distant cousin of his predecessor and who had just died without issue] will cannot be got at till it is proved. A caveat now lies against that proceeding. ... If any *reasonable* grounds for contest appear, it may be a matter of speculation whether an attack upon Mr and Mrs Kaye [Augusta Henrietta Kaye, sister and heir-at-law of the recently deceased 3rd Earl] might not produce a compromise: namely, to permit them to enjoy for life on condition that they will settle the reversion on you and your heirs agreeable to the original settlement of Thomas [1st Earl of Strafford]. ...'

He suggests that, if the present collector of Drogheda is dismissed, Conolly should recommend Cromie for the post. 'I could always get leave of absence for a short time to attend to your business here, which *no emolument* under government should tempt me to forego. It would be something to give up for a better, and my son could attend to it when I was away.'

29 Sep. 1799 Cromie, London, to Conolly, Castletown.
'I this day had the honour of an audience from the Duke of Portland and delivered your letter ... . I stated to his Grace how near I was to preferment during his administration in Ireland in 1782, in Lord Northington's in 1783 and in Lord Fitzwilliam's reign in 1795; that for 22 years I served in parliament, I never was absent for one debate of consequence, and never swerved from the line of politics you supported which, together with a knowledge of me since I was fourteen years old, inclined you to make that

F/5/7 *contd.*

application in my favour. ...' Portland responded with expressions of goodwill but did not commit himself.

23 Oct. 1799 Cromie, London, to Conolly, Castletown.
He refers '... to a demand of Lord Howe's [Sir William Howe had succeeded to his family's Irish viscountcy earlier in the year] for *two* years' interest of the £8,000 to midsummer last ...'.

15 Nov. 1799 Cromie, London, to [Conolly].
'... I have examined the act of parliament and can find no mention of any settlement made by Thomas, [1st] Earl of Strafford, but in consequence of the settlement made by Sir Henry Johnson of his estates [in 1711], the Earl promised to settle £2,000 a year on the issue of that marriage, and you will see he provides for that in his will. ... I think it possible that some estates might have been settled *before* the time of Earl Thomas by his father or grandfather. I will get copies of *their* wills and follow up this investigation. It may be very material for you.

Lady Strafford has retired to Henbury [Dorset, a house and estate owned by the late (3rd) Earl, her husband, prior to his succession to the earldom in 1791] and given up the possession of the Strafford estates to the Kayes, whose people are now at Wentworth Castle. But Mrs Kaye is with her husband in a dying state at Abbey Park, Edinburgh. ...

The expenses at Toddington are dreadfully heavy, but you have now a capital estate in a ring fence; and, great as the expenses have been, it [sic] will repay you tenfold ...'.

15 Dec. 1799 Cromie, London, to Conolly, Castletown.
'... I am strongly inclined to think ... that the most likely method to secure the reversion of the Wentworth property *is to treat* with Mrs Kaye on the ground of inaccuracy of the recovery. Mr Kaye is incompetent and not considered long for this world. ...'

He thinks that the advowson of the rectory of Toddington is worth '... £5,837 17s., allowing for the life of the present rector aged 57. ...

Vernon wishes much that you would apply for the title of Raby with reversion to him in failure of issue in you. I said, if the title came to you by descent, you would feel it incumbent on you to assume it, but I conceived you would not apply for a new creation in your own person, thinking that "Mr Conolly" was a more respectable appellation than the King could bestow. How far you might be induced to ask for the title for him, it was impossible for me to pretend to say. Vernon will be a material witness on the trial with Lord H[owe]. ...'

F/6/1 Jan.–Dec. 1800 Letters to Conolly from Cromie, London and Toddington.

13 June 1800 Cromie, London, to Conolly, Castletown, discussing at length his views of Conolly's possible entitlements under the marriage settlement of his mother's father, Thomas, [1st] Earl of Strafford, and Anna Johnson [in 1711]. He reports that the Duke of Portland and Lord Townshend had both '... praised your address [to his Co. Londonderry constituents on his retirement from the seat] in words of high encomium ... . I told you in my last how much that publication was admired by everybody I see or hear of. ...'

30 Aug. 1800 Cromie, London, to Conolly, Castletown.
'... All the leases [of Toddington] are ready for your signature, which from March 1801 will secure you a rental of £2,542 16s. 11d. Your former rent previous to the enclosure was £1,855 2s. 0d. ...'

He discusses the heavy remittance charges which Conolly has been paying. '... This extortion of the bankers in the two kingdoms suggested to me the idea of forming two houses, one in London, the other in Dublin, to deliver my countrymen from such imposition. The plan is ripening fast and [is] to extend much further than I had first conceived. Here let me ask you, which would be most conducive to your ease and comfort, that I should pitch my tent for life in England or Ireland. ...'

30 Sep. 1800 Cromie, London, to [Conolly] refuting Conolly's charge that '... I disobeyed your orders last summer in *not* taking possession of Wentworth Castle in your name, that through such neglect you are deprived of a chance of compromise with Mrs Kaye, involved in a greater expense to sift your title to the bottom, Mr Byng allowed an opportunity to coalesce with her, and Boodle leisure to bribe your solicitor, Bridges. ...' Cromie demonstrates that everything he has done and not done has been pursuant to Conolly's instructions.

13 Dec. 1800 Cromie, Lincoln's Inn, to [Conolly] announcing that the Lord Chancellor has made a decree in the lawsuit between Conolly and Lord Howe and the others which fully vindicates Conolly's character and conduct but requires that he pay £30,000 to his three surviving sisters. [The £10,000 to William Conolly Staples had presumably lapsed with Staples's death.] This means that Conolly's title to Toddington and the detached estates is now clear, and Cromie will immediately proceed to sell the latter.

[late 1800?] 'Note of Sir Michael Cromie on sale of detached estates ...'. This shows that they fetched at least £6,300.

F/6/2 Jan.–May and Sep.–Oct. 1801 Letters to Conolly from Cromie, London and Toddington.

6 Jan. 1801 Cromie, 19 Piccadilly, to [Conolly] about the decree and about Cromie's bank.

'... I cannot say I approve of English equity in this case, or see how it can be equitable to conclude a man bound by letters written under a complete misapprehension of the circumstances of his property, and unsuspecting that his generosity should be tortured into evidence against himself. ...

It will give you pleasure to hear this new establishment is much approved of by the public and likely to answer my expectations, but like every other infant scheme will require time to bring it to maturity. Every accommodation that you wish for and that can fall within my power shall always be at your command. ...

As you informed me of your having given the next presentation of the advowson of Toddington to Colonel Napier's son, I have given directions for the drawing a deed to specify that gift previous to the sale. ...'

23 Feb. 1801 Cromie, 19 Piccadilly, to [Conolly], endorsed 'Dissolution of partnership in the Union Bank.'

'... Your advice to me was equally friendly and sensible and I never lost sight of it. But having two children grown up to maturity and naturally looking for establishment, the present undertaking seemed to me likely to produce the means, and it was the only one I could adopt unaided by friends or government. So far as the prospect could reach my son, I have succeeded. He is for the present provided with an honourable method of maintaining himself without *risk* and of fitting himself for any employment that may require a perfect knowledge of business. ... But as to myself, I could not conceive without a trial the great anxiety attached to this business, the hazards that attend it and the confinement it requires; and, if those apprehensions could be calmed, the speculations some of the firm wished to adopt alarmed me to such a degree as to render me the most unhappy of men. I took my resolution and carried it into effect. On Friday the 20th instant the deeds of dissolution were perfected and bonds of *indemnity* to the amount of £50,000 passed to me for the use of my name for six months, as the declaring the firm altered in so short a time would defeat the hopes of those that remain and prevent them probably from getting another partner, which is now their object. ...

Lord Rossmore sat an hour with me this morning. He was yesterday at the Duchess of Gordon's when Mr Dundas came in. Her Grace asked him if he and his colleagues were pledged to Marquess Cornwallis upon the Emancipation. He replied in the

F/6/2 *contd.*		negative. The Duchess then said, why have you all resigned. I suspect there is a great deal more in the business than the public yet know. Mr Dundas evaded the question. ...'
	11 Apr. 1801	Cromie to Conolly. 'Your letter of the 7th inst. I have this moment received. Your sensible determination not to sell your estate at a period of such universal despondency as the present has relieved my breast from a load of anxiety not to be described. I flatter myself that my exertions would put £10,000 in your pocket. An estate so improved ought to sell at the lowest at 32 years' purchase. ...'
	22 Apr. 1801	Cromie to Conolly. 'The Wakefield commissioners have at length made up their report, as I am informed this moment by Mr Allan, one of the Duke of Leeds's solicitors. The amount in value about £24,000. This account cannot be relied on as *accurate*. We must wait the official statement, which is now expected every post. ... Be assured, experience will convince you how prudent it was to postpone your sales. Even two months will make a great change in the value of lands. ...'
	7 May. 1801	Cromie, Upper Fitzroy Street, [London], to [Conolly]. '... The Wakefield property will turn out more valuable to you than was expected .. . I conceive the copyholds *only* that were the right of William, [2nd] Earl of Strafford under the first settlements gavel, and all those acquired by Thomas [1st Earl] are yours *exclusively* in right of your mother. ... It may be a matter ... for your consideration to enfranchise those copyholds, thereby to turn them into freeholds – a transaction which the Duke of Leeds possesses the power no less than the will to perform. It will cost you about two years' purchase and you will sell for at least five years more. ...'
F/6/3	1802	Two letters and an enclosure to Conolly, Richmond House, Whitehall, London, from Cromie, Stacumnie [sic – Stacumny] Lodge, [Leixlip, Co. Kildare. (Stacumny, Cromie's Irish seat, was leased by him in perpetuity from Conolly and was part of the latter's Leixlip estate.)]
	18 May 1802	Cromie, Stacumnie [sic] Lodge, [Leixlip], to Conolly, Richmond House, Whitehall. '... I am much obliged to you for the accurate statement of Mrs Kaye's disposition of her property, as I feel very warmly interested in everything which concerns you. But [I] am sorry I can perceive no grounds to congratulate you upon. £20,000 would be a dear purchase for a *life interest* in Wentworth Castle upon the demise of

F/6/3 *contd.*		Mr Kaye, as I believe the late Lord Strafford cut down much timber ...'. He apologises for having mislaid some important Toddington accounts, and laments that the '... *load* of apprehension on my mind caused by my unfortunate bank connection, rendered me very unfit for your severe scrutiny into vouchers, some of which were stolen and others lost by the above embarrassments; but sixpence of your money did not remain unaccounted for. ...' He will search a large box of papers which are being stored for him in Dublin.
	7 Sep. 1802	Cromie, Stacumnie Lodge, to Conolly. '... It grieves me to the soul to find that you, for whom I have from my earliest youth felt more than a filial love and respect, and whom I have always considered as my first friend and patron, should now be the *only one* who frowns on me because I have been unfortunate. Am I the single man that ever made a mistake in speculation or was seduced by the sophistry of a deceiver? Are all my services to be forgotten and my error only remembered? But I have many enemies with you because I was your steady friend. Your sisters and all their great and numerous connections know well how industrious I was in your cause against them. Mr Vernon, by turns capable of the meanest and the most generous sentiments, never forgets that you received his private correspondence with Bridges through my hands. Lord Ossory and General Fitzpatrick hate me. Through the misrepresentations of all this host of enemies, you became yourself my accuser. ...' He goes on to recite his labours in building houses, carrying out enclosures, sinking drainage, etc. '... I went to Toddington every month while these works were going on ..., to view, measure, pay and direct ... . Besides, there was scarcely a day for six years that either your money or your law business did not require my attendance in London. The rent I paid for a house there for those purposes would have paid for a farm, by which I could at least have lived. These were not the duties of an agent: they were the ardours of a heart devoted to you. ...'
F/6/4–7	1801–27	Four folders of letters and case papers about the sale of the advowson of the rectory of Toddington.

G/	**DATE**	**DESCRIPTION**
G/1–18	**1682–1937**	**DEEDS, VOUCHERS AND OTHER PAPERS RELATING TO SETTLEMENTS, MORTGAGES, DEBTS, WILLS AND GENERAL MATTERS OF FAMILY FINANCE, AS FOLLOWS:**

G/1/1 –c.35	1682: 1690: 1698: 1707–8: 1718–19: 1723: 1725	Very miscellaneous business and other papers of William Conolly, as follows: account and receipt concerning the Upper Iveagh, [Co. Down], estate of William Hill, 1682; account of money spent on Conolly's personal account, 1698; two letters from Thomas Smith, Lisgoole, [Co. Fermanagh], to his 'brother', William Conolly, Dublin, about family matters, N.D. and 1718; conveyance by Conolly to Robert Lowry of Aghenis, Co. Tyrone, of the lands of Altedesert [Pomeroy] for £2,850, 1719; and letter from George Conyngham, Springhill, [Moneymore], to Conolly, Dublin, thanking him for complying with Conyngham's request about the commons, 25 May 1723.
G/2/1	1694	Marriage settlement of William Conolly and Katherine Conyngham, by which he settled 'Radinstown', Co. Meath, in consideration of a marriage portion of £2,300.
G/3/ 1–17	1695–7: 1725–8	Very rough jottings and memoranda by William Conolly, apparently about his estate and financial affairs.
G/4/1	1705	Settlement by William Conolly of the interest on £2,000 on his only brother, Patrick.
G/5/ 1–67	1707–29	Letters and legal case papers about Dr Ezekiel Burridge and Mrs Frances Burridge, of Sligo, mainly relating to William Conolly's role as Mrs Burridge's executor after her death in 1725; correspondents include Owen Wynne of Sligo and Henry Ormsby of Cammin, Co. Sligo, Mrs Burridge's brother.
G/6/1	1725	Settlement by William Conolly of all his estates in Cos. Donegal, Dublin, Fermanagh, Kildare, Meath and Westmeath and in North and South Wales: trustees, Sir Ralph Gore [4th Bt], Thomas Marlay and Charles Campbell.
G/7/ 1–c.50	1731–40	Letters, receipts, etc, to Mrs Katherine Conolly (widow of William Conolly) and to William Conolly junior (his nephew and principal heir) from members of the Burton, Carleton and Dickson families, relating to Conolly's legacies to them.
G/8/ 1–*c.* 15	1692–1750	Half-box of deeds, leases, wills, receipts, etc, all relating to the provision made by William Conolly, during his life and by his will, for his sister, Jane, wife of Thomas Pearson of Beamore, near Drogheda, and their children. Included is a lease of premises in Thomas Street, Dublin, 1740, and the will of Mrs Pearson, 1749.
G/9/ 1–2	1733	Settlement on the marriage of William Conolly junior and Lady Anne Wentworth, with related statement of title to the Conolly estates.

G/10/1	[*c.* 1740]	Schedule of deeds relating to the Conolly estates and the encumbrances upon them.
G/11/1	1758	Vast deed whereby Nathaniel Clements assigns to Sir Sampson Gideon of London in consideration of £25,000 sterling the mortgages he holds on parts of the estates of Thomas Conolly and the Earl of Shannon.
G/12–13	1759–1801	Two boxes of deeds and related papers (*c.* 35) whereby Thomas Conolly borrows large sums of money by a mixture of mortgage and annuity, mainly for the purpose of securing his sisters' marriage portions. G/12 contains deeds of 1759–73, and G/13 deeds of 1774–1801.
G/12	1759–1773	Box of deeds and related papers (*c.* 15) whereby Thomas Conolly borrows large sums of money by a mixture of mortgage and annuity, mainly for the purpose of securing his sisters' marriage portions, and also including an executors' account for his late father's estate, 4 January 1754–9 February 1759 and an abstract drawn up *c.* 1772 of Conolly's title to the manors of Ballyshannon and Leixlip following the passing of the act of parliament of 1766 for the sale of part of his estates.
		The deeds and papers include the following:
	12 June 1761	Mortgage from Thomas Conolly to Henry Fox of the manor of Grocers, Co. Londonderry, for £12,450 at 5 per cent.
	8 Aug. 1765	Letter from Michael Clarke, Dublin, to [Thomas Conolly]. '... As to your directions about preparing a plan for an act of parliament for changing the securities from one estate to another, I am much afraid it will be attended with greater difficulties than you seem to think of, as I understood from Counsellor Radcliffe when you borrowed the money in England to pay Clements, etc, that he never was in greater distress with regard to the security that was to be given by you for it, that what he did on that occasion was not only liable to exceptions to his own knowledge but was really excepted to by the counsel on the other side, and that if the money had not been paid before the security had been agreed to, you never would have got it. This I understand is all owing to your own marriage settlement, wherein your father's debts, portions and jointure are so blended with those several particulars and as auxiliaries the one to the other in your own settlement, that your whole estates are made liable thereto, and therefore no safe title I am afraid can be made to a purchaser. ...'

17 Jan. 1771 Indenture between Thomas Conolly and Michael Clarke of the first part, and William McGuire of Valans, Kent, of the second part, whereby Conolly borrows £16,000 British on mortgage from McGuire to pay the portions of Mrs Staples and Mrs Byng.

[*c.* 1772] Abstract of Thomas Conolly's title to the manors of Ballyshannon and Leixlip.

'... 14 December 1738. The said William Conolly made his will and devised the several estates in his power to his son, Thomas, for life with remainders over, and by codicil dated 27th December 1753 reciting the power in his settlement charged £4,000 apiece for his six daughters ..., and further charged his unsettled estates with £6,000 for his daughter, Catherine, and £4,000 apiece for his other five daughters. ...

29th and 30th December 1758. By indented deed of settlement of this date ... the said Thomas Conolly did pursuant to his powers charge the devised lands with £2,500 [per annum jointure] for the said Lady Louisa Augusta; and in order to free the devised lands from encumbrances and the manor of Castletown and Castlefinn from Lady Anne's jointure and from debts, the said Thomas Conolly did grant to trustees the manors of Ballyshannon and Leixlip among other lands in trust, by sale thereof to raise a sum sufficient to pay said original and additional portions and all the other debts affecting the devised lands of Castletown and Castlefin, and the remainder to be conveyed to said Thomas Conolly and his heirs.

1765 [*sic* – 1766], 6th George III, an act of parliament passed in Ireland for sale of part of the devised lands for payment of encumbrances and for settling other lands in lieu thereof, whereby several lands therein enumerated then of a clear yearly value of £2,948 7s. 2d. are vested in trustees to be sold for the purpose aforesaid, and the manor of Rathfarnham, Co. Dublin, of equal value is given in reprisal, discharged of Lady Anne Conolly's jointure, which devised lands, together with Raddinstown, etc, the Co. Meath estate, then amounted in yearly value to £4,117 11s. ...

By this act of parliament the Ballyshannon estate of the present yearly value of £3,711 and the Leixlip estate of the yearly value of £1,400 are vested in fee in Mr Conolly, subject to the jointure of Lady Anne, his mother, and to the uses and trusts concerning the same declared in and by the settlement of 1733. ...'

The act of parliament, however, provides only for the discharge of those debts which by its terms are charged on the estates earmarked for sale. It does not provide for the payment of two mortgage debts of £10,000 each, one charged on the manor of Rathfarnham and one on the Vintners' Proportion, nor for the payment of the additional portions (amounting in total to £24,000) for Conolly's sisters, which were charged on unspecified,

G/12 *contd.*		unsettled estates (but not specifically on the lands earmarked for sale by the act of parliament). Conolly now proposes to place the manors of Ballyshannon and Leixlip in the hands of trustees for the payment of the £44,000, although it is noted that they are also currently liable for his own debts of £31,400.
	19 Jan. 1773	Lease for a year from Conolly to Thomas Hunt of Mollington, Cheshire, of Conolly's Meath, Roscommon and Leitrim estates.
	20 Jan. 1773	Assignment from the Duke of Leinster and Ralph Earl of Ross to Thomas Hunt and Colonel Samuel Townshend of the manors of Ballyshannon and Leixlip, with a then annual rental of £3,712 and £1,397 respectively. The purpose of the deed is to release these lands from the settlement charges placed on them by Thomas Conolly's marriage settlement of 1758, and make them subject to Lady Anne Conolly's jointure of £3,000 per annum British plus £16,000 British of the additional portions of £26,000 left to his daughters by the will of William Conolly junior. It is recited that several lands and premises vested by the act of parliament of 1765 in the Duke of Leinster, Nathaniel Clements and Michael Clarke had already been sold to answer the purposes of that act (and in particular to raise the original portions of £24,000 provided for the daughters of William Conolly junior in his marriage settlement of 1733). The lands sold seem to include the 'Raddinstown' estate and other lands in Co. Meath which together had a rental of £1,170 per annum. It is also recited that 'only' £43,333 remains to be raised by the sale of lands specified in the act of parliament, and that the remaining lands so specified are sufficient for this purpose. The deed then proceeds to vest Ballyshannon and Leixlip in Hunt and Townshend, who are to mortgage them to Lord Cavan [presumably by assigning the mortgage previously held by William McGuire] for £16,000 British. The clause for redemption provides that Conolly is to pay Hunt and Townshend principal and interest amounting to £17,010 British or £18,427 Irish. Alternatively, he may discharge the mortgage by conveying to Hunt and Townshend lands of equivalent value [to Ballyshannon and Leixlip?], viz. £1,600 per annum in Great Britain or £2,000 per annum in Ireland. There is also a clause binding Hunt and Townshend, on the same terms as Conolly is bound, Conolly's '... heirs and all and every other person and persons whatsoever having or lawfully claiming ... any estate, right, title, trust or interest, charge or encumbrance either at law or in equity of, in, to or out of the said manors or lordships ... from ... him ... or under the said William Conolly, his father, or any of his ancestors ...'.

G/12 *contd.*	20 Jan. 1773	'Deed of assignment of the portions of Mrs Staples and Mrs Byng ...' [which are to be paid by the £16,000 borrowed by Hunt and Townshend and so remotely become a charge on Ballyshannon and Leixlip. £8,000 of the £16,000 represents 'original' portions charged on 'Raddinstown', and the other £8,000 additional portions not specifically charged on anything and lying outside the terms of the act of parliament.]
	20 Jan. 1773	Two originals of an indenture between Conolly, of the one part, and Hunt and Townshend of the other, much shorter in length but apparently covering the same ground as the mortgage of the same date. This deed describes the estate act of 1766 as 'An act for the sale of part of the estates devised to the Rt Hon. Thomas Conolly Esq. for life with remainders over by the will and codicil of his father ..., for the payment of several encumbrances affecting the lands so devised and for the settling of other estates in lieu thereof to the uses in the said will and codicil and in the marriage settlement of the said Thomas Conolly ...'.
G/14	1773–87	Box of accounts, receipts, etc (*c.* 500), for payments of jointure, annuities and mortgage interest charged on Thomas Conolly's estates. These papers all relate to his dealing with Dublin banks: Sir Annesley Stewart, Bt, & Co. (an 11–page statement of account, 1773); David Latouche & Sons [who forced the sale of the Westmeath and part of the Co. Dublin estate in 1782]; and John Stewart & Co.
G/15	1790–1803	The same except that only Latouches and Stewarts are involved. A letter of 17 September 1802 from John Stewart, Dublin, about Conolly's overdraft, is addressed to Conolly at Wentworth Castle, Barnsley, Yorkshire [whither he had presumably gone to try to assert his claim to the Yorkshire estates of the Earls of Strafford].
G/16	1793–1803	The same, except that this box contains accounts, receipts, correspondence, etc, between Thomas Conolly and his London bankers, Nesbitt & Stewart.
G/17	1778–c.1829	Box containing folders of accounts, correspondence, bonds, judgements, statements of the position, etc, all relating to the volume of debt affecting Thomas Conolly's estates and the general financial mess which came to light at his death in 1803 and complicated the task of his executors and trustees, as follows:
G/17/1	1791	Statement of the locations and tenures of Thomas Conolly's various estates.

G/17/2 1793–1803 Letters to Thomas Conolly about his debts, mainly to his relations on his mother's side, his nephew, George Byng of Wrotham Park, Middlesex, and his brother-in-law, General Sir William Howe, later Viscount Howe.

24 Aug. 1797 Sir William Howe, Wivenhoe, near Colchester, to Conolly ('Dear Sir') about Conolly's debt to him. '... As these embarrassments would be totally removed by the payment of the fortune which has been so many years delayed, I must repeat my solicitations that you would discharge that debt.'

30 Jan. 1801 George Byng, St James's Square, to Conolly ('My dearest uncle'), Castletown.
'When I left Ireland about three years ago, you informed me that *perhaps* in two years you might find it convenient to pay interest for the £12,000 [by bond dated 26 February 1792] due to me, and the £2,000 due to Lord Strafford's estate. As my brother Robert is going to be married, and as I owe him 5,000 three per cent consols, which would not now cost above £2,700, and which *must* be paid in the names of trustees for the benefit of younger children, you would oblige me if you could pay it now, or after the sale of the Bedfordshire estate, if you mean to dispose of it. But if it is not convenient for you, I would not desire it for the world. I would sooner live upon bread and water for a twelvemonth than appear unkind to you, for as long as I live I shall continue to feel the most sincere and disinterested affection for you, and never can forget the *many* marks of kindness you have so repeatedly shown ...'.

13 Feb. 1801 Byng, Wrotham Park, to Conolly, Castletown.
'As I have many debts to discharge, I shall of course be happy to receive what money you can spare with convenience to yourself after the sale of the Bedfordshire and Yorkshire estates. But, alas, the pressing necessity of replacing 5,000 three per cent consols on my brother's account, no longer exists, as his marriage is not likely to take place. *They* have had a quarrel. She appears irreconcilable. Her first husband was a brute, and she is afraid of embarking a second time into the holy estate.

As you wish it, I shall of course deduct the £248 Irish paid by you for these three last years to Mr C[otter]. It is very singular, and I must add rather unfortunate for the country, that in the course of *nearly* 19 years you should never have had sufficient interest with the government to procure so trifling a place as was required by Mr Cotter.'

22 Dec. 1802 Edward Bulkeley [Conolly's Dublin man of business] to Conolly, Castletown, about the rents and arrears of 'Newtown'. '... By the

G/17/2 *contd.*		mortgage account, there appears a very slow progress in the sales. From 4 May 1801 to 6 September 1802, above a year and a quarter, no sale was made. The amount of the sale is only a fourth part of the interest incurred in the time, unless the £350 17s. refers to something significant. Perhaps it may to Mr Hamilton's purchase of the Largy wood, of which no mention is made. ...'
G/17/3	*c.* 1795–1805	Papers about the debts which Thomas Conolly left at his death in April 1803, including details of debts paid off since 1795. One undated list, in Conolly's handwriting, is of principal money paid off since 1795. This includes £8,000 to Lady Buckingham[shire], £16,000 to Latouche, 'besides Newtown to Latouche, £10,000 at least', etc. The total comes to £63,700.
G/17/4	1803	List of deeds sent to Castletown.
G/17/5	1803–4	Letters to Lady Louisa Conolly and to Thomas Conolly's trustees from Edward Bulkeley, the Conolly man of business in Dublin, about the debts and general financial mess.
G/17/6	1803–6	Pocket-sized account book kept by Lady Louisa Conolly.
G/17/7	*c.* 1806–13	Statement of the case for promoting a private act of parliament to enable Thomas Conolly's trustees to sell Castletown, in breach of the provisions of his will, together with other papers of a general nature relating to the post-1803 financial situation, including:
	[1806–7]	Reasons [in Lady Louisa Conolly's handwriting] justifying the trustees in applying to parliament for legislation to enable them to sell Castletown. 'The testator, under the most ardent wish for a discharge of his debts, directs the disposal of such parts of his property as the trustees shall deem fit for the purpose, *tyeing up only* (from such sales) his fine mansion house and demesne of Castletown with Celbridge estate adjoining it. The trustees have sold a large estate in Bedfordshire ... and two estates in Ireland, in the counties of Leitrim and Londonderry, and would willingly proceed on with more sales, could purchasers be had in these times. But the major part of the remaining estates in fee being let forever, does not invite them. The College and Church lands would prove very unproductive sales proportionably to the value of their income, and therefore the trustees most reluctantly are induced to come before parliament to pray for a release of the testator's injunction to preserve Castletown for his heirs. Two considerable disappointments have taken place since his death, and ... the will ... cannot now stand upon the same ground that it did before. ...

G/17/7 *contd.*

The testator, with the most affectionate and benevolent intentions towards his native country, endeavours at establishing an *independent family* in it that is not likely to desert it. ... [The trustees consider that] the expected rise on the estates will be slow and distant, and therefore, looking on Castletown (in the present moment) as an unproductive encumbrance, they strongly recommend it to all parties to part with it, which a proposal from government to purchase it for a barrack gives them an opportunity of doing. Lady Louisa, whose consent is necessary during her lifetime, gives it, under an impression that *in effect* it is fulfilling the will better than if she resisted the necessary forms for obtaining permission to part with Castletown.'

The 'two considerable disappointments' referred to are: (1) a debt to Colonel Harcourt of £10,000 charged on the Vintners Proportion, Co. Londonderry. The testator's father, William Conolly, bequeathed this estate 'to his daughters in the event of his son's leaving no heir. The testator uniformly believed, to the end of his life, that his sisters (upon succeeding to him) would be liable to that debt ..., [but] a consultation was held on it, in which Counsellor Ball gave it as his opinion that an act of parliament which passed in the year 1766 (for the purpose of arranging the sale of some estates) had exonerated the Vintners Proportion from the charge ...'. (2) The testator had assumed that he was the sole heir to the Wakefield estate in Yorkshire under the will of his grandfather, Thomas [1st] Earl of Strafford, 'and expected ... to sell and raise £60,000 upon it'. But litigation initiated by the representatives of his mother's sisters, resulted in 1804 in an adverse decree that the estate should be divided into three shares, thus reducing the testator's inheritance from £60,000 to £20,000.

12 Nov. 1813 'Statement of the trust funds of the late Rt Hon. Thomas Conolly.' This shows that the rental of the trust estates is £18,801 and the outgoings – in the form of interest payments, chief rents, annuities, 'permanent charges', etc – come to £14,848, leaving a surplus of only £3,953. Total debts amount to £194,158, including legacies under the will of Thomas Conolly (principally £10,000 to the Napier family). Lord Clancarty is owed £40,000, Lord Eardley £15,925, George Byng £16,000, Lord Cavan £17,550, John Clements £10,830, Colonel Harcourt £10,000, Messrs Latouche £13,264, Messrs Stewart £14,408, the executors of William, Lord Strafford, £1,733, and the legatees of the late Miss Fitzgerald *c.* £1,300. The permanent charges on the Castletown estate (£584 per annum) are included, so presumably the act of parliament had been obtained, the Castletown/Celbridge estate was now part of the trust estate, and its rental was therefore included in the £18,801.

G/17/8 1791–1827 Bond, judgements and statements of account, all relating to Thomas Conolly's debt to Colonel Thomas Staples.

G/17/ 9–10	1788–1829	Two folders of bonds, judgements, statements of account, etc, relating to miscellaneous debts of Thomas Conolly.
G/18	1801–1937	Box of deeds, correspondence and accounts relating to the financial and estate affairs of the Conolly family, including the settlements made on the marriages of Miss Louisa A. Conolly (1846) and Miss Margaret Mary Conolly (1854).

H/	**DATE**	**DESCRIPTION**
H/1–17	**1684–1945**	**RENTALS (MAINLY OUTSIZE) OF THE CO. KILDARE ESTATES, RENTALS (MAINLY OUTSIZE) RELATING TO ESTATES IN MORE THAN ONE COUNTY, AND MAPS, PLANS AND SURVEYS, ARRANGED AS FOLLOWS:**
H/1	1684–5: *c.* 1700–1830	Box of surveys and rentals of the Co. Kildare estates, including: Castletown estate rentals, 1710–28 (mentioning Lord Limerick and Bartholomew Van Homrigh); list of Leixlip estate arrears, 1731; Leixlip estate rentals, 1774–1830 (the earliest mentioning Richard Guinness, father of Arthur); rentals of Castletown and Leixlip combined, 1761–82; Colonel Pakenham's rental of Castletown estate for the half year ending 1 May 1815; etc.
H/2	1753–1831	Box of outsize rentals, with a couple of maps, covering all estates or estates in more than one country. Included is an account of *c.* 1760 between Thomas Conolly and his agent, Charles Davis, which states the half year's rent of Leixlip as £478, of Castletown as £515, of Rodanstown, Co. Meath, as £588, and of 'Westmeath' and 'Roscommon' as £533 and £416 respectively.
H/3	1767–76	Outsize account book balancing disbursements on various accounts against rent receipts from all estates.
H/4	1787–92	Outsize rent book for the Castletown and Leixlip estates (127ff).
H/5	1815	The same – but a different format and fairly empty (50ff).
H/6	1821–40	Outsize account book of Edward Conolly, balancing disbursements on various accounts against rent receipts from all estates.
H/7	1902–03: 1905	Five rental and account books for the Castletown estate, for the half years ending Dec. 1902, June 1903, Dec. 1903, June 1905, Dec. 1905.

H/8	Mar. 1906–Dec. 1907	Four rental and account books for Castletown for half years ending Mar. and May 1906 (rental), and June (accounts) 1906, Sep. and Nov. 1906 (rental) and Dec. (accounts) 1906, and as above for 1907.
H/9	1908–10	Four rental and account books for Castletown for half years ending Mar. and May (rental) 1908 and 1910 and June 1908 and 1910 (accounts), and Sep. and Nov. 1908 and 1909 (rental) and Dec. 1908 (accounts) and Dec. 1909 (accounts).
H/10	1910–12	Four rental and account books for Castletown for half years ending Sep. and Nov. 1910 and 1911 (rental) and Dec. 1910 and 1911 (accounts), and Mar. and May 1911 and 1912 (rental) and June 1911 and 1912 (accounts).
H/11	1912–14	Five rental and account books for Capt. E.M. Conolly's estate at Castletown for half years ending Sep., Nov. and Dec. 1912, Mar., May and June 1913, Sep., Nov. and Dec. 1913, Mar., May and June 1914, Sep., Nov. and Dec. 1914.
H/12	1917–18	Three rental and account books for Colonel E.M. Conolly's estate at Castletown for half years ending June 1917, Dec. 1917, June 1918.
H/13	1918–24	Three rental and account books for Colonel E.M. Conolly's estate at Castletown for half year ending Sep., Nov. and Dec. 1918, for half year ending Sep., Nov. and Dec. 1921, and Mar., May and June 1922, and for two years ending Mar., May and June 1924.
H/14	1924–25: 1938: 1942–1943: 1947: 1938–45	Six rental and account books for the Castletown estate for half years in 1924, 1925, 1938; statement of accounts and auditors' report to shareholders for years ending Dec. 1942, 1943 and 1947; volume recording receipts and expenditure (monthly) of the Castletown Estate Co. Ltd, 1938–45.
H/15	[early 18th century]	Portfolio of *c.* 12 maps taken from the Down Survey by Patrick Guerin, Deputy Surveyor General. Includes various parishes in Co. Kildare, with details of parish and proprietors of land, and refers to Co. Westmeath.
H/16	[1709–80]	Maps (c.14) relating to Leixlip, Dunsink, Rathfarnham and the Roscommon estate, some drawn by Henry Roe; including a survey of Rathfarnham certified by Thomas Taylor.
H/17	[1742]	Maps (c.13) relating to Conolly lands at Ballybrack, Leixlip, Rathfarnham and in Co. Roscommon.

J/	DATE	DESCRIPTION
J/1–11	1697–1938	ACCOUNTS AND ACCOUNT BOOKS RELATING TO PERSONAL, HOUSEHOLD AND DEMESNE EXPENDITURE, MAINLY AT CASTLETOWN, ARRANGED AS FOLLOWS:
J/1	1697: 1723–8	Folder of personal accounts of William Conolly, mainly relating to his coach, including a letter to him about apple trees [for Castletown?].
J/2	1720–33	Folder of personal accounts of Mrs Katharine Conolly, including an undated letter to her about the state of the house at Rodanstown, Co. Meath.
J/3/1–3	1730s–40s	Three folders of personal accounts of Lady Anne Conolly.
J/4/ 1–10	1742–8	Ten folders of personal accounts of William Conolly junior. One is stated to be 'Dublin accounts' and two are stated to be 'Leixlip accounts'. [William Conolly junior and Lady Anne lived at Leixlip Castle because Mrs Katherine Conolly had a life-interest in Castletown.]
J/5	1798–1801	Folder of personal accounts of Thomas Conolly.
J/6	1761–6	Folder of vouchers from William Coane, steward at Castletown, for disbursements made by him.
J/7	1762	Folder of monthly returns for various works carried out on the house and demesne at Castletown.
J/8/1–3	1762–81	Three account books recording household and demesne expenditure at Castletown.
J/9	1767–90	Box of Castletown household and demesne accounts and account books (*c.* 12 documents and 12 volumes), including a series of settled accounts, 1767–78, between Thomas Conolly and William Coane.
J/10	[*c.* 1790]	Two outsize plans for, respectively, a hothouse and a gardener's house at Castletown
J/11	1796–1803: 1898: 1906–38	Box containing: account book outlining sundry expenses in relating to Castletown (1796–1803); inventory of Castletown taken in conjunction with the resettlement of the Castletown estate in 1898, with index, detailing rooms such as beer cellar, boudoir and stillroom; and visitors book (1906–38).

PART II

THE CONOLLY PAPERS IN TRINITY COLLEGE DUBLIN

THE CONOLLY PAPERS IN TRINITY COLLEGE DUBLIN (TCD MSS 3939–84)

Reference*	Description
MSS 3939–3973	Household accounts, personal accounts, receipts and rentals mostly pertaining to Castletown, 1684–1893.
MSS 3974/1–109	Miscellaneous financial, household and personal papers of William Conolly, Katherine Conolly and William Conolly junior, 1685–1748.
MSS 3974/109–3975/349	Letters, receipts and other miscellaneous papers of Thomas Conolly 1758–70
MSS 3975/350–3976/444	Letters, receipts and other miscellaneous papers of Thomas Conolly 1771–76
MSS 3976/445–3977/715	Letters, receipts and other miscellaneous papers of Thomas Conolly 1777–80
MSS 3977/716–3978/956	Letters, receipts and other miscellaneous papers of Thomas Conolly 1781–88
MSS 3978/957–3979/1063	Letters, receipts and other miscellaneous papers of Thomas Conolly 1789–95
MSS 3979/1064–3980/1303	Letters, receipts and other miscellaneous papers of Thomas Conolly 1796–99
MSS 3980/1304–3981/1439	Letters, receipts and other miscellaneous papers of Thomas Conolly 1800–03
MSS 3981/1440–3983/1695	Letters, receipts and accounts and other miscellaneous papers of the trustees of Thomas Conolly 1803–21
MS 3983/1696–1717	Letters, receipts and accounts of Edward Michael Conolly 1821–48
MS 3983/1718–35	Letters, receipts and accounts of Thomas Conolly MP 1848–1876
MS 3984/1736–1923	Undated letters and accounts mostly relating to Thomas Conolly 1738–1803

* TCD MS numbers do not correspond to discrete section of archives but rather correspond to the contents of a TCD Manuscript box.

MSS	DATE	DESCRIPTION
3939–3973	**1684–1893**	**TCD Conolly miscellaneous volumes of accounts etc, as follows:**
3939–41	1778–1806	Three volumes of tradesmen's receipt books, with receipts pasted in some cases; in others the printed forms in the volumes are used.
3942–3	1763–1770	Two volumes of servants wages receipts
3944	1770	Survey of part of Trinity College Dublin estates in the parish of Drumholin, bar. Tirhugh, Co. Donegal leased by Thomas Conolly
3945–47	1781–92	Three volumes of rentals relating to the Conolly estates in Counties Dublin and Kildare.
3948–50	1782–95	Three volumes detailing prices of groceries consumed at Castletown
3951	1783–7	Memoranda of the consumption of different foods at Castletown tabulated.
3952	1758–78	Accounts, monthly, of household bills, servants' wages and tradesmen's bill.
3953	1767–77	Accounts, quarterly, of house bills, servants' wages and tradesmen's bills.
3954–6	1768–93; 1 778–88;	Three volumes of detailed accounts 1786–90 in the handwriting of Lady Louisa Conolly often with receipt numbers corresponding to MSS 3939–41 above,
3957	1791–1803, 1821–3	Volume containing servant's wages and miscellaneous household accounts.
3958	1854–6	Volume of Castletown household accounts
3959	1885–93	Volume of Castletown household accounts
3960	N.D.	Alphabetical catalogue of the Castletown Library.
3961	1684–5	Letterbook of a Dutch merchant in Dublin [Possibly Bartholomew Van Homrigh] in Dutch and English.
3962	1787–8; 1792–7	Volume containing expenditure on hounds, mostly wages and food, 1787–8, as well as miscellaneous Castletown expenses, 1792–7.

3963–65	1766; 1767–70; 1775–84	Personal accounts of Thomas Conolly.
3966	1766–75	Personal account book of Lady Louisa Augusta Conolly.
3967	1847–53	Personal account book of Arthur W. Conolly 51st King's Own Light Infantry, with a list of his belongings including books.
3968	1818–21	Workmen's bills on account of the Castletown rents.
3969	N.D	Accounts of the servants, windows and hearths at Castletown for tax purposes.
3970	1803–11	Entry book of details of drafts and bank notes and to whom paid.
3971	1798–9	Castletown dairy accounts
3972	May 1815	Account of Colonel Pakenham's first rent collection.

MSS	DATE	DESCRIPTION
3974/ 1–109	**1709–48**	**Miscellaneous financial, household and personal papers of William Conolly, Katherine Conolly and William Conolly junior, as follows:**
1	1709	Draft indenture between Garrett Nangle of Co. Westmeath, gent., and Bruen Worthington of Dublin gent. Transferring a rent charge granted to Nangle by Francis Nugent late of Co. Westmeath, esq., 9 Nov. 1685 on lands in Co. Roscommon. Worthington was acting on behalf of William Conolly, who acquired these lands in 1703.
2/A–D	13, 15 Apr., 6 Oct., 20 Nov. 1714	Four letters from William Conolly, Dublin, to Rev. [ ], about his nephew, William Conolly junior's inheritance in England. Conolly junior was born in 1706, the son of the Speaker's brother Patrick and his wife, Frances Hewett of Dunton Bassett, Leicestershire. These letters are damaged/illegible in places.
2A		Dublin 13 April 1714 Rev. Sir, I received both yours of the [ ] instance and the 30th ult and am sorry upon the whole matter to find my nephews and nieces circumstances so bad in all particulars I shall not enter into the debate how liable my brothers small assets are to the debts you

3974/2A
contd.

mention for I think every just debt ought to be paid and to prevent anything further then affecting the mortgage effecting the little estate. It is but just the plate etc should be sold and all debts paid and I doubt not but you will take particular care that the debts be justly due and made as easy as possible and the plate sold to the best advantage. When this is done you can in a very narrow compass show what will remain to both my nephew and niece and then I beg Colonel Hewetts and your thoughts as to the estate. I will tell you my opinion very candidly that though the estate near inheritance and came to my nephew I should think it very hard he should have it without a reasonable portion to his sister and since it's the case of a brother and sister who are equally related to Colonel Hewett and me, he shall find me very just and reasonable in anything he shall think so I can say little more till I receive your answer to this and then matters will be near a determination. I am sorry for Col. Hewett's indisposition though I have not the honour of being known to him pray give him my service and accept of the like from… WC [In Katherine Conolly's handwriting]

2B

Dublin 15 Apr. 1714
Sir,
My patience is clear worn out in not hearing from you about my nephew's affairs having long since expected according to your several letters, that before this the account should be sent [to] me. I have not drawn a farthing on your lands…there is now two years rent to be accounted for besides the [ ] this I let by to make a sum to pay a part of the debts on the estate and I cannot justify letting matters stand as they now are and hope you will make me easy by getting in all that is due and transmitting the accounts that I may do what is proper. I am sensible it is your multiplicity of business that retards matters and I fear this will find you entangled in parliamentary affairs but I hope you will set a little time apart to answer my expectations and hope as you formerly wrote me that the tythes are paid with all care and also the rents and that if they are not that you have proceeded as you designed as well about them as the derelict lands in which you were resolved to prepare a bill. Pray mind these severally and let me have your answer for I hate trouble and writing as much as I can. I left it to your judgement and information whether it was not proper to sell the [ ] and I hope you have not [ ] proper time. I am informed that the landlord and tenants of Marchton parish have a desire to apply to you for consent or have to drive their several through our con[] I hope you will not nor will not consent to this upon any account but on the contrary to take all methods to oppose it, for I am very apprehensive it will extremely prejudice my nephews estate and fall the rents thereof and [] have [ ] time it must be our interest to suffer no encroachment. I could say a good deal more on this

3974/2A *contd.*		subject but I am sure you understand it so well I will say no more…WC [In Katherine Conolly's handwriting]
2C		Conolly to? 6 September 1714 'I had the honour of yours of the 27th of August last and heartily condole you on the death of Colonel Hewett whose loss after consideration will affect his friends as well as his country. I pray make my respects to his lady this melancholy occasion. When he wrote to me he gave me the account of £2000 of my nephews which I then [ ] him that I hoped the sum was laid out at interest.' Conolly goes on to enquire about the disposal of his brother's plate. He also asks when his nephew left the school he was at and went to London. [This letter very difficult to read.]
2D		20 September 1714 Same to Same This letter is again about his nephew's affairs, but extraordinarily hard to read.
3/A–C	8 Dec. 1720–10 Feb. 1721	Accounts of the office of the cursitor in the Court of Chancery following the death of Thomas Carr, the incumbent in this office. William Conolly junior succeeded Carr in this office.
4	13 Nov. 1723	William Colvill to David Nixon at the Court of Exchequer. Endorsed with reply from John Young certifying that a search had revealed no judgement against Philip, Duke of Wharton. [This relates to Conolly's purchase of the Rathfarnham estate from Wharton in 1723, for which see Section D of the Castletown papers.]
5–7	9, 21 Nov. 1728	Captain Thomas Dickson's accounts with Conolly for the May 1728 rent of the manor of Ballyshannon, the church lands at Ballyhanna and the College lands at Bundrows and Tirhugh, Co. Donegal. Thomas Dickson was Conolly's brother-in-law and his agent for the Ballyshannon estate. Also included is a letter from Dickson to Robert McCausland, Conolly's agent at Limavady, about the delay in receiving payment from the dragoons stationed at Ballyshannon.
8	21, Nov. 1728	Robert McCausland, Limavady, to Conolly, about Ballyshannon estate affairs, and Conolly's recovery from illness. 'I am heartily glad you have recovered of your last inflammation of St Anthony's for we had various accounts here of your disorder, but praise be to God it is over, or will soon. And that it may pass to good in relieving your [ ] of your former disorder.' He then proceeds to discuss estate affairs.

3974/9 23 Nov. 1728 Robert McCausland [Limavady] to Conolly about the emigration of 'Men of substance and poor men' from Conolly's estates to the West Indies:
'They are all mad, and those tithes all over the north are the great occasion of this cry in going to the Western plantations.... I fear if the government put a stop to any person that has a mind to transport themselves to the Western plantations who will pay all their just debts and demands before they leave the place where they reside. That such a loss will put them for disgrace...God knows how those designs and affairs will end: but they looks gloomy at present in most parts of Ulster as I am told.'

10 23 Nov 1728 McCausland [Limavady] to Henry Downes, Bishop of Derry.
He suggests that the collectors of the tithes stop their collections because the tenants are unable to pay due to the rising price of grain. He doesn't want a repeat of the 'debates that happened last year'. 'I am as little fond of being concerned in such debates as any man of my own station: and had it not been for several letters I had from my Lord Justice Conolly and your Lordship and daily complaints from the people I should not give myself the least trouble had they broke others bones, six days in the week, as I fear it will come to that in the end.'

11 25 Nov. 1728 McCausland [Limavady] to Conolly.
'This day the [tithe] farmers of Mr Rothery of Ballykelly and your petitioners came to an agreement to leave the debates to Colonel Cary and me.'

12 26 Nov. 1728 Bishop Henry Downes [Londonderry] to Conolly.
'I take the opportunity by the first post to let your Excellency know what the Corporation (which is not a rich one) has cheerfully and unanimously done towards their support of the poor under the apprehension of scarcity of corn by reason of the great shake it received on the 24 August last, and the advantage proposed to be made of fifty engrossers and forestallers of the market: these measures they readily came unto upon my bare intimation of the charitable scheme that was setting on foot in Dublin in favour of us in the north and my order to promote what my Lord Primate proposed that I thereto became a subscriber as I readily expressed my willingness to come in and to be a subscriber somewhere to be so good and charitable an end but did not desire to become a subscriber here in case the corporation (as they had formerly done with great success) should set on foot any method to the same purpose. What they have thought to do your Excellency will perceive by the enclosed and I this day proposed to throw in my might vis an £100 pound upon the same charitable design and we hope that running of the risk of a little loss to bring

3974/12 *contd.*		in great gain to the poor and by prudent management to keep the markets down to a moderate degree and to prevent their being made a prey to such as would devour them. It is with pleasure also that I can acquaint your Excellency that by a letter I received from Colonel McCausland I am in hopes that the affair of Ballyikilly [*sic*] may at last be accommodated between the tythemen and the tenants having come to a resolution to submit their differences for determination to Colonel Carew,[*sic* – Cary] which is agreeable to what was recommended by your Excellency. Ps. I hope to hear soon that your rheumy [*sic*] which robbed you of the use of your eyes (which you have employed too much on your private and public affairs) is happily gone off and carried off an stammer that might have been troublesome in some respects.'
13–16	30 Nov., 2, 9 Dec. 1728	Four further letters from Robert McCausland to Conolly about Conolly's estates at Limavady, Co. Londonderry, and Ballyshannon, Co. Donegal.
16a	19 Jan. 1731/32	Accounts of voyage to Stockholm in the ship 'Mars' of Dublin. It is unclear why this document is in the collection. [There is no obvious Conolly connection.]
17–28	10 July 1732– 20 July 1734	Correspondence and other documents including a draft deed of sale (no. 26) relating to the purchase of Stretton Hall, Staffordshire, by William Conolly junior from William Congreve in 1733 Includes references to various charges payable out of the estate. The total sum paid for the estate was £15,535, which included a mortgage of £7,300.
29	16 Dec. 1735,	Katherine Conolly (Dublin) to [George Bubb Dodington, Clerk of the Pells in the Irish Exchequer] Sir, I had 2 packets ago the favour of yours of the 28th of November, not long before that your affair [the emoluments of the Clerkship of the Pells] was in the House of Commons. When I heard it was to be mentioned I assure you, Sir, I was not neglectful of it. I sent to my friends both in town and country, for my nephew Conolly and some more of my friends was out of town, but came time enough to do your services and I am truly glad to tell you it went as you and your friends could wish. You may depend I shall ever have a true regard for every man that belongs to your uncle [the late George] Dodington for whom my dear Mr Conolly had such a regard. I had and always shall have a pleasure to serve you but as my power is far short of my inclination (none) to serve my friends I shall be silent and give you no further trouble than to assure you I am with great respect your most obedient humble servant Katherine Conolly.'

3974/30	2 June 1736	Katherine Conolly, Dublin, to an unknown recipient. 'Sir, the last letter I had the honour to receive from you was so obliging and filled with such kind expressions encourages me to beg your [ ] and friendship in an affair I am to acquaint you with. Mr [William] Harrison the [Revenue] Commissioner being just a dying or dead I have nothing so much at heart as that my nephew Conolly may succeed Mr Harrison – I made application to Sir Robert Walpole on the death of my dear Mr Conolly but my sorrows made my request come to[o] late and then I had most obliging messages from Sir Robert that, that commission was disposed of but [he] would be glad of any opportunity to serve me and I cannot think any of the King's friends can forget the many true and faithful services my dear husband for many years of his life did for the protestant succession and for the Kings service and it is well known in this kingdom what he suffered in the Queen's reign – and as I never applied for any mark of royal favour for myself, which many thought I had a just right to do, both on my husband and my own family's account I never did – but now I beg your friendship and interest in this affair – and give me leave to say [that although] my nephew Conolly's fortune or the best part of it is in this kingdom, he is an Englishman by birth and education – and I may add because I am no stranger to the affairs of this kingdom that a man of his fortune and interest in this country would be the greatest service to the revenue – and I dare say he would be a constant resident at the Board when his attendance in parliament in England was not necessary – and I am sure that Board is often wanting on many occasions – this I do not say by inducing my nephew's friends to serve him on this occasion, for I hope he has many other qualifications – his fortune, his own merit, and the services and memory of his uncle I hope will engage his friends to serve him, and Sir I have not the assurance to write myself to Sir Robert Walpole but must entreat your making my most humble services acceptable to him and that I am very sensible of the friendship he had and always expressed for my dear Mr Conolly and myself for which I retain a just sense so I shall give no more further trouble now ….'
31	12 Dec. 1738	M. Pelham's promise to pay Mr Birch the sum of £30. Unclear who either party is.
31a	22 Nov. 1740	Receipt for £60 received from Thomas Pakenham by John Smyth for carrying out several transactions in London.
32–50	7, 8, 10, 13, 14, 16, 17 Apr. 1744	Nineteen receipts for various items and services, including a surgeon for the cook and nurse, various groceries and glazing. Mostly signed by William Conolly junior.

3974/51	Apr. 1745	Wyatt's valuation of the estate of Thomas Lane at Stretton, Staffordshire. The total valuation was £165 18s
52	8 Mar. 1745/46	Katherine Conolly to Lady Anne Conolly, London, 'With great joy I had my Lady Anne Conolly's of the 27th of February when it brought me the good account of your being better. Your letter came last Thursday night late and mine to Miss Conolly was gone to the post office before the packet came in or I had opened her letter to tell her I had yours. I was in great uneasiness about you but I thank God you has made me happy – I find by Mr Conolly to Mr Clark[e] he has been ill which I am glad I did not know till he says he is quite well again – or it had been an addition to my concern. I pray God keep him, you and all yours in perfect health and happiness is my sincere wish. I believe my last to my dear Katy surprised you the match I told her of but so it is and what with weddings, balls, drums, assemblies and plays three times a week never was such a gay term. I hear of them but I can have no pleasure in anything (but the health of my friends) till I hear the rebels are entirely dispersed. Since I wrote this far the packet due last Thursday came in, no letter from anybody to me as I wrote twice to Kitty Jones this day sennight I have not a word of news to entertain you with; is Lady Strafford clear of her gout? Capt. Curry and Mr Brock both very ill with it. Doctor Grattan is recovering to my great joy for whenever I am ill he is here at least twice a day and when well never misses coming once a day and all this without fee or reward except true love and friendship which he has sincerely. My love and best wishes attend Mr Conolly your Ladyship and all yours. Tell [Nancy?/Fanny] she must not marry Master Clements till she has my consent and they shall be married at Castletown and I'll give them a fine large plum cake. We had very fine weather for 4 or 5 days but now its very bad great rain and hail. Lady Santry and Miss Netting[?] desires me to make their compliments as doth my sister, Mrs Nesbit, Cashel and twenty more.
53–109	13 Apr. 1747–25 Apr. 1748	Various household receipts mostly signed by William Conolly. The items receipted include candles from William Rathborne.

MSS	DATE	DESCRIPTION
3974/ 110– 3975/349	1758–70	**Letters, receipts and other miscellaneous papers of Thomas Conolly (1738–1803), only son of William Conolly junior, who took over the management of the Conolly estates in 1758, the year he married Lady Louisa Lennox, 1758–70.**

3974/ 110–13, 119	30 Sept. 1758.– 21 Nov. 1758	Four receipts signed by Thomas Conolly, detailing personal expenditure, including the freight of a horse and chaise.
114–16, 118	1–17 Nov. 1758	Four receipts relating to annuities left by Mrs Jane Pearson [nee Conolly] in her will. She was Speaker Conolly's sister, and the widow of Thomas Pearson MP.
117	5 Nov. 1758	Abraham Hamilton, Bellaghy, to Michael Clarke on the subject of the valuation of church lands leased from the Bishop of Raphoe in the barony of Boylagh and Banagh, Co. Donegal.

'I send you the return and valuation made to me of the bishop's lease in Boylagh. I have set them down by the parishes that they are situated in. And I believe you may depend on the return to be the best that can be got. I make no doubt but it will be of service to you in the setting. You may judge the measuring of this has been both troublesome and expensive and all the favour I demand for both is to show some regard to R. Nesbitt that was at the trouble and at my earnest suggestion procured it. If there be occasion he [will] write [to] make good his returns. As to the tenants about Killybegs and Claggan I could not as yet get a particular return but it is promised to me soon.

I am told most of the tenants have made proposals, which is to give in rent a fifth penny and two year's rent fine, which is less I believe than the Bishop now demands upon a renewal, for I am told his demands are the same as the Bishop of Derry gets, which is a year's rent for every year that is lapsed and if you suffer seven years to elapse then he gets eight year's rent as a fine. I believe you will find my friend has made the best proposal for the farm he holds and I believe a fine return at what it is set for, for by return I had from other people they don't value it so high as he does himself.

By the enclosed return you may observe it to be the value that it would, or is set for, and you know what part you will fine down, or whether you will take fines or not. I believe your granting leases yourself will keep that knowledge of the rise you intend from the Bishop or his agent and I think it would be advisable to renew with the Bishop before you conclude bargains with the tenants. Pray pardon these hints for you must be a better judge than I am. You may be assured I would do everything in my power to serve the son of the late Mr Conolly who I loved and honoured more than any man whatsoever and I make no doubt but the young gentleman will deserve the like from every one of his acquaintance.'

120	1 Dec. 1758	Receipt from Thomas Monck for Conolly. Rental of bishop of Clogher's lands of Ballyhanna, Co. Donegal.

3974/ 121–125 28 Dec. 1758– 12 Dec. 1759 Various receipts signed by Conolly. Includes a receipt for hearth money collected on Conolly's Capel Street house (no. 124), which had 26 taxable hearths. There are also two tickets (engraved) for a benefit at St Andrews's Church for Mercer's Hospital. Signed by Isaac Steele. Price: half guinea each. (no. 125).

126 31 May 1760 Affidavit of Michael Daily, Terence Gorman and Thomas Faucett taken by John Dickson about the interference caused by a flax mill to the Abbey river salmon fishery, Ballyshannon, Co. Donegal.

127 20 July 1760 Samuel McCrea, Lifford, to Conolly enclosing a survey of part of the Castlefin estate, Co. Donegal.
'Enclosed according to your desire you have a survey and valuation of lower Dungorman and Bealalt nigh Castlefin which I hope are very just. The tenants in both are busy reclaiming the barren improvable grounds and on that account deserve to be encouraged: but the Bealalt tenants are too numerous and mostly poor. On that account, though they are desirous of separate leases, I rather advise to bind them in one, for in that case if any of them run in arrears, or break, the rest will on their own account take care to see your rent paid which in the other case they would not be liable to pay. The value I have laid on each is suited to the time, and in Bealalt is very little over the present rent, but I believe they will pay or promise to pay more for it, if you require it, though I think it high enough. I hope the whole will be to your liking …'
Two sheets including survey. Lower Dungorman contained 90 Scotch acres valued at £18 5s. while Bealalt contained 44 Scotch acres valued at £37 7s.

128–129 12 Sept– 2 Nov. 1760 Two receipts from William Clements for Conolly. One is a Kildare Hunt subscription of £5 13s. 9d.

130 5 Dec. 1760 Abraham Hamilton, Bellaghy, to Conolly about the corporation of Newtown-Limavady and Bellaghy estate affairs.
'Since I had the honour of seeing you I received the enclosed list of the members of the corporation of Newtown from the gentleman I mentioned to you at Derry (but he begs his name may not be made use of). He informs me that the four eldest burgesses may be secured in your interest. Robert Johnson one of them is a gauger in the county of Donegal, and was put in the revenue either by your Uncle or Aunt Conolly. My friend says he can't give a particular account of the illegal proceedings of the corporation but advises you to write to Conolly McCausland Esq. to make a more exact enquiry into them which he is certain he will very readily do, and as that gentleman lives on the spot, and was bred a lawyer I believe he would be a proper person and one that you may depend upon.

3974/130 *contd.*

In the list of the new members, I believe several of them would rather serve you than his Lordship [Lord Conyngham] particularly Mr Montgomery a clergyman in Co Fermanagh, who your father provided for, by procuring the parish he has now.

This affair ought to be well considered and carried on with great secrecy before any proceedings, and whether it will be mot prudent now or after his Lordship's death. These are some of the members that are legal who are old and infirm particularly William McCausland. I suppose you have the charter of that corporation amongst your papers for there can be no opinion or advice taken without seeing it.

During my being at Derry there came a pheasant into the park, a farm I hold from you, but the poor bird was soon killed by Capt. Rankin or one in his Company, before I returned home, which gave great concern because it was the only one that has been since I came to this country and I would have endeavoured to preserve it, for which reason I would have prosecuted the person that killed it only Mr Rankin says he has leave to kill the game in any part of your estate, which I cannot credit, for I can't believe you would license him or any person to break into any of the inclosures I have made wherever he pleases. He does not only do this often but invites several others to attend him on these occasions which I think very hard for though I am a sportsman, yet would willingly reserve what game are on my own farm for any friend that came to see me. I never denied that gentleman's leave to divert himself on the rest of your estate but I will not satisfy him. Therefore I must entreat the favour of you to let me know whether he has your leave to plague me in this manner and I hope for your assistance in putting a stop to it for the future.

There are several parks about this town that are only held from year to year, which may be raised, particularly about eighteen acres held by Mr Spotswood for which he pays no rent. This farm the late Mr Conolly intended for the minister of this parish and as Mr Spotswood's father was our parson he held it during his life without any rent and on his death Mr Conolly continued it to the rest of his family, but as the widow is now dead, Mr Spotswood is willing to take a lease of it as he must build a house and leave the rent to you…'

131 5 Dec. 1760 James Huey, Derry, to Conolly about a proposed takeover of Newtown Limavady Corporation from Lord Conyngham.

'I heard some short time ago that you had an inclination to get the borough of Newtown Limavady in your power if possible and my information gave me to understand that in the borough there are only six legal burgesses, that all the others are admitted contrary to the express words of the charter as not being sworn. Three of those legal burgesses were at this time looked upon as your friends…

3974/131 *contd.*		Ensign John McCausland, Mr William McCausland of Dublin and Mr William King of Newtown. So out of those six you had an equality, but among the six there is one Mr Robert Johnson, who is in the Excise at Castlefin. I immediately went to this gentleman and I have secured him in your interest, which gives you two-thirds of the good burgesses. You may depend on this man, therefore I apprehend you may have the borough if cautious and proper steps be taken there…So that your measures may be better brought to bear, the copy of the charter may be a had at the Rolls Office in Dublin. I am thus far on my road home to Castlefin, and thought it prudent to stop here and give you the earliest report of my proceedings. I shall write to Mr Clarke by next post and remit some money. If you think of doing anything towards getting the borough in your own power, or getting new burgesses in the place of those who have been irregularly chosen and admitted. I think you should be cautious in the choice of and if it should seem agreeable to you either myself or my son, or both would be always ready and willing to serve you, but of this you are the best judge.'
132, 134–37, 139–42	Apr. 1761–15 Nov. 1762	Receipts relating to Conolly's personal expenditure, mostly relating to horseracing, including a receipt for his subscription to the Jockey Club for April plate. Includes an account of Conolly's cattle (no. 137). There were 105 cattle and 917 sheep at Castletown, Killadoon and Montpelier (part of Rathfarnham estate).
133	24 June 1761	Nathaniel Clements [Deputy Vice Treasurer and Irish MP] to Conolly, about interest payments due to Clements. 'I was in hopes I should have received the interest before this, as you wrote to me months ago that I should be paid. There is now above two and twenty hundred pounds due to me and I am paying interest at the rate of six per cent, which lays me under great inconvenience. If therefore you will be pleased to give me a bill on Mr Clarke for it you will much oblige me; if it is not very inconvenient to you to come to town tomorrow morning in order to settle it I would take it as a very particular favour. I would wait on you, but that I am to sail tomorrow at three o'clock. You were so kind as to tell me you would be one of my security but I never troubled you to sign the bond. As I am going to England to settle some affairs, I am to take over the securities to the Vice Treasurers for my faithful discharge of my office [as Deputy Vice-Treasurer for Ireland]. If therefore you will be good enough as to join me in a bond with them for five thousand pounds I shall esteem it as an obligation, and have sent one by Willy that you may perfect it if you can not spare time and come to town. If you have any commands that I can execute there I hope you will favour me with them …

3974/ 138	16 Feb. 1762	James O'Neill to Conolly on the subject of the rent of the Ballyhanna estate, Co. Donegal, which Conolly leased from the Bishop of Clogher.
143	27 Jan. 1763	Arnold Nesbitt & Co., London, Conolly's London bankers, to Conolly. 'The 13th instant we paid Mr William Chaigneau on your account, £50 and this day to the Vintners Company £212 due Xmas. These two sums making together £262 English and Irish £286.4s 8d.'
144	31 Jan. 1763	Thomas Crane, Melton, Conolly's agent for the Stretton Hall estate, to Conolly. 'I hope you had a good passage to Ireland and that you found Lady Louisa well. I have sent you my half year's account ending 5th instant. The balance being eighty-four pounds one shilling and nine pence for which sum I have sent Lady Anne Conolly a draught on Mr Hoare, I was in hopes I should have had the pleasure of waiting upon you at Stretton…'
145–49, 151	2 Feb. 1763–31 Mar. 1763	Letters to Conolly from his bankers, Henry Mitchell in Dublin and Arnold Nesbit in London, as well as his agent Michael Clarke, about the need to settle his accounts.
150	30 Mar. 1763	William Knaresborough, Purcels Inch, to John Cramer Esq., at Ballyvilla near Naas, discussing forthcoming races at the Curragh.
152–161	29 Apr.–26 Sept 1763	Receipts for Conolly's personal expenditure, mostly relating to his horse racing interests, including subscriptions to the Jockey Club and receipts relating to the purchase of horses.
162	31 Jan. 1764	Petition of Hercules Ellis to Trustees of the Linen Manufacture for financial support for his mill at Innishrush, Co. Londonderry, with a schedule of the money spent in erecting it and a signed testimonial. His mill was located on the Vintners' Proportion, Bellaghy.
163	6 Feb. 1764	[Henry Conyngham 1st Viscount] Conyngham to Conolly 'I have been lately informed that my brother [Williams Conyngham] mortgaged the Bishop's lease to my Uncle Conolly, but did not sell it. I shall therefore take it as a favour if you will satisfy me in this doubt by showing me the deed of sale. The reason that I proposed purchasing your reversionary chance of the Newtown estate or to sell you the borough is that I am determined to sell the latter, if I cant purchase the former, therefore gave you the preference….'

3974/ 164	13 Feb. 1764	Receipt signed by Alex. Hope from A. Drummond for Conolly in relation to the Redburn Hunt.
165	11 Apr. 1764	Thomas Crane, Melton, to Conolly informing him that the roof of Conolly's English house Stretton Hall in Staffordshire is in bad repair and lets in water, and that he has ordered repair work to begin as soon as the weather permits. It should have been done during the previous summer, but the weather was too bad.
166–170	23 Apr.– 17 June 1764	Various receipts for expenditure on Conolly's horseracing interests. Includes a receipt for Conolly's subscription to the Curragh Coffee House scheme.
171	4 July 1764	Thomas Crane, Melton, to Conolly. Lady Anne Conolly is at Stretton, where Crane has settled the accounts for 1763 with her.
172	22 July 1764	Michael Clarke to Conolly about the state of Conolly's finances. 'I came to town yesterday and settled accounts with Mitchell and exchanged the vouchers. The balance due to him amounts to £5387 3s for which I have signed a note to him. I was in hopes to have seen you here today but on inquiry I find you have met with a disagreeable accident which will prevent your intended jaunt to England. I hope you will soon get the better of it, but I am afraid it will be tedious. If you find it so, I wish you would call in somebody else besides your Scotch surgeon, for he has the character of keeping people in his hands longer than he should do. Enclosed, is an abstract of your income [not found] and the several deductions payable out of it, by which you will find that you have £8,320 clear exclusive of the mountain park and the Archbishop of Dublin's lease which came into your hands from March last. I send you likewise a list of the debts distinguishing those of your father, and yours and also your sisters' fortunes, with the annual interest on each particular and the totals of principal and interest under each head. I have been as accurate as possible in this, and hope it will be to your satisfaction. There is near £1,600 interest due to Clements at March last and I wish you would contrive to pay him out of the English money, and I think after that we shall with your intended scheme be without any distress for the future. I assure you I am happy at the thoughts of it, and have not the least doubt from the plan that you are now upon, but you will find more satisfaction to yourself than you have hitherto done. You must forgive me if I at any time plague you on this subject, as it proceeds from my sincere zeal for your welfare. I am beginning my northern expedition tomorrow and as I expect to be back in less than three weeks, perhaps I may have the pleasure of seeing you before you embark…'

3974/ 173	29 July 1764	Part of a bill of J. Burgoyne (crossed out) Kilkenny for John Clarke addressed to Conolly at Castletown.
174	17 Oct. 1764	Mr Calcraft, Lancaster, to Conolly about hunting and racing at the Curragh.
175	19 Oct. 1764	Charles O'Hara, Nymphsfield, [Collooney, Co. Sligo], to Conolly about racing at the Curragh.
176	31 Oct. 1764	Thomas Crane, Stretton to Conolly. He has settled the accounts for Stretton and Water Eaton, Conolly's estate in Oxfordshire.
177	16 Nov. 1764	Receipt from James Finnegan for Conolly
178	20 Dec. 1764	Receipt in relation to a huntsman's bill from Bart Nowlan to Conolly
179	2 Feb. 1765	Michael Clarke to Conolly. Mr Daunt who holds a mortgage on the Trinity College leases in Co. Donegal is offering to lend Conolly a further £1,700 at six per cent interest. Clarke leaves the decision to Conolly, but points out the various upcoming payments including £1,000 due to Lady Anne Conolly.
180	5 Feb. 1765	Henry Mitchell, Conolly's Dublin banker, to Conolly asking Conolly to raise six or seven thousand pounds in London to settle his account with Mitchell.
181	12 Feb. 1765	Michael Clarke to Conolly writing about the need to settle Conolly's account with Mitchell and he notes that Mitchell and his predecessors have been bankers to Conolly's father and great–uncle.
182	15 Feb. 1765	Michael Clarke to Conolly. Conolly needs to borrow up to £10,600. The only estate clear of any charge and able to be used as security is the Rathfarnham estate in Co. Dublin.
183–84	30 Apr – 14 May. 1765	Two letters from James Glascock, Conolly's solicitor, to Conolly, about Colonel Burton's case relating to a charge on the Newtown Limavady estate.
185	3 July 1765	Michael Clarke to Conolly. The May rents from estates in Counties Donegal and Derry are coming in by degrees.

3974/ 186	27 July 1765	A. Staples, Killymoon, to Mr Cowan at Castletown sending two foxes, with James Rathe's receipt for payment for carrying the foxes.
187	8 Aug. 1765	James Wier, Dublin, to Conolly about the recovery of some lands in Co. Sligo by Mr William Coane.
188	2 Sept. 1765	Michael Clarke to Conolly. He has been discussing with Conolly's lawyer Mr Radcliffe which debts should be paid first, Conolly's own or those inherited from his father. He recommends paying off the former first.
189	26 Sept. 1765	Receipt for hunting expenses from Thomas Ennis for Conolly.
190	8 Oct. 1765	Draft receipt for Conolly (endorsed: McSorley) for taking the young hounds to the mountain.
191	10 Oct. 1765	Michael Clarke to Conolly about the possible sale of some of Conolly's estates. He lists those which were not included in Conolly's parents' marriage settlement in 1733, with their yearly value.
192–3, 196–9	2 Dec. 1765– Apr. 1766	Various receipts relating to Conolly's personal expenditure on his horse racing interests.
194–5	23 Jan. 1766	John Patterson, New Burlington St., London, to Conolly about the preparation of a private parliamentary bill to sell some of Conolly's estates. Enclosed is an abstract of the title of Conolly's estates prepared by Patterson. (no. 195).
201	27 July 1766	Lord Conyngham, Slane Castle, to Conolly about uniting their political interests to challenge the Ponsonbys. 'I received yours with Mr Mitchell's receipt for a £1,000 drawn on my account as per agreement. If it is agreeable to you to unite your interest with mine, both in England, and Ireland, I think we shall show a power that will check the present absolute power in one family [The Ponsonbys]. I foresee nothing rational that can prevent this union, but my reasonable desire to have the original settlements of my estates, and to see my brother's deed of sale or mortgage of the Bishop's lease to my Uncle Conolly. A short bill in Chancery must bring them all into court but I hope you will not lay me under the necessity of such proceeding, as I am convinced you neither want or desire any more than your legal property....'
202–204	6–19 Sept. 1766	Receipts relating to Conolly's horses

3974/ 205A–C	13 Dec. 1766; 16 Dec. 1766; 10 Jan 1767	Copy of three letters between Mr Partington and General Howard about the Water Eaton estate and Sir Henry Johnson's will. [Johnson (d.1711) was Lady Anne Conolly's maternal grandfather]. Mr [Charles] Yorke has been consulted for a legal opinion.
206–249	8 Dec. 1766–Oct. 1767	Various receipts, mostly relating to Conolly's racing establishment at the Curragh.
250	17 Oct. 1767	Henry Cole, Cutslow, to Lady Anne Conolly about the rents of Stretton and Water Eaton. Lady Anne co-owned the latter with her sisters, Lady Lucy Howard and Lady Harriet Vernon.
251–57	26 Oct – 30 Nov. 1767	Various receipts mostly relating to Conolly's racing establishment at the Curragh.
258	12 Dec. 1767	Lord Conyngham to Conolly about the disputed settlement of the Limavady estate, and Colonel [William] Burton's [Conyngham's nephew] claims. 'You promised to Colonel Burton above three years ago that you would not make use of privilege in the Newtown-Limavady affair. A year or two after you insisted on privilege except Colonel Burton would relinquish one of the two £5000. He laid the case before the Solicitor General, who would not take upon him to advise in so material a demand. I then spoke to Mr Glascock to advise you to file a short [ ] bill in order to bring that affair into the general [ ] of the cause. He promised me for two years that it should be done, but has not done it though the determination of that cause is so material to all parties, especially to me, who have no time to lose. I should be very sorry to be under the necessity of moving the House of Commons to oblige you to waive your privilege, which I must do if you make use of it.'
259	31 Dec. 1767	Conolly, Bangor, [Wales] to Lord Conyngham in relation to the settlement of Limavady. 'I received your Lordship's letter of the twelfth instant but the day before yesterday, from Ireland, where it had been directed, having been confined in this country above a fortnight by an illness occasioned by a horse falling with me. Your Lordship, or Mr Glascock, must have mistaken me very much, if you imagine that I meant to take any step to prevent Colonel Burton, whom I wish very well to, from getting whatever sum of money he was entitled to upon the Newtown Limavady estate by my Uncle's will. My directions to Mr Glascock were to facilitate anything as far as lay in my power for the Colonel's satisfaction but to take care that no further sum should be raised than what my Uncle's will directed.

3974/259 *contd.*		You seem to threaten me my Lord with moving the House to make me waive my privilege. I can assure you my Lord, though you know that it is a thing that has sometimes been obliged to be done to make some members do justice to their creditors, yet there never was nor never will be a time when Mr Conolly would ever show the least desire to prevent any person of any rank from coming at his property either by this or any such dirty measure.'
260–291	20 Jan.–29 Sept. 1768	Various receipts mostly for stables etc.
292	7 Oct. 1768	John Mayor, Londonderry, to Conolly. In relation to the possibility of Conolly gaining control of Derry Corporation. He is not always clear in his meaning. 'As I know you have the county of Derry and the interest thereof all in your favour. I do think an opportunity offers that you may have also the City which should you lose the present opportunity will never during your life have another. The case is this: that the Corporation was contested for by Mr Henry Hamilton and Mr Andrew Knox. Upon Mr Hamilton's absence so long in England [he] was forgot by his friends who chose Mr Hill for member which so much offended him that he has withdrawn his wanted regard for the friends he had in the Corporation and desired them to choose a new leader for he will be it no longer. Lord Donegall offered his service which they accepted of for their patron and one try claim interest upon the election which comes on the 20th of this month for an Alderman. At foot you have the names of the members your agent Mr George Ash can bring over all Lord Donegall's friends to your interest. If you can prevail on him to vote for Mr Hill his vote will bring them upon equality. The mayor will then have the casting vote and he can give the corporation into your hands if you please to accept of it. I have thrown you out this hint have for you may incline to be a burgess in that Corporation as there will be one vacant upon this election of Aldermen being filled up is most humbly submitted to your own consideration… Enclosed is a list of burgesses of the Corporation divided between those in Lord Donegalls interest and those in Mr Knox's interest.
293–321	12 Oct. 1768–20 May 1769	Various receipts mostly relating to Conolly's establishment at the Curragh
318, 322	2 May; 4 June 1769	Two letters from William Christy, the first from Edinburgh Infirmary and the second from Falkirk, to Mrs Gilbert at Castletown. She must have been a guest at Castletown, and Christy, one of her servants. He reports that he is very weak and unable to work, and asks her to relay this information to his master.

3974/ 323	6 June 1769	Thomas Lee, General Post Office, to Conolly. Conolly's bill for a year and a quarter's English newspapers is overdue.
319, 325, 326	9 May; 12, 16 July 1769	Three letters from Benjamin Harenc, Sproughton near Ipswich, to Conolly Conolly was assisting Harenc in obtaining information on Lord Kerry's estate in Co. Kerry. Conolly's agent William Coane was dispatched to report on the state of the leases on the estate.
327	18 July 1769	Thomas Sheppard, Carrick on Shannon, to Conolly about his military career, which Conolly has helped sponsor.
328–48	26 July 1769– 5 Dec. 1770	Various receipts mostly relating to Conolly's establishment at the Curragh
349	1770–77	Note, possibly an extract from a common-place book, in an unknown hand about visits to great houses near Nottingham Forest: 'Of the four great places near one another in Nottingham Forest I have seen three of the houses new built. The four are Worksop, Welbeck, Thoresby and Clumber. Welbeck is the worst and oldest house. Added in 1777: 'Welbeck considerably altered and improved.'

MSS	**DATE**	**DESCRIPTION**
3975/ 350– 3976/443	**23 Jan. 1771– 31 Dec. 1776**	**Letters, receipts and other miscellaneous papers of Thomas Conolly, 1771–76.**
350– 352	23 Jan–11 April 1771	Three receipts relating to Conolly's hunting exploits.
353– 357	20 May– 18 June 1771	Five letters to Conolly in relation to Newtown Limavady corporation and the election of new burgesses. These show that political control of the borough was still formally in the hands of Lord Conyngham, but that Conolly was becoming increasingly important.
	20 May	Robert Johnson, Castlefin, to Conolly. When the provost of Newtown, McCausland, died Johnson assumed his place as oldest burgess. No time to consult Conolly, who was in England. Protestations of loyalty and respect.

3975/ 353–357 *contd.*	23 May	Rev. William Nesbitt, Dublin, to Lt. Colonel [William] Burton, Limavady. Agrees to be elected burgess of Newtown. This is appropriate because he is a trustee for Lord Conyngham 'and on, his Lordship's decease without issue for Mr Conolly'.
	28 May	Conolly McCausland to [Burton]. Johnson should be re-elected provost and McCausland will have the notice posted 16 days before the election. Procuring a mandamus now is the only way to make Burton's future election unquestionably good. McCausland is glad that harmony in corporation matters now prevails between Lord Conyngham and Conolly.
	4 June	Hugh Montgomery, Castle Coole, to [Burton]. Will attend at Newtown on the 24th and will discharge his trust to the satisfaction of Lord Conyngham and Conolly.
	18 June	[Rev.] James Montgomery, Cloverhill, to [Burton]. Ditto. After being elected a burgess he will do his utmost to preserve the borough to Lord Conyngham and, on his death without issue, to Conolly.
358	28 June 1771	Conolly, Bellisle [Lisbellew, Co. Fermanagh, seat of Sir Ralph Gore, Viscount Bellisle, later Earl of Ross] to [the 2nd] Lord Strafford, Conolly's uncle. Mostly about family affairs including the death of Conolly's sister Catherine Lady Bellisle. 'My lord, I have been here with Louisa this week past as poor Lord Bellisle seemed very desirous [to have] us both with him and although I always regret leaving home yet I could not resist his entreaties of having us some time with him and we shall stay until the beginning of next week. He is very much improved since I saw him at Castletown and I hope will soon regain his former spirits. He goes the end of the next month to see a sister of his that lives at Preston in Lancashire from where he means to go to York and Scarborough and he will very likely call upon you at Wentworth Castle for a day or two. I am sure if you knew him you would esteem him as all his acquaintances do for a better or more sensible man hasn't lived. Mr [John] Staples [Conolly's brother-in-law] was very ill at [ ] so when I saw him he is gone to his house in the county of Tyrone and from there will return to town to take possession of his employment which Lord Townshend has at last given him, and which I hope will be of some comfort to him, being worth upwards of £1,000 a year. I have now my Lord given you an account of the situation of the remainder of your unhappy family in Ireland except of Louisa and

3975/358 *contd.* myself, who are thank God very well in health though I cannot help [ ] very terribly of being situated in a country without any near relations when I was so lately in a very different situation. It will certainly make me live more in England where the remains of my family now live, though I shall always quit my own place with regret as it is now very complete and almost all of my own making.

I think your ideas about horse racing very right and I will never run for any sum of consequence for the future though I lost very little by my match with Mr Blake and would not have lost a farthing as it was a national affair though the horse was quick and would have won had he not been lamed.' Greetings to Lady Strafford etc.

359 30 June 1771 Colonel William Burton [Lord Conyngham's nephew and heir], Henry Street, to Conolly about Limavady Corporation.
I am just returned from Limavady where I had the honour of assisting to make you one of our burgesses, with Staples, Conolly McCausland, Hugh Montgomery of Castlecool, the Rev. Mr Nesbitt, Capt. Shaw and Mr James Montgomery of Donegal, a very worth clergyman who I sent for express having received a letter from Mr Corry that he could not possibly attend. I enclose you the letter of Lord Conyngham's friends who attended by which, and that of Mr Nesbitt that I forwarded to you before I left Dublin. You will see fully the intentions of Lord Conyngham who ordered me to do every thing to your satisfaction. I hope my dear Conolly I have done it, and again repeat those assurances I before made to you, that in case of the event of Lord Conyngham's death, you may dispose of me and my friends as you wish. That Lord Conyngham may be satisfied of my having executed the trust he reposed in me to his satisfaction I have desired Staples and Conolly McCausland to write me each of them a letter, to show to Lord Conyngham, that they understand the trust reposed in them to be the preserving the borough to his lordship for his life, to be handed over to you and your heirs with the estate.

May I beg therefore you will take the trouble of writing me three lines to the same purpose and I hope this thorough reconciliation that has taken place, will lead to that kind of union of the two families, which heretofore made them so respectable in this country, and which I make no doubt a little attention could restore them so. I confess I think there is a particular case that a union of that sort could be more considerable.

I could wish whatever opportunity of waiting on you and Lady Louisa to receive your commands for England but as I expect to get away on Wednesday and have much business to do, I fear it will be impossible. I beg my best respects to her ladyship…'.

3975/ 360a–370; 372–79	4 July–1771–1 Jan.1773	Receipts and accounts relating to Conolly's hunting establishment at the Curragh.
371	31 Apr. 1772	Arnold & Albert Nesbitt, London, to Conolly informing Conolly that his drafts on Major Clifford and Sons of Amsterdam have been drawn and put into his account with Nesbitt. He has been 'very lucky in this transaction owing to the rise in the Dutch Exchange since we drew on the Cliffords as you will have had the use of the money for five or six months at a less rate than 1½ % all expenses included, but this happens very seldom.'
380	4 Mar. 1773	Conolly to Lord Strafford about his financial affairs, and the nature of his inherited debt. 'My Dear Lord, From what passed between us this morning you seemed to doubt not only the veracity of the sketch of my affairs that I mentioned to you, but likewise my punctuality in money matters. The adherence to truth in one and the exactness in the other instance certainly constitutes the character of an honest man. As to the first I believe the enclosed [No. 381] account of my affairs will justify me, as I give it to you for fact and as to the latter I thought the interest due to you which Mr Nesbitt though he requested my written order to pay remitted my mothers half year jointure which he did not then for standing to agreement. I can [ ] to report that I did not owe one farthing interest or money due upon the last pay day when I left Ireland nor any bills in the whole country above one hundred pounds to my tradesmen. The money I owed the bank was not the consequence of any extravagance whatever or money lost by horses or otherwise but solely owing to my endeavouring by degrees to pay the following debts without laying my fortune under such encumbrances, £10,000 Mrs B[yng]'s fortune, £4,300, my house in Dublin and two other debts of my own contracting upon making purchases some years ago. One to Mrs Wogan of £3,500 and the other to Messrs Nesbitt of £5,000. All this money was paid for me by the bank within two years and if the credit of the country and yours had not received the shock it has. I can hasten to say upon the receipt of three half years rents more I should have been clear with the bankers. The state of my affairs they knew upon the advancing of the money and they now only desire payment, as the partnership with Sir George Colebrooke will be disposed the 25th of this month and my wishes to pay them at that time induced me to trouble you this morning looking upon you as the only friend here. And I had a light to speak to you upon such a subject. Had I sold my estates when I got the act of parliament for that

3975/380 *contd.*		purpose some years ago, this disagreeable situation would have been avoided. But no man living could have imagined that a peace of eleven years would produce a greater scarcity of money and want of confidence than in the rebellion and an almost impossibility of selling in Ireland even with the best titles and them under sanction of an act of parliament. However sell I will every farthing under the act of parliament and that by public auction…for half value sooner than soon run the risk of a similar situation. I must beg pardon for troubling you with this, but in justice to my own feelings and desires of retaining your good opinion I could not refrain from taking up so much of your time…'
381	4 Mar 1773	Account of Conolly's estate since his coming of age enclosed with no. 380 above. 'The estate in Ireland let me by my father was sixteen thousand six hundred pounds a year The debts affecting that estate, my sisters fortunes included were one hundred twenty four thousand pounds The estate I am now possessed of in Ireland is £21,651 7s 4d The debts now remaining due of my fathers are £43,333 6s 8d and my own including the bank debt £42,5051 7s 2d a year more than my father left me and I owe £38,666 13s 4d less than when my father died. I had no occasion to save money having no children and I flatter myself the money I have spent annually was rationally employed by living not extravagantly but like a gentleman.' Detailed breakdown of expenditure follows including the purchase of house in Dublin for £4,300, and one in London for £5,000; 'in finishing my house and furnishing buildings barns, stables dog kennels, kitchen garden, buildings, planting, and laying down the whole demesne upwards of £25,000.'[Castletown]. His total expenditure was £85,000, while his income included £10,000 received with Lady Louisa; for Water Eaton, £16,000; and for several lands sold since Act of Parliament, £31,000.
382	9 Mar. 1773	Lord Strafford to Conolly. In response to above letter, acknowledging scale of his inherited debt and Conolly's need to have at least £8,000–£10,000 per annum to live like a gentleman. Suggests Conolly mortgage his English property to raise money: 'there is your house in London and estate in Staffordshire that may be mortgaged for a good deal, till you have time by your large income to be paying off by degrees.'
383–394	13 Apr. 1773–23 Aug. 1774	Receipts and accounts mostly relating to Conolly's hunting and racing activities. Also included is an account of the death of the Duchess of Norfolk [no. 386].

3975/ 395 19 Oct. 1774 Note, in an unknown hand, of a visit to Worksop, Thoresby and Kniveton.
'I went from Wentworth Castle and called on William Mason then got to Worksop Manor by dinner and found the Duke of Norfolk (who is at 69) quite well, the Duke of Portland sent me a letter about the Bedfordshire election the 15th sent to Welbeck and then went to Thoresby and stopped at Clumber as I came back to Worksop with the Duke of Newcastle who had Lord Lincoln and his youngest son with him: Lord Chancellor Apsley dined at Worksop. The 16th came home by Kniveton the Duke of Leeds' and sent to Lord Rockingham at Wentworth. In these three days I saw genius, beautys of nature and art, riches and nobility.' [See also no. 349.]

396 10 Nov. 1774 Arnold Nesbitt, London, to Conolly enclosing a copy of a letter from Nesbitt to Conolly of 18 October 1774.
In his first letter Nesbitt suggests that Conolly consider mortgaging some of his estate to raise the money he needs. He recommends a Mr Smith who is interested in taking a mortgage on an Irish estate.
In the second letter Nesbitt presses Conolly for an answer, as Smith is very eager to employ his fortune, and has been calling frequently.

397 1774 Receipt from the [2nd] Duke of Leinster for Conolly's subscription to the Kildare Hunt

398 1774 Note, in same hand as no. 395, about the opening of the tomb of Edward I by the Society of Antiquaries.
'On the 2nd of May last the Society of Antiquarians got leave of the Dean of Westminster to open the tomb of Edward. They found him wrapped in crimson silk, and under that the body was near perfect in a coat and waistcoat of gold tissue, with a silver gilt crown on his head, and a sceptre in one hand, and a cross in the other. He was a very tall man, [with] an ugly face, the eyes were taken out, a long nose and chin. These particulars were told by the man that saw him (who shows the abbey).'

399 13 Mar. 1775 Edward Bulkeley [Conolly's 'man of business' in Dublin], Dublin to Conolly about his financial affairs and remitting money to England.
Conolly is being overcharged by his bankers, the Latouches, for the money he is remitting to England, something which needs to be remedied considering the increasing sums he is remitting each year.
He has been examining Conolly's financial affairs concluding: 'that which has chiefly injured your credit and occasioned a great

3975/399 *contd.*		and needless expense has been the neglect of providing for the successive demands as they became due: the consequence of which was borrowing in a hurry and complying with extravagant terms…'
400	5 July 1775	Robert Maxwell [Earl of], Farnham, Hunston, to Conolly about racing, and the form of his horses.
401	29 Aug. 1775	Arnold & Albert Nesbitt, London, to Conolly about money drawn on his account.
402–06	10 Sept. 1775– 15 Apr. 1776	Receipts and accounts relating to Conolly's stables at the Curragh. Included is a glazier's account for 1775–6.
407– 412	16 Apr.–2 May 1776	Four proposals for leases of woods on Conolly's estate at Bellaghy, Co. Londonderry. [the Vintners' Proportion].
413	2 May 1776	Andrew Spotswood, Bellaghy, to Conolly about the proposals for the woods on Conolly's estates in Co. Londonderry. Since Conolly previously sold his woods at auction, perhaps he might 'choose that way of sale' again. (nos. 407–12) Also references to forthcoming elections in the county: Richardson has been canvassing Conolly and Dawson's estates, but Conolly's tenants stand firm. Dawson and Staples think it the height of opposition in Richardson to stand a poll. There is to be a meeting at Colonel Cary's of the above plus McCausland, Ash, Sterling and the law agent. How does Conolly want him to vote in Derry City?
414	20 June 1776	Arnold Nesbitt to Conolly sending Conolly his account, and desiring that Conolly honour his debts as soon as possible
415	21 June 1776	Robert McClintock, Dunmore, [Carrigans], Co. Donegal, to Conolly. '…I observed your orders with the tenants in regard to their votes and did everything in my power for Mr [Robert] Clements: they every man voted for him but we were afraid [that] pressing them for a single vote might work some bad effect: therefore we gave up that point. They in general were for Mr Clements and Mr Hamilton.
416	24 June 1776	Sir John Blaquerie, Chief Secretary of Ireland, Dublin Castle, to Edward Bulkeley informing Bulkeley that he has lost the agency of the half pay officers but has got a pension instead
417–19, 421–2	30 June– 1 July1776	Five letters about a pension for Capt. John Staples obtained by Conolly, his brother-in-law. Correspondents include Staples, Conolly and Robert Waller.

3975/ 420	2 July 1776	Stephen Popham, 7 Dorset St., to Conolly. He is going to London on Conolly's behalf to pay a bill of £3,000.
423–425	11–12 July 1776	Receipts ands accounts relating to Conolly's stables at the Curragh.
426	21 July 1776	Sir John Blaquerie, Dublin Castle, to Thomas Shepard, Celbridge I received the favour of your letter of the 16th .You must have misapprehended Mr Staples – my recollection is perfect that I told and by my Lord Lieutenant's command to him not that the pension could be recommended in your name only – could it have been otherwise I should have been very instrumental in any degree to your accommodation and convenience…
427	24 July 1776	Benson & Co., Cork to Conolly about importing Madeira wine through Cork for Conolly. General Howe has sailed to America with 8,000 men.
428	31 July	Receipt to Conolly from Thomas Cockayne for Castletown wages.
429	15 Aug. 1776	Ralph Knox & Samuel Mercer, bankers, London, to Conolly about payment of his mother's jointure.
430	29 Aug. 1776	John Nesbitt to Conolly stating payments on Conolly's account.
432	28 Sept. 1776	Ralph Knox & Samuel Mercer, London, to Conolly about payment of Lady Anne Conolly's jointure.
433	1 Oct. 1776	John Nesbitt to Conolly stating payments on Conolly's account
434	5 Oct. 1776	Ralph Knox & Samuel Mercer, London, to Conolly about payment of Lady Anne Conolly's jointure.
435	15 Oct. 1776	[The 1st Earl] Harcourt, Lord Lieutenant of Ireland, Dublin Castle, to Conolly. Harcourt seeks to ease Conolly's worries about his brother-in-law General Sir William Howe's actions at New York. Harcourt is still waiting for definitive accounts of the army's progress.
436–38	22 Oct.– 2 Nov. 1776	Three letters from Ralph Knox and Samuel Mercer, London, to Conolly about various payments on Conolly's account including the half yearly rent of the Grocer's Proportion (£300).
439	19 Nov. 1776	[John Hobart 2nd Earl of] Buckinghamshire [who was married to Conolly's sister, Caroline] to Conolly About his forthcoming appointment as Lord Lieutenant of Ireland and his hopes that politics will never interfere with their

3975/439 *contd.*		friendship. 'Though you have for reasons most kind to myself wished that my so long reported and so frequently contradicted appointment to the lieutenancy of Ireland should take place, I cannot forbear giving you the earliest intelligence of a circumstance which amongst all the ideas of unavoidable anxiety which attend it, offers the one most pleasing prospect that of frequently enjoying your society, and availing myself of that cheerfulness which attends you. Politics can never interfere in our friendship either in England or Ireland. The propriety of the measures in each country should alone determine such a man as you; my most sanguine hope is only that in a doubtful point the scale might be turned by your goodwill.' PS Our best love to Lady Louisa, Caroline's present situation [She was pregnant] will not admit of her accompanying me.'
440	26 Nov. 1776	John Nesbitt to Conolly stating Conolly's accounts and the need to remit money to Nesbitt.
441	Post Nov. 1776	Conolly to Buckinghamshire. Copy. About the state of Irish politics and the need for Free Trade. 'I wish you joy of your appointment as I am sure it is what you have been desirous of and I wish myself of being likely to partake in your company and Queen Caroline's, for that is the name she always went by in the family from a child. You do me justice in being very sure that our private friendship can never be broke into by politics on either side…This country must always depend upon yours for its welfare or undoing. It is certainly in the power of Great Britain to make this kingdom of much greater use to the British Empire than she has hitherto been by granting us a power to make use of the situation for trade which providence has given us, and which hitherto the limited way of thinking of those that have governed in England has prevented in order to please the representatives of a few cities whose trade might be injured by any advantage given to us, forgetting that ultimately any wealth that the kingdom should acquire would all settle in Great Britain. But I trust that the wisdom and bold way of thinking of your friend Lord George Gemaine who knows this country so well will advise a very different mode of conduct for the future. Even if the present critical situation of the British Empire did not oblige government to look seriously into all her resources she might then have four million industrious well clothed useful subjects adding to her wealth instead of building up idleness and of course continuing in misery, and want without any spur to their industry, or good will to a country which has always treated them with contempt and burdened them with taxes which has been put out of their power to pay by repeated fetters on her trade.

3975/441 *contd.*

Lord Townshend came over here to overturn the old aristocracy of the first families of parliamentary right which he certainly [ ] lost the kingdom in unhinging all the old connections and making new ones at a great sum.

My Lord Harcourt who found a government in possession of a dignity sufficient to do all the King's business has laid more upon us than even Lord Townshend who had a [ ] point of the British government to carry and he has continued to raise the price of members so that in the new parliament which contains more men without landed property who have bought in for the purpose of making the best interest of their money will make it difficult for a lord lieutenant who has nothing but the ordinary supplies to demand to get even that done without pay, which must temporarily ensure great trouble, your predecessors having cut off the spring from which they were to be supplied and which has made Lord Harcourt in such a hurry to avoid another parliament.

After having given you this sketch of what I take to be the situation of this kingdom respecting the mother country and of that of the person appointed to govern it, I must beg your pardon for taking up so much of your time which nothing but my good wishes for your credit and representation in the arduous task you have undertaken would have led me to do and [which] I shall endeavour at all times to promote, as far as I am permitted by my first connection with a country in which I was born and in the prosperity of which I am so deeply interested. I belong to no party here. I never did nor never will and I am and have been at all times at liberty to vote in favour of such measures and ministers which according to my judgement are best calculated to do good to this kingdom.'

Goes on to extend good wishes and invite Buckinghamshire to Castletown to escape the 'smoke and dirt of Dublin'. Lady Louisa will stand in for his wife 'if any female honour is to be done'.

442 10 Dec. 1776 Coote Molesworth, Chichester, to Conolly.
In favour of his nephew William Molesworth who seeks a place in the Custom House, in Dublin.

443 31 Dec. 1776 Henry Major, Ballyshannon, to Conolly about payment of Ballyshannon rents.

444 *Blank in sequence*

MSS	DATE	DESCRIPTION
3976/ 445– 3977/ 715	**2 Jan. 1777– 31 Dec. 1780**	**Letters, papers, and other miscellaneous papers, including his correspondence with his brother-in-law Lord Buckinghamshire while the latter was Lord Lieutenant of Ireland, 1777–80.**
445	2 Jan. 1777	Knox & Mercer to Conolly stating their accounts
446	4 Jan. 1777	Lord Buckinghamshire to Conolly announcing his departure for Ireland. He is pained by the forthcoming separation from his 'queen'.
447	13 Jan. 1777	Receipt for Conolly for wages at his Curragh establishment
448–50, 452, 463		Copies of correspondence of Major Apollos Morris [late of the 27th Regiment] relating to his attempted peace negotiations with General Sir William Howe and George Washington. [See also nos. 477,479and 484]
	20 Jan. 1777	Apollos Morris, Philadelphia to Sir William Howe asking what terms would be offered to the Americans 'That there may be no objection to the perusal of this letter on account of the place whence it is dated, I beg leave to inform you that I was taken and sent in by the Congress privateer of this port; and though indulged with more liberty than came to the share one deemed an enemy, have ever professed my earnest wish for a reconciliation between G. Britain and the Colonys. In this spirit and with an affection for the inhabitants of both countries not to be altered by change of fortune, I address myself to your Excellency, rather than to his lordship to whom I have not the honour of being known. The times require explicitness and the magnanimity of the Howes will ever disdain the mysterious style of officers and though I cannot suppose the gratifying me will appear of mighty consequence, I must believe it is your inclination that all here should be clearly informed of what the country has to hope from a return of dependence. His Majesty's most gracious promises, be the reliance of them never so great, can give no security beyond their own extent. This after pardon is limited to the revisal of Acts and Instructions: a submission thus circumstanced has to the Americans the appearance of leaving them in all they contended for, to the mercy of that majority which has already divided against them, and wholly in the dark in respect of the principal subject of the contest, the right or rather in future exercise of parliamentary taxation. I therefore humbly request that satisfaction from you, which no publication has hitherto given. Submitting the following questions:

3976/448
contd.

Are His Majesty's Commissioners now empowered or were they empowered supposing independence out of the question,

Firstly, to treat and come to any settlement with persons treating on behalf of the colonies jointly?

Secondly, to fix on any particular acts or instructions: to give assurances (satisfactory at least in honour) that administration will do what depends thereon to effect the repeal and alteration of the acts and instructions so fixed on, or by public or private articles to accept submissions on conditions of such repeal?

Thirdly, to give assurance that a free offer of a certain proportion of the dutys arising from foreign imports (allowed or to be allowed by some relaxation of the trade laws), or of a certain sum in lieu (unalterable but with the growth of trade or by consent) will be accepted as the American quota towards the common exigencys of the Empire. All others to be applied by requisition.

Fourthly, or to agree to a cessation of hostilities till such powers can be obtained.

Settlement of establishment. If the principles of the laws of England and the respective civil and religious charter rights of the Colonys are to be the guide, will not be matters of insurmountable difficulty.

The desire of a reconciliation implies a desire that the mode should be consistent with the dignity of the King and of the Parliament, but in taking the law, they will wish to see their rights secure which are in their [ ] against, what the yeomanry fears more than a just proportion of necessary expense, rents, tythes, and internal taxes. And to that desire by all I can understand they are not likely to be brought by means which have the appearance of mere force. Whether their acquiescence under such would be of any lasting advantage to the King or G. Britain is also most humbly submitted....

PS. An answer to this letter will be deemed a great condescension. I have accepted no employment as reported, nor am under any influence in writing it (though from the nature of the conveyance tis liable to inspection), but that of my wish expressed in the first paragraph.

26 Jan. 1777

Apollos Morris, N. Bromley Mills to General Washington, draft. Sir, I send the letter promised to which if a favourable answer (which from anything known yet from the ministry can hardly be expected) is not given, I shall consider myself at one of the country and gladly follow your fortune and doers as the best means of showing my attachment to it. If I have not suddenly engaged myself from personal motives, till fully convinced no equitable terms or accommodation can be had, I hope it will be in earnest of my perseverance. [this first paragraph is crossed out in]

But since I speak of these matters, I cannot dismiss them

3976/448
contd.

without adding one wish, that you would add, to the honours you have already gained; that of doing what is in your power for bringing about such an accommodation as I have mentioned or at least for making some offer not only of a mutually advantageous commerce but of taking a part of the national debt when able in lieu of independence. It will ever look ungenerous to part from Britain merely because we fear to share her necessary burdens, part of which were undoubtedly used in the defence of this country and of which the people of it are likely to enjoy the everlasting benefit: for no other people have so fair an inheritance.

Tis glorious to guard against slavery and corruption and there is a grandeur in the design of keeping them out of this vast continent, but tis submitted to you if it would not be worthy the cause of liberty and to the immortal honour of the Colonys to have their proceedings founded not only on the oppression attempts of the ministry, but on their own justice and even generosity.

31 Jan 1777

John Fitzgerald ADC [to Washington], Headquarters, to Apollos Morris at New Bromley Mills within 3 miles of Pouckimin.
'I saw your letter of yesterday to His Excellency, and am sorry to find you of opinion that returning your letter intended for General Howe was meant to cast the least slight or reflection on you, as I can assure you it was not. I now by the General's consent invite you here tomorrow (to dinner) that matters not easily adjudged at a distance or indeed fit to be committed to paper may be cleared up by a personal interview.

On the reverse of this letter is an unfinished draft [copy of one from Washington?] dated Morris Town, 29 Jan. 1777 repudiating Morris's attempts to mediate as a private person – with a draft letter from Morris.

17 Feb;

Apollos Morris, Philadelphia to Sir William Howe
'Not having the honour to be personally known to his lordship nor taking on me to speak to him as a commissioner, I address myself to your Excellency: first declaring that I write under the influence of no person, nor have any political connection whatsoever.

Though brought in by a privateer, I own, I have been indulged with more liberty than came to the share of one deemed an enemy. This however has not hindered me from professing myself a friend to G. Britain as well as to the Colonys and an advocate for a reconciliation looking on an equitable one as most desirable to both and to G. Britain itself preferable whether in point of honour or of interest.

I cannot suppose that what I think will appear of any importance, but from your character I must believe you inclined

3976/448
contd.

to have every individual here informed of what the country is to expect from a submission.

The significance of His Majesty's most gracious disposition, can give no assurance beyond its own extent, which in the apprehension of most here reaches after pardon, only to a revisal. A submission so circumstanced has the appearance of leaving all they contended for, to the mercy of a majority, which has already decided against them and of an implied surrender of every civil and religious right. For its real extent the only good authority must be in those acquainted with the powers given. I therefore humbly request from you that satisfaction which no publication here has given. Submitting the following questions.

Are His majesty's Commissioners empowered or were they of if indolence was out of the question

1. To treat with any persons treating for all the Colonys jointly?
2. To fix on any act or instruction proper to be repealed or altered and to give assurances (satisfactory at least in honour) that the repeal and alteration fixed on should as far as depended on administration be carried into effect?
3. To come to a settlement about taxation so as by like assurances of acceptance of a stipulated quota (unalterable but with increase of foreign trade) or otherwise, to remove all just fear of oppression from a Parliamentary exercise of it?
4. Or to agree to a cessation of hostilities, till such powers can be obtained?

If you condescend to give an answer or to signify by the bearer if I am to expect one it will be esteemed a favour.

27 Apr. 1777. Apollos Morris, Allen Town, to Mr Allen.

Sir, I never had the least account of a letter which I some time since sent enclosed to you by Mr Gibbs, who lately resided at Philadelphia.

On my design in taking that letter by person to be certain of its delivery from authority so good as yours, I cannot think of any objection (except the trouble) which you or he could have to give me some indication since, I apprehend either mistake or miscarriage.

I have therefore obtained permission to ask if it has been received and if any answer has or will be given as this may be the only opportunity of enquiring. I entreat you to take the best means of informing me you can. Had ambition, interest, resentment, good or ill fortune moved me I should not have taken so much time or pains for information. But true to the character which, by common comment of my superiors, I have taken, that of knights errand. I have been requested merely by my idea of right and wrong by such public motives must even my most natural propensity be regulated.

3976/ 451	11 Feb 1777	Arnold & John Nesbit to Conolly, about money drawn on his account.
453	20 Feb. 1777	Rev. Anthony Weldon, Athy, to Conolly. He seeks Conolly's interest with the Lord Lieutenant to exchange his benefice in the Diocese of Tuam for one at Killeban, near Killcullen in the Diocese of Leighlin. They are both of the same value, but his family have been in residence at Killcullen since the 'establishment of this kingdom.'
454	22 Feb. 1777	Arnold & John Nesbitt, London, to Conolly seeking payment of money paid out on Conolly's behalf.
455	8 Mar. 1777	Arnold & John Nesbitt, London, to Conolly, stating their account including a half years rent of the Vintners' proportion (£212).
456	15 Mar. 1777	Receipt to Conolly for spending at the Curragh establishment.
457–59	18,19, 27 Mar. 1777	Three letters from Arnold & John Nesbitt, London, to Conolly, stating accounts and money due to them from Conolly.
460	29 Mar. 1777	Edward Bulkeley, Dublin, to Conolly about the need to perfect a bond for £1,200 as security for the money which Conolly has borrowed from a Mr Exshaw.
461	30 Mar. 1777	William Sherlock, Sherlockstown, Co. Kildare, to Conolly about racing at the Curragh and foxhunting.
462	26 Apr. 1777	Knox & Mercer, London, to Conolly stating Conolly's accounts. Samuel Mercer is dead and Ralph Knox is carrying on the business, on his own, from the end of April 1777.
464–68	27 Apr.– 3 May 1777	Receipts for Conolly's racing expenditure, including one for his subscription to the Jockey Club.
469	10 May 1777	Ralph Knox & Co., London, to Conolly about the payment of Lady Anne Conolly's jointure, and Conolly's account.
470	23 May 1777	Ralph Knox, Crosby Square, London, to Conolly stating Conolly's account.
471	23 May 1777	Andrew Spotswood, Bellaghy, to Conolly about the Bellaghy estate, and the affairs of the tenants. Reference is made to a letter from Lady Louisa Conolly written on 16 April to Spotswood.
472	27 May 1777	Ralph Knox, London, to Conolly about payment of a bill drawn on Lord John Manners

3976/ 473	30 May 1777	Robert Henry Drummond, London, to Conolly stating payment of £300 to Conolly's account.
474	31 May 1777	Ralph Knox, London, to Conolly stating Conolly's account.
475	1 June 1777	Andrew Spotswood, Bellaghy, to Conolly about the activities of the mob at the late election at Derry. Asks Conolly to take note of the spirited and active behaviour of Francis Doherty, publican, of the Water Side of Londonderry, '…in protecting several of your voters on the late election from the fury of a tumultuous mob, and particularly myself. When leaving Derry the day after the election was finished, judging all would be quiet, my son and I was [sic] attacked from behind an hedge…by a number of fellows who pelted us with stones…'
476	7 June 1777	Thomas Thoroton, Belvoir Castle, [Leicestershire], to Conolly. The brood bitch is ready to travel, 'but will soon to be too big with whelps to travel.'
477, 479, 484		Copies of further 'American' correspondence of Major Apollos Morris.
	9 June 1777	B[endict]. Arnold, Headquarters, Philadelphia, to Major Apollos Morris 'In compliance with an order of the honorable Continental Congress to put you under immediate arrest and confinement, I have ordered two sentinels placed at your lodgings, who have directions to give you the liberty of the house and yard. No person (the family excepted) will be permitted to visit you without liberty – the guardian you will doubtfully soon be acquainted with.' Endorsed with a draft of no. 479 on the rear.
	12 June 1777	Memorial of Apollos Morris to John Hancock, President of the Congress of the United States. 'Sheweth, that memorialist came to this country to share not its riches but its distresses and even take up arms for its peace, liberty and safety, which he thought consisted in restoring it to the situation of 1763 and against an unconditional submission. In doing this he thought himself a friend both of Britain and the Colonys believing the liberty of the former could not subsist with such an appendage enslaved. Memorialist found on his arrival matters on a new ground: independence being declared. To this he had no objection, did he know the limit of its claims, believing a friendly parting preferable to an uncertain or ill humoured union. But had just before in print declared it was not the wish or interest of the Colonys and thought his taking up arms against for it against great Britain (of

3976/477
contd.

which he had at the same time professed himself the friend) could not be consistently justified except by her refusal of an equitable accommodation. For this purpose he took the best means he could to know the disposition of the Commissioners; not underhand and has reason to suppose they would depart from their injurious claims.

Memorialist at same time acknowledges nothing has been by authority to his knowledge held out to the United States to decide them on any alteration of their measures. He has therefore confined his internal opinions to himself, and so far from declaring them to any individual but to those whom he ought to declare them to the General and two of the members of the Congress, he has in all company condemned the measures of the British ministry and believes that in respect to the contents of this paragraph the Congress has been misled or misconstrued his conduct, or would not have been induced to put him under any restraint.

Until he sees these internal opinions belied by [the] ministry in words or facts he cannot defensibly take a commission. However, thought himself as much bound in honour as ever not to abandon this country were it in distress or till equitable terms are fairly and explicitly opened. But would certainly rather quit any country than live under suspicion.

What degree of confidence the Honourable Congress chooses to put in him is their own power. But he cannot be under stronger ties than the above. He has done much to deserve nothing (knowingly he is certain) to forfeit it. And so little conscious was he of anything traitorous [treacherous] in his disposition or that he could be suspected that it is provable he would now have offered himself as a volunteer, though it was necessary to let the General know he could not as an officer.

He loved the people of the country and the prospect of their extending liberty and the pillory of the English name over this continent was his common topic of exultation. At the same time no man can say it is an ungenerous principle to wish to avoid disgracing Britain in doing this, if she is not bent on disgracing herself, when it seems clear the result of obstinacy on both sides will be a peace made by the enemy of both at the expense of both.

Memorialist owns when he was refused asking the questions he proposed, he would have left the country if he could without obligation to ministry. But he thought it equally disgraceful at the time of its distress and under the proclamation held out. It was the latter indeed which inclined him to stay and when the fortune of the country took a more favourable aspect he must have appeared a time server to have come into the service on any terms but those he had in the worst circumstances possible.

Memorialist therefore prays to know how the Honourable Congress will be pleased to dispose of him. Believing that a true

3976/477 *contd.*		consideration of the above as well as that candour which has cost him every personal interest here and good intention to this country by which he incurred the forfeiture of his fortune in Europe will dispose it rather to act with generosity than to let him lay under the public stigma…'
	15 June 1777	Pass from Vice President Robert Morris of the Marine Committee of Congress for Apollos Morris to board the brig. 'Friendship' for Europe.
478		*Blank in the sequence*
480	13 June 1777	John Spotswood, Bellaghy, to Conolly re payment of Bellaghy rents.
481	14 June 1777	Robert Henry Drummond, London, to Conolly about the remittance of Stretton rents by Henry Cole.
482	15 June 1777	Receipted account from Bar. Senior Dep. Ranger [at the Curragh] for Conolly for entrance fees for horses.
483	15 June 1777	Receipt from J. Long for Conolly for rent.
485	18 June 1777	Robert McClintock, Dublin, to Conolly stating his accounts. He is a little uneasy because it is so long since they settled their accounts.
486	18 June 1777	Richard Woodward, Dean of Clogher, London, to Conolly, about his audience with Lord North. 'I hope you received my letter which was left for you at Hart's in Chester. You would have heard from me much earlier on my coming to town, but that I wanted to give you an account of my reception by Lord North to whom I was yesterday introduced by Sir Robert Hamilton. He received me very cordially and graciously ate a very hearty breakfast in my presence. The interview was rather of his seeking as he wanted to ask some questions about the general state of Ireland. They related principally to the temper of the people and their disposition towards administration but, a little to my surprise, he was very particular in his enquiries about the probability of Mr Flood getting a seat in parliament. On my being unable to clear up that point he concluded with a decisive sour face that Flood must not expect to keep such a place [as a Vice Treasurer for Ireland] (looking still sourer) without being in parliament. I did not wonder at the sentiments but was amazed at his delivering it to a man who might have been connected with the person concerned. I had the honour of seeing Lady Buckingham[shire] to deliver His Excellency's picture and had the pleasure of seeing her look perfectly well and exceedingly handsome…'

3976/ 487	20 June 1777	George Ash to Conolly about racing at Derry, where Conolly has provided a cup.
488	20 June 1777	Walter Hussey Burgh, MP, Dominick St, Dublin, to Conolly about his political conduct, and favourable attitude to Buckinghamshire's administration. 'My anxiety for your approbation of my conduct will I hope be a sufficient apology for my giving you this trouble. I am afraid you understand the conversation that I lately had with Mr [Richard] Heron [Buckinghamshire's Chief Secretary] in a light very different from that in which I intended it – far from expressing or indeed feeling any degree of pique or resentment I declared in that conversation that the failure of the intended arrangement should make no manner of difference to my parliamentary conduct – the truth is I have just the same favourable disposition towards Lord Buckingham's administration and the same inclination to support it so far as is conversant with the true interest of the country as I could have in the most lucrative employment, and the whole of what I have said amounts to this, that I mean to act the very same part without emolument instead of with. This seems to me to be a matter in which no human being is concerned but myself. The reason of my making such a decision is no other than this – that during a course of I believe near two years since the matter was first mentioned I have felt an awkwardness in my situation that wounded something in my mind – call it niceness or pride or what you will. I was not anxious for employment but I was anxious to have an end to all negotiation about it and to be able to say (with some evidence of the truth of what I said) that I was not an expectant for office – a declaration such as I have made seemed to me the only means of wincing the truth of such an apparition – with that view I made it and not with a view to express the most distant idea of dissatisfaction at the part Lord Buckingham had acted – on the contrary I have the most grateful sense of the kind dispositions he has shown towards me and the greatest confidence in his good intentions towards the country – for my own part I have only allotted my future life to the more private walk of my profession instead of engaging any further in the bustle of politics….'
489	22 June 1777	Thomas Thoroton, Belvoir Castle, to Conolly. He has sent the hounds and discusses their merits.
490	24 June 1777	Henry Major, Ballyshannon, to Conolly about conveying the Ballyshannon rents to Conolly. He is worried about being robbed while on his way to meet Conolly at Cavan or Clones.

3976/ 491	24 June 1777	William Ellis, deputy barrack master, to Conolly, seeking a coastguard job for his brother.
492	1 July 1777	Henry Major, Ballyshannon, to Conolly about remitting Ballyshannon rents.
493	1 July 1777	John Spotswood, Bellaghy, to Conolly about rental of Vintners' proportion.
494	3 July 1777	Ralph Knox to Conolly stating accounts.
495	14 July 1777	Henry Major, Clones, to Conolly, about remitting rent from Ballyshannon
496	17 July 1777	[The 1st] Lord Clifden, Gowran, [Co.Kilkenny], to Conolly about hunting and hounds. Offering Conolly some hounds.
497	19 July 1777	Thomas Casker to Conolly in relation to the provision of land for Lady Massereene's garden at Leixlip Castle, which she rented from Conolly.
498	24 July 1777	Edward Bulkeley, Dublin, to Conolly. 'Mr Glascock is preparing the papers necessary for the conveyance of the Newporton estate', Co. Fermanagh.
499	26 July 1777	Francis Savage, Hillsborough, to Conolly, about racing.
500	4 Aug. 1777	[Charles Watson-Wentworth, 2nd Marquess of] Rockingham, Wentworth [Woodhouse, Yorkshire] to Conolly. Asks Conolly to recommend [the 5th] Earl of Inchiquin as Governor and Custos Rotulorum of Co. Clare. Sneering reference to the previous Governor [the 5th Earl's uncle, the 4th Earl of Inchiquin], whose 'Whig' principles were softened by courts. Conolly may not like to make to make the request even of this lord lieutenant.
501	28 Aug. 1777	Arnold & John Nesbitt, London, to Conolly seeking payment of money paid out on Conolly's behalf.
504	25 Sept. 1777	Caleb Powell [Collector of the Revenue], Limerick, to Conolly enclosing a return of the exports of Limerick and Waterford for year ending 25 Mar. 1777.
505	10 Dec. 1777	[Sir] James Caldwell [3rd Bt], Castle Caldwell, [Belleek], Co. Fermanagh, to Lord Buckinghamshire sending debates of the House of Commons in the Duke of Northumberland's administration [1763–4] and a part of a further imminent publication. Hoping Conolly will honour Caldwell's part of the country with a visit.

3976/ 506	20 Dec. 1777	Sir William Howe, Philadelphia, to Conolly. Recommending a Captain Boyd. He plans to leave his command to return home to answer his attackers in England.
507–10	Ante 25 Jan. 1778	Various receipts and accounts, including George Faulkner's account for printing notices of race meetings in 1777, as well as stable accounts.
511	27 May 1778	William Conolly Clarke, 43 Montgomery St., Dublin seeking preferment.
512	29 May 1778	[Henry Thomas Fox-Strangways, 2nd Earl of] Ilchester, Blandford, to Conolly. He cannot pay money he owes Conolly just yet. He hopes this is not an inconvenience.
513	30 May 1778	Henry Cole, Stretton, to Conolly about tenants at Stretton, and minor repairs to roof of the house at Stretton.
514	2 June 1778	Andrew Spotswood, Bellaghy to Conolly about the problems with collecting the November rent due to scarcity of money. 'I have been using my utmost endeavours to bring in the November rents and assure you Sir, when I have impounded the tenants' cattle [I] have been obliged to return them again for want of purchasers, and little or no money given for cloth or yarn so great is the distress of this part of the country…' He also encloses a valuation of the oak and ash in the deer park at Bellaghy by Mr Frith of Co. Fermanagh.
515	8 June 1778	John Coghill, Coghill Hall, Yorkshire, to Conolly about the payment of the fees for Coghill's baronetcy, as well as some friendly gossip. 'There has happened by a mistake of Mr Drummond's people that I have been put to the blush as I requested you would give me credit on Drummond for £250 to pass my patent and you mentioned to me that you had drawn on him for £100 to be ready. His answer was that he had got no directions from you or any of his people. I will be much obliged to you to write to him as it might appear to him that I have acted a very improper part in naming your name. I wrote to Crofton to pay my agent the money which he has found the time to pay and I have given orders to my agent to pay it on your account to Mr Latouche. To my great surprise I met Pierpoint Burton in my walks. He is come to Harrogate for the waters. He says Lord Conyngham is bearing it away at Bristol.

3976/515 *contd.*		In a very few posts this long promise is to take place [he was created a baronet on 31 August] by my letters from Lord North's friends. It has been long on the carpet. This will find you at the Curragh races…
516	9 June 1778	William Grueber, Phrappes Lane, to Conolly. He had taken a lease of a farm at Posseckstown, [on Conolly's Castletown estate], Co. Kildare, but due to a change in circumstances he no longer feels he has the 'moral certainty of having a fund to build it'. He has made various improvements, but hopes to be released from his tenancy. He has ten children to support.
517	13 June 1778	Edward Bulkeley, Dublin, to Conolly. 'I understand from Mr Major that a Mr Dillon has leave to bring in a bill relative to the salmon fisheries of this kingdom and that this gentleman was concerned with Mr Adderley in the year 1773. He desires therefore that this matter should be attended to, lest the fishery of Ballyshannon should be injured…'
518	14 June 1778	Receipt from William Bell to Conolly for Bell's salary as steward of the Jockey Club.
519	14 June 1778	George Ash, Ashbrook, [Co. Londonderry], to Conolly about racing at Derry, but also making reference to the 'the distressed situation of this starving country.'
520–21	18–23 June 1778	Two letters from John Nesbitt, London to Conolly about the payment of a bill of 2,000 guineas on Mr Brooks. Reference is also made to Nesbitt taking advice from Mr Clements on this matter.
522	23 June 1778	Henry Major, Ballyshannon, to Conolly about the dismal economic situation in the north of Ireland and the difficulties in collecting rents. Reports that he has impounded tenant's cattle and been forced to release them. '…I must beg that you will as soon as you can conveniently honour me with your directions whether or not you approve of my receiving whatever sums the tenants can at present afford to pay, or that I should proceed to sell the distresses on the land to the amount of the whole rent… 'The necessities of the people in this country are really very great occasioned by the bad markets for black cattle and for yarn and also by the failure of the late harvest, which has obliged almost every individual of them to purchase meal for the support of their families, which has been conveyed to this place from Derry, Sligo and Scotland. Several families who were in tolerable circumstances

3976/522 *contd.*		a year ago are reduced to beggary and many of them have nearly exhausted whatever money they had and will very shortly be in want of the necessities of life unless you shall be pleased to order them some relief.'
523	25 June 1778	James Boyle, Newtown Limavady, to Conolly about the formation of an independent Volunteer company at Limavady. 'At this present conjunction when there are so many independent corps forming for internal defence in the northern parts of Ireland, we hope Mr Conolly will not disapprove of an address from 100 young men in the country part of the manor of Limavady – the inhabitants of Newtown are not concerned – all freeholders who with his approbation, will form themselves into an independent company at their own private expense furnish themselves with arms and uniforms, and having perfectly learned their exercise, will march to any part of the county Government pleases to appoint them when there shall be occasion. We hope it is agreeable to Mr Conolly that they should be called Conolly's Independent Volunteers. Also that he would please to advise them how to act with regard to Government orders as they are quite ignorant of the propriety of the measure [the Militia Bill?], yet sensible of the necessity...'
524	25 June 1778	Francis Savage, Mount Pottinger, to Conolly about accommodation for horses at the Co. Down course.
525	26 June 1778	James O'Neill to Conolly about his son's work enlisting men to join the army. His son's first name is Conolly.
526	1 July 1778	William Congreve to Conolly about the Stretton Mortgage. He wants to buy an estate in Staffordshire for his nephew, but is finding it difficult to raise money and therefore wants to call in the £7,300 mortgage he holds on Stretton, since its purchase by Conolly's father in 1733.
527	2 July 1778	John Knox, Waringsford, to Conolly seking a commission of the peace for Hamilton Moore, who is planning to reside in Co. Derry.
528	4 July 1778	John Frith, Enniskillen, to Conolly about his valuation of the woods at Bellaghy, which Conolly hopes to sell.
529	5 July 1778	Henry Major to Conolly about the collection of the Ballyshannon and Killybegs rents. He has not been very successful due to the scarcity of money.

3976/ 530	7 July 1778	James Every, Dublin, to Conolly about the state of the Dublin public coal yards, which the poor tradesmen have no access to despite the provisions made by parliament 'some years ago'. He encloses a petition [not found] which he urges Conolly to lay before the Irish privy council, as the petitioners missed the opportunity to lay it before parliament.
531–34		*Blanks in the sequence*
535	14 July 1778	Henry Major to Conolly sending 100 guineas for Conolly's use.
536	17 July 1778	Archibald Grant, Manchester Sq., London to Conolly. He is buying a commission for his son in the Foot Guards, and as a result needs to call in money owed to him by Conolly. Conolly should pay the money through Theophilus Bolton in the Treasury Office in Dublin. He apologises for the short notice he is giving.
537	18 July 1778	Charles Dawson, Limerick, to Conolly seeking to dispose of his employment.
538	22 July 1778	Bill remitted to Conolly's account at Latouche's bank, Feb. 1782
539	31 July 1778	Andrew Spotswood, Bellaghy, to Conolly about the lack of money in the country, and his hopes for a market for their cloth and yarn.
540	1 Aug. 1778	John Powell, [accountant at the Pay office under Henry Fox, 1st Lord Holland, when the latter was Paymaster-General, and Holland's executor], Pay Office, to Conolly. 'Mr Bulkeley in his letter of the 25th past desires I would give you the following information. The sum due from you to the estate of Henry Lord Holland deceased is £12,450 sterling at interest 5 per cent premium due and payable 12 June and 12 December… NB Poor Lady Holland has been and is very bad indeed.'
541	6 Aug. 1778	William Tighe, Ballyshannon, to Conolly about the lease of part of a farm at Creevy formerly held by the late Thomas Dickson.
541a, 549	7 Aug. 1778	Katherine Sterling, Sligo, to Conolly. Seeking employment for her husband. Her husband due to 'his thirst for fame' would prefer a career in the navy, but she hopes Conolly can find a civil employment in the revenue, as she has four small children ranging in age from six days to six years, and does not want to be parted '(perhaps for ever) from the best of husbands' if he joins the navy.
	25 Sept. 1778	Katherine Sterling to Conolly about her husband's employment. She is accompanying her husband to Dublin, where he wants to meet Conolly to take up his offer of a career in the navy. She wants

3976/549 *contd.*		Conolly to assist in persuading him to take up a place in the revenue instead. She believes separation will be worse than death.
542	16 Aug, 1778	Henry Major to Conolly. The market was plentifully supplied with oaten meal and new potatoes, but 'the markets for black cattle and yarn are still very bad and the scarcity of money so bad I cannot get a shilling from any of your tenants…'
543	16 Aug. 1778	Wray Babington, Derry, to Conolly seeking an army career for his brother. His late father was the incumbent at Bellaghy.
544	17 Aug. 1778	Capt. Thomas Loftus, Armagh, to Conolly. He wants to purchase a majority of dragoons. He has already obtained the support of Lord Ely for his application, but also wants Conolly's assistance in making an application to the Lord Lieutenant.
545	30 Aug. 1778	John Ferguson, Mayor of Londonderry, to Conolly about the Derry races, for which Conolly has provided a silver cup as a prize.
546–7	8–13 Sept. 1778	Two receipts relating to Conolly's racing exploits.
548	17 Sept. 1778	William Cashell, Berwick on Tweed, to Conolly seeking employment. He is a half-pay officer who was severely wounded by a musket ball, losing the sight of one eye, but he is still capable of employment, and seeks Conolly's intercession with Lord Buckinghamshire. He formerly served in Lord George Lennox's regiment. [Lennox was Lady Louisa's brother]
550	1 Oct. 1778	John Nesbitt to Conolly. They need to draw on Conolly for £600 sterling in order to pay bills on his account.
551	10 Oct. 1778	Richard Heron, Chief Secretary for Ireland, Dublin Castle, to Conolly about the appointment of a Mr Anthony Lestrange to an ensigny in the 36th Regiment of Foot on Conolly's recommendation.
552	18 Oct. 1778	Arch. Murray, Ballyshannon, to Conolly enclosing a chart of the river from the bar to the town [not found]. He has built a new quay.
553	7 Nov. 1778	J. Hamilton, Custom House, Dublin, to Conolly. Dawson, port surveyor of Limerick, wants to exchange for the collection of Loughrea.

3976/ 554	1778–79	Account from George Faulkner to Conolly, for the cost of printing racing advertisements at the Curragh.
555	4 Jan. 1779	Mary Cotter, Old Church St., Dublin, to Conolly. She wants her second son brought out, her first already serving under General Howe thanks to Conolly's support.
556	15 Jan. 1779	George Ash, Ashbrook, to Conolly about racing at Derry, and the valuation of woods on Conolly's estate at Bellaghy.
557	19 Jan. 1779	William Conolly Clarke, 43 Montgomery St., Dublin, to Conolly. He wants Conolly's support to obtain the clerkship of the 'stationary wares'. The vacancy has occurred because the incumbent, a Mr Green, has been declared insane.
558	22 Jan. 1779	Receipted account from John Scott for Conolly's horses.
559	1 Mar. 1779	Letticea Mervyn, 79 Capel St., to Conolly enclosing a copy of her and her sister's petition to the Lord Lieutenant and a note from Lord Annaly supporting her case: she is the daughter of an old sportsman and is reduced to misery. The petition cites their family's services going back to Sir Audley Mervyn, Speaker of the Restoration parliament.
560	4 Mar. 1779	D[awson]. Downing [of Rowesgift, Bellaghy], Drogheda to Conolly. Enclosing a copy of his petition to the Lord Lieutenant seeking a place in the revenue.
561	6 Mar. 1779	Daniel Toler, Beechwood, [Nenagh, Co. Tipperary], to Conolly apologising for the poor foxhunting at Nenagh, when Conolly and Lady Louisa came to stay.
562	7 Mar. 1779	H. Warren, Summer Hill, [Dublin], to Conolly. He wants the clerkship and treasurership of the 'Circular Road' for a friend.
563	7 Mar. 1779	James Ash, Hermitage, to Lady Louisa Conolly citing the various hardships the labours under. He wants her help in procuring an employment from Lord Buckinghamshire.
564	20 Mar. 1779	Robert Johnston to Conolly about an application he made to Conolly through Mr [George] [Conolly's brother-in-law] Byng.
565	20 Mar. 1779	Edward Bulkeley, Dublin, to Conolly about a mortgage on his estate held by Sir Sampson Gideon. Reference is made to Mr [Henry Theophilus] Clements, who 'is very urgent.' Clements wants to extricate his security.

3976/ 566	21 Mar. 1779	Her[cules] Langford Rowley, Summerhill, [Co. Meath], to Conolly Expressing thanks for some service provided by Conolly and Lady Louisa during a time of suffering.
567	21 Mar. 1779	George Ash, Derry, to Conolly. This town is in joy at the expectation of having the honour of having you and your lady at our races, where you and she will meet every mark of respect and attention that can be shown you and attach every person to your interest on a future occasion….'
568	23 Mar. 1779	John Spotswood, Bellaghy, to Conolly. He is writing on behalf of his father [Andrew] who has sore eyes and is unable to write himself. He has received Conolly's directions from Mr Bulkeley to stop all renewals on the Vintners' proportion. They have been busy examining all the tenants' leases as instructed.
569	23 Mar. 1779	John Scott to Conolly about the upkeep of his horses at the Curragh.
570	27 Mar. 1779	Robert Sterling, Dublin, to Conolly. He has joined the navy, and is gone to Liverpool. He intends setting up his wife with a small business at Sligo. He seeks a letter of introduction to Admiral Keppel, or any other officer, from Conolly.
571	6 Apr. 1779	William Smith, Newtown Limavady, to Conolly about the sale of woods in the manor of Limavady. There is a newspaper cutting with the advertisement of sale enclosed.
573	15 Apr. 1779	David Latouche to Conolly about Conolly's 'exorbitant' overdraft on his account with Latouche's bank. 'I am much concerned to acquaint you that the balance of your account is so exorbitant, being above £21,000, that I am under the necessity of giving directions to confine your drafts and expect that you will speedily enter some method of reducing this enormous balance. You will know, when I consented to open an account with you that you, assured me you never would exceed the amount of the security then deposited which was £7,000. How far you have complied with this agreement it is unnecessary to mention. In hopes of a satisfactory answer.
574	16 Apr. 1779	John Hatch, Dublin, to Conolly. He is a tenant of thirty acres on the Rathfarnham estate. He wants to renew his lease and insert the names of his two daughters. Enclosed is a portion of his lease.

3976/ 575 17 Apr. 1779 Thomas Conolly to David Latouche (draft) about his overdrawn account at Latouche's bank.
'I received your letter, which I must take for granted you well considered before you wrote. I certainly never meant to exceed the security of £7,000 first given to you, but the situation of affairs having taken such a turn as to prevent the raising of money upon any other terms than usurious ones, and the situation of [being] a man in debt to many who could only sell and not mortgage, occasioned several of my creditors to call in their money, which has been paid to a very considerable amount through your means. Your house was appraised of this circumstance and in possession of a real security for £7,000 and a personal one for upwards of £15,000 which I offered to strengthen with one of the Duke of Leinster. I own I was surprised to have my credit stopped at so respectable a house as yours before I had drawn without any previous notice to prepare elsewhere. You know Sir that in order to reduce the balance due to you, I offered my Dunsink estate at a lower rate by three year's purchase than I sold at to Mr [Toon?] who was advised not to buy. I now offer it to you to whatever value you set upon it, with this reserve [that], provided your price does not amount to twenty-four year's purchase you will give your word of honour that I may be at liberty to redeem it in two years allowing you legal interest for your money. I shall offer you, your choice of several other estates upon the same terms. If you do not accept this proposal, I shall only add that no effort of mine shall be wanting to procure you immediately money at payment due and you may be assured no further drafts of mine shall be brought to your house.'

576 19 Apr. 1779 Messrs David Latouche to Conolly
In response to no. 575 above. They think that there has been some misunderstanding and sets out their case as follows: 'At a time when money was extremely scarce you desired to open up an account with our house. The terms were that you would not overdraw but perhaps at a particular season of the year and then but for a few thousands; that our advancements would be reimbursed in a short time; and [that] in order that we might be perfectly secure you would mortgage to us the amount of £8,000. This was agreed to from a just sense of your character and personal regard for yourself. We believe you will allow these were the previous conditions to opening of the account. Now, upon examining into the accounts, it will appear almost from the commencement of them our advance exceeded the securities and when the balance accumulated beyond whatever we could have conceived we thought it advisable to take your bond for it, as a better security than a mere book debt, as a temporary expedient, till you had raised the money elsewhere, but by no means as an advance that we had acquiesced under.

3976/576 *contd.*		We flattered ourselves that our conduct towards you had demonstrated a sincere friendship and regard and perhaps carried us further than a strict prudence could justify, having never in the course of business for a series of years ever advanced such sums of money on the best specified securities. With respect to your offer of the lands of Dunsink or any other of your estate's money is too scarce to afford a thought to such expectations, though at the same time we are much obliged to you for your intention. We make no doubt of your taking every step in your power to extricate us and procure for us at least part of our debt, which we consider not properly secured…'
577	21 Apr. 1779	Conolly to David Latouche & Sons (Copy) responding to Latouche's letter above. 'I always considered myself under obligations to you for placing so much confidence in me as to permit me to overdraw my first security to so great an amount, but the distress of individuals in these bad times made me the more serious to be punctual in all my payments and not to make that apology to others which has for these two years been made to me, thinking that it was more honest as well as more consistent with my own feelings to be at the expense of paying an interest for sums due to me which I could not immediately come at, and satisfied that you could at no time be sufferers in case of immediate death the sum in my tenant's hands and the rich security is gone securing you in that case beyond a doubt. My debt to you, though great, was the only one I had in the world and if I may be permitted to say so when I owe no interest of money or bill to any man beyond the commencement of this year. These circumstances induced me to trespass so much upon a house that I considered so opulent as yours. But you may rest assured every effort in my power shall be made to reduce my balance within its original bounds, and I have no doubt of effecting it in a very considerable degree in a short time. I have directed my agents to pay in as normal all my rents to your house and, as Mr Bulkeley informed you we desire my account, though great, to continue open however exceeding the present balance which, at this time of year, was always the most considerable as the interest and rents due…my half years rents gale of rents besides considerable arrears…'
578–580a	24 Apr.– 1 May 1779	Humphrey Turner's accounts for Conolly's stables at the Curragh.
581	6 July 1779	Henry Major to Lady Louisa Conolly about the difficulty in collecting Ballyshannon rents due to the failure of the flax crop last season. He hopes to see both Conollys in Ballyshannon this year where Mr Conolly has 'much business to do with his tenants, which cannot be so well executed in a hurry'.

3976/ 582	8 July 1779	Richard King, Mulkeeragh, [Limavady], to Conolly. '...what with the number of Independent companies in the North etc. and the marching and counter-marching of the King's army[things] make an odd appearance and many conjectures on this [but] different opinions...' [See also nos. 1782–8.]
583	9 July 1779	Andrew Spotswood, Bellaghy, to Conolly about the state of the leases on the Bellaghy estate, and the Conollys' planned summer visit to the north, when that business can be taken care of.
584	14 July 1779	M. McDonnell, Newhall, [Co. Clare], to Conolly seeking a commission in the army.
585	15 July 1779	Edward Bulkeley to Conolly enquiring whether Conolly dines near town the following day as he wishes to speak to him.
586	16 July 1779	Henry Major, Ballyshannon, to Conolly on the difficulties of collecting rents due to the scarcity of money.
587	16 July 1779	Receipted account from William Brophy to Thomas Conolly for tailoring.
588	18 July 1779	Henry Major, Ballyshannon, to Conolly. He has remitted £600 to Messrs Latouche.
589	18 July 1779	George Ash, Bellaghy, to Conolly about the sale of woods at Bellaghy and the Derry races, where they have taken the liberty of appointing Conolly a steward.
590		*Blank in the sequence*
591	July 1779	Receipt relating to entrance fees for Conolly's horses at a race meeting.
592	3 Aug. 1779	Dawson Downing, Rowesgift, [Bellaghy, Co. Londonderry], to Conolly seeking assistance in procuring an employment in Dublin. He is waiting for confirmation of the resignation of the incumbent Mr Buttle.
593		*Blank in the sequence*
594	8 Aug. 1779	Francis Savage, Scarva, [Co. Down] to Conolly about the state of his horses following the journey to Co. Down.
595	9 Aug. 1779	Apollos Morris, Cork, to Conolly on the formation of volunteer corps in Cork

3976/595 *contd.*

'As I have publicly said that neither in this country nor in England the precautions necessary for a country likely to be invaded are taken, it is right to mention some of the particulars, that you might mention them to the Lord Lieutenant…

1st interesting the commonality of the kingdom for 'tis evident a great majority is no way interested in its defence

6th organising the independent armed societies as to put some of them on a footing to co-operate with the troops.

I have not the usual fate of prophets, for I cannot complain of the behaviour of my own countrymen. I am offered a high rank in Cork and total command in Bandon. The number enrolled in the different societies in Cork exceeds 1,000. 900 assembled in June, when the alarm was given, but there are not above 6 or 7 hundred well exercised. In Bandon near 300 on the rolls about 200 exercised. But to make a certain military force many things are requisite…'

596 29 Aug. 1779 Apollos Morris, Cork, to Conolly on the defence of Ireland and the deficiencies of government. See also NLI Conolly Papers MS 41,341/6/19.

'In obedience to your letter I proceed to say something on the heads which I laid before you, respecting the defence of Ireland.

But first I must lament the situation of a chief governor who has not only an external enemy to contend with but also the faults of ages: of a series of administrations without any system but that of procuring grants and places for friends; of short sighted legislatures which occupied with like objects never made a law for the regulation of government except in the fever of some party struggle; of a gentry whose selfish passions have kept it constantly at work from the time of Henry II cutting down the branches upon which it stood; of a clergy who (a few excepted) have as such, scarce anything to do in the world; and whose only road to the next seems to be through a court; of a people so corrupt as after the manner of their betters to prevent every public trust into a job, and to know no public spirit, unless chained into the narrow views of a party. He is to bring them to act in concert in war though so avowedly ill policed as be scarcely manageable in peace; and what is worse than all to struggle with the circumstances which the remains of the absurd system of laws (if the ruins of a system can be so called) have thrown them into which make the interests of the majority almost incompatible with public tranquillity and make it unapt for the regulations of any policed country ancient or modern.

I mention those things not as reproaches but to show the ground we and the enemy are on, that we take better if possible, and thereby defeat him. For the same purpose I enclose a sheet entitled Irish Complaints [no. 1801] but had I not written them

3976/596 *contd.*		before I would not have taken up time with them now. Dispatch and decisive action are now more wanted than discussions. I therefore confine myself to hints such as immediately occur under each head. I wish you had pointed out what was not understood and what was provided for. The 4th article may seem to be provided for by the proclamations addressed to justices of peace: I look on those proclamations as mere matter of form, except that they may legally serve to justify a minister in one of our courts, but would make no military or historical defence before such as were acquainted with this vague part of our executive power. The inactive will not stir and they may give a pretence to some too active to run away with their neighbour's cattle without account and be productive of resistance and concealment. The strokes may appear bold but are they not necessary; if you do not bring the people to act for you they will act against you; if you will not give a method they will give you more trouble than service; if you are not generous to the people the enemy will. One proclamation irrecoverably may break the hold of hands which for want of address we keep too tight.'
597	13 Sept. 1779	Receipted account from William Bell for entrance fees for horses.
598	20 Sept. 1779	Dawson Downing, Rowesgrift, to Conolly reminding him of his promise to Downing of a tidewaiter's place at Belfast. Conolly is to speak to Chief Secretary Heron.
599	4 Oct. 1779	Audley Fanning, Lifford, to Conolly seeking employment for a son.
600–602: 604	9 Oct.–16 Nov. 1779	Receipts from James Finegan and Humphrey Turner for wages and stable accounts at the Curragh.
603	12 Nov 1779	Dawson Downing, Rowesgrift, to Conolly seeking the position of land waiter in Limerick which has become vacant due to the transfer to Dublin of the incumbent Mr Charles Dawson.
605	26 Nov. 1779	Robert Johnson, Magherafelt, to Conolly seeking a job in the revenue service.
606	30 Nov. 1779	A list of the officers of the Castletown Union [Conolly's Volunteer Corps] Captain Commandant — Thomas Conolly Captain — Hugh Cairncross Captain Lieutenant — Andrew Mills Lieutenants — Alex Law Richard Phillips

3976/606 *contd.*		Ensign Chaplain Surgeon	Edward Harper Rev. Patrick Sands Thomas Taggart

607 30 Nov 1779 List of the 'the gentlemen of the vicinity of Celbridge who got notice to attend at Castletown the 30th of November 1779.' There are 74 names, 37 of them stated to be Roman Catholics.

608 22 Dec 1779 Return of the Celbridge division of the Castletown Union There are 24 names, (15 Catholics and 9 Protestants) and indications of their attendance record.

609–625 *Blanks in the sequence.*

626 1 Jan. 1780 Hugh Drake, HMS Victory, Spithead, to Hamilton Drake, Bellaghy.
This letter was originally enclosed in no. 630 below. See also NLI Conolly Papers, MS 41,341/5/16.

627 2 Jan. 1780 Michael Spence, Donaghmore, Co. Donegal, to Conolly about the demise of his family, who have long enjoyed the patronage of Conolly and his father. He seeks Conolly's assistance in securing a living under the Bishop of Raphoe.

627a 6 Jan. 1780 [Simon Luttrell,1st Lord] Irnham, Lutrellstown, [Clonsilla, Co. Dublin], to Conolly.
'Your apology is very sufficient for unhinging any park gates. Their being so closely shut up was owing to the terror my wife and family live in from a lawless banditti armed with clubs, bludgeons and headed by Colonel Luttrell [his son] with his sabre, which at present surround this place, I was preparing my departure for England but was obliged to postpone it till I can put Lady Irnham under proper protection in my absence…'.

628 14 Jan. 1780 Lord Buckinghamshire to Conolly about his impatience to talk to Conolly about the drafts of the intended 'Free Trade' bills, which have just arrived.
'An express arrived last night from Mr Hamilton [John Hamilton, under-secretary, Dublin Castle, 17778–81, and a relation and protégé of Lord North] with drafts of the intended bills. Lord North seems inclined to go beyond his engagements and do everything in the most extended and liberal manner.

I am impatient to talk to you upon the subject and wish, as the nights are light that you would dine with me either tomorrow or Monday.

If it was not for my confidence in your friendship, support and assistance my spirits would sink under the difficulties of my situation…

3976/ 630	14 Jan. 1780	Eliza Drake, Bellaghy to Conolly. She is worried about her brother [Hugh Drake] who wants to transfer to a smaller ship, where he has a better chance of greater pay. He got his career in the navy through Conolly, and she seeks Conolly's assistance in this matter.
631	15 Jan. 1780	Thomas Dilkes, Warden, Biggleswade, [Berkshire],to Conolly seeking employment in England
632	19 Jan. 1780	Lord Buckinghamshire to Conolly. Though the breaking either into your business or amusements is a most unpleasing task to me, yet in the present anxious [ ] I cannot help expressing my wish that for a few days to come you should be in Dublin. 'I want your advice and assistance upon every point the determination of which they decide upon the existence of every species of government in this kingdom and the comfort of the few remaining years…'
633	4 Feb. 1780	James Barclay, Ballyshannon, to Conolly seeking to be appointed super numerary gauger in the revenue at Killybegs.
634	9 Feb 1780	Hamilton Gorges, Ballygalway, [Co. Tyrone], to Conolly seeking a better living for his brother and asking Conolly to intercede with Lord Buckinghamshire on his behalf.
635	11 Feb. 1780	Richard Woodward, [Dean of Clogher], Clogher, [Co. Tyrone], to Lady Louisa Conolly He is seeking the bishopric of Kilalla. He has heard that the current bishop's life is very precarious. ' The whole object of my troubling your Ladyship with this, that as two bishoprics are likely to become soon vacant, and the first is promised to Mr Beresford, he may be obliged by Lord Buckingham to content himself with the first, whatever it may chance to be, and not be allowed to wait till the death of a second bishop gives him the option, and leaves to me the least desirable, which would be marking a second time the superiority of Lord Tyrone's interest to that of Mr Conolly as well as subjecting me the second time to mortification and perhaps real loss and inconvenience. To explain this matter to your Ladyship who are but lately entered into the study of bishoprics: if the Bishop of Raphoe dies, he will be succeeded by the bishop of Dromore and Beresford will succeed to Dromore worth £1,800 a year. Killala is worth at least £2,200 a year and Mrs Woodward (though she hates the thought of Connaught likes the odd £400) joins with me that Mr Beresford may not be allowed to stay to get the best. We want the odd money the more having bought Lord Carlow's house and this day sent the money to pay for it. Till a bishop dies I shall not

3976/635 *contd.*		think of leaving Clogher, for having now two houses in town we think it (naturally for Irish people) doubly prudent to live in the country. Our own house is advertised and until it is disposed of we chose to keep the purchase of the other secret and let Mr Dawson remain in it. We got it monstrous cheap at £1,550 and only 11 pounds and some shillings ground rent. An apology for this letter would only make it longer, I shall therefore conclude myself with the greatest respect…'
636	12 Feb. 1780	John Powell, Bennet St, London, to Conolly 'I am under the necessity of soliciting the payment of the debt of £12,450 due from you to the executors of Henry Lord Holland deceased and to inform you that if I do not receive satisfaction on or before the 8th of April next I shall be under the necessity of taking the most speedy and effectual legal steps to enforce payment….'
637	17 Feb. 1780	J Braughall, Kildare to Conolly, seeking an employment to enable him to pay off a debt he incurred by standing security to another man since declared a bankrupt.
638	18 Feb 1780	Bartholomew McNaughten, Coleraine, to Conolly about the utility of the Volunteers. See also NLI Conolly Papers MS 41,341/6/7. 'The utility of the Volunteers appeared to you much earlier than it did to my poor mean capacity, but my conviction of the rectitude of your conduct made me resolve to lend my small aid when I saw you take the lead, and my wish to be under Mr Conolly's protection induced me to request it for my company. The great use of these societies is now I think conspicuous to even poorest understanding and for their continuance at least for some time. I gave my reasons in a former letter why I was convinced you intended to gratify my request of guns at a proper time. I continue of the same opinion, and I did keep between sixty and seventy men learning the exercise for three months past at some expense to myself, with the hope of getting arms from you every ensuing week; and I can aver that had arms for an hundred come down two months since I would now have as many stout young fellows tolerably trained to add to the defence of the kingdom and political catalogue, that the most patient have refused to assemble any more until the arms come. Then as I believe you have this matter at heart, let me beg of you to order arms.'
639	22 Feb. 1780	Arch. Murray, Ballyshannon, to Conolly about changes made to the harbour at Ballyshannon.
640	10 Mar. 1780	John Downing, Rowesgrift, to Conolly about a dispute with his son Dawson Downing over the reversion of the writer's employment.

3976/ 641	11 Mar. 1780	Rev. William Percy to Conolly seeking an improvement in the income from his living in the diocese of Ossory.
642	14 Mar. 1780	Richard Morgan, Newcastle, [Co. Dublin] to Conolly. about the dishonesty of bakers in Celbridge and the need to extend the Dublin assize of bread to that town to stop such irregularities.
643	28 Mar. 1780	William Trench [of Garbally, Ballinasloe, Co. Galway. MP for that county], to Conolly. He encloses an address which he and Denis Daly received from a meeting of the gentlemen, clergy and freeholders of Co. Galway, chaired by Lord Clanricarde, about the forthcoming supply bill. This requested them to vote only for a six month supply bill until Poynings' Law was modified and to work for a repeal of the 6th of George I and a retrenchment of public expenditure. Although it was signed with 155 names, Trench claims that more than half of these names have been inserted without the consent of the people concerned '…we [Daly and he] have acted a strong and indeed rather violent part with our constituents, and I am very sure if Daly had not come down I should not have been able to have done anything with them, but as it is, I think myself now free; but at the same time I hope if I go with government that my Lord lieutenant will insist on Nimble Dick [Heron] going through in any matter in which he makes his friends show themselves and insist on all placemen going with them…'
644	31 Mar. 1780	Sir Robert Staples, [7th Bt] Dunmore, [Co. Laois] to Conolly seeking employment for a friend.
644a	n.d.	Instructions for the review or field day of the Dublin Volunteers under the Duke of Leinster on 2 April 1780.
645	4 Apr. 1780	[Frederick Hervey, Bishop of Derry and 4th Earl of] Bristol to Conolly Long letter about the repeal of Poyning's Law. 'As to Poynings' Law….it is like the leading strings of a child, which are often left tacked to the garment of that child, long after the governess has no occasion to hold them, but which if continued after the child had reached a certain degree of stature and strength would be sure to produce a struggle between the child and its parent…'
646	7 Apr. 1780	J. Braughall, Kildare, to Conolly following up on his previous letter [no. 637], which has gone unanswered.
647–8	10 Apr. 1780	Henry Cole, Stretton to Conolly about the 'Division of Widow Day's farm.'

3976/ 649	15 Apr. 1780	[Sir] John Coghill [1st Bt], London, to Conolly 'In a hurry I write to say I came here last night. The papers will tell the business in the Lords. In the course of the debate the Lords in administration declared they would throw out every thing that was passing in the Commons, The Lords in opposition are to secede and leave the House to administration. Mr North and Sir Grey's hopes were locked out on the question that was carried by two….'
650	16 Apr. 1780	David Young, Londonderry, to Conolly. Long letter detailing an abduction case recently heard at the Londonderry assizes and seeking for Conolly's intercession to prevent the execution of a Mr David Millar. 'To a gentleman of Mr Conolly's liberality of mind, and humanity of temper no apology need be made for the following letter. At our last assizes a young man David Millar committed by one of your Volunteer companies in the parish of Comber was prosecuted for forcibly entering a neighbour's house after sunset and taking away his daughter with an intention of marriage without the consent of her father and mother. It appeared on the trial, that though the young people were together for a night and day and had all the aid that secrecy and concealment afforded, yet Millar never hinted at nor attempted anything improper. By the ignorance of his prosecutor, who had no mind to affect his life, an indictment was laid against him as well for breaking into the house, as carrying off the woman. On trial his character from infancy was ascertained spotless the nigh fault excepted and hence the jury wanted to give in their verdict "damages to the amount of £4 11s". The judge (Mr Lill) sent them away and desired them to bring him in guilty or not guilty. They could not avoid returning the former. Sentence was therefore pronounced against the unfortunate young man and his execution appointed on the sixth of May. The grand jury would have recommended him as an object of mercy but the judge prevented them by assuring several of the members that he would certainly obtain a pardon. From Mr Lill's correctness as a judge and humanity as a man there is reason to believe the man's life may be safe, but the last of these principles pleads strongly for expedition in this business. As duty leads me I have attended the hapless man in confinement and a being so unhappy I never beheld. Your colleague [as MP for Co. Londonderry] Colonel Cary assured him of pardon and between hope and uncertainty of life he is wretched in the extreme. His father, a respectable freeholder, a healthy vigorous man of fifty years, has died of grief on the sons account since sentence was passed against him, as if the distress arising from his own situation had been insufficient to complete his misery. I saw a judicious friend who was at his father's funeral yesterday who assured me that the widowed mother and three children were likely to lose

3976/650 *contd.*

their reason with the accumulation of their misfortunes. From your connexion with the Lord Lieutenant I have no doubt of your power, and from the benevolence of your heart I have a little of your inclination, to hasten at least to secure his reprieve.

No man serves the laws of his country more than I do and no man can have a stronger desire to punish the guilty but justice as well as humanity compel me to take this liberty aided as they are with the pleasing hope of being successful when I apply to Mr Conolly.

Though I have the honour of being known to you yet I cannot plead a sufficient knowledge on your part to trust your confidence in my representation. If you would take the trouble of sending this letter to Sir H[ugh] Hill whom I have the honour to call my friend he will satisfy you that I would not interest myself or trouble you in favour of an unworthy object.

Amidst the important business in which you are engaged I cannot expect the honour of an answer but your application in favour of the young man will not be inconsistent with your endeavour to obtain the greater object of your country: prosperity'.

651 21 Apr. 1780 George Ash, Ash Brook, to Conolly bout the Derry races, and the Conollys' attendance at them. The Bishop of Derry has invited Conolly and Lady Louisa to stay at Downhill.

652 29 Apr. 1780 Conolly to [the Whig opposition leader, the 2nd Marquess of] Rockingham.

Copy of a long letter about the debates over Poynings' Law and the need for free trade.

'I never was more obliged to any person than I feel myself to you for the great pains you have taken amidst the intricacies of your own domestic business to write me so long a letter, upon the subject of our national affairs: and the hurry in parliament for these last few days never permitted me to answer you sooner.

You certainly overrate my importance, and my opinions being totally different from yours, I shall in a few words give reasons why they are so.

In the first place I think no resolutions of our parliament here can secure us from any attempt in future of the British legislature: it may bind us to resist but it cannot secure us success, even with the assistance of France and Spain. Our House has already unanimously, and between ourselves I think wisely adjourned the debate on the declaratory resolutions: and I know it's understood that it shall not be taken up again this session. The statute of Sir Edward Poynings is nonsense in its original, and all the explanatory ones that follow in Elizabeth and Philip and Mary are the same. But I hope the House will likewise adjourn the consideration of it until a time of peace, when both countries can

3976/652 *contd.* meet the subject calmly and see what is proper to be done away and what to remain.

The starting these subjects now evidently shows the want of gratitude in a country that has by their words strongly expressed it and shows a determination in us to quarrel with Great Britain at any rate, must sour the people of England, can do us no good, but to make them impatient to take back what they have so generously given – I mean the restoration of our trade and participation of her own. If we now endeavour to establish the precedent of might makes right, Great Britain will some day or other have it in her power to return the compliment and your Lordship very well knows the situation and circumstances of this kingdom will not admit of the contest. France and Spain may help us for a time but even if they succeed this country will be obliged to change religions and to enjoy a worse constitution than the present, even with all the horrors and fetters of Poynings. I was as active and strenuous as any man to obtain a Free Trade and I shall now do everything in my power to promote and secure it: but in my poor opinion we can do neither by quarrelling with the mother country that at present it is in her power to sink; but we must go down first.

If we live to have peace, you will see many people with their capital come and settle in this kingdom for these reasons. Great Britain's rent roll – I mean the produce of her land – is now valued at fifty millions: and her debt two hundred increasing at a rate of 12 millions annually. The produce of the land here is about four million and a half, likely to increase, and her debt two millions, including expirable annuities. You will therefore see that people will settle in a country, possessing equal trade, and having only taxes to pay, according to the proportionable interest of our comparative debts and establishments, instead of Great Britain. And I look upon it that our lands here will rise proportionally.

The difference of the situation and treatment of America and this country are such that need not be mentioned, but the loss of the former will oblige England, by making it her interest, to advance this country in every particular, if our ingratitude does not prevent it, and this country in another century will carry five millions industrious rich inhabitants instead of four and a half idle and half starved. Such is the political creed of your much obliged and sincere friend…'.

653 23 Apr. 1780 Pat Haly, Ballyshannon, to Conolly outlining his fears about been moved in the revenue service from Killybegs district. Appeals to his 'great friend and only patron'.

654 25 Apr. 1780 Robert McClintock, Dunmore, [Carrigans, Co. Donegal], to Conolly.

3976/654 *contd.*		Had accidentally remitted the wrong amount to Latouche's bank on Conolly's account, but has since made up the difference.
656	3 May 1780	Sir John Coghill, London, to Conolly enclosing a study of the costs of the army in America. Coghill and Ponsonby have been drinking Conolly's health and happiness.
657	9 May 1780	Thomas Burke Dunlevy, Galway, to Conolly. He wants to take holy orders and seeks Conolly's help in securing a living in the Church.
658	20 May 1780	Conolly to Rockingham (Copy) advising Rockingham to let the separate Mutiny Bill (which will pass in Ireland 'on Monday) return without suppression or alteration. 'The desperate situation to which this kingdom is reduced will plead my excuse for troubling your Lordship with this letter. The mutiny act which is to be introduced into our House on Monday next, and which will inevitably pass by a majority of above two to one, is likely to affect this country with the most serious consequences which are perhaps more numerous than you can be aware of though I am convinced you have already had official information. I have seen this matter big with all its fatal consequences from the time and manner in which it was first started in the House, and have opposed it to the utmost, as a measure not only likely to separate the two kingdoms, but likewise to expose everybody here to the immediate loss of property by the disbanding of the army. As many of our estates are settled by English Acts and many gentleman have been so imprudent already as to declare that they will use their utmost influence as magistrates and jurors to prevent the execution of any English act, many, great and immediate would be the bad affects should these heads of a bill be suppressed in either Council. But if the wisdom of Great Britain should suffer them to pass into a law, it is my belief that all would be quiet, and that the real well wishers of the peace of this country and the prosperity of the whole Empire would be able to prevail against those members who from various political and interested motives would risk the loss of both, and who have engaged others better intentioned to go further than they now wish they had gone. Neither Lord Buckinghamshire nor any man of business know of my writing this letter, which I thought it my duty to send, for your Lordship's use, and those only to whom you may think it necessary to be made known.'
659	20 May 1780	Alex Young, Snowhill near Lisnakea. [Co. Fermanagh], to Conolly seeking employment, he is a tenant of Conollys.

3976/ 660	22 May 1784	*This letter is out of Date sequence* Mr [Thomas] Orde [Chief Secretary to the Duke of Rutland, 1784–87] Dublin Castle, to Conolly Wants to meet Conolly before his return to England.
661	30 May 1780	Andrew Spotswood, Bellaghy, to Conolly about the valuation of Eden Wood on the Bellaghy estate.
662	2 June 1780	John Ferguson, Londonderry, to Conolly explaining why Conolly was not chosen as Reviewing General for the forthcoming review of the Volunteers of Derry, Tyrone and Donegal to be held in August. 'When this review was first set on foot your friends here intended to propose you as Reviewing General, and we had the greatest hopes of being able to carry our point; but there came in such numbers from Tyrone and Donegal that I was afraid I would not have a clear majority, as all those were strongly attached to Mr [James] Stewart of the county of Tyrone, who they proposed as Reviewing general. In this dilemma I was forced to change my ground as I would not by any means have your name mentioned unless I could have brought you in quite hollow…I then determined to oppose Mr Stewart with all my power…and set up Lord Charlemont…as less offensive to you than the Member of [*sic* –for] the adjoining county…it would have cut me to the heart to see my General, Governor and representative of this county outvoted by anyone…' Concludes by assuring Conolly that this is not to be taken as a sign of ingratitude '…I know you to be one of the very best friends of Ireland, and that your endeavours have been great, not only in the senate, but in the closet to procure Free Trade…'
665	23 June 1780	[Sir] Richard Heron, Dublin Castle, to Conolly Paul Canning is to be Deputy Governor of Co. Londonderry.
666	23 June 1780	Edmund Bannerman, Londonderry, to Conolly seeking a promotion for Lieutenant Wylde of the 30th Regiment of Foot.
667	28 June 1780	Lord Buckinghamshire, Dublin Castle, to Conolly 'The consideration of the army bill will come on in Council upon Monday next. I can tell you in confidence that it is put off till that time in hopes of receiving more explicit instructions.'
668	30 June 1780	George Byng junior, Westminster, to Conolly [his uncle]. He has just left school and is off to Gottingen to attend a military academy. He is slightly uneasy about leaving his family, 'however, it was [what] you did and all other men must do…'

3976/ 669	4 July 1780	Charles Kennedy, Johnstown, [Naas, Co. Kildare], to Conolly. Has fox cubs from Co. Waterford for Conolly, and desires instructions regarding their collection.
670	4 July 1780	Buckinghamshire, London, to Conolly Giving news of a naval engagement, involving Admiral [George Brydges] Rodney. Moves on to Irish affairs, especially the mutiny bill 'Yesterday the bill for the better regulation of the army was submitted to the Privy Council, which Richard Heron with very little support ineffectually opposed. The bill with several others was transmitted last night. As the business will not be ready for the House of Commons by Saturday, a further adjournment of a fortnight will be proposed. Lord Camden dined with me yesterday… He is going to the north where I hope he will preach the doctrine of real whiggism without any republican sophistication.' Goes on to trade family gossip.
672	12 July 1780	Anne Taylor, St Stephen's Green, to Conolly. She wants her son, Matthew Beresford Taylor, to succeed Henry Archdall on the Linen Board, and desires Conolly's assistance.
673	23 July 1780	Geo. Fall, Dublin to Conolly about the debt owed to him by John Fenaghty of Celbridge, and seeking Conolly's assistance in recovering this debt.
674	4 Aug. 1780	David Latouche & Sons to Conolly stating payments on his account.
675	9 Aug. 1780	Buckinghamshire to Conolly asking him to solicit several named individuals to support the government in the House of Commons on the vote on the mutiny bill. 'Though by such accounts as reach us there is little cause to doubt of the carrying of the army bill., yet the deciding the question by a respectable majority is so partial to the tranquillity of the kingdom, and to the credit of my administration, that I cannot help requesting that assistance which I am persuaded you will most cordially give. Will you therefore solicit Mr Trench, Mr Smith and Mr Prendergast, and if you could try a word to Captain Skeffington who must necessarily lose all chance of advancement as a soldier if he opposes in so an exceptional a question as this immediately relative to his profession. If these gentlemen cannot be induced to vote with us at least persuade them for the sake of the kingdom, and to prevent its now openly[?] propensity from being checked by intestine connotations, at least not to oppose. [See no. 1784]

3976/ 676	12 Aug. 1780	Buckinghamshire to Conolly strongly urging Conolly to use his interest in the matter of the previous letter, if only for Buckingham's 'peace of mind'.
677	16 Aug. 1780	General Sir William Howe, Cholderton, [near Amesbury, Wiltshire]. to Conolly requesting payment of his wife's [Conolly's sister Frances] fortune which would be very acceptable to 'a poor cast off general with a plump wife.' 'My narrative with some remarks on [Joseph] Galloways' pamphlet [*Letters to a nobleman, on the conduct of the war in the middle colonies.* London, 1780] is in the press. This should have been out sooner had we not waited to see if there would be anything more to answer as this will [be] the last and the first of my publications. I will send you half dozen of them before they are given to the public.'
678	19 Aug. 1780	Robert Clements, MP, Killadoon, [Celbridge, Co. Kildare], to Conolly. Wants Conolly's assistance in removing a gauger, Parke, to another walk, because he has got himself into 'a scrape'. Parke's father is a Ballyshannon man, who has always attached himself to Conolly's interest.
679	27 Aug. 1780	George Tompkins, Limerick, to Conolly. Wants to be revenue collector at Kilkenny. He refers to the 'steady and zealous attachment of my ancestors to the interest of your family on all occasions that offered but more especially on their election in Co. Londonderry.'
680	8 Sept. 1780	John Staples, Lissan, [Cookstown, Co. Tyrone], to Conolly [his brother-in-law] about Conolly's non-appearance at the assizes. 'Yet still I wish you had come down, were it for no other reason but to counteract Cary, who is just come down, [and is] setting up for a very great patriot, and if what I have heard be true cares not how much it is at the expense of yours (I mean as to parliamentary conduct) [that] he acquires such a character…'
681	8 Sept. 1780,	John Hamilton, Brownhall, [Ballintra, Co. Donegal], to Conolly. Montgomery will oppose Hamilton in Co. Donegal with all his might Would Conolly be prepared to speak to the Youngs and Lord Conyngham in his favour?
682	10 Sept. 1780	Thomas Bateson, Londonderry, to Conolly. As there will soon be an election in Co. Londonderry 'my vote and interest for that county is at your service, which amounts to 45 to 50 voters, and as sure a tenantry as any in the kingdom.' Praises Conolly for his conduct in the House on 21 August. '…when the present factious spirit, which cannot last any time, blows over, you will then appear conspicuous as a friend to Ireland.'

3976/ 683	12 Sept 1780	Apollos Morris, Cork, to Conolly about the delay in Colonel [William Hull] Tonson's promised peerage and deception on part of Sir Richard Heron. Tonson required to give Mr Beamish a pension in return for the peerage. Lord Shannon active on Tonson's behalf. [Tonson became Lord Riversdale in 1783 after years of agitation.]
684	14 Sept 1780	Sir William Howe, Cholderton, to Conolly. He has withdrawn as a candidate for Nottingham, because his interest is 'distracted and divided' over the American War. His pamphlet [*The narrative of Lieut. Gen. Sir William Howe, in a committee of the House of Commons, on the 29th of April, 1779, relative to his conduct,* ... London, 1780] has been published, although he feels he has overlooked some of Conolly's remarks on Galloway's pamphlet in the final printing. 'I find that you have decided to have nothing to say to our parliament except (as I suppose) that you may at the head of your Paddys give them law from Ireland instead of their giving it to you.' Again requests payment of Lady Howe's fortune.
685	15 Sept. 1780	Sir Richard Heron, Dublin Castle, to Conolly about the proposed appointment of a first commissioner of the revenue. 'My Lord Lieutenant being of opinion that the appointing one of the commissioners of the revenue to be first commissioner (as at the Boards of Treasury, Admiralty and Trade in England) and to be in a more especial manner responsible to government for the transaction of business at that Board, would have a beneficial effect in the conduct of the business, and establish a degree of responsibility in one commissioner which can hardly be expected from many among whom authority is equally divided. As such a measure may be of very great importance to the kingdom His Excellency judged it necessary to consult you and other persons of consequence in this kingdom; and will be much obliged by your sentiments upon the idea. P.S. I am to observe to you, that it is not intended to make any alteration in the mode of disposal of revenue employments.'
686	23 Sept. 1780	James Browne, Brownhall, to Conolly about horse racing
687	7 Oct. 1780	Sir John Coghill, Dublin, to Conolly. 'I landed last night and the night before we on shipboard were ready to take the chance of leaping on the Rock of Howth or drown, ninety on board and saved by no more than five minutes and made then for Ireland's Eye, behind which we lay for twelve hours as no wherry dare stir after that, one came from Howth where I landed at six o'clock and was obliged to walk to town.' He has brought seeds for Lady Louisa as requested.

3976/ 688	14 Oct. 1780	Apollos Morris, Cork, to Conolly. Appeals for remission of imprisonment of Mr Conner's son. Sends abstract of the suit Wade versus Conner.
689	15 Oct. 1780	Conolly, Castletown to Buckinghamshire, requesting that his friend Dean [George] Marlay be given the Deanery of Derry, '…and I think his relationship with Grattan over whom he has no influence, should not weigh against your good wishes to me, in strengthening my interest in Derry, which you must be sensible has of late and particularly in the last question of the Mutiny Bill, received a considerable shock.'
690	17 Oct. 1780	John Ferris, 40 St Mary's Lane, Dublin, to Conolly reporting fraud over the corn premium.
691	22 Oct. 1780	Sir William Howe, Cholderton, to Conolly. He wants his wife's fortunein order to invest it in the funds. He refers to the new lord lieutenant, 'Your new lord lieutenant [The 5th Earl of Carlisle] will please the ladies whatever he may do the men, but his white livered secretary [William Eden] I hope may please neither. He is a diabolical fellow with a smooth tongue and a foul heart.'
692	24 Oct, 1780	Francis Gervais, Portarlington, to Conolly seeking his interest to assist a friend, who wants to resign his office in favour of another.
693	1 Nov. 1780	Humphrey Turner's account re. Conolly's stables at the Curragh.
694, 700	2, 29 Nov. 1780	Two letters from Rev. Thomas Norman, Iniskeen,[Carrickmacross, Co. Monaghan], to Conolly. He wants to resign his living [of Inniskeen] in favour of his son [Robert].
695	3 Nov. 1780	Buckinghamshire to Conolly in response to no. 689 above. Marlay's politics are so extreme and Buckinghamshire's influence in England so shaken that he doubts if he could obtain the Deanery of Derry for him.
696	6 Nov. 1780	Thomas Phelan Martin, Ballyshannon, to Conolly. He wants an army promotion. He is a great grandson of Thady Coane of Ballyshannon, many of whose descendants have been promoted by Conolly.
697	11 Nov. 1780	Conolly McCausland, Fruithill, to Conolly about the sale of the Collectorship of Armagh to his brother-in-law's son-in-law.

3976/ 698	17 Nov. 1780	John Downing, Rowesgift, to Conolly seeking a pension in the revenue, after thirty-three years service. He cites his father's and his own service including his father's participation in the siege of Derry and the Boyne. 'Your great uncle from his particular regard to my father for such service knowing him to be a staunch whig (as he was himself) appointed him his lt-colonel of militia dragoons and only deputy governor of this county in the year 1715 at the time of the rebellion and procured for his friends and at his recommendation commissions in the Revenue.'
699	27 Nov. 1780	Robert Johnson, Magherafelt, to Conolly seeking employment.
701	1 Dec. 1780	J. Stanley Monck , Dunboe House, to Conolly enclosing a newspaper cutting from the *Belfast Newsletter* about the 'Dunboe protest'. This was the protest of the Dunboe Volunteers which appeared in the Belfast Newsletter on 19 September, protesting against certain resolutions of the assembled officers and captains of the Coleraine Battalion [possibly those censuring the Dublin Merchants' Company]. Monck drew up a resolution for Isaac Hazlett, Captain of the Dunboe Volunteers to the effect that he had in a hasty moment allowed his name to be signed to the Dunboe protest, but having carefully read the resolutions of the Coleraine Battalion, he finds he agrees with them perfectly and thinks the Dunloe Protest unwarranted. This resolution Monck 'laboured to get signed but it could not literally effect it', whereupon another version had to be prepared to the effect that Hazlett had signed the Coleraine Battalion's resolutions on his own behalf., and not in the name of the Dunboe Company, and this was accepted and 'has effectively silenced the popular applause the Dunboe Protest had universally gained in this country.'
702–703	3 Dec. 1780	William Greene, Cork, to Conolly enclosing no. 702, the 'Memorial of William Greene author of 'Some Observations on the harbour of Cork' Greene has heard it has been declared of some use and is seeking a reward from Lord Buckinghamshire.
704	5 Dec. 1780	Thomas Venables, Derry, to Conolly seeking employment.
705	6 Dec. 1780	[Richard Boyle, 2nd Earl of] Shannon, Castlemartyr, [Co. Cork], to Conolly. He has being thrown while foxhunting.
706	6 Dec. 1780	George Byng senior, Wrotham Park, [Middlesex], to Conolly About his daughter Anne's 'peremptory' refusal of Mr Bagwell [sic-Bagenal] though he was strongly recommended by the Conollys and Lady Buckinghamshire. 'I have invariably made up my mind on the subject of my children's marriage. Let them judge for

3976/706 *contd.*		themselves. I would rather they should see with false eyes than act under control from me. All I would have asked on this occasion from her would have been to have given the matter some consideration…'. [See no. 1738 below.].
707	8 Dec. 1780	Mr Mayne, 39 Abbey Street, [Dublin], to Conolly recommending a John McGrath for a career in the navy.
708	10 Dec. 1780	Lord Buckinghamshire to [his brother-in-law] Sir Charles Hotham Thompson [8th Bt]. Copy letter in which Buckinghamshire gives a long-winded vindication of his conduct in Ireland. Lays most of the blame on Lord Hillsborough; complains of his advice being neglected or ignored by Lord North and his ministers, of their carelessness in issuing instructions, and their general willingness to listen to 'the low intrigues of interested emissaries'. Overall he paints a picture of Ireland in a state of unrest and points to 'the conduct of those who formerly never presumed to form an opinion' becoming so fluctuating as to make steady government impossible. But above all he complains of Hillsborough. '…he addressed me in a style very unusual in the composition of letters to men in high office. The terms of a dispatch containing instructions from the king, are however, to be received with respect and deference but Lord Hillsborough is not to address Lord Buckingham in the style which Doctor Busby with birch under his arm, would have used to a King's scholar.' A particular grievance was that Hillsborough sent circular letters to the magistrates of every corporation informing them of the intended commercial concessions, without consulting him, the Lord Lieutenant – 'a most glaring unofficial act', which even the Irish regarded as a slight to him. Half the peers and privy councillors recommended by him have been rejected; recommendations for employments traditionally in the power of the lord lieutenant have been ignored; and he has not even been informed of the official date upon which Lord Carlisle will arrive.
708a	18 Dec. 1780	Receipted account from a Sergeant Griffin for Conolly for subsistence.
709–10, 714	23, 30 Dec. 1780; 7 Feb. 1781	Three letters from David Latouche & Sons, Dublin, to Robert McClintock, Strabane, about remitting money on Conolly's account.
711–713, 715	31 Dec. 1780–24 Feb. 1781	Accounts and receipts relating to Conolly's racing establishment at the Curragh, including a list of mares covered in the year 1780.

MSS	DATE	DESCRIPTION
3977/ 716– 3978/ 956	**26 Feb. 1781– 28 Dec. 1788**	**Letters, receipts and miscellaneous papers of Thomas Conolly, 1781–88**
716	26 Feb. 1781	Lieutenant General Robert Cunningham, Dublin, to Conolly about the sale of an army commission.
717	17 Mar. 1781	Executors of Edward Sneyd, Sackville Street, [Dublin], to Conolly 'The executors of the late Edward Sneyd Esq., sensible of the favour and partiality with which you honoured Mr Sneyd in the wine trade, beg leave to request the continuance of your countenance to his family for whose benefit you can with certainty be supplied as formerly on the best terms from the largest and most excellent stock of wines in this country.'
719	29 Mar. 1781	A record of a days events in London [by Lady Louisa?] 'Went in the morning to Sir Joshua Reynolds and Copley painters and topical sculptors, then to Mrs Damer's, Mr Mackenzie's and Sir W. Howe's, then to the House of Lords (the King was there). Lady M Coke dined with us in the evening. I was at Sir G Howard's and Lady Petrie's assembly.
720	5 Apr. 1781	Robert and Henry Drummond,[bankers], London, to Conolly about money drawn on his account.
721	15 Apr. 1781	Conolly McCausland, Fruithill, to Conolly about the death of Lord Conyngham and enclosing a list of burgesses of Limavady. William Burton is a man of honour and will observe the agreement. Conolly should write to all the burgesses reminding them of it and asking for a guarantee in writing. One burgess's place is to be filled because of the death of Robert Johnston, so the Provost and at least six burgesses will be needed to make a Common Council. Conolly should delay sacking his agent lest he should offend his brother, Rev. James Montgomery, the present provost. Mr Jones is anxious to resign as a burgess. See also NLI Conolly Papers MS 41,341/7/3
722	18 Apr. 1781	William Eden, [Chief Secretary], Dublin Castle, to Conolly Assures him that he has laid before the Lord Lieutenant, Conolly's objections to Edward Cary MP becoming joint governor of Co. Derry in place of the late Lord Conyngham. Eden has acquainted Cary that it is impossible for the Lord Lieutenant to accept him in this position, because of Conolly's superior claims.

3977/ 723	26 Apr. 1781	William Burton to Conolly about calling a meeting of the burgesses of Limavady.
724	1 May 1781	Humphrey Turner's accounts for the stables at the Curragh
725	5 May 1781	Charles Isdill to James Hanly at Cargins near Roscommon and Thomas Morton, near Strokestown, [Co. Roscommon] – Conolly connection unclear, except that Conolly owned a small estate in that county.
726	19 May 1781	Robert and Henry Drummond, London, to Conolly about money drawn on his account.
727	May 1781	Rent roll of the Cloghard estate, Castlefin, Co. Donegal, sent by Robert McClintock.
728	3 June 1781	Rev. James Montgomery to Henry Major. Hurt that Conolly should be distrustful of him. Will give Conolly no cause. Notice for election of Jones's successor [as burgess of Limavady] cannot be posted until after Jones's resignation has been accepted by the Common Council.
729	6 June 1781	Thomas Throrton, Screveton near Newark, Notts, to Conolly about hounds he is buying for Conolly at Tattersalls.
730	9 June 1781	Rev. James Montgomery, Woodhill, to [Conolly McCausland] He has received a letter from Conolly, which has cleared up the possibility of disagreement over Limavady corporation, where Montgomery was provost.
731	10 June 1781	Conolly McCausland, Fruithill, to Conolly. Is handling Conolly's interest in regard to the election of new burgesses and a provost for Limavady. The town is 'murmuring and complaining' that they need a resident provost to supervise the markets, and McCausland recommends to Conolly that he acquiesce in this.
732	15 June 1781	Unsigned receipt from Thomas Dunn to Conolly.
733–35	19–21 June 1781	Three letters from James Glascock to Conolly giving legal advice on elections to Limavady Corporation.
736	26 June 1781	David Latouche & Sons to Robert McClintock, Strabane, about remitting money on Conolly's account.
737	27 July 1781	Robert and Henry Drummond, London, to Conolly about money drawn on his account.

3977/ 738	6 Aug. 1781	Receipted account from a Sergeant Griffin to Conolly for subsistence.
739, 741,745, 749	17, 30. Aug., 14 Oct. 1781, 8 Feb, 1782.	Four accounts signed by Robert McClintock relating to surveying and advertising farms on the Castlefin estate.
740	18 Aug. 1781	David Latouche & Sons to Robert McClintock, Strabane, about remitting money on Conolly's account.
741–43	21 Sept.– 2 Oct. 1781	Copies of correspondence between John Courtney, London, and Francis Fetherston, who is seeking an East India commission for his son, sent by Courtney to Conolly.
742	23 Sept. 1781	Frances, Lady Howe, Cholderton, to Conolly, her brother about hunting and family affairs.
744	12 Oct. 1781	Mrs Anne Byng, Wrotham, to Conolly, her brother about hunting and family affairs.
746, 748	15 Dec. 1781, 8 Jan. 1782	Two letters from David Latouche & Sons to Robert McClintock, Strabane, about remitting money on Conolly's account.
750	23 Mar. 1782	Solomon Martin, Culmore, Co. Londonderry, to Conolly. Petition about his holding on Conolly's Limavady estate, which first came into his family during Conolly's granduncle's time.
751– 53, 755	13, 29 Apr. 1782	Four receipts relating to renewals of leases on Conolly's Limavady estate.
754	14 Apr. 1782	Henry Major, Ballyshannon, to Conolly with a valuation of Conolly's farms out of lease at Castlefin.
756, 759	28 June, 22 Aug. 1782	Two letters from Robert and Henry Drummond, London, to Conolly about money drawn on his account.
757	29 June 1782	[Thomas Robinson, 2nd] Lord Grantham, London, to Conolly about the rent paid by Conolly to him for his London house. He was mistaken in the account he sent Conolly, and has overcharged him.
758	6 Aug. 1782	Henry Major, Ballyshannon, to Conolly about the Ballyshannon Volunteers. 'I beg leave to assure you that the Ballyshannon Volunteers have since the arrival of Capt. McBride's commission used their utmost endeavours to enlist men for His Majesty's sea service, in which we have not been in any degree successful. The lower class of people in this country seem to have a very great

3977/758 *contd.*		dislike to that service, but we hope by persevering to overcome their objections….I take the liberty to say that we cannot well attend Mr Archdale's review without the Colours which you were pleased to give us reason to expect.'
760–62; 770	29–Aug.–22 Sept. 1782	Two letters from William Bruce, Leixlip, to Conolly About the enclosed petition of George Walker Bruce regarding Derry Corporation. (no. 762). Also included is a letter from Alexander Crookshank to Bruce (no. 760).
763	6 Sept. 1782	Edward Bulkeley, Limavady, to Conolly enclosing: 1. An account of Lesley Alexander's losses by the erection of other bleach greens on the River Roe. 2. Abstracts of leases and the valuation of the lands contained therein. [part of the Limavady estate].
764	6 Sept. 1782	Robert and Henry Drummond, London, to Conolly about money drawn on his account.
765	6 Sept. 1782	Charles Powell Leslie, Glaslough, to Conolly. about his [successful] candidature in the forthcoming Monaghan election, and seeking Conolly's support. 'The last time I had the honour of meeting you at Mr Alexander's you were so kind to express an inclination to serve me if in power as to the approaching election for the county of Monaghan. Neither of the former representatives offers themselves. Mr John Montgomery offers himself as a candidate in the room of his father. With him I am joined and indeed we have every probability of success. However Lucas of Castleshane says he will oppose us and the canvass is begun. Colonel Marlay, who I am informed resides principally at Celbridge, has an interest in the county – your kind assistance there would very much oblige me. I shall write to him as soon as I think you may have paved the way. The present bishop of Clogher [Sir John Hotham 9th Bt] has not as yet signified a wish to see company. I have not therefore the least acquaintance with him: if you could by any of his connections [ie. Lord Buckinghamshire] get him to give the least hint that he wished me success it would have a pleasing effect upon the conduct of his clergy. But for the kind encouragement you gave me I should think many apologies necessary for the liberty I have taken…' See NLI Conolly Papers MS 41,341/8/19] for Buckingham's recommendation of Leslie to the Bishop of Clogher.
766–67	21 Sept. 1782	Regnier & Penstone, Leicester Fields, to Conolly enclosing a tailoring bill dated 1 May—17 June 1779.

3977/ 768	21 Sept. 1782	Paul Canning, Garvagh, [Co. Londonderry], to Conolly about Limavady Corporation affairs.
769	22 Sept. 1782	Petition from William Haslett to Conolly about his leases from Mr Smith at Limavady.
771–73	25–30 Sept. 1782	Three letters to Conolly from tenants on the Limavady estate about renewing their leases.
774	25 Oct. 1782	John Shannon, Londonderry, to Conolly seeking an army commission for his son, Frederick.
775, 777	27 Oct., 5 Nov. 1782	Two letters from Rev. William Nesbitt, Drogheda, to Conolly. He wants to succeed Dr Thomas Foster in the living of Dunleer
776–776a	2–4 Nov. 1782	Two letters, one from James Glascock, and one from Alex Boyle about a dispute between Conolly and a Mr Conyngham over a bog near Limavady.
778	15 Nov. 1782	George Ash, Derry, to Conolly about horse racing at Derry.
779	19 Nov. 1782	George Faulkner, Parliament Street, to Conolly seeking payment for printing advertisements [for Curragh races?]
780	23 Nov. 1782	John Hamilton of Brownhall, to Conolly seeking support for his [unsuccessful] campaign in the forthcoming Donegal election. He thinks his interest in Donegal is bound up with Conolly's and that they can give each other mutual support.
781	23 Nov. 1782	Edward Bulkeleyy to Conolly about his purchase of a lottery ticket.
782	29 Nov. 1782	Thomas Lear, Winton, to Conolly about his engagement to a Miss Howett.
783	3 Dec. 1782	James Glascock to Conolly. Matters re Lord Conyngham's estates and financial affairs are now adjusted amicably except the question of whether the sum of £15,000 is to remain charged on the Limavady estate. This is to be referred to arbitration.
784	4 Dec. 1782	George Byng, Wrotham to Conolly about family and military affairs. He also refers to Conolly's struggle over the borough of Limavady: 'I hope you have settled to your mind your corporation borough of Limavady. If such things are to be endured in any free country I would rather see them in your hands than in any other. Though

3977/784 *contd.* the thing itself is an abuse you will not abuse it. It is by the change of proprietor rescued from the venal market so let it rest with you till the good sense or the *ultimatum populi* shall occur to themselves a more just and equal distribution. At present both kingdoms are misrepresented.'

785 4 Dec. 1782 B. Henfrey, 43 Essex Street, Dublin, to Conolly.
He wants encouragement for his plan to set up a factory for silver plated wares.

786 10 Dec. 1782 Andrew Spotswood, Bellaghy, to Conolly about the remittance of rents.

787 15 Dec. 1782 Henry Major, Ballyshannon, to Conolly about the remittance of rents.

788 20 Dec. 1782 George Byng, Wrotham, to Conolly.
His son George's regiment, [Abercromby's] is due to go to India, and he would like his son transferred to another regiment so he doesn't have to go.

789 29 Dec. 1782 Richard King, Mulkeeragh, to Conolly about the bog at Limavady.

790 1783–84 Account of Conolly's subscription to the *Racing Calendar.*

791 21 Jan. 1783 Affidavit of Mary Holmes, nurse in the infirmary in Kildare, of the reasons of her leaving her employment.

792 2 Feb. 1783 John Dillon, Lismullin, Co. Meath, to Conolly.
Wants Conolly to visit so that they can 'enjoy the fox chase in its perfection.'

793 2 Feb. 1783 Patrick How, Killybegs, [Co. Donegal], to Conolly about his pension from the Chatham chest.

794 6 Feb. 1783 John Powell, Pay Office, London, to Conolly about Conolly's debt to the estate of the late Lord Holland.

795 14 Feb. 1783 John Ferguson, Londonderry, to Conolly about the forthcoming elections in counties Donegal and Tyrone. He will support Hamilton in Co. Donegal to utmost of his power. In Tyrone he has virtually no registered freeholders and did not trouble to re-register because he thought the election would take place during his shrievalty and was anxious to demonstrate his impartiality. Alexander told him in confidence that he was very sorry not to be able to vote for Knox in Tyrone as Conolly wished, but that he felt bound in consistency with the independent line he had always

3977/795 *contd.*		pursued to support Stewart and Montgomery. However he would not press his tenants to vote for the latter. If Lord Belmore sets up Eccles, Montgomery will resign; in which case Alexander's tenants will vote for Stewart and Knox.
796	17 Feb. 1783	John Hamilton, Brownhall, to Conolly. Asking him to get the 'considerable' interest of Mr [Andrew] Downes, son of the bishop [Robert Downes, bishop of Raphoe, 1753–63]. Hamilton did not apply to him because he thought he was about to sell his Donegal property.
797	28 Feb. 1783	Cadogan Keating, Frederick St, Dublin, to Conolly inviting him to dinner.
798	28 Feb. 1783	John Spotswood, Bellaghy, to Conolly about Conolly's subscription to a mass house and a proposal to plant Scotch firs on the estate at Bellaghy.
799	14 Mar. 1783	Sir Hugh Hill, [1st Bt], to Conolly. He wants the Collectorship at Strangford, [Co. Down].
800	30 Mar. 1783	Thomas Young, Loughlaske, to Conolly about his son's dismissal from the barrack master's place in Derry.
801	4 Apr. 1783	Robert Hamilton Hill to Conolly about racing at the Curragh
802	4 Apr. 1782	Claud Pottinger, Craigavade, [Co. Down], to Conolly. He wants to become the Duke of Leinster's agent at Strangford.
803	9 Apr. 1783	John King, Clondalkin, Co. Dublin, to Conolly about his rent of the mills at Leixlip
804	19 Apr. 1783	James Glascock, Dublin, to Conolly. 'I have just now got Dr Radcliffe's opinion upon the article with Henfrey. I find he is under the same difficulties I was to make this article legal and binding – I shall beg to know your sentiments upon it by Monday's post…' PS I think at least you should have the nomination of the workmen to be employed in the building to avoid being charged with work not executed.
805	2 July	James Dickson, ensign in the 67th regiment, to Conolly. He is unable to pay back the money he borrowed from Conolly to purchase his commission.
806	29 Aug. 1783	John Ponsonby MP, Bishopscourt, [Co. Kildare],to Conolly. About the recent general election, and Conolly's support for his

3977/806 *contd.*		campaign for the speakership. I have been very much out of order since I returned from my election campaign [on behalf of his son in Co. Kilkenny] which ended perfectly well as to success but the fatigue of it was too much for me. I am now beginning to recover and propose setting out for Mallow to drink the waters for a month. They have always done me service and I have great faith in them. How can I in terms sufficiently expressive of my feelings return you my thanks for the kind letter I received from you upon the subject of the chair. I do assure you I have the most lively sense of your friendship. I had many proofs of it and I shall never forget your kindness so repeatedly manifested to me and to my family at all times and on all occasions. I know you don't love long speeches. I shall therefore only add I am with the most sincere affection....'
807	17 Sept. 1783	Andrew Spotswood, Bellaghy, to Conolly about remitting rent to Conolly.
808	17 Oct.1783	Lord Bristol, Bishop of Derry, Londonderry, to Conolly. He wants to take a farm on Conolly's estate [at Bellaghy] to square his [Ballyscullion] demesne, and he also wants to build a bridge at New Ferry
809	19 Oct. 1783	Henry Major, Ballyshannon, to Conolly about remitting rent to Conolly.
810	19 Oct. 1783	Richard Norris, Drogheda, to Conolly seeking a clerkship in the Stamp Office for a nephew.
811	25–Oct. 1783	James Plunkett, Kinnard, [Strokestown, Co. Roscommon], to Conolly, about his rent.
812	27 Oct. 1783	Address of the inhabitants of the town of Leixlip assembled at a court leet to Conolly requesting a market house.
813–18	27 Oct.–10 Dec. 1783	Six letters and accounts relating to a case involving Richard King of Mulkeeragh, a tenant of Conolly's at Limavady. [See also nos. 1782–88.]
819	15 Dec. 1783	John Beresford [Chief Revenue Commissioner] to Peter Holmes, London. About a job application for a position in the revenue service, the applicant will need to prove he is of age, i.e.: over fourteen years old. The Conolly connection is unclear.

3977/ 820	23 Dec. 1783	John Spotswood, Bellaghy, to Conolly about remitting money to Conolly.
821	28 Dec. 1783	George Ash, Ashbrook, to Conolly. 'I think the Lord Bishop [Frederick Hervey, Earl of Bristol] much the better of the little address the [ ]sent him. I have not had the least communication with him since he became so violent a Volunteer. I am told he has said he will no longer interfere in politics. I see the people are cooling very much towards him.'
822	4 Jan. 1784	Richard King, Mulkeeragh, to Conolly seeking a coast surveyorship for his son.
823	7 Jan. 1784	Anne Thornhill, Cork, to Conolly about the welfare of the orphaned children of Lieutenant Francis Greenfield. She is their grandmother. The late lieutenant served under the Duke of Richmond [Lady Louisa's brother]. The eldest son is named John Conolly Greenfield.
824	7 Jan. 1784	John Staples, Lissan, to Conolly He is coming to Dublin and hopes to dine with Conolly at Castletown. He refers to events in England. 'I confess I have great fears that our friends in England [the Foxite Whigs] will not be able to stand their ground as I think there is the strongest reason to believe that a certain person [the King] is determined to keep them out at all events…'.
825	20 Jan. 1784	W. Walker, Londonderry, to Conolly seeking the payment of money owed too him.
826	21 Jan. 1784	Henry Major, Ballyshannon, to Conolly about remitting money to Conolly.
827	24 Jan. 1784	Receipt from James Finnegan to Conolly.
828	3 Feb. 1784	Henry Major, Ballyshannon, to Conolly about remitting money to Conolly.
829	14 Feb. 1784	Spencer Huey, Londonderry, to Conolly. Reports a meeting with Alderman Alexander, who 'does not disapprove of a reform' but thinks 'the present warm pursuit [of it] is doing great injury to the nation.' Also reports that the Earl-Bishop's son and young Alexander wished to attend a freeholders' meeting in Londonderry, the purpose of which was to elect delegates for a reform meeting at Dungiven. The Earl-Bishop has announced his intention of trying to promote provincial addresses which he will personally present to the King. In view of this, Huey

3977/829 *contd.* set out to Dungiven to quash what he knew 'would be displeasing to Mr Conolly'. At the meeting he was prevented from doing very much by a group of enthusiasts from Derry who regarded Cary as their chief, and young Harvey as his principal assistant. Despite this, however, an address 'for the reform, without either censure or applause to our representatives' was eventually carried. The evening concluded with much mirth and good fellowship, 'and bawdy songs by the clergy'. Almost all the clergy of the county were there, the Earl-Bishop having written to request their attendance. After the meeting too, many kind things were said about Conolly, although Huey observes that 'it would be serving him [Conolly] more effectually if these opinions were declared in public and to the freeholders throughout the county. [Conolly] McCausland [the younger] said that he never blamed Mr Conolly for anything but for not returning thanks to the friends who had laboured so much at Dungannon to have him appointed a delegate to the Convention. I said their friends mistook their service very much for they would have served him much more if they had voted against that measure, and that I heard of some people who voted for it in hopes it would turn out to his disadvantage, which it had done. I do believe little McCausland sincerely regards Mr Conolly and would serve him if he knew how, or could do it without giving up his popularity with the Volunteers or the Bishop…'

Huey concludes with a few observations on the meeting. The first is that 'the constitutional [plan of] reform was not read at Dungiven, nor does the tenth [of the] freeholders that attended know a single line of it. Two other county meetings were held for the same purpose…but the meetings were so inconsiderable that it would have been ridiculous to have resolved, and even in the present meeting not the sixth part of the freeholders attended, probably from a dislike to the measure – and therefore Mr Conolly cannot suppose the present resolutions the sense of the county, nor that the principal managers had acted candidly in not reading them what they were to adopt…'

830 14 Feb. 1784 Huey's account of the meeting at Dungiven, 12 February 1784. The meeting was held in the parish church and Alderman Lecky opened proceedings by proposing that an address of thanks should be addressed to the King for removing the late ministry. Huey opposed this on the grounds that it had never been done at any other meeting and that strict neutrality had always been observed before; and advised against making enemies in either England or Ireland by espousing the cause of parties with whom there was no previous connection. Lecky, however, read his address, which was constructed with much art, so that the address itself was coupled with the order for the Earl-Bishop to forward it, and many people

3977/830 *contd.* voted for the address – which contained 'the stale subject of the Fencibles to make it palatable' – in order to compliment Lord Bristol without regard to the address itself. Huey's was the only negative.

A committee consisting of a delegate from each barony was then appointed to sift and consider all the resolutions brought to the meeting and digest them. They returned after an hour's deliberation with what were basically Lecky's resolutions. '...The resolutions and petition seem to be warm and inflammatory. The address to Mr Conolly cold and impertinently positive. And that to Mr Cary grateful and flattering...' After this a committee was appointed to make a return of the state of the representation in the county. '...When the address to Mr Conolly was read it could not be determined whether the ayes or noes held it, though the question was several times put, but at length Mr Atchison, the secretary, explained and said that he supposed many people gave it a negative because they imagined it was a compliment to Mr Conolly, whereas there was none intended...' and apparently it was passed on those grounds. Coming out of the church each man was supposed to pay six pence towards the cost of advertising the meeting, which occasioned a rush and numbers escaped over the church wall to avoid paying. Two and a half guineas were collected.

831 15 Feb. 1784 Spencer Huey to Conolly
Forwards 829 and 830 above. Reports that the addresses to the King were entirely fabricated by the Earl-Bishop with a view to ingratiating himself with the new ministry. The meeting itself was composed largely of the tenants of Cary and Beresford, and not many from Conolly's estates. Some of those present explained they had been 'sent for'. Huey advises that Conolly in his answer to the address should show 'his disapprobation of armed citizens interfering in acts of legislature.' He also mentions a pamphlet he has written entitled 'The New Year's gift to the freeholders' apparently extolling moderation.

832 25 Feb. 1784 Henry Downing, 19 Strafford Street, London, about the cutting of timber at Rocktown, [near Bellaghy].

833 29 Feb. 1784 Pierce Simpson, Mount Campbell, [Drumsna, Co. Leitrim] to Conolly
Applying for a road through Cloncurry demesne [Co. Kildare] at next assizes.

834 2 Mar, 1784 Leslie Grove and T. Hood, London to Conolly drawing money on his account to pay off debt due on a bond to the late Mr Knox. They praise Conolly for his punctuality in making payments.

3977/ 835	14 Mar. 1784	Peter Holmes to Conolly seeking a position for his nephew, Alex Holmes, and enclosing no. 819.
836	14 Mar. 1784	John O'Neill, Park Hill, Ballyshannon, to Conolly about rent he owes Conolly.
837	16 Mar. 1784	Henry Major, Ballyshannon, to Conolly concerning interest payments and enclosing a note about principal and interest.
838	16 Mar. 1784	Simon Davenport's certificate that Richard King faithfully discharged his duty as a coast officer.
839	4 Apr. 1784	Thomas Bateson, Derry, to Conolly. '…in this place we are very quiet , and what is a little extraordinary, since the Reform Bill was thrown out by the Commons, we have not had a word about it here more than if such a thing had never been agitated. …Had the Parliament been irresolute and complied with the petition in all probability we would have had civil war, as the next thing the Republicans would have proposed would be to abolish tithes and a reform of property. Our bishop has not been here for upwards of two months and I think we shall not see him for some time; all his efforts could not get the Volunteers to take up arms and I think he will lose his popularity very soon with as much rapidity as he gained it – which cost him a deal of pains and money…'
840	10 Apr. 1784	Edward Bulkeley, Dublin, to Conolly about the payment of the Leixlip estate rent.
841	23 Apr. 1784	Anne Byng, Berkeley Square, London, to Conolly and Lady Louisa, giving the results of the Brentford election, where George Byng senior was a candidate. He came third, despite polling well. He is thinking of demanding a scrutiny against another candidate, Wicks, but she believes this will be unsuccessful. The rest of the letter is given over to family gossip.
842	27 Apr. 1784	Charles Tew's proposal to rent Killgreag, part of Conolly's estate in Co. Meath.
842A	1 May 1784	J.J. Ashenhurst to Conolly inviting the Castletown Union to take part in a Volunteer review in the Phoenix Park on 31 May and 1 June. The Volunteers of the city and county of Dublin '…would esteem it a very great honour…and will be ready to attend on a similar occasion in your vicinity at any time which shall hereafter be agreed upon.'
843	1 May 1784	James Glascock, York Street, Dublin, to Conolly about money owed to him.

3977/ 844 | 12 May 1784 | Henry Cole, Peterborough, to Conolly. He is going to Stretton to collect Conolly's rent.

845 | 21 May 1784 | Mrs C. McGhee (née Blackhall), Muff, Co. Londonderry, to Conolly. She is seeking a better living for her husband. [Muff, alias Eglinton, was the principal town on Conolly's leasehold estate held under the Grocers' Company of London.]

846 | 23 May 1784 | Richard Woodward, Bishop of Cloyne, to Conolly '...God be praised, the spirit of Volunteering is at an end. The Imokilly Blues (my corps) disbanded. One or two factious corps in Cork recruit blackguards, like their brethren in Dublin; but there too the admission of the rabble offends the respectable Volunteers. If we keep clear with France we have nothing to fear at home....'

847 | 26 May 1784 | *This letter and the following one are catalogued in the wrong order.* Conolly to Messrs Latouche in reply to no. 848. Copy. 'Mr Bulkeley was sent by me to your House this morning by one o'clock with a letter expressive of the terms upon which I meant to dispose of my Meath estate. This estate I had promised to let you know the value of before I entered into a treaty with any other person. The valuation I put upon it and the mode I proposed treating upon was such as I did imagine would upon investigation have met with your approbation, but since it has not, I shall immediately enter into treaty with others and advertise it to be sold in the whole or in parcels. The balance of that estate and a part of my Roscommon one will liquidate my debt at your House. This Sir is the method in which I propose to reimburse you and my debt shall not be of a moment longer continuance than the sale of those estates. I have no other mode to offer you for payment, much to your impatience, but conscious that my character will not suffer when no delay upon my part is intended, I am careless what steps you may take to force a more speedy payment. And had I my return sent to me monthly the debt would not have been permitted to grow to its present magnitude. Upon no account shall any future be debt incurred and I am prepared to pay those bills that are under my acceptance when they become due.'

848 | 25 May 1784 | David Latouche to Conolly. 'I must acquaint you that the balance of your account is now the enormous sum of £34,000 exclusive of interest, besides bills from England under your acceptance to a very large amount. What your scheme may be to liquidate this great sum I know not, but neither prudence nor friendship can suffer me to permit either its continuance or increase. I therefore request it may be immediately settled and that you will not draw any further on the House as I have give directions to refuse your drafts. I await your answer with much impatience.'

3977/ 849	27 May 1784	Conolly Lepper, Whitehouse, Belfast, to Conolly seeking a tide waitership at Ross.
850	28 May 1784	George Ash, Ashbrook, to Conolly answering accusations made about his stewardship of Conolly's estate at Limavady. [See also the Castletown Papers, A/10/3.]
851	30 May 1784	Abraham Creighton, Castle Dawson, Co. Londonderry, to Conolly about his surveyorship in the revenue service.
852	12 June 1784	Receipt for rent from John Long to Conolly.
853	23 June 1784	Francis Harpur to Conolly seeking a job in the new post office
854	2 Sept. 1784	W[illiam] Digby, [Dean of Clonfert], Philipstown, King's County, to Conolly. He has come to town to perfect the conveyance of Conolly's estate at Ballynakill, Queens County, but Mr Glascock is not available.
855–57	7, 14 & 15 Sept. 1784	Three receipts addressed to Conolly in relation to his horseracing establishment at the Curragh.
858	1 Oct. 1784	Richard King Mulkeeragh, to Conolly about schemes against Conolly on his Limavady estate.
859–62	1,2,12 &13 Oct. 1784	Four receipts addressed to Conolly in relation to his horseracing establishment at the Curragh.
863	21 Dec 1784	Richard Woodward, Bshop of Cloyne, to Conolly. 'As far as your political sentiments affect any views of mine I feel as I wrote to Lady Louisa perfectly indifferent. So entirely satisfied am I with my present situation that in truth I am rather easier at the idea that I am not likely to change it. What is called prudence I have and that is enough. But in a public view I cannot read your letter without anxiety, as the countenance of a man of your sort to opposition in these factious times, seems to me to threaten consequences of the worst kind. I am a very bad judge of the legal regularity of proceeding by attachment, but I own a trial by jury in the instances of the sheriff appears to me worse than nugatory. By failing, as it certainly would, of procuring justice, it would have encouraged attempts still more and serious till the business had ended as it evidently began, like that in America. I have lately read Smith's tour, ill wrote and yet in some respects worth reading. The similarity of proceeding from less to more general meetings of insignificant persons frightened me. I was not before aware how near we were to the brink of the precipice. Your observation on the inconsistency of ministers is striking and their favours to the

3977/863 *contd.* Bishop of Derry infamous. Yet I should be sorry to see any government run down at this period. In this disposition of yours to me I think it best for me to remain where I am for a time at least for I could not reconcile to my feelings not to act with you as to my ideas of the safety of the kingdom to add to that distress of government, which while arises from opposition not quite so pure and disinterested as yours. The violence of our people appears to me to have forced the minister to recur to the mode of attachment and the court in levying the fine seemed rather desirous to show the power of the law, than to inflict the penalty. In the present independent state of the judges I own I do not fear star chamber processes, as we have more to fear in this kingdom from the people than the crown. I shall therefore prefer the quiet of the country which in other respects is more convenient. I shall be glad to hear that you have paid off Mr Day's mortgage on the Grocers' Proportion on my own account, as you may then get it assigned for my security.'

864 8 Mar. 1785 George Ash, Ashbrook, to Conolly about turf bogs on Conolly's Limavady estate.

865 12 Mar. 1785 Committee of Brooks' Club, London: resolutions on the payment of subscriptions since the death of Brooks.

866 26 Mar. 1785 Gareth Tyrell, Mullingar, Co. Westmeath, to Conolly seeking a subscription to a new gaol for the county. [Conolly had an estate in Westmeath].

867 1 Apr. 1785 Alexander Ogilby, Limavady, to Conolly seeking employment.

868 2 Apr. 1785 Henry Heatly, Larstown Lodge, to Conolly about a point of fairness in drag hunting.

869 6 Apr. 1785 John McIntire, Ballyshannon, to Conolly seeking a better tide waitership in the revenue service than his current position.

870 17 Apr. 1785 William Swetenham, Derry, to Conolly
He is dissatisfied with his position and feels he has lost Conolly's interest because he went to Dublin with 'the Bishop' against Conolly's express wishes.

871 23 Apr. 1785 J. Hendrick, Ballymena, [Co. Antrim] to Conolly.
'As I had the honour to experience your countenance on a former occasion, I beg to take the liberty of sending you the enclosed papers [not found]. The work is dedicated to Mr O'Neill and I have the honour of his patronage.

3977/871 *contd.*		If I may be so happy as to have your support in behalf of my intended publication, I shall consider it with the utmost gratitude and particular honour conferred…'
872	24 Apr. 1785	John Britton to Conolly sending a man who stops the earths.
873	30 Apr. 1785	Receipt from James Finegan to Conolly for Conolly's establishment at the Curragh.
874	28 May 1785	Nat. Nichols, Queen Street, Cheapside, to Conolly about the payment of part of a mortgage debt due to the executors of the late Archibald Grant Esq. of Manchester Square, London. He asks for a payment of £1,000.
875	28 May 1785	Richard King, Mulkeeragh, to Conolly about turf bogs on the Limavady estate.
876	29 May 1785	Conolly McCausland. Limavady, to Conolly seeking the provostship of Limavady Corporation.
877	24 June 1785	Henry Cole's account of the Stretton rent for 1784.
878	30 June 1785	Robert and Henry Drummond, London, to Conolly stating their account and seeking payment.
879		*Blank in the sequence*
880–81	9 Sept. 1785	Two receipts for harnesses sent by Agnes Read to Conolly.
882	14 Sept. 1785	Lord Buckinghamshire, Blickling, [Norfolk], to Conolly 'Accept my best thanks for your most obliging communication. Your public or private conduct will ever be dictated by such honourable feelings as to render justification unnecessary. The paper, however, is an excellent one and the premises of it gave me real satisfaction. Under such disgraceful ministers where obstinacy, self conceit and ignorance direct the cabinet, the miserable subalterns in office must suffer from the folly and inconsistency of their principals…it is reported that Ireland is to have the honour of being governed by the Marquis of Buckingham.'
883–87	17 Sept, 18 Oct., 4, 6 Nov. 1785	Five receipts addressed to Conolly in relation to his horseracing establishment at the Curragh.
888	N.D. [1785]	Petition to parliament from the Incorporated Society in Dublin for promoting English Protestant Schools in Ireland.

3977/ 889	4 Jan. 1786	Robert and Henry Drummond, London, to Conolly stating their account and seeking payment.
890	20 Feb. 1786	Joseph Henry, Straffan, [Co. Kildare], to Conolly about problems of access to his estate during a foxhunt, and the measures needing to be taken to prevent similar problems in the future.
891	28 Feb–15 Mar. 1786	Account of the riots in Ballyshannon on 28 Feb. 1786. A party of soldiers belonging to the 49th Regiment searching for illicit stills mutinied and began firing at random at the townspeople of Ballyshannon. A mob retaliated '...with stones, no firearms being used...although many Volunteers were among the people...On 7 March it was proposed "to call together the Volunteers of this and the neighbouring counties" to conduct the guilty soldiers to prison. But this was overruled at a meeting of the gentlemen and principal inhabitants of the district.'
892	28 Mar. 1786	Two receipts sent by James Spencer, the Duke of Leinster's agent, to Conolly for the rent of Conolly's hunting lodge in Kildare which Conolly leased from the Duke.
893	16 Apr. 1786	William Glascock, Lifford, [Co. Donegal], to Conolly giving an account of the trial of the murderers of Ballyshannon. The trial lasted seventeen hours and saw the soldiers acquitted, but their actions censured. The riot took place in the market place on Shrove Tuesday, where many drunken people were gathered.
894	25 Apr. 1786	Henry Major's account of the same trial.
895	25 Apr. 1786	John Patterson, [attorney], New Burlington Street, London, to Conolly. 'Your frequent absence from London and the few opportunities I have of knowing when you are there, will I hope apologise for my delay in sending you the enclosed account (No. 896) of so old a date, which in truth I had forgot till looking over my books, I found that it still remained undischarged. I find that the last money I received from you was on the 6th of December 1761, and that my absent bills were £28 7s for the purchase of your house in Whitehall, £31 10s for the Irish act of parliament and May 1765 Miss [Frances] Conolly's settlement £44 – in all £64 1s. This sum I shall be very glad to receive ...'
896		Bill for law costs from 1765–66 formerly enclosed in No. 895.
897	27 June 1787	Receipt from James Keegan to Conolly for his racing establishment at the Curragh.

3977/898 11 July 1786 Richard Woodward, Bishop of Cloyne, to Conolly.
'Your return to Ireland is always pleasant to your friends. At this time it is critical. The friends of the constitution were never more wanted. You ask particularly of the Whiteboys. It is very fit you should ask them. The reduction of tithes is the bait to the short-sighted protestants and they have swallowed it. It is a pretext for calling a popish mob to arms, who cannot be trusted with the greater objects in view. These may be guessed at by their beginning with disarming the protestants in many parishes. Did they fear that the protestant farmers would fight in favour of tithes?

I will give you a short history. Sir John Colthurst and Mrs Jefferies [*sic* Jeffereyes] caught at the proposal to reduce tithes and the former suggested to the Whiteboys a plan to swear the parishioners of every parish not to pay above a certain rate. The latter gave out that her brother [John] Fitzgibbon would protect them. This led them to conceive that they were protected by government. Their numbers and audaciousness increases. The newspapers informed you of many of their outrages. I shall mention a few which are not to be found there, for the patriotic news writers are friends of these patriots. On Saturday night (the 10th of June) they took Dr Atterbury of the Great Island and the gentleman whose post chaise conveyed us to Cove in the hour of distress out of his bed and swore him to obey their tithe law. The following Saturday was appointed for a visit to me. Their harbinger sent to friend's houses for the party was apprehended and the plan disconcerted. I had provided some kind of arms and having for my agent an old lieutenant of a man of war, I made him commander of my little garrison. This alarm lasted only a few days as Lord Shannon procured an order for a company of foot to be quartered here, half of whom are arrived. My cartridges are therefore of no use and from the opposition given to the Whiteboy spirit in this barony I have not the smallest personal apprehension but my fears for the Established Church and for the peace of this kingdom are greater than I can express in the compass of a letter. You may judge whether I have reason by the following facts: besides the lawless attack on the property of the clergy they have forced one to take an illegal oath. They have commanded another, with menaces of a horrible nature, to attend at the mass house door on a Sunday morning and in the presence of the popish congregation to subscribe to their laws. They sent a message to one of my clergy attending my visitation at Cloyne to return home the following Sunday to receive their orders. In a parish in the Diocese of Cork they forced the vestry not to levy any [money] for the repair of the church unless an equal sum was raised for the repair of the mass house. In one parish of my diocese they forced the vestry not to provide for anything but the repair of the church so that the bread and wine for the sacrament was not to be provided

3977/898 *contd.* and on last Saturday night they shut up the church of Donaghmore in my diocese and forced the curate at his peril to open it and swore the clerk and sexton not to attend him. Here you see the cat is out of the bag, tithes are out of the question. Many of the clergy in the dioceses of Cloyne and Cork have left their parishes. I have done with facts. I write to you my fears.

I apprehend that there is a plan at bottom to make a law in favour of popery. I apprehend that the protestants caught by the hopes of raising rent by lowering tithes will make such a commutation as will reduce the income of the parish minister so low that a large proportion of the parishes will be unoccupied and the churches shut up. I fear much that Fitzgibbon, Parnell and Foster have persuaded Mr Orde that such a commutation (as must produce that effect, though they do not see it) is advisable. I fear that the bulk of the gentry, struck with the inconveniences attending tithes, are not well aware of the fatal consequences of innovation [and] may adopt a measure which must [not] only stop the building of churches to extend the protestant religion, the erection of glebe houses for the residence of the clergy and consequent civilisation of the kingdom, but [also] shut up a large proportion of the churches now existing, extinguish the protestant religion in Munster and Connaught, raise the expectation of the papists of a religious war and separate Ireland from Great Britain. All these evils are at the end of my telescope. I hope there is a flaw in the glass or a disorder in my eyes, but I am not naturally a croaker. Let me entreat you to consider the subject. I shall lay my thoughts more at large before you. It is a moment and a subject to call forth a real friend of his country. Of the Duke [of Rutland]'s intentions I have a good opinion, of Mr [Thomas] Orde some hopes, of the triumvirate very little if any. By this post I send to government official information that one of my churches is at the moment shut up by Whiteboys and many parishes deserted by the clergy. Pray acknowledge the receipt of this. I shall be anxious to know that it came safe to hand, that you did and other people did not read it. Not that I [ ]my opinions. I will speak out let the consequences be what they may. It is not a time to consider personal interest or even safety…
P.S. A proclamation from government did some good. Read on. It might have been better if it had mentioned the clergy who were attacked exclusively. Proclamations on private occasions specify which persons whom they are intended to protect. Why not the class of men attacked. Fitzgibbon drew it I suppose.'

899 22 July 1786 Mrs Sydney Fitzgerald to Conolly reporting the death [by hanging] of her husband [George Robert 'Fighting Fitzgerald, of Turlough, Castlebar, Co. Mayo, who had previously been married to Conolly's sister Jane d.1779]. See nos. 1771–2 and 1850–1 below.

3977/900 25 July 1786 E. O'Brien to Conolly.
He wants to get his son into Woolwich Military Academy.

901 9 Aug. 1786 Sir Michael Cromie, Au petites Capucines pres de Tours, France, to Conolly reporting Louis XVI's journey to Cherboug, and Cromie's establishment in Tours where he seems to have temporarily settled.

902 9 Sept. 1786 Thomas Behan's stable receipt to Conolly.

903 12 Sept. 1786 Richard Woodward, Bishop of Cloyne, Cloyne, to Conolly.
More about Whiteboy disturbances. He thinks Sir John Colthurst is the leader of the Whiteboys, as they are led by 'men well versed in the law'. However, 'Mobs however well tutored will occasionally break discipline. Some parties have touched gently on the subject of rents. Some have hinted at hearth money and one (on Sunday morning last at 2 o'clock) rescued cattle levied for quit rent at Blarney.' The letter is addressed to Lady Louisa for fear of post office tricks.

904 16 Sept. 1786 Receipt for horseshoeing sent by Richard Colton to Conolly.

905 14 Oct. 1786 Leslie Grove and J. Hood, London, to Conolly seeking payment of money owed to them.

906 17 Oct. 1786 Michael Fenton, Sligo, to Conolly.
He is dealing with the late George Fitzgerald's property.

907 26 Oct. 1786 Receipted account from Charles Watson to Conolly for stabling.

908 28 Oct. 1786 Thomas and James Flanagan , near Piercetown, Co. Longford, to Conolly offering to prove his title to a disputed property.

909 4 Nov. 1786–13 Sept. 1787 Receipts from Mary Hunt to Conolly for his Curragh establishment.

910–11 5 Nov. 1786 Two receipts relating to Conolly's horseracing establishment.

912 19 Nov. 1786 Conolly, Castletown, to Lord Strafford. Copy.
He has been ill, with a cold and a bad rash, which he caught while in the north surveying his estates. 'Lady Louisa stayed a fortnight with me to lay out a small place I have got at Newtown Limavady in the County of Derry by Lord Conyngham's death. It is a beautiful spot near the sea, with wood in copses, waterfall and distant mountains. It is about ten miles from the Downhill where the present Lord Bristol has built an extraordinary mansion, upon a high cliff near the sea, without trees, open to the Atlantic, but

3977/912 *contd.*

with distant views of the Giant's Causeway, some parts of Scotland and the islands of Isla and Jura, part of the Hebrides where I think I see old Johnson and Boswell travelling like fools in the autumnal months of the year, when the climate is bad and the sea tempestuous. He has filled this house with bad pictures and statues at an amazing expense from Italy, and from the frequent appearance of Ganymede I should suppose his Lordship fonder of boys than of girls, the latter of which are incomparably tall and handsome in that wild country and I believe approach nearer to the size of giants than any except the Patagonians.

My nephew young [George] Byng is just come over to stay until March. I am pleased to find the expense old Mrs Byng and myself went to for his education and travels has not been thrown away. He is very well bred, well informed and reads a great deal and I think he will never be devoted to politics like his father. Popularity is the most idle pursuit in the world; you generally acquire it by demeaning yourself and you lose it often when you best deserve the good wishes of your country.

Young [William Conolly] Staples joined us at Shanes Castle in the North upon his return from the fleet and stays with his father till near Xmas when we hope to see him at Castletown. He is a high spirited, shrewd, ingenious boy, very fond of his profession in which he must make a figure and will be a credit and a happiness to all his friends and relations. Indeed, though very different, they are both very promising young men. I am glad my poor mother stands this cold weather so well and I have wrote to her my opinion about her nephew young Staples, which I am sure will please her.'

913 7 Dec. 1787 James Glascock, York Street, Dublin, to Conolly seeking payment of money owed to him.

914 18 Dec. 1786 Buckinghamshire, Blickling, to Conolly.
'Lord Strafford is now an old man, there is little probability of his having a child and you stand the nearest upon the line of succession. He cannot be totally divested of family pride and must naturally wish that a splendid seat [Wentworth Castle, Stainsborough, Yorkshire] and an extensive demesne should not when he is no more be totally abandoned. Ireland and England presently to the misfortune of both stand not in the same degree of connection as formerly. Not to disgust him therefore you should manifest a divided duty. He will not expect that Castletown should be given up, but he must suppose that a proportion of your time may be given to Wentworth Castle. When you are in England it is impossible for you not to be sensible of the number of your wellwishers, nor does it occur to me the ever having seen you happier in Ireland than in London. Further let me observe without detailing public calamity that in times similar to the present, it may be better to have two homes than one.'

3977/ 915	27 Dec. 1786	Henry Aaron Baker, Dublin, to Conolly. He has served an apprenticeship under the architect Thomas Ivory and wants to succeed him in the Academy. He encloses a certificate of support from James Gandon.
916–19	3 Feb.–16 June 1787	Four receipts to Conolly all connected with his horseracing establishment at the Curragh.
920	17 Apr. 1787	Nesbitt & Stewart, bankers, London, to Conolly stating their account.
921	11 May 1787	Mr Beaufort to James Glascock. He will take a packet to George Boggs in London on Glascock's behalf.
922	12 May 1787	James Glascock to Conolly. Enclosing no. 921. The packet was Henry Fox, Lord Holland's will.
923	12 May 1787	David Ross, Londonderry, to Conolly seeking employment.
924	5 June 1787	Rachel Alesbrook to Conolly. She has delivered hackles to the Linen Board and seeks her payment.
925	28 June 1787	Robert, Henry, George and Andrew Drummond, London, to Conolly seeking payment of money on his account.
926	16 July 1787	R. Johnston, Ennis, to Conolly about the disagreeableness of his post office job.
927–28	13 Sept. 1787	Two receipts to Conolly both connected with his horseracing establishment at the Curragh.
929	1 Oct. 1787	Messrs Drummond & Co. to Conolly seeking payment of money on his account.
930–34	19, 20 Oct., 3, 8 Nov. &17 Dec. 1787	Five receipts to Conolly all connected with his horseracing establishment at the Curragh.
935	27 Dec. 1787	George Ash, Ashbrook, to Conolly seeking a subscription for the navigation at Coleraine.
936–38	28 Dec. 1787, 1 Mar., 9 Apr. 1788	Three receipts to Conolly all connected with his horseracing establishment at the Curragh.

3977/ 939	20 May 1788	Henry Major, Ballyshannon, to Conolly noting the fines paid upon the renewal of leases on the Ballyshannon estate.
940		*Blank in the sequence*
941	15 June 1788	State of Conolly's account with Thomas Behan for feeding horses, etc.
942	27 June 1788	Benjamin Harenc, Cloyne, to Conolly, detailing his journey from Castletown to Cloyne.

Your horses seemed not sensible of the heavy hearts they were drawing from Castletown, and went as cheerfully as you engaged they should, setting us down at Kildare within three hours. We then summoned up all our resolutions and determined to be as merry as we could, taking leave of everything visible belonging to your kind and friendly entertainment of us at Castletown. It was not so with the Kildare horses. They kindly entered into our feelings and reluctantly put us further from our fiends, but our postillion more obdurate than these poor animals began regularly from the nose to the tail to find out a sensible part, and by diet of whipping, his arm keeping constant pace with their legs we got to Emo in good time. The postillion from this inn calculated that the former had bestowed whipping enough for the next and he depended so much on this that he drove without any whip, and told me he had left it at home. His calculation proved right, I never went a stage more briskly to Ballyroan. Where we lay and were entertained tolerably well as to meat and drink but extraordinarily well with paintings in the room we sat, the master of the inn being related to Stokes the painter. Many beauties of Ireland were exhibited and among the celebrated persons was the portrait of Mrs Maguire, the high flier, as you call the family opposite to you. It appeared to me that this gentleman was nearly in as great danger as we were going over Durrow bridge or rather half-bridge. Half a loaf I have heard was better than no bread, but while I was passing over Durrow bridge, I was clear that half a bridge was not so good as no bridge. Johnstown was the first place which made us regret English post horses, we were five hours going 17 miles. At Cashel we were much struck with the ruins of the castle on the rock, but had not time to go up to it. We got to Cahir in good time, a new town and handsome, the improvement of which was owing to the late Lord Cahir from hence they obliged us to take 4 horses to Mitchellstown, new built likewise by the good direction and well understood liberality of Lord Kingsborough, making now a very beautiful and handsome appearance. About a mile from hence we descended the highest mountain we met withy on the road, and our leaders on the descent of this vast mountain took the advantage of our wheel

3977/942 *contd.* horses. In military order the van, I believe Mr Napier will tell you, is the post of honour, but I who have been Sheriff for Kent know that the rear is the post of honour. The leading postillion's horse sensible of this slipped down with his rider and so far carried his point that the wheel horse bestrode him, and for long time the conflict lasted, my wife even got out of the chaise, in order to be better judges of the matter, however the wheel horse kept the station, he sat out in and the leader gave up the point and submitted, a conscious blush of inferiority however appeared on his knees, which I look on the true mark of humility and lowliness of disposition in a horse. We were anxious to have done with these horses so we asked the postillion if it was far to Rathcormack after we had travelled some time, and if there was any more hills. He told we should soon be there, it was quite flat, and that after we got over the next hill we should have but a mile or two to travel. From hence we got to Cloyne at seven o'clock. Every individual well in their family. Mary had many lines in the name of Lady Louisa and you in our mouths, Mr Napier and Lady Sarah have their friends and the younger part of your amicable family. My wife and I with grateful acknowledgement for all your kindness to us, and all individuals of this family join in every expression of respect and heartiest affection…'

943 27 June 1788 Receipt for wages from James Heir to Conolly

944 4 Aug. 1788 James Hamilton, Manor Waterhouse near Lisnakea, Co. Fermanagh, to Conolly seeking a job as a 'preventing officer.'

945 15 Aug. 1788 Buckinghamshire, Blickling, to Conolly.
'It gives me great pleasure to inform you that by the last accounts Caroline's fever has entirely left her and we too expect to see her in a few days perfectly recovered. Her disorder has been tiring but is no degree dangerous.

The progress of our gracious sovereign into the heart of his kingdom and necessarily into the hearts of the subject must give general satisfaction, and the salubrious spring of Cheltenham purify the royal bowels which otherwise might with difficulty have digested that most bitter pill, the event of the Westminster election. Unless he should travel very assiduously indeed as far as it may be permitted use to prerogative should Mr Pitt's administration live to the changing another parliament, it will not be exactly similar to the former. The ministry is so completely at variance that unless an improbable conciliation should take place, a partial though perhaps not a total change must happen.

From the uniform tenor of every newspaper, English and Irish, your Lord Lieutenant is as a statesman, a moralist and a citizen irreproachable, in short that perfect monster which till his age was

3977/945 *contd.* never such. Is it for me to cross the sea and risk a retrospective comparison. If you and Lady Louisa will come over once more to Blickling your eloquence may perhaps give me resolution once more to cross the Irish channel and to experience if my real goodwill to Ireland is totally forgotten....'

946 16 Aug. 1788 Henry Cole, Stretton, to Conolly stating his accounts.

947 18 Aug. 1788 Messrs Drummond & Co. to Conolly seeking payment of money on his account.

948 6 Sept. 1788 Benjamin Harenc, Footscray Place, Kent, to Conolly further describing his trip to Ireland. See no. 942 above.

I cannot my dear friend so soon after my return home which happened only last Tuesday keep Ireland out of my thoughts, and surely when I think of Ireland, you and all the amiable inhabitants of Castletown must be very present to my mind sand sensibly affect my heart. I wrote you a letter from Cloyne which crossed your kind mark of friendship to me.

I do not mean to draw you into a regular correspondence which I know the habit of writing on particular and extraordinary occasions only had made irksome to you. I feel I want once more to thank you for the kind reception Lady Louisa and you gave us and to tell you which I know you will feel pleasure from, that every moment we passed in Ireland was without the least inconvenience or the least disappointment.

The Bishop's family seem comfortable and happy in every respect, his abilities considerable as I always knew them to be, I think rather stronger, at least I found them sop actively exerted in my behalf and so successfully that I was led perhaps from that circumstance to think more highly of them than ever. Many reasons led him to remain at Cloyne, instead of making another tour with me to Kerry, though this was a disappointment to me, yet he made it up to me by sparing me his agent Mr Haines, whom I found very active in my interest and useful to me, and whose friendship I regard, far from the plainness of his manners and frankness of his behaviour I found myself sincerely attached to him although from a short acquaintance. He is an old friend of Mrs Woodward, being a Gloucestershire man and the Bishop has comfort in him as a person he can open himself up to without reserve, he was an old lieutenant of a man of war and I understand well known to Captain Pakenham. I believe you as well as I have naturally an affection or at least a partiality to an brave sailor.

I was made very happy in finding my estate had received its share of improvement with the rest of Ireland, surely there never was a county so much altered for the better in eleven years time. I left everything on the farms finished and a plan I suggested will I

3977/948
contd.

hope have further extent as it took place in a small degree in several farms. I offered all the more needy tenants sums of money on their raising their rents at the rate of 6s 6d which in cases where extensive draining was wanting I was well informed would return them very considerable profit, under the direction and inspection of my agent whom I had a real reason to be satisfied with. I followed your advice in filling up the lives where they had fallen off and I hope to make a considerable advance of rent in one instance, but the treaty in this case is not quite concluded. One life out of two being of the age of 83 will in the course of nature soon force it to a conclusion on my terms which are moderate.

In compliment to Mr Haines I visited once more the Lake of Killarney. Every scene there was delightful as we found it 11 years ago, there is however no waterfall from Mangerton, but one island is beautiful and decorated by the present inhabitants of Muckross. I was detained much longer at the Bishop's than I intended; by getting solid securities on land for a debt of £1,600 owing me by Harnett, the man who gave up lease to me, had granted to Lord Kerry and which he had bought of him. Of course I saw all the neighbourhood of Cloyne, many of whom were very pleasant companions. I was particularly glad to see Dean Erskine, a very old acquaintance.

The Harbour of Cork which extends 10 miles is very beautiful, I think superior to that of Dublin, which I saw on the water and from the different shores. I came a different way from Kerry, where by the bye, Mr Ponsonby was very obliging in his invitation to me to spend my time at his house. I should have called on him on my first going into Kerry but I was informed he was out of the country. I owe his attract to me to you and I told him I should write to you. Blennerhasset was ill, I returned to Cloyne by Mallow and the Blackwater, which is a line of great extent and by much the most beautiful part of Ireland for its extent, allowing the remaining part of the river to be as well decorated as far as Youghall, as what I saw was, which is certainly the case. There is a noble road making from Cappoquin to Waterford40 miles, on a good and solid plan under the direction and partly by the labour of the military, Waterford, I think by the accounts I received is the most enriched of late and in the most improving state of any port of Ireland I saw. Mr [Cornelius] Bolton [of Faithlegg] whom I made acquaintance with here is very active in everything which may benefit this city and its environs, he has built a noble house for himself, an excellent inn at Checkpoint for the passengers going on board the Packet. He is third part owner of the Packet, he is building a quay at Checkpoint of considerable extent, he has set on foot a stocking manufacture, in which the prices of the labour, and workmanship and of the stockings, silk, cotton,

3977/948 *contd.* thread, and worsted are in every particular regulated by the tariff of Nottingham, and it is in a very flourishing condition.
Mr Bolton loaded us with peaches and pineapples for our voyage. You know this very worthy citizen of Ireland, that is a new word in application, but you will know my meaning. There is a very high mountain above Checkpoint or Bolton (for I think it has taken name now), from whence you see the whole line of the Waterford river from the city far into the open sea, the river being 20 miles from Waterford to the sea. I think this view is superior to anything I ever admired. The packet not ailing the day following my arrival at Bolton, I went twice up this mountain.
On Sunday the 24th of August I sailed and landed at Hubberston on Monday after 17 hours navigation. I wish I could give you a notion of South Wales but that beggars description. And there after three months absence from home I am returned without a single inconvenience with every gratification which friendship , civility and success in objects of business could afford…'

949 8 Sept. 1788 Receipt from Thomas Behan to Conolly for stabling.

950 28 Set. 1788 Richard Woodward, Bishop of Cloyne, to Conolly.
He has a curacy for a Mr Carson. He has recently presented Mr Delaney with a living worth £300. Whiteboyism has subsided except near Mallow and Cork city. His son, also Richard, has set out for Lausanne.

951 24 Oct. 1788 William Ross, Limavady, to Conolly enclosing a certified return of the produce of the Roe Mills in Limavady for the year 1788.

952 31 Oct. 1788 Receipt from Michael Igoe for Conolly for stabling.

953 10 Nov. 1788 Lady Anne Conolly, London, to Conolly.
'We are in great uneasiness about the King, who is no doubt very dangerously ill. On Friday there was little hopes of his life, Saturday he was much better, this morning it was reported he was dead, but I hear at Lord Sydney's a messenger is just arrived from Windsor, he is alive and rather better. His death will be a dreadful calamity to the country when you consider how unworthy his successor is, though I hear the Prince is in a fright having made many promises while they appeared distant, that now they approach so near, he neither can nor wishes to fulfil. Many think the opposition will be disappointed.' Goes on to discuss the letting of Stretton to a Mr Lloyd.

954 20 Dec. 1788 Sir John Coghill, Coghill Hall, [Knaresborough, Yorkshire], to Conolly.
He writes about a plan to regulate alehouses citing the English example. He plans to send Conolly a master key that will open all gates.

3977/ 955	28 Dec. 1788	E. Tisdall, Dublin, to Conolly recommending a painter called Elmer.
956	n.d	[The 1st] Marquess of Buckingham, [Lord Lieutenant of Ireland], Kilmainham to Conolly, sending him resolutions of English parliament on King's illness. He had hoped to call on him at Castletown, but was delayed by the late arrival of the mail.

MSS	DATE	DESCRIPTION
3978/ 957– 3979/ 1063	**6 Jan. 1789– 26 Dec. 1795**	**Letters, receipts and other miscellaneous papers of Thomas Conolly, 1789–95**
957	6 Jan. 1789	Bishop Woodward, Cloyne, to Conolly about his intentions regarding the forthcoming parliamentary session. He hopes not to have to come to Dublin too soon. Recommends various issues to Conolly including ongoing Whiteboy disturbances, and the need for a committee to examine the management of the charter schools.
958	21 Feb. 1789	George Byng senior, Berkeley Square, London, to Conolly. 'The King is certainly so much better that a new turn is given to everything, and we expect by Tuesday that he will by his servants be thought in condition to send a message to the House. If so probably the physicians will be re-examined and possibly a new Regency Bill of another nature brought forward. The King can if out of the kingdom appoint a regency or justices in his absence; probably he will be made to apply for similar powers though in the kingdom. Had you arrived a few days ago I so much agreed with you in opinion about the not accepting in a hurry, but waiting for investment of the power hear that in the doubtful state the King was in during the beginning of the week, that there was the finest occasion for moderation in the Prince's answer to Ireland, that I almost lament the loss of it. The giving Ireland, all the credit of loyalty and affection to the King receiving their offer to him as grounded in that affection and loyalty and to have declined the immediate acceptance of it till he would with more certainty ascertain the uncertainty of his father's recovery. I have heard much of the Marquis's saying he will now wreak his vengeance on those who have not supported him, but he will wreak his vengeance in vain, if they are firm. Thank God you are out of his reach. I hope you will all stand by one another. I write this in

3978/958 *contd.* expectation that you are in Ireland, though possibly it may not reach you in time, but I hope you have found some excuse for delay that may prevent your journey – I mean only delay your journey – as I still entertain hopes of seeing you in the spring. I hear George [Byng junior] is as warm as his father. I am glad of it as I rejoice at his eagerness. William [Byng, another son] writes me word that George is with the spirit of the Paddys. I hear he improves in argument and that it is admitted by those with whom he argues.'

959–60 8,9 May 1789 Two receipts to Conolly both connected to his horseracing establishment at the Curragh.

961 29 May 1789 [Sir Ralph Gore, Earl of] Ross to Conolly.
In case there is a change in the ministry, he will be very obliged if Conolly will mention that he is keen to return to the army despite his age.

962 1 June 1789 John Hamilton, Brownhall, to Conolly.
He wants to stand for election again for Co. Donegal, if only for the sake of his son. He failed last time because Mr Conyngham's friends declined to support him at the last minute. Had the junction been kept up Mr Conyngham would have been sure of success and Hamilton very likely to succeed even though Conyngham's freeholders were so few. Hamilton's brother Harry Stewart has since bought McCausland's estate which was formerly against Hamilton, and is now agent for Stiles's estate which was likewise. His prospects are brighter as long as he still has Conolly's support.

963 12 June 1789 Invoice for Bristol cider addressed to Conolly

964 17 June 1784 Receipt from Thomas Kearns for Conolly's subscription to the Kildare St Club.

965 21 June 1789 Edward Monckton, Upper Grosvenor Street, to Conolly.
He wants to rent Stretton for a Mr and Mrs Russell recently returned from India, and is enquiring under what terms it might be available.

970 15 Aug. 1789 Edward Monckton, Somerford near Wolverhampton, to Conolly offering to purchase Stretton for 35 years purchase at the present rent.

971 19 Aug. 1789 George Byng junior, Scarborough, to Conolly.
Excitable letter about his intended marriage to Lady Charlotte Leveson.

3978/ 972	22 Aug. 1789	George Byng junior, Scarborough, to Conolly She has refused him to his despair.
973	1 Sept. 1789	George Byng senior, Wrotham Park, to Conolly about his son's love affair, and giving his approval of the sale of Stretton.
974	6 Sept. 1789	Lord Buckinghamshire to Conolly. 'There have been various reports respecting the return of your Marquis [of Buckingham] to Ireland. My opinion is that you may depend upon possessing him sometime longer, as nothing would distress his cousin Pitt more than his residence in England. Persons in France are obliged to write with so much caution that very little authentic intelligence is received. The greatest confusion certainly prevails and the prospect of a settlement of any permanence seems remote.'
975	10 Sept. 1789	William Howe, Fifeshire, [Scotland], to Conolly about the sale of Stretton. Howe gives his permission to sell but suggests,'That the purchase money be invested in trustees, in answer to the purposes of your fathers will. For the purchasing of lands in Ireland with the surplus after the debt is paid could not be otherwise than very troublesome to those who might inherit it according to your father's will. I am therefore of the opinion that the trustees should place the surplus in the English funds.'
976	15 Sept. 1789	Henry Cole, Hull, to Conolly about the sale of Stretton. He is sorry Conolly is selling but urges him to get the best possible price for it, by valuing every tree in the wood etc.
977	23 Sept. 1789	William P. K. Trench [MP for Co. Galway] to Conolly seeking the payment of money owed to him.
978	25 Sept. 1789	Buckinghamshire to Conolly giving his permission for the sale of Stretton. Still believes 'Ireland's darling,' the Marquess of Buckingham, is still returning to Ireland.
979	28 Sept. 1789	Edward Monckton, Somerford, to Conolly. He rather than Mr Russell will be purchasing Stretton. He is glad Conolly has the consent of all the other parties concerned. [See no. 1795.]
980	2 Oct. 1789	William. P.K. Trench to Conolly about his daughter Anne's marriage to William Gregory of Coole Park, [Gort, Co. Galway].
981	11 Oct. 1789	Thomas Dickson, Woodville, near Ballyshannon, giving his consent to the sale of Stretton.

3978/ 982	15 Oct 1789	[Edmund Boyle, 7th Earl of] Cork, Shanes Castle, [Randalstown, Co. Antrim], to Conolly. As an original member of the Whig Club in London, he wishes to join the Irish Whig Club. [Conolly was secretary of the Dublin Whig club founded in 1789.]
983	2 Nov. 1789	Edward Monckton to Conolly about the sale of Stretton. He has received a rentroll from Mr Cole.
984	9 Nov. 1789	James Long to Conolly. He wants to be accountant to the Royal Canal.
985	Nov. 1789	James Glascock, York St Dublin, to Conolly reciting the state of the title to Stretton. The current annual rent is £835 10s 11d, but the real annual value is only £175 10s 11d after taxes and charges are deducted. He calculates the purchase price at £29,244 from which a mortgage debt of £7,000 must be deducted, giving Conolly a return of £22,244 on the sale.
986	27 Jan. 1790	Edward Monckton, Somerford, to Conolly about his purchase of Stretton. He is still waiting for Conolly's title deeds, which seem to have been in [William] Congreve's possession.
987	Jan. 1790	Note about costs of sending a chariot by the pacquet.
988	12 Mar. 1790	Sir Edward Newenham, MP, No. 23 Grafton Street, [Dublin], to Conolly about the Co. Dublin election. There will be a close contest between, Talbot, Finlay and himself. Mr Hamilton is not much spoken of, 'reports say that there cannot be but a very trifling majority in favour of the two that may prove successful.' He asks Conolly to apply to Sir P King, Mr Sheppard, Mr Wilkinson, Mr James Somerville, Conolly's tenants at Rathfarnham, and above all Mr Domville, who voted for him on the last occasion. The Cramers could get him many votes around Dunlavin, and Kilcullen.
989	13 Mar. 1790	George Gaven, Custom House, to Conolly about the payment of custom duties owed by Conolly.
990	25 Mar. 1790	Envelope formerly containing a letter from the Duke of Portland to Conolly.
991	28 Mar. 1790	J. Turvey, Leixlip to Conolly about his threatened eviction by Conolly.
992	29 Mar. 1790	Henry Cole, Peterborough, to Conolly about remitting interest to Mrs Congreve.

3978/ 993	9 Apr. 1790	Sir Edward Newenham to Conolly about the Co. Dublin election. There is some confusion amongst prospective voters because of Newenham's previous support for Finlay. Wants Conolly to assist in convincing his tenants to vote for Newenham rather than Finlay.
994	11 Apr. 1790	Peter Tyrell, Leixlip, to Conolly seeking employment.
995	19 Apr. 1790	Edward Monckton, Upper Grosvenor Street, to Conolly about the sale of Stretton. He is sorry Conolly's trip to London will be delayed. Refers to Co. Londonderry election. 'I hope you will not have much hard drinking in Londonderry at your election, other trouble you cannot have for the county knows you do them more honour than they do you.'
996–97	9, 12 May 1790	Two letters from [George de la Poer Beresford, 2nd Earl of Tyrone and 1st Marquess of] Waterford, Curraghmore, [Co. Waterford], to Conolly thanking him for the support he gave to [his son] Lord Tyrone [Henry de la Poer Beresford] in the recent election in Derry.
998	13 May 1790	Receipted account to Conolly for horse shoeing.
999	23 May 1790	James Miller, 10 Harris St, Grafton Street, to Conolly. He has lost a letter of recommendation from Edmund Burke, but still seeks Conolly's patronage.
1000–1001	9, 12 Sept. 1790	Robert Jackson, Grosvenor Square, London, to Conolly enclosing a receipt for a case of books sent to Conolly.
1002	22 Sept. 1790	George Ash, Ashbrook, to Conolly about the favourable reception, Lords Waterford and Tyrone received at Derry.
1003	1 Oct. 1790	Mary Hunt, Kildare, to Conolly. She has been accused wrongly of stealing George Ponsonby's watch, and wants Conolly to help clear her name.
1004	12 Oct. 1790	Benjamin Harenc, Footscray Place, Kent, to Conolly. He informs Conolly of his recent visits to Oxford and Stowe, where he wishes 'the character of the possessor of Stowe corresponded with the charms of his house and gardens.' He also reports news from Paris, 'houses, pictures and such like valuables have no price, the houses being untenanted at Paris, and the arrears of their public funds are paid in paper at a great discount, so that he [Harenc's cousin] has reduced his system of living prodigiously and in the expectation of further deductions being necessary. The Brabantines are likely to be obliged to submit to

3978/1004 *contd.* terms, their game is almost over; the French I think cannot go on long in their present state of anarchy. What a world of misery have these inconsiderate people brought upon themselves, but perhaps it may all end well and the future generations may be benefited, for I think some alterations for the better must take place, even if a counter-revolution should succeed.'

1005 26 Oct. 1790 William Cruise to Conolly about the difficulty of raising a loan of £12,500 secured on the Grocers' Proportion because of the present financial situation, 'which has put a stop to every kind of transaction except stock jobbing.'

1006 2 Nov. 1790 William Conolly Staples, Chatham, to, his uncle, Conolly.
He hopes to become a lieutenant in the navy soon, and is quite excited about the prospect of a Spanish War.

1007 1 Dec. 1790 Edward Monckton, London to Conolly about the mortgage on Stretton, and the payment of annuities.

1008 1 Dec. 1790 H.P. Warren, London to Conolly reporting political gossip, and news of the opening of parliament, and of changes in Pitt's cabinet.

1009 12 Dec. 1790 William Tredennick, Camlin [Co. Roscommon], to Conolly about the state of the mills, which need to be rebuilt. He is prepared to meet the cost of this, if Conolly renews his lease.

1010 13 Dec. 1790 George Byng junior [who is now the only George Byng, his father having died in 1789], London, to Conolly.
He has been acting on Conolly's behalf renewing the lease from the Grocer's Company. Much of letter is taken up with family gossip, and references to various ladies Byng has been paying court to.

1011 20 Dec. 1790 Lady Anne Conolly to Conolly about the case of books sent to Conolly.

1013 25 Dec. 1790 Rev. John Alcock, Murvagh, Ballyshannon, to Conolly seeking relief for the poor inhabitants of the parish, who live in misery.

1014 25 Dec. 1790 Mrs Locke's abstract account for 1790 [of the £7,000 or £8,000 she had lent to Conolly – see no. 1030].

1015 29 Dec. 1790 Henry Darlot, Foreign Post Office, London, to Conolly about his subscriptions to French newspapers.

1016 2 Jan. 1791 Edward Monckton, Somerton, to Conolly about the sale of Stretton.

3978/ 1017	5 Jan. 1791	Messrs Drummond & Co. to Conolly stating their account.
1018, 1021	9, 19 Jan. 1791	Two letters from William Byng [younger brother of George Byng junior], Feversham, to Conolly [his uncle] about his company in a regiment of the line, with a reference to his 'Ballyshannon boys'.
1019	15 Jan. 1791	Robert Lawe, Robert's Ville, to Conolly requesting a coronership for Edward Read of Leixlip.
1020	16 Jan. 1791	Pierce Simpson, Mount Campbell, to Conolly enclosing the decision of arbitrators, Major Mahon and Henry Irwin in a dispute about the bounds of an estate near Elphin, Co. Roscommon. The dispute was between Conolly and a Mrs Walcott [of Donamon, Tulsk, Co. Roscommon].
1022	7 Feb. 1791	Conolly to Lord Strafford. 'Dear uncle, I wrote you a long stupid letter about two months ago, at the setting in of winter and I made the season an apology for the dullness of my letter and should not trouble you now, but that you are always so kind to Louisa and myself to wish to ask of us and from us. We are thank God both well although we have had bad colds, which few in this country have escaped as I never knew so unwholesome a season, a continual hurricane, with cold wet weather till within this week past when it is unusually warm and foggy. Our parliament has met which brings me once or twice a week to town but I never stay a moment longer than I can help. Town does not agree with me as I am inclined to be asthmatic in hot foggy air and particularly in the House of Commons. At Castletown I enjoy myself and am delighted with the birds who now begin to sing in the mornings and evenings. Our parliament have undertaken a very laudable measure, that of getting rid of spirituous liquors, particularly a kind of whiskey (something better than gin) and substituting ale in the room of it. An Irishman has a great deal of good nature in his composition when sober, but when drunk with this spirit is a cruel savage and capable of any enormity. I wish we had another Hogarth to give us a sketch of whiskey street, as he did in London of Gin Street in 1754. If our ministry do not expect too great a duty on malt, made into beer, I think a few years will make this a sober industrious rich kingdom, and our inhabitants have certainly increased to above four million. I know this to be a fact by inquiring into the numbers that paid hearth money, a tax that I wish our poor here to be relieved from as yours in England were in King William's time. If I thought that I should not be considered as a Boar and that I should take up so much of your time, I should write to you upon

3978/1022 *contd.*		every subject to which I turn my mind, not that I should ever expect an answer, but I have always and particularly lately received such strong marks of your particular affection that I like you should know my thoughts upon all subjects. I have hung your picture of Wentworth Castle that came from Stretton in my dressing room, and I always thought I saw you admiring the prospect of the place. May you long continue to do so in health and comfort is the prayer and sincere wish of your friend and nephew….'
1023	7 Apr. 1791	Charles Brodrick, Bath to Conolly about money drawn on Conolly's account.
1024	26 Oct. 1791	Dr H. Zouch, Sandel, to Conolly about Lord Strafford's will. One of Strafford's servants was likely to know of its existence, as this servant was Strafford's close confidant.
1025	30 Oct. 1791	Dr H. Zouch, Sandel, to Conolly. Dr Ellison {the servant mentioned in the above letter?] says that there was a will in which Conolly was 'to succeed to the principal part of Lord Strafford's fortune of which he had the power to dispose…a considerable bequest fell to Lady Anne Conolly, but which was to devolve upon Mr Conolly at her demise…'.
1026	1 Nov. 1791	Lord Bristol, Berlin, to Conolly. He wants Conolly to move his mill at Bellaghy upstream so that he can create a canal on his adjoining demesne.
1027	3 July 1792	Nesbit & Stewart, London, to Conolly stating their account.
1028	23 July 1792	General Richard Vyse, Ipswich, to Conolly. Vyse informs Conolly of developments on [their joint] Suffolk estate. [Vyse, in right of his wife and Conolly and Henry Vernon (see no. 1033 below) were co-heirs to roughly half of the Wentworth/Strafford estates following the death, childless of the 2nd Earl of Strafford in 1791.] He also suggests that a vacant vicarage should be let out during the 'bathing season'.
1029	11 Oct. 1792	Messrs Hood & Co., London, to Conolly stating their account.
1030	27 Nov. 1792	Mrs Locke, Dorset Street, to Conolly. She is happy to continue to place her fortune of seven or eight thousand pounds in Conolly's hands at 5 per cent.
1031	9–13 July 1793	John Stewart's account for wine purchased by Conolly.
1031a	2 Aug. 1793	Receipt from Latouche's bank to Conolly.

3978/ 1032	13 Dec. 1794	John Stewart's account for wine purchased by Conolly.
1033	30 Apr. 1794	Henry Vernon, [Conolly's cousin], Hilton Park, to Conolly. 'I most sincerely sympathise with you and Lady Louisa on your loss [probably the death of Miss Mary Anne Fitzgerald of Turlough]. Where the master string is broke, all is discord, until reason returns to our aid and brings comfort. Lady Anne Conolly has no doubt informed you of my comfort, and it is known to you that I am married to Miss Fisher, whose amicable qualities make her the admiration of all who have the happiness of knowing her. I long for the honour of presenting her to Lady Louisa and you, my dear friend. Before I left town Lord Strafford [Frederick Thomas Wentworth, 3rd Earl of Strafford, their more distant cousin] called to congratulate me and at the same time told me he had passed a fine to enable him to dispose of his property as he thought proper; that he [had] since made his will, and followed the words of Thomas [1st] Earl of Strafford in your favour. I informed Lady Anne of his friendly disposition towards you and I think it my duty to inform you of it, from the affection I entertain of your goodness to me…'
1034–35	21 May–20 July; 17 June–15 Dec. 1794	Two notes of bills paid on Conolly's account.
1036	1794	Note of agricultural produce for this year.
1037	19 Jan. 1795	[William Wentworth Fitzwilliam, 4th Earl] Fitzwilliam, Lord Lieutenant of Ireland, Dublin Castle, to Conolly. He wants him to engage Mr [Robert] Stewart [Conolly's nephew-by-marriage, the future Lord Castlereagh] to second Grattan, who will move the address to the King.
1038	6 Feb. 1795	J[ohn] Armit to Captain Stark about the remittance of Conolly's Bellaghy rents.
1039	13 Mar. 1795	Colonel Darby, Old Jury, London, to Conolly. The writer has escaped from a French prison.
1040	21 Mar. 1795	C[harles] L[ionel] Fitzgerald, Turlough, Co. Mayo, to Conolly enclosing his rent for Turlough, [i.e. he was renting it from his and Conolly's niece, Miss Mary Mary Anne Fitzgerald]. .
1041	22 Mar. 1795	General Richard Vyse, Cloppenburg, to Conolly about the Suffolk estate and the military situation in Europe.

3978/ 1042	24 Mar. 1795	Nesbit & Stewart, London, to Conolly stating their account.
1043	27 Mar. 1795	G. Renny, Surgeon, Royal Hospital, Dublin, to the Commander in Chief. William Murray, a member of the Londonderry militia, was injured during a field day and is now a patient in the hospital.
1044	30 Mar. 1795	Brook Bridges, Red Lion Square, London, to Conolly about a petition signed by General Vyse [for a private act partitioning the joint estates?].
1045	31 Mar. 1795	Stephenson Bateson, London, to Conolly seeking payment of money owed to him.
1046	31 Mar. 1795	Messrs Hood & Co., London, to Conolly stating their account, but also lamenting the departure from Ireland of 'your most excellent friend Earl Fitzwilliam'.
1047	3 April 1795	Sir Michael Cromie, Dublin, to Conolly about the private bill to partition the joint estates, and the aftermath of the Fitzwilliam affair. 'By yesterday's packet I received a letter from Mr Bridges to inform me that his clerk was returned from the continent with the papers duly signed by General Vyse and that he would present the petition forthwith so that no doubt now remains of this business going before the judges after the Easter recess. I will hold myself ready to set out at a moments notice and think I should attend all the readings of the bill through the Houses, lest any clerical error should present itself, or a necessity of amending any clause where a cloud might appear that would damp a purchaser, which perhaps might not strike a person less warmly interested in anything that concerns you. My attention to this kind of business is the reason why I am put into the chair when bills of consequence are passing through committee here. The very day your bill receives the royal assent I ought to go and take possession of your dividend in your name and ascertain the means and bounds beyond the possibility of future dispute. The repairs must be attended to with great industry and economy and every consideration employed to turn that property into most money; what might be prudent to do if you did not intend to sell may be the reverse under your present idea. You have some detached property allotted to your share and some agreements to make with Harry Vernon as to timber and a particular farm he wishes to have. All those circumstances require much thought and close inspection, and I believe you are sufficiently convinced that my heart and head are yours.

3978/1047 *contd.*

I thought it right to state those matters fully to you at this time, when I know your mind is so occupied with a multiplicity of affairs. You will therefore determine where my services can be most useful to you at this particular crisis in Dublin or London.

The newspapers give you as exact an account of political matters as I possibly could. Lord Camden at present I understand seems not inclined to attach himself to any particular party or description of men, Mr Beresford is gone to Bath under pretence of ill health but prudently to escape the storm he fears would burst over his head here. Claudius Beresford boasts of having shot with his own hand the poor wretch who died of a wound yesterday. This will ensure that family more odious to the people than they were before and the people are not always unmindful of injury. It is impossible for any administration to govern this country if the Beresfords compose their cabinet, and the principles of the Chancellor [Fitzgibbon] are ill calculated for the present times. Desperation and oppression are bad remedies to apply to a heated and disappointed people; his politics are tyranny – always stiff in opinion though frequently wrong. On the other side may be found much talent but little common sense and no temper with a total ignorance of men, and too often we admire what is glaring before we discern what is sensible. To spend one's whole life in study may give knowledge but can never furnish sense.

We now need some great national character to stem the torrent between both parties and a moment of such difficulty and danger to the state as this will unite them all in one common cause in one common interest for the salvation of the kingdom…'

1048 4 Apr. 1795 Nesbitt & Stewart, London, to Conolly about money drawn on his account

1049 4 Apr. 1795 Henry Hoare & Co., London, to Conolly about money drawn on his account and credited to Lady Anne Conolly

1050 6 Apr. 1795 Sir Michael Cromie, Dublin, to Conolly.
'Since my last I have taken pains to find out the plan the new government here intend to pursue, and believe you will find the following to be nearly the truth, which information I conceive will not be unacceptable to you so far from the fountainhead.

The Speaker [John Foster] is chief counsellor and has been closeted with Lord C[amden] every morning since his arrival. The Chancellor is to be second, when occasion demands, but the Beresfords are to be totally left out. The Catholic question is to be resisted.

At this moment the government are preparing a strong military force, which is to be quartered in and near the city to prevent insurrection. Mr Hume's great uninhabited house in Merrion

3978/1050 *contd.*

Square is to be the rendezvous for that quarter of the town. It is already engaged and other situations are fixed, and cannon prepared. The police is be new-modelled, not disbanded, the patronage lessened and the peculation stopped. The Treasury Board is to be confirmed according to Forbes's bill. Sackville Hamilton is restored to his office and is to keep all the emoluments allotted for his resignation by Lord Fitzwilliam. Doyle is not to be displaced. [Edward] Cooke is in high dudgeon, and to mend the matter, his wife wrote him a letter a few days ago to say she was so much in love with Mr Fane, Lord Westmorland's nephew, that she could not live without him, and was determined to fly to him immediately, in which Cooke is determined to indulge her.

My letters from London state that Mr Pitt is persuaded that the Catholics had made up a great sum for Mr Grattan, whose god is money, and that he duped Lord Fitzwilliam and damned his administration to gratify his inordinate love of gold. As far as I can judge from my own poor speculation, we shall not divide 60 upon that question.

They have some better expectations of peace. By the last accounts from France. Charette is in strong force and has beseeched aid from England – if not men, arms. A treaty is on the tapis between him and the Convention, in which he holds some strong language and insists in [sic] being considered as the general of Louis XVII. Mr Beresford, I understand, never intends to resume his office and will remain at Bath until this brush is over. It is said for certain the Commander in Chief is to resign, and that his successor is shortly to arrive from England, of less years but more experience. Lord Mornintgton's friends and relatives fill the several departments in the Castle, Comptroller, Steward, etc. Everything seems perfectly tranquil here at present, but some money failures of consequence are much apprehended in England. Sir William G. Newcomen sailed a few nights ago, to return before the 20th, I suppose to guard against losses…'.

1051 30 Apr. 1795 William Sandford, New Bond Street, to Conolly about overdue interest payments, on a loan from a Mr Christie, [secured by mortgage on the Strafford estate in Bedfordshire which was due to fall to Conolly's share].

1052 18 Aug. 1795 Messrs Hood & Co., London, to Conolly stating their account.

1053 10 Sept. 1795 Thomas Staples, Madden, Co. Armagh, to Conolly requesting more time to pay two bills due to Conolly.

1054 18 Sept.–15 Jan. 1795/96 List of bills drawn on Conolly's account.

3978/ 1055	22 Sept. 1795	William Sandford, New Bond Street, to Conolly about overdue interest payments, on the Christie mortgage.
1056	26 Sept. 1795	Robert, Lord Hobart, Fort St George, [Madras, India], to Conolly about his health, and his daily routine, which he compares to Conolly's at Castletown. He informs Conolly of his travels, and the conditions of famine, he has seen. He compares the situation in [Madras] to Ireland. He has taken the Dutch settlements on the Coromandel coast.
1057	3 Oct. 1795	Messrs Hood & Co., London, to Conolly stating their account.
1058	3 Oct. 1795	Michael Cooke, Morristown, [Co. Kildare], to Conolly about his son's disgrace in the army, and looking for Conolly's assistance.
1059	31 Oct.–24 Dec. 1795	List of bills drawn on Conolly's account.
1060	6 Nov. 1795	Nesbitt & Stewart, London, to Conolly. '…We are much concerned to find that your business in future is to be transacted by another house here. It was our wish at all times to accommodate you as far as in our power and we believe if you revert to your accounts you will see that we have oftentimes entered into very large engagements for you, much greater than we should have done for almost any other person, and our motive could only be to serve you. As we never made a charge of commission for any business we did for you as the matter now stands we have only to lament you should have taken the resolution without first intimating to us your intentions, as it gives us real concern to be compelled to close accounts with a gentleman foe whom we have so high a respect. As this house is security for the greater part of the payments we make for you it will be necessary to have them given up to us. We must therefore request you will be so good as to direct the different particulars to do so…'
1061	14 Dec. 1795	Mrs A[nne] Byng, Mount Ephraim, [Tunbridge wells], to Conolly about family affairs. Their mother is in town, as she found the fog at Twickenham bad for her health.
1062	26 Dec. 1795	Puget & Bainbridge, [bankers], London, to Conolly about money owed to him.
1063	1795	Account of agricultural produce for the year.

MSS	DATE	DESCRIPTION
3979/ 1064– 3980/ 1303	**22 Jan. 1796– 21 Dec. 1799**	**Letters, papers and other miscellaneous papers of Thomas Conolly, including correspondence about the 1798 rebellion 1796–99.**
1064	4 Jan. 1797	[Robert Stewart, Lord] Castlereagh, [lt – colonel commanding Conolly' regiment, the Co. Londonderry Militia, in the absence of Conolly because of age and infirmity], Bandon, [Co. Cork], to Conolly about the attempted Bantry Bay invasion in December 1796. *This letter is listed out of sequence.* 'Your regiment has at last had two days rest. We have laid up by the fatigue about 20 men; the rest are again fit for any service. Yesterday morning General Smith reported himself surrounded by enemies and called in reinforcements, the drums beat to arms and the cavalry of Sligo marched immediately. Other corps at a distance were directed to move to his assistance, but the whole in the course of 12 hours were halted, the enemy having sailed from the Shannon, he thinks they are returning to Bantry. The wind will not admit of it, [they are] more probably gone to Galway or the north, if they have any sense, which their reported state makes doubtful, there are certainly 8 ships still in Bantry, but more probably 14. That number having been there the day before yesterday, the whole, 2 disabled ships excepted, dropped down the night before last and were concluded to have gone off, but 6 came to off Bear Island and the others cannot be far off. No farther movement of the troops will take place till the enemy more clearly disclose their intentions. Valentine and Crawford are arrived; I hope Sterling is on the road. Whenever the enemy lands you shall have the earliest notice. Till then I think your health is the first consideration and there is no occasion for exposing it in marching and counter marching. We are all well, Emily [his wife, the daughter of Conolly's sister Lady Buckinghamshire] I hope is well and in tolerable spirits. What is become of dear Lady Louisa….your affectionate nephew...'
1065	22 Jan. 1796	Henry Vernon, Conolly's cousin, 10 Lower Wimpole St, London, to Conolly (Marked 'Private'). 'I called this morning on Lady Anne and found her very well. She told me Boodle [her London attorney and adviser] was coming to concert measures with her to prevent your success in your journey to London; that Lady Howe had informed her yesterday no less than three of your most intimate friends had met you in London who had each come and informed her of your being there. In the course of our conversation came in the post with a letter from you to inform your mother of Miss [Henrietta] Staples being to be

3979/1065 *contd.* married to Mr Trench's eldest son [Richard, later Lord Dunlo] which she showed me, wherein you stated her father gave her £3,000, Miss Fitzgerald had left her £2,000 and that you intended to make the whole £10,000 which you desired might be made known by Lady Anne to your sisters. Your mother was much pleased with this news, not only on Miss Staples' account, but because it proved to her that there were people in your family who were capable of strongly misleading her mind about you. She immediately sent your letter to Lady Howe, with a very proper letter on the subject of the news sent her the day before which had caused her many uneasy hours. I think it right to inform you of this but request you will not speak of it [as] of course [it] would be known from whence it came. Mr Boodle came whilst I was in the room. Lady Anne informed him the whole information was false and showed your letter.

I called today on Sir Michael Cromie but learnt he was gone to Ireland. I have desired him some time past to state to you how very happy it would make me if you would be so good to take the timber at £800 and let me have your draft for that sum payable at your convenience. I have some money to pay at Lady Day. If not agreeable to you to pay it then, make your note payable at your own convenience and my bankers will advance me the money which will be of the <u>most material service to me</u> for I gave notice to pay off a debt I cannot discharge without this help, which is so very material to my comfort and future happiness that I trust and humbly beg you to comply with it. ..'

1066 22 Jan. 1796 Lady Anne Conolly, London, to Conolly
She is happy for Miss Staples. She does not want to speak of business, except that 'Lord Thurlow has entirely stopped our business in chancery'. [This was a lawsuit brought by her to overturn her late brother, Lord Strafford's will.] She is worried about her 'great friend' [and brother-in-law, Field Marshal] Sir George Howard who is so ill.

1067 26 Jan. 1796 George Ash, Ashbrook, to Conolly about candidates seeking appointment to various local offices including surgeon to the infirmary and inspector of the gaol. Also reports that every freeholder has to register anew under a late act of parliament.

1068 28 Jan. 1796 William Cruise, Lincolns Inn, to Conolly.
He has made an application to Mr Boodle to lay before him the papers relating to Conolly's title to the Leixlip estate. 'In consequence of the death of Marshall Conway [one of Lord Strafford's executors] the suit respecting Lord Strafford's private estate is abated, the consequence of which is that Lady Anne does not receive one shilling of her dividend and nothing can be done

3979/1068 *contd.*		until Lord Thurlow either takes the executorship upon himself or renounces…' This will take time and Lady Anne may be distressed and need her jointure.
1069	8 Feb. 1796	Dazarin, 4 Rue de Paris, St Germain, to Conolly. In French. An old servant begs for help.
1070	20 Feb. 1796	Henry Vernon, Lower Wimpole St, London, to Conolly about Conolly's dispute with his mother over the payment of an addition of £30,000–£40,000 to his sister's portions and the withholding of her jointure. She has stopped Conolly from selling his Bedfordshire estate. Lord Thurlow has taken on the executorship of Lord Strafford's will. He also mentions that Lady Anne has made William Conolly Staples her heir.
1071	21 Feb. 1796	George Byng , Wrotham Park, to Conolly. 'I am sorry, very sorry that you should be engaged in a dispute with your mother, which I am much afraid will only end on her death….'
1072	25 Feb. 1796	Henry Vernon, Lower Wimpole St, London, to Conolly in relation to the division of the Bedfordshire estate.
1073	9 Mar. 1796	Brook Bridges, Red Lion Square, to Conolly about his case with his mother over the Bedfordshire estate.
1074	20 Apr. 1796	William Cruise, Lincolns Inn, to Conolly in relation to Conolly's case in Chancery, and the payment of his mother's jointure. Mr Hoare, the banker, has made enquiries about purchasing Conolly's Whitehall house. Cruise has suggested a price of £5,000.
1075	27 Apr. 1796	John Kipling, Rolls Chapel, to Lord Castlereagh in relation to the purchase of a house in Bond Street by a Mr Parsons from Lord Castlereagh, which a suit in Chancery has delayed.
1076	2 May 1796	Thomas Dickson to Conolly about the renewal of his leases at Ballyhanna.
1077	4 June 1796	Anne Byng, Berkeley Square, to Conolly Her son [George] was elected for Middlesex the previous day. Sir William Howe has gone to his command at Newcastle. Their mother keeps well and will go to Twickenham when the warm weather arrives. 'The chancellor [Lord Loughborough] has decided that my sister Staples, Lady Vernon and myself should have the £1,000 mentioned in Lord Strafford's will.'

3979/1078		*Blank in the sequence*
1079	27 June 1796	John Clements [A cousin of Robert Clements 1st Earl of Leitrim and colonel theRt. Hon. Henry Theophilus Clements], Portland Place, London, to Conolly seeking Conolly's assistance in raising £5,000 to fit out his new Ship, Royal Charlotte.
1080	19 July 1796	George Ash, Ashbrook, to Conolly about the valuation of the woods at Cumber on the Limavady estate.
1081	21 July 1796	Nesbitt & Stewart, London, to Conolly about payments outstanding on Conolly's account.
1082	27 July 1796	John Clements, Portland Place, London, to Conolly in relation to his proposal that Conolly should perfect a bond of £10,000 for his use. He has discussed this with Conolly's London bankers.
1083	29 July 1796	George Byng, St James Square, to Conolly seeking the payment of money owed by Conolly.
1084	2 Aug. 1796	George Ash, Ashbrook, to Conolly enclosing a valuation of the woods at Ervey, Aughlagh and Listress. Lord Clare has visited Derry, where the corporation entertained him. He stayed with Mr Richardson.
1085	6 Aug. 1796	William Jones, Cherrymount, Ballyshannon, to Conolly. He wants to rent the salmon and eel fisheries at Ballyshannon.
1086	6 Aug. 1796	William Jones' proposal to rent the Ballyshannon fisheries enclosed in no. 1085. He proposes the sum of £700 per annum.
1087	12 Aug. 1796	Copy of a bill of £1,000 paid on Conolly's account by Edward Bulkeley to Henry Sandford Esq.
1088	19 Aug. 1796	James Kernan's proposal for the Ballyshannon fisheries. He proposes the sum of £750.
1089	23 Sept. 1796	Capt. D. Stack, Limerick, to Conolly about money due to Conolly from Stack.
1090	24 Sept. 1796	James Johnston's proposal for the Ballyshannon fisheries.
1091	29 Sept. 1796	Jo. Francillon, London, to Conolly about money owed to him by a bond secured on Conolly and the late Arnold Nesbitt.
1092	30 Sept. 1796	John Josselyn, Belstead near Ipswich, to Conolly seeking expenses for acting as a commissioner in the division of the late Lord Strafford's estate.

3979/ 1093 1 Oct. 1796 [The 1st Earl of] Londonderry [to whom Conolly had recently sold the parliamentary borough of Newtown Limavady], Magherafelt, to Conolly

We had a full common council on Thursday at Newtown-Limavady and I got all my business very well transacted. I am sorry my stay in this part of the country will be so short I have no chance of seeing you. But in truth before I left home, I found the minds of my people so much poisoned with the infection of the times, I am very uneasy to get back among them to try whether I can by personal application gain over a few to enrol themselves as yeoman cavalry and take the oath of allegiance. From the difficulty they seem to make about swearing it is pretty evident all those we can bring to consent may be depended on, for the Presbyterians, whatever mischief they may have in their heads are not without religion and although they may aim at subverting the government the people in general will not by their present wicked guides be persuaded to perjure themselves. Wishing you better success among your tenantry in arming for the defence of our lives and property than I have had as yet with mine…'

1094 2 Oct. 1796 James Corry, Linen Office, Dublin, to Conolly requesting his presence at a meeting of the Linen Board, of which Conolly was a member. Enclosed is a list of board members who have defaulted on their attendance including Conolly.

1095 4 Oct. 1796 Thomas Conolly, Belleisle, Co. Fermanagh, to John Major [Henry Major's son].

'The scheme proposed by government for the arming of the yeomanry is in some points not so explicit as it ought to be and in particular it is doubtful whether the receiving pay for two days in the week and clothes and taking the oath of allegiance does submit the takers of them to the mutiny act, but as it is afterwards expected that that shall not be the case till they have marched beyond the second barony by their own offer or in case of invasion I take it for granted that the yeomen are not subject to the mutiny act upon being embroiled. But this shall be inscribed into it they shall be informed of it.

The district of Ballyshannon should at most furnish one hundred men, forty of whom should be mounted, the remainder dismounted cavalry. Each horseman in case of riot or disturbance at a distance could take one man behind him with his firelock. The remaining twenty to be left in the town, for the protection of its inhabitants.

I am sorry Mr [Henry] Major's illness and the necessity I am under of returning immediately to my own regiment and parliament will prevent my personal application to my tenants and friends at Ballyshannon. But I trust that their own good sense and

3979/1095 *contd.*		loyalty will sow them the necessity of this armament. That they will agree this with cheerfulness and alacrity and thereby prove to government that the tenants of a gentleman who has uniformly opposed the extravagance and profligacy of government will with their landlord be at all times ready to defend the king, constitution and property of individuals, as those that have profited by a contrary conduct.'
1096	5 Oct. 1796	[John Jeffreys Pratt 2nd Earl] Camden, [the Lord Lieutenant], Dublin Castle, to Conolly 'My relation, Mr [Thomas] Pelham has informed me of your progress in the north of Ireland and the steps you are taking to ascertain the sentiments of your tenants and neighbours and to form corps of the nature of those recommended by government. I trouble you with these few lines to express you my view of the advantage which is likely to accrue to the country by your active exertions upon this occasion…'.
1097	8 Oct. 1796	Thomas Pelham, [the Chief Secretary], Phoenix Park, to Conolly He has written to Henry Major about the Ballyshannon yeomanry. He expects the next parliamentary session to begin on 13 October.
1098	8 Oct. 1796	Thomas Pelham, Dublin Castle, to John Major, Ballyshannon asking him to stop recruiting for the yeomanry. He has already recruited a sufficient number of suitable men.
1099	9 Oct. 1796	Catherine Dickson, Jackson's Hall, Coleraine, to Conolly seeking payment of the annuity promised to her sister by Conolly.
1100	10 Oct. 1796	John Major, Ballyshannon, to Conolly. His father [Henry Major, Conolly's agent] is still very ill and incapable of doing any business. There are several tenants whose leases need to be renewed
1101	12 Oct. 1796	Thomas Conolly, Coleraine, to Lord Camden. (Copy). 'My Lord, I have many thanks to return your Excellency for your very kind letter approving of my humble services at Ballyshannon. I have now the pleasure to tell you that I have had a meeting at Clandermott and at Muff of Mr Richard Ponsonby's tenants, Mr Scott's, son of the late Judge Scott, and my own, and I found them to a man as peaceable and as loyal as I could wish. I yesterday had a meeting at Newtown Limavady of the principal gentlemen of the neighbourhood with a great body of my own tenants though the weather had prevented some from coming there. The gentlemen and all that attended seemed perfectly disposed to support the king, the constitution to maintain the peace and protect the property of the kingdom.

3979/1101 *contd.*		I have at these places appointed days of enrolment for my own tenants and have recommended the doing of the same to the different agents of Lord Waterford and Mr Beresford and the other gentlemen present. When their lists are made out they will be sent to Mr Pelham for your Excellency's information. I shall see my tenants at Bellaghy next Friday and shall then proceed to Dublin when I will communicate to your Excellency any further information I may receive, hoping however that a very refractory spirit that Mr Richardson informs me has broke out in this town may not affect the other part of this county hitherto well disposed…'.
1102	13 Oct. 1796	Hood & Company, London, to Conolly about sundry payments made on his account.
1103	15 Oct. 1796	John Major, Ballyshannon, to Conolly about the Ballyshannon yeomanry.
1104	19 Oct. 1796	Archibald Boyd, Londonderry, to Conolly. He has received the parish of Tamlaghtacreely's contribution to the augmentation for the Londonderry Militia.
1105	22 Oct. 1796	Henry Lease, Bushfield, to Henry Major, Ballyshannon reporting the presence of a suspicious Frenchman calling himself Count Toumak mapping the north Mayo coast.
1106	29 Oct. 1796	Henry Major, Ballyshannon, to Thomas Pelham. He can enrol more yeomen at Ballyshannon than the government requires if it is so desired. He encloses no. 1105 and reports that the man calling himself Count Toumak passed through Ballyshannon. He agrees with the view of Lord Altamont 'that he had neither the manners nor the address, nor the appearance of a gentleman'.
1107	Oct. 1796	Lord Camden, Dublin Castle, to Conolly 'The zeal and anxiety you expressed when I had the honour of seeing you upon your return from Limerick to show your determination to support his majesty and the constitution and contribute to the defence of the country in times of danger, has induced me to take the liberty of enclosing you the plan upon which it has been thought many useful Corps for defending the security and the peace of the neighbourhood might be formed. The great stake you have in this country and the manner in which you were so good as to express yourself relative to the necessity of taking measures of defence renders it unnecessary for me to make any apology for enclosing this plan…'.

3979/ 1108	2 Nov. 1796	William Sandford, Castlerea, Co. Roscommon, to Conolly about interest due from Conolly on a bond which the writer has inherited from his father.
1109	15 Nov. 1796	Rev. Henry Bruce, Finlagan, Co. Londonderry, to Conolly. He reports the difficulties encountered raising yeomen cavalry at Newtown Limavady and fears the neighbourhood may be 'disgraced'. He also writes that 'the potato diggers have shown themselves in this county; several thousand assembled on Thursday last near Dungiven, many of them from the counties of Down and Antrim, to dig the potatoes of the mother of McClung now in jail for the inhuman murder of McClusky, and though they dispersed on the military being brought against them from Derry, after many threats and entreaties from the sheriff and other magistrates who conducted the party, as soon as the soldiers were withdrawn they almost all returned and did not separate until they effected their purpose. The gentlemen here are very anxious to have a troop of horse quartered at Newtown. I sincerely hope we shall get them, as with their assistance the magistrates may be much more active in endeavouring to preserve the peace of the country which is now in a most disturbed state…'
1110	13 Dec. 1796	Nesbitt & Stewart, London, to Conolly sending their bill on his account.
1111	21 Dec. 1796	Magistrates of Co. Londonderry to Conolly: circular letter to non-resident gentry seeking their assistance in enrolling yeomanry.
1112	23 Aug.–23 Dec. 1796	John Stewart & Company's bill for wine addressed to Conolly.
1113	28 Dec. 1796	John Spotswood, Bellaghy, to Conolly about his success in getting Conolly's tenants to enrol in the yeomanry.
1114	31 Dec. 1796	Thomas Dickson, Woodville, Co. Donegal, to Conolly seeking payment of £500 owed to him. He also recommends his nephew Gilbert Eccles, who wishes to join the navy, to Conolly, asking Conolly to intercede with Captain [Thomas] Pakenham who has recently married Miss [Louisa] Staples, Conolly's niece.
1115	31 Dec. 1796	John Major, Ballyshannon, to Thomas Pelham seeking arms for his yeomanry company. 'They are ignorant of the cavalry discipline: however, as old volunteers they are familiar with the musket and bayonet.'
1116	1796–7	Produce of oats for 1796–7. It is unclear which part of the Conolly estate this document comes from.

3979/ 1117	10 Jan. 1797	Nesbitt & Stewart, London, to Conolly stating their account.
1118	11 Jan. 1797	Dean Christopher Butson, Waterford, to Henry Major, Ballyshannon.mostly reporting family news and gossip but also commenting on the good behaviour of the Fermanagh Militia while stationed in Waterford.
1119	19 Jan. 1797	Address of the Corporation of Smiths, Dublin to Captain Thomas Pakenham, praising his exertions in defence of the empire especially at the Battle of Ushant, 1 June 1794.
1119a	20 Jan. 1797	William Conolly Staples, London, to Conolly about Conolly's ongoing case in Chancery over the £30,000-£40,000 allegedly due his sisters.
1120	21 Jan. 1797	Nesbitt & Stewart, London, to Conolly stating their account.
1121	21 Jan. 1797	Copy of a bill of £1,000 payable to George Sandford due on this date.
1122	24 Jan. 1797	George Sandford to Conolly enclosing no. 1121.
1123	31 Jan. 1797	Nesbitt & Stewart, London, to Conolly stating their account.
1124	3 Feb. 1797	George Byng, Wrotham Park, to Conolly stating the money owed him by Conolly and requesting payment of at least £500 because his creditors are coming after him for his own debts. He adds; ' if at the death of your mother I have the command of money there will be no sacrifice I should think too great for your ease and comfort.'
1125	9 Feb. 1797	Memorial of Anthony Coane to Lord Camden asking to retire as port surveyor of Rutland.
1126	9 Feb. 1797	Anthony Coane, Rutland, to Conolly enclosing No. 1125 above. Conolly had procured him his entry into the revenue service.
1127	9 Feb. 1797	Richard Trench, [husband of Conolly's niece, Henrietta Staples], Merrion Square, to Conolly stating his account of household expenses.
1128	9 Feb. 1797	Nesbitt & Stewart, London, to Conolly stating their account
1129	9 Feb. 1797	J. Clark Jervoise, Hanover Square, London, to Conolly recommending Mr Thomas Fleet's medicine for sheep rot.

3979/ 1130	14 Feb. 1797	A[ndrew] Knox, Dublin, to Conolly. He is writing as an executor of the late Lord Conyngham seeking payment of two bonds totalling £14,000 and 'the considerable arrear of interest, upwards of £2,500' due to the late Lord's estate from Conolly.
1131	18 Feb. 1797	Nesbitt & Stewart, London, to Conolly stating their account.
1132	23 Feb. 1797	Austin Cooper, Dublin, to Conolly seeking payment of the £14,000 mortgage due to the late Lord Conyngham's estate and charged on Limavady.
1133	4 Mar. 1797	Dean Christopher Butson, Waterford to Henry Major, Ballyshannon about the benefice of Ballyshannon.
1134	9 Mar. 1797	Nesbitt & Stewart, London, to Conolly stating their account.
1135	11 Mar. 1797	Henry Major, Ballyshannon, to Conolly enclosing no. 1133. Major's clergyman son's currently has a benefice in a distant county, but would prefer the benefice of Ballyshannon currently held by the Dean of Waterford.
1136	13 Mar. 1797	George, Prince of Wales, London, to Conolly, with royal seal attached to the cover.[1] 'Dear Conolly, I return you my best thanks for your letter with the account of the state of affairs in Ireland, which in consequence of your permission I submitted to the consideration of His Majesty's ministers. I was impelled by the affection I bear that kingdom and by a sense of the duty I owe my father and the state to submit to them about the same time my opinion on the measures to be adopted to unite all distinctions of Irish subjects against our foreign enemy. I will freely acknowledge to you, that encouraged by the many kind invitations I have received from some of the first and best men in that kingdom and by the gratitude I must ever feel for the distinguished marks of kindness I have received from the Irish nation, I was led if my opinion had being adopted to make an offer of my personal service, willing to share the fate of that generous and loyal people. I am anxious though that this offer on my part should not be considered in any point of view as conveying the smallest censure upon Lord Camden, or in the least personal to him, but as proceeding from a [ ] from the loyalty of the people and the measures proposed, my presence might have had a tendency to strengthen a good understanding between the two kingdoms, to extinguish party divisions and to have animated

1 This letter does not appear in Arthur Aspinall's *The correspondence of George, Prince of Wales 1770–1812,* Vol. III, 1795–98 (London, 1965).

3979/1136 *contd.* the current strength of the state against a foreign invasion if the desperate attempt should be repeated. I trust that every friend of mine will feel the necessity of strengthening the hands of government at this critical period and I feel a confident hope that no circumstances will ever diminish the loyalty of Ireland, or its attachment to the Crown or slacken its exertion in the hour of danger, as the affectionate regard His Majesty feels for every description of his faithful subjects ought to inspire them with the fullest reliance on his beneficent protection. As to myself I can only say that in every situation Ireland may be assured of my gratitude and affection.

Having said this much my dear Conolly I shall not perhaps any longer linger upon your patience, except to assure you of the personal regard…'

1137 16 Mar. 1797 John Hood, London, to Conolly about the urgent need for Conolly to remit money to him through Latouche's bank to pay off the outstanding balance on Conolly's account.

1138 18 Mar. 1797 Nesbitt & Stewart, London, to Conolly stating their account.

1139 24 Mar. 1797 M. Burroughs, Limerick, to Conolly seeking his influence with Captain [Thomas] Pakenham for a job at the latter's disposal.

1140 24 Mar. 1797 Joseph Courtney, Grange, to Conolly seeking a navy commission for his son.

1141 1 Apr. 1797 Conolly, Castletown, to George Prince of Wales. Copy.[2]
Though time whilst I can live [ ] my gratitude to your Royal Highness for your gracious condescension in writing to me as well from the benign sentiments your letter contains to the people of this my native country as from the kind expressions of your regard, which I trust I shall never forfeit.
I shall ever lament that your Royal Highness's opinion was adopted as from its conciliatory tendency and your presence amongst us the present alarming state of the this kingdom might have been avoided and His Majesty's government might have confided with reason in that loyalty and attachment to the Crown so much to be wished for at this awful crisis. I should desire your Royal Highness if I told you that such an event is likely now to happen but I fear the revenue as the disappointed catholic is growing unmindful and careless about his discipline as a [ ] and the active republican looks for more success to his principles from this indifference of the catholic from the exhausted state of our Treasury and credit which may not long continue to pay our army. The credit of Great Britain affords no better prospect. Lord

2 This letter not in Aspinall.

3979/1141 *contd.* Camden I must always personally wish well but the system of parliamentary corruption that has ruined both kingdoms. I ever have and must oppose the acts to strengthen his majesty's government. I have through my influence worked though I have lamented the cause that made them necessary. I shall continue to offer my earnest prayer that the greatest empire ever known may thrive and flourish under your illustrious family…'

1142 1 Apr. 1797 Dive Downes, London, to Conolly demanding payment of an annuity due to him from Conolly.

1143 3 Apr. 1797 Conolly Coane, Kinsale, to Conolly about the renewal of his lease of part of Conolly's Ballyshannon estate.

1144 8 Apr. 1797 John Hood, London, to Conolly about Conolly's outstanding bill drawn on his bank.

1145 10 Apr. 1797 Will. Nesbitt, Drogheda, to Conolly
'I see by the Dundalk papers that the Prince of Wales laid letters to him from Ireland before Mr Pitt with his offer to come here as lord lieutenant in hopes of guiding the country among which your letters must be principal and I recollect you desired his R.H. to make what use he pleased of it but the infatuated father and the delusive Pitt rejected the offer. I am thoroughly satisfied if his R.H. had been permitted to come over, the salutary effects would have instantly appeared….

I am convinced nothing less than a reform in parliament and some other matters to which now with common sense and prudence government ought not to object can re-anglicise this country and continue its connection with Great Britain. I take the liberty of enclosing [not found] a few hints for a reform in parliament which are as gentle as the subject will admit and I freely submit my first and last essay on politics to your friendly eye…'

1146 17 Apr. 1797 Henry Major, Ballyshannon, to Conolly about the renewal of leases on the Ballyshannon estate.

1147 3 May 1797 David Babington, Ballyshannon, to Conolly.
Lord Belmore wants Conolly to write to the burgesses of Ballyshannon requesting them to resign, following the formers purchase of the borough. Conolly should send all the letters to Babington and he will enclose to each burgess the form of resignation for signature.

Enclosed is a list of the burgesses as follows: Henry Major (Provost), Conolly, Lord Ross, John Staples, Thomas Dickson, John Hamilton, John Atkinson, James Dickson, Anthony Coane, Patrick Haley, John Major, Conolly Coane and John O'Neill, who is dead but has not been replaced.

3979/ 1148 13 May 1797 Ransome Morland, London, to Conolly reminding Conolly of an outstanding bill.

1149 20 May 1797 John Hood & Company, London, to Conolly about the payment of overdue bills. Mr Latouche is becoming 'quite impatient'. Enclosed is a copy of no. 1144.

1150 20 May 1797 Henry Major, Ballyshannon, to Conolly.
'I am extremely concerned to be obliged to tell you that your tenants in general do not show a proper inclination to pay the last November rent, nor, in my opinion, would they though the markets which are at present very low should enable them to do so. This I attribute to the rebellious state of almost the whole of this county. Hardly a night passes that different houses within three or four miles of Ballyshannon are not broken open by considerable bodies of United Irishmen, well armed and abundantly supplied with ammunition, who carry off all arms and ammunition without distinction and invariably demolish the doors and windows of every house where they meet with the shadow of opposition. The Ballyshannon Corps who are as spirited and as zealous as possible have been out several nights but could never contrive to come up with any of the deluded insurgents, and yet I find from unquestionable information that different houses have been robbed of arms and ammunition about half an hour before or after my patrol entered them. In their depredations they are dreadfully successful as you will conceive from the following circumstances: On last Sunday night they attacked the house of counsellor Johnston in the very centre of a corps of yeomanry which he commands and after demolishing all the windows they robbed it of twelve hundred ball cartridges and some of the arms belonging to his corps; on the same night they forcibly entered Captain Caldwell's house at Bundoran from which they took six muskets and four blunderbusses; and on the same night many other houses in this neighbourhood shared the same fate: in short such excesses have they committed that if our garrison be not speedily and strongly reinforced, I am confident they will attack Ballyshannon….'

1151–52 3, 14 June 1797 Two letters from John Spotswood of Bellaghy to Conolly about the lack of money available to pay rents. Spotswood's account with Conolly is enclosed with no. 1151.

1153 16 June 1797 William Conolly Staples, Cheltenham, to Conolly about the valuation of the family plate he has inherited from Lady Anne Conolly.

3979/ 1154	19 June 1797	George Byng, St James' Square, London, to Conolly. He is marrying and settling his estate. He wants to settle part of his inheritance from [the 2nd Earl of] Strafford, and thinks that 'if I lose my suit in Chancery. £100,000 would buy off my brother and the next of kin….'.
1155	29 June 1797	William Elliot, Trim, to Conolly about a bill drawn on Conolly's account.
1156	3 July 1797	Arthur McGwire, Dawson Street, to Lady Louisa Conolly. He sends drawings of a new 'intended kitchen'. He includes detailed descriptions of the various ovens and boilers including a hot hearth, a fish kettle and a roaster. Included is an elevation of the planned kitchen.
1157	6 July 1797	[General] Henry Eustace, Royal Hospital, Kilmainham, to Christophilus Clinch listing the names of individuals a Mr Colman has lodged examinations against. Those named appear to be tenants of Conolly's at Celbridge.
1158	7 July 1797	David Ross, Grand Hotel, Covent Garden, to Conolly about money owed to him by Conolly.
1159	16 July–20 Feb. 1798	Account of money received for timber.
1160	23 July 1797	George Byng, Wrotham Park, to Conolly about his recent marriage and his outstanding debts.
1161	25 July 1797	Dive Downes, London, to Conolly about the annuity due to Downes.
1162	26 July 1797	Brook Bridges, Red Lion Square, to [Sir Michael Cromie?] about Conolly's legal bills.
1163	11 Aug. 1797	Martin Stones, London, to Conolly about the payment of Lady Conyngham's jointure.
1164	12 Aug. 1797	Lucas Waring, Kilkeel, [Co. Down], to Conolly demanding payment of a bond of £2,000 with interest by the following February.
1165	29 Aug. 1797	John Staples, Ballycastle, [Co. Antrim], to Conolly about a debt of £2,000 owed by Staples to Bishop Woodward's executors. Staples claims that Conolly promised to assume responsibility for this debt when Staples lost his government pension in 1789 following the regency crisis.

3979/ 1166	30 Aug. 1797	Michael Hanley, Ballyshannon, to Conolly about a disputed lease of a tenement in Ballyshannon, which has been forfeited by a 'papist' under a ' bill of discovery'. Conolly's [great] uncle, 'the Speaker', had granted Hanley's grandfather the lease of the property, for lives renewable forever.
1167	2 Sept. 1797	Joseph Courtney, Grange, to Conolly seeking information about 'Arsbald your old ensign' who had served with Captain Pakenham.
1168	4 Sept. 1797	Messrs Drummond & Company, London, to Conolly stating their account.
1169	9 Sept.1797	John Harrison, North Strand, [Dublin], to Conolly seeking payment of money due to him from Conolly.
1170	9 Sept. 1797	Conolly, Dublin, to [his brother-in-law, the Rt Hon.] John Staples. Copy 'I am very unfortunate indeed in having told Mr Benjamin Woodward that I did not consider myself liable to the debt of £2,000, the price of the seat for the borough of Carlow, having totally forgot the letter in question written eight years ago; and I was the more confirmed in that idea when I talked over Mr B. Woodward's claim upon you for the interest last spring, and you did not say anything against the payment of it but the want of money at that time. The acquisition of Mr Gore's employment [the joint examinatorship of Dublin Customs in 1794] and your voting in consequence of it with the administration likewise made me conceive that there was no such engagement on my part, nor did I ever think I should be able to fulfil it till my mother's death who has left everything she could from me with an attack on my integrity and a lawsuit for my birthright into the bargain. At any rate, however, my written promise must not be broken, though you see the disagreeable situation I am left in, not only to lose my patriotic friends' support but to have him and his son provided for at my expense and an arrear of eight years interest, above £1,000, into the bargain which I should never have permitted to have accumulated had I had the smallest idea that I was to have paid it. I now cannot pay it and much wonder at Mr Woodward's hurry. I should be much obliged to you to send me the original letter when convenient...'
1171	13 Sept. 1797	Henry Major, Ballyshannon, to Conolly about the sale of salt, and his losses by it. He also refers to a brig carrying salmon to Cork which has been stranded and the necessity of informing the insurers.

3979/ 1172	15 Sept. 1797	P.D. Latouche, Dublin, to Conolly about payments on Conolly's account.
1173	18 Sept. 1797	Cath. Chaigneau, Young Street, Kensington, to Conolly about the payment of her annuity.
1174	23 Sept, 1797	Henry Major, Ballyshannon, to Conolly about the wreck of the brig carrying the salmon. He encloses an account of the cargo salvaged from the ship signed by Michael Hanley and John Britton.
1175	28 Sept. 1797	Richard Friend, Paradise Row, [Dublin], to Conolly seeking an army commission for his son.
1176	2 Oct. 1797	John O'Regan, pastor of Faughanvale, Muff, Co. Londonderry, to Conolly seeking the promised subscription for the erection of a new chapel in the parish.
1177	2 Oct. 1797	Elizabeth [Lambart, Countess Dowager of] Cavan [widow of the 6th Earl (d.1774)], Clifton, Bristol, to Conolly about her finances and wish for a pension on the Irish civil list.
1178	7 Oct. 1797	John Spotswood, Bellaghy, to Conolly about remitting rents to Conolly and a new lease for a Dr John Sheil.
1179	9 Oct. 1797	Henry Major, Ballyshannon, to Conolly about the payment of the head rent due to the Bishop of Raphoe.
1180	9 Oct. 1797	William Cheshire, Ardfinan Camp, [Co. Tipperary], to Conolly seeking payment of an outstanding debt.
1181	10 Oct. 1797	Elizabeth Lady Cavan, Clifton, to Conolly. Her son [the 7th Earl of Cavan] wants to call in the mortgage held on Conolly's estate.
1182	10 Oct. 1797	Dive Downes, London, to Conolly asking for the payment of money owed to him.
1183	11 Oct. 1797	Edward Cane to Conolly about the payment of interest payments due to the Dowager Lady Cavan.
1184	12 Oct. 1797	Widow Linn, Londonderry, to Conolly about a debt of two guineas owed to her.
1185	13 Oct. 1797	Charles Norman, 14 Gardiner Street, to [Luke Gardiner, 1st Viscount] Mountjoy about money owed by Conolly to Mountjoy.

3979/ 1186	18 Oct. 1797	Henry Major, Ballyshannon, to Conolly about the payment of rent due to Trinity College, Dublin for the Bundrows and Tirhugh] estates held by Conolly under TCD. Enclosed is a letter from Dr Thomas Elrington, the College bursar, to Henry Major.
1187	18 Oct. 1797	T. Lear, Downton near Sarum, to Conolly about the death of his wife. He wants a draft owed by Conolly exchanged for a bond, which will benefit his wife's two sons.
1188	21 Oct. 1797	Copy of a letter from Conolly to John Staples. 'I am more concerned at the idea that the debt of £2,000 to Mr Woodward was yours not mine, as upon talking over the matter this day with him he says that in many conversations with him and in many letters since he has pressed for the payment of the money you acknowledged the debt and never mentioned me as the person to be looked to for the money, and he particularly remembers last spring your having said to him that you considered yourself entirely at his mercy without ever naming me to him as implicated in the transaction.'
1189	21 Oct. 1797	John Daniel, Ballyshannon, to Conolly about the loss of the salmon brig.
1190	25 Oct. 1797	John Clements, Ramsgate, to Conolly asking for money [see no. 1196].
1191	30 Oct. 1797	John Daniel, Ballyshannon, to Conolly. The eel fishery will do better than expected. Eels are usually sold at Belturbet on Ash Wednesday.
1192	31 Oct. 1797	Nesbitt & Stewart, London, to Conolly stating their account.
1193	1 Nov. 1797	William Hamilton, Bessbrook near Limavady, to Conolly desiring to be agent for the game in Conolly's woods.
1194	4 Nov. 1797	William Conolly Staples, Coleraine, to Conolly. He wants Conolly's help in securing an estate for himself and his pregnant wife. He cannot wait until the conclusion of the lawsuit with Mr Byng.
1195	6 Nov. 1797	John Daniel, Ballyshannon, to Conolly about a bill drawn by a Thomas Champion on Conolly's account. Enclosed is a letter from Champion to Daniel.
1196	10 Nov. 1797	John Clements, Ramsgate, to Conolly about the replacement of £9,000 in stock, with which Clements wants Conolly's assistance.

3979/ 1197	15 Nov. 1797	Nesbitt & Stewart, London, to Conolly stating their account.
1198	21 Nov. 1797	Thomas Elrington, Bursar, Trinity College, to Conolly about the renewal of Conolly's leases of the College estates in Co. Donegal.
1199	25 Nov. 1797	John Rogers to Conolly seeking payment of an outstanding debt.
1200	26 Nov. 1797	Peter Gervais, Armagh, to Conolly demanding payment of overdue interest payments.
1201–03	15, 18, 23 Dec. 1797	Three letters from John Daniel, Ballyshannon, to Conolly about the salvage of the salmon from the wrecked brig, and his dealings with the insurers.
1204	1797	John Latouche, Dublin, to Conolly. 'When I had the pleasure of seeing you last year I made you a proposal on the subject of the large sum due to the banks and I do confess that I was equally concerned and surprised that it should meet your disapprobation before you had given yourself any or at least sufficient time to judge of the propriety of it. I shall choose to take the liberty of laying it before you once more explaining in a few words the principles on I which I offered it to your consideration. The very large sums advanced by the bank to you have been for many years a very heavy burden on them and in fact attended with very considerable loss on them insomuch as it confined them in other pursuits infinitely more profitable than the loan of money at the legal interest. They have in consequence for many years pressed you very much though certainly in the kindest and most friendly manner to reimburse or to reduce the debt, which you have often attempted to do, but the large balance now due so appears by the schedule annexed shows that little or nothing has been effectively done. This being I believe a true state of the case on this we founded the proposal offered to you, being as follows: that you should appoint the sum of £5,000 per annum by assigning over tenants to this amount on any estate you should choose to be appropriated to the liquidation of the debt. This was thought reasonable and could not be inconvenient for the following reasons: because it would not diminish your income from what it had been as a jointure of £3,000 had fallen into you and that the interest you paid on your account generally amounted to £2,000. This measure would likewise tend to diminish the debt till you could find an opportunity of selling and of course in the interval lighten the burden on the bank….'

3979/ 1205	6 Jan. 1798	John Daniel, Ballyshannon, to Conolly. The arrival of troops in Ballyshannon has meant that the eel fishery, which had taken over the horse barracks for stores, coopers' workshop, etc., must vacate the barracks. Daniel asks Conolly for his assistance in securing new premises.
1206–09	6 Jan. 1798– 12 Jan. 1799	Four accounts for threshing oats and wheat submitted by Patrick Derby to Conolly. [See alsp nos. 1212, 1216–17, 1222 and 1226 below.]
1210	20 Jan. 1798	John Daniel, Ballyshannon, to Conolly about the shipping of salted salmon to Dublin. Enclosed is a letter to Hamilton & Maxwell, merchants, ordering them to deliver some of the salmon to Conolly at Castletown.
1211	6 Feb. 1798	John Daniel, Dublin, to Conolly about the lawsuit with the insurance company over the loss of the salmon brig in 1797.
1212	6 Feb. 1798	Account from Patrick Derby to Conolly for threshing oats.
1213–14	15, 16 Feb. 1798	Two letters from C[harles] L[ionel Fitzgerald, [brother of George Robert Fitzgerald] 21 Sackville Street, to William Glascock, York Street, about the sale of his estate. [See also no. 1171.]
1215	28 Feb. 1798	John Daniel, Ballyshannon, to Conolly about the disappointing demand for the eels, and the lawsuit with the insurers of the salmon brig.
1216–17	2, 14 Mar. 1798	Two receipts from Patrick Derby for threshing.
1218–21	14, 17, 21	Three letters from John Daniel to Conolly about the Ballyshannon fisheries. no. 1220 enclosed in no. 1219 is addressed to a Mr Taylor.
1222	28 Mar. 1798	Account from Patrick Derby for threshing.
1223, 25	2, 4 Apr. 1798	Two letters from John Daniel to Conolly about the Ballyshannon fisheries.
1224	2 Apr. 1798	J. James, Deputy Receiver of Crown rents', account of rents due from Conolly for his house in Whitehall.
1226	7 Apr. 1798	Account from Patrick Derby for threshing.

3979/ 1227–34	9, 21, 25, 30 Apr., 5, 7, 30 May, 4 June 1798	Eight letters from John Daniel to Conolly about the Ballyshannon fisheries.
1235	13 June 1798	John Daniel, Ballyshannon, to Lady Louisa Conolly about the eel fisheries. This letter addressed is to Lady Louisa because he assumes Conolly is busy with his militia regiment 'at these critical times'.
1235a	15 June 1798	J.D. Nesbitt, Medlycott Burroughs, W Miller and Fleming McNeill [officers of the Co. Londonderry Militia], Kilcullen, [Co. Kildare], to Conolly. 'When we represented Major Smith's [of the Londonderry Militia] conduct to you our most sincere wish was that you would not take any active step against him, further than a suspension of his command, or a removal from this place. We thought it not proper to mention our wishes relying on your humanity and your knowledge of his distressed circumstances. We now feel ourselves called on to beg you will not bring him to a court martial as in our opinion nothing could save him, and being broke to a man of feeling must be worse than death in the present times.'
1236	18 June 1798	John Daniel, Ballyshannon, to Conolly. The lease of the eel weirs is coming up for renewal. The curfew imposed by the 'civil war' almost halted the eel fishing as the fishermen tended to go out early in the morning and late at night, but Colonel Urquhart relented.
1237–38	4, 9 July 1798	Two letters from John Daniel, Ballyshannon, to Lady Louisa Conolly about the eel fishery.
1239	17 July 1798	John Stewart, Dublin, to John Major, Ballyshannon about bills drawn on Henry Major by Conolly.
1240	28 July 1798	John Daniel, Ballyshannon, to Lady Louisa Conolly about the eel fisheries and reporting the death of Henry Major, Conolly's Ballyshannon agent who was succeeded in the ahency by his son, John].
1241	1 Aug. 1798	John Daniel, Ballyshannon, to Lady Louisa Conolly about the eel fishery.
1242	18 Aug. 1798	John Hood, London, to Conolly demanding payment of Conolly's outstanding balances. He has been forced to borrow to keep his business afloat.

3979/ 1243	22 Aug. 1798	John Daniel, Ballyshannon, to Conolly about the Ballyshannon fisheries.
1244	23 Aug. 1798	Conolly, Bellisle, to John Major, Ballyshannon desiring him to send £80 sterling to the Earl of Ross at Belleisle. Copy.
1245	24 Aug. 1798	John Daniel, Ballyshannon, to Conolly. 'Since I wrote to you at Belleisle things have taken a considerable change here, the French landings etc, and the post just arrived says that they have thrown up entrenchments at Ballina. Above 2,000 rebels are already gone in, whom they are putting in uniform, but we have so many accounts I can't give you anything for certain.' The rest of the letter relates to the fisheries.
1246	4 Sept. 1798	Brook Bridges, Red Lion Square, London, to Sir Michael Cromie desiring the payment of Major Christie's half years interest [on Christie's £10,000 secured on the Toddington estate, Bedfordshire]..
1247–53	10,15, 17, 24, 26 Sept., 6, 23 Oct. 1798	Seven letters from John Daniel at Ballyshannon to Conolly about the fisheries, including references to the insurance of the ships carrying the salmon.
1254	6 Nov. 1798	John Stephens, Barrack Office, [Dublin], to Conolly about the temporary accommodation of the army in Celbridge Market House.
1255	14 Nov. 1798	Brook Bridges, Red Lion Square, to Conolly about the lawsuit over Lord Strafford's will.
1256	17 Nov. 1798	Will. Uniacke, Barrack Office, [Dublin], to Conolly about the temporary accommodation of the army in Celbridge Market House.
1257	8–24 Dec. 1798	Account of cash received and paid between these dates for attention of Lady Louisa Conolly.
1258	11 Dec. 1798	Conolly to John Major, Ballyshannon. 'I told you I was indebted to Major Dickson in the sum of £1,000, as you will see by the enclosed bill which I send you, as a memorandum, and as I have desired you to allow him £120 on account of his rent you will find then he will be paid two years interest, which will not be due till the 19th of February and 19th of March next. So that if I die in the meantime these cancelled notes which I enclose will be a memorandum of the transaction done to accommodate Mr Dickson…' Copy.

3979/ 1259	27 Dec. 1798	John Daniel, Corbett's Hotel, Dublin, to Conolly about the allyshannon fisheries.
1260	5 Jan. 1799– 11 Jan 1800	Conolly's accounts with Crask, mostly disbursements of petty cash.
1261	9 Jan. 1799	[Francis Rawdon-Hastings 2nd Earl of] Moira, Donington, [Park, Leicestershire], to Conolly seeking support for an Irish state pension for [Admiral] Sir John [Borlase] Warren.
1262	15 Jan. 1799	Captain Medlycott Burroughs [of the Londonderry Militia], Balbriggan, [Co. Dublin], to Conolly rejecting charges that he is an inefficient officer.
1263	18 Jan. 1799	Conolly, Castletown, to John Major, Ballyshannon, about the renewal of a lease on the Ballyshannon estate.
1264	26 Jan. 1799	John Daniel, Ballyshannon, to Conolly. He is building a fifty-ton ship which will be the first such vessel ever built at Ballyshannon. He hopes that Conolly will name it when it is done.
1265	26 Feb.–30 July 1799	Receipt for charcoal from a Mr Fawcett addressed to Conolly.
1265a	27 Feb. 1799	Map of woods at Drumlamph and Parabanes island, part of Conolly's Bellaghy estate, by Stafford Hunter.
1266	28 Feb. 1799	Richard Trench, Merrion Square, to Conolly stating Conolly's accounts both in his capacity as executor of Miss [Mary Anne] Fitzgerald[of Turlough] and in his own capacity.
1267	4 Mar. 1799	John Daniel, Ballyshannon, to Conolly. He wants to build a quay at Ballyshannon.
1268	6 Mar. 1799	John Spotswood, Bellaghy, to Conolly about the value of the woods mapped in 1265a.
1269	18 Mar. 1799	John Daniel, Ballyshannon, to Conolly about the security on his bond with Conolly as his partner in the Ballyshannon fishery.
1270	19 Mar. 1799	Conolly, Castletown, to John Major, Ballyshannon. Copy. 'This part of the country being so disturbed makes my going to Ballyshannon next month doubtful. However I will certainly go there if I can. In the meantime I would have you go round the tenants whose leases are out or will be out next year and let me know whether

3979/1270 *contd.* they are willing to pay the rise (sic) rent that you think might be out upon them from May next. Make out a new rent roll accordingly if they agree with you and let them know that I will have their leases made out the College and Bishop's lands for 20 and my own estate for three lives or thirty-one years. When you have got their answer, let me know them and send me as soon as you can an account of your valuation. I shall stay some days at Bellisle on my way down. You can meet me there and we can arrange the answers to be given….'

1271 6 Apr. 1799 John Hood & Co., London, to Conolly.
They are sorry to hear about the failure of Conolly's insurance suit relating to the salmon brig at Ballyshannon. 'We were likewise very sorry the boon [the Union] held out to your parliament for which you were so able an advocate was so opposed, which in its effect may have been the cause of many of the horrid crimes which have been since committed and also bring many people to the same resolution as yourself in seeking a quiet abode elsewhere – a dismal reflection for a country when its best friends forsake it. However we now with pleasure see it is likely to be prevented.' They go on to discuss payments due on Conolly's account.

1272 19 Apr. 1799 Benjamin Harenc, London, to Conolly.
'My good Colonel, worshipful justice, active constable but above all my dear and faithful friend I am much concerned you should find a necessity of exerting yourself in the three first capacities you mention in your letter but as you have found it so I find much consolation in your having performed your duty with so much laudable exertion and spirit and to so material effect as to have brought to punishment the two culprits you mention. Virtue has its own reward and your reflections on having probably saved many good people from becoming victims to these wretches and having materially contributed to restore order in the country by the executions of two of the leaders of your misguided countrymen will support your mind against the many vexatious occurrences which from your situation are unavoidable. From the late accounts I have had from General Hunter's aide-de-camp I hope that public tranquillity is taking place. He says that they travelled together in their regimentals without any escort and without any conceived danger from Kilkenny to Dublin.' He goes on to relate gossip and news of various mutual friends.

1273 27 Apr. 1799 Copy of a letter from Conolly, Castletown, to Dominick McCausland, law agent to William Conolly Staples' executors.
'The account you sent me I believe is right and as soon as my bonds come over I will replace them with fresh security to Mr William Conolly Staples' executors. My mother's jointure was

3979/1273 *contd.* £3,000 but there was a clause in her marriage settlement to reduce it to £1,500 if she did not settle Lord Strafford's estates upon my father or his heirs male upon getting a half-years previous notice. This notice was never served as I never expected that my mother and sisters since would persevere in an unjust lawsuit for a part of my birthright which they could never succeed in, in law or equity, but at the expense of my character which I thank God they cannot hurt. Had they trusted my honour, they would have got much, but they now have nothing but what the law awards.

Whilst this lawsuit is persevered in I cannot nor ought not to pay the full jointure awarded by my father's marriage settlement unless my mother or her executor comply with their part of it. This you must let Mr Staples know. My sisters have as yet made no reply to my answer in Chancery, so that I must only make my debt to my mother's jointure conditional…'

1274 27 Apr. 1799 Draft of a letter from Conolly, Castletown, to Dominick McCausland. (Marked 'not sent').

'My mother's jointure was £3,000 Irish chargeable upon my Irish estates and was changed by an act of parliament in 1766 from one division of them to another. My mother at her own request was paid quarterly until 1793[when] I paid her a whole year in one sum as you can see by her receipts up to August 1794. There was an article in her marriage settlement of 1733 that reduced her jointure to £1,500 provided that upon giving her half a year's notice she did not settle any estates in England that she should come to in right of her mother's marriage settlement upon my father and his heirs male. Now my mother, upon the disappointment I experienced in not finding that parchment will which he [the 2nd Earl of Strafford] had twice put into my hands in 1785 and lastly when I was an ambassador in 1789, prevailed upon me not to enter a caveat against the present will of 1774, a paper one written by himself, and made over the estates she got by her brother's death conditionally to pay £10,000 apiece to my sisters out of the produce of them unless she lived to save that sum out of the interest of Lord Strafford's personal property [which was] near £400,000 in the funds and other securities. She did live to have saved this sum before I went to London in May 1795 and accordingly gave me a deed in the most handsome manner according to that promise which I have. However she was afterwards prevailed upon, certainly I believe by her attorney Boodle, to write that she meant only to exonerate the small detached estates not worth £10,000. Thus she has left a Chancery writ to her daughters for £10,000 apiece on these estates which they can only succeed in by proving me a swindler and a rogue and getting the better of her own marriage settlement of which she had the one part and the other was kept by the late Lord Strafford

3979/1274 *contd.* which I now have. She knew or might have known the contents of her own marriage settlement. I did not and only found a copy of it at Glascock's [his Dublin attorney] in August 1795 when I was looking for papers in order to give my sisters at my death a charge of £10,000 apiece on my Irish estates to keep the English ones free for mortgage or sale so as to extricate myself from debt by selling at 34 years purchase in England instead of 20 here.'

1275 29 Apr. 1799 John Daniel, Ballyshannon, to Conolly about the lease of the fisheries.

1276 2 May 1799 Conolly, Castletown, to John Daniel.
'I have received this day your two bills of £500 British each at par upon Thomas Keogh Esq., Townsend St, and George Adamson & Co., Dublin, for the rent of my fishery of salmon and eel at Ballyshannon for this season. Mr Major has my orders by this post not only to give you possession of the fisheries for this season but to take an inventory of the utensils and the vinegar, salt, etc., on hand which belonged to our former partnership now dissolved…'

1277 2 May 1799 Conolly, Castletown, to John Major, Ballyshannon.
He has received Mr Daniel's bills. He asks Major to take over the Belleek fishery on his behalf, and to make the inventory mentioned in no. 1276. He goes on to discuss the re letting of the Ballyshannon estate: 'I have heard from you about the new letting of my land but the bad weather has prevented everything and you are in the right not to hurry and please God the French will be so subdued by the present coalition against them that they will not trouble us any more in this kingdom.

Whenever I go to Ballyshannon I shall certainly go to your mothers but it is upon the express condition that she will let me keep house while I stay there and that she will manage for me…'

1278 17 May 1799 Conolly, Castletown, to John Major.
'I approve of what you have done about the letting of my land and shall be ready to sign leases accordingly when I go to Belleisle and Ballyshannon in the course of next month or July if our politics and my health will permit. I will give at least a weeks notice. Tell your brother Captain Ashford[?] that I am obliged to him for the offer of his house but shall decline the offer. I have recommended you to the Secretary at War Mr Elliot to succeed him as Captain of the Ballyshannon Yeomanry. You will have no invasion this year and I fear the French will do more mischief to Great Britain by going to Lisbon, Cadiz, or the Mediterranean…'

3979/ 1279	16 June 1799	Conolly, Castletown, to Richard Trench. 'If it shall please God suddenly to take me away before I have otherwise provided for my friend Mrs Jennet [Conolly's mistress] I request that you would see the contents of the enclosed codicil fulfilled in the manner best suitable to my affairs. An annuity upon Ballyshannon the least encumbered of my estates, seems the most preferable and I mean that it should be paid to her solely for her own use and not to be transferable to another person, who might by marriage or friend cheat her out of it…'
1280	27 June 1799	John Hood & Co., London to Conolly about payments made on his account.
1281	19 June 1799	John Daniel, Ballyshannon, to Conolly about the need for repairs to Sir John Caldwell's eel weirs.
1282	2 July 1799	A[ndrew] Knox, acting on behalf of Messrs Latouche, to Conolly enclosing his balance.
1283	6 July 1799	John Hood & Co., London, to Conolly about payments due to Latouche's bank.
1284	24 July 1799	John Daniel, Ballyshannon, to Conolly about his lease of the Ballyshannon fisheries. The rent is to be adjusted if the proposed Union takes place.
1285	16 Aug. 1799	J. James, Deputy Receiver, to Conolly about the crown rents due on his house in Whitehall.
1286	16 Aug. 1799	Formal printed notice of the crown rent due, enclosed in no. 1085.
1287	20 Aug. 1797	Henry Vernon, Woodhead, Yorkshire, to Conolly. He has visited Wentworth Castle, where Lady Strafford was still in residence. The butler could not tell him who actually owned the house. Vernon believes Lord Strafford left the estate to Conolly.
1288	27 Aug. 1797	Benjamin Harenc, Footscray Place, to Conolly. 'I lament with you sincerely the alarming state of Lord Ross. He has always been the same towards you. He was a kind and tender husband towards your amiable sister; I saw him so many times since her tender frame called for his gentle attentions and he answered the call. I hope you will not lose him yet. When I saw him last his strength of body was above his years.'…He goes on to describe the Kentish volunteers and his financial affairs.
1289	31 Aug.–28 Sept. 1799	Bill for turnpike and carter's charges.

3979/ 1290	17 Sept. 1799	John Clements, Tunbridge Wells, to Conolly thanking him for sending him two bills and wishing Conolly well in his court case. 'For by what I know of the business I think in justice you certainly should' succeed.
1291	30 Sept. 1799	Sir William Howe [now 5th Viscount Howe], Seymour Place, to Sir Michael Cromie seeking the payment of two years interest due from Conolly.
1292	6 Oct. 1799	Lord Howe, Highfield, to Sir Michael Cromie. He was mistaken in his previous letter; only one year's interest is due.
1293	7 Oct. 1799	Conolly, Castletown, to John Major, Ballyshannon. 'I enclose you a letter from Mr Conolly Coane to whom I have wrote to inform him that I would though contrary to my rule give him a deed for ever of Drimnagrath at the value that you should have put upon it. You will therefore get it surveyed and valued and a lease drawn accordingly...' Enclosed is Conolly Coane's letter from Bath dated 19 Aug. 1799.
1294	14 Oct. 1799	John Daniel, Ballyshannon, to Conolly about the costs of the fishery business and the falling price for cattle.
1295	2 Nov. 1799	John Hughes, Barrack Office, to Conolly about the size of the coal measure used at the barracks in Maynooth, and enclosing affidavits about delivery of coal to the barracks.
1296	6 Nov. 1796	John Daniel, Ballyshannon, to Conolly about the bad market for the salmon.
1297	14 Nov. 1799	Henry Vernon, Hilton Park, Wolverhampton, to Conolly. '...Lady Strafford has gone to live at Henbury [Dorset] and has given up the York, Nottingham and Lincolnshire estates to Mrs Augusta Henrietta Kaye sister of Lady Strafford's late husband, the 3rd Earl], who has taken possession by her servants, but she resides with her husband who is in a dying state at Abbey Park near Edinburgh...' She will probably give no trouble in the Wakefield suit. 'I understand that opinions have been taken and that you seem to have a just right to your grandfather's estates, but you have been by one means or other so shamefully ill-used that I fear you will not succeed to your birthright.'
1298	3 Dec. 1799	Nesbitt & Stewart, London, to Conolly stating their account.
1299	14 Dec. 1799	John Daniel, Ballyshannon, to Conolly about the problems surrounding salvage claims.

3979/ 1300	17 Dec. 1799	Conolly, Castletown, to John Major, Ballyshannon, about arrears of rent due to Trinity College.' I am sorry to inform you that I have had this day a formal complaint from the bursar of the College, Mr Brown by their express command of the backwardness of payment of their rent. Pray rectify this without delay. I thought that the money due for arrears and was kept for that purpose. I must likewise think of an immediate renewal which will cost a great deal...I desired your mother to wish you joy of your intended marriage with Miss Nesbitt.'
1301	21 Dec. 1799	Henry Vernon, Hilton Park, Wolverhampton, to Conolly. He starts by telling Conolly news of various military movements, and his continued desire to visit Ireland when his son gets leave from his regiment. He then moves on to business and Conolly's lawsuit over his Strafford inheritance. He has discovered that the late Lord Strafford did nothing to bar the entail, so the lands settled on the heirs general and on the heirs male will all go one-third each, to Conolly, Vernon and the infant Vyse, not to Mrs Kaye as the heir-at-law. This will be double what they had expected. This applies to the Wakefield copyholds too. He wants the barony of Raby or the earldom of Strafford and 'earnestly begs' Conolly to apply for the title, which will then pass on to Vernon's family. 'I well know title is no object to you, but to me and my family it is, and I think the titles belonging to your ancient family should not be lost for want of a little trouble to establish your right particularly when you call to mind that it cost Thomas 1st earl of Strafford his life. Add to this it will be probable to make Mrs Kaye more inclined to leave you her property.'
1302	N.D. 1799	Patrick Grogan's account with James Clark.
1303	N.D. 1799	Two accounts of Andrew Fawcett for Conolly.

MSS	**DATE**	**DESCRIPTION**
3980/ 1304– 3981/ 1430	**1 Jan. 1800– 23 Apr. 1803**	**Letters, receipts and papers of Thomas Conolly. This section stops at Conolly's death in April 1803.**
1304	1 Jan. 1800	John Toler, Attorney General, to Colonel [Edward] Littlehales. About the trial of three men, John Coyle, George Coyle, and Flanagan accused of robbery and cattle stealing. They are not to be tried as rebels.

3980/ 1305 | 3 Jan. 1800 | [Colonel] Edward Littlehales [private secretary to Lord Cornwallis], Dublin Castle, to Conolly.
'Mr [Alexander] Marsden having laid before the Lord Lieutenant your letter of the 9th instance and its enclosures relative to John and George Coyle and Flanagan, I was directed to refer the same through the regular channel to the Attorney General for his opinion, a copy of which I enclose [no. 1304] and in consequence I am enjoined to mention that His Excellency is concerned that we cannot comply with your request upon this occasion in ordering these offenders to be tried by a court martial.'

1306 6 Jan. 1800 Patrick Sands, 52 Sackville Street, to Conolly about cattle stolen from Lord Leitrim.

1307 9 Jan. 1800 Alexander Lindsay, 107 Grafton Street, to Conolly.
He advises Conolly that he should not attend parliament 'this misty foggy weather' because of his asthma. He encloses a prescription which Conolly should take.

1308 9 Jan. 1800 Mark Napier, Edinburgh, to George?
He details the situation of Mr and Mrs Kaye, who have inherited Wentworth Castle, and are resident in Edinburgh. He does not know whether they will take up residence at Wentworth Castle.

1309 14 Jan. 1800 John Latouche, Dublin, to Conolly.
Declines Conolly's proposal that they should pair off for the Union vote in the House of Commons: '...I am so deeply interested in the business that I cannot reconcile it to my duty to absent myself from the House when the question of a Union may be debated.'

1310 16 Jan. 1800 Benjamin Harenc, Footscray Place, to Conolly.
He wishes him good health and praises Conolly's military activity, before enquiring of Conolly's suit in Chancery. He also refers to the proposed Union: 'I hope the Union you have so much at heart will not meet with the resistance you apprehend. The effect of it will I trust have all the advantages the wisest people I have conversed on the subject expect from it. I remember our friend Woodward's opinion of it. He always thought it the greatest advantage to both countries...'

1311 23 Jan. 1800 Conolly, Dublin, to John Major, Ballyshannon.
'As there is £2,100 short of your acceptance in favour of Mr John Stewart and bills are so doubtful and hard to be had and I am losing the interest, I beg you will be so kind as to pay your guineas to Mr Hamilton at Brown Hall and the advice of such payment will be acknowledged as cash by Mr Stewart...'

3980/ 1312 27 Feb. 1800 Conolly, Castletown, to John Major.
'As I have not heard to the contrary I take it for granted that you have settled with my tenants for the renewal of their leases according to the terms offered last summer. You will therefore bring such leases with you to be perfected when you come up with the new rent roll from May 1799 and 1800. I wish to know what money has been paid to Mr Hamilton of Brown Hall in guineas upon Mr Stewart's account.

Let Mr Daniel know that I am satisfied that he should continue this year upon the same terms as the last for the fishery, but that if the union will please God take place from January 1801 I shall advertise it to be let for a long term from that date unless he and I agree upon terms for such a lease beforehand. Tell him I shall expect bills payable in November and December next upon Dublin merchants to be approved of for this year's rent on or before the first of April next. Let me have his answer and your opinions private upon the terms to be demanded for a lease of 31 years…'

1313 4 Mar. 1800 Arthur Browne, [Bursar], Trinity College, Dublin, about Conolly's leases from the College. The College want £2,000 from Conolly for renewing the leases. He also refers to the union, which he thinks is the best thing 'under the existing circumstances for Ireland.'

1314 8 Mar. 1800 John Hood & Co., London, to Conolly about payments on Conolly's account.

1315 5 Apr. 1800 Lord Howe, Seymour Place, to Sir Michael Cromie about interest payments due from Conolly.

1316 10 Apr. 1800 John Daniel, Ballyshannon, to Conolly about his surrender of the lease of the fishery.

1317 10 Apr. 1800 Lord Londonderry, Mount Stewart, [Newtownards, Co. Down], to Conolly.
'The conversation you have had with Castlereagh respecting the county of Londonderry has been communicated to me and nothing can mark your kind attachment and friendship for me and Charles [Stewart, his second son] than the inclination you have expressed to withdraw from your own situation, the better to assist and facilitate his succeeding in your lifetime to a seat which you have honourably to yourself and satisfactorily to the county so long occupied.

However flattering and important such an object is to a young man it is what neither he nor I would have did we not understand from Castlereagh that you have consulted perfectly your own

3980/1317 *contd.*		convenience. With this impression, we shall avail ourselves of your good intentions and while at the assizes take some steps to sound Mr Beresford and other gentlemen we may meet there, by communicating to them your solicitude and readiness to vacate in his favour should be so fortunate as to meet with general concurrence…'
1318	13 Apr. 1800	John Daniel, Ballyshannon, to Conolly about the fishery at Ballyshannon.
1319	13 Apr. 1800	Samuel Montgomery, Deputy Advocate General, Naas, to Conolly about the trial of a Michael Foley, at which he requests the attendance of Conolly's gamekeeper.
1320	15 Apr. 1800	Samuel Montgomery, Naas, to Conolly about the trial of Michael Foley and the crime committed by a Thomas Talents.
1321	16 Apr. 1800	Edward Littlehales, Dublin Castle, to Conolly about the trial of Foley.
1322	21 Apr. 1800	Conolly, Castletown, to John Montgomery, High Sheriff of Co. Kildare. Copy. 'I am very glad that I shall not be wanted to attend your grand jury. However I would venture that, or anything else, to serve this my native county which I am sorry to see taking an active and a decided part against a legislative Union with the best regulated, most industrious, most loyal and happy nation in the world, and being so absurd from the violence of party, disappointed ambition, or from worse motives such as emoulments produced to individuals by our parliament and the continuance of the dread of fresh commotion which we [ ] keeping up the present enormous military establishment, makes the fortunes of a few agents, bankers and contractors and falls heavy upon the honest and industrious landed proprietors of the kingdom. Pray God grant us Union and peace. To our own parliament I can pay no compliment, and to tell you the truth those that support its existence now are those that have abused its infamy the most heretofore. I always used my poor efforts to preserve its character and thereby its consequence, but finding that in vain I have nearly quit it for ever as well from infirmity as inclination. Make what [use] you please of this letter…'
1323, 24,27	21, 22, Apr., 4 May 1800	Three letters from John Daniel to Conolly about the Ballyshannon fishery and his creditors.
1325	22 Apr. 1800	John Major, Ballyshannon, to Conolly. He is still waiting for Daniel to give up possession of the fishery.

3980/ 1326	26 Apr. 1800	Henry Vernon, Hilton Park, Wolverhampton, to Conolly about his discussions with the late Lord Strafford's servants about the latter's will.
1328	7 May 1800	Two newspaper cuttings featuring Conolly's letter of resignation as MP for Co. Londonderry.
1329	7–30 May 1800	Letter listing Conolly's resignation address and related documents.
1330	8 May 1800	Benjamin Harenc, Footscray Place, to Conolly about Conolly's lawsuit, with his sisters.
1331	9 May 1800	Edward Littlehales, Dublin Castle, to Conolly about the trial of Coyle and Flanagan.
1332	14 May 1800	Copy of a letter from John Daniel to John Major about the fishery.
1333	14 May 1800	[George Townshend, 1st Marquess], Townshend, Weymouth Street, London, to Conolly. 'I cannot deny myself the satisfaction of thanking you for your excellent address to your county which I hope will have its due effect throughout Ireland and make some impression upon the opponents of the measure here, though their disapprobation I believe arose chiefly from that opposition which disappointment for power creates in every ambitious mind. The havoc which the late desperadoes have made in your country, where almost every man of property was obliged to garrison his house, and the devastation which followed it, might have been expected to have recommended a restitution of order and cultivation. The latter I think will result from a frank and cordial communication and intercourse of commerce between both countries, as our parliament wisely rejected the monopolising proposals of some manufacturers here, and our future contests with Ireland will I hope consist only in which shall furnish the best and cheapest for our mutual consumption. A line that your health is better and that Lady Louisa is well, will give me as well as Lady Townshend great satisfaction and believe me, my most worthy friend, that I shall never be so ungrateful as to forget my during my residence in Ireland [as lord lieutenant, 1767–72]…'
1334	17 May 1800	Damaged letter from John Hood & Co. to Conolly stating payments on his account.
1335	17 May 1800	Edward Bulkeley, Dublin, to Conolly seeking payment of outstanding sums of interest.

3980/ 1336	19 May 1800	William Brabazon Ponsonby, MP, to Conolly. He is indignant that Conolly kept him in the dark about resigning his seat for Co. Londonderry and naming [Charles] Stewart as his successor. He wants Conolly to support his son George Ponsonby.
1337	19 May 1800	Conolly to William Brabazon Ponsonby. Copy. He had intended to support Ponsonby's son after the failure of young Staples. But after Conolly's vote on the Union it was impossible to support Ponsonby's son, and this he told [Denis] Bowes Daly a month or five weeks ago. He tells him that 'we are both to honest for politicians, as the world has gone of late years'.
1338	19 May 1800	James Scott to Conolly. He will gladly propose Stewart at the hustings just as he proposed Conolly last time. Stewart's canvas is going well. He laments Ponsonby's 'leaden shafts' against Conolly. Their election address has offended virtually every resident gentleman, since virtually every one signed the address in favour of Union.
1339	19 May 1800	[Colonel the Hon.] Charles Stewart to Conolly. He is confident of success though the contest will be expensive. Spotswood, Conolly's agent, is lethargic and his nephew Brown supports Ponsonby and is seducing Conolly's tenants at Bellaghy. Ponsonby's policy is to try and separate the tenants from their landlords.
1340	20 May 1800	Denis Bowes Daly MP to Conolly. He regarded Conolly's remark about the Ponsonbys being 'Defenders or United Irishmen' as a joke and not as a serious declaration of intent re Co. Londonderry.
1341	22 May 1800	Conolly to Denis Bowes Daly. He did not regard their conversation as 'a loose one' but on the contrary as very explicit. As he never sees Ponsonby, he spoke to Daly as his oldest friend, Lords Londonderry, Ross and Leitrim excepted.
1342	22 May 1800	Charles Stewart, Derry, to Conolly announcing that Ponsonby has declined the contest and thanking Conolly in fulsome fashion.
1343	24 May 1800	Charles Stewart, Londonderry, to Conolly. Praising Conolly's decision to come to Derry, in spite of the warnings of alarmists. Ponsonby has done himself great harm by appealing to tenants against the wishes of their landlords and by paying no calls on gentlemen. 'Old George' has been trying to secure pledges for the next election but without success. Conolly's Muff tenantry were with Stewart to a man; a few of the Bellaghy

3980/1343 *contd.* tenants had been led astray, but were coming round. Conolly's agents Spotswood and Ash could not have done more for Conolly himself.

1344 27 May 1800 John Stewart to John Major enclosing a sketch of his account [not found].

1345 28 May 1800 John Spotswood, Bellaghy, to Conolly.
He will communicate the contents of Conolly's letter to all the freeholders '…which will be very necessary from the reports of Mr Ponsonby's friends and his addresses since the election, one of which I think right to enclose [not found]….'

He vindicates the conduct of his kinsman Alexander Browne. '…I observe the contents of your favour, wherein you say the expense of your tenants who go to Derry to vote for Colonel Stewart is to be paid by you, which I fear you will find a very expensive business, first being desired by Mr Patterson [see no. 1353] to let no expense be wanting and next being ordered three days before we set off to bring twenty the first day into Derry, then the day after to bring the whole, which I brought to Dungiven last Thursday night except a very few, and all that would have gone against you on the whole estate were five disciples of Glendy's in the townland of Ballynacross…,who have all lives renewable forever, and who you may be assured I will have a strict look-out when they come across me, but not one of them can I distress for bog or by making them pay their rent on the day, nor indeed fifty freeholders on the estate.

Some have died since the last registry in '96 and I shall make the first quarter sessions register above sixty freeholders or from that to a hundred.'

1346 28 May 1800 William Brabazon Ponsonby, Dublin, to Conolly pointing out the success of his son George's canvass and asking Conolly to support him once the question of the Union has been decided one way or the other. Conolly has underlined Ponsonby's reference to the 'wonderful encouragement and support' which Ponsonby junior received.

1347 29 May 1800 Amended copy of a letter from Conolly to William Brabazon Ponsonby declaring Conolly's intention of supporting Charles Stewart and a member of Lord Waterford's family at the next general election, and citing as his reasons the expressions in young George Ponsonby's address and the canvassing of Conolly's tenants, which he the more resents because Ponsonby had specifically stated to H[amilton] Ash that all Ponsonby's tenants were to vote for G. Ponsonby. He points out that his intention to resign his seat was a secret, even to the Stewarts, until the night

3980/1347 *contd.* before he made it public; even Lord Waterford knew nothing about it, '...though his steady and uniform attachment to my interests in the county at all times and in all situations of politics entitled him to that information...'. He goes over again the business of the misunderstood conversation with Daly and refers, to the Ponsonby property in Co. Londonderry as 'your late acquisition'. [It had been left to W.B. Ponsonby and his brother George, by their elderly bachelor uncle, the Hon. Richard Ponsonby, who had died earlier that year.]

1348 30 May 1800 Copy of a letter from Conolly to William Brabazon Ponsonby explaining that he has heard from William Burton that Ponsonby has interpreted his address of thanks as a reflection on Ponsonby's public or private character, and denying that this is so.

1349 1 June 1800 William Brabazon Ponsonby, Dublin, to Conolly acquitting Conolly of any intention of reflecting on Ponsonby's character, public or private, but pointing out that this is the general impression which the address has created, and asking Conolly to contradict it publicly.

1350 9 June 1800 John Spotswood, Bellaghy, to Conolly.
'I am honoured with your favours of the 2nd and 4th instant and when you will consider the situation of the country and the independence of your tenants at the election, you will not blame me so much as appearances are against me. I never experienced such distress as the people are in general in, and assure you there are very few on your estate have their bread unbought, and you will not be surprised at it when I can with truth inform you there are but four who live on your estate have above 50 acres of land in their own occupation, and not twenty who occupy 20 acres and the general average of this estate do not occupy more than 7 acres, so you may judge our situation.

The expense attending the election for the people who went from this estate amounts to £196 6s 8d. I took 200 to Dungiven and was obliged to hire carriages, some cars and horses for people who had not horses of their own, were infirm, etc. This I did on the advice of Mr Patterson, who said he would account with me for all expenses, and not to spare any, and indeed I must say our appearance and steadiness being so early in the field put a stop to the election, as did the Bellaghy tenants in the year 1776. I registered 234 freeholders on this estate in May 1796. above 25 are since dead or gone to America, a very few stayed at home and five only went to vote for Mr Ponsonby, whose names, etc, I informed you of. I can I believe now register 100, which I will do next month at the quarter sessions in Magherafelt. Most of your Roman Catholic tenants who you gave lives to would not take the

3980/1350 *contd.*		oath prescribed by the law to enable them to vote, but many came in when they heard you were anxious for Colonel Stewart and offered to take the oaths and I am in hopes I will get all Catholics to register votes in July next. I am well informed Mr Ponsonby's friends near Derry are busy electioneering for him, and from the Marquess of Waterford's state of health a new election for this county appears not a very distant look forward. However, Sir, I fear not that your tenantry on this estate will show the attachment they ever did when called upon by you. I am also informed that copies of a letter from you to old Mr Ponsonby are handing about. However I think I have satisfied your friends in this country how much it was for the advantage of the kingdom your throwing that party off…'
1351	17 June 1800	Brook Bridges, Red Lion Square, to Sir Michael Cromie about Conolly's lawsuit with [the 3rd Earl of] Strafford's executors.
1352	19 May 1800	John Hood & Co. to Conolly about payments on his account
1353	25 June 1800	James Patterson, Ards, [Co. Donegal] to Lord Castlereagh. Denying that he or his brother was responsible for instructing John Spotswood '…to expend nearly 20 shillings a man in one night on 200 freeholders in Dungiven…' and discussing the forthcoming registry of Lord Londonderry's freeholders.
1354	29 June 1800	John Staples, Ballycastle, to Conolly seeking payment of money
1355	30 June 1800	Brook Bridges, Red Lion Square, to Sir Michael Cromie about Conolly's lawsuit with Lord Strafford's executors.
1356	30 June 1800	John Staples, Ballycastle, to Conolly seeking payment of money.
1357	1 July 1800	Andrew Knox on behalf of Latouche's Bank to Conolly about money owed by Conolly.
1358	1 July 1800	John Spotswood, Bellaghy, to Conolly expressing regret at Conolly's dissatisfaction at the level of election expenses. He explains that arrangements for the pubs in Dungiven were made by Colonel Boyle, acting on Colonel Stewart's instructions, and that Spotswood had nothing to do with this, though he will now in company with Boyle endeavour to get the bills reduced. '…I have the vanity to think that I rather deserve some degree of merit for my exertions in bringing them [the freeholders] forward, considering the circumstances of the times and the season, when everyone was busily engaged with their potatoes, flax and barley, and when on account of the scarcity and badness of provender with the greatest difficulty could a horse be procured that was fit

3980/1358 *contd.*		to travel, and assure you there was not a horse my brother and I were masters of were [sic] not employed on the occasion…'
1359	4 July 1800	Sir John Coghill, London, to Conolly about a cure for Conolly's asthma which Coghill has procured the cure from his doctor, who suffered violently from the 'disorder' until he has discovered this cure, which Coghill claims was highly successful. He laments Conolly's departure from parliament, as he had hoped to have Conolly and Lady Louisa annually in London for the parliamentary season.
1360	4 July 1800	General Richard Vyse, Edinburgh, to Conolly. A long letter about the state of Ireland, and his belief that the Act of Union will 'be ultimately productive of national prosperity and happiness'.
1361	5 July 1800	John Spotswood, Bellaghy, to Conolly. 'I have sent you a rentroll of this proportion as it was let in 1734 and November 1779 showing the situation of each lease by the different columns, where they are determinable, the acre of lands, and acres of bog and mountain, are set forth, as also what I think each man ought to give in case of a perpetuity is on paper, and should times alter, I would not be afraid to put £5,000 in your pocket, and not lessen your rentroll £250 per annum. Some places might be fined down, but very few among the number and the principal would be the castle and demesne, the ferry quarter of [?Ballycombs], both Lord Bristol's…' etc. Few of the Roman Catholic tenants (if any) are able to fine down to the rent of the lands granted in 1734. The farms each man occupies are so small, it is impossible for them to be rich, and it is by the linen manufacture all live….'
1362	23 July 1800	Alexander Browne, 159 Great Britain Street, to Conolly giving a detailed breakdown of the election expenses which come to just over £200.
1363	Endorsed July 1800	Lord Castlereagh, [Phoneix] Park, to Conolly about Conolly's resignation of the Londonderry Militia and informing him that he is called 'the father of the Union.'
1364	26 Aug. 1800	John Spotswood, Bellaghy, to Conolly about the distressed condition of his tenants.
1365	7 Oct. 1800	John Daniel, Ballyshannon, to Conolly about the Ballyshannon fishery.

3980/ 1366	12 Oct. 1800	General Richard Vyse, Edinburgh, to Conolly relaying information about Mrs Kaye [Henrietta Augusta Kaye, the 3rd Earl of Strafford's sister and heir-at-law], the other claimant to the Strafford inheritance, who was resident in Edinburgh.
1367	27 Oct. 1800	Jefferys & Gilbert, King's Goldsmiths, London, to Conolly offering him the opportunity to purchase a silver dessert service and some silver dressing plate put up for sale by the Countess of Strafford.
1368	5 Nov. 1800	John Alcock, Murvagh, to Conolly about acquiring a lease of a turf bog on the Ballyshannon estate.
1369	15 Nov. 1800	Edward Bulkeley to Conolly about the renewal of his Trinity College leases.
1370	22 Nov. 1800	Edward Bulkeley, Dublin, to John Major, Ballyshannon about the payment of rent to the College.
1371	24 Nov. 1800	John Major, Ballyshannon, to Conolly about the payment of rent and Mr Talbot's survey of Bundoran, Co. Donegal.
1372	29 Nov. 1800	Draft of a letter from Conolly to Mr [William] Cruise, London about his inheritance. 'How could you think any compromise admissible on my part, when my mother had impeached my character. The law suit must be pushed to an immediate hearing, but it will be impossible to have William Conolly Staples' answer ready by the 6th of next month. The not producing it before then shows the trick and rascality of the business. He having given up his claim in his lifetime and his executors have for him as they made no claim knowing he had given it up. My mother cheated me when she gave me what was my birthright by her marriage settlement conditionally. She restored me to it when she exonerated me from the charge. When she wrote her assertion and published it, she again adhered to her original thought. I have no fear from the assertion of an angry influenced old woman for my character and integrity. I am sure my sisters know she has called them and written them whores except Mrs Byng that she otherwise always abused.'
1373	29 Nov. 1800	Second draft of a letter from Conolly to Cruise, London about his inheritance. 'If my sisters were to offer to compromise the matter for one guinea each I would not consent to it. My mother's attack upon my character makes a public trial necessary and I have no doubt nor fear of the result. My mother first *robbed* me when she gave

3980/1373 *contd.*		me the estates *conditionally* and then a month after she had exonerated me from those conditions she accuses me of *fraud.* Equity will clearly give me up those estates *free*, if the court will only read my letters. I would have given the whole 10,000 [each] to my *sisters* with pleasure when I knew the contents of my mother's settlement, *in the manner most suitable to my affairs.*'
1374	2 Dec. 1800	L. Shiel to Conolly about taking a lease of a farm at Tullygallen near Donegal.
1375	13 Dec. 1800	John Spotswood, Bellaghy, to Conolly promising to use all his influence to get Conolly's tenants to vote for John Beresford and stating his expectations of success. He assumes all election costs will be borne by Conolly.
1376	20 Dec. 1800	John Major, Ballyshannon, to Conolly about the establishment of a rival mill and the renewal of leases on his estate.
1377	1 Jan. 1801	L. Shiel, Ballyshannon, to Conolly about the canal from Lough Erne to Ballyshannon and the excessive duty charged on salted fish.
1378	1 Jan. 1801	[Sir] John Mitford, [later 1st Lord Redesdale], Lincoln's Inns, to Conolly. He would be happy to represent Conolly and 'this day cannot but remind me of the obligations the United Kingdom has to him'.
1379	6 Jan. 1801	John Major, Ballyshannon, to Conolly about Ballyshannon estate affairs. Enclosed are two letters from Dominick McCausland to Major, about the lease of the Belalt portion of the estate.
1380	6 Jan. 1801	Conolly, Castletown, to John Major, Ballyshannon. 'I hope you will be able to come to town with your accounts, leases, lists of arrears and of those tenants who agreed in 1799 for their renewals on the College lands and who are gone off from their bargains, for as I have renewed with the College, I shall not think myself bound to them unless they pay the full rent from the date of the renewal of their leases. Mr Stewart is very impatient for the arrears upon the bills now due and I soon will be obliged to give him some.'
1381	4 Feb. 1801	John Spotswood, Bellaghy, to Conolly reporting that Lord Londonderry and Conolly have now divided the election expenses, each paying £100 11s 2d.
1382	5 Feb. 1801	Edward Bulkeley to John Major, Ballyshannon about payments made on account of interest due on the Conyngham mortgage on Newtown Limavady.

3980/ 1383	14 Feb. 1801	Tim Francillon, banker, London, to Conolly about the overdue payment of bills owed by Conolly.
1384	22 Feb. 1801	William Hamilton Ash, Ashbrook, to Conolly about money owed to him by Conolly.
1385	9 Mar. 1801	John Staples, St James's Coffee House, London, to Conolly about a business involving Mr Hood, the banker, and Staples' fears that Conolly has fallen out with him.
1386	16 Mar. 1801	Copy of a letter from Conolly, Castletown, to his brother-in-law John Staples Referring to '…the attack upon my character on the trial with my sisters…' and discussing Staples' debt to Bishop Woodward which Conolly took on himself because Staples lost his pension during the regency crisis, and which Staples never offered to pay when he was restored to office.
1387	23 Mar. 1801	Staples, London, to Conolly vindicating himself from these charges and pointing out that the payment of the debt of £2,000 had nothing to with the loss of Staples' pension which in any case cost him £3,000, and stating his determination to repay the £2,000 since it now transpires that in spite of Conolly's large fortune, this gift was not made ungrudgingly.
1388	26 Mar. 1801	W. Brebner, Dublin, to Conolly acknowledging the payment of money owed by Conolly.
1389	27 Mar. 1801	George Darby, No. 46 Upper Norton Street, Fitzroy Square, London, to Conolly about money owed to him in his capacity as executor to his father Colonel Darby.
1390	31 Mar. 1801	John Stewart, Dublin, to John Major, Ballyshannon about the remittance of rents.
1391	3 Apr. 1801	Copy of a circular issued by Colonel Morrice, aide de camp to the Lord Lieutenant [Lord Cornwallis] seeking authenticated information from magistrates of outrages committed by rebels in their neighbourhoods since 1 September.
1392	10 Apr. 1801	Copy of a letter from [William Fitzgerald, 2nd] Duke of Leinster to General Needham refusing to act upon no. 1391.
1393	16 Apr. 1801	George Darby, London, to Conolly about his father's annuity.
1394	5 May 1801	Richard Trench, 37 St James's Place, London to Conolly about his dealings with Mr Cruise on Conolly's behalf. The Wakefield copyholds could fetch £50,000 which at the worst means £16,000

3980/1394 *contd.*		to Conolly. The Duke of Leeds could be got to enfranchise them at small additional cost, which would make them sell better. He also refers to his enquiries about purchasing a coach for Conolly.
1395	14 May 1801	Richard Trench, London, to Conolly about a dispute over a boundary with a Mr Bacon on Conolly's estate at Barnet (?). Enclosed is a sketch of the disputed boundary.
1396	19 May 1801	John Spotswood, Bellaghy to Conolly. '…I have received from Messrs Glascock and Blacks Counsellor French's opinion and instructions respecting taking fines and making leases in perpetuity to that part of your estate not let in perpetuity by the late Mr Conolly, which I fear will throw difficulties in the way not easy to persuade the tenant in possession to go through. However, I shall do everything in my power to forward the business, and if anything occurs worth communicating before you return to Ireland, shall inform you. The estate is so thickly inhabited and so many men joined in a lease and the dreadful distresses at least five out of eight have suffered for eighteen months last past, that it has rendered many bankrupts [sic] and numbers obliged to sell part of their farms, many the whole, to keep them and their families from starving…'
1397	30 May 1801	John Spotswood, Bellaghy, to Conolly bout the distressed state of his tenants.
1398	6 June 1801	Richard Trench, London, to Conolly about the value of the Wakefield copyholds which Conolly is trying to sell.
1399	10 June 1801	Captain Medlycott Burroughs, Belfast, to Conolly about attacks on Burroughs's character from within the regiment.
1400	13 June 18801	Richard Trench, London, to Conolly. He has secured the loan of a house in London for Conolly's use.
1401	1 July 1801	Copy of a letter from Conolly to Captain Burroughs. 'You were ordered by me to Kilcock in your tour of duty and I did express myself to you in warmth when you seemed to think I had ordered you there out of turn. What Major Stark has said I know nothing of but through your statement in your letter (no. 1399), but I am certain he is too much of a man of honour to have misstated my words or to have aspersed your character ...'.
1402	4 July 1801	Henry Vernon, Hilton Park, to Conolly congratulating him on his good fortune and hoping it will be 'a forerunner of many much happier events.'

3980/ 1403	9 July 1801	General Richard Vyse, Edinburgh, to Conolly about the Wakefield copyholds.
1404	8 Aug. 1801	Glascock & Black, Conolly's solicitors, York Street, Dublin, to Gilbert Jones, solicitor, Salisbury Square, London informing him that Conolly intends to raise most of the £8,000 due to Lady Howe and charged on his estate, by selling the lands of Cloncuna, Co. Roscommon and Ballynakill, King's County. '…At the rate of purchase paid in this country which is twenty years, calculating only on the rent and four years on the renewal fines payable on the fall of each life, you will find the property to be worth £7,611 1s…'.
1405	8 Aug. 1801	Glascock & Black, Dublin, to Conolly, London about the sale of the estates in Roscommon and King's County and Conolly's success in gaining the rights to the Wakefield copyholds, and enclosing no. 1404.
1406	18 Aug. 1801	J. James, Crown Rent office, to Sir Michael Cromie about the rent owed for Conolly's Whitehall house.
1407	15 Sept. 1801	Conolly, Brighton, to General Vyse, Edinburgh. 'My Dear Vyse, when you look over the will of my maternal grandfather, Thomas Lord Strafford, you will have no doubts that all the Yorkshire property whether freehold or copyhold is mine that was not included in the recovery suffered by the late Lord, Frederick William. And this was the opinion at the time that I wrote to you of Mr Cruise and Mrs Kaye's lawyer, Mr Henry Martin. Mr Bridges had however always wrote me word that it went share and share alike amongst the three. When brought to the point he alleged that though Lord Strafford had not made himself master of [ ] according to the custom of the Manor of Wakefield. These rolls being searched and investigated it turned out that he had done everything requisite. I then thought that I had nothing to do after the commission was confirmed but to pay my fine and to be admitted and had prepared everything accordingly, when Mr Tooker, the Duke of Leeds's steward, wrote me word that I could not be admitted with propriety till the Chancellor had directed not only the amount of the fines payable to the Duke of Leeds but likewise the heirs of those that were to be admitted and that the next term would bring this business to a conclusion. I think this is a lucky circumstance as the lawyers who were fishing for a lawsuit for their own sakes, would endeavour to set the best friends at variance and now the Chancellor might well have the whole case before him. All I wish therefore is that that your lawyer Mr Bridges, or his more proper director, the Master, may join as we have hitherto done with the Duke of Leeds in

3980/1407 *contd.* bringing this matter next term to a conclusion. I have written to the Duke of Leeds's Steward Mr Tooker and to Vernon to this purpose, to which I have no doubt of his agreeing as he has already wished me joy in the handsomest manner [no. 1402], being certain as I am confident you are that I would not infringe for a shilling on any of your rights in favour of my own. I have since added Mr Hargrave's opinion to the others, which my solicitor Mr Jones, Salisbury Square, has orders upon a written order from you to show to Mr Bridges. The completion of what appears to me so simple and plain a business has been made so tedious that I could not write to you in an intelligible manner before. I stay here till the 27th and shall then go to Cleveland Row, London, to Toddington, the 8th of October, and to Yorkshire, both to Wentworth Castle and Wakefield, about the 13th or 14th…'.

1408 13 Sept. 1801 Vulliamy & Son, watchmakers, London, to Conolly about repairs being made to Conolly's 'repeating watch.' He has a number of Irish gentlemen amongst his clients.

1409 15 Sept. 1801 E[llen, CountessDowager] Conyngham, Hitchenden House, High Wycombe, Bucks., to Conolly regarding new arrangements for paying her jointure.

1410 16 Sept. 1801 John Spotswood, Bellaghy, to Conolly about the renewal of a lease on the Bellaghy estate.

1411 16 Sept. 1801 Brook Bridges, Red Lion Square, London, to Conolly about the current status of the various legal cases involving Conolly.

1412 19 Sept. 1801 General Vyse, Edinburgh, to Henry Vernon enclosing a letter from Conolly for Vernon's use.

1413 21 Sept. 1801 General Vyse, Edinburgh, to Conolly about the Wakefield copyholds. Goes on to discuss the state of both Ireland and England.

1414 22 Sept. 1801 Brook Bridges, Red Lion Square, London, to Henry Vernon giving an account of the various suits he has an interest in.

1415 25 Sept. 1801 Henry Vernon to Conolly about the letters he has received from Bridges and Vyse relating to the Strafford lawsuit. He also mentions that his son wishes to become aide de camp to [Lord] Cornwallis, if the latter is to stay in Ireland.

1416 27 Sept. 1801 John Spotswood, Bellaghy, to Conolly about the renewal of leases on the Bellaghy estate.

3980/ 1417	29 Sept. 1801	John Staples, Ballycastle, to Conolly about the Hood business.
1418	1 Oct. 1800	General Vyse, Edinburgh, to Conolly about the Strafford lawsuit.
1419	15 Oct. 1801	Edward Bulkeley to Conolly about payments due on Conolly's account.
1420	22 Oct. 1801	Edward Kivlington, Ossett, near Wakefield, Yorkshire, to Conolly. He wants to buy a copyhold, where he intends to build a house and he includes a sketch of the site in the letter.
1421	16 Nov. 1801	J. James, Gray's Inn Place, to Sir Michael Cromie seeking payment of rent due for Conolly's Whitehall house.
1422	12 Dec. 1801	Henry Vernon, Hilton Park, to Conolly about the Wakefield Copyholds lawsuit.
1423	16 Dec. 1801	Sir Michael Cromie, at Mr Lygons, to Conolly about th lawsuit with Conolly's sisters. He has also dispatched some hops for Lady Louisa at Castletown.
1424	18 Dec. 1801	C. Vernon [brother of Henry], St James's Place, to Conolly about a codicil in Lord Strafford's will pertaining to his family.
1425	19 Dec. 1801	Conolly, Richmond House, London, to Mr Holden regarding his title to the Wakefield Copyholds.
1426	26 Dec. 1801	John Clements, Portland Place, London, to Conolly about money owed to him by Conolly, which he needs to fit out the Royal Charlotte.
1427	n.d. 1801	Copy of a letter from Robert Lumb, Wakefield, to William Cruise, Lincolns Inn about a search he conducted in the court rolls of the manor of Wakefield.
1428	26 Feb. 1802	L.A.C. [Lady Louisa Conolly], Richmond House, to Miss Byng about the dispute between Conolly and his sisters which went on from 1796 until 1800 over their perceived failure to disavow Lady Anne's attack on his character. This dispute has prevented Lady Louisa from writing to Miss Byng.
1429	20 July 1802	Messrs Glascock & Black, Dublin to Conolly about his account with Mr Stewart.
1430	4 Apr. 1802	Bob Balderdash, Blackrock, to Conolly. Poem written by Robert Jephson MP using the pseudonym Bob Balderdash, gently mocking Conolly's health problems.

3980/ 1431	27 Apr. 1802	Conolly, Whitehall, to John Major, Ballyshannon about John Daniel's bankruptcy.
1432	16 Sept. 1802	Poem written by Robert Jephson to Conolly about the latter's sojourn in England and desiring his return to Ireland.
1433	16–17 Nov. 1802	Two further poems; one from Conolly to Jephson and then Jephson's answer, together with the original wrapper which formerly tied them together.
1434	24 Dec. 1802	Conolly, Castletown, to John Major, Ballyshannon about interest payments due to the Archbishop of Cashel [Charles Brodrick].
1435	n.d.	Valuation of the furniture in Wentworth Castle divided into 3 columns titled respectively; Earl Thomas, Earl William and Earl Frederick.
1436	25 Jan. 1803	Edward Cane to Conolly about interest due to Lady Cavan.
1437		*Blank in the sequence*
1438	15 Apr. 1803	Richard Trench, now Lord Dunlo, London, to Conolly about the Strafford lawsuit, which is due before the court of Kings Bench.
1439	23 Apr. 1803	William Cruise, Lincoln's Inn, to Conolly about the Wakefield copyholds lawsuit.

MSS	**DATE**	**DESCRIPTION**
3981/ 1440– 3983/ 1695	**2 May 1803– 2 May 1820**	**Accounts and correspondence of Thomas Conolly's executors, primarily Richard Trench, Lord Dunlo, and Admiral Thomas Pakenham, who took over the management of Conolly's affairs after his death. Most of the correspondence dates from 1803–04 and deals with Conolly's extensive debts. *c.* 150 items. These papers include the following:**
1447	17 May 1803	[Richard] Lord Dunlo, London, to Admiral [Thomas] Pakenham. 'I am glad you have opened the letter addressed to me, which was found in the will. This clears up everything, and shows the poor Squire had never entertained even the most remote intentions of being guilty of such gross indelicacy as to make a gift of £5,000 to his niece, that she should divide it with his concubine. It seems to me from your statement that the codicil and letter are now of no avail, the latter explaining the former and directing it only to be

3981/1447 *contd.*		used in the event of Mrs J[ennet, Conolly's mistress] not being otherwise provided for. Now the bond for £3,000 to you I take to be a subsequent provision, and as such completes the purpose of the codicil and letter…'
1448	20 May 1803	Dunlo, London, to Admiral Pakenham. 'I have carefully perused the letter from Mr C. and the codicil, both relevant to Mrs Jennet, and am fully of opinion, *that the intentions* of Mr Conolly as expressed in that letter and codicil, have been fulfilled by the bond given to you, if this bond, as I believe it does, bears date subsequent to the date of the letter and codicil. There are, however, two awkward circumstances attending this transaction, which if the woman is, as I suspect, a bitch, will probably involve us in a lawsuit with her. First that by the attestation to the codicil itself it appeared that he had actually executed a counterpart of it and delivered it to her, and secondly, that although the letter to me is conditional, the codicil is absolute. I should, however, have no doubt at all of the result of such a suit. That, however, is not the question: the question is, if possible to avoid any suit at all in which her name would become implicated with Mr Conolly's concerns, and thereby more than probably come to Lady Louisa's ears. At present I see no further advice to give on the subject, than that you would carefully put up the original codicil in the letter which contained it and enclosing them in an envelope under your seal and with your initials endorsed, keep them carefully in your possession until we meet. By the bye I perceive that the letter to me is dated June 15 whereas the codicil bears date June 16. Is this fact so, or is it a mistake of yours or Louisa's?'
1457	3 June 1803	Admiral Pakenham, Ballyshannon, to Dunlo. Describing '…all the miseries heaped on me at this damned place, where Conolly has been picking up money by the expedient of promising renewals which we have not now the power to fulfil. The distress arising of many poor people who have borrowed money for these purposes is not to be described; it is heartbreaking to witness it. […] Conolly anticipated by drafts all his income and Lady Louisa will have at least £10,000 of interest to pay with the half year's rent of this estate […] I see no chance of your legacies being ever paid or of Edward [Pakenham's son and Conolly's great-nephew and ultimate heir] having one farthing from the property or Castletown and everything else escaping the creditors. In my mind there will not be enough to pay all except the Wakefield [copyhold estate] sells well and soon.
1462	3 June 1803	Dunlo, London, to John Heywood, Wakefield, about 'the very extraordinary conduct of Mr [Henry] Vernon in taking possession

3981/1462 *contd.*		of Wentworth Castle with his family without any permission either from Lady Louisa Conolly or Mr C's trustees…'. Lady Louisa had decided to sell it to Vernon for the same consideration for which it was received, and if Vernon refused, to shut it up and let the land.
1468	15 June 1803	[Charles Lennox 3rd Duke of] Richmond, Whitehall, to [his sister] Lady Louisa Conolly.about her husband's debts to his sisters. Lord Howe and Conolly's sisters have agreed to reasonable terms regarding the payment of the £30,000 plus interest. The Bedford estate is subject to a mortgage to Mr Christie for £10,000.
1571, 1576	13 Dec. 1803; 8 Jan. 1804	Two letters from Simon Armstrong, Tootheville, Manor Hamilton, Co. Leitrim, to Admiral Pakenham. He will buy Conolly's estate in Leitrim for 22 year's purchase. He seems to be acting on behalf of Luke White, of Woodlands, Co. Dublin.
1593	20 Feb. 1804	Dunlo, London, to Admiral Pakenham. On '…the supposition of Luke White's purchasing the [King's County], Leixlip, Leitrim and Limavady estates there will still remain a debt… of £131,774…' [White, the father of the 1st Lord Annaly, in the end only purchased the Leitrim estate.]
1609	30 May 1804	Colonel Richard B. Harcourt, London, to Dunlo. His £10,000 mortgage on the Vintners' Proportion (Bellaghy) is at 6%.
1619	May 1805	Half year rental of the Conolly estate in Co. Leitrim. [The half year's rent was £136, so at 22 years purchase it fetched £5,984.]
1634	15 Sept. 1808	Counsel's opinion re. Leitrim lands of Boynay, Ardfarne etc., sold to Luke White. They adjoin the College lands of Bundrows, Co. Donegal, and the tenants of the latter had customary rights on the Leitrim lands. See nos. 1571–6 above.
1653	5 Feb. 1814	Gilbert Jones, Salisbury Square, London, to Lady Louisa. The Duke of Leeds is to receive £10,560 for 'accommodations' re. the sale of the Wakefield copyholds.
1671	1817	Statement of what the residuary legatee of the Dowager Countess of Strafford, Rev. Robert F. Gould, is entitled to out of Wakefield since 1799: £7,779.

3981/ 1683	23 June 1818	John Boodle, Brook Street, to Lady Louisa. The late Viscountess Howe's fortune of £8,000 remains unpaid, as also a bond debt of £3,000 from Conolly to her.

MSS	DATE	DESCRIPTION
3983/ 1696– 1717	**11 Feb. 1822– 7 May 1847**	**Letters, receipts and accounts of Edward Michael Conolly, formerly Edward Pakenham, eldest son of Admiral Thomas Pakenham and Louisa Staples, Thomas Conolly's niece, who inherited Castletown upon the death of Lady Louisa Conolly in 1821, and in accordance with the terms of Thomas Conolly's will took the name Conolly.**
1696– 1698j	11 Feb. 1822– 31 Mar. 1826	Fifteen bills and receipts for household expenditure including one hotel bill for Admiral Thomas Pakenham.
1699– 1703	5 Mar.–26 July 1827	Six letters about a legacy due to Thomas Staples from Thomas Conolly. The correspondents include Edward Conolly, [Richard] Lord Clancarty and Thomas Staples.
1704	20–27 May 1828	Bill from Cooke & Minchin, Lucas & Co. for Colonel Edward Conolly for carpeting.
1704a	21 Oct. 1828	John H Smith, Elphin, to the Conolly trustees about head rent due to them from the representatives of the late Edward Simpson.
1705	23 Jan. 1829	Copies of five letters written by Colonel [William] Gossett private secretary to the Lord Lieutenant, the [1st] Marquess of Anglesey certified to be correct by Sackville Lambart, Chief Secretary's office, about the livings of Celbridge Co. Kildare and Kilbarron, Co. Donegal. One Letter is addressed to Colonel Conolly, while the others are addressed to Lord Cloncurry, John Hely Hutchinson and Rev. Walter Burgh (two letters).
1706	23 Jan. 1829	Rev. Walter Burgh, Celbridge to Colonel Conolly about the disputed livings of Celbridge and Kilbarron.
1707	12 May 1829	[General John Byng [Thomas Conolly's nephew, (a younger brother of George Byng of Wrotham Park), currently serving as Commander of the Forces in Ireland], Dublin, to Colonel Conolly about the agency for the Rathfarnham estate.
1708	12 May 1829	[Richard Trench, formerly Lord Dunlo, now 2nd Earl of] Clancarty, Dublin to Colonel Conolly about the agency for the Rathfarnham estate.

3983/ 1709	26 June 1829	Return of the plate belonging to the Donegal Militia inspected and repacked in a chest with two hanging locks in Ballyshannon for the purpose of being deposited in the Bank of Ireland.
1710	13 May 1831	G.V. Hart, 54 Harley Street, London, to Colonel Conolly. Asking him to stand for parliament for Co. Donegal. 'My dear Colonel Conolly, I do not recollect to have ever enjoyed more gratification than your most kind letter of the 29th of last month (after having seen my son George, I hope, at Castletown) has ever since afforded me. Had I however suspected what is this morning confirmed to me, that our friend Sir James Stewart does not offer himself a candidate for our county in conjunction with Sir Edmond Hayes, as you mentioned to me, and as I had reason to hope and to believe he would not flinch from offering himself to us, I should have hesitated in writing my last letter, and rather have ventured to spend my last breath in the service of such minds as yours and in the service of our most deservedly respected county, as well as our country at large. My dear Colonel if it be possible can you offer yourself? To prevent any improper person to succeed? You could at any moment almost afterwards obtain the "Chiltern Hundreds" and secure to us some person of your proper choice and otherwise eligible to succeed you...'
1711	13 Oct. 1831	Redmond? O'Neill, 9 Lincoln Place, London, to Major General Shortall about his health and making reference to the loss of the Reform Bill. [The Conolly connection is unclear.]
1712	29 Dec. 1831	Lord Clancarty, Garbally, [Ballinasloe, Co. Galway], to Colonel Edward Conolly. 'My dear Ned, I received yours of the 26th instant this morning and hasten to assure you that I can perceive no possible objection to the increase of income it mentions, according to the amount, and method, you have proposed. It would be well indeed for all trustees if their [cesticque?] trusts were like you. You have therefore my full consent and approbation for your execution of your very reasonable desires. We wish you had come here in person to have negotiated your object. If I had been wise I should have made difficulties and then you must come and explained them away. However if you will now come, the favour will be greater, as it will then be voluntary and not a compulsory visit.... Endorsed by Thomas Pakenham: 'I agree to the increase of allowance of £1,000 a year as proposed by Colonel Conolly and agreed by Lord Clancarty.'
1712a	1 Nov. 1834	Receipt from William Pakenham to Sir Thomas Pakenham

3983/ 1713	4 Jan. 1838	Samuel Law, Clare St., to Colonel Conolly about the late Sir Thomas Pakenham's account with Messrs Hallet, Robinson & Child & Co., London.
1713a–c	2–6 May 1838	Three letters from the Duke of Wellington to Colonel Conolly making an appointment to discuss the Poor Law Bill.
1714	5 May 1841	Edmund Davy, Professor of Chemistry, Royal Dublin Society, to Henry Hamilton about a chemical examination of ore from Conolly's Donegal estate.
1715	8 Jan. 1845	[General John Byng, now 1st] Lord Strafford [of a new creation] to Colonel Conolly about the sale of some jointly owned property (not specified).
1716	12 Sept. 1846	Benjamin H. Holmes, Glenties, Co. Donegal, to Colonel Conolly expressing his views on the existing constabulary force for the protection of the transmission and storage of India corn and meal.
1717	7 May 1847	Richard Cane, Dawson Street, [Dublin], to Daniel Simmonds, Conolly's agent, about interest payments.

MSS	**DATE**	**DESCRIPTION**
3983/ 1718–35	**1849–1900**	**Letters and papers mainly of Thomas Conolly (1823–76) eldest son of Colonel Edward Conolly, who succeeded his father as head of the Conolly family upon the latter's death in 1848 including letters from his brothers Arthur, John, and Richard describing their travels across the British Empire. [Most of Thomas Conolly's papers have not survived, and his diaries are to be found in the Castletown Papers and in a private collection (q.v.).]**
1718	28 Jan. 1849	[George Villiers, 4th Earl of] Clarendon, [Lord Lieutenant of Ireland], Dublin Castle, to Sir George Grey [2nd] Bt., [The Home Secretary] about the need to extend the suspension of the Habeus Corpus Act.
1718a	5 July 1851	Arthur W. Conolly, Argostoli, Cephalonia, Greece, to his brother, Thomas Conolly. He wants to exchange his commission and is planning a voyage in the Eastern Mediterranean.
1719	27 Apr. 1853	Motion for debate on the income tax in the House of Commons.

3983/ 1720–24	7, 11, 13, 26 Oct. 1853: 16 June 1854	Five letters about the construction of gasworks at Castletown.
1725	15 Apr. 1855	Sermon preached at Celbridge on Colossians, 3.1.
1725a	24 Apr. 1856	Thomas Conolly, 19 Hanover St., London, to Mr Legh. 'My dear brother Arthur sent home just before the Battle of Inkerman his swordknot which he wished to have conveyed to Miss Wright. I have therefore had it enclosed in a bracelet of suitable [ ] bearing his name inside and the date. The bracelet is now ready and it would be a great satisfaction to me to have it conveyed safely to Miss Wright and there is no one else who could do me this kind service so well or as suitably as you. May I therefore beg you to say where I can leave it for you in London and I trust in your goodness to permit Miss Wright to know the respectful and deep regard with which I offer to her this small tribute of my dear brother's memory and affection.'
1726	13 Dec. 1856	Teague Gallagher to Thomas Conolly seeking the post of chief boatmen at Killowen, Carlingford, Co. Down for his brother-in-law, Francis Cunney.
1727	4 July 1857	Statement of Lord George Hill, Mr Nixon, Mr W. Olpherts, Mr Stewart of Ards, Mr Stewart of Horn Head, Mrs Russell and Mr Woodhouse proprietors in the 'now disturbed' Gweedore, Co. Donegal. 30 pages.
1728	7 Jan. 1860	J[ohn Augustus] Conolly, St Petersburg, to Thomas Conolly about his elk hunting exploits and a parade of 30,000 troops before the emperor at the Winter Palace in St Petersburg. Incomplete.
1729	4 Dec. 1862	James Howard, Office of Woods, etc., London, to Thomas Conolly about the reclamation of lands along the shore in Co. Donegal.
1730	19 Aug. 1863	Thomas Conolly, Aux Quartiers Imperiales, Camp de Chalons, France, to Harry? containing a description of the camp, and his breakfast with Emperor Napoleon III.
1731	18 May 1866	Richard Conolly, Hotel des Ambassadeurs, Cairo, to 'Jack' [John Augustus Conolly describing his voyage from Malta to Cairo.
1732	14 June 1866	Richard Conolly, Pavillion, Kandy, to 'Tom' Conolly describing his voyage from Malta to Ceylon via Egypt.

3983/ 1733	10 Nov. 1866	Richard Conolly, Peking, China, to 'Tom' Conolly. 'Your letter did my heart good. Thank God a sale of the portion of the property will set you right. That infernal word "sale"! I hope and trust that from this on it will be banished from our family vocabulary. Your account of poor Uncle Bo[?] is indeed pitiable but even he is better off than the Pope, Austria and the Irish Church. What a lucky fellow I am to be out here, safe from the risk of being shelved by Bismarck's sweeping annexations! His campaign in February is the finest thing since the 100 days. Even his old friend the Emperor had to kowtow as we say here, before him! Life here is certainly [ ] but nevertheless very interesting. What with Chinese and our own work the day is not half long enough. I have had but one disappointment and that is the stories about sporting are all myths. The distances are too great for sport, and expeditions of any duration are too expensive to be repeated often. My Chinese teacher with the curiosity which characterises his race, is always corking me about Bismarck and his [ ] gun. This last he cannot understand so what I will explain it to him. This is not to be wondered at here where a gun requires two men, one to carry it and one to fire it off. If the weapon does not burst the operation of loading takes about twenty minutes if done rapidly. Our winter has begun with a vengeance, heavy snow and hard frost will soon shut us out from the civilised world till February. We shall be thrown on our own resources for amusement, but as we have a bowling alley, a fives court, a gymnasium, a billiard table and a skating pond within the legation we are not much to be pitied. …'
1734	1884–5	Account of Mrs [Sarah Eliza] Conolly's jointure for three years
1735	23 July 1900	Message of sympathy from the inhabitants of Celbridge to Mrs Sarah Eliza Conolly, 'Tom' Conolly's widow, on the death of her eldest son Thomas in the Boer War. Amongst the signatories is the Catholic parish priest.

MSS	DATE	DESCRIPTION
3984/ 1736– 1923	1733–1804	**Mostly undated letters and accounts which derive mainly from Thomas Conolly (1738–1803). Because they were, or appeared to be, undated, they were kept separate in the original TCD list, which is arranged in strict chronological order. Attempts have been made to date them, where possible, but their original order has been retained.**
1736	26 Mar. 1777	George Ash, Mrs Walshe's, 144 Abbey St, Dublin, to Conolly stating accounts.

3984/ 1737 [c.1730s] Part of an incomplete draft marriage settlement between Ralph Babington and Rebecca Scanlan with counsel's corrections.

1738 [Dec. 1780] B[eauchamp] Bagenal to Conolly about his son's proposed marriage to Miss Byng, Conolly's niece, and his problems raising a sufficient dowry.
[See no. 706 above.]

1739 c.1778 W. Brooks to Conolly about his accounts with Brooks' banking house.

1740 [Nov. 1800] Dr Arthur Browne, Trinity College Dublin, to Edward Bulkeley about the renewal of Thomas Conolly's College leases.

1741 24 Aug. [1785] Lord Buckinghamshire, Blickling, to Conolly.
Dear Brother, your respected attention after so long a silence is flattering to me. From the very commencement and, still more, during the progress of the now departed bill [the Commercial Propositions], it was my firm opinion that the consequential catastrophe would be just that which we experience. The prevailing idea is that Mr Pitt must sink under the decided proof of his ignorance and indiscretion, especially as, from the very beginning of his administration, he has [not] brought forward any one measure in which he has not been more or less disgraced, yet there is a glorious persevering spirit in the Closet which may determine him to weather even this storm.
Lord Belmore arrived here yesterday with his son who is a most pleasing boy. Every day increases my concern at Harriet having separated herself from so amiable a husband. This place is in high beauty but has never again been so cheerful as during the short period when you and Lady Louisa enlivened it.
I am entirely out of political intelligence, but can assure you of one pleasing circumstance, the unprecedented influx of money into this country which has still increased for the last six months Bills are now discounted in London at 4½ %

1742 [1780] Lord Buckinghamshire, Dublin, to Conolly.
He wants Conolly to secure the support of the independent gentlemen for his policy.

1743 Dec. [1776] Lord Buckinghamshire, London, to Conolly
'I have a thousand things to say to you and very little time to express them. You must therefore excuse my bringing them into so small a compass as possible. I am fully sensible that Ireland has been too little attended to and to the real disadvantage of this country, nor do I know any event which would give me such real satisfaction as to be the happy minister of measures which might

3984/1743 *contd.* tend to the permanent advantage of both countryies. I must however avoid dwelling upon a subject where very little is in my power. The man you mention may do much and he knows how happy it would make me to cooperate with him. You will have heard of my secretary, I will say nothing but that he is in affluent circumstances and too honourable, too honest and too disinterested a man to disgrace my choice. I some thoughts of appointing Mr [Henry] Meredyth a gentleman who has been particularly recommended to me, to be the under secretary, but as this is not determined you will keep it to yourself till it reaches you from other hands. I who with pleasure accepted the use of the house now Lord Harcourt's [St Wolstan's, Celbridge], as it is luckily so very near you then offer to embrace you at Castletown, Mr Gardiner came to London this morning who did the honour of presenting himself unexpectedly at my levee; from the character I have heard of him nobody would have made a better first minister to a lord lieutenant. It gives me great pleasure to hear that the present state of the treasury will make it unnecessary to come to parliament with new demands, and I must hope that some allowance may be given to a man who from the circumstances which have attended the preceding administration has less to give than those who went before him. Sir John Blaquerie has done me the honour to attend my levee, but nothing past between us but great civility. Queen Caroline [Lady Buckinghamshire] descends from her dignity to love you and says that if the running footmen are ready for her majesty's arrival in July she shall be satisfied…'

1744 17 Sept. 1789 Caroline [Countess of] Buckinghamshire, Conolly's sister, to Conolly about the sale of Stretton.

1745 c.1764 Edward Bulkeley to Conolly about the value of leases on his Co. Meath estates.

1746 4 June [1781–96] William Burton, Slane Castle, to Conolly seeking Conolly's cooperation in road building at Lettermacaward and the Rosses, Co. Donegal.

1747–1752 [1781] Six letters from William Burton to Conolly about Limavady Corporation and Conolly's inheritance of the estate and borough under the terms of Speaker Conolly's will and following the death, childless, of Burton's uncle, Lord [Henry] Conyngham .

1753 Feb. 1789 George Byng senior to Conolly about the King's health and its implications. He wants to get his son George out of the army. He also refers to Lord Edward Fitzgerald, who is in Quebec.

3984/ 1754	[c. 1784–5]	Signed memorial of the calico printers of Dublin to the Lord Lieutenant, [Charles Manners, 4th] Duke of Rutland for some reward for Thomas Harpur of Leixlip who has invented a new machine for printing on calico and linen. [See no. 1778]
1755	[c. 1790]	Major Hugh Cairncross to Conolly about his sons army career, which he owes to Conolly's patronage.
1756	23 July [1744]	P. Cashell to Katherine Conolly. About the secret marriage of Miss [Jane] Gore, Sir Ralph Gore [4th Bt]'s daughter to Mr [Chidley] Coote whose mad father lodges at Mr Tipper's within 2 miles of Castletown. Endorsed with a letter from Katherine Conolly to Lady Anne Conolly. 'My dear daughter Lady Anne, I am 2 letters in your past and when I rose this morning I was fully resolved to write to you but so many people came in and so much distress I could not, and I go this evening to Castletown with poor Sir St George Gore [5th Bt], he has got an addition to his trouble which grieves me so. Farewell god bless you. Your Mr Conolly is very well; he stays in town till Saturday. I am most affectionately your dear madam Katherine Conolly.
1757	7 Mar. 1780	H[enry] T[heophilus]. Clements, MP, Longford, to Conolly. Lord Buckinghamshire's failure to do him small favours has injured his interest in Co. Leitrim.
1758	[Spring 1777]	H.T. Clements to Conolly asking him to act as Clements's security as deputy vice treasurer.
1759	[pre 1784]	Robert Clements, MP, Killadoon, to Conolly about Mr Pierce Simpson's proposals for lands in Co. Leitrim.
1760	[1781?]	Memorial of William Coane of Celbridge to Conolly. He wants his rent of Ballycreagh and Ballycullen reduced.
1761–62		1733–4 Two letters from William Congreve, Grange Court, [Staffordshire], to William Conolly junior about the purchase of Stretton Hall.
1763	[1860s?]	J[ohn]. A[ugustus] Conolly, Celbridge, to [his brother] 'Tom' about a hunt in Co. Kildare.
1764	[post 9 Aug. 1780]	Thomas Conolly to Lord [Buckinghamshire], in reply to no. 675 'You cannot doubt the sincerity of my wishes not only for the prosperity of this kingdom but likewise for the credit of your administration. But I own a perpetual army bill staggers me much

3984/1764 *contd.*		especially as I was one of those that never saw the necessity of any, wishing this kingdom and its army at all times to be considered as part of Great Britain's at least in everything that could add to their mutual strength. I always cursed the introduction of the bill, and if it now passes in its present state, which is giving such an additional power to the Crown more to be dreaded by even an Englishman than an Irishman it must certainly be understood, that for the future their parliament will vote no money unless the perpetuity is taken off and the bill to go always hand in hand for the time which the money and troops are granted. This strikes me upon consideration as the only political salve for the very disagreeable situation our wise men here have brought us into, and in my conscience I think they may deserve to be reduced to the alternative of either having an army kept here in defiance of them, or having a perpetual mutiny bill. Though there may be true wit in the minister that sent it, I dread very fatal consequences from it, and it is hard to punish the kingdom for the misbehaviour of a few individuals. As it is now plain that the minister has dared give as a mutiny bill without the leave of the parliament of England why then not give us a constitutional one? These are my personal sentiments and what I wish to throw out in the House unless I see cause to alter my opinion and which I mean to talk over with you when we meet either this morning or on some other day….'
1765	Aug. 1779	Conolly, writing in his capacity as governor of the county, to Mr Fanning, Dublin. See also NLI Conolly Papers, MS 41,341/6/3 John Paul Jones has appeared off the Co. Londonderry coast with six frigates.
1766	[Autumn]1789	Conolly to Lord [Buckinghamshire] about the sale of Stretton, and the terms of his father's will.
1767	26 Feb. 1802	Conolly to John Staples. about Mr [John] Boodle's [his late mother's solicitor] variable advice regarding the sale of the Bedfordshire estate.
1768–1768a	1733–4	Two copies of a letter from William Conolly junior to John Jacob about leases [probably on the Rathfarnham estate].
1769	10 Jan. [1780?]	Mrs Crew, Dungannon, to Thomas Conolly seeking to borrow money. She is not personally known to Conolly, but appeals to his charity on basis that 'you protect orphans, feed the hungry and cloth the naked'.
1770	[1780s?]	Bill from John Ferns, 44 Abbey Street to Conolly for wine.

3984/ 1771	[c.1798]	Anonymous but believed to be from Charles Lionel Fitzgerald to Conolly about the sale of [George Robert] Fitzgerald's lands to pay for his daughter Miss Mary Anne Fitzgerald's [d.1794] legacies. 'Sir, having been in the Four Courts a few days ago and in conversation with some of the most eminent lawyers I heard that the sale of Mr Fitzgerald's lands is nearly concluded to pay the legacies of [your] niece. As your friend I can't help telling that the eyes of the public and particularly the respectable part of the public is on your conduct with respect to this gentleman. Remember your niece was his also and that she lived in your house and as might rationally be expected was under the immediate control of her aunt and you. She died at Castletown and makes a will but never signs it in which she leaves her entire fortune to you and your relatives – nay even leaves her nurse £500 – but passed by all her other uncle's [Fitzgerald] family except indeed by leaving his daughter her cousin a watch valued at the utmost thirty guineas. A third part of this gentleman's property is sold to discharge the debt and in every way he is put to an enormous expense to convey the titles. He has a family. Consider then Sir whether the world will not form a very unfavourable opinion of you if you don't do something handsome on the occasion. The character you have held hitherto coined will lose considerably in the estimation of the public as I assure you it is the conversation of the whole town and even your friends consider it a great hardship on the part of Mr Fitzgerald's family. From a friend.'
1772	[*c.* 1784]	[George Robert] Fitzgerald to Conolly. Defending himself against the charges laid against him in the public newspapers including accusations that he kept his father in confinement.
1773	[Post 1803?]	Petition of Louisa Foley, wife of James Gallagher, a discharged soldier, to Lady Louisa Conolly.
1774		Mr Gay's claim for deduction of his rent for Collinstown, Co. Kildare.
1775	[1778?]	William Grueber to Conolly about losses on his lease.
1776		Miss Hamilton to Lady Louisa Conolly seeking money.
1777	May–July 1769	Benjamin Harenc to Conolly about Lord Kerry's proposal to sell his lease of the estate he had sold to Harenc.
1778	[1784–5]	Thomas Harpur's petition to the Irish House of Commons to make his inventions known to his fellow cloth printers. [See no. 1754]

3984/ 1779	14 Oct. [1780?]	Sir William Howe, Seymour Place to Conolly thanking him for three letters.
1780	[1758?]	Petition of Denis Kelly and Joshua Lumley etc., tenants in Celbridge demanding the use of a market house and expressing grievances over tithes.
1781		Petition of Archibald Kerr of Terrydremont, Limavady to Conolly about his bargain with a John Smith about a bleach green.
1782–88	[*c.* 1782–5]	Nine memoranda from Richard King, Mulkeeragh, Limavady about his troubles and Conolly's Limavady estate.
1789–90	1799	Two sets of accounts from Dominick McCausland for Conolly relating to the late Lady Anne Conolly's jointure.
1791	[1783?]	Petition from John Martin, Culmore, Co. Londonderry, to Conolly concerning a dispute about his land.
1792	[1783?]	John Martin, Culmore, to Richard King about the same dispute.
1793	24 Sept. 1790	Mr Miller, 70 Great Georges St, to Conolly about an expedition to Ballyshannon.
1794		Petition of Cornelius Molony, a labourer wrongfully imprisoned for assault, to Conolly. [Damaged]
1795	6 Oct. 1789	Edward Monckton, Somerford, to Conolly about the sale of Stretton.
1796	29 May [1780s?]	Hamilton Moore, Trinity College Dublin, to Conolly seeking his intercession with the Provost over some disciplinary matter.
1797	July 1777	Apollos Morris to Mr John Allen enclosing a letter to Sir William Howe. Copy endorsed with cipher and other notes. [See also nos. 477, 479 and 484.]
1798	July 1777	Apollos Morris to [General Cuyler] a member of Sir William Howe's 'family'. Seeking an acknowledgement of his letter to the general. 'As you are the only person of Sir William Howe's family with whom according to my information I have the pleasure of being acquainted I beg leave through you to have the herewith enclosed transmitted and an answer from yourself if any letter from me to General Sir William Howe has been delivered. Having no intimation of its receipt I apprehend some miscarriage or misconstruction; for though I must look on an answer as a great condescension I do suppose the General on such a subject will despise etiquette. …'

3984/ 1799	July 1777	Very rough draft of a letter from Apollos Morris to the American Congress vindicating his conduct in attempting to mediate between Howe and Washington..
1800	1777	Cover of a letter addressed to Major Apollos Morris afterwards used to wrap his American correspondence.
1801	21 Aug. 1779	*On Irish complaints against English restrictions with a summary of the circumstance of the Irish and the means to better them.* By A[pollo] M[orris] for the Rt. Hon. Thomas Conolly MP. 13 pages. Formerly enclosed in no. 596.
1802	9 Aug. 1779	*Hints in respect to the defence etc… of Ireland.* For Thomas Conolly by Apollos Morris. 20 pages. Formerly enclosed in no. 595
1803		*Blank in the sequence*
1804	[1780s]	Christopher Nicholson, Stephens Green, to Conolly. He has sent hounds for Conolly's use to Mellifont Park near Drogheda.
1805	post 16 June 1780	Petition of Jonathan Pasley to the Governors of the Kildare Infirmary seeking to be restored to his position as steward of the infirmary, to which he was elected on 16 June 1780.
1806	27 Oct. 1775	[General] W[illiam]. A[ugusus]. Pitt, Commander in Chief in Ireland, Queen St., London, to Conolly. I have deferred answering your kind letter in hopes every day, to have some news from our friend Howe to send you, that my letter might be more acceptable. But no accounts are come since the 21st of August. It is supposed that our troops are to evacuate Boston judging it to be an improper situation for them to winter at with our enemy surrounding them, and to take possession of Rhode Island or some other place to the southward. We are waiting with impatience for the account of this movement which must be attended with some difficulty. Government seem determined to carry their point, to which purpose more troops are ordered to be in readiness and Howe will have a powerful army under his command next spring. Great debates in both Houses yesterday on the King's speech, the Commons sat till near 5 o'clock the division was 278 to 108. Lord Townshend moved for the address in the House of Lords and Mr [John Dyke] Acland in the Commons. Lord Shelburne, Lord Lyttleton and the Duke of Manchester spoke well on the side of opposition. The Duke of Grafton also spoke and voted with the minority. General Conway spoke well on the side of the opposition in the Commons. At the close of the debate Lord

3984/1806 *contd.*		North threw out that it was intended to send over a commission to America with powers to treat, and to offer terms of reconciliation to the colonies and (as Lord Gower said in the House of Lords) they are to go with the sword in one hand and the olive branch in the other. I hope the terms will be such as the Americans ought to accept of, and that a reconciliation may take place before more blood is shed. I am much obliged to you for your account of your Curragh meeting. I am sorry poor surveyor was beat by poor riding. Had he won it would have been a glorious meeting for you. I hope we are to see you soon in England, we have been hunting in Hampshire for a fortnight. I am now in town for a few days to kiss hands for the Carbineers which possibly you have heard that His Majesty has done me the honour to appoint me colonel of. This will probably occasion us another visit to Ireland next spring. Mrs Pitt desires her love to Lady Louisa, Lady Sarah and yourself...'
1807	[1771 onwards]	Clotworthy Rowley, MP, to Conolly recommending Rev. James Whiteside, dissenting minister of Tobermore, Co. Londonderry, as a good tenant.
1808	10 June 1777	E[dward] Sandford, Southampton, to Conolly about a mortgage.
1809	*c.* 1781	General Robert Sandford, Carton Cottage, [Maynooth, Co. Kildare], to Conolly seeking a government job.
1810	Dec. 1776	Robert Sandford to Conolly about Sir John Blaquiere, Chief Secretary, and government jobs. He refers to the case of a Colonel Brown who wanted to sell out when the 28th was ordered to America.
1811	30 May [1780?]	Mrs L. Shepherd to Conolly thanking him for the pension for herself and her children.
1812	*c.* Apr. 1761–c. Apr. 1763	Petition of Alice Starrat [widow of the surveyor William Starrat?] to the Lord Lieutenant, the [2nd] earl of Halifax. She was left destitute by her husband whose property passed to his heirs at law and therefore seeks charity.
1813	[post May 1800]	James Stewart [of Killymoon, Co. Tyrone], Clare St., [Dublin], to Conolly seeking to reconcile Conolly with [W.B.] Ponsonby [Stewart's brother-in-law] after Conolly's and Ponsonby's quarrel over the Co. Londonderry by-election.
1814	[1780–82]	Petition of Catherine Stuart, widow of Thomas Stuart, to the lord lieutenant, the earl of Carlisle for charity. Her husband, a sergeant, served with distinction at Fontenoy and Dettingen.

3984/ 1815	16 June [1780?]	Lord Tyrone to Conolly seeking a meeting.
1816	[*c.* 1759–83]	Agmondisham Vesey, MP, to Conolly about a debt of £500 he owes Conolly.
1817	[1781 onwards]	Petition of James & George Wilson, Abraham Scott and Samuel Anderson of Lower Corndale, Limavady, seeking a reduction in their rent due to flooding on the River Roe.
1818	1804	B.B. Woodward, Cavan Regiment, Nenagh, to one of Conolly's executors about a debt by Conolly's estate.
1819	1799	A child [Emily Napier?]'s letter to her brother [Thomas George Napier?] describing the time of the 1798 rebellion in Celbridge. Incomplete. '…we have not forgot that you were a good little fellow and I hope you continue good, I think you will be glad to hear all about your friends which I will write because your father has no time. He is very well but a little old and greyheaded. Your sister is well at service in Dublin. The rebellion was a sad thing for many a poor innocent man was killed by villains on both sides, for Orangemen and United Men are both bad and destroy poor Ireland and between these rogues all honest men suffer but Lord Cornwallis has saved Ireland. He beat the French. He pardoned the rebels that were sorry and he punished the Orangemen that were cruel!… Papa [Colonel George Napier] and Charles [Napier] built a fortification in Celbridge against the rebels and they never have dared to set their feet in it since. Uncle Conolly's regiment is here now. It is the Londonderry Militia. Your father gives you his blessing and hopes you are a good by. The maids send their love to you. Papa, Mama and brothers will want to know how you like the 10th and if you are happy…
1820	25 June [1786]	Letter describing a hunting party at Leinster Lodge.
1821	[1779]	Part of a letter from John Staples seeking a government job?
1822–31	*c.* 1779–84	Ten papers relating to the Castletown Union Volunteer Corps including details of reviews by the Duke of Leinster and a weekly return of the members of the Castletown Corps attendance.
1832	[1767–9?]	Abstract of the proposed augmentation of the army.

3984/ 1833	1782	Note of the Loughlinsholin Battalion's desire to accede to the Dungannon resolutions and asking their officers to meet at Castledawson on May 1 for that purpose.
1834–41	1733–4	Various papers connected with William Conolly junior's purchase of the Stretton estate from William Congreve.
1842	1778	Draft resolutions of a committee of the Commons about military expenditure on the American War.
1843	1789	Copy of a printed dispatch from Paris on the start of the French revolution. In French
1844	*c.* 1782	*Paddy's hints for making a fortune and for raising his own dear country and her sister country along with her… collected from the Hibernian and Volunteer journals – 18 aphorisms intended ironically.*
1845–90		Miscellaneous undated accounts and other fragmentary material. Many of these relate to Conolly's racing establishment at the Curragh.
1891–1923		Collection of titles and wrappers showing how the correspondence and accounts were originally organised. This organisation had broken down before the papers arrived in the TCD Library.

PART III

THE CONOLLY PAPERS IN THE PUBLIC RECORD OFFICE OF NORTHERN IRELAND

THE CONOLLY PAPERS IN THE PUBLIC RECORD OFFICE OF NORTHERN IRELAND (D/2094)

Reference	**Description**
D/2094/1–11B	Miscellaneous seventeenth century deeds relating to estates later acquired by William Conolly
D/2094/12–34	Leases and rent rolls relating to William Conolly's estates in Counties Donegal and Londonderry, 1697–1729
D/2094/35–42A	Leases of portions of the Limavady estate granted during the Conyngham family's stewardship of the estate, 1731–1754
D/2094/42B–81	Leases, rentals and other papers relating to Thomas Conolly's estates in Counties Donegal and Londonderry, 1759–1802

D/	DATE	DESCRIPTION
D/2094/ 1–11B	**30 Mar. 1612– 20 Sept. 1692**	**Miscellaneous seventeenth century deeds relating to estates later purchased by William Conolly. Most of these deeds refer to the Manor of Limavady, county Londonderry purchased by Conolly in 1697 from the Philips family.**
1	30 Mar. 1612	Letters Patent granting corporate status to Limavady, Co. Limavady
2	30 June 1616	Letters Patent granting to Sir Thomas Phillips the right to hold fairs and markets in Limavady
3	28 Oct. 1618	Lease for seven years of State of Coagh, Bar. Tirkennedy, Co. Fermanagh from Shane McGilpatricke Magintyre of [Kilressell] Co. Fermanagh, to Sir Henry Folliott of Ballyshannon, Co. Donegal
4	17 May 1634	Agreement to redeem £3,000 bond of Statute Staple, Robert, Lord Dillon with Thomas, Lord Folliott
5	– Chas. II	Fragment of indenture between Roger Moore of Dublin and Sir John Edgeworth of Lissard, Co. Longford
6	11 Chas. II	Copy of Indenture of Fine re castle and manor of Trim Co. Meath. Robert Digby and others –v– Adam Loftus and others.
7A	19 Chas. II	Copy of Indenture of Fine re Manor of Trim Co. Meath. [Morvagh?] Dowling of Rathfarnham –v– Adam Loftus and others.
7B	1670	Copy of recovery re Manor of Trim, Co. Meath, Robert Boyle –v– Adam Loftus
8	24 Chas. II	Copy of Indenture of Fine re manor of Pynnar, Co. Cavan, Sir John Cole, etc, –v– Richard, Lord Rosse, etc.
9	6 Dec. 1682	Appointment of George Deyos as collector of alnage for Co. Tipperary.
10	1682	Marriage settlement of Gustavus Hamilton of Castletown, Co. Fermanagh with Margaret Cooper, of Drumederdraulagh, Co. Sligo. The settled property is the Hamilton estate in the barony of Magheraboy, Co Fermanagh. William Conolly represented Margaret Hamilton in a later court case, hence its presence here. [See also Castletown Papers B/2/1–16]

D/2094/ 11A	10 Feb. 1684	Lease for ever of a tenement in Limavady, George Phillips, Governor of the city of Londonderry, to Simon Broster of Limavady, tanner.
11B	20 Sep. 1692	Lease for 41 years from George Phillips of Limavady to Walter Williamson of same, merchant. The property consists of a tenement in Limavady with eight acres in Ballyclose.

D/	**DATE**	**DESCRIPTION**
D/2094/ 12A–34	**24 June 1697– May 1729**	**Leases and rent rolls of William Conolly's estates at Ballyshannon county Donegal, Limavady county Londonderry, and the Vintners' and Grocers' proportions, county Londonderry. Also included are surveys of the Vintner's Proportion (1718) and the Ballyshannon estate (1728).**
12A–C	24/25 June 1697	Conveyance by lease and release, with indenture of fine of the manor of Limavady; William Phillips of Limavady to William Conolly of Rawdenstowne [Rodanstown], Co. Meath.
13A–D	1697–1705	Bundle of accounts relating to mortgages on the Phillips estate at Limavady.
14	*c.* 1700	Chancery bill re Hamilton estate in the barony of Magherboy, Co Fermanagh; Margaret Hamilton, widow of Gustavus Hamilton, with Sir William Gore –v– William Hamilton and others.
15	4 Apr. 1700	Copy of lease of Lower Culmore, Co. Londonderry; William Conolly of Newhall, Limavady, to Robert Patton of Lower Culmore.
16	22 June 1705	Lease for 41 years of Clonmoghane and Corcreagh in Co. Roscommon; William Conolly to Edmond Kelly of Ruthnalogleygh, Co. Roscommon.
17	*c.* 1707	Draught of Mr Hody and Mr Barton's and Mrs Tazewell's deed to Mr Conolly and Mr [Oliver] McCausland. The property is the manor of Castlefin, Co. Donegal.
18A	30 July 1709	Copy of late Mr Conolly's 'minnit' to Mr Nathaniel Hornby of the house and lands he then possessed at Muff [Grocers' Proportion, Co. Londonderry], for 41 years.

D/2094/ 18B	1710	Mortgage of the manor of Mount Charles Killybegs, Co. Donegal [estate of William Conolly's late brother-in-law, Henry Conyngham d. 1707].
19	Early 18th century	Memo of leases granted by Phillips in Back and Ballyhenry, Co. Londonderry, in 1639 and 1640
20	1713	Conveyance of rent charge arising out of manor of Castlefin, Co. Donegal; Hody, Barton and Tazewell to Conolly and McCausland.
21	18 Oct. 1718	'Copy of rent roll of the Vintners' Proportion sent by Amos Strettle.' This is an unusually detailed analysis of the rents, tenants, land use, etc, of the Vintners' Proportion at Bellaghy, etc, in Co. Londonderry with some comment on the estate in 1673. Rent £593 19s. Lands in Parishes of Ballyscullion. Killelagh Maghera, etc., Bar. Loughinsholin.
22	12 Dec. 1721	Memo and accounts drawn up by Oliver McCausland relating to Dr Edmund Evans' fourth part of the Castlefin estate.
23	1721–24	Rent roll of the Castlefin estate with details of holdings over the estate and tenants in Castlefin town. This is probably a copy made relative to proposed litigation by Dr Evans against Mrs Tazewell's freeholders. Rent £75 7s.
24A–C	1718–26	Wrapper endorsed, 4 June 1726 and containing: early 18th century rent roll of the manor of Ballyshannon, Co. Donegal, with details of tenants and 'old' and 'new' rents; 1718 survey and valuation [by Hogan] of the manors of Ballyshannon, Co. Donegal and Newporton Co. Fermanagh; this provides a detailed review of these estates under the headings of 'tenants names', 'Denominations', Acreage value per acre and per annum and observations. John Cunningham printed a version of these documents in *Donegal Annual*, vol. 33 (1981), pp 27–44.
25	15 June 1728	Copy of Robert Cunningham's lease of the mills of Mulanboy and Monella set by Samuel Sinclair and Johnston Mansfield ... This relates to the division of the manor of Castlefin by order of the Court of Exchequer.
26	Nov. 1729	'Rent roll for the manor of Limavady with denominations of lands per deeds and leases' 'Oats, hens, muttons, spangles of yarn' 'and money in lieu' Rent £591.5.9 Lands in parishes of Carrick Drumachose and etc. Barony of Keenagh.

D/2094/ 27	Nov. 1729	Rent roll of the manor of Limavady with an account of the deeds and leases with their dates.
28	May 1729	William Conolly's executor's accounts of the manor of Limavady, Grocers' proportion, Church Lands and Vintners' proportion, Co. Londonderry.
29	1729	Detailed rent-roll of the Vintners' proportion, Co. Londonderry.
30	1729	Detailed rent roll for the Vintners' proportion at Bellaghy, Co. Londonderry, 'exactly compared with the leases by George Downing and Robert McCausland. This was probably connected with Conolly's negotiations to renew the lease of the Vintner's estate from the Irish Society at this time.
31	1729	Rent roll of the Grocer's manor, Co. Londonderry for May and All Saints 1729.
32	1729	Rent roll of the Grocers' manor, Co. Londonderry with an account of the leases laid out, May and All Saints 1729.
33	1729	Lord Justice [William] Conolly's Ballyshannon accounts for All Saints 1728.
34	1729	Ballyshannon accounts for May rent, 1729.

D/	DATE	DESCRIPTION
D/2094/ 35–42A	**14 Jan. 1731–1754**	**Following William Conolly's death in 1729, the manor of Limavady passed into the successive possession of his nephews Williams and Henry Conyngham before reverting to the Conolly family following the death of Henry Conyngham in 1781 with no direct heir. Also included here is a survey of lands in county Leitrim acquired by the Conolly family c. 1731. These lands were adjacent to the Conolly estates in county Donegal.**
35	14 Jan. 1730/31	Map and survey of Aghaderard, Co. Leitrim, by William Starrat of Strabane.
36	20 Jan. 1740	Twenty year lease of lands in Terrydremont, Co. Londonderry; John and Robert Smith of Limavady to John Torrens, Robert Speer and James Wilson of Lower Terrydremont; endorsed is the transfer of one-third part of the lease, 1754.

D/2094/ 37A–B	30 Oct. 1740	Lease of lives or 41 years of land in Corndale, Co. Londonderry; Thomas Smith of Limavady on behalf of Henry Conyngham of Slane, Co. Meath. To John Wilson senr., John Scott, John Anderson and John Wilson jnr., all of Corndale. With counterpart.
38	20 Apr. 1742	Memo of lease for lives of or 41 years of tenement in Limavady; same to Joseph Dick and Nathaniel Rankin of Limavady.
39	28 Sep. 1742	Lease for lives or 41 years of land in Lomond, Co. Londonderry; same to William Patton of Culmore.
40	Mid-eighteenth century	'A copy of the No. of acres reclaimed of bog in the manor of Limavady and the valuation of the same.
41	18 Nov. 1754	Memorial of deed between John Patton of Culmore and Thomas Smith of Limavady re land in Ballyhenry, Co. Londonderry.
42A	30 Mar. 1754[?]	Memorial of lease of Terrydremont, Co. Londonderry, from George, James and Mary Glen of same to Bernard Dogherty of Limavady.

D/	DATE	DESCRIPTION
D/2094/ 42B–81	*c.* **1759– May 1802**	**Leases, rentals and other papers relating to Thomas Conolly's estates in counties Donegal and Londonderry, 1759–1802. Most of these papers relate to Conolly's Limavady estate but there are also rentals from the Vintners' and Grocers' Proportions, which Conolly leased from the Irish Society.**
42B	c. 1759	An exemplification of recovery suffered by Thomas Conolly of lands in Co. Meath.
43	1 Nov. 1760	Lease of 18 years of land in Terrydremont, from John Smith of Magilligan to John Torrens and others of Terrydremont.
44	14 May 1763	Memorial of lease of Crindle, Co. Londonderry. John Patton of Culmore and John Martin of Culmore.
45	*c.* 1770–*c.* 1780	Bundle of agent's observations and calculations relating to the state of leases, etc. of the various townlands making up the Limavady estate; with particular reference to Terrydremont, Lomond, Crindle and Ballyhenry.

D/2094/ 46	June 1774	Examination of freeholders of Tamlaght Finlagan {Limavady, Co. Londonderry] who allegedly subscribed to a resolution appearing in the *Freeman's Journal*. The resolution protested against Thomas Conolly's support for 'the late Act of Parliament by which dissenters are precluded voting at vestries'; it was argued that it would cause unrest and encourage emigration. The signatories threatened to aid 'our independent brethren in the county' at the next election. The freeholders, 196 in all, were each examined c. July 1775 by Thomas Conolly, Conolly McCausland and Richard King as to whether they in fact supported the resolution and their replies are given. E.g. Rev. Benjamin McDowell 'acknowledged the contents and gloried in it'; Michael Crisswell of Ned 'declared that he would not give any satisfaction, that Richard King had no business to ask him questions, but thrashed and beat that he did not value Mr Conolly or Mr King apart, etc.'. [Reproduced in W.H. Crawford and Brian Trainor, *Aspects of Irish social history* (Belfast, 1969), pp 156–62.]
47	Nov. 1774	Rent account from Thomas Conolly's estate at Newporton, Co. Fermanagh. Rent £280 6s 4d.
48	July 1775	Note from Thomas Conolly to Andrew Spotswood at Bellaghy requesting that he pays £200 to Conolly McCausland.
49	Nov. 1775	Note from Thomas Conolly to Andrew Spotswood requesting that he pay £72 15s. To the Bishop of Derry. Endorsed are the Bishop of Derry [Frederick Hervey]'s instructions that Robert Alexander should have £50 for 'the new chapel at Tamlat and £22 15s for the new spire at Maghera.'
50	May 1775	Rental of Vintners' proportion at Bellaghy. Rent £2,867 13s. 8d.
51	May 1776	Rental of the Vintners' proportion at Bellaghy.
52	*c*. 1773–*c*. 1780	Bundle of Mr Spotswood's vouchers etc., re rents for Vintners' proportion.
53	May 1775	Rent account for Vintners' proportion. 'Settled this account, 9 Feb. 1779.'
54	Nov.1775–May 1776	Rent account for Vintners' proportion. 'Rt. Hon. Thomas Conolly's account current.'
55	6 Feb. 1775	Certificate of Messrs Latouche payments made on Mr Spotswood account November 1774 to May 1775. Rents of the Vintners' Proportion.

D/2094/ 56	*c.* 1781	Bundle of calculations etc., re leases in Limavady area from Lord Conyngham to Lesley Alexander.
57	*c.* 1781	Map of Limavady mill by Patrick Roe, with survey calculation.
58	*c.* 1780	Abstract of various leases on the Limavady estate from *c.* 1700.
59	1781	'Leases in ... Limavady estate expireable ... according to the term of years.
60	8 Nov. 1782	Letter from William Haslet to Edward Bulkeley [Conolly's solicitor] asking that he be allowed to continue in his tenancy from Mr Conolly in preference to Smith.
61	1782	'Valuation of lands in...Limavady estate per – Calhoun, land surveyor' Value £982 4s 9½d. Area 1795 A 3R 17P.
62	1782	An account of lives dropped in the respective deeds in the Limavady estate.
63	1782	Recommendation of freeholders of manor of Limavady by Robert McClelland as seneschal of said manor. Addressed to Rt. Hon. Thomas Conolly.
64	1782	An account of the lands out of lease in Limavady with reference to the map.
65	22 Dec. 1782	Letters from Henry Hewy in Limavady to Edward Bulkeley asking to be considered as a tenant of certain properties in Limavady town.
66	14 Jan. 1782	Assignment of title to lease of tenement in 'Rowmill' Co. Londonderry, from Mary Witherow of same to John Lamond, her son-in-law, and to his son Thomas Witherow-Lamond.
67	1782	Alphabetical list of denominations in Limavady estate.
68	Nov. 1781– May 1782	Bundle of accounts for the Vintners' proportion, Bellaghy. 'Settled 13 Apr. 1784.'
69	25 Oct. 1782	Award of Rt. Hon. Thomas Conolly on the partition of Back between himself and Mr Church.
70	3 Feb. 1787	Receipt for interest due on bond from Thomas Conolly to Angel Hamilton.

D/2094/ 71	6 Dec. 1788	Receipt for rents paid by Thomas Conolly to Trinity College, Dublin re Rossnowlagh and Cowlowdown, Co. Donegal.
72	29 Oct. 1787	Receipt for interest due on bond from Thomas Conolly to Matt. Montgomery.
73	22 Mar. 1789	Receipt for annuity due from Thomas Conolly to William Coane.
74	1788	Bundle of payment instructions from Thomas Conolly to Henry Major in Ballyshannon, Co. Donegal.
75	1788–90	Rental of Vintners' proportion.
76	1788	Rental, with accounts, for Vintners' proportion.
77	1787	Deed of mortgage of Limavady estate, Rt. Hon. Thomas Conolly to David Latouche.
78	1791–93	Rental of Vintners' proportion.
79	*c.* 1800 [?]	Yearly rent roll of Limavady estate. Rent of £1,521 8s 3d. Lands i n parishes of Carrick, Drumachose etc. Bar. Keenagh.
80	*c.* 1800	Map of Carrowclare, Co. Londonderry.
81	May 1802	Half yearly rental of Thomas Conolly's Limavady estate.

PART IV

THE CONOLLY PAPERS IN THE NATIONAL ARCHIVES OF IRELAND

THE CONOLLY PAPERS IN THE NATIONAL ARCHIVES OF IRELAND (M 6917)

Reference	Description
M 6917/1–67	Rentals and accounts relating to Thomas Conolly's estates in counties Donegal and Londonderry, 1748–1795
M 6917/68–106	Leases, accounts and deeds relating to William Conolly, 1684–1729
M 6917/107–13	Legal papers and deeds relating to William Conolly junior, 1729–54
M 6917/114–42	Deeds, leases and settlements relating to Thomas Conolly, 1758–1803
M 6917/143–238	Deeds, leases, and settlements of Edward Michael Conolly and his son Thomas 1819–68

M/	DATE	DESCRIPTION
M/6917/ 1–67	**1728–95**	**Rentals and accounts from Thomas Conolly's estates in counties Donegal and Londonderry. Most of these accounts relate to the Ballyshannon estate in Co. Donegal and include letters from Conolly's agents Henry Major and John Spotswood. Also included is a stray account from 1728.**
1–18	1748, 1773–92	May and November rentals of Ballyshannon estate, Co. Donegal, College Lands of Bundrows and Tirhugh, and various lands in the Barony of Boylagh and Bannagh, Co. Donegal. The main series begins with November 1773. There is one stray rental for May 1748.
19	1728	List of insolvent cabins in Ballyshannon for the May rent 1728, and account between Thomas Dickson and Robert McCausland, 1728.
20–62	1 Nov. 1773– 1 May 1794	Mr Henry Major's accounts with Thomas Conolly for the Ballyshannon estate. Includes biannual accounts dated May and November respectively as well as accounts of cash payments out of the rents collected.
63/1–285	1775–95	Miscellaneous bills and receipts. No. 1 is a bill for advertising Mr Conolly's address to the freeholders of Co. Londonderry requesting their votes at the next general election, 1776, and his thanks on being re-elected.
64/1–74	1779, 1782–94	Cheques and bills of exchange
65/1–60	1777–93	Correspondence to John Spotswood and Henry Major, Conolly's agents on his Donegal estates.
66	Nov. 1776– May 1777	Rent roll for the Vintners' Proportion, Co. Londonderry
67	1 May 1777	Account for the Vintners' Proportion, Co. Londonderry

M/	DATE	DESCRIPTION
M/6917/ 68–106	**1663–1729**	**William Conolly's leases, accounts and deeds. Included are papers relating to Conolly's acquisition of estates from the Trustees of Forfeited Estates in 1703. There are also papers relating to his complicated purchase of the Castlefin estate in county Donegal. Also included in this section is a stray map of the Conolly estates in the Barony of Tirhugh in county Donegal dating from 1777.**
68–77	1703	Decrees of the Trustees for Forfeited Estates (entered in n the series of Decree books, formerly in the P.R.O.I. See Wood, *Guide*, p. 153) No. 67 (vol. 4) in favour of Elinor Nugent No. 68 (vol. 6) in favour of Bridget Nugent No. 127 (Vol. 6) in favour of Major Garrett Nangle No. 644 (Vol. 4) in favour of Dame Alice Mulledy No. 736 (Vol. 5) in favour of Robert earl of Roscommon No. 860. (Vol. 5) in favour of Terence McDermotroe No. 874. (Vol. 2) in favour of Thomasin Nugent No. 1234. (Vol. 4) in favour of Margaret Nugent No. 2459. (Vol. 3) in favour of William Handcock No. 2617. (Vol. 7) in favour of Benjamin Chetwood
78	1777	Map of lands at Rossnowlagh, Barony of Tirhugh, Co. Donegal, held by Thomas Conolly on a lease from Trinity College Dublin, by Richard Frizell. MS parchment 40p. Marked 'Fabulous I suspect' in a modern hand.
79	Btw. 1742–62	List of determinable leases in Co. Meath. Mostly leases for terms of years or three lives on portions of the Rodanstown estate, Bar. Deece, Co. Meath.
80	24–May 1663	Deed of sale between Sir Charles Coote the younger, of Castle Coote, Co. Roscommon, and Sir Robert and Dame Ellinor Loftus of Monasterevin, Co. Kildare. Includes the lands of Dunsink and Scribblestown, Bar. Castleknock, Co. Dublin purchased by William Conolly *c.* 1700.
81	18 June 1684	William Viscount Dungan [Dongan] of Clane to Francis Leigh of Rathbride, Co. Kildare, esq., Simon Luttrell of Luttrellstown, esq., and James Talbot of Templeogue, Co. Dublin. Settlement of Viscount Dungan's estate viz. the manors of Kildrought, Castletowne and Clane, other lands in Co. Kildare, and lands in Counties Meath, Longford, Dublin, Queens County, Co. Carlow, Co. Kilkenny and Tipperary. William Conolly later purchased part of the Dongan estate, including Castletown in 1709.

M/6917/ 82	3 Oct. 1693	Phelim Conolly of Edinbrone, Co. Monaghan, gent., to William Conolly of Dublin, esq. Bond of £1,000 to observe the covenants of a deed of even date 'Know all men by these presents that Phelim Conolly of Edinbrone in the County of Monaghan gent. Am [be]holden in and ...bound unto William Conolly of the city of Dublin Esq. in the sum of £1,000 pounds sterling good and lawful money of England to be paid to the said William Conolly or his lawful attorney executors and administrators or assigns. To which payment well and truly to be made good. Bind me by those...this third day of October 1693 The condition of this above obligation is such that if the above bonder Phelim Conolly his heirs and assigns or any of them shall and do well and truly... Witnessed by Patrick Conolly and Thomas Atkinson.
83	30 Oct. 1703	Richard Jones of Dallanstowne [Dollanstown], Co. Meath to William Conolly of Dublin esq. Release, Consideration £180, of 77a 3r 36p in Dollanstown, Bar. Deece, Co. Meath.
84	19 Mar. 1700/01	Trustees of Forfeited Estates to William Conolly of Dublin esq. conveyance of lands formerly granted to [Arnold] Joost [van Keppel] Earl of Albermarle. Includes lands in counties, Meath, Westmeath, and Wexford, which are listed on the reverse of the deed
85	14 Junc 1703	Thomas Jones, son of Nicholas Jones of Dublin, and Benjamin Chetwood his trustee, to Edmund Stafford [MP] of Dublin Esq. assignment, consideration £400, of a decree of the Trustees for Forfeited Estates allowing to him certain judgements against Sir John Nugent of Taghmon, Co. Westmeath and Richard Nugent of the same.
86	14 June 1703	Warrant to confess judgement in £260, by Sir John Nugent of Taghmon, Bart., and Richard Nugent of same, esq., in favour of Nicholas Jones.
87	14 June 1703	Warrant to confess judgement in £140, by Sir John Nugent of Taghmon, Bart., and Richard Nugent of same, esq., in favour of Nicholas Jones.
88	16 June 1703	Alice Mulledy alias Nugent, widow of Sir Anthony Mulledy and daughter of Francis Nugent of Dardistown, Co. Westmeath, esq. deceased, to Edmund Stafford Esq. Assignment, consideration £300 of a decree in her favour, being her portion chargeable on Dardistown and other lands in Co. Westmeath and Corkagh etc. Co. Roscommon, late the property of Christopher Nugent attainted.

M/6917/ 89	3 Mar. 1703/ 04	William Cairnes of Dublin, merchant, to William Conolly of Raddenstowne [Rodanstown], Co. Meath, esq. Release consideration of £2,400, of Cloncuma alias Clonsoma etc. in B. and Co. of Roscommon, formerly the property of Christopher Nugent attainted and Code and Ticknock in B. Shelburne formerly the property of John Itchingham attainted, Dirpatrick Bar. Deece Co Meath formerly the property of Thomas Plunkett attainted and one half plus one third of Abbotstown and part of Blanchardstown, Co. Dublin formerly the property of Edward Swetenham, attainted, conveyed to the grantor by the Trustees for Forfeited Estates.
90	17 Oct. 1705	Henry Philips of Wanborough, Wiltshire, gent., to William Philips of Eaton Hastings, Berkshire and William Phillips of London, distiller. Mortgage of the lordship of Castlefin Co. Donegal and other lands and other rents in the barony of Raphoe to secure a debt of £320 owed by Grantor to Phillips of Eaton Hastings and one of £50 to Phillips of London. The premises were formerly mortgaged to one James Tazewell for £688 but he failed to hand over the principal. Grantees are now to proceed to prosecute him and obtain the money, pay £10 to one Margaret Hopkins a spinster, and hand over the balance to the grantor. This deed and the two following it relate to the Castlefin estate, Co. Donegal, purchased by Conolly and Oliver McCausland in 1711.
91	20 Apr. 1706	James Tazewell of London to James Young of Castlefin. Assignment of certain debts due to Tazewell, in consideration of Young's taking over Tazewell's liabilities with regard to Castlefin.
92	11 June 1707	James Tazewell to James Young of Castlefin. Assignment of a rent charge of £120 out of Castlefin.
93	17 June 1707	Settlement by James Tazewell of a Rent charge of £80 out of Castlefin on Anne his wife, Humphrey Hody of St Clement Dane's Middlesex and Stephen Barton of Andover being trustees, and James Young of Castlefin having a right to redeem it for £1200.
94	9 Aug. 1707	Deed of defeasance of a bond for £1700 on William Conolly of Rawdenstown [Rodanstown], county Meath held by John Pearson Alderman, said sum being the intended marriage portion of Jane sister of William Conolly who is to marry Thomas Pearson, son of John Pearson. £1,700 to be paid on Conolly's death.
95	1 Sept. 1708	John and Michael Steevenson of Cooleslin and Hugh Steevenson Mullanbuey, Co. Donegal, with the Rt. Hon. William Conolly of

M/6917/95 *contd.*		Dublin, esq. Agreement by which Conolly releases the Steevensons from any obligations to have their corn ground at any mill other than Mullanbuey, they undertaking always to grind at the latter. (Damaged).
96	28 Mar. 1709	James Tazewell the younger, of Lyons Inn, gent. to John Dowdall of the Middle Temple, esq. Conveyance of the manor of Castlefin in trust for William Conolly and Oliver McCausland of Strabane.
97–98	1 & 2 Apr. 1709	William Phillips of Easton Hastings Berkshire, to Edward Riggs of London lease and release of his interest in Castlefin, in trust for William Conolly and Oliver McCausland.
99	13 Feb. 1710/11	William Conolly to Richard Jones of Dollanstown, county Meath. Lease for one year of the Church meadow alias Forestane Meadow B. Deece Co. Meath. In consideration of the sum of 5 shillings.
100	8 Dec. 1713	Conveyance by Humphrey Hody of St Clement Dane's, [London]. and Stephen Barton of Andover to William Conolly of Dublin and Oliver McCausland of Rash, county Tyrone, of their interest in Castlefin Co. Donegal. Anne, widow of James Tazewell being a party.
101	1 Mar. 1718/19	Nicholas Cashell of Cashellstowne, Co. Louth, to John Pearson (Dublin) alderman. Lease for one year of Cashellstowne, Rulestowne, and ½ a corn mill and tuck mill, in Bar. Ardee, county Louth.
102	17 Apr. 1742	William Conolly of Dublin to Henry Crawford of Carrow McMeagh, Co. Fermanagh, gent. Lease for lives of Relagh in the Manor of Newporton, in county Fermanagh.
103	3 June 1725	Assignment by Thomas Fortescue of Reynoldstown, Co. Louth, trustee of Matthew Plunkett commonly called Lord Louth, to Henry Rose of Dublin, of a mortgage of Killadowan, [Killadoon] Co. Kildare formerly made by Matthew Lord Louth, grandfather of said grantor to Sir Joshua Allen. William Conolly purchased Killadoon from Lord Louth in 1725.
104	4 Dec. 1729	William Conolly of Dublin, esq., nephew of William Conolly of same deceased, and Katherine, widow of the latter, to George Finey of Celbridge, Co. Kildare. Fee farm grant of Killadoon, Co. Kildare.
105	1729	William Conolly of Newhall, Co. Londonderry to William Rogers of Carrowclare. Unexecuted lease of Carrowclare in the manor of Limavady.

M/6917/ 106	7 Feb. 1729/30	William Conolly of Dublin to Christopher Carleton of Newry. Lease for 15 years of lower Rossnowlagh, Bar. Tirhugh, Co. Donegal.

M/	**DATE**	**DESCRIPTION**
M/6917/ 107– 142	**27 Apr. 1733– 1 Sept. 1803**	**Legal papers and deeds relating to William Conolly junior and his son, and heir, Thomas Conolly. Included are their marriage settlements of 1733 and 1758 respectively.**
107	27 Apr. 1733	Settlement on marriage of William Conolly and Lady Anne Wentworth, eldest daughter of Thomas earl of Strafford.
108	27 Apr. 1733	Counterpart of above deed.
109	16 Sept. 1740	Thomas Smith of Newtownlimavady, gent., on behalf of Henry Conyngham of Slane, to Thomas and Christopher Moor of Roe Mill, Co. Londonderry. Lease for 41 years of 3 tenements in Limavady.
110	1742	Draft of a memorial of a conveyance (not clear if ever executed) of lands in Barrackstown, Co. Kildare, by Robert, earl of Kildare, to William and Katherine Conolly, in exchange for lands at Kilmacredock in the same county.
111	12 Sept. 1748	John and James Brown of Magherykellaghan, and other tenants in Castlefin, Co. Donegal. Attornment to William Conolly.
112	22 Feb. 1754	Settlement on the marriage of Sir Ralph Gore St George, 6th Bart., and Catherine, eldest daughter of William Conolly, deceased, and Lady Anne Conolly.
113	20 Aug. 1757	John Finey of Killadoon, Co. Kildare, gent., to Alexander and Robert Montgomery of Dublin, merchants. Mortgage of Killadoon.
114	Michelmas 1758	Recovery suffered by Thomas Conolly of his lands in county Kildare.
115–16	1 & 2 Nov. 1758	Deeds of lease and release of Thomas Conolly's property in county Kildare, for the purpose of the above recovery.
117	30 Dec. 1758	Settlement on the marriage of Thomas Conolly and Lady Louisa Augusta Lennox, sister to Charles, 3rd duke of Richmond.
118	30 Dec. 1758	Counterpart to above deed

M/6917/ 119	28 Jan. 1760	Thomas Conolly to George Daunt esq. Mortgage of Rossnowlagh etc. Bar. Tirhugh, Co. Donegal, held by grantor on lease from Trinity College, Dublin.
120	28 Mar. 1760	Thomas Conolly to Michael Clarke. Mortgage of the 4 quarters of Lettermacaward and other lands in Boylagh and Bannagh, Co. Donegal, and Glencolumkille etc., Bar. Raphoe, held by grantor on lease from Bishop of Raphoe.
121	28 Mar. 1760	Counterpart of above deed
122	25 Dec. 1764	Thomas Conolly to William Coane of Dublin, gent. Lease for lives or 31 years of lands in Drumnagroagh, Bar. Tirhugh, Co. Kildare.
123	6 Mar. 1767	Viscount [Henry] Conyngham of Slane to Lesley Alexander of Newtownlimavady. Lease of reclaimed lands in the Largy Wood in the manor of Limavady.
124	31 Aug. 1769	Thomas Conolly to Robert Clements of Dublin, gent. Lease of lives of part of Killadoon, Co. Kildare, with map, and a renewal dated 25 March 1779.
125	31 Aug. 1769	Thomas Conolly to George Tew of Kilgreage, Co. Meath. Lease of lands in Black Bog, Bar. Deece, Co. Meath.
126	2 Nov. 1769	Thomas Conolly to Sir Marcus Lowther Crofton. Lease for 31 years of lands in Ardkinagh, Bar. And Co. Roscommon.
127	10 Feb. 1770	Settlement on marriage of George Robert Fitzgerald, esq., ["Fighting Fitzgerald"] eldest son of George Fitzgerald of Rockfield, Co. Mayo and Jane Conolly of London, spinster, daughter of the late William Conolly, esq., and ward of her mother, Lady Anne Conolly.
128	23 Nov. 1772	Thomas Croker of Bankstown, Co. Kildare, to Thomas Conolly. Conveyance of 1A 22P in Parsonstown, Co. Kildare.
129	20 Jan. 1773	Thomas Hunt of Mollington, Cheshire, and Lieut. Colonel James Townshend of the 34th regiment of foot, to Richard, earl of Cavan. Declaration that a sum of £16,000 lent by Hunt and Townshend to Thomas Conolly, for which Conolly has mortgaged the lordships of Ballyshannon and Leixlip, was not their proper money, but was a sum procured by sale of securities held by them as trustees of the marriage settlement of the earl of Cavan and Elizabeth, countess of Cavan, his wife.

130	20 Jan. 1773	Trustees of Thomas Conolly to trustees of the earl and countess of Cavan. Assignment of the portions of the late Mrs Harriet Staples, wife of John Staples and daughter of the late William Conolly, and of Anne Byng, 2nd daughter of same, and wife of George Byng, charged on Thomas Conolly's lands, as security for the loan referred to in no. 129 above.
131	20 Sept. 1773	Sir James Caldwell of Rossbegg, Co. Fermanagh, Bart., to Thomas Conolly. Renewal of lease of Belleek salmon fishery, Co. Donegal (original lease 9 May 1751).
132	2 June 1777	Thomas Conolly to William Meaghan of Collinstown, farmer. Lease for 31 years of lands in Collinstown, Co. Kildare.
133	2 June 1777	Thomas Conolly to Thomas Coony of Killcorragh. Lease for 31 years of lands in Killcorragh, Co. Kildare.
134	2 June 1777	Counterpart of no. 132 above.
135	12 Dec. 1780	Trinity College Dublin, to Thomas Conolly. Lease of Rossnowlagh etc. Bar. Tirhugh, Co. Donegal for 21 years.
136	20 Jan. 1784	Thomas Conolly to Henry Pyne of Cashel, merchant. Lease for lives of bog land, Newtownlimavady.
137	30 Dec. 1785	Sir John Caldwell, Bart., to Thomas Conolly. Renewal of lease of Belleek salmon fishery (see no. 131 above).
138	Nov. 1790	John, bishop of Clogher, to Thomas Conolly. Lease of B allyhanna, Parish of Innismacsaint, Co. Donegal, for 21 years.
139	27 Aug. 1791	William Fitzgerald, 2nd Duke of Leinster, and Thomas Conolly. Deed of exchange, by which the Duke gives Conolly a plot in Donaghmore Bar. Salt N, Co. Kildare, in exchange for a plot in Kilmacredock adjoining it.
140	1 Oct. 1800	Thomas Conolly to Robert Brown. Lease for 41 years of Skeaghghutta, Co. Kildare.
141	28 July 1801	Thomas Conolly to John Yates, Anna Maria Yates, [ ] Godfrey and Frances Godfrey. Renewal of lease of Kildrought, Co. Kildare.
142	1 Sept. 1803	Trustees of the will of Thomas Conolly deceased to Messrs Richardson, Little & Co. Lease for lives of salmon and eel fisheries at Ballyshannon.

M/	DATE	DESCRIPTION
M/6917/ 143–238	1 May. 1807– 23 Aug. 1868	**Deeds and leases of Edward Michael Conolly (formerly Pakenham) who inherited the Conolly estates in 1821, and his son Thomas. These papers include their respective marriage settlements dating from 1819 and 1868, but the bulk of the papers relate to lands leased by the Conolly family from the dioceses of Clogher and Raphoe in county Donegal. Also included are some deeds made by the trustees of Thomas Conolly, 1807–18**
143	24 May 1819	Settlement on marriage of Edward Michael Pakenham esq., only son of Thomas Pakenham of Coolure, county Westmeath and Catherine Jane Ponsonby, only daughter of Chambre Brabazon Barker of Kilcooley Abbey, Co. Tipperary.
144	20 Oct. 1819	Jeremiah Houghton to Edward Michael Pakenham. Lease for 99 years of the fever hospital, Celbridge, for the use of the subscribers or governors of the hospital.
145	26 Dec. 1811	John [Porter], bishop of Clogher to trustees of the will of Thomas Conolly. Lease for 21 years of lands in Ballyhanna, Parish of Innismacsaint, Co. Donegal.
146	19 Nov. 1813	John, bishop of Clogher to trustees of the will of Thomas Conolly. Lease for 21 years of lands in Ballyhanna, Parish of Innismacsaint, Co. Donegal.
147	10 Feb. 1817	John, bishop of Clogher to trustees of the will of Thomas Conolly. Lease for 21 years of lands in Ballyhanna, Parish of Innismacsaint, Co. Donegal.
148	5 May 1818	John, bishop of Clogher to trustees of the will of Thomas Conolly. Lease for 21 years of lands in Ballyhanna, Parish of Innismacsaint, Co. Donegal.
149	12 Apr. 1822	Percy [Jocelyn], bishop of Clogher to Thomas Pakenham and Richard, earl of Clancarty, trustees of Thomas Conolly's will. Lease for 21 years of lands in Ballyhanna.
150–59	3 Apr. 1824– 20 Aug. 1833	Lord Robert Ponsonby Tottenham, bishop of Clogher to Thomas Pakenham and Richard, earl of Clancarty, trustees of Thomas Conolly's will. Annual leases for 21 years of lands in Ballyhanna. Usually renewed in February.
160–63	19 Feb. 1834– 7 Feb. 1837	Lord Robert Ponsonby Tottenham, bishop of Clogher, to Edward Conolly. Annual leases for 21 years of lands at Ballyhanna, Co. Donegal.

M/6917/ 164	1 May 1807	James [Hawkins], bishop of Raphoe, to John Staples, Thomas Pakenham and Richard, 2nd earl of Clancarty, trustees of the will of Thomas Conolly. Lease for 21 years of Lettermacaward, Co. Donegal.
165	1 May 1807	Same to Same. Lease for 21 years of Inniskeel, Co. Donegal.
166–211	3 Jan. 1826–12 Dec. 1833	William [Bisset], bishop of Raphoe to Richard, earl of Clancarty and Thomas Pakenham, trustees of the will of Thomas Conolly. 46 leases for 21 years of church lands at Inniskeel, Lettermacaward and Glencolumbkille, Co. Donegal.
212	23 Oct. 1831	Trinity College Dublin to trustees of the will of Thomas Conolly. Lease for 21 years of Cowlowdown, alias Magheryear alias Bundrows, Co. Donegal.
213–214	31 Oct. 1833	Trinity College Dublin to Edward Conolly of Castletown, Co. Kildare. Lease and counterpart for 21 years of Cowlowdown, alias Magheryear alias Bundrows, Co. Donegal.
215	31 Jan. 1835	Edward Conolly of Castletown to Susannah and Anne Hume of Claremount Cottage, Co. Down. Lease for 19 years lands in the parish of Glen, Co. Donegal.
216–23	29 Oct. 1836–31 Oct. 1840	Trinity College Dublin to Edward Conolly of Castletown, Eight 21 year leases of College lands at Cowlowdown and Rossnowlagh, Co. Donegal.
224	14 Jan. 1840	Edward Conolly to Nathaniel [Clements], 2nd earl of Leitrim. Lease for lives of part of Killadoon, Bar. Salt N, Co. Kildare. (Damaged).
225–32	30 Oct. 1841–31 Oct. 1845	Trinity College Dublin to Edward Conolly of Castletown, Eight 21 year leases of College lands at Cowlowdown and Rossnowlagh, Co. Donegal.
233	1 May 1851	Clotworthy, Lord Langford, and Louisa, Lady Langford, to [her brother] Thomas Conolly of Castletown, Richard and William Pakenham of Coolure, Co. Westmeath, and Daniel Simmonds of Collinstown, Co. Kildare. Release of Lady Langford's portion charged in her marriage settlement on lands in Celbridge, Co. Kildare and Ballyshannon, Co. Donegal.
234	23 Aug. 1868	Settlement of marriage of Thomas Conolly of Castletown, MP and Sarah Eliza Shaw of Temple Mills, Co. Kildare.

M/6917/ 235/a–d	28 Sept. 1835	Certificate of the Ecclesiastical Commissioners for Ireland to Thomas Conolly of his right to purchase the fee simple of the termon lands of Inniskeel, Co. Donegal under the Church Temporalities Act of 1833. With notice, receipt for purchase money, and an unsealed certificate dated 4 Aug, 1835.
236/a–d	28 Sept. 1835	Certificate of the Ecclesiastical Commissioners for Ireland to Thomas Conolly of his right to purchase the fee simple of the termon lands of Killybegs and Glencolumbkille, Co. Donegal under the Church Temporalities Act of 1833. With notice, receipt for purchase money, and two certificates dated 4 Aug, 1835 (unsealed) and 28 Sept. 1835 (sealed).
237	28 Sept. 1835	Certificate of the Ecclesiastical Commissioners for Ireland to Thomas Conolly of his right to purchase the fee simple of the termon lands of Lettermacaward, Co. Donegal under the Church Temporalities Act of 1833. With notice, receipt for purchase money, and an unsealed certificate dated 4 Aug, 1835.
238/a–b	28 Sept. 1835	Certificate of the Ecclesiastical Commissioners for Ireland to Thomas Conolly of his right to purchase the fee simple of the termon lands of Ballyhanna, Co. Donegal under the Church Temporalities Act of 1833. With receipt for purchase money.

PART V

THE CONOLLY PAPERS IN THE NATIONAL LIBRARY OF IRELAND

THE CONOLLY PAPERS IN THE NATIONAL LIBRARY OF IRELAND

Reference	**Description**
MS 41,341/1	Letters to Thomas Conolly from Rev. Richard Woodward successively Dean of Clogher and Bishop of Cloyne, 1760–94
41,341/2	Letters to Thomas Conolly from miscellaneous correspondents on miscellaneous topics, 1763–69
41,341/3	Letters to Thomas Conolly from Michael Clarke, his head agent and man of business, mainly about the letting of Leixlip Castle, 1765
41,341/4	Original bundle of correspondence relating to Thomas Conolly's relations, personal and financial, with his mother and the Strafford family, 1766–93
41,341/5–8	General correspondence of Thomas Conolly arranged by date on political, financial and personal matters, 1778–1782.
41,341/9	Miscellaneous letters to Thomas Conolly, 1784–95
41,341/10	Three letters and papers about Leixlip Castle, demesne and estate, 1811–22

MSS	DATE	DESCRIPTION
41,341/ 1–10	**1760–1822**	**Box of *c.*150 letters and papers relating to the estate, business, political and family concerns of Thomas Conolly of Castletown, arranged as follows:**
1/1–26	1760–94	Letters to Thomas Conolly from the Rev. Richard Woodward, successively dean of Clogher and bishop of Cloyne, writing from Bristol, Clogher and Cloyne, together with some other correspondence of Conolly about promotion in the Church for Woodward. Many of Woodward's letters are about his promotion but others relate to politics and Conolly's financial affairs.
1	6 June 1760	Woodward, Bristol, to Conolly giving advice on the management of Conolly's estates, and on books he should read: 'with regard to books relating to the affairs of Ireland, I think that after Sir John Davies's tract that you should take Coxe's [sic Cox's] History beginning with the reign of James the first, then Archbishop King's State of the Protestants in Ireland in the reign of James II, and after that Harris's Life of William III. This (as well as Coxe's) is a heavy work, but being the best or rather the only one on that period, the thread of Irish history cannot be kept up without reading at least as much of it as relates to that kingdom. These are the only books of an historical kind which it would be at all useful for you to read immediately. After them enquiries of a political nature will come on regularly and I shall be glad if it be in my power to forward them by recommending books and or any other method…'
2	30 Mar. 1762	Woodward, London, to Conolly seeking the deanery of Lismore, which has become vacant.
3	9 Mar. 1762	Woodward, London, to Conolly about the Irish septennial bill, which he thinks Conolly should support, not least because it will increase his political interest: 'Your interest seems to be particularly affected not principally on account of Ballyshannon, which is filled by members who will never counteract you in the House, but for the probability of Newtown [Limavady] coming to you long before a new reign. In which case you will have a certainty of naming members for it in a few years after Lord Cunningham's [sic] death and this will add so great a weight to your parliamentary influence…'
4	10 Apr. 1763	Woodward, London, to Conolly about Lord Halifax's [George Montagu Dunk, 2nd earl of Halifax Lord Lieutenant of Ireland, 1761–3] failure to find a promotion for Woodward in the Irish Church despite Conolly's applications on his behalf.

5	11 Mar. 1763	Woodward, London, to Conolly reporting political news and gossip, and wondering when Conolly will next travel to England. 'I fear that as you are every day making Castletown more beautiful, you will every day grow less inclined to leave it…'
6	15 July 1763	William Hamilton [Chief Secretary, 1761–3], Hampton Court, [London], to Conolly announcing Woodward's appointment as Dean of Clogher.
7	28 Aug. 1763	Woodward, Bristol to Conolly about his promotion and his forthcoming marriage, 'which is now almost a certainty'. [He married Susanna Blake (*d.* 1795) on 6 October 1763.]
8	20 Sept. 1763	Woodward, Bristol, to Jack Handcock asking him to find some accommodation in Dublin preferably on or near Capel Street, as he wants to be near Conolly.
9	14 June 1764	Woodward, Bristol, to Conolly reporting gossip and sending congratulations to Mr [John] and Mrs [Harriet, Conolly's younger sister] Staples upon their marriage.
10	16 Sept. 1764	Woodward, Bristol, to Conolly reporting news from Bath, where 'a considerable part of the Irish government' are in residence including the lord lieutenant [Hugh Percy, 2nd earl of Northumberland], lord chancellor [John Bowes], and the primate [George Stone].
11	8 June 1769	Woodward, Bristol, to Conolly about his 'poor' chances of getting a bishopric during Lord Townshend's administration, despite the promises, both public and private, that were made to him.
12	25 July 1779	Woodward, Clogher, to Conolly about the diminishing prospects of invasion and the Volunteers: '…The minds of the people are much quieter than last year. The hatred of France and Spain gets the better of their affection for their Presbyterian brethren in America. This is a disposition that should be encouraged, and no individual could do so much towards it as yourself. I should rejoice to see you in your Volunteer uniform…'
13	3 Sept. 1779	Woodward, Clogher, to Conolly about his Volunteer corps. He is determined to dilute the Presbyterian influence by encouraging members of the established church to join. He also wonders how 'Lady Louisa is reconciled to a husband that carries a musket.'
14	5 Oct. 1779	Woodward, Clogher, to Conolly about promotions in the church, and his continuing hopes for a bishopric.

15 12 Oct. 1779 Woodward, Clogher, to Conolly enclosing a copy of a letter he has sent to Lord Buckingham[shire] about the promotions detailed in the previous letter.

16 30 Oct. 1779 Woodward, Clogher, to Conolly about the growing membership of the Volunteers. He reckons there are 16,000 in Ulster alone. He also refers to the death of Conolly's sister Mrs [Jane] Fitzgerald: 'you cannot but feel on the occasion and yet you must at the same time reflect that, every circumstance considered, her change is a very happy release.'

17 30 Nov. 1779 Woodward, Clogher, to Conolly giving his views on the proposed repeal of the test act: 'I am persuaded you concur with me in thinking that nothing should be done which can give reason to the Protestants of the establishment to think that any innovation is intended prejudicial to the establishment. Such a step would alienate others who are of approved attachment to the constitution in order to gratify the Presbyterians who are almost universally *republicans* and *levellers.* No man living has a more liberal idea of toleration than myself, but as for the sake even of order some religion should be established, it surely is repugnant to that principle to give to any other sect such a countenance as may indulge their hopes of being able to overturn the ecclesiastical establishment and to encroach on those revenues with which the state has thought proper to endow it. Such hopes in a mutinous country like this lead to violent attacks on the persons as well as property of the clergy, as was evident in the proceedings of the Oakboys in 1763.'

18 24 Jan. 1781 Copy of Conolly's letter to Lord Buckinghamshire thanking him for Woodward's promotion to the bishopric of Cloyne.

19 25 Jan. 1781 William Eden [Chief Secretary, 1780–82], Dublin Castle, to Conolly announcing Woodward's appointment as bishop of Cloyne.

20 23 Sept. 1781 Woodward, Cloyne, to Conolly about renewed invasion fears and the Volunteers. He has joined the Imokilly Blues, where he seconded a motion to allow Catholics 'of property and character into our corps'.

21 4 Mar. 1783 Woodward, Cloyne, to Conolly about peace being declared in America, and its consequences; these include a reduction of the army, which he regrets.

22 12 Mar. 1794 Woodward, Cloyne, to Conolly on the renewal of Whiteboy activity in his neighbourhood: 'The mode of proceeding to tender

22 *contd.* the oath is quite different from that of former Whiteboys. They go in the daytime without arms, [not] even a stick, use no threats but take down in writing the names of those who refuse to swear. The oath is to obey the rules which will be given out on St Patrick's day. We shall know next Monday what to expect but I am confident that there will not be any formidable gathering in this neighbourhood, though a watchful eye will be kept in all quarters on that day…'.

23 5 Mar. 1794 Woodward, Cloyne, to Conolly about Conolly's financial affairs and disturbances in Co. Cork.

'... I perfectly concur in opinion with you that it is essential to the happiness of your life to give up the (vain) pursuit of Lord Strafford's [Conolly's maternal uncle] fortune and to render your own, which is a noble one, more easily manageable by selling a part to pay off debt... Take the instance of Newtown Limavady. Lord Caledon's £60,000 applied to pay off 6 per cent creditors would have taken off a burthen of £3,600 per annum, of which you receive only £2,200. The wood stands and produces nothing; fines occur but now and then. It is certainly vexatious to sell for £60,000 what is (or rather was) worth £70,000. But we must all yield to [the] times, and to you who have no children to scheme for, a year's comfort is a considerable object. If I were in your place, I would undoubtedly sell at the price, which I could get, especially as in your estimation (and indeed in mine, as you have no son), the borough is of no value ...'

He also writes about his continuing fears regarding the 'Black boys': 'On both sides of Cork there are numerous mobs calling themselves Black Boys, who swear the people not to pay tithes or rent and to imitate in all things the behaviour of the French. They have a guillotine with them. They fly when the military make their appearance. Several are committed to Cork Gaol. It is supposed that they have French emissaries at their head. I suspect, but it is only my fancy, that when the French squadron was off Cape Clear, the officers tampered with the people, promised to come with a great force to support them, and exhorted (and bribed them) to raise a general spirit against the government. They could hold forth as an encouragement that they were masters of the seas, which was countenanced by them shutting up at that moment a line of battle ship, a 50 gun and a frigate with the West India convoy in the harbour of Cork. The magistrates of Cork and the gentlemen of the county are exerting themselves, and as it does not appear that any persons above the lowest class are concerned, I am persuaded it will die away. No man of (even a small) property, much less a priest, will wish to disseminate *French manners.* They threaten death to those who refuse to join them, but have not yet employed the guillotine, except on a dead horse, to show its operation.

23 *contd.*		We are quite quiet in this immediate neighbourhood and likely to remain so. Lord Kingsborough's [militia] ballot does not disturb us. In this parish and the adjoining one a sum is raised for substitutes, for which his lordship engages to provide them for four years. This would have been universal, if he had kept to his terms, but he [flew] off and only a few parishes to which gentlemen stood pledged to his name are admitted. Cloyne luckily was one. We furnish 13 men and I made up the deficiency of the subscription. This has put me in great favour with the people. The Roman Catholics were pleased with my charge and an offer of a piece of ground for a chapel. I am quite in the *odour of sanctity* with them. But alas! That is no guard against the guillotine but I am as safe as the priest only that I am richer...'.
24	5 Mar. 1793	Woodward, Bath, to Conolly about the Catholic question and their differing views on the subject. Woodward opposes opening up the franchise particularly in the potwalloping boroughs, as this will turn Ireland into a 'popish country'.
25	21 Aug. 1793	Woodward, Cloyne, to Conolly about a loan of £3,000 he has made to Conolly.
26	17 May 1794	Benjamin Harene, London, to Conolly reporting the death of Bishop Woodward.

MSS	DATE	DESCRIPTION
2/1–5	**1763–9**	**Letters to Thomas Conolly from miscellaneous correspondents on miscellaneous topics.**
1	1 Feb. 1763	John Neal, Limerick, to Conolly seeking financial support. He has been ill and has run up substantial debts.
2	17 Apr. 1764	Anne Byng, Charles Street, London, to Conolly (her brother) forwarding a message from Lord [George Harry, later 5th earl of Stamford] Grey that 'Mr [Thomas] Jenkins has finished your picture and begs to receive your orders'.
3	27 May 1764	James Finnegan, Kildare, to Conolly about his horses and his establishment at the Curragh.
4	15 Aug. 1765	Nathaniel Clements, Dublin, to Conolly: 'I have the favour of your letter. I really am pleased that you think of parting with your Roscommon and Westmeath estates, as they never can rise, and [I] am persuaded they will sell very well. Anything you have occasion

4 *contd.*		for me to do in regard to my consent to transfer the securities and debts that affect them to other part[s] of your estate, I am very ready and willing to do it, and you may depend upon my giving all the assistance in my power to have the bill carried through the House of Commons here. ... I was the other day at Castletown. You are making it an exceeding good house. Bob [Clements' son Robert, later 1st earl of Leitrim] is much obliged to you for your kind remembrance of him. He has retired to Killadoon and has been there ever since he was married.'
5	27 Oct. 1769	George [4th Viscount later 1st Marquess] Townshend [Lord Lieutenant, 1767–72], Dublin Castle, to Conolly promising to do his best to promote Mr [John] Staples and to obtain a deanery for [Richard] Marlay.

MSS	**DATE**	**DESCRIPTION**
3	**1765**	**Letters to Thomas Conolly from Michael Clarke, his head agent and man of business, mainly about the letting of Leixlip Castle. Present in the folder are modern transcripts of these letters by the late Mrs Lena Boylan. She notes that Clarke had been appointed in 1754 under the late William Conolly's will (from which she quotes) to '... state and audit all accounts relating to my estates real or personal and that he shall from time to time and as often as he is requested by my other executors, guardians of my children, give an account of all matters and things relating to all or any of the said affairs under his care and management and shall from time to be time be accountable to my son and other executors and guardians for such sum or sums of money as he shall receive out of my real and personal estate'; in consideration of which £200 was to be paid to Clarke half yearly.**
		The letters are as follows:
	1 Jan. 1765	Clarke to Conolly, then in England. He is forwarding £500 to Lady Anne [Conolly, Conolly's mother] as requested. He has borrowed £1,300 and will pay several drafts that are due with the balance. '... As to Leixlip not one word about it since I wrote last; they have given possession of the land and Coane tells me your cattle are on it.' [Coane was Conolly's kinsman and agent, and lived in Kildrought House, Celbridge.] The letter also mentions Mr Fraigneau [Conolly's former tutor and companion on the Grand Tour].

19 Jan. 1765 Clarke to Conolly. '... Leixlip was advertised the Tuesday after you went away and to my great surprise nobody has bid for it since, or taken any notice about it except Sir Harry Cavendish, who I had some discourse with today, and by what I can find he is deterred from bidding anything for it, as he says your demand is so very large and he would not offer any rent that might have the appearance of undervaluing anything belonging to you, and as for Mr Trevor I am well assured that he has not the least thoughts of taking it on any terms. Sir Harry told me that he had spoke to Will[iam] Clements about it, and between you and me I make no doubt but he has undervalued the land and is in hopes of getting it for his brother for much less than you offered it to him for, though you paid him a compliment about it. I begin to despair of getting it off our hands so soon as we had reason to expect, yet I would not recommend it to you to be too hasty in parting with it except Clements should close with you for what you first proposed, as his father [Nathaniel] told me that he had wrote to him, and that if he had any thoughts of matrimony, he would consent to his taking it, and that he would enable him to keep it.'

30 Mar. 1765 Clarke to Conolly. 'I got your letter of the 14th two days ago about the things at Leixlip, and as I hear you intend being here before the Curragh races, you will then be best judge yourself of what things should be kept for your house use. As to what is out of doors, to be sure no body ought to buy them but you.'

4 May 1765 Clarke to Conolly. 'I am glad you have ordered *Bowers* [carpenter at Castletown] to be discharged, which Coane did yesterday; he is a good-for-nothing vain fellow. Mrs Stone and I have consented to Cooper Walker's valuing such things as are to be paid for in the house by you, and I hope we shall settle it next week. Not a word of any bidding for Leixlip. I am afraid people are terrified at so great a rent. Yet I hope this summer will induce some of the great folks to offer something for it.'

1 June 1765 Clarke to Conolly. 'I hope in a few days I shall get the valuation of the fixtures, etc, at Leixlip which I am sorry to find there are no bidders for as yet. Mrs Stone (previous to your directions to have the flowers, shrubs, etc, bought for you) had made a present of five pots of the Magn'ola [sic – magnolia] to Lady Betty Ponsonby, but the Speaker [John Ponsonby, Lady Betty's husband], hearing that I had said Lady Louisa would be much disappointed in not getting them, sent for me and told me that she should have three of the pots, and that Lady Betty was determined to keep but two of them. The Speaker begged I would let you know this and that you would acquaint Lady Louisa with it.

Pray are we to see you here this summer. Though Castletown is not habitable, Leixlip is and may very soon be fitted up for you.'

	6 July 1765	Clarke to Conolly. 'I wish with all my heart you may let Leixlip to some of those people you mention. I am sorry Lord Kildare has resigned. I fear he has done a hasty thing, but he knows his own business best. Castletown by all accounts will take more time to fit it up for your reception than you imagine, but since the work is begun, the best way is to complete it and have done with the expense at once, and I hope when that is over we shall see ourselves gaining ground and no distresses presenting to our view which is now daily the case and for which I can't tell you how much I suffer, but no man will be more happy when I find your affairs mend, for I do solemnly declare, I have it as much at heart as if you were my own son to see you live in the world with the splendour that your fortune entitles you to. I have in three covers sent to you the inventory of the furniture, etc, at Leixlip, and which Mrs Stone begged might be sent you, as I suppose she wants you to buy all the furniture as they are valued, but I think you will want nothing but the chimney pieces, locks, etc, and everything that is their property which might damage or deface the house by taking them away. All the fixtures and brewing utensils in the brew house will be necessary for you to keep.'
	8 Aug. 1765	Clarke, Castletown, to Conolly. 'I must observe to you that what money I have directed to be paid to tradesmen that are now actually employed has been done in order to keep them going on with the work, which they declared they would leave if they had not some subsistence to pay their journeymen and maintain themselves.'

MSS	**DATE**	**DESCRIPTION**
4	1766–93	**Original bundle of correspondence relating to Thomas Conolly's relations, personal and financial, with his mother and the Strafford family.**
1	21. Jan. 1766	Copy of a letter from Conolly to [his uncle William 2nd earl of] Strafford. 'I this moment received your very kind letter from London, and I think I can safely say that you do me but justice in thinking my mother and sisters may safely trust to my honour and integrity, as I can assure you nothing upon earth could ever prevail upon me to do anything that should injure any of them in the smallest degree, and even in regard to preferring Lady Louisa's interest to Lady Anne's, ... you will find by my answer to Lady Anne's queries [this] was by no means the case, but had been at first wrongly stated to

1 *contd.*		Lady Anne. In regard to diminishing the load of my debts, I intend to do that in what degree I find most expedient, being entirely of your opinion that the less I can sell the better. But it is always right to put these affairs upon the clearest footing, and I am sure, if I had no debts at all, mine have been so perplexed with wills and settlements that it would have been worthwhile to get an act of parliament on purpose to make them intelligible. ...' He will not, however, allow this to interfere with his attendance in the House of Commons, if Lord Strafford wants him to go over.
2	5 July 1775	George Byng senior, Wrotham Park, to Lord Strafford about the sale of annuities which have been laid out in the purchase of lands in Herefordshire.
3	19 Jan. 1787	Lady Anne Conolly, London, to Conolly. '... Since poor Lady Strafford died, my brother has often begun to talk of his affairs and has expressed the kindness of his intentions towards me, but I always put an end to the subject by saying (with truth) that I was glad my being so much older than him made it improbable I should feel so great a misfortune as that of losing so kind a friend and a brother I loved with so much affection. And as to what Mr B[yng] wanted you to propose, I declare from my heart I had rather live on a bare subsistence with a clear conscience than in the highest affluence with the thoughts of having wronged another of their lawful inheritance. I am very glad you are now well and am sorry 'tis necessary for you to attend the horrid House of Commons, as it don't agree with you, but there are duties that a man of property owes to his country and must go through. ...'
4	3 Nov. 1791	George Byng junior to Lady Louisa Conolly formerly enclosing a letter from General [Henry Seymour] Conway to Byng's mother, Anne, written in 1775 suggesting that her children should represent him [presumably as executors of Lord Strafford's will]. The meaning is slightly unclear, as the enclosure is missing.
5	21 Mar. 1791	Lady Anne Conolly, London, to Conolly. '... As to your coming to England, that must depend on your affairs where you are, and there is nothing here that requires your immediate presence; and as to your note to me for £5,000, you are very welcome to let it remain a year longer ... Mr Staples's is but a shabby excuse for his strange conduct to his son, and ... as William [Conolly Staples, the son] never has a farthing from him, *he* has nothing to do with that. He [W.C. Staples] is very well and is backwards and forwards between his ship and home. ... I ... abhor George Byng's public conduct, though I have forgiven his injuries to myself and let him use the furniture he so cruelly made me pay for. As the [late Lord Strafford's] house in St James's Square is yours, I am glad you don't disapprove of his being in it in your absence. ...'

6	16 Dec. 1793	Lady Anne Conolly, London, to Conolly. '... I had spoke to Mr [Thomas] Pakenham and begged him to assist me, which he promised me to do, but he deceived me, and I shall never henceforward depend on his friendship. I am glad of Mr Napier's appointment on this expedition that Lord Moira commands. It may put him in the way of doing something towards maintaining his very large family ... . I wish your letter to Lord Bristol in favour of his son may prove successful, but he is so uncertain a man, one can't flatter one's self much. ... You said when you came home the beginning of November you would order Mr Latouche to pay my jointure. I must entreat you to do so. With your large landed property in Ireland and what you have here, it can be no inconvenience to you to do this common act of justice ...'.

MSS	**DATE**	**DESCRIPTION**
5	1778	**General correspondence of Thomas Conolly for that year on political, financial and personal matters. Included are letters from his brother-in-law, General Sir William Howe, about the possibility of a parliamentary attack on Howe for his lack of success in North America. A letter from Edmund Burke, Beaconsfield, 27 August 1778, congratulates him 'most heartily on the success of the Irish toleration act'. There are also a number of letters about naval affairs, Co. Londonderry estate affairs (the correspondents in this instance being George Ash of Ashbrook and John Spotswood, Conolly's agent at Bellaghy) and, as usual with Conolly, horses and hounds.** **Also included is a précis by Mrs Lena Boylan of the contents of the bundle**
1	23 Mar. 1778	George Byng senior, Berkeley Square, London, to Conolly about the forthcoming parliamentary session. He notes that Sir William Howe is going to bring in his business after the holidays but that he does not desire Conolly's attendance, as Conolly has recently suffered a bad neck injury. Enclosed is a list of members who voted with their party. There are 194 members listed as well as a further twenty who were abroad.
2	31 Mar. 1778	Sir William Howe, Seymour Place, to Conolly about the forthcoming parliamentary enquiry into his conduct during the American War.
3	14 June 1778	Lord Buckinghamshire, Dublin Castle, to Conolly about his fear that the 'opposition to the Roman Catholic Bills grows so formidable...' and seeking Conolly's assistance and influence.

4	12 July 1778	Sir William Howe, Marble Arch [Twickenham], to Conolly announcing his return from America. : '... I am truly yours either in prosperity or adversity ... . Your attention to me, as mentioned to me by Lady Viscountess Howe, "not to throw myself upon any *party* for my justification against the attacks of Lord George", is a mark of the sincerity of your friendship and of your opinion that I am not in need of any additional strength to the *facts* that I shall produce in the House of Commons when the time comes. I am in an odd state here – most graciously received by the K[ing] and still censured in the Ministerial paper or *Morning Post.* By your Lord Lieutenant's [Lord Buckinghamshire] goodness we are most comfortably situated at this place, but ready to quit it on the first intimation of her Ladyship's return from Ireland. How goes horses and hounds? I hope with the same success as at Almack's, from whence I hear you waddled off (for it was as much as you could do to walk under the weight) with £8,000, and I hope never to return where you may be subject to the frowns of Madam Fortune, who was so propitious last winter. I find Fanny [his wife, Frances, Conolly's sister] in charming health, and as partial to the old gentleman [himself] as she was in her younger days. ...'
5	3 Aug. 1778	Thomas Weldon, Exeter, to Conolly about Admiral [Augustus] Keppel's naval battles with the French: 'Our losses were considerable.'
6–9	31 July; 13, 16, 25 Aug. 1778	Four letters from George Ash (2), John Spotswood and Thomas Boyle about Co. Londonderry estate affairs and about invasion fears.
10	27 Aug. 1778	Edmund Burke, Beaconsfield, to Conolly, about the toleration bill, the American war and a patronage request.* 'Dear Sir, I congratulate you most heartily on the success of the Irish toleration act. I wish it had been attended with all the circumstances which might tend to put everybody in good humour with a measure so proper in itself. But I hope this may be so managed in future as to reconcile the whole people of Ireland to the means of their common prosperity. I think you are pleased with an act, which will contribute a great deal to the happiness of a country that you do not love the less because you have a great interest in it. I am sorry to say that this is not very common. You will be the more satisfied, because is particularly your own. It is the legitimate issue of yours and Lord Richard Cavendish's bill. I am sure you must love both the measure and your association in it. I had a letter from Admiral Keppel from Mount Edgcumbe. Among many things like himself in it, he says "Lord Richard

* This letter does not appear in the otherwise comprehensive John A. Woods, *The Correspondence of Edmund Burke, Volume IV, July 1778–June 1782* (Cambridge, 1963).

10 *contd.* Cavendish is the young man I envy most in the world; so much humour, so much temper, and indifference for his own person will ever be a bright star in his family names," I do believe no man was ever more deserving of such a panegyrick. It is no mean honour to have it upon the hand on which the honour and the being of the country depends.

Keppel is now out and a second action is hourly expected. It was a most astonishing piece of good fortune that Estan [D'Estaing] did not arrive on the coast of America a few days before he appeared in that quarter. If he had come when every thing from Philadelphia was afloat, nothing could have given the army the chance it now has of returning free to England. Lord Howe is in an ugly way about it. It is remarkable that when the army had marched through the Jerseys and arrived at their place of embarkation for New York, the moment they saw the fleet they cried out – it were with an involuntary emotion – " a Howe, a Howe, we see one of the Howes again!" This was no treat to Clinton. This I have had from very good authority and you may believe, it gave me pleasure.

I don't know whether you remember that I made an application to you to get leave for a Roman Catholic friend and relation of mine Mr Garret Nagle of Ballyduff in the county of Cork, to carry arms and keep them in his house. He had the honour of attending you and Lady Louisa in his boat on the Lake of Killarney. This may put you in mind of him. He is obliged sometimes to ride rather in a wild and lawless country, and he does not like to be knocked on the head. You will forgive the odd humour in him and may be assured that he will not aid Mr Arnold or Mr Washington in the conquest of Munster, or help the descent of M. D'Orvilliers. If it be no great matter as I conceive it is not, I shall be extremely obliged if you will have the goodness to direct the notice of license to him at Killarney.

Present my most sincerely respectful compliments to Lady Louisa ...'

11 13 Sept. 1778 John Downing, Rowesgift, [Bellaghy, Co. Londonderry], to Conolly seeking arms for his Volunteer company, and reminding Conolly of the high regard in which Speaker Conolly held Downing's father in. [See also TCD Conolly Papers, no. 698.]

12 18 Oct. 1778 Sir John Coghill, Coghill Hall, [Yorkshire] to Conolly congratulating him on the success of his horses at various race meetings.

13 20 Oct. 1778 William Caldbeck, French Street, [Dublin], to Conolly asking him to be the Colonel of the Caldbecks' Volunteer corps.

14	After 20 Oct. 1778	Conolly's draft response to William Caldbeck, turning down his offer, because of the pressures of his other commitments in England and in other parts of the country.
15	25 Oct. 1778	Sir William Howe, Cholderton, to Conolly thanking him for sending over a grey mare for Howe's use. He also reports war news from America, and from Admiral Keppel's fleet in the English Channel.
16	29 Mar. 1779	Hugh Drake, 'Victory', Portsmouth Harbour, to Conolly informing him that Admiral Keppel does not accept the command of the fleet, which has instead been given to Admiral Hardy, and also seeking naval preferment for himself. Drake was a tenant of Conolly's at Limavady. [See also TCD Conolly Papers, nos. 626 and 630.]
17	11 Apr. 1779	Thomas Weldon, Exeter, to Conolly seeking military preferment, on the occasion of new regiments being raised in Ireland.

MSS	DATE	DESCRIPTION
6	**1779**	**General correspondence of Thomas Conolly for that year on political, financial and personal matters, with a précis by Mrs Boylan.** **Several letters relate to Volunteering and military preparations generally in Co. Londonderry [of which Conolly was Governor], and also the raising of (hitherto inadequate) subscriptions in Yorkshire for similar purposes of defence.**
1	3 July 1779	William Rowley, Harley Street, London, to Conolly about a commission he has received to raise a volunteer corps in Ireland, and wondering whether Conolly has any candidates for preferment.
2	9 July 1779	J. Turner to Conolly seeking preferment for a relative in the army.
3	1 Aug. 1779	Copy of a letter from Conolly to Audley Fanning, Lifford, [Co. Donegal], to deliver arms for the use of Mr Dawson's Company. [See also TCD Conolly Papers no. 1765.]
4–5	22, 24 Aug. 1779	Copies of two letters from an anonymous correspondent at Sidmouth to Sir John Coghill, which have been forwarded to Conolly, about the activities of the fleet in the Channel.

6	20 Aug. 1779	Arthur Dawson, Castledawson, [Co. Londonderry], to Conolly, about the defence of the county: 'I should be much obliged to you if in the distribution of arms as Governor of the County you would let me have what number you can spare and [I] hope on your return to this part of the country to have a well appointed body of men turned out to pay their compliments to you.'
7	30 Aug. 1779	Bartholomew McNaughten, Coleraine, to Conolly offering Conolly the command of the Co. Derry Volunteers. [See also TCD Conolly Papers no. 638.]
8	31 Aug. 1779	Audley Fanning to Conolly about arming the Volunteers, in response to no. 3 above.
9	31 Aug. 1779	Richard Jackson, Coleraine, to Conolly stating Jackson's readiness to respond in case of an emergency.
10	After 4 Aug. 1779	Copy of a letter from Conolly to Lord Buckingham[shire]. 'At a meeting held at Newtown Limavady on Saturday last, the 4th instant, the captains of the independent companies of this county signed the endorsed association, which I hope you will approve of. They have likewise entered into resolutions to form themselves into different regiments about their respective cities and towns, of which I likewise endorse a copy. They are to get this association signed by their officers and men. As there is no order from government to provide for them when they leave their own homes, upon service, and as an emergency might arise before any such provision could be made, sooner than run the risk of so considerable body not acting in defence of their country, I have taken that upon myself at the risk of my own private property, not doubting of repayment whenever the circumstances of the kingdom will admit, and I make no doubt but that parliament when it meets will not only take this into consideration, but likewise point out some method of procuring the arms that have been purchased by individuals to be laid by in some proper place of security. Otherwise when all danger of a foreign enemy is over, they may be made an improper use of, and as this is a very *delicate subject* I shall converse more upon it when we meet. Not having as yet got authentic copies of the different companies, I have deferred sending them, until I can do it altogether in an official manner. The number however is much greater than I had any idea of and many more are willing to join them, provided that they are furnished with arms. Indeed the spirit is so great *just at present*, that I could have any number I pleased, upon condition of being furnished with arms and provisions, when upon service.

10 *contd.*		The number of this body, being upon an average at least 50 men a company, the thousand arms belonging to this county are already disposed of, and I should be happy to be able to promise about 300 more. Those to whom I have delivered them had (all but one company) taken the oaths of allegiance before I came down and I should not deliver out any without making this bargain. Those who have purchased their own arms, have not taken this oath, but have signed the association, which must do for the present, though it is not exactly what I could wish, and I had no hand in the wording of it, not thinking it prudent to appear a principal, as the people here are easier led than drove. I beg you will make my apology for sending all these particulars immediately to you, instead of Mr Richard Heron, to whom they should go with more propriety, but my hurry is too great to send duplicate. I mean to go to Ballyshannon, 40 miles west of Derry on Saturday next about some private business of my own, if there is no apprehension of [John] Paul Jones. If there is I shall defer it, meaning however to stay within call of my troops till I can leave this part with honour and safety, in which part I hall be regulated by your opinion and intelligence…'
11–13	After 23 Aug. 1779	Copies of three letters sent by Conolly to Conolly McCausland, Andrew Spotswood and Richard Jackson respectively. As Governor of the County he informs them of a sighting of six frigates commanded by Paul Jones off the Kerry coast, and orders them to have their companies ready to march at a moment's notice.'
14	Aug. 1779	Incomplete copy of an invitation from Conolly to Captain Tracy, Captain Downing and Captain Spotswood to dine with him and other Volunteer officers at Limavady.
15	2 Aug. 1779	Sir John Coghill, Coghill Hall, [Yorkshire], to Conolly about the raising of Volunteer companies in Yorkshire.
16	3 Sept. 1779	Sir Hugh Hill to Conolly reporting that [John] Paul Jones' squadron are still 'hovering off the Skelligs on the coast of Kerry'.
17	9 Sept. 1779	Buckinghamshire, Dublin Castle, to Conolly about a misunderstanding over the disposal of commissions in the army.
18	14 Sept. 1779	Buckinghamshire to Conolly reporting military news from the West Indies, and expressing the hope that Conolly will be in Dublin for the forthcoming parliamentary session. He also reports the death of [Richard Chenevix] the Bishop of Waterford.
19	17 Oct. 1779	Apollos Morris, Bandon, [Co. Cork], to Conolly about the defence of the country. [See TCD Conolly Papers no. 596.]

19 *contd.*		'To comply with the directions of your letter in the manner most agreeable to what I conceived to be its intentions, I on receipt of it sat down and gave the outlines of a plan for putting the kingdom in defence, and without waiting to copy, or even arrange the several heads, I enclosed it to you, under cover to his Excellency not as lord lieutenant but as your friend. I followed it a few days after with a sort of recapitulation with some additional hints. Of neither have I received any acknowledgement. I have therefore taken the following postulation on the soundest principles of military policy *that the kingdom is not in a posture of defence* ... If the steps I recommend or similar are not taken a country in which one person in 20 is not interested in its preservation will be lost. And in which those are most interested in its preservation do not reform their mode of governing, which scarcely answers any end of government their enemies will come to do it for them.'
20	17 Oct. 1779	Buckinghamshire, Dublin Castle, to Conolly, wondering whether he can expect Conolly's assistance in 'carrying out the King's business for the future'.
21	17 Oct. 1779	Conolly to Buckinghamshire in answer to no. 20 above. '... I told you of my fixed determination to remain a freeman in parliament. The carrying on of the King's business, which is in truth the business of the kingdom, I never wished to give any opposition to in any administration, much less in yours who have behaved so honourably by this country, as will be confessed by everyone. ...'
22	25 Oct. 1779	'A true son of Milesius', London, to Conolly about the need to push for free trade during the current session of the Irish parliament.
23	9 Dec. 1779	William Rowley, Harley Street, London, to Conolly seeking a Volunteer commission. Rowley was the son of a Suffolk baronet, whose family held a lease of the Drapers' Proportion in Co. Londonderry.

MSS	DATE	DESCRIPTION
7	1781	**General correspondence of Thomas Conolly for that year on political, financial and personal matters, including some correspondence about Conolly's succession to the estate and borough of Newtown Limavady, and some letters praising the conduct of William Conolly Staples [as a midshipman] and commenting on the conduct of Conolly's brother-in-law, George Robert Fitzgerald.**

1	26 Feb. 1781	Buckinghamshire, London, to Conolly reporting political and naval news from London, including the prospects of an imminent peace with France.
2	7 Mar. 1781	Sir William Howe, Lumley, [Durham], to Conolly about his hunting exploits, and reporting political gossip.
3	13 Apr. 1781	Conolly McCausland, Fruithill, [Limavady, Co. Londonderry], to Conolly congratulating him on his imminent succession to the 'estate of your ancestors' at Limavady upon the death of Lord Conyngham. [See also TCD Conolly Papers no. 721.]
4	7 June 1781	[The 2nd] Lord Conyngham [nephew of the deceased], London, to Conolly resigning as one of the burgesses of Limavady.
5	21 May 1781	Buckinghamshire, London, to Conolly. Mostly about military affairs, but also advising Conolly to visit England more frequently, I greatly apprehend that for the future you mean rarely to visit England. It is not selfishness which directs …the expressing that you may hereafter regret the withdrawing yourself from the society and connection with your friends on this side. As you advance in life you must share the common fate of becoming less active and finding fewer resources in yourself. Whatever may be your determination remember hereafter it is my advice to give a large proportion of the alternate spring and winter to this kingdom. It is a matter that merits your attention…I lately saw Lord Strafford, in confidence let me tell you that he will not give credit to my repeated assurances that you are easy in your circumstances and attentive to them. This leads me to express my real satisfaction at your late acquisitions by the death of Lord Conyngham.'
6	22 Oct. 1781	Sir William Howe, Cholderton, to Conolly mostly about hunting and racehorses.
7	19 Oct. 1781	[Constantine Phipps, 2nd] Lord Mulgrave, 'The Courageous', to John Staples praising the latter's son William Conolly Staples, who is serving under his command.
8	19 Oct. 1781	William Conolly Staples, 'The Courageous', to John Staples describing his enjoyment of his naval career.
9	8 Nov. 1781	Lady Anne Conolly, London, to John Staples about the enclosed letters she has received from William Conolly Staples (see above). She goes on to enquire about George, 'Fighting', Fitzgerald who was married to her late daughter Jane (d.1779): 'I am come down to town for a day to inquire after poor Lady Mary Fitzgerald, and in hopes of getting some intelligence from her family of what is

9 *contd.*		likely to be the fate of her unfortunate son. I should be very much obliged to you , if you would let her know whether he is to be tried soon and what is the general opinion of his crimes as to their being capital, for worthless and bad as he is, the thought of his coming to an ignominious death is very shocking to me…'
10	9 Nov. 1781	John Staples, Lissan, [Cookstown, Co. Tyrone], to Conolly enclosing the three previous letters and asking him to send her the information she requires about 'that unfortunate man, Fitzgerald'.

MSS	**DATE**	**DESCRIPTION**
8	**1782**	**General correspondence of Thomas Conolly for that year on political, financial and personal matters. Included are letters on Volunteering and the political situation in Ireland including a long letter from Conolly to Lord Rockingham.**
1	Post 27 Mar. 1782	Copy of a letter from Conolly to Lord [Charles Watson-Wentworth, 2nd Marquess of] Rockingham, on his appointment as prime minister. 'Permit me to wish you joy upon your recent appointment, not so much upon your own account, as upon that of the kingdom of Great Britain, which has long wanted both integrity and ability to direct it. I flatter myself likewise that under your auspices this country may survive a storm that has been long gathering owing certainly to that cursed American war, which in its consequences ruined both the merchant and the squire, and in their ruin involved the state. Point d'argent, Point de Suisse was our motto in June 1779. Lord North lent us 50,000 and gave us 50,000 more out of the sum voted by the parliament of Great Britain for the support of the dependencies, which enabled a frugal government to go on, till our parliament met, but in the mean time every man armed, not only for fear of a foreign army, but more so, for his own defence against confusion, which was likely to arrive from the want of credit and of course of governing amongst ourselves. Every success of the Americans advanced the spirit of the Irish, who grew anxious of their emancipation when they thought their own loyalty deserved a better fate. The acquisition of free trade, given us unexpectedly, without explanation, as it was linked in consequence of the thanks of the Commons and Lords to the Volunteers, being given at the instance of that body gave rise to other constitutional demands, which to me appeared ill timed, as we had expressed our satisfaction and content, upon obtaining a

1 *contd.*

freedom of trade. I for one always objected to them upon that ground. Two years ago one Volunteer corps arraigned the conduct of the parliament and the papers here were filled with the same paragraphs and sentiments that preceded the burning of London. I thought it my duty as a member of parliament and as a citizen to endeavour to stop both the one and the other. The House was of my opinion unanimously. No more Volunteer resolutions then appeared and the printers and publishers were ordered by the Lord Lieutenant at the request of the House to be prosecuted. From whatever reasons I know not the prosecution was dropped … Hence the resolution at the different reviews, hence the meeting at Dungannon and hence the resolutions of almost every Volunteer corps except my own to arraign that very parliament that obtained a freedom of trade and who expressed every wish for emancipation, concomitant with that subordination that is necessary to be maintained in the government of the two kingdoms under one king. Our declaration of rights may hurt us much unless Mr Yelverton's bill, for quieting possessions should be permitted to pass, but pass it now will as the whole kingdom is determined upon it at any rate. If the Duke of Portland could bring us over a repeal of the obnoxious part of the 6th of George the first in his pocket, I am convinced it would keep us quiet and we might then new model Poyning's Law and make a biennial mutiny bill at our leisure.

I have no motive in troubling you with this long detail, but that of duty to my country and love for your administration and its principles. The latter as they invigorate the constitution of Great Britain and give independence to America, cannot consistently refuse the same to a long neglected, loyal, spirited and armed people. Use therefore your influence in the cabinet and save the lives and fortunes of thousands whose blood and treasure may be better spent in the defence of her sister country, curtailed in point of trade and history by your predecessors, but strengthened so much in her constitution, so much, in the very dawn of yours, as to be still a match for her European enemies.'

2 25 March 1782 George Byng senior, London, to Conolly passing on news about the Rockingham's ministry difficulties in forming a cabinet. Included is a list of the cabinet members.

3 29 May 1782 George Byng junior, Hill Street, London, to Conolly giving family gossip, and discussing his forthcoming trip to Ireland. He also refers to the political situation in Ireland: 'I dare say the Irish are mighty happy to see with what justice and moderation the present ministry act towards them. I suppose you had a great deal of drinking and bonfiring in the neighbourhood of Dublin as they have had probably an account of everything that has passed on this

3 *contd.*		side [of] the water. I went into the House of Commons yesterday. I found it looked very different from what it did when I left England; it smelt of independence, instead of a sleepy [Lord] North, an active [Charles James] Fox shined upon the Treasury bench.'
4	26 July 1782	[George] Nugent Temple, [3rd Earl Temple], Pall Mall, London, to Conolly about his forthcoming appointment as Lord Lieutenant of Ireland and his hopes for his ministry: 'The only inducement with me to quit a life of pleasure and of ease in England, must be the hope of being able to secure to Ireland the continuance of those blessings which her own fortitude and the magnanimity of England have given to her: I am too much interested in that country not to feel most warmly for her prosperity and you will remember that I was in very early days an eager advocate in the House of Commons for the extension of that commerce and those rights which are now happily secured to her. Under these impressions, it is with peculiar satisfaction that I am called to convey the most explicit and unequivocal assurances of the intention to pursue inviolate those engagements, which must ever be held most sacred, and under these impressions I may, I am sure, venture to hope for the support of every honest man in Ireland, to the great objects of improving that commerce, reforming the expenditure and reducing the baleful influence of the crown. I have only to add my hopes that these measures will meet your ideas …'.
5	5 Aug. 1782	John Richardson, Castle Ward, Co. Down, to Conolly giving a detailed account of the proceedings of the Belfast review of the Volunteers, and their address of thanks to Lord Charlemont.
6	27 Aug. 1782	Buckinghamshire, Blickling Hall, to Conolly about the replacement of the Duke of Portland by Lord Temple as Lord Lieutenant of Ireland. The latter is 'generally deemed conceited, unaccommodating and unsociable. My opinions lean that way, and I hope they are not illiberally biased by my resentment at his attempt to deprive me of my title. [Lord Temple later became 1st Marquess of Buckingham]. He goes on to report news of the war and Lord Howe's attempt to take Gibraltar.
7–9	15–24 Sept. 1782	Two letters from William P. K. Trench, Galway, to Conolly about the Volunteers and the Galway assizes. There is also a letter from a J. Kelly of Castle Kelly [Co. Galway] to Trench declining a majority in the Volunteers.
10	26 Sept. 1782	George Byng senior, Berkeley Square, London, to Conolly reporting naval news and political gossip. Amongst the individuals mentioned are Sir William Howe, Charles Fox and Admiral Keppel.

11	2 Oct. 1782	William P. K. Trench, Garbally, [Co. Galway], to Conolly about his Volunteer corps.
12	7 Oct. 1782	Buckinghamshire, Blickling Hall, to Conolly about his wife's illness, and the grim prospects of peace with France. He also reports his suspicions that 'Lord Shelburne is becoming a second Lord Bute in the closet'.
13	28 Oct. 1782	Andrew Armstrong, Gallen near Banagher, [Kings County], to Conolly about Conolly's stallion, Lenox, enclosing a printed description of the horse's pedigree. He recommends that Lenox should stand at Castletown where he will earn more money.
14	16 Nov. 1782	Robert Smith to George Ash, [now Conolly's agent at Limavady] seeking a new lease on Conolly's Limavady estate.
15–16	19 Nov. 1782	James Boyle, Dungiven, [Co. Londonderry], to Conolly explaining his absence from the Newtown Limavady review which had caused Conolly some annoyance. He encloses a list of the names and subscriptions of the Limavady 7th Battalion.
17	26 Nov. 1782	George Byng senior, Berkeley Square, London, to Conolly about the prospects of peace with France which he attributes to [Charles James] Fox's resignation: 'which drove Lord Shelburne to the necessity of renouncing his vain hope of retaining America'.
18	3 Dec. 1782	William P. K. Trench, Garbally, to Conolly about his efforts at recruiting and enclosing a list of men who have enlisted for the 1st Connaught [Fencible] Regiment under his command.
19	7 Dec. 1782	Buckinghamshire, Bond Street, London, to Conolly about peace with France and the forthcoming elections in Ireland, where he promises to write to the bishop of Clogher, to secure the latter's support for Charles Lesly [sic Leslie of Glaslough, Co. Monaghan]. He expresses his concern about the role of the Volunteers: 'The irrational, impolitic, and one might almost say the illiberal conduct of many of your countrymen, in some instances has given me serious uneasiness. It has ever been my opinion that if the existence of the Volunteer corps lasted till a general election a county contest would produce a battle'. He also asks if it is necessary to solicit Conolly's interest for Mr [John] Foster to succeed to the chair of the House of Commons in the event of Mr [Edmond Sexten] Pery's resignation.
20–21	16 Dec. 1782	William P. K. Trench, Garbally, to Conolly again on recruiting and enclosing a list of the men raised for the 1st Connaught Regiment under his command.

22	26 Dec. 1782	George Ogle MP, Dublin, to Conolly on Ogle's possible candidacy for the speakership of the House of Commons, if Pery is called up to the House of Lords, and if [John] Ponsonby does not have 'it again in his contemplation.'
23	N.D. 1782	Fragment of an account of Lord Howe' challenge to Lord Hervey about accusations made about Lord Howe's character.

MSS	DATE	DESCRIPTION
9	**1784: 1795: N.D.**	**Three miscellaneous letters and papers, including a letter of 22 May 1784 to Conolly from Edmund Garvey, a landscape painter, and a letter of 15 Nov. [1795?] from the Hon. Robert Stewart [later Lord Castlereagh;' husband of Conolly's niece, Lady Emily Hobart], writing from London.**
1	22 May 1784	Edmund Garvey, London, to Conolly about his landscape paintings of Castletown: 'The four views of Castletown are finished. The Earl of Strafford did me the honour to come to see them and also Lady Anne Conolly. They (with great condescension) were so good as to approve of and seem very much pleased with them. Notwithstanding I should wish to submit them to your and Lady Louisa Conolly's well known accurate judgement…'.
2	15 Nov. 1795	Robert Stewart, London, to [his uncle by marriage] Conolly about the proceedings of the Westminster election, 'tomorrow we are to have a Westminster meeting, which will end as their elections generally do without knowing on which side the majority is' and the bills before parliament: 'the material; one which is the that one before our House for preventing seditious meetings', which he goes on to discuss in detail.
3	N.D.	Fragment of a paper on 'the value of man'. Author and recipient unknown.

MSS	DATE	DESCRIPTION
10	1790: 1811: 1822	Three letters and papers about Leixlip Castle, demesne and estate. The second is a valuation of the estate made for Thomas Conolly's executors and trustees on 18 July 1811. This mentions that the castle and demesne are let in perpetuity to the Hon. George Cavendish at a rent of £400 per annum, plus a fine of £50 for each renewal, and that part of Stacumny is let to Sir Michael Cromie on the same tenure at £40 and £19. The sale value of the whole property, calculated at 20 years' purchase of the rent and 4 years' purchase of the renewal fines, amounts to £10,897.

PART VI

THE CONOLLY/NAPIER PAPERS IN THE NATIONAL LIBRARY OF IRELAND

THE CONOLLY/NAPIER PAPERS IN THE NATIONAL LIBRARY OF IRELAND

Reference	Description
MS 40,242	Correspondence of Thomas and Lady Louisa Conolly with members of the Napier family, 1783–1815, including a number of letters about the 1798 rebellion
MS 34,922	Correspondence of Thomas and Lady Louisa Conolly with miscellaneous correspondents including John FitzGibbon, 1st Earl of Clare, 1795–8, mostly about the 1798 rebellion.

MSS	DATE	DESCRIPTION
40,242/ 1	12 Mar. 1783	Lady Sarah Napier [daughter of Charles Lennox, 2nd Duke of Richmond, and previously married (1762–76) to Sir Thomas Charles Bunbury; married George Napier in 1781] to Conolly, about the British political situation, a bon mot of the King, etc. 'You will get no newspaper tonight, for it is ten o'clock at night and 'tis not printed yet, owing to the very late House of Commons yesterday. I therefore will endeavour to supply it about all that is material. At a late hour, everybody being tired and sleepy, Lord J. Cavendish proposed a motion of no sort of consequence, saying that those ministers were blameable who made so bad a peace when they had the means of making better, and the question being put, it was carried by 17 against the ministers. This second defeat is supposed to threaten Lord Shelburne's downfall, and all his lower orders of friends look very melancholy about it, but if he keeps his seat in the saddle, it will be more owing to the confusion of his opposers than his own genius; and that they are in confusion is evident, for a whole week is elapsed and no plan formed. I cannot give you the least guess at what makes the rub, for it's attributed to a variety of reasons. Some say Lord N[orth] wants to be premier and that Charles [James Fox] won't consent to it, but wants the D. of P[ortland] or Lord Fitzwilliams [sic] to take it, and they both say they are not fit for it, and want Charles to have it. Charles won't refuse it, certainly, if it's offered, but the King seems in no hurry to offer it to any of them. The ministerial party abuse Charles *pis que pendre* for joining with Lord North, and they won't admit that to follow or lead Lord North are two very different things. The Duchess of Richmond today re–echoed the cry against him to me. I told her I could not call it any disgrace to Charles to follow my brother Richmond's system, viz. to mind measures not men. She said, Oh, but there is a difference. Lord North is the very essence of bad; Lord Shelburne is quite another thing. Not a pin to choose between them, Duchess. My brother thought himself right, I daresay Charles thinks the same, and those who differ from them think both equally wrong, I daresay. I hope, dear Mr Conolly, that you agree with me. Why should it be such a crying sin in Charles to do what every politician does for ever? Don't you think they are all alike? Louisa says she is afraid none of them think of the good of their country. Pray ask her if ever she heard that politicians made it their first point. If it's their second or third, surely we are well off? To return to news. The D. of Grafton has resigned; Lord Camden also. Lord Ashburton shams sick, not to vote with Lord Shelburne. Mr Conway talks of resigning. In short, the present doubtful state of things puts all the trimmers to a non-plus. I

40,242/1
contd.

flatter myself my brother is not one of them, though I hate Lord Shelburne. Yet, since my brother will be imposed on by him, I hope he will go through with it, and go out with him. It's reported the King is angry, but my idea is that it's only a sham, for that a firm ministry would not suit his purposes, and these will o'the wisp ministries are just the thing for his purpose. My brother won't believe Lord Shelburne has made money by the stocks, and denies that he sent to Lord North. The first part is generally believed, and the latter Lord Advocate avows, and says he was the messenger to offer Lord North anything. See what a gudgeon my brother is in politics! But it's no disgrace to him, I think, not to credit with ease that people will lie and flatter and deceive with such perseverance.

I am sorry to tell you that our dear Lord Howe (for he must be dear to us all as a great officer) has fallen most terribly in most people's opinions by last Monday's speech. You know that Lord K[eppel] had shown him every kind of respect and attention, and more, for he had shown him kindness on all occasions. No sooner is Lord Howe in his place than (in order to support Lord Shelburne, and to give himself credit, I suppose) he says in the House that the fleet and stores and everything is in bad order, and to give height to the colouring, he adds, Nay, the very ship I came home in and the "Ocean" were in a ruined state. Little Lord Keppel could contain his anger no longer, and up he got, and said True, so it was; and God forbid the English fleet should be all in perfect order, for then they would be all rotten at once. But let me ask the noble lord: he came home in October, and the "Victory" is now in perfect order and repair, and the "Ocean" will be so in May. Is not this true? Lord Howe looked ashamed, and confessed it was true. *Fi donc, c'est indigne d'un héros!*

Bon mot of the King's. He said to Mr Conway at the levée, Pray how is poor Lord Hertford since Lady Hertford's death? Mr Conway answered, Tolerably well, Sir, considering it so immediately followed the severe misfortune that preceded it. King: what misfortune? General Conway: Your Majesty's dismissing him from your service. King: I dismiss him! Not I, Mr Conway, you dismissed him yourself, not I indeed. Is it not a good one for the old gentleman? The papers are just arrived, so I give place to them, and shall only tell you that my sister Leinster's friend, Mrs Rudd, has taught me to lose no time in asking favours, so to follow her good example who wants me to obtain a favour from Mr Minister Fox, *nous nous recommandez á vous,* pour Monsieur Ministre Portland.

2 16 Jan. 1784 Thomas Conolly, Castletown, to George Napier [husband of Lady Sarah Napier], Whitehall, London, testifying to his regard for Napier and referring to British and Irish politics.

40,242/2 *contd.*		'Be assured that, though no man writes or says less to you, that no one values and esteems your honest, disinterested principles and way of acting more than I do, though they sometimes carry you beyond what wordly prudence would admit, but which I admire. I shall not trouble you with my opinion about the state of politics of this country, which must so immediately depend upon yours, and if some permanent administration is not soon fixed in Britain, anarchy will immediately ensue here, and the mob and the Bishop of Derry command. All this is the more deplorable, as this kingdom, if it had had but the good sense to know, and to enjoy, her [sic] comparative situation with other countries, had nothing to wish for. ... The only comfort we have is that English government seems to be as well inclined to support despotism as our mob is to produce anarchy. The latter may produce a constitutional remedy, but the former being once established, cannot. I wish I could turn my mind to my horses and hounds, as my knowledge of mankind in the political world neither agrees with my spirits or my peace of mind, and your frequent changes in England and the manner of them, leaves one with little to hope and everything to fear, and all about nothing, but a strange desire of governing a country contrary to the principles and just within the forms of the constitution. ...'
3	16 Jan. 1784	Conolly, Dublin, to Lady Sarah Napier, Stretton Hall, Wolverhampton, discussing family movements and visits during the coming year, giving her a free hand with Stretton [Conolly's house where the Napiers were living], expressing regard for Napier and referring to Irish politics. ' ... I know your heart and your husband's integrity and honour. His manly, open behaviour is what I admire and should always be happy to have such men for my friends. Indeed, I can never speak my mind [to] or place any confidence in your fine folks, who are always acting upon [text defective] watching your words, and inventing speeches to insinuate themselves into favour, without one atom of real friendship or sincerity. You will be glad to hear that the paroxysm of the popular frenzy in this country is at an end, and though a croaker, I will venture to assure you that all will now be quiet here, and that we shall quit politics and the firelock and return to industry and the plough. Much pains have been taken, and some French money certainly spent here, but Paddy, feeling no real grievance, will be quiet. ...'
4	2 May 1790	[Lady] L[ouisa] C[onolly], London, to Lady Sarah Napier, Castletown, Leixlip, describing her reception in London, and making some reference to Irish politics and Thomas Conolly's part in them. '... my dear brother [the Duke of Richmond] is exactly the same to me that he always was, and you would think he had

40,242/4 *contd.* seen me but t'other day – quite at his ease with me, and talks of the Whig Club and the politics of Ireland with such temper and good humour as prevents its being the least distressing, and I see plainly is unalterable in his good opinion of Mr Conolly, laments the part he has taken, thinks it dangerous in these times, when the spirit of revolution (he thinks) is so universal, and only hopes that Mr Conolly will not have cause to repent the part he has taken by being made the dupe of people not so well-intentioned as himself. ... My party yesterday was dining with my sister Leinster to meet Charles Fox, who looks in perfect health, and you may be sure inquired most kindly after you. ... The Prince, I find, is so vastly interested about Ireland that the fear of omitting any civility to an Irishman makes him often countenance those that don't deserve it from him, from not knowing who they are. This is vastly amiable in him, and Mr St Leger, or other Irish people that are about him, ought not to let his kindness be flung away upon those that have used him ill. ...'

5 15 May 1790 Lady Louisa Conolly, London, to Lady Sarah Napier, Castletown, Leixlip, describing the social successes enjoyed by 'Emmy' [Lady Sarah's daughter, Emily, who had been adopted by Lady Louisa], particularly at Lady Spencer's ball.

6 25 May 1790 Lady Louisa Conolly, London, to Lady Sarah Napier, Castletown, Leixlip, describing the Duchess of Leinster's reunion with [Lord] Edward [Fitzgerald, her son] on his return from military service overseas, and referring to the election of a Speaker of the Irish House of Commons. '... my dear Sal. This postponing the meeting [of the Irish parliament] till the 8th is a sad thing, but I was more prepared for it than Mr Conolly or you imagined, for I heard of it here, and also found that the D[uke] of P[ortland's] chief dependence in Ireland is in Mr Conolly (between ourselves), and therefore, if the contest was close, that Mr Ponsonby could not let off Mr Conolly; so that I was only vexed and not surprised. If Mr Ponsonby was sure of a defeat, I should have taken it unkind of him not to let Mr Conolly off, but I have great hopes of his success from all I hear. ...'

7 15 June 1795 Lady Louisa Conolly to Thomas Conolly about the proposed sale of Newtown Limavady estate and borough. '... I hope your mother means to give you the whole £72,000 which, with the sale of your Newtown estate, would make you very comfortable indeed. Mr Alexander has been at [?Donny's] these two days past, and dined here yesterday. He told me that he thought it a pity you should sell the Newtown estate, which he considered as very cheap, and that if you would have patience till the war was over, he was sure you would get more for it. The borough he says is so circumstanced

40,242/7 *contd.* that he conceives it one of the safest in the kingdom, and one that could not be affected by the change of representation, should that business ever be in question. He is so convinced of the value of lands in Ireland that he and his brother are buying all they can afford to purchase now, in the expectation that lands will rise. I do not know how far he is a judge, but I thought it right to tell you this conversation. ...'

8 16 June 1795 Lady Louisa Conolly, Castletown, to Thomas Conolly, 4 Cleveland Row, St James's, London, referring to the failure of the expedition against France by emigré forces, discussing the family's financial situation, describing her farming activities and mentioning British and Irish politics, particularly the idea of a union. '... I hope you will be able to get your mother to fulfil her original promise to you of releasing you from the £40,000, if she lived long enough to do so, which she certainly has done. If she does do it, I think you will have nothing more to wish for in the money way, as the sale of N[ew]town estate (should it produce but £60,000) added to the £72,000 in England would clear your debts so nearly that the other £30,000 (that I reckon you would owe still) might easily be cleared off by a sinking fund appropriated for the purpose; which out of the income you would have after paying off £130,000 debt, probably would allow you to do with ease to yourself [sense]. I am certain that £8,000 a year to spend is as much as you can ever wish for at Castletown, and would be a great income in the way we live here. ... Your account of my brother's observation upon the Irish I fear is too true. With respect to the Irish parliament I grant he is right. But I hope it is not so out of the Houses of Parliament. If the whole country was like the parliament, it would be surely despicable; and indeed the same compliment may be returned for the British parliament, for if the people of England acted as basely as they do, the nation would not be worth much. As to any union with England such as the present cabinet would make with us, I hope never to see. We have had too much experience of Mr Pitt's duplicity ever to trust him, and yet I fear the thing is intended. I am certain that the idea of such a thing is in this country now, but it's too long to tell you in a letter of all the little circumstances that have come across me, upon which I found that opinion. I am glad Lady Spencer was so pleasant to you, but how can she make out that, when they coalesce with Mr Pitt that [sic] it was we that left them? I am, like you, hoping never to live in London, but if we [should] ever inhabit our Whitehall House, what Mrs Cornwall [sic] means to do to it would make it much pleasanter. ...'

40,242/ 9	27 June 1795	Lady Louisa Conolly, Dublin, to Conolly, 4 Cleveland Row, about the family's financial affairs. Conolly's enquiries have revealed that his mother has only about £30,000 left out of her riches instead of £50,000 and thus has been 'terribly cheated'. Conolly's sisters will be the losers unless he comes to their assistance. Lady Louisa urges submission to this severe trial.
10	10–11 July 1795	Lady Louisa Conolly to Conolly, 4 Cleveland Row, about the family dispute over money, in which she thinks Lady Buckingham[shire] the most reasonable of Conolly's sisters. ' ... Your situation in this business stands (I think) in a very simple point of view. Your mother, when she gave you her estates, feared she might not live long enough to provide as well for her daughters as she wished to do, consequently (and very properly) reserved the power of charging you with £10,000 apiece for them. She has lived to save near £20,000 above that sum, and upon the final settlement of your receiving those estates, she fulfils the promise she made you of releasing you from the sum charged upon those estates. Nothing can be clearer, and how were you to suppose that she was not as rich as she ought to be? But upon finding that she is not so (although she has the £30,000 that would pay off your sisters), you very properly offer to charge yourself with the £30,000 she wishes to leave to them. I say properly because it is kind in you to do so (being much more gratifying to one's heart to be kind than to be rich), but in strict justice you were not called upon to do it, as your mother in releasing you from the £40,000 only fulfilled her promise, and upon the terms that she had told you she would do so. Lady Anne might with justice say to her daughters that they had no right to ask her to break her word with you. However, I easily enter into her distress about it, for she loves you all, and is torn to pieces by you in different ways and by the different parties. I only hope that when she has time to reflect upon all this transaction, that [sic] she will distinguish your conduct from the rest of her children, and see it in the true, kind light that it deserves, wishing as you have ever done to be good to everything belonging to you. ... July 11th. I have just received yours of the 7th, and my heart is absolutely oppressed upon reading the account you gave me of your mother's treatment. But I trust that the consciousness of rectitude in your own mind supports you against the cruel attacks upon all your affectionate, tender, natural feelings, which though the cause of so much distress to you at times from your own family, have so completed my happiness through life that I cannot wish you without them.'

40,242/ 11	20 July 1795	Lady Louisa Conolly, Castletown, to Conolly, re-directed to Dublin, describing an attack by 150 defenders on the Napiers' house, and Lady Louisa's measures to put Castletown into a state of defence.
12	20 July 1795	Lady Louisa Conolly to Lady Sarah Napier, at William Ogilvie's, Harley Street, Cavendish Square, London: the same.
13	7 Jan. 1797	Lady Louisa Conolly, London, to Conolly, Merrion Street, Dublin, about the failure of the French invasion attempt, her optimistic view of the disposition of the Irish people, family movements and news and with references to British politics. ' ... I hope God is with us in this natural defence of our country, and I wish the French no other harm than to send them home without arms. What a desperate plan this has been of theirs, and how happily for Ireland has it ended in the best possible manner, viz. the goodwill of the people, of which I am not a little proud, having always thought that, when it came to be between French and Irish to fight against Irish, the country would not divide itself. I even think that Belfast would turn out fewer traitors than is imagined. Happily, there is enough national feel that at the moment does operate with most people, however they may detest and abhor the wicked, corrupt system that our government are daily practising. I expect to see Charles Fox today. He comes through town on his way to Norfolk to see me. I dined with Mr and Mrs Grey on Wednesday. I am sorry to say that he is as gloomy as you about England being a bankrupt nation. ... Charles Fox has just been here – very well but very desponding about politics. Delighted about the escape that Ireland has had. Frank thought that, as Charles Fox was here, he was not to let in anybody and so denied me to the D. of Portland, who called here. I was sorry for it. ...'
14	28 May 1797	Copy of a letter [in Lady Louisa Conolly's handwriting] from Conolly, Castletown, to the Duke [of Leinster] declining to sign a petition to the King to dismiss [his British or Irish ministers?]. 'I have looked over the printed papers which you have enclosed, and shall take care it [sic] shall not be seen by anyone except Lady Louisa. I got another copy left here last night by Mr Wogan Browne. I shall not sign it, as I do not see any good it can possibly do, and [it] will only add fuel to fire by making the poor people (going nightly about in a cruel manner, frightening and plundering the peaceable inhabitants) suppose they have supporters or abettors in the higher orders of the community. His Majesty not having complied with the petitions of his English subjects legally convened by their sheriffs, although not in open or smothered rebellion, will scarce listen to his Irish ones in the

40,242/14 *contd.*		contrary predicament. I wished for the landed interest of this and other counties in Ireland to be called to take their own peculiar situation into consideration, but not in Ireland to pray for the dismission of English ministers who do not belong to this country, and by naming them, make the cause of the landed interest sorely aggrieved appear a party cause, which will in times like these weaken a better one. I am always sorry when we differ, though I am always most truly and affectionately yours ...'.
15	20 Dec. 1799	Pamela, Lady Edward Fitzgerald [widow of Lord Edward] to Colonel [George William Richard] Harcourt, M.P. [her lover], Hamburgh about her sorry situation. Enquires whether he remains the same for her and whether she still has *'cette bonne place dans votre coeur'*. She describes her attachment to him. She can apply herself to nothing and can see nothing other than him. The letter is written in French.
16	[1799]	Lady Louisa Conolly to Lady Sarah Napier, Kildare Street, expressing the hope that the murder of the French ministers was not politically motivated and the fear that its consequences will be as serious as the attack of General Duff on the rebels negotiating a surrender on the Curragh, and discussing a visit of the Londonderrys and other social news.
19	26 July 1803	Lady Louisa Conolly, Castletown, to Lady Sarah Napier, Comptroller of Army Accounts Office, Merrion Street, Dublin, about the widow of an officer killed in Emmet's insurrection. 'My heart wrings with distress at the sufferings of the afflicted widows and families. Poor Lady Kilwarden, being at home, must have friends innumerable to attend to her, but it may not be the case with the unhappy Mrs Browne, whom I take to be either an English or Scotch woman, and but lately come to Ireland. If so, she must be here almost destitute of friends, for although I make no doubt of her having received all the attention possible from the females of the regiment, yet they may be but late acquaintances, and although I am still a greater stranger to her, it has come into my head that, as soon as she can be prevailed upon to relinquish those precious remains, the removing her from that dreadful scene of misery to the country, and to a house of mourning [following Conolly's death in April], might be the best place for her, until her friends from England or Scotland should have consulted on the best manner of removing her from this country, which she must so naturally abhor. If you will have the goodness to go to the barrack, and in my name (if you find the circumstances make it advisable, and that I shall not appear an officious intruder upon her) to make her this proposal, and you can tell her truly, how much her sorrows are felt

40,242/19 *contd.*		here, and being partners in affliction, she will find this house one of entire liberty to pass her days, if she pleases, solely in her own room; and if she has children, she will of course bring them, and I would send my carriage to bring her down here. There are cases sometimes where such a proposal might be of use, and if this should turn out to be one, you cannot say too much for me, in the gratification I should feel, could I but alleviate one sigh in such a deeply wounded heart. You will also explain the safety of this house (which at least we consider as such), notwithstanding the disturbances. All was quiet here last night.'
20	1 Aug. 1803	Lady Louisa Conolly, Castletown, to the Duke of Richmond, re-directed to Brighton, Sussex, explaining that Lord Dunlo, Admiral Pakenham and herself, who are the three people principally concerned in her estate affairs, are of one mind that the Bedfordshire estate should be sold and that the details of the sale should be entrusted solely to Richmond, and referring to her precautionary measures at Castletown, the deplorable murders which were committed in the course of the recent insurrection, and the ill-health of Napier.
28	5 July 1815	Lady Louisa Conolly, Castletown, to [Lady Sarah Napier], commenting on the battle of Waterloo, particularly the casualties among friends of theirs, but with a reference to the Duke of Wellington's proclamation on entering France, of which Lady Louisa approves and Lady Sarah does not.

MSS	DATE	DESCRIPTION
34,922	1795–1802	**Correspondence of Thomas and Lady Louisa Conolly with miscellaneous correspondents including John FitzGibbon, 1st earl of Clare, 1795–8, mostly about the 1798 rebellion**
1	3 Mar. 1798	Clare, Dublin, to Lady Louisa ('My dear Madam') in reply to MS 34,922/2.* 'As yet nothing has appeared in print as what fell from me in the late debate on Lord Moira's motion, which is not full of inaccuracy and misstatement. Of course, I need not tell you that nothing printed on that subject has been published by my authority. At the very earnest importunities of many of my friends here and in England, I have endeavoured to correct a very bad note which was sent to me, and probably it will be printed on Monday. I will send

* This and the following letter is printed in D. A. Fleming & A.P.W. Malcomson, *A Volley of Execrations: The letters and Papers of John FitzGibbon, Earl of Clare, 1772–1802* (Irish Manuscripts Commission: Dublin, 2005), pp 280–81, although reference is only made to copies in the McPeake Papers in PRONI rather than originals calendared here.

34,922/1 *contd.*

you a copy by post on that night, if it should be then published, by which you will see that nothing fell from me which could carry with it a shade of imputation on the fidelity of your servants; and I shall thank your Ladyship extremely if you will, in my name, set their minds at perfect ease on this subject. Be assured that I never can think or speak of you without affectionate admiration, and that I am with the truest respect and regard, always your Ladyship's faithful humble servant, Clare C.'

2 2 Mar. 1798 Copy of a letter from Lady Louisa [Conolly], Castletown, [Celbridge, Co. Kildare], to Clare ('My dear Lord') about his speech in the Lords in which he reflected on the fidelity of the Conollys' servants.

'The Evening Post having given an account of that part of your speech relative to the disturbances here last May, different from what yours (published by authority) does, and our faithful old servants thinking themselves injured thereby, we have judged it necessary to publish an acknowledgment of their good conduct upon that occasion, and at the same time considering it a good opportunity for inserting what appears to us to be just in the case of the prisoners, whose evil intentions towards us (as reported at the time) neither Mr Conolly or I ever gave the least credit to, and therefore are anxious that no impression of that sort should remain to their prejudice, or make it possible that it should affect their trials; in which we feel certain of meeting with your approbation, and wishing sincerely (as I am sure we all three do) that nothing but justice should take place. Your very partial mention of me, my dear Lord, I can say nothing to, conscious that I can owe it only to the friendship you have ever been so good as to profess for me, and which is returned with equal regard ... .

[Copy of the public declaration mentioned in the foregoing:] From some reports having been circulated through the channel of the several n[ews]papers injurious to the character of our servants in general, we think ourselves called upon to declare our firm reliance on the fidelity, attachment and courage of those who so eminently distinguished themselves at the time of the disturbances in our neighbourhood last May, when surmises of an unpleasant nature accompanied the first breaking out of those riots, but which surmises we never considered as authenticating a belief of particular danger to our persons. One servant and a helper (among others) taken up at that time, were found guilty upon their trial of administering the Union Oath, and sentenced to transportation. The want of time at those same assizes have [sic] left the rest yet to be tried. The grievous circumstance of being obliged to detain them in prison so many months beyond the limit of their first commitment renders a silence the more imposing [sic]. As to what their guilt may or may not prove to be, they ought not to be pre-judge [sic].'

34,922/ 22 Mar. 1798 E[mily, Duchess of] L[einster] to Lady Louisa Conolly,
3 Castletown,

'... Thank God I have nothing to fear for my beloved Eddy [Lord Edward Fitzgerald]. I am not the least nervous'. Recovery from a fever by Lady Sarah's husband. Is glad that Lord Edward's wife is near them: 'I dread her health being sadly affected by his absence and uncomfortable situation. ... I enclose a letter to her as those directed to her might perhaps be stopt [sic] at the Port and not delivered to her? ...'

4 [May 1798] Paper in Lady Louisa Conolly's handwriting, endorsed by her, 'Attempt to keep a journal of the rebellion, too full of misery to continue it.

On Thursday 24 May, the first insurrection broke out at Naas, Prosperous, Kilcullen Bridge and Clane. A company of the Cork Militia quartered at Prosperous had their sentinels killed, upon which the insurgents rushed into the place where the soldiers lay and destroyed their officers and themselves by murder and fire. It is feared that the women and children of the company shared the same fate. The insurgents then went to Clane, where Mr Wogan Browne, with yeomanry and part of the Armagh Militia, defeated them. At Naas the insurgents proceeded with more skill, having secured the different entries into the town, where the Armagh Militia had their headquarters, under their commander, Lord Gosport [sic – Gosford]. After losing about 20 of their soldiers and two pieces of cannon rescued two or three times from the insurgents, the Ancient Britons and the Armagh Militia defeated the insurgents. At Kilcullen Bridge the insurgents rose likewise, but were defeated by General Dundas, who commanded that district that took in Kildare. He however retreated for that night to Naas. The loss of the rebels at those four places that day is reputed to be about 200.

Friday the 25th, the insurgents broke out at Dunboyne, which was considered serious enough to bring General Craig from Dublin with 1,600 troops, who defeated them at their camp, supposed to contain some thousands. 130 of the rebels were killed without the loss of one soldier.

The rebel camp then changed their position [sic] to Tara Hill, where they were attacked on Sunday 27th by Lt Scobie of the Ray [sic Reay] Fencibles and some yeoman cavalry, where 250 of them were found dead in the field, and their commander in full uniform among them. Two days previous to this business, a sergeant and 12 men attending the baggage of the R[e]ay Fencibles were taken, and all killed but two men. But it was reported that the baggage and ammunition was re-taken by the R[e]ay Fencibles, who at Tara Hill lost 9 soldiers killed and 16 wounded, but dispersed the insurgents. On Saturday morning, 26th, about 3 o'clock, a party

34,922/4 *contd.*		of 200 broke through Mr Conolly's gate at Celbridge, marched across the lawn and joined three other parties coming different roads to the town of Leixlip, which they attacked, lost 21 killed, and were dispersed by a party of the Inverness Fencibles, a small party of the Derry Militia and the Leixlip yeoman [sic].'
5	8 June 1798	Copy of a letter from Lady Louisa Conolly, Castletown, to Lord Camden On arrangements for the funeral of Lord Edward Fitzgerald. '… I cannot forbear from assuring Your Excellency that so earnest was my wish to preclude any possibility of a riot on that melancholy occasion, that I claim not the smallest merit in having ordered such a private funeral for my beloved nephew as accorded *very ill* with my feelings towards him. But thinking no sacrifice too great for the attainment of that important end, I had desired that three persons only should attend – two of the Duke of Leinster's oldest servants and Mr Leeson the agent. By the neglect before alluded to Mr Leeson was deprived of his attendance at the ceremony in the Church. However, a complaint against Mr Cook[e] upon *that score*, which only regards my feelings, I consider as entirely beneath my notice, but I think it right that Your Excellency should know that after my kind friend the Chancellor (with whom I conversed) had approved of my plan, and Lord Castlereagh too, whom I sent to apprize of it, the effect was the same as if no orders had been given. …'
6	26 May 1798	T[homas] C[onolly] to [his wife], Lady Louisa Conolly, about the progress of the rebellion. 'All well here, and our Grand Army returned, having killed about 50 unfortunate people, scarcely armed or deserving the name of soldiers. General Needham came and took the command in the barracks about 9 o'clock with two fresh regiments. I think it useless to harrass the soldiers so much, and I hope a few days' reflection will bring these poor deluded men to their senses, and a proclamation of pardon set all again to rights. I will endeavour to obtain it. ... I have got all your despatches and my letters by Mr Marlay.'
7	[28 May 1798]	Lady Louisa Conolly to Lady Sarah Napier enclosing no. 7a and praising God for the news.
7a	[28 May 1798]	[Thomas Conolly] to Lady Louisa Conolly. 'Sallins, near 6 o'clock, Monday morning. Lest you should be frightened at not finding me in Dublin, I send the boy to tell you the joyful news of peace with the rebels, who are to surrender 15,000 stand of arms to General Dundas. If possible I will go home today or tomorrow.'

34,922/ 8 7 June1798 [The 3rd Duke of Richmond], Whitehall, to his sister, Lady Louisa Conolly, Castletown, describing the composed state of the Duchess of Leinster and the distracted state of Lady Edward Fitzgerald, at the news of Lord Edward's death.
'... a more generous, good-hearted soul I believe never existed than poor Edward possessed. His thoughts were errors of his imagination, but I am sure no man acted more from principle (mistaken as it was) than he did. I am glad that you and Henry saw him before he died. It must have been a happiness to him and a comfort to you both to have witnessed that calmness of mind and warmth of affection which never forsook him.
His poor mother set off last night with Mimi [her youngest daughter] and his boy for Ireland, in hopes that her presence might do some good in retarding his trial till the heat and prejudice of the moment were a little subsided. ... The King appeared ... very feeling to me yesterday when I had an audience to state to him the grounds on which I had, with Mr Pitt's permission, written to Lord Camden to beg a delay in the trial. ...'
Lady Edward has received intimations that it was wished that she should go to Hamburgh.

9 18 June 1798 Lady Louisa Conolly, Castletown, to the Duke of Richmond, Midhurst, describing the effects of Lord Edward's death on all the members of the Leinster family in Ireland, discussing the characters of Lord and Lady Edward and describing the progress of the rebellion in Co Kildare.
'... the poor D[uke] of Leinster is all gratitude [to Richmond]. His distresses are great indeed. I do not believe that his excellent and amiable wife can live, by all I hear, his distress about the whole of poor Edward's business (and end) is of that nature that it must give him the deepest affliction, and with his immense family, the derangement of his property for the present is a most alarming prospect – the Co Kildare, where his whole estate is, in a manner laid waste, and no chance that I can foresee of his getting in his half year's rents. He is worse off in that particular than any of us, and I do not know what he can do. By his letter to me, he does not seem aware of that distress, and I fear does not know how very bad things are. His agent [James Spencer of Rathangan, Co. Kildare] (whom [sic] had lately resigned, but not yet given up his accounts) has been murdered in his own house, so that I dread confusion from that quarter. ...

Your character of that dear Edward is precisely the same that I would give him, with the addition of the most undaunted spirit and courage, which by being on the spot I have had opportunities of knowing. The total carelessness of his own life, and his firm adherence to those whom he considered as under his protection, made him sacrifice himself in the manner he did. He could have

34,922/9
contd.

saved himself over and over, but spurned at the thought, and no entreaties of the tenderest kind would have kept him out of the scrape. That he originally flattered himself with the vain hope that a redress of grievances might be effected without bloodshed, I am convinced of. How far he may have seen the impossibility of such a measure lately, I cannot say; but this I know, that whatever danger was attached to the plan, he was to meet it and to sacrifice himself to save others. This valuable and charming character is what we have to lament the loss of, and to grieve that his most excellent qualities were bestowed on a set of people not worthy of the cause he undertook for them. For his cause was a benevolent one, and not what the mischievous persons he was engaged with would have made it. At least, if we are told true of the sad conspiracy against Dublin, it was a dreadful one, and such as his heart could never have brought itself to. I therefore do not consider myself as uncharitable by separating him from the mass of them, and the less so when I recollect that it was by them that he was betrayed. But thank God, he is at peace, and from my knowledge of him, I have the happiness of thinking that he appeared before his God in full security of having acted to the best of his judgement. What more, dearest brother, can any of us hope to do? Had he lived and everything turned out according to our most sanguine expectations, I do not think he would have been happy. His mind was too much worked up with the idea of the sufferings of his country to be at ease, and he probably would have quitted Europe forever. ...'

She goes on to discuss Lady Edward, who she says had much prejudice to contend against in Ireland because of the family she came from. Lady Louisa participated in this prejudice at first, but was soon won over by the excellence of Lady Edward's character. She is convinced that Lord Edward's decision to join in the plan to bring in the French had nothing to do with Lady Edward's influence. She implores Richmond to continue his protection to Lady Edward.

'... I am necessarily engaged with the business of this sad rebellion. Wexford is the worst, the county of Kildare next, in which we live, and we are surrounded by different posts of the insurgents. The grand camp is about 9 miles from us, at a place called Timahoe, upon the borders of the Bog of Allen. At Prosperous, a place about the same distance, there is another settlement of them. Kilcock, six miles from here, was taken possession of last night, so that we may be annoyed from any one of these places. Poor Castletown is turned into a garrison. We have 18 soldiers sleeping in our drawing-rooms, and the house put into such a state of defence at night with the help of the servants, as they tell me would stand a good siege, and a sentinel constantly on the roof of the house to watch the approach of the enemy. There

34,922/9
contd.

are 80 men at Celbridge and 300 at Leixlip, the conjunction of which I hope will make a stand sufficient against them. This is certainly a most anxious moment, when all seems at stake. But I think that you will approve of Mr Conolly's determination and mine to meet it, whatever it may turn out. We are both old enough not to expect to live many years more, so that the anxiety about life must lessen, and the only cordial that can be given to the last portion of our existence is the employing it (to the last) in the good of our fellow-creatures, as far as lies in our powers.

It would be too long to go back to the history of last year, when the first certainty of this evil spirit having crept into our own house came to our knowledge. You heard how much it affected my spirits and how little communicative I was about it. My feeling so much as I did arose from the very great mortification I felt at having spent near 40 years (in what I considered a laudable pursuit) in vain. After having shown the greatest goodwill to the different classes around me, without ever once being conscious of a moment's feel of pride or severity towards them, and not even suffering my amusements to be independent of their advantages, I had flattered myself with the hope of possessing their friendship and confidence, and that when ill-advisers came to them with new proposals, that they would at least have consulted me before they engaged in so deep a business, particularly as (so long ago as '95) when Col[onel] Napier's house was attacked for arms (he and Mr Conolly being both in England), I went myself to every house, spoke to every poor person to explain the nature of this mischievous manner of proceeding, entreated them to desist and repose some confidence in two such old friends as Mr Conolly and myself, who never had nor ever would deceive them. From that time our pains were unremitting to get as many out of the scrape as we could, and even last year, when the violence broke out that committed so many of them to prison, and a general indignation seemed to prevail against them, Mr Conolly and I (though censured by many for doing so) determined to ward off every attack upon them that appeared to us a stretch beyond the laws of the land. In this state of mind have we both gone on, sometimes hoping that things were not so bad, at others fearing the worst. When the positive discovery of the existence of the pikes brought along with it the conviction of intended attack or resistance, either idea proved that war was in contemplation with the people of Ireland. A retrospect into the conduct of all those on either side who have brought these calamities upon us (one, through the very terrible misuse of power, sad, sad extravagance and the most unjustifiable goading acts upon the feelings of the great majority of the Irish, opposed now by the most uncontrolled spirit of revenge on the other part), are not points for present discussion. We are plunged into a most dreadful civil war, and it is the business of

34,922/9
contd.

everybody to endeavour to extricate the country from it as soon as possible.

We mean, my dearest brother, to do our best, for which reason we stay here, as Mr Conolly thinks that by his presence he has some chance of influencing this district, and is at hand to receive the returning allegiance of many that are said to wish to come in with it. Our situation is a little awkward, for we cannot think of refusing protection to those who say they wish for it, and yet we are not quite sure of their sincerity, the infatuation about this business has spread so far and is so deep. However, we think it right to risk the danger that may attend it for the sake of those who are sincere and who would be reduced to the most desperate situation if we withheld it from them. For your comfort, I must tell you that I was very well treated 10 days ago, when Mr Conolly had marched from Dublin with his regiment, and that I was here (without any gentleman in the house or soldiers) and saw 200 of the insurgents at 3 o'clock in the morning walk across our lawn in the front of the house, in their way from Celbridge to Leixlip, where they joined other parties from different sides of the country and attacked Leixlip, where they were defeated. In passing through our gates, they took the keys with them, and locked us in, leaving word that they would not hurt me nor anybody in the house, and that they only took that road because the high road was not safe for them to go on. They marched in great order and quietness, and did not molest me, but it was not a pleasant sight. Mr Conolly was at that time at Sallins, seven miles off, marching with his regiment to Kilcullen Bridge, and came home two days after in the greatest joy, thinking that we were going to make peace with these insurgents. General Dundas thought so too, and went to receive many arms on the Curragh the next day. A number did come in, and the people who brought them were thought to be their leaders. It is since imagined that their own leaders went off to Wexford, and that they were not in earnest. On the other hand, the insurgents complain of a breach of faith, and say that while they were delivering up their arms to General Dundas on one side of the Curragh, that Sir James Duff was firing at them from the other. An unfortunate mistake in some degree, I fear, did take place, for Sir James Duff, by a very clever forced march from Limerick, came upon the rear of these people before General Dundas had intelligence of him. However Sir James very fortunately at first required them to lay down their arms, which had an effect upon some of them, but a number either thought themselves betrayed or chose to make it an excuse for not surrendering their arms, and accordingly run away as fast as they could; so that this wished-for peace stopped there, and there has been no overtures since.

34,922/9 *contd.*

Happily, the accounts (upon the whole) from the north are good, and we do not apprehend much from the south, though we have reason to think the disposition of the people is not favourable to us. I am obliged to say us now, for although Mr Conolly has ever opposed the votes of the government, he will stand by any existing government rather than none. Connaught we really believe will remain quiet. We have just heard that Lord Cornwallis is expected to land today or tomorrow as Lord Lieutenant. It is quite a surprise upon us, not having heard more than a report of such a thing being in contemplation only the day before yesterday. We must hope that the change will be for the better. Lord Cornwallis being a soldier, is certainly what we want most at present, and as he has always had the character of being a good man, the two things going together may be of use to us. I shall long to hear whether he adopts new measures.

This business is too deep for such a political head as mine to judge of, but I still think that it does not proceed from a religious cause, such numbers of the greatest and best catholics are so unhappy about it, behave so well and take such pains to discountenance anything of the kind. At Wexford there has, so far back as 36 years to my knowledge, existed a violent protestant and catholic party. Consequently those engines were set to work for the purpose of rebellion. In other places, that of electioneering parties, and so on. Every means has [sic] been received that could answer their design. The free quarters, whipping the people and burning the houses have just been stopped, which rejoices me, for although in some places (where these terrible sentences were executed with great caution by humane and discerning officers) the object did answer for discovering the pikes and arms, yet upon the whole it was a dangerous measure in regard to the licentiousness that it produced among the soldiers, the fury and madness that it drove the insurgents to and the lukewarmth that it threw upon the well-disposed persons, who found themselves equally aggrieved by the free quarters as the rebels were; so that 'tis a blessing to have it all stopped.

We have just got an account of a skirmish at Kilcock having happened this morning, where the rebels were dispersed, 100 men with their general killed (a Mr Elmer, who was an officer in the Kildare Militia) and we have lost 12 men of an excellent Scotch regiment. An officer also, we fear, is killed, and two or three wounded. It is dreadful to be brought to that point that the destruction of so many people must be considered as game. ...'

10 4 July 1798 Copy of a letter [in Lady Louisa's handwriting] from Lord Cornwallis, Dublin Castle, to Conolly, endorsed by her, '... who wrote him word of the doubts that were entertained of the validity of the proclamation, for want of the Lord Lieutenant's name and signature of the Privy Councillors to it.'

34,922/10 *contd.*

'It is my most earnest wish to adopt such measures as may be most likely to induce the deluded people to submit without having further recourse to the horrors of war. It was thought that the proclamation issued from the generals commanding in the different districts in which there are still rebels in arms, would have the best effect. If however I should find that the operations should not succeed from any doubts that may be entertained of their validity, I will endeavour to remove the objections that are made to them. Lord Castlereagh tells me that he has explained to you that the mistake that you mention will have no bad consequence.'

11 26 July 1798

The Duke of Richmond, Goodwood, [Sussex], to Lady Louisa Conolly, Castletown: a long, philosophical letter about the rebellion and the wise and humane part which the Conollys have played, concluding with a further character-sketch of Lord Edward and report of Lady Edward's state of mind.

'... from what I personally knew of his conduct formerly, I was satisfied that he had that sort of weakness of character which, at the same time that it is amiable in its manners and affections, is liable to draw into great errors, and equally does mischief with what proceeds from bad principles. He had no steadiness to resist where he could be persuaded that friendship intervened, and those consequences which prudence should have persuaded him to dread, became the greater incentives if any personal danger to himself was attached to them. It was these sentiments that led him to rejoin opposition after he had allowed me to tell the King and Mr Pitt that he had determined not to be any more concerned in it, and that he would not take his seat in the House, wherein he had been chosen contrary to his express request, and while he was in America, and that he meant for the future to stick wholly to his profession. But the idea of abandoning his friends and party got the better of the other alternative of breaking his word, and I believe chiefly because he felt his interest might go with and be deemed the cause of his keeping it. How much more noble was the conduct of the Earl of Scarbrough in the late reign, who having been drawn in by Lord Chesterfield to say he would vote for an address to the King to inquire the cause why an officer had been turned out of his regiment for a vote in parliament, on reflection found he was wrong, and openly avowed it; but to prevent its being thought that he voted with the court from interested motives, resigned his regiment of guards and his place of Master of the Horse to the King. But poor Edward had a weak mind, and was easily led by those who worked upon the noble points of his disposition, and accordingly, by what I hear of the late trials, was probably drawn in to go to horrid lengths indeed – lengths that would have sacrificed all his family and country and all that was

34,922/11 *contd.*		dear to him; for it was still weaker if he could believe that his influence could have stopped any of the excesses to which his measures tended, and still less to those which the introduction of the French must have produced. But yet, even admitting all this, can you and I who knew the natural goodness of his heart, his family affections, his love for his friends, say that this deluded amiable young man deserved no compassion? We cannot. Law would not, could not, have made any distinction in his favour. But we may and do, not because he was our nephew only, but because at bottom we knew his intentions, however misled they might have been, to be good. ...' Copy of that part of the former item expressing Richmond's views on Divine providence.
12	12 Aug. 1798	Copy of a letter from Lady Louisa Conolly, Castletown, to Lord Cornwallis asking for an audience to discuss the bill of attainder against Lord Edward as it will affect his widow and children. She refers to a letter from the Duke of Leinster in which he states that he has been given permission by Lord Castlereagh, at Lord Cornwallis's command, 'to apply in favour of the widow and children of his late brother Lord Edward Fitzgerald against the bill of attainder'. Lady Louisa wishes to thank the Lord Lieutenant in person: 'I have not the courage to name Castletown, the house at present being little better than a garrison and an hospital ...'
13	15–16 Aug. 1798	Lady Louisa Conolly, Castletown, to [Conolly] describing her audience with Lord Cornwallis. The importance of making an example of Lord Edward and his family has been impressed upon Cornwallis, but Lady Louisa still thinks that it is harsh to visit the sins of one who has already paid for them with his life, on his innocent family. Lady Louisa has sent George Ponsonby the Duke of Richmond's opinion on how they should proceed, and she hopes that this will be acted upon, if counsel thinks proper. Returning to the subject of Lord Cornwallis, she exclaims: '... how he does hate being Lord Lieutenant! I do not wonder at him. He has made a bargain with us not to call him Excellency. What a good man he must be, to undertake so horrid a situation for the sake of doing right! ...' She concludes with references to estate and family affairs.
14	24 Aug. 1798	[The 1st Earl of] Charlemont, Dublin, to [Lady Louisa Conolly] about her request that he oppose the bill of attainder in the House of Lords. 'When your Ladyship in your goodness shall reflect upon the affection I have ever felt for the unhappy object of our present regret, an affection which even his misconduct has not been able to obliterate, and shall duly estimate the respectful love I have ever borne towards the family of which he was a member, you will, I

34,922/11 *contd.*

am confident, entertain no doubt of the real concern with which I find that his guilt is now become so notorious as to render it almost impossible for a man of public feelings to hazard any measure in his defence.

The wonderful abilities and laborious endeavours of his counsel, Mr Curran, have not been able to make out for him any case so plausible as to obtain a single vote in his favour, even among those who with reason are likely to oppose the bill as an unconstitutional measure. But the proofs to which I principally allude are contained in the report of the secret committee of the House of Commons, which has now been publicly read and is ordered to be printed, and which must be allowed authentic, as the information proceeds, not from perjured informers, but from the voluntary confession of accomplices. Under these circumstances, I find myself involved in the most distressing difficulty. On the one hand, I am pushed forward by the remembrance of an old affection and by my ardent wish to obey your Ladyship's commands and to act in conformity with the desires of a family which I have always loved and respected, while on the other I am forcibly restrained by a consciousness of the weakness of our cause, by the dread of acting from partial and not from public motives, by the improbability of meeting with any support, and by my shameful inability to express myself in public so as to give any plausible colour to an opposition which, if left unaccounted for, would undoubtedly be discreditable to the opponent. Of this my unfortunate dilemma, the difficulties of which are farther increased by the miserable state of my health and spirits, I have thought it my duty to inform your Ladyship, in order that if, as will too probably be the case, the causes already mentioned should disable me from proceeding in a manner conformable to your wishes and to my own, I may obtain a pardon from your goodness ... .

If it shall be thought proper to lay a petition before the Lords, I am still ready and willing to present it, as I most assuredly am to do everything within the limits of my powers. We have been surprised by the intelligence that the French have landed at Killala. There are however only three frigates with 700 men, a few cannons and some small arms.'

15 28 Aug. 1798 Copy of a letter from Lady Louisa Conolly, Castletown, to Lord Charlemont. She respects Charlemont's views and situation, '... although my unshaken opinion remains that those very accomplices who have screened themselves behind his departed shade, have more to answer for than himself, and prove (what I always dreaded would happen) that his name and character being necessary to their banner, they would put him foremost, as the best covering for themselves. ...' She thanks him for his kindness in still offering to present a petition, but says that she would not wish to stretch his friendship so far.

34,922/16	27 Nov. 1798	Lord Cornwallis, Phoenix Park, to Conolly announcing his intention of offering the Comptrollership of Army Accounts to Colonel Napier.
17	9 Sept. 1798	The Dowager Duchess of Leinster, Stikenor[?], Chichester, [Sussex], to Lady Louisa Conolly, Castletown: family losses and bereavements, particularly the death of 'Eddy'.
18	10 Sept. 1798	Lady Louisa Conolly, Castletown, to the Duke of Richmond, about the passing of the attainder bill and about the French surrender at Ballinamuck. 'I was meditating to write you an account of the fate of the attainder bill (which passed the House of Lords last Thursday) and all the circumstances that attended it, but in truth, our anxiety has been kept so much alive since the landing of the French, and particularly the last four or five days, when we have been in hourly expectation of hearing from Lord Cornwallis, that it was not easy to collect my thoughts sufficiently to give you the detail of the business alluded to. But I cannot lose one moment in telling you of the happy event of last Thursday at Johnstown in the county of Longford, where the French surrendered and were made prisoners. General Hulse in his way to town yesterday was so good as to call here and tell us of the victory over the French, which he had got a short, hasty account of from General Lake. The particulars he had not learnt, nor did a messenger that came from Dublin to us in the course of the day bring many more. However, such as they were, you shall have them. ...' She goes on to give such information as she has, and concludes by attributing the defeat of the French and the good conduct of the Irish Militia to Lord Cornwallis's conciliatory measures, and by expressing sorrow at the extent of the slaughter which must have taken place.
21	[Sept. 1801]	[Elizabeth, Lady Holland], Brighton, to [?] introducing a physician and naturalist much patronised by Napoleon called Pietit and discussing Lady Louisa Conolly and Lord and Lady Edward Fitzgerald. She goes on at great length extolling Lady Louisa's virtues, lack of malice, persistant ability to see only good in others and therefore bring the best out of them, etc. She even finds 'old Conolly' likeable 'in his hubble-bubble way', and says that, if anybody could overcome her aversion to Ireland and the Irish and induce her to visit that country, it would be the Conollys. '... as a witness of the progress of poor Lord Ed's delusion, her [Lady Louisa's] testimony carries weight, and her complete acquittal of Pamela either as promoter or accessory in his proceedings is sufficient. She ascribes the origin of his feeling and acting upon the principles that caused his ruin to his wandering

34,922/21 *contd.*		among the savages in America, where his ardent imagination was captivated by beholding what he thought the charms of liberty and independence; displeasure against his uncle for refusing his marriage with his cousin on account of poverty made him execrate wealth and property. His dismissal from the army for a foolish, drunken toast soured a disposition already tainted with the novelties of philantrophy, etc, and when once ill-inclined, he found numbers themselves ready either from the discontent of obscurity, poverty [?] or ambition, ready to foment his disloyalty and avail themselves of so great and popular [a] name as his. During his confinement, she saw him but once a few hours before he expired. He was then rambling, but knew her, praised Pamela, hoped Eddy would comfort his mother and rejoiced at the success of the rebels, whom he said would finally succeed. Lady L said he was dissatisfied with his adherents and persuaded they betrayed him. Neilson was supposed to have given him up, and McNevin was also a false friend. ...'
22	6 June 1795	Frances [Countess] Camden, [wife of the newly arrived Lord Lieutenant], Phoenix Park, to [Lady Louisa Conolly] expressing the hope that in spite of political difference the Conollys and Camdens will meet socially.
23	7 June 1795	Copy of a letter from Lady Louisa Conolly, Castletown, to Lady Camden responding in like manner.
24	7 June 1795	Copy of a letter from Lady Louisa Conolly, Castletown, to Lady Londonderry [Lord Camden's sister] explaining how embarrassing it is to her that the Camdens will be visiting the Bishop of Waterford, [Richard Marlay], who lives almost at Lady Louisa's own door, since she does not yet feel able, on political grounds, to invite the Camdens for a visit to Castletown. She hopes that Lady Camden will not feel that this is contrary to the spirit of Lady Louisa's letter [of 7 June 1795].
25	6. Jan. 1802	Lord Cornwallis, Amiens, [France], to Lady Louisa Conolly regretting that it will not be in his power to do all that she wishes for a Mr Cannon, whose property has been sequestered by the French. He refers to the important services performed by Colonel Napier as Comptroller of Army Accounts.

APPENDIX

MISCELLANEOUS CONOLLY PAPERS IN VARIOUS LOCATIONS

1. IRISH ARCHITECTURAL ARCHIVE

98/79	1864–71	Five volumes of diaries of Thomas Conolly (1823–76) detailing his travels in America (the first four volumes) and Italy as follows:
	26 Nov. 1864–19 Jan. 1865	Soft bound volume detailing a voyage to Bermuda via Madeira. Included are a series of sketches in colour ink depicting various people in Bermuda.
	7–16 Dec. 1864; 4–13 Jan. 1865.	A log book containing the proceedings on board the Emily & Florence from the port of Cardiff and Madeira and St George Bermuda.Thomas Conolly a passenger on this voyage. Enclosed are nine loose documents including newspaper cuttings relating to events in America.
	23 Feb.–4 May 1865	Hardbound volume entitled 'Log of 1st expedition to America beginning 23rd day of February 1865 being two days before my birthday, Thomas Conolly'. This diary details his trip to Virginia during the American Civil War, and has been published as Nelson D. Lankford, (ed.), *An Irishman in Dixie: Thomas Conolly's diary of the fall of the confederacy* (South Carolina, 1988).
	1865	Hardbound volume containing newspaper cuttings and other ephemeral material from Conolly's trip to America. It is inscribed 'Thomas Conolly, Richmond, VA. Included are sheet music and song lyrics for pro southern marching tunes.
	23 Nov. 1870–30 Mar. 1871	Hardbound volume detailing a journey to Italy made by Conolly in 1870–71, which was mostly spent in Rome. 23 Nov. 1870–30 March 1871. Included are 32 loose documents, mostly ephemeral material including concert programmes, business cards, advertisements etc. There is also a coloured ink drawing of the death of Ceasar, in Conolly's hand.

2. NATIONAL LIBRARY OF IRELAND

MS 15,549	Aug.–Oct. 1707	Eight letters dealing with the discharge of a bond charged on the estate of the late Sir Albert Conyngham. Includes letters from William Conolly to Lady Shelbourne.
MS 15,550	1707–08	Five letters to William Conolly of Dublin from Thomas Knox of Mount Charles [Murray agent in Donegal], William Pinkstan of Donoughdee, Lady Shelbourne and Murray of Cally in Scotland.

MS 17,302	1728	Rental for part of William Conolly's estate in Ballyshannon, Co. Donegal, 1728
MS 17,858	1708–26	Letters from Robert McCausland [Conolly's agent] to William Conolly, about the Co. Londonderry Militia, included are lists of officers.
MS 14,342	1828–65	Castletown account book
MS 14338 –41	1803–15; 1813–19	Three ledgers of miscellaneous accounts of Lady Louisa Conolly.
MS 15,397	n.d.	Essay on the plantations of trees presented by John Walker to Lady Louisa Conolly
MS 22,005	1853	A volume containing the ordnance survey sheets showing the several townlands of Thomas Conolly (1823–76)'s estate in Co. Donegal, in which he has granted mineral working rights to the great Donegal Mining Company.

3. PUBLIC RECORD OFFICE, NORTHERN IRELAND

D/663	1659–1806	The Newtown Limavady corporation records.
D/1062/1	1734–1900	A solicitor's collection of Bellaghy, Co. Londonderry, estate papers including:
D/1062/1/5	*c.* 1850	Return of leases renewable forever on the Bellaghy estate
D/1062/1/ 8–12	1730–1870	Leases and fee farm grants on the Bellaghy estate.
D/1567/F/ 11, 17	1817–20	Letters and papers of Richard Staples as agent for the Bellaghy estate.
LR1/1010/ A/20/B	1817—75	Land Registry of Northern Ireland. Bellaghy estate papers and testamentary material including a copy of the will of Frances Lady Howe dated 20. Sept. 1817. The copy dates from 1875 and is included in a mortgage from female members of the Trench/Clancarty family reciting previous transactions. From a codicil of 24 July 1804 to Lady Howe's will it appears that Thomas Conolly's four surviving sisters had each inherited an undivided fourth part of Bellaghy in fee.
T/3110	**1817–42**	Further Bellaghy estate papers.

4. PAPERS IN PRIVATE COLLECTIONS

A. A bundle of political letters to Thomas Conolly, 1796–1800, in PRONI's Register of Irish Archives (Pakenham Papers, G/2/20). Including the following:

G/2/20 4 Dec. 1796		[Henry] Grattan to Conolly About the improper use of Conolly's name and Conolly's replacement as secretary to the Whig Club. 'Whenver I ever differ from you even in point of time 'tis always with deference to your opinion and diffidence in my own... . We entirely agree about the two great measures, reform and emancipation, ...[except as to their timing]. I really believe that, if the government had agreed to the catholic question and the reform when you brought in the latter and supported both, the country would now be united and tranquil. ...' He still thinks them 'not unreasonable' as a counterpart to oppressive measures. The resolutions of the Whig Club should at least 'show the public' that we have not abandoned their favourite measures and that they are still to look to a British constitution and Irish gentlemen, not to France and a convention.'
	20 Mar. 1798	[Sir Laurence] Parsons, [5th Bt], to Conolly. Upon his resigning the command of the King's County Militia. His regiment was 'well conditioned', but guilty of the 'atrocious crime' that 'most of them are papists –none of them Orangemen.'
	20 Apr.–7 May 1798	Correspondence between Conolly, Lord Camden, Lord Castlereagh and Sir Ralph Abercromby [Commander in chief in Ireland] over Conolly's resignation of the colonelcy of the Derry Militia and then his withdrawal of it. Conolly is convinced that Sir G.E. Hill would be no more full time as his successor because of his new 'place' [clerkship of the House of Commons] and Dublin yeomanry corps. 'I am confident it would be better for the regiment for me, old, infirm, broken-indeed as I am to remain...' There was an initial shortage of resident gentlemen of property to come forward and take commissions.
	25 Apr. 1798	Abercromby to Conolly. Praising his 'exertions in forming so fine a regiment'.
	2 Oct. 1798	James Scott, Willborough [Co. Londonderry], to Conolly about Orangemen in his militia regiment.
	19 Jan. 1799	Scott to Conolly. About the act of Union.

B. A survey of the Grocers' Proportion in Co. Londonderry, *c.* 1760, in private possession in Co. Londonderry.

C. Four diaries of Thomas Conolly (1823–76) covering the years 1853, 1857, 1863 and 1864 in private possession in Co. Kildare.

INDEX

ARAKCHEEV

Count Alexei Andreevich Arakcheev
Portrait by George Dawe. Courtesy of the British Museum

ARAKCHEEV

Grand Vizier of the Russian Empire

A biography by

Michael Jenkins

Faber and Faber
24 Russell Square
London

First published in England in 1969
by Faber and Faber Limited
24 Russell Square London WC1
Printed in Great Britain by
Latimer Trend Whitstable

SBN 571 08222 X

For Penny and Tony
in memory of a Russian campaign

CONTENTS

Introduction

It has been said that no man ever held as much power in Russia under the dynasty of the Romanovs as did Count Alexei Andreevich Arakcheev during the reign of the Emperor Alexander I in the first quarter of the nineteenth century. Foreigners saw him as the Grand Vizier of the Empire, and in the eyes of the Russians he reached the status of a Vice-Emperor, if not higher. For everyone, he was the very symbol of autocracy.

Arakcheev became a legend in Russia in his own lifetime. There were qualities in his character which both fascinated and repelled his contemporaries, many of whom vied with each other in relating often quite apocryphal stories about his harshness and brutality. The judgments of those who had direct dealings with him were frequently no less extreme. "He was a man," wrote one of his adjutants, "who in my eyes so blotted the name of citizen, father, brother and friend, that he was unworthier than the most unworthy, about whom we are taught by history which he had never read." A priest who served for a time in the church on Arakcheev's estate at Gruzino remarked that "his name should be written not in ink but in blood." In some peasant communities they said that he was a cannibal.

The verdict of historians has been no kinder to him. "At the very mention of his name thousands of our ancestors trembled and crossed themselves in terror," observed the Russian historian Kizevetter at the end of the last century, while Professor A. G. Mazour in his book *The First Russian Revolution*, published in 1937, writes that "in the history of the nineteenth century the name of Arakcheev stands as a symbol of the darkest reaction and the cruellest oppression. . . . Tactless, bigoted and unsympathetic with suffering, he was hated by more people than was any other statesman of his time."

Arakcheev was to a large extent his own worst enemy where his reputation was concerned. He would never make a concession in order to make a friend. With one isolated exception, he never joined a group or clique in order to further his career, nor was he interested in surrounding himself with his own party of supporters. He stood alone, disliked and feared by the courtiers and ministers whose influence he had supplanted, and mocked by a society whose conventions he flouted with contempt. He deliberately encouraged people to think that he was uncultivated as well as exigent and heartless. He began his career as a cadet in the Saint Petersburg artillery cadet corps, where the boys had instilled in them, as Arakcheev said himself, "the fear of God and the fear of the whip," and his early successes were achieved by his ability to impose an iron discipline on the officers and men who came under him. Whatever tactics he subsequently adopted in order to get his way, he always suspected that in the last resort people obeyed him because they were afraid of him, and all too often he played on this knowledge. He had no illusions as to his unpopularity. "I have been given much happiness in my life, but the affection of my comrades was not granted to me. I was never loved during my years of service because of the discipline I demanded," he once wrote to a friend. But as long as he retained the favor of the Emperor, he was prepared to be philosophical about everyone else's opinion.

The key to Arakcheev's career lies in his relationship with Alexander I. The Emperor's affection for him and trust in him baffled Arakcheev's contemporaries as much as it has puzzled historians. General Mikhailovsky-Danilevsky, the soldier-historian who was an eyewitness to many of Alexander's campaigns, spoke for most people when he asked himself how it was that "without brilliant achievements, without special natural gifts from nature, having studied nothing but the Russian language and mathematics, without even the charm which sometimes attracts people unconsciously, Arakcheev, alone of fifty million subjects, was able to gain the unlimited trust of an Emperor who had a highly educated mind, charming manners, and whose chief qualities were secretiveness and perspicacity."

Put in these terms, the question seems scarcely soluble, but the terms are misleading. For Alexander, despite the liberal reputation which he had when he came to the throne, proved to be in many ways as great an autocrat as his father, the tyrannical Emperor Paul, albeit a more attractive and successful one. Alexander needed a strong man who would be obeyed unquestioningly in order to execute policies which he knew would be unpopular in Russia, and the clearest instance of this was his creation of the military colonies. This project for settling the Russian army on the land in closed communities where soldiers were to learn the art of farming, and peasants to be turned into soldiers, was entrusted entirely to Arakcheev. The Emperor knew that his plan was regarded with suspicion at all levels of Russian society and with outright hostility by his own general staff, but he gave full rein to Arakcheev's energy and drive, and the results were remarkable. Moreover, there were several moments of crisis during the reign when Alexander felt secure only with a man of undeviating loyalty at his side. He was an attractive and intelligent monarch, who was borne to the throne on a wave of enthusiasm for what was known at the time of his politics and personal qualities, but on various occasions during his reign he aroused fierce hostility: after the agreement at Tilsit, when he seemed to the Russians to have sold out to Napoleon; at the lowest point of the war of 1812, when Moscow was in ashes; and toward the end of his life, when a number of young officers in his regiments were actively plotting his assassination. Some people have maintained that Alexander deliberately used Arakcheev to take the blame for a number of the unpopular policies and measures for which he himself was responsible, but this would be going too far. It meant a great deal to Alexander to know that a man who would never turn against him and who could be relied on to get things done, stood firmly beside him.

This fierce personal loyalty to his Emperor was at once the mainspring of Arakcheev's character and his most attractive quality. When the Emperor Paul succeeded to the throne in 1796 and brought with him to Saint Petersburg a young and virtually unknown artillery officer, Arakcheev had already shown his worth. At every task with which Alexander in his turn entrusted him, he succeeded triumphantly. He built up the Russian artillery from the most neglected arm of the Russian forces to a formidable instrument with which Napoleon could be faced. As Minister of War he conducted, at the Emperor's behest, a campaign in Finland after Russia's generals had condemned the proposed strategy as unworkable and had thrown in their hand. During the Napoleonic campaigns he stayed by Alexander's side as his counselor and friend. In the second half of the reign he surmounted enormous obstacles in order to set up the military colonies. In accomplishing all these tasks Arakcheev gained more and more of the Emperor's confidence, until Alexander would do state business with no one but him. All decisions of the Committee of Ministers were submitted to Arakcheev before being passed to the Emperor. During Alexander's many absences abroad, from 1815 until the end of his reign a decade later, the government was in Arakcheev's hands. A man in his position could scarcely have avoided becoming an object of envy and suspicion.

Yet the remarkable feature of Arakcheev's handling of the great power entrusted to him was his reluctance to exercise it. Even toward the end of the reign he repeatedly declared that his only official responsibility was the military colonies. He made no attempt to sway the Emperor in one direction or another where state policies were concerned. It is true that he was fiercely jealous of his position, and when he behaved dishonorably it was in order to keep at a distance or bring down potential rivals. Yet he did not seek power in order to realize any political or ideological design of his own, for he had none. His concept of government was essentially executive. His sole aim was to serve his Emperor and friend to the best of his ability.

The term "Arakcheevshchina" has been applied to the last period of Alexander's reign to denote reaction and oppression. But although it was a time of great tension in Russian society, and many influential people attempted to clamp down on the growing pressures for change, this was none of Arakcheev's doing. He was not, for example, responsible for the disgraceful purge of the universities; and he was only too slow to see the dangers that the conspiracies which were being hatched in Saint Petersburg and in the south during the last years of the Emperor's life represented to the regime. Alexander could not bring himself to take repressive measures against the young officers who by this time were deeply disappointed in him, nor did Arakcheev ever urge the Emperor to do so.

A closer examination of Arakcheev's career, therefore, does something to destroy the image of the arch oppressor. It is true that his methods of government were stern and frequently even brutal; he did not mind telling people that he would "scatter them like dust" if they did not carry out his orders, and they discovered often enough that he meant what he said. But he was not the sadist indulging in orgies of cruelty, nor the ideological reactionary of popular history. In the late eighteenth and early nineteenth centuries a small section of the Russian governing class was strongly influenced by the Prussian way of life and Prussian habits of thought, for which many other Russians felt the deepest antipathy. Arakcheev was an extreme product of this influence.

Peter the Great was first to employ foreign advisers, usually of German origin, in many important fields of government, and his successors followed his example. Catherine's son Paul was much impressed by Frederick the Great and, as Grand Duke, built a small private army on the Prussian model on his estate at Gatchina, outside Saint Petersburg. The years Arakcheev spent at Gatchina constituted the formative period of his life. Will and discipline became his governing principles. Naturally enough, his rigid authoritarianism was hardly likely to endear him either to the individualist and arrogant Russian nobility, jealous of the power and independence they had won for themselves in the previous century, or to the peasantry, who were accustomed to poverty and suffering but remained conservative in their ways and put up a determined resistance to the kind of regimentation which Arakcheev imposed on them. Not only did Arakcheev's abrupt manners, his insistence on obedience to the letter of his instruction, and his refusal to discuss his decisions arouse the hostility of his colleagues and subordinates: they found his meticulous habits of work, the methodical arrangement of his home and estate, and his Spartan way of life all profoundly alien. Visitors to his estate at Gruzino said that the house was like a museum and the garden like a cemetery, while the paved roads and stone houses of the peasant villages on the estate smacked to them of the barracks and the parade ground.

It was, however, these very qualities which attracted Alexander to Arakcheev. At the beginning of his reign Alexander appeared to be reacting against Paul's whole way of life and government, but he had unconsciously absorbed many of his father's characteristics, and this became more and more obvious as his reign progressed. Alexander was as intolerant of criticism and jealous of his own authority as Paul had been; and having an almost manic obsession with order and neatness, nothing aroused his enthusiasm as much as a sparkling regiment on parade. When the Emperor paid his first visit to Gruzino, his admiration knew no bounds: at last he had found someone who might sweep away the morass of mud and the clouds of dust in which, according to the seasons, the Empire floundered; someone who could apparently tidy up and discipline the peasantry; and who might even bring some order into the ramshackle imperial administration.

But discipline was neither a practical nor a desirable remedy for Russia's ills. The events of Alexander's reign were of such magnitude that Russia more than ever before needed imaginative and reforming statesmanship. This was the period when the Russians, for the first time in their history, discovered themselves as a nation. The epic of the Napoleonic invasion, with its attendant devastation, suffering, and drama, stirred in all sections of society a feeling for their country that went even deeper than their detestation of the invader.

No country was more rent with divisions than Russia on the eve of the Napoleonic wars. The social structure consisted of a number of closed groups, the aristocracy, the country landowners, the merchants, and the peasants, whose only concern was to extend their own privileges or defend their own rights at the expense, if need be, of the interests of the state. Indeed, the court and aristocracy, who spoke French more naturally than Russian and followed French fashions in every detail, seemed like some foreign caste quite divorced from the rest of the Russian people. But Napoleon's penetration to the heart of Russia, the destruction of Moscow, and the bitter fighting on Russian territory began at last to close the divided ranks of Russian society. Not for nothing did the campaign of 1812 become known as the Great Patriotic War.

The Russian victory which followed this campaign provided a unique opportunity for the Emperor to draw his nation together and promote measures, such as the abolition of serfdom, which could have carried Russia out of the feudal world in which she had lived for so long. But Alexander now became more interested in European politics than in events at home. During the last critical decade of his reign he spent much of his time in Western Europe, while the centrifugal forces in Russian society began to reassert themselves more vigorously than before. The war had increased discontent with the state of affairs in Russia, but at this difficult time Alexander chose virtually to ignore the fundamental problems of his country and to rely for the day-to-day government of the Empire on the one friend he could always trust, Arakcheev. The single major project on which the Emperor and Arakcheev did embark after the war, the creation of the military colonies, showed how far they both were from understanding Russia's real needs.

Arakcheev was, of course, ill-fitted to advise the Emperor on the explosive situation that was building up inside Russia toward the end of his reign. He had no taste for constitutional reform and he made no attempt to understand the impassioned debate on the future of the imperial government which everyone knew was taking place in many regiments and sections of society. Indeed, it is arguable that had he been of a more inquiring and independent disposition, Alexander would never have given him the high position he held for so long. As it was, Arakcheev faithfully executed the Emperor's wishes without raising his eyes from the immediate horizon to the storm clouds massing overhead. If the Emperor was not concerned by the impending crisis, then it was no concern of Arakcheev's either.

Nonetheless, Arakcheev's personality and his unique position were enough for the ills of the reign to be laid at his door, rather than with the Emperor, where they more truly belonged. When one reads contemporary or secondary accounts of Arakcheev's life, one is struck by their lack of objectivity. Nearly all of them are written in the manner of the pamphleteer, who portrays his subject in the darkest colors. "The historian is not a judge, still less a hanging judge," Dom David Knowles has written; nor, of course, does he wield a pot of white paint. In this account I have done my best to adopt a more dispassionate approach toward Arakcheev, and I have tried to allow him to portray himself, warts and all, as a man who was above all the loyal servant of his Emperor.

The material available on Arakcheev does not make this an

easy task. He wrote no memoirs, and no one has ever attempted to write his biography, although in the 1860's Colonel Ratch collected a great deal of useful information on his early life. There are, however, a number of valuable collections of Arakcheev's letters, and he scrupulously preserved for history his voluminous correspondence with Alexander. But the bulk of the material consists of the great quantity of short memoirs and sketches of Arakcheev written down by those who knew him; indeed, few people seem to have worked with him for long without feeling impelled to write something about him. Many of these sketches, which have done much to give Arakcheev the reputation he has, are highly colored and unreliable; they are so inaccurate in dealing with facts that can be checked that one is bound to treat with some suspicion a number of the unverifiable stories which the writers relate with such gusto. Yet the material is rich, it is based on personal observation, and much of it has the ring of truth.

As Voltaire said, "*On ne doit aux morts que la vérité.*" It is a good maxim, but a great challenge to the biographer.

This book was written in such calmer intervals as came my way during an eighteen-month tour of duty at the British Embassy in Moscow. The work is based entirely on printed sources. Unfortunately, I was not granted permission to consult the Arakcheev papers which are listed as being contained in the Soviet historical archives.

Without the help of a number of people the book would never have been completed when it was. I should like to thank firstly the staff of Reading Room 1 in the Lenin Library, where nearly all my research was done, who were always friendly and helpful in dealing with my requests for material. I also wish to thank the Keeper of Printed Books in the British Museum for his great kindness in allowing me access to the stacks at a moment when my time was very short.

I am grateful to Timothy Binyon for some most useful initial advice. I am much indebted to Edward Thomas and to Mary-Kay Wilmers for reading my manuscript and for the very constructive comments and criticisms they made.

I should also like to thank Miss Angela Sargeant for her kindness and perseverance in typing an often illegible manuscript.

But man, proud man,
Dress'd in a little brief authority,
Most ignorant of what he's most assur'd,
His glassy essence, like an angry ape,
Plays such fantastic tricks before high heaven,
As makes the angels weep. . .

—William Shakespeare
Measure for Measure

I advise those who have this book after me to remember that it is always difficult for an honest man to hold important posts in the state.

—Note by Arakcheev, on the flyleaf of his Bible

All dates in the text follow the Julian calendar, which in the eighteenth century was eleven days behind the Gregorian calendar in use in Western Europe, and twelve days behind it in the nineteenth century. The Julian calendar remained in force in Russia until 1918.

I have transliterated Russian names and phrases as phonetically as possible, except in cases where there is already an established English spelling.

The RUSSIAN EMPIRE (Europe) After the Treaty of 1815

ARAKCHEEV

1
The Corporal of Gatchina

You don't get things done by talking softly in French.
—ARAKCHEEV

The self-made man is not a phenomenon unique to our times. Even in the strictly hierarchical society of eighteenth- and nineteenth-century Russia it was possible by a combination of luck, ability, and ambition to reach the most powerful positions in the state without the help either of the money or of the ready-made influence which were normally at the command of the established families. At the beginning of the nineteenth century, the period described by Tolstoy in *War and Peace*, when the Russian aristocracy seemed stronger and more firmly established than ever before, two such men made their own way to the pinnacles of power under Emperor Alexander I. One was Mikhail Speransky, the brilliant son of a country priest, who knew a brief moment of glory while Alexander toyed with the constitution which Speransky had drafted for him. The other was Alexei Andreevich Arakcheev, who was often contrasted with Speransky, although the two were never truly rivals. Pushkin once remarked to Speransky, "You and Arakcheev stand in opposite doors of this reign, as the genius of good and the genius of evil."

Arakcheev always insisted on the simplicity of his origins and liked to boast about his lack of education. Yet he was born into a family of country landowners, and he received the same kind of tuition as most Russians of his station in the eighteenth century. In the general absence of schools and textbooks, the country gentry made do with the village priest; the more privileged families usually employed foreign tutors for their sons. Alexei's early education was certainly rudimentary, and he retained a complex about it all his life. He would frequently and sarcastically assert that "as a poor uneducated nobleman" he could scarcely be expected to converse with the clever people at court and in society. Yet in the course of his career, education became one of his chief passions. In the same way, he used to claim that he was not interested in reading, yet he collected a library of more than eleven thousand volumes. "I am not very literate. My father paid a brass farthing for my education," he announced characteristically as he introduced himself to the members of the War Ministry on his appointment as Minister.[1] To a friend he once wrote: "As a poor nobleman, I had all my education in the old Russian style. I learned to read by using the prayer book, and not by modern methods. Then, when I had been taught to read the Psalter for the repose of the souls of my parents, I was sent to serve the Czar and was entrusted to the miracle-working icon of Kazan, having been ordered by my parents to begin anything I undertook with its approval, which I do to this day."[2]

Arakcheev's family were without rank or influence and led an uneventful country life in the province of Tver. However, they had the status of *dvoryane*, or noblemen, and thus belonged to the privileged serf-owning caste, which included both the richest princes of the Russian Empire and the most obscure country gentlemen, who might possess only a few acres of land and a handful of serfs. The Arakcheev family had been assimilated into the nobility in March, 1695, when Ivan Stepanovich Arakcheev, "for the services of his forebears and of his father, and for his own services in the Polish war," was granted an estate by the Crown near the town of Bezhetsk, which lay roughly midway between Moscow and Saint Petersburg. Thereafter the male line served as army officers. One of Ivan's descendants, Vassili Arakcheev, reached the rank of major-general and fought with distinction in Field Marshal Münnich's famous campaign of the 1730's against the Turks and Crimean Tartars; Vassili's brother, who was Alexei's grandfather, was killed in the same campaign.

Alexei's father, Andrei, resigned his commission as lieutenant in 1762 under Peter III's manifesto releasing the nobility from compulsory state service, and went to live on his estate at Garusovo, some one hundred kilometers from Bezhetsk. Andrei was never rich. He had only twenty serfs to his name, but he also had a town house in Bezhetsk to which he and his family moved once a year in order to escape the worst rigors of the winter. His relatives, who also lived in Tver province, were better off. The family as a whole owned more than five hundred serfs in the Bezhetsk district, and Andrei's wife had property of her own.[3]

Alexei was born on September 23, 1769, at Garusovo. Two more sons were born, Petr in 1776 and Andrei in 1778. His father, who had little energy and less ambition, was content to lead the existence of a small provincial landowner. He left the education of his children and even abdicated the running of his properties to his more active wife, Elisaveta Andreevna.

Elisaveta Andreevna had a strong influence on Alexei in

his childhood, and he was always devoted to her. Nicknamed "the Dutchwoman" by her neighbors because of her unusual obsession with tidiness and cleanliness, she instilled in her son at least one quality for which he later became renowned throughout Russia—a pedantic love of discipline and order, which he applied ruthlessly in both his public and private life. Unable to read or write herself, Elisaveta Andreevna hired a priest at Garusovo to give her son a basic education in return for "a quarter of rye and two quarters of oats." The priest cannot have been a very gifted teacher, however, for Arakcheev never learned to write easily or correctly, and all his life he remained unable to string three words together without making some mistake in grammar or spelling. His father, who did not want to see his son enter the army, but hoped that he would make an official career through one of the state chanceries, was disappointed at Alexei's slow progress and would make him copy out long official documents to improve his handwriting and spelling. But the boy, who did not lack application, preferred arithmetic, and one of his favorite occupations as a child was the multiplication of huge sums.[4]

There was one other person who attracted the admiration of Arakcheev in these early years: his aunt, Nastasia Zherebtsova. She had her own house just outside Bezhetsk and was by all accounts a woman of character who played a prominent part in the life of the town. Arakcheev's early affection for Nastasia proved as warm and as lasting as his affection for his parents. When they died he still enjoyed returning to Bezhetsk to stay with her and would take a gracious if condescending interest in local politics, receiving petitioners and officials and on occasion helping them with their problems or putting right some local injustice. As his aunt's guest he was careful never to show the harsh side of his nature, for which by this time he had acquired a terrible reputation in Saint Petersburg. Nastasia even allowed herself to send certain petitioners to Arakcheev in the capital, and he always received them with kindness and consideration. They were, after all, an agreeable reminder of the distance he had traveled.[5]

When Alexei reached the age of thirteen, a decision had to be made about his career. He did not really know what path he would like to follow and was unenthusiastic about his father's proposal to send him to stay with a relative in Moscow who would help him enter state service as a clerk in one of the chanceries. One day he went with his father to visit a neighbor whose two sons had just returned on leave after passing out of the Shlyakhetny artillery school. They made an instant impression on Alexei. He was envious of their smart red uniforms and drank in every word of their stories about camp, their studies, and firing cannon. "They seemed superior beings to me. I did not leave them for one moment." He pleaded with his parents to let him apply to join the school, but they considered it unwise to send their son to Saint Petersburg without money or protectors. Finally, in the face of Alexei's insistence, they relented.

There was never much ready money in Andrei Arakcheev's pocket, but he somehow managed to find a hundred rubles and with this sum he and his son set off in the spring of 1783 for Saint Petersburg. Alexei was "in transports of delight." They found a cheap hotel on Yamskaya Street, where they rented part of a room, separated from the rest by a partition. Alexei put in his request to join the corps, but then, as they had neither friends nor influential contacts, their difficulties began.

Arakcheev later described this first crisis in his life to Speransky. "There was a good deal of walking about," he said, "and we needed a lot of patience while our request was being considered. There was no word of an answer, and every day we went from Yamskaya Street to the Petersburg side of the town* and waited on the staircase of the Director of the Corps, Pyotr Ivanovich Melissino, in order to greet him and remind him of our request. During this wait my father's small reserve of money melted away and was finally exhausted: we did not have a kopeck left. The position was desperate. My father had heard that the Metropolitan Gabriel gave assistance to the poor, and our need forced him to ask for help. We went to the monastery. There was a crowd of paupers at the entrance. My father requested that his Holiness be informed that a nobleman wished to see him. We were shown in. My father related his unhappy position and asked for assistance. His Holiness sent us to the treasurer and we were given a silver ruble. Coming out into the street, my father held up the ruble and burst into tears. When I saw him do this, I cried as well. The three of us (that is, including our servant) lived for nine days on one ruble. Then the ruble was gone! Again we went to the Petersburg side and again we took up our positions on the Director's staircase. Melissino appeared, and before my father could speak, I stepped forward and said in despair, 'Your Excellency, accept me as a cadet. If we wait any longer we shall die of hunger. I will be grateful to your Excellency all my life and will pray to God for you. My father can last no longer and will die here, and I with him!' Tears were pouring down my face. Melissino looked at me searchingly. I was sobbing, and my father was crying helplessly. Melissino asked me my name and the date of my application. Then he returned to his room,

* "The Petersburg side" was a district of the town on one of the principal islands in the mouth of the Neva. The north bank of the Neva was known as "the Viborg side."

telling us to wait. A few minutes later he came out, and handing me a note, said: 'Take this to the chancery; you are accepted into the corps.' I tried to kiss his hands, but he slipped past, got into his carriage and drove off. Before going to the chancery my father and I went into a church, and as we had no money to light candles before an icon, we prayed to God, bowing low to the ground, and left the church with joy in our hearts.

"On the next day I joined the corps. It is an old saying that good and bad luck never come singly. On the same day my father met a relative who had arrived from Moscow, and whose purse was fat. He gave my father enough money for the return journey to the country. God had taken pity on us! This first lesson of poverty and helplessness made a strong impression on me."*

So on July 19, 1783, Arakcheev enrolled as an artillery cadet and took the first step on the road of his official career. He was in some ways fortunate to have chosen this branch of the army, which was still very much the Cinderella of Russia's armed forces. As a result of years of neglect, the artillery was in a bad state of decay, but it was soon, in the face of French gunpower, to become a vital part of the army. Meanwhile, for a cadet without money or influence, a successful career in the artillery could be achieved by hard work

* This story was written down by Bulgarin, the first editor of the Saint Petersburg newspaper *The Northern Bee*, after he heard Arakcheev telling it to Speransky on the balcony of Arakcheev's house at Gruzino (see F. Bulgarin, "Poezdka v Gruzino v 1824," in *Novoselye*, 1846). Arakcheev was fond of this story, but there were several variants. One was that his father found that he did not have enough money to pay the entrance fee to the school. General Maevsky (*Russkaya Starina*, 1873) quotes Arakcheev as telling him that his father could not afford to buy the frock coat which every pupil needed to enter the school, and that an old friend, Madame Gurieva, lent him the seven rubles he needed. Whatever the truth, the episode seems to be an illustration of Andrei Arakcheev's improvidence rather than of his poverty.

and expertise. The more influential families preferred, as in other European countries, to place their sons in the guards and the cavalry regiments. The gunners were considered merely an unattractive adjunct of the infantry, whose fire, as Prince Orlov loudly remarked, depended entirely on luck. Training was poor, guns were heavy to transport, and the gunpowder was frequently impure. Indeed, the most spectacular function of the artillery was the organizing of firework displays, for which General Melissino was much in demand in Saint Petersburg.

There were, however, one or two people in the reign of Catherine the Great, including the Empress herself, who were aware of the growing importance of the artillery. One was Count Peter Shuvalov, adjutant general of the army and a powerful figure in the 1750's. Although no expert on the subject himself, Shuvalov was particularly anxious that artillery should cease to be the almost exclusive province of German military advisers; and to this end he amalgamated the largely neglected schools of artillery and engineering in Saint Petersburg, thus founding the Shlyakhetny Corps for training sons of the nobility in the technical side of warfare. It was just before the Arakcheevs arrived in Saint Petersburg that Catherine appointed General Melissino head of the corps and in a burst of enthusiasm asked him to increase the number of pupils from one hundred and fifty to one thousand. Catherine had suggested as well that the elementary classes be closed and the school reserved for those who had already acquired a knowledge of language and science. Melissino, more aware of the difficulties of attracting recruits from the nobility, contested these proposals and maintained instead that the school should aim at giving a broad education to children of the poorer nobility. He won his point, but the fact that this discussion was taking place in the first six months of his tenure of office may have accounted for the delay in considering Alexei's application.

Arakcheev's progress in the school was spectacular. After only seven months he had reached the top classes, won all the existing medals for excellence, and was given a noncommissioned rank in the artillery. Work was his only occupation. He had neither money nor friends, and he made no attempt to acquire friends either in or outside the school. A tall, lonely figure, he was unable in his first months to afford even a uniform of his own, and was to be seen in a worn-out uniform which belonged to the school, his long arms protruding awkwardly from the sleeves. But if he appeared ungainly and even comic, it did not occur to his companions to make fun of him. Already he was beginning to inspire in his fellows the mixture of awe and repulsion with which many of his contemporaries regarded him for the whole of his life.

It did not take Melissino long to spot the abilities of his outstanding pupil and to decide that they could be put to good use in the corps. Melissino himself was intelligent and ambitious and was doing much to promote the cause of the artillery. He could certainly have enjoyed an even more illustrious career were it not for certain defects of character which made him appear less serious about his profession than was in fact the case. He had a reputation of being vain, weak, and a spendthrift. He was a prominent figure in Saint Petersburg society; he spoke several languages, fenced and danced well, and was an authority on the theater. But it was difficult to take him seriously, and society had nicknamed him "le grand seigneur manqué." Nonetheless, the school rapidly acquired a name under him, and in very little time the number of cadets more than doubled. The sensible changes in the studies which he introduced with the help of his abler pupils bore fruit; and the major reform in the artillery which subsequently took place was largely the work of his former pupils.

From the day when Melissino personally opened the doors of the school to him, Arakcheev treated the general as his benefactor and set him in the small category of people to whom at all times in his life he gave unchanging loyalty. Melissino showed him no special favors at the outset, but one day when Alexei was walking in the Director's garden, a privilege reserved for cadets who had been promoted to a noncommissioned rank, Melissino came up to him with a smile and exclaimed, "So soon!" After less than a year the instructors were giving him backward pupils to coach, with highly successful results. Melissino thought so highly of him that he sent him a note which said, "From today you may attend classes or study in your room. You will make your own plan of work and will be responsible for it to your own conscience." But success, allied perhaps with his loneliness, was breeding less attractive qualities in him. The harsh strain in his character now found its first outlet, and a contemporary in the school wrote that "he exercised a revolting brutality over the cadets."

Four years after entering the school, Arakcheev achieved the rank of lieutenant instructor. Following the advice of Melissino, he decided to stay on, and Melissino now considered him an authority on artillery training. Arakcheev drafted some *Short Artillery Notes* on the subject of training and maneuvers, which were published under the Director's name.

In July, 1788, when the Russian army was already fully engaged in fighting the Turks in the south, Gustave III of Sweden suddenly declared war on Russia. Saint Petersburg, temporarily undefended, appeared to lie at the mercy of the Swedish fleet and army. Melissino was asked to train three artillery battalions from raw recruits in six weeks, and he called on his instructors and pupils to help. The Comte de Segur, French Minister at the Court, recalled "the enormous and grotesque recruits who were instructed in marching and in exercises by children drawn from the military school, who climbed onto chairs and benches in order to straighten the heads, necks, and chests of these gigantic brutes."

The war dragged on for two years; and in the end the Russians acquitted themselves better than either they or the Swedes had imagined they would. They denied Sweden the quick victory for which she had hoped, and a peace was eventually signed in which Sweden settled for a return to the position which had existed before the war began. Meanwhile, the performance of the three artillery battalions further enhanced the prestige of the school, and this may have induced Count Nicolai Saltikov, a prominent Saint Petersburg figure in charge of the education of Catherine's two grandsons Alexander and Constantine, to turn to Melissino in his search for a tutor who would provide military instruction for his own son. Arakcheev, the star pupil, was the obvious choice.

As it turned out, Saltikov rather than Melissino proved to be Arakcheev's first real patron. Melissino found his young lieutenant useful as an assistant, but Saltikov was intrigued by his character and took pity on him in his straitened circumstances. He obtained leave for him for the first time, and after nearly seven years' absence Arakcheev, now aged twenty, returned to Bezhetsk in the red uniform he had coveted as a boy, and with a gold watch given to him by Countess Saltikov on his departure. He received a hero's welcome from his family. Arakcheev later liked to recount how his father at once confiscated the watch and hung it over his own bed. He gave it back only when the time came for Alexei to return to Saint Petersburg, and then with the words, "Remember that you owe it to me. If I had not entered you for the corps, you would not have been given a watch." "So now," Arakcheev would say, "I keep it as a present from my father." A short time afterward the Arakcheevs returned their son's visit. When she saw his rooms in the school, his mother remarked with pleasure on their cleanliness and tidiness. His father, surveying the writing table, the leather-covered sofa, the armchair, and the mahogany cupboard, said with a frown, "Listen, Alexei, tell me straight, as a son should speak to his father, you are not stealing or taking bribes?" Indeed, Andrei's ambition for his son continued to be very limited. When he was at the height of his power, Arakcheev once told a colleague, "My father would often say to me, 'Alyosha, you will reach the rank of major and retire with a pension; then we shall all be happy.' But what would he have said if he could see me now?"[6]

Arakcheev used his own initiative to take the next step in his career, which was to have far-reaching consequences. Although he had never penetrated Saltikov's household beyond the classroom, he was encouraged by the Count's friendliness to ask his help in securing his appointment to the vacant post of adjutant and assistant director of the school. Melissino was surprised and annoyed by the approach. He preferred to have rich and sociable men as his close collaborators, and had regarded Arakcheev as a reliable subordinate, too dependent on the goodwill of his commanding officer to push for promotion. But he dared not refuse a request from a person of such influence as Saltikov, and in July, 1791, Arakcheev was given the post. Melissino remained outwardly friendly, but he began to look for an opportunity to push Arakcheev out of the school. The occasion arose only a year later.

In 1790 Melissino had been appointed commander in chief of the Russian artillery, while retaining his post as director of the corps. Despite his high position and his love of society, he was never entirely happy in Catherine's court. The Empress's favorites regarded him as a somewhat comic figure, and he returned their contempt with good measure. One day he was heard to express unflattering views on one or two members of the court and was summoned by Prince Potemkin, Catherine's famous general, who received him lying in bed and rudely told him to watch his tongue.[7] Melissino's hostility toward the court circle was increased by the insult, and from this time he began to draw closer to the only rival center of influence, the small court of Catherine's son, the Grand Duke Paul, who was living on his country estate at Gatchina, some sixty kilometers from Saint Petersburg.

In 1792, when Paul wanted a qualified artillery officer to join his establishment at Gatchina, he turned to Melissino: Arakcheev's career was decided. Melissino must have been confident that Arakcheev was well qualified to satisfy the Grand Duke's exacting demands, but despite his subsequent claims to the contrary, he could have had no conception of the glorious course on which he was launching his hard-working but unattractive lieutenant.

When Arakcheev arrived at Gatchina on September 4, already dressed in the dark green uniform of Paul's troops, he found himself in a Prussian military encampment. The estate was laid out with parade grounds, barracks, and sentries at every point, who challenged visitors in the Prussian style. The peasants who lived on the estate were under camp discipline. Daily life revolved around the strict routine of the Grand Duke himself, who rose at 4 A.M. for his first parade and spent the day organizing the training and maneuvers of his little army. "By ten in the evening the whole estate was already asleep, and the only sounds to be heard were the footsteps of the patrols and the cries of the sentries," wrote a bored visitor. "Everything is organized on Prussian lines, and on old Prussian lines at that," noted Princess Kobirskaya. "The worst part is that the soldiers are Russians turned into Prussians and dressed in the old uniforms of Frederick William the First."[8]

Paul, at the age of thirty-eight, was a frustrated and bitter man. He had been a clever, charming child, full of promise, but from birth he was isolated from his mother by his great-aunt, the Empress Elizabeth, and he never subsequently achieved a satisfactory relationship with Catherine. After Catherine had seized the throne from her own husband, the feeble Peter III, she continued to keep her son at a distance, refusing to allow him any role in the administration of the Empire or even to take part in the numerous military campaigns of her reign. Catherine's uncertain claim to the throne and her fear that her son might achieve a popularity which would impinge on her own absolute power were undoubtedly the major reasons for this ostracism. Moreover, Paul's devotion to the memory of the father he had never known was scarcely likely to please the woman who had played a direct part in his assassination. It was perhaps this irrational worship for his father, who had himself been a strong admirer of the Prussians and had even begun to drill the Saint Petersburg garrison in Prussian fashion during his short reign, which inspired Paul to look in the same direction. Certainly a visit which the Grand Duke paid to the Prussian court in Berlin at the age of twenty-two was a turning point in his life. Frederick II did his best to flatter the Russian delegation, and Paul's predilection for things Prussian now turned into something of a mania. "I can see what hands the Empire will fall into after my death," Catherine once observed ruefully after a talk with Paul. "We shall be turned into a province dependent on the will of Prussia."

Arakcheev's mother,
Elisaveta Andreevna Arakcheeva
Courtesy of the British Museum

The Emperor Paul
*Courtesy of
the British Museum*

Paul's frustration grew with the passing years, and it had an increasingly noticeable effect on his character. He became moody and subject to fits of ungovernable temper, which he would vent over the most trifling matters. His wife, Maria Feodorovna, formerly Duchess of Württemberg, whom Paul had met on his visit to Berlin, always did her best to calm him, but only rarely did she have any real influence. Princess Kobirskaya echoed a general sentiment when she said that "the Grand Duke is clever and knows how to be pleasant when he so wishes, but there is much about him which is strange and incomprehensible." The Comte de Segur wrote that it did not take a long period—above all, when he spoke of his present and future position—to perceive his restless, mercurial, distrustful, and very sensitive nature, which was later to be the cause of his faults, injustices, and misfortunes; and at another time he remarked, "Never was a man more uncertain, timid, and capricious, and less capable of making either others or himself happy."[9] Paul was miserable in Saint Petersburg. Catherine's favorites treated him with open contempt, and he was forced to witness a system of government which was anathema to him. Indeed, he did not trouble to conceal his dislike of his mother's government, and said openly that as soon as he gained power he would turn out her advisers with a whipping. When Catherine bought Gatchina for him in 1784, he moved to it with relief and returned as little as possible to the capital.

The Gatchina estate was a marshy terrain which contained several small hamlets, two lakes, and a spacious country house built in the classical style by the Italian architect Rinaldi for Catherine's favorite, Gregory Orlov, to whom the property belonged until his death in 1783. Paul, who had written unhappily to a friend in 1784, "I am already thirty and have nothing to do," now released some of his pent-up energies, turning his estate into a model kingdom. His first concern was the welfare of the peasants, for whom he built in quick succession a school, a hospital, and four churches. He organized a system of loans for those who fell on hard times and set up glass and china factories to reduce the villagers' dependence on agriculture as a livelihood. His chief interest, however, was centered on the miniature army which he created. He conducted experimental maneuvers and made on a small scale changes of drill, equipment, and administration in preparation for the day when he might apply these reforms to the whole Russian army.

The genesis of the notorious Gatchina troops, which on Paul's accession to the throne numbered twenty-four hundred officers and men, was the personal guard of sixty marines, originally attached to the Grand Duke as admiral of the fleet. Catherine was aware of the advantages of keeping her son amused in a way that had become almost a tradition for the heir to the throne since the days of Peter the Great's boy soldiers, and she allowed Paul gradually to increase the number of his men. Paul began by building into his small force detachments from every branch of the armed forces; he even included a small armed flotilla on one of the lakes.

A posting to Gatchina was not, however, very popular with Russian officers. They were expected to train and drill according to Prussian regulations, to abandon their cherished light-green infantry or red artillery uniforms and put on the detested dark green of Frederick's troops, and to obey the orders of a number of German advisers who were assisting the Grand Duke. No one who could avoid it would volunteer for service at Gatchina, and in consequence Paul's men were an ill-assorted collection of officers and soldiers, many of whom could find no other home in the army. Some of the officers were foreigners who had served in Prussia or elsewhere, and others came from small landowning families in distant provinces who were prepared to gamble on serving the Grand Duke as a shortcut to the top. Foreign in spirit and discipline to the regular regiments, the Gatchina force was regarded with a mixture of scorn and suspicion by Catherine's officers, and particularly by the guard regiments. The general view was reflected by a contemporary who wrote that the Gatchina troops were mostly "rough and quite uneducated people, the dregs of our army. Expelled from their regiments for bad conduct, drunkenness, or cowardice, these people found asylum in the Gatchina battalions. . . . There were some extremely evil people among these villains. From the Gatchina marshes they looked out enviously on those who were proudly and bravely marching along the path of honor."[10]

Paul became increasingly interested in artillery experiments and was at first ably assisted by a young lieutenant called Aprelev, but Aprelev had invented a process for eliminating the flaws that frequently occurred in gun barrels and was in great demand all over Russia. Arakcheev therefore arrived to take over Aprelev's duties in organizing the artillery detachment, and he had the good fortune to make an immediately favorable impression on his capricious master. At his first parade, he behaved as if he had been at Gatchina for many years. He conducted a maneuver before Paul within a month of his arrival and was rewarded with promotion to the rank of captain and the privilege of lunching at the Grand Duke's table. After that it didn't take long for him to become Paul's chief assistant in all military affairs. He was zealous and skillful in carrying out the Grand Duke's many intelligent ideas for creating a new artillery, chiefly based on autonomous units of guns and devices to achieve their greater mobility. A room was set aside in the palace, where he taught the junior officers mathematics and gunnery for two hours a day. By the end of 1795 he had composed detailed training instructions, which were subsequently published and remained in force for years in the Russian artillery.[11]

Alexei had a genius for getting quick results, and his energy was inexhaustible. He applied himself to all aspects of garrison life and was rewarded in 1795 with the appointment of "Governor of Gatchina." But his success was achieved by the liberal use of punishment rather than by exhortation and persuasion. His subordinate officers would make efforts to resign from time to time, but Paul didn't allow anyone to defect.

Arakcheev remained very poor. Paul himself was restricted by Catherine to an annual allowance of ten thousand rubles, which he received in two installments, on his birthday and name day. The sum was in sharp contrast to the riches which Catherine poured on her favorites, but she was deaf to her son's appeals for more funds. "I can only think that you are being robbed incessantly," she once wrote to him, "for I cannot understand how otherwise you should be in such continual need of money, when by rights you ought to have enough for everything." But as the Empress well knew, Paul received no state grant to support his Gatchina troops, and he had therefore to pay them out of his own pocket. It was an effective way of ensuring that the Grand Duke's army did not grow dangerously large. As it was, Paul was forced to borrow in order to pay the men, and he lived on credit to keep them equipped. His debt to the artillery paymaster alone reached sixteen thousand rubles by 1795, but Arakcheev's close contact with Melissino assured that Gatchina was never short of supplies.

Arakcheev's own income consisted solely of the modest pay he received from Paul, which he supplemented by giving private coaching when he could find the time. "I had only one uniform and one pair of buckskin breeches. At night I would take them off, whiten them, and put them on damp in the morning. This was bearable in summer; but in winter I was almost in tears when the breeches froze to my body and the bitter cold pierced me right through," he recalled later.[12] Moreover, his poverty and background made him ill-fitted for the society world in which he now found himself, and he kept his distance from the small court around Paul, which was inclined to make jokes about him. Rostopchin, the Grand Duke's chamberlain, nicknamed Arakcheev "the corporal of Gatchina," a sobriquet which stuck throughout his career; and another courtier wrote that "Jamais poète pyndarique ne fut plus impérieusement tourmenté de son Apollon que cet homme ne fut obsédé de son démon martial."[13] He was still ungainly and unprepossessing, "like a big ape in uniform," recalled General Sablukov, who as a young man used to accompany his father to Gatchina when the latter, an official in the state treasury, went there to pay Paul his allowance. "There was nothing handsome about his figure," continues this unkind description, "since he was round-shouldered and had a long thin neck on which one could study the anatomy of his sinews and muscles. He was in the habit of making jerky contractions with his chin. His ears were big and fleshy and he had a round ugly head, which he always held on one side. His face was sallow, his cheeks were hollow, his nose was broad but angular, with big nostrils. He had a large mouth and a low forehead. To complete the portrait, he had deep-set gray eyes, and the whole expression of his face was a strange mixture of intelligence and evil."[14]

He did not even draw close to "the men of Gatchina," Pleshcheev, Obolyaninov, Kushelev, the Kurakin brothers, and Kutaisov, all of whom, like himself, were to be given power in the new reign. His only friend was the Grand Duke himself, but Arakcheev, too, was liable to be the victim of

Paul's temper. Once he was fiercely rebuked by Paul for some negligence on the part of the officer of the guard. "In my grief I rushed into the church and started to pray and make vows. I felt I was innocent but thought I had deprived myself of the Grand Duke's favor forever. I could not hold back my tears and even began to sob. There was no one in the church except the sexton, who was beginning to extinguish the candles. Suddenly I heard footsteps behind me and the sound of spurs. I jumped up and wiped away my tears, and when I looked around I saw the Grand Duke. 'Why are you crying?' he asked me kindly. 'I am grieved to have lost your Imperial Highness' favor.' 'But you have not lost it at all,' returned the Grand Duke, putting his hand on my shoulder, 'nor will you ever lose it if you continue to conduct yourself and serve me as you have until now. Pray to God and be faithful in your service, for prayers to God and service to the Emperor are never wasted.' I threw myself on my knees in front of the Grand Duke and in my emotion exclaimed: 'All I have is God and Yourself!' The Grand Duke ordered me to stand up and follow him in silence. At last he stopped, glanced at me, and said, 'Go home; in time I shall make a man of you.' "[15]

Paul's remark was more true than he could have known. Arakcheev eagerly absorbed the Prussian way of life, and the time he spent at Gatchina had a lasting effect on his character. It gave form and expression to the austerity and ruthlessness of his nature and cast him in a mold which finally set him apart from his fellows, earning him the distrust of those who could not understand him and the hatred of colleagues and subordinates who were victims of his harshness. He made no approaches to others and, although aware of his unpopularity, no attempt to explain himself to any but a few intimate companions. "I know many people do not like me because I am strict," he once said, "but what can I do? That's how God made me." Since he had so few friends or supporters, his position depended to an unusual degree on the personal trust and favor of the emperors he served. He never breathed a word of criticism of Paul's growing eccentricities, nor, later, of his chaotic policies. At Gatchina he deliberately limited his role to that of a faithful executant, and he was the first to admire Paul's attention to the minutiae of drill, training, and military affairs. For his part, Paul continued to show his confidence in Arakcheev's qualities, and on occasion his affection for him. Among a number of dry instructions and reproofs from Paul which Arakcheev religiously preserved and later had printed for himself and a few friends, there is a touching handwritten message from the Grand Duke on the death of Arakcheev's father in August, 1796, which runs, "I have just learned of the sad news you have received. You know my affection for you and will have no doubt of my sympathy, all the more since I knew him and he was a man of the old school. May God console you."[16]

Arakcheev had little contact with the stream of outsiders who came and went at Gatchina, but there were two distinguished visitors whom he saw with increasing frequency during the last two years of Catherine's reign. In the spring of 1795 Paul's elder sons, Alexander and Constantine, began to make the journey from Saint Petersburg to Gatchina and the nearby estate of Pavlovsk four or five times a week in order to take part in the exercises organized by Paul. This rapprochement between the Grand Duke and his children had been initiated by Alexander's Swiss tutor, La Harpe, who, little as he sympathized with Paul's views and way of life, had always been disturbed by the gulf between the father and his sons. The rift had been deliberately created by Catherine. She had virtually abducted Alexander and Constantine in order to remove them from the influence of their father and to supervise personally their upbringing.

Catherine lavished on Alexander the care and love which she had never been able to show to her own son. She devoted unlimited attention to his education, seeking the advice of French philosophers such as Grimm and Diderot, with whom she was in regular correspondence. The liberal principles of the French enlightenment were instilled in the boy; and even if his tutor was careful never to question the basis of Russian institutions, such as serfdom and the absolute power of the Crown, Alexander acquired under La Harpe an awareness of the ideas abroad in Europe and a wider education than any Russian prince before him. At the same time, frequenting as he did two mutually hostile courts, Alexander developed at an early age the habit of concealing his thoughts and of using the arts of diplomacy. It was not only a question of reading the French constitution with Catherine and then acquiescing in silence when he heard his father end a tirade on the French Revolution with the words, "You see, my children, you have to treat people like dogs!" He also had to endure the mutual recriminations of two people, both of whom he respected, and of their entourages. Alexander's loyalties were genuinely divided. He sympathized with some of Paul's criticisms of Catherine's policies, such as the unscrupulous partitions of Poland which resulted in that country being wiped off the map in 1795–96, and he cordially disliked many of the courtiers who surrounded the Empress, of whom he once said that he would not like to have them around him as footmen. He was, on the other hand, aware of Paul's shortcomings, and fear of his father kept his filial love at bay; yet despite the fact that many aspects of his upbringing combined to set him apart from Paul, there was never in fact a complete separation between the two. The young Prince's real loyalty to his father finally became clear in these last two years of Catherine's reign.

As Alexander's remarkable charm and intelligence became more apparent to Catherine and the court, and Paul seemed ever more eccentric and foreign to the image which Catherine had tried to stamp on her reign, it became increasingly clear that Alexander was the more suitable successor to the throne.

One day in 1793 Catherine sent for La Harpe and in the course of a long conversation hinted at what she had in mind. The tutor was horrified. It was true that under a law of Peter the Great the sovereign had the right to nominate the successor to the throne, but La Harpe was convinced that any procedure other than strict adherence to the hereditary principle would be a source of chronic weakness for the Crown. He did his best in guarded terms to convince Catherine of her mistake; and when in the ensuing months the Empress realized that she could not alter his view, she decided to dismiss him, for fear that he might succeed in arousing Alexander's hostility to her plans for him. By this time Catherine's enthusiasm for La Harpe was in any case waning. When the Empress had taken the throne she had thought ambitiously in terms of giving Russia a constitution and abolishing serfdom. But her liberalism dwindled in the course of her reign, and the French Revolution finally buried it. In her last years Catherine was a disenchanted autocrat, and in dismissing La Harpe she cut off Alexander's education at a vital moment in his development.

La Harpe made one final effort to save Alexander and Russia from what he saw as a possible catastrophe. In April, 1795, on the eve of his departure, he overcame his repugnance for Paul, who had not spoken to him for more than three years, and drove to Gatchina, where he obtained an interview with the Grand Duke, in which he hinted at the dangers of the situation, urging Paul to see more of his sons. The interview went well. Paul, surprised that a hated Jacobin should talk such sense, accepted the advice with gratitude and showed his appreciation by inviting the tutor to stay the night for a ball at Gatchina. He even lent him a pair of white gloves for the occasion, which La Harpe preserved for the rest of his life.

The results of La Harpe's intervention were soon apparent. The two princes were to be seen far more frequently at Gatchina. They came chiefly to take part in maneuvers, although Alexander, despite his remarkable good looks, was scarcely martial in spirit or figure. Deaf in his left ear from having stood too close to some guns, shortsighted, lame as a result of a fall from his horse, he also had a pronounced stammer; and these physical handicaps were underlined in his father's presence by evident nervousness and lack of assurance. Both he and Constantine were genuinely frightened of Paul. "When he looked at all angry, they went white and trembled like aspen leaves," noted General Sablukov.[17] Alexander began to lean on Arakcheev, relying on his help in maneuvers and using him as a shield against his father's excessive fits of rage. This was how the foundation was laid for the friendship which was to prove so useful to Alexander during his father's reign.

So passed the year 1795, and as the months of 1796 went by, the tension at Gatchina, never quite absent, markedly increased. At the beginning of the year Catherine had still not spoken to her grandson of her plans for him, but all the talk at Saint Petersburg was of the succession, and the situation was increasingly weighing on Alexander. In May he wrote to his friend Alexei Kochubey, "There is an unbelievable disorder in our affairs. In such circumstances, can one man rule the state, still less correct the abuses in it? This is beyond the strength not only of a man gifted with ordinary abilities like myself, but even of a genius, and I have always kept to the rule that it is better not to attempt something than to do it badly. My plan is to settle on the banks of the Rhine with my wife, where I shall live peacefully as a private individual, finding my happiness in the society of friends and the study of nature."

During June and July he assiduously attended Paul's maneuvers, arriving at Pavlovsk every morning at six and staying until one. "This summer I can really say I have done my military service," he wrote feelingly to La Harpe. Then, on September 16, Catherine had a talk with Alexander, during which, it is generally supposed, she at last told him of her plans. Alexander never revealed the details of this conversation. In response to Catherine's proposals he wrote a characteristically diplomatic letter to her in which he expressed his gratitude for her kindness and faith in him—"even with my blood I should be unable to repay all you have done and still wish to do for me"—but avoided committing himself to any specific plan. In Saint Petersburg the rumors increased. People seemed to think that the Empress would issue a manifesto on New Year's Day announcing Alexander's title to the succession, and that Paul would then be arrested and imprisoned. Alexander's position was more intolerable than ever. Maybe it was in order to ingratiate himself with Gatchina that in a note to Arakcheev on administrative matters, dated September 23, he made the gesture of referring to his father as "His Imperial Majesty," a habit to which Arakcheev was himself addicted.

November 5 began as a normal day at Gatchina. The Grand Duke rose, attended parade, and inspected some mounted exercises before lunching at a mill on the estate with his wife and a group of officers which included Arakcheev,

Pleshcheev, and General Kutlubitsky. As they were returning from lunch, the party met a hussar on his way to inform the Grand Duke that Count Nicholas Zubov, the brother of Catherine's current favorite, had arrived from Saint Petersburg. Everyone sensed that this must mean important news. Paul at once asked the hussar if Zubov had come with a big escort. On learning that he was alone, Paul said, "Well, we can cope with one," and taking off his hat, he crossed himself.[18]

Zubov brought the news that Catherine had suffered a stroke that night and was seriously ill. Paul at once ordered his carriage, and together with Maria Feodorovna, hastily set off for Saint Petersburg. A messenger was sent ahead to inform Alexander of his impending arrival. Paul ordered Arakcheev and a number of other officers to follow as soon as possible. On the journey he met Rostopchin with a message from Alexander asking him to come to the capital. Rostopchin, overcome with emotion, seized Paul by the hand and exclaimed, "Ah, Monseigneur, what a moment for you!" "Wait, my dear fellow, wait," replied Paul. "I have lived forty-two years. God has given me his help, and maybe he will give me the strength and mind to occupy the position for which he has destined me."[19]

In the course of his journey Paul met twenty-three other messengers with similar tidings. These turned their horses and swelled the Grand Duke's escort as his carriage hurried on through the clear frosty night, passing through the gates of the Winter Palace shortly before midnight. Alexander and Constantine, dressed in their Gatchina uniforms, were standing on the steps of the palace to greet their father, and Paul was escorted inside with candles. Rostopchin noted that "the reception he received was already that of an Emperor rather than a Grand Duke."

2
Brief Authority

Alexei is like a wolf; however much you feed him, he still looks into the wood.—ANDREI ARAKCHEEV

During the night of November 5 the Winter Palace gradually filled with officers and courtiers from Gatchina. The polished floors rang with the unfamiliar sounds of jackboots, swords, and spurs. To Catherine's courtiers "it was as if the palace had turned into a barracks." The small but powerful group of her favorites and advisers made no last-minute attempt to keep the Grand Duke from the throne, but Paul took no chances.

He wasted little time in asserting his authority, and established himself that night in a small study adjoining Catherine's bedroom. When he learned from her doctors that his mother had no chance of recovery, he set about collecting together her personal papers, aided by Bezborodko, one of her advisers. Some papers were at once destroyed, and others were put under seal; no documentary evidence remained as to Catherine's intentions over the succession. It had indeed been lucky for Paul that her sudden illness had taken the form of depriving her of the power of speech.

Arakcheev arrived from Gatchina hard on Paul's heels. He was at once escorted through the bedroom of the dying Empress to the little study, where he found the Grand Duke in conversation with Alexander. Visibly affected by the drama of the day's events, Paul greeted Arakcheev with a theatrical gesture. He seized him by the hand and exclaimed, "Continue to serve me as you have done so far." Then he joined Arakcheev's hand to that of Alexander and solemnly said, "Always be friends." Next they settled down to discussing the immediate question of changing and strengthening the palace guard. This was an important security measure, but the change was also designed to symbolize the accession of a new sovereign. Arakcheev was instructed to put Paul's orders into effect as soon as possible. Characteristically, he inquired how much the new arrangements were likely to cost. "Don't worry," Paul replied. "Remember that now we shall have not thirty thousand rubles, but seventy million."* At the end of this conversation, Alexander, noticing that Arakcheev's collar was spattered with mud as a result of his hasty journey, took him to his apartments and gave him one of his own shirts. Arakcheev was deeply touched by this mark of affection; he kept the shirt until the end of his life and finally had himself buried in it.[1]

Catherine died on the evening of November 6, and the next day a stream of new appointments issued from the Emperor. Arakcheev was made Commandant of Saint Petersburg and given a commission in the Preobrazhensky regiment, the senior of the three guards regiments. On the following day he was promoted to the rank of major-general and awarded the "Anna," the most coveted of imperial decorations. As Com-

* This remark is quoted without explanation by Ratch in *Svedeniya o Grafe Arakcheeve* (Saint Petersburg, 1874), and the thirty thousand rubles may refer to Paul's total income, as opposed to his personal allowance of ten thousand rubles from his mother.

mandant of the city he was entitled to rooms in the Winter Palace and was allotted the apartments recently evacuated by Catherine's favorite, Platon Zubov. Paul also invited him to choose one of the estates in the imperial gift, and Arakcheev asked at once for the village and land of Gruzino, an estate on the Volkhov River, eighty kilometers from Novgorod, which at the beginning of the century had belonged to Peter I's favorite, Menshikov. The house and park had been totally neglected since Menshikov's disgrace, and the land was situated in flat, marshy country frequently flooded by the Volkhov. But Arakcheev, who must have passed by the estate on his journeys between Bezhetsk and Saint Petersburg, had set his heart on it. Despite a rival claimant in the former governor general of the Novgorod and Tver provinces, Arkharov, he received the formal title to the land and two thousand serfs a month after Paul's accession.

At the age of twenty-eight, a wave of the imperial wand had transformed Arakcheev overnight from a poor and unknown colonel to a major-general, a close confidant of the Emperor, and a substantial landowner. It was a vertiginous rise, and his success now spurred him to apply even more energetically and rigorously than before the methods of command which had found favor with his master at Gatchina. He became the very symbol of the new order, imitating Paul in his open scorn of the old court, his harsh parade-ground manners, and his lack of concession to the ways and customs of Saint Petersburg society. During Paul's short and chaotic reign he played virtually no part in the formation of the Emperor's domestic and foreign policies. Indeed, Paul relied little on personal advisers; and although, at the start of his reign, he made use of the great organs of state, such as the Supreme Council, he was always an ostentatious autocrat. Once when someone dared to contradict him and supported his case with a reference to the law, Paul struck himself on the chest, crying, "Here is your law." This style pleased Arakcheev and made easy his self-imposed role as the Emperor's unquestioning servant, loyal and indifferent to unpopularity in circles whose influence he could safely choose to ignore. Indeed, he almost courted the hatred of those whom he knew at heart disliked the new regime.

He appeared to revel in the image of unlettered drill sergeant. On the barrack square he struck and swore at officers and soldiers alike as he inculcated the new methods of training; he tore at the soldiers' moustaches and on one occasion even bit a soldier's ear like an enraged bulldog. At his first guards' parade he outraged all the officers within earshot by referring contemptuously to the colors as "Catherine's petticoats." A. M. Turgenev recalled that when the Horse Guards marched with their colors to the Winter Palace after taking their oath of loyalty to Paul, they found the solitary figure of Arakcheev waiting for them on the square. He at once began to tell the standard-bearers how to hold the colors and present them to the Emperor, accompanying every instruction with some insult, and turning and pushing the regimental adjutant as if he were a valet. "Arakcheev ordered 'March!' but as the new words of command had not yet been announced, we did not understand and therefore did not move. Arakcheev cried again, 'Standard-junkers, forward march!' But this rank did not exist in the regiment. So Arakcheev honored us with a new rank, shouting at the top of his voice, with foam on his lips, 'So, you scum, you won't march. Forward march!' This time we did move, having understood that 'march' had replaced the old word '*stupai.*' "*[2] In the

* "*Stupai*" was the Russian word in force in the army until that time as the command for "March!" The new command was taken from the Prussian orders.

palace Arakcheev's conduct was considered equally gross. When Countess Golovine burst into tears at the sight of Catherine's body being carried into the throne room for the lying in state, "This person, who had been pulled out of the mire by the Emperor to become the factotum of his severities, pushed me violently and told me to shut up."[3]

Saint Petersburg had much to worry about during the first month of Paul's accession. The Gatchina officers, to whom Catherine had always forbidden the Winter Palace, now stood about uneasily in the corners and doorways of the palace like representatives of an occupying power. Their clumsy uniforms, high boots, and thickly powdered hair distinguished them sharply from the elegant courtiers; they would sit silently at table, eat mechanically, and disappear like ghosts at the end of the meal. But the Emperor was at home with them. It was apparent from the start that he was determined to rule Russia as he had run Gatchina, and he subjected Saint Petersburg in particular to an iron discipline which applied to nobleman and peasant alike. Paul's foibles and obsessions, which had made him the laughingstock of society when he was safely secluded in the country, became a very bad joke now that he was in a position to impose them on everyone. A stream of decrees issued on the day following Catherine's death dealt with such matters as the number of horses to a carriage, the banning of round hats and tailcoats, and the obligatory appearance of officers at all times in uniform. Large parties were frowned on by the Emperor, and special permission to hold them now had to be obtained from the palace. Paul continued to rise at six, and the chanceries and departments of state were compelled to follow his example. More alarming for the nobility were decrees which threatened their unfettered privileges by making them liable to corporal punishment, as well as purporting to regulate the days of work of the serfs and to prohibit the sale of serfs without land, an evil which frequently led to the break-up of serf families. Not surprisingly, however, Paul's hand fell heaviest on the army.

Despite the numerous campaigns fought in the previous reign, there is no doubt that on Catherine's death the army was in a very neglected state. Under Catherine's benevolent command, officers had enjoyed the same personal freedom as the rest of the nobility: they were in the habit of absenting themselves from their regiments for months at a time and took to living in Saint Petersburg or on their estates. Colonels treated their regiments as personal possessions, frequently employing soldiers for their own private purposes. Paul put a rapid end to this state of affairs. He did not feel strong enough to reverse the manifesto of 1762, which had released the nobility from compulsory service to the state, but all serving officers were required to return at once to their regiments or justify their absence, and Arakcheev was instructed to interview every officer in Saint Petersburg who was not with his regiment. Meanwhile, the troops throughout Russia were expected to lose no time in acquiring the new forms of training and discipline.

On the day of his accession, the Emperor had appointed himself colonel in chief of all the guards regiments, and now saw that the new order was swiftly adopted there. On the morning of November 8 he appeared at a parade of the guards accompanied by Arakcheev and the other "men of Gatchina." Alexander and Constantine were also present, dressed in their new uniforms and looking, to at least one officer, like "old portraits of German officers which had jumped out of their frames."[4] Paul at first appeared to be very discontented and kept shrugging his shoulders and shaking his head, but then he was told that the "Gatchina army" had arrived in the city.

He left the parade drawn up, rode off to meet his troops, and returned at their head. The new men were divided up on the spot and assigned to the guards regiments with the task of instilling the Gatchina ways as soon as possible. Paul measured the progress of the guards by continuing to take the daily "watch parade" every morning, a ceremony to which his officers went as to a place of execution. No one knew what awaited him there—promotion, exile to Siberia, imprisonment, or dismissal from the service. Retribution for the smallest error was instantaneous. General Sablukov recounted how he and his brother officers clubbed together to ensure that whoever was on duty had several hundred rubles about him so that he should not find himself exiled without a kopeck.[5]

Masson, a Swiss who acted as Alexander's secretary until he was sent away by Paul, has left a vivid picture of the daily appearances at the watch parade of this Emperor who was trying to run Russia like a regiment. "Dressed in a simple dark green uniform, large boots, and a great hat, he would spend his mornings at the parade exercising the guards. Here he issued his instructions, received reports, gave out pardons, awards, and punishments, and had every officer presented to him. Surrounded by his sons and his aides-de-camp, he would stamp his feet to keep warm. With his bald head uncovered and his nose in the air, one hand behind his back and the other beating time with his cane, and crying 'One two, one two' all the while, he made it a point of honor to brave fifteen or twenty degrees of frost without an overcoat. Soon no officer dared show himself in his fur coat, and the old generals, tormented by coughs, gout, and rheumatism, had to stand around Paul dressed in the same way."[6] It is small wonder that officers now began to resign in droves.

But the reforms went deeper than parades and ceremonies. Prussian tactics were introduced, even though the old school of Russian officers, such as Catherine's illustrious General Suvorov, considered them as impractical as the pomaded hair and black lacquered boots in which the soldiers now appeared. These tactics, which rested on the principle of troops rigidly holding the line and advancing with the precision of a well-oiled machine, had been effective against badly trained and slow-moving soldiers. By the end of the eighteenth century they were hopelessly out of date, and Napoleon finally buried them in 1806, when he forced the Prussian troops to fight on broken ground at Iena and Auerstadt. Within six weeks Prussia and her famous army were completely destroyed. But Paul did not live to see this humiliation.

On his accession, Paul immediately ordered Rostopchin to draft a completely new set of regulations for the Russian army, and Rostopchin worked with such speed that they were published at the end of November, 1796. Based as they were on a translation of Frederick the Great's regulations, they were fiercely opposed by the senior Russian officers, headed by Suvorov, who described them as "a blind Russian translation of a motheaten manuscript found twenty years ago in the ruins of an old castle." Paul also created a new rank called "Inspector" and sent these inspectors to the regiments to make sure that the regulations were being properly enforced. The opposition the regulations aroused is illustrated by the fact that in the course of three years, seven field marshals, more than three hundred generals, and more than two thousand other officers were dismissed from the service, although many of them were subsequently reinstated.[7]

Again Paul set the example by ordering Arakcheev to establish daily classes in the White Hall of the Winter Palace. Colonel Kannabikh, a Prussian who had formerly commanded the horse artillery at Gatchina, lectured in broken Russian on tactics to the staff officers. Paul attended regularly himself and liked to see his senior generals there. Only Suvorov was ostentatiously absent. "The blind teaching the lame," he remarked scornfully, and indeed Kannabikh was such a comic figure that people were said to turn up to watch rather than listen. Arakcheev was embarrassed, and chose the first convenient occasion, the departure of Paul for his coronation in Moscow the following spring, to put an end to the classes. Meanwhile, Suvorov's own position became increasingly invidious, and in the end he resigned rather than apply what he regarded as a disastrous code. "Suvorov the conqueror has fallen into the clutches of the corporal of Gatchina, who has taken it upon himself to subdue the arrogance of Catherine's generals," remarked Rostopchin on learning of the resignation, but the old General was clearly only too thankful to go.[8] When he was called back by Paul two years later to fight his brilliant campaign against Napoleon in Italy, he simply went back to his own tactics.[9]

Alexander, now heir to the throne and first Grand Duke of the Empire, was particularly bewildered and nervous during the turmoil of his father's reign, and he relied more and more on Arakcheev to help him through his duties. As commanding officer of the Semenovsky Guards regiment, he was expected to see that his men were imbibing the reforms, but Arakcheev exercised this supervision for him and even trained the officers and men himself. Alexander had also been appointed one of the two military governors of Saint Petersburg, and in this office was responsible for drawing up a report twice daily covering the state of the garrison and the arrival of foreigners or prominent Russians in the town. Once again Arakcheev was indispensable. As commandant he was well placed to draft these statements, and since Paul expected to see the overnight report when he rose at five A.M., Arakcheev would go into the Grand Duke's bedroom at this hour and take Alexander's signature, while his wife, Elizaveta Alexeevna, hid under the bedclothes.[10] Despite the obvious risk of this little stratagem, Paul does not appear to have detected it, and services of this kind strengthened the growing friendship between Alexander and Arakcheev. Alexander increasingly respected the authority and reliability of the young general. Moreover, he was flattered by Arakcheev's ardent expressions of devotion to him. In a perilous world he seemed a bedrock on which to rest, and Alexander now began to close his eyes to the brutality which Arakcheev exercised in carrying out the royal will, evident as it was to everyone else. In the carefully preserved collection of letters and notes from Alexander to Arakcheev, there is only one belonging to this time which seems to contain a note of reproof. "I much regret that my major and officers are being punished for such a trifling matter; I hope that in future they will be more zealous." More typical is the message which runs, "Do me a favor and be here when my guard is mounted so that they get nothing wrong."[11]

Even had they wished otherwise, there was no choice for those nearest the Emperor but to bow to his obsession with the minutiae of daily life. For Arakcheev this was no problem: his passion for detail, order, and smartness was equal to Paul's. His valet recounted how one night when there was a fire in the town Paul sent for Arakcheev so that they could inspect the damage together. Arakcheev jumped out of bed and began to dress quickly, but the valet let a few drops of wax from the candle fall on his yellow breeches. Arakcheev at once took them off and sent for another pair, which was several rooms away, thus making the Emperor wait another five minutes. "He was in such a hurry," the valet related, "that he did not strike me once, but afterward he had me whipped."[12]

He was now in a position to enforce his old love of cleanliness on others. As commandant he set about cleaning up the city, particularly around the barracks, where the refuse was piled so high that the streets had become impassable. The effect was noticed at the time, although only a few years later an English visitor was still struck by the contrast between the grandeur of the palaces and public buildings in Saint Petersburg and the squalor of the courts and side streets, "which are more filthy than it is possible for an Englishman to conceive."[13] The city guards were also strengthened and subject to unexpected visits from the commandant at any hour; these impromptu inspections were so frequent that it was rumored among the soldiers that Arakcheev never undressed at night.

Yet even in the fire of his enthusiasm, Arakcheev was not always merciless. Early one morning a young officer arrived from his regiment to make a report to Arakcheev but was so drunk that he could hardly stand and was unable to utter a word. Arakcheev instantly ordered his arrest, and he was taken off to the guard room. Toward the end of the morning, however, Arakcheev called his adjutant, Prince Dolgoruky, and said, "I cannot get that young man out of my head; how could he have got drunk so early, particular when he knew he had to report to me? Something doesn't add up. Go to the guard room and try to find out what this means." Questioned by Dolgoruky, the officer admitted that members of his regiment had made him terrified of Arakcheev, saying that the slightest mistake on his part would mean the end of his career. "I never drink vodka, but swallowed several glasses at a gulp to give myself courage. The fresh air was too much for me, and I appeared before him in this unhappy condition. Please save me if you can." When Arakcheev heard this, he at once ordered the officer's release and invited him to lunch. He went out of his way to be agreeable, and at the end of the meal said, "Go back to your regiment and tell your comrades that Arakcheev is not as terrible as they think."[14]

On the day of the Emperor's coronation, April 5, 1797, Arakcheev was granted the title of Baron and received the Grand Cross of the Order of St. Alexander Nevsky. When the new Baron's coat of arms was submitted for approval, Paul himself wrote under it the motto which was to become notorious throughout Russia: "Devoted without flattery."* He was chosen to accompany Paul on his first progress through the Russian provinces. "This will be a great consolation to me and will do something to soften my grief at being parted from my wife, whom I must admit it pains me to leave," wrote Alexander when he learned that they would be traveling together. The journey took the Emperor west of Moscow to Smolensk, then north to Riga and Narva. Paul was delighted to find himself greeted in each town by troops drilling in the new Prussian style, until he reached Kovno, where the Tavrichesky Grenadiers, who were commanded by the deaf and nearly blind General Yakobi, seemed quite unaware of the new regulations. General Yakobi was dismissed on the spot, and Arakcheev stayed behind and devoted six weeks to training the regiment. "I nearly went out of my mind after you left," he wrote to Alexander. "The regiment know nothing, march and handle their rifles badly; in fact, everything is terrible. I have been training them every day from morning to night, and have made up a battalion by

* By an untranslatable pun, the motto, which in Russian reads "*Bez Lesti Predan*," was popularly turned into "*Bess, Lesti Predan*"—"a devil devoted to flattery." A typical lampoon runs:

> Your motto says you serve but do not flatter.
> I can believe it.
> But what do you serve?
> Perfidy, spite, revenge.

taking sixty men from each company. Now they look like something."[15]

Away from the strained atmosphere of the capital, he allowed himself to relax for once, and the officers of the regiment found him friendly and even expansive when he gave them tea in the evenings at his quarters. Alexander, suddenly deprived of his friend and adviser, bombarded him with letters in which he sought advice on a mass of detailed administrative and military points. "Forgive me for troubling you, my friend, but I am young and badly need your advice," ends one of these missives. Arakcheev was delighted at this renewed evidence of Alexander's confidence. "Ah, how pleasant it would be for me to receive matters of this kind more often," he wrote back. "Then I would not need to worry and would know that poor Alexei has not been forgotten in Latvia." The adjutant who was instructed to make copies of these letters for Arakcheev's archives was not a little surprised at Arakcheev's odd warmth of expression.[16] One letter ended: "As I cannot see your Highness personally every day, I would at least like to be able to look on a portrait of your Highness, which I would then prize more dearly than anything else in the world." The adjutant noted that the General wrote twice a week to the Grand Duke.

"It is time you came back to us," wrote Paul in a note describing an unsatisfactory inspection at Pavlovsk. Arakcheev returned and was appointed colonel of the Preobrazhensky regiment in the place of Prince Golitsyn, who had been unable to drill his men satisfactorily. "This will be excellent for the regiment, and I can foresee that they will be better than all our other regiments," Alexander wrote to him. But the Preobrazhensky officers did not agree. Arakcheev was, anyway, unpopular with the regiment, since they held him responsible for the dismissal of Suvorov, and after a few weeks of his command bitter complaints reached the Emperor's ears. However, Paul had no sympathy. "I hear that your officers are saying everywhere that they cannot satisfy you in any way," he wrote to Arakcheev. "They forget that if they worked like officers in other regiments, they too would give satisfaction." But the unhappiness was not confined to the guards. The Prussian envoy, Count Bruhl, recorded that he could find no words to describe the general disgust in the army. "The uncertainty as to whether they will find themselves in the same place from one day to the next, and the incessant innovations, are driving them to despair. . . . The junior officers are at the end of their tether. The continual exercises which they do not begin to understand are overloaded with minutiae which have been abolished in all other services. God knows where all this will end."

Paul pressed on. That autumn he held big maneuvers at Gatchina. The men moved into battle formation like automatons while the Emperor personally orchestrated the action. By now there were enough well-trained soldiers to put on a brave show, and Paul was well pleased. "I realize, gentlemen, that the new training of the troops has not been agreeable to everyone," he announced to the assembled officers at the end of the exercises. "I have waited until the autumn for you to see the results for yourselves. You have now witnessed the first fruit of our work for the honor and glory of Russian arms."

Most saw through the facade, not least Alexander, the strain and tension of whose life was in direct proportion to his proximity to the Emperor. "Strange things are going on here, and there is one alarm after another," he wrote to Arakcheev from Pavlovsk. "Yesterday's had unhappy consequences: two Preobrazhensky officers were reduced to the ranks, but later, thank God, they were pardoned." In the autumn of 1797

Alexander went through one of his recurring periods of depression and disillusionment. He confided in Arakcheev and again spoke of his longing to abandon all his responsibilities and retreat with his wife into isolaton. After one quarrel with Paul, he told Arakcheev that the Emperor had "sent me kind messages through my wife, saying, for example, that I must not be angry with him, etc. But this does not change my desire to go into retirement, although I fear it is unlikely that this can happen."

Alexander often toyed with this dream, but it does not seem as if he ever took it very seriously. Only a month later in a remarkable letter to La Harpe he came to a quite different conclusion. The feelings of frustration and the sense of chaos which he expressed were now weighing on many young officers. "The army wastes almost all its time on the parade ground. There is no kind of properly worked out plan for anything else. . . . Business is done without any thought for the welfare of the state. Power is simply unlimited, and exercised perversely. Add to this severity deprived of all justice, a large dose of prejudice, and complete inexperience in affairs of state. Subordinates are chosen out of favoritism, and real worth is quite irrelevant. In a word, my unhappy country is in a situation which is beyond description. Agriculture has been damaged, trade hampered, freedom and personal well-being have been destroyed. This is the picture of contemporary Russia, and you can judge how I am suffering. Personally, I have become very unhappy. Tied as I am to all the trivialities of military service, I find myself carrying out the duties of an under-officer and have no time for the academic work which is my favorite occupation. It seems to me that if my turn to reign comes someday, rather than voluntarily exile myself I shall do incomparably better to devote myself to the task of giving freedom to my country and thus preventing her from becoming a toy in the hands of some future madman."[17]

Arakcheev's authority had been extended even further in April, 1797, by his appointment as quartermaster general of the army. There were few people on whom Paul could rely both to attack energetically the disorder which prevailed in the supply departments of the army and to remain untouched by the temptations of peculation which ran through these departments from top to bottom. Arakcheev could now savor the experience of being sought after and petitioned by those on whose favor he himself had formerly depended. "Your fame flatters my pride," Melissino wrote to the young general in June, 1797. "Long ago I could tell from your talents what was to become of you. I expect you still remember what I said to you after that examination when your knowledge astonished Mr. Epinas, and also what I hoped and foretold when I released you to serve the Emperor." Later that year Melissino wrote to his former pupil to ask for his assistance over the construction of a laboratory for artillery research.[18]

Arakcheev did not, however, succeed in grappling with the fundamental problems of organization during the short period he held this post. Perhaps his other duties took up too much of his time. Certainly he had not yet developed the administrative gifts which were later to be the basis of his authority; and the tangled supply question undoubtedly needed qualities other than those associated with his heavy hand. "You have gone to sleep and do nothing; this is unworthy, and I am sometimes inconsiderate when I wake people up," he wrote to one unfortunate major in the department. It was in the supply department that early in the following year a dramatic event first checked Arakcheev's swift upward course.

The central office of the department was in the Winter

Palace immediately under his apartments, and Arakcheev was in the habit of making sudden descents on the officers working there. He would storm in and berate them for minor errors in language worthy only of the parade ground. One day toward the end of January he poured a stream of abuse on a foreigner working in the department, an officer called Colonel Lehn, who had served with distinction in the Russian army and had been decorated with the order of St. George. Lehn was deeply wounded by this public humiliation. He returned home, took a pair of loaded pistols, and then reappeared at the palace, asking for Arakcheev. The officer of the guard dissuaded him from entering, and Lehn went home once more, wrote letters to the Emperor, Alexander, and Arakcheev, and then shot himself. When the scandal reached Paul's ears, he ordered Arakcheev's temporary retirement while the affair was investigated; and on February 1, Arakcheev was sent on leave "for reasons of health." Six weeks later he was officially retired from the army with the rank of lieutenant general.

"In these painful circumstances my one consolation is that I may still turn to Your Imperial Highness," he wrote to Alexander from Gruzino, but it took the Grand Duke six weeks to reply. However, when it did arrive the answer may have shown him that he was not likely to be out of favor for too long. "When I arrived at Vishny-Volochek* I very much wanted to see you and tell you that I am your true friend, as before. I admit that I am guilty in not having written for so long, but this is because I have not had a spare minute, and I hope you know me well enough not to have doubted me. If you have, you will have sinned against my honor and I will feel much insulted, but I hope you haven't. Farewell, my friend. Don't forget me, and send me the letter which you owe me." Less than three months later Alexander

* The town was not far from Gruzino.

wrote again with welcome news. "The Emperor has asked me to write to you to say that he needs you and that you should come to him. I am very glad that I shall have this opportunity of seeing you again, as I have long been wanting to."

On his arrival in Saint Petersburg Arakcheev was reinstated to his former position of seniority in the army and appointed to the Emperor's suite. After an absence of only six months he found himself closer to Paul than before. The Emperor had missed the zealous and efficient officer who never questioned orders from above. Moreover, he neither trusted nor understood the Grand Duke and hoped to be able to make use of Arakcheev's friendship with him. Shortly after Arakcheev's reappointment, Paul asked him privately if he would make it his task to watch over Alexander "like a favorite grandchild" and report anything which he felt the Emperor should know. Arakcheev, foreseeing the potential embarrassment for himself and the long-term dangers for his position, refused. He asked Paul to find someone else. "I replied that I could not serve as a weapon between father and son, and Paul did not refer to the matter again, although he was not annoyed," Arakcheev recounted many years later.[19]

With every month that passed his position seemed to grow stronger. At the end of 1798 he was reappointed quartermaster general, and in January of the following year he was made inspector general of the artillery. In May he received a further distinction, when Paul gave him the title of Count. He began to consider marriage. He was strongly attracted to Avdotya Savelevna Vaksel, the young daughter of a former official in the admiralty. Unfortunately, the girl considered herself already engaged to General Kutlubitsky, who had been Arakcheev's adjutant at Gatchina and was now an adjutant to the Emperor. Avdotya's mother saw in Arakcheev a man with a brilliant future and tried to push her daughter into the match, but Arakcheev never stood a chance. "I was at Uncle Alexei Ivanovich's and at last saw the Count," Avdotya wrote to Kutlubitsky in July. "He paid me the most extravagant compliments during dinner and said that as you always considered him your friend, he hoped I would be nice to him. How nasty and vicious he is! What a vile and mean face he has! I found him very disagreeable." And again: "If only you knew what Mother does with your fruit. She sends it every time via Uncle Alexei Ivanovich to the Count, to that beastly Arakcheev!"[20] Kutlubitsky married Avdotya in August, but the two men remained friends. Kutlubitsky, who was always fond of Arakcheev (and teased him by saying, "You ought occasionally to praise someone, if only by a slip of the tongue"), later went out of his way to help his former senior officer.

There are few records of Arakcheev's activities during this period, and nothing about his work as inspector general of artillery which anticipated the important reforms he was to carry out in Alexander's reign. Systematic administration was in any case virtually impossible under Paul, who had refused to appoint anyone to head the military collegiate which ran the army, preferring to occupy this post himself. As head of the artillery's disciplinary courts, Arakcheev recommended a number of acts of clemency, which have been presented as examples of the true sense of justice that was hidden behind his harsh exterior, but to the modern historian these cases are more revealing of the haphazard and savage nature of the justice of the day than of Arakcheev's leniency.[21] A certain Staff Captain Lopatin, for instance, was sentenced to temporary demotion to the ranks "for various illegal activities"; "in view of the fact that he had already spent ten years under arrest and in irons while his case was sub judice," Arakcheev recommended no further punishment.

By the end of 1799 few of those who had received high positions from Paul on his accession were found to have stayed the course. The Swedish Ambassador wrote in a letter home: "I would never finish if I tried to make a list of the people whom I have seen appear at court, shine in favor, and then disappear. Ministers, generals, and favorities change constantly, almost daily." The rapid sequence of elevations and demotions threw the administrative machine into chaos and swept away the Emperor's most loyal servants, including early friends such as Pleshcheev and Alexei Kurakin. Only Kutaisov, the Emperor's valet, chamberlain, and confidant; the detested Obolyaninov, head of the secret police; Rostopchin; and Arakcheev appeared invulnerable. Then another thunderbolt, this time entirely of Arakcheev's making, and provoked by an act of family loyalty, brought about a second disgrace.

Arakcheev's rising fortunes had enhanced the careers of his two brothers, both of whom were made guard officers on Paul's accession. In 1799 his younger brother, Andrei, was promoted to the rank of major-general and put in charge of a battalion of field artillery. In September this battalion was guarding an arsenal in which stood an old gun carriage. One night some thieves slipped past the guard and succeeded in stealing some of the gilded standards and gold braid with which the carriage was decorated. It was clear that the theft must be reported to the Emperor; but Arakcheev was anxious to save his brother from disaster. He declared in his report to Paul that the investigating officer had discovered that "the windows of the magazine, through which the officers in charge of the arsenal suppose that the theft took place, were broken earlier. People therefore have reason to believe that the theft may have taken place not on that night, but on a previous occasion." Whether or not Arakcheev prompted him to do so, the Emperor, always hasty in his judgments, at once dismissed from the service Colonel Vilde, the officer who had been on duty the night before. But the thieves, three artillerymen, were swiftly apprehended and admitted that the theft had been committed on the night Andrei was on duty. Vilde sought redress through Kutaisov, who interceded with the Emperor. Paul was equally prompt to reverse his judgment, but angry at having been, as he thought, badly advised, he laid the blame on Arakcheev. On the evening of the day Kutaisov spoke to Paul, Arakcheev arrived at Gatchina, where the Emperor was giving a ball. As soon as he caught sight of him, Paul sent Kutlubitsky with a message to say that he must leave at once.

On the next day, October 1, he was retired for the second time in his career. The order specified that he had made a false report about the night of the theft and had named as duty officer a staff officer other than the one who was on guard. Major General Tuchkov described Alexander's strange reaction to the news. When he was told by Tuchkov that Arakcheev's successor knew little drill but was "a good honest man," Alexander exclaimed, "Well, thank God. These appointments are a real lottery, and they could have picked another blackguard like Arakcheev."[22] People both at the time and subsequently have tended to interpret the remark as a spontaneous expression of the Grand Duke's true feelings about a man he disliked but always found indispensable.[23] It seems more likely that this impression was the very one which Alexander, who was no mean diplomat, intended to produce, given Arakcheev's unpopularity with his brother officers and the fact that his own close relationship with him had been generally known. For although he had gone out of his way to vilify Arakcheev in public, he did not attempt to break off relations with him.

Two weeks later the Grand Duke wrote to Arakcheev from Gatchina: "I hope, my friend, that under these unhappy circumstances I do not need to send you renewed assurances of my unshakable friendship. You know it well enough, and I am sure you have no doubts of it. Believe me, it will never change. I have inquired everywhere about the false report which you are alleged to have made, but no one knows anything about it, and no paper of this discription has been sent by anyone to the Emperor's chancery. If anything was written, it was done behind the scenes. The Emperor called Lieven* and indicated himself the words which stand on the order. I can see from the way the whole affair has been conducted that the Emperor thought that the theft was perpetrated at foreign instigation. The thieves have already been caught, as I think you know, and he was very surprised that he had been wrong in his deductions. He sent for me at once and made me tell him how the theft took place; after which he said to me, 'I was quite sure that this was a foreign initiative.' I did not reply that foreigners would have little use for five old standards. So the matter has ended. He did not say one word to me about you, but it is clear that strong allegations against you have been made to him."

Arakcheev did not justify himself in reply. Instead he made a plea for his brother, who had been dismissed from the service at the same time as himself. "Now he has been blamed on my account, and as a young man finds himself idle and excluded from the service. Since the guard and the officer of the guard have been acquitted of the arsenal theft by the military court, I tearfully beg Your Imperial Highness to intercede for the Emperor's pardon and for my brother's

* Paul's aide-de-camp.

reappointment in the service, since he is young and could work and sacrifice his life in return for all the favors shown to our family."[24]

Arakcheev did not leave Saint Petersburg at once. Now that he had completely fallen from his position of influence, many people tried to settle old scores, although in fact only minor charges could be leveled against him. One charge came from the auditors' department. Arakcheev was accused of negligence in buying poor horses for the Guard's Artillery Battalion and in the arrangements he made for the construction of new barracks for the same battalion. He was required to defend himself, but the accusations were never convincingly substantiated and the charges were eventually dropped.

His old enemies, however, did not give up easily. They were eager to pursue him in his disgrace, fearing perhaps that he might yet again be called to power. In the following year he was nearly tripped up by Kutaisov, one of his fiercest rivals in Paul's small circle, and was saved from serious trouble only by his old friend Kutlubitsky. Kutaisov was a Turk who had been captured by the Russians as a boy during the wars of the 1770's and given to Paul by Catherine as a domestic servant. Paul had sent Kutaisov to the court of Louis XVI to learn hairdressing and medical duties, but his influence with the Emperor went well beyond these menial tasks. Ever since their days at Gatchina he and Arakcheev had regarded each other as serious rivals and never lost an occasion to discredit each other in Paul's eyes. It so happened that Kutaisov now learned that Arakcheev was taking advantage of his old position in the artillery to employ artillery soldiers in building his house at Gruzino. He reported this to Paul, who at once sent an aide-de-camp to investigate. Kutlubitsky learned what was afoot and showed the aide-de-camp a circuitous route to Gruzino, while dispatching his own coachman by the direct road with a warning note to his friend and the injunction to burn it after reading. "Tell him I have not burned the note but eaten it in your presence," exclaimed Arakcheev with tears of gratitude in his eyes. He proceeded to swallow the paper in front of the startled messenger.[25]

Arakcheev's career appeared to have ended with the same speed as it had begun. He had retired to his newly acquired estate at Gruzino, and his contacts with the capital ceased almost completely. It is true that he did not lose touch with Alexander at once; the Grand Duke wrote to him at the end of the year suggesting that he come to Saint Petersburg for a talk about "some rather important matters concerning you." He added: "Your friendship will always be agreeable to me and you can be sure that mine will never cease." But no further correspondence between the two over the ensuing months has survived; and in view of Arakcheev's habit of meticulously preserving the briefest note he received from any member of the imperial family, it must be supposed that Alexander, increasingly preoccupied by the events of the last troubled year of his father's reign, did cease to pay attention to his friend.

The year 1800 was marked by a progressive deterioration in Paul's character. His mistrust of his entourage and in particular his own close family increased. A new series of unreasonable and repressive decrees was issued that alienated the nobility and the army even further. The importing of foreign books was totally forbidden. Foreign travel was barred. Provincial assemblies of the nobility were disallowed. Both the army and civilian society were outraged by the flogging of a staff captain, who was sentenced to a thousand strokes and the loss of his status and privileges as *dvoryanin.* A pastor was knouted for possessing forbidden books; a lieutenant had his tongue cut out and was sent to Siberia for writing an epigram on the construction of St. Isaac's Cathedral. Kotzebue, the German dramatist, who at the time was the director of a theater in Saint Petersburg, later described this year of terror in the capital. He said that every time his wife and children were late in returning home, he was frightened lest they had been arrested on their walk for omitting to salute a member of the imperial family; and during the cold months he found that he had to run past the long walls of the Winter Palace, since it was now obligatory to take off one's hat when in sight of it. After nine in the evening the turnpikes in the city were closed, and only doctors and midwives were allowed in the streets. Kochubey wrote to a friend that "the fear in which we are all living is indescribable. People are terrified of their own shadows. Everyone is afraid. Denunciations are an everyday matter: true or false, they are always believed. All the fortresses are overflowing with detainees. A deep melancholy has taken hold of everybody, and people no longer know what it is to be happy."

More seriously, Paul turned a complete somersault in his foreign policy. Instead of continuing to participate in the anti-French coalition, he made advances to Napoleon and placed an embargo on British shipping, simultaneously arresting more than a thousand British sailors. This was a most dangerous step. Apart from the reprisals it would inevitably invite, virtually the whole of Russia's foreign trade was in the hands of the community of some four thousand British merchants resident in Saint Petersburg.

It was this erratic conduct of foreign affairs which seems to have convinced Panin, a former diplomat who in 1800 occupied the post of Vice-Chancellor of Foreign Affairs, that Paul must be made to abdicate in favor of his son. Possibly he had in mind the precedent of the British King, George III. In the fevered atmosphere of Saint Petersburg, alive with police informers, he shared his thoughts with Count von Pahlen, the man whose cooperation was essential if the plan were to have any chance of success. Pahlen was, with Alexander, joint military governor of the capital, and the two men agreed that the Grand Duke must be sounded out before any step was taken; accordingly, Pahlen arranged for Panin to have an interview with Alexander.

Alexander recoiled from the thought of being embroiled in a conspiracy to remove his Emperor and father, and for six months after Panin had spoken to him he refused to commit himself. But events were inexorably forcing him to a decision. In November, 1800, when Paul accidentally discovered how far his Vice-Chancellor disapproved of the anti-British foreign policy he was supposed to be executing, Panin was suddenly exiled to his estate. Paul's attitude to his own immediate circle, including the Empress and Grand Dukes, was becoming even more hostile; at the beginning of the year 1801 the position of the imperial family had become virtually untenable. They were frequently placed under house arrest, they were insulted in public by the Emperor, and there was even talk that Alexander was to be disinherited and imprisoned in the Schusselberg fortress.

In these circumstances, Alexander finally consented to the idea of establishing a regency, although he stipulated emphatically to Pahlen that his father was in no way to be harmed. He even seems to have thought that after his abdication Paul could continue to live in the Winter Palace and enjoy the use of the royal residences outside Saint Petersburg. Pahlen was under no such illusions. From the outset he was convinced that Paul would never agree to abdicate, but it was essential that Alexander should be a party to the coup, and he accordingly gave his word to the Grand Duke.

With Paul becoming more dangerous and unpredictable at every moment, Pahlen now began quickly to forge the links of his conspiracy. He was fortunate in that after a somewhat checkered career he had come to enjoy the complete trust of the Emperor, largely thanks to his friendship with Kutaisov and to his efficient administration of the capital. He filled Saint Petersburg with officers who could be relied on to support him in the event of a move in Paul's favor and even used his position to engineer the pardon of Platon Zubov, Catherine's favorite at the time of her death, and of his brother Nicholas, both of whom had been exiled by the Emperor.

By February, 1801, Paul was feeling increasingly insecure in the Winter Palace, and he moved with his family into the Mikhailovsky castle, a gloomy fortress with innumerable defenses and safety devices which the Emperor had constructed for his own protection. As the plot ripened, so did Paul's suspicions increase. One day at the beginning of March Paul suddenly eyed Pahlen suspiciously in the course of a conversation and asked him whether he recalled the events of 1762 when Peter III had been assassinated, and whether he thought they could be repeated at the present time. Pahlen kept his head and coolly replied that a plot against the Emperor's life was indeed forming, but that he had placed himself at the head of it in order to keep himself informed of the conspirators' activities.

Paul was now thoroughly frightened. Suddenly he felt that there was no one in the capital whom he could trust, and in this crisis he tried to retrieve the only man on whose undeviating loyalty he had always been able to rely. On March 9, without informing Pahlen, he sent a note to Arakcheev at Gruzino, asking him to come at once to Saint Petersburg. But by now he could not move a step without Pahlen's knowledge; and the Governor was confident enough to intercept the note, confront Paul with it, and suggest that as the Emperor had not informed him of his intention, it must be a forgery. The Emperor insisted that the message be sent off, and also scrawled a note to Rostopchin, who was living on his estate near Moscow, "I need you. Come at once."

Pahlen was disturbed at the Emperor's attempts to summon his old supporters and knew that he must strike before they arrived. He decided to act on March 11 when men from Alexander's Semenovsky regiment were due to form part of the guard at the Mikhailovsky Palace. The atmosphere was tense in the palace during the whole of that day. Paul seemed to smell treason all around him and had the door between his bedroom and that of the Empress locked, while Alexander and Constantine were taken by Obolyaninov to swear an oath of loyalty to the Emperor, and then placed under house arrest. For his part, Pahlen suggested to Paul that the regiment of Horse Guards, which was guarding the royal apartments under the command of the loyal Colonel Sablukov, was untrustworthy since it was penetrated by Jacobinism. The maneuver was successful; in the early evening Paul stood down the guard, and his only protection was two valets dressed in hussar's uniform but unarmed, who stood at the door of his bedroom while a new regiment was summoned.

Some sixty young officers, many of whom had undergone humiliating punishments at the hands of the Emperor, were chosen by Pahlen to take part in the coup. That evening he assembled them, and plying them heavily with wine, he explained that the Emperor must be made to abdicate at once in favor of Alexander, if Russia was to be saved from disaster. One officer asked what would happen if the Emperor tried to

Gruzino

Peasant homes at Gruzino

resist. "Gentlemen, you do not make an omelet without breaking eggs," Pahlen dryly replied.

The night was cold and wet. Silently the conspirators made their way through the dark, empty streets to the castle and occupied the entrances, under the direction of an officer of the Preobrazhensky regiment who was already waiting for them. Once inside the castle the ringleaders split into two groups: Pahlen went to Alexander's apartment, while General Bennigsen and Platon Zubov led eighteen other officers to Paul's bedroom. After a short scuffle with the two valets, in which one was wounded, they burst into the room with drawn swords. The room was lit only by a candle, and to their dismay it appeared at first to be empty. Someone exclaimed, "The bird has flown!" But General Bennigsen soon noticed the terrified Paul, who had heard the clash of arms outside his door, and was standing barefoot in his nightshirt behind a screen. "Sir, you have ceased to reign," cried Bennigsen in French. "Alexander is now Emperor. We are arresting you on his orders. You must abdicate the throne." As Paul was apparently struck dumb with fear, Platon Zubov repeated the words in Russian. "Arrested, what does this mean, arrested?" exclaimed the Emperor at last. "What have I done to you?"

Paul either would not or could not understand what was happening, but the officers were half-crazed with drink and excitement and were in no mood to argue with him. In the ensuing confusion, someone knocked over the candle, and as the Emperor began to shout for help, the giant Nicholas Zubov, the man who four years previously had brought the news of his accession to Paul at Gatchina, seized a heavy gold snuffbox and dealt a violent blow to his left temple. Someone else found a scarf hanging by the bed, and a few moments later the Emperor was lying strangled.

Alexander was thrown into a paroxysm of despair and grief

by the arrival of the drunken Nicholas Zubov with the news that his father had "died of a fit of apoplexy." However inevitable the Emperor's death may have been to the leading conspirators, Alexander had refused to see the reality of the situation and had somehow remained persuaded that his father could be induced to abdicate. Once again it was Pahlen who took charge. Sharply rousing the prostrate Alexander, he said roughly, "Stop behaving like a child. The peace of millions of men now depends on you. Come and show yourself to the soldiers." Alexander obeyed. Choking with grief, he made a brief announcement to his regiment from the palace steps: "My father has died from an attack of apoplexy. Everything during my reign will be done in accordance with the spirit and principles of my beloved grandmother, the Empress Catherine."[26]

On the evening Paul died, Arakcheev arrived at the gates of Saint Petersburg, but he was denied entry. Pahlen had given orders that he should not be allowed through without the express command of the Emperor. He was thus spared the supremely difficult choice that would have faced him, blindly loyal as he was to both his masters, once Pahlen had secured Alexander's acquiescence to the plot. He returned quietly to Gruzino and set up a bust of Paul in the church he was building in front of his house. The bust was cut in white marble by the sculptor Martos, and along the wall above the memorial ran the following inscription in gold letters: "My heart is pure and my spirit just before you."

Alexander never recovered from the terrible guilt he felt over his father's death. "The grief and remorse which he was continually reviving in his heart were inexpressibly deep and troubling; his mental tortures never ceased," wrote his friend and minister Adam Czartoryski. It was in this way that Arakcheev, the man who had never betrayed his Emperor, became for Alexander the very symbol of loyalty and devotion. It would be wrong to see Arakcheev as deliberately playing on Alexander's feelings of guilt, though it is often alleged that he did so.[27] He had always worn his loyalty to his sovereign on his sleeve. But he became well aware of Alexander's haunting remorse and was happy to see his own former devotion to Paul become an unshakable bond between himself and the new Emperor.

3

The Master of Gruzino

We must build and build, for buildings become a memorial to us after our death. Without them our very name vanishes when we die.—ARAKCHEEV

Arakcheev's power had been reduced by his disgrace to his little kingdom of two thousand souls. But it was his own, his authority over it was complete, and he had a very definite idea of what he wanted to do.[1] In order to understand the nature of his work at Gruzino, how he turned it into the most celebrated estate in Russia and deeply impressed the Emperor with what he achieved, it is necessary to have some conception of the institution of serfdom, which was at the time the foundation of the whole social and economic structure of Russia.

Serfs were the personal possessions of the landowners, like the slaves who belonged to the planters in the West Indies. They were virtually human cattle, or, in the words of the Marquis de Custine, "des hommes-plantes." In the sixteenth and seventeenth centuries the jurisdiction of the landowners over the peasants who worked on their land was gradually increased, the original purpose being to tie the peasants to the land, but they came to be regarded as belonging to the landowners absolutely. Although there was no clear formulation of the legal basis of serfdom, the landowners' rights were extended piecemeal, while more and more landowners acquired serfs. For Peter the Great, serfdom was only one element in a state system where all levels of society, including the nobility, had obligations to serve in one form or another. But with the emancipation of the nobility under Catherine the moral justification of serfdom, if one can call it that, finally disappeared, and the gulf between landowner and serf became intolerably wide. A census taken at the end of Catherine's reign revealed that half the ten million male peasants in Russia were serfs who belonged with their families to private landlords, while the other half were state peasants tied to the land but not owning it, and paying taxes to the exchequer.

The peasantry never reconciled themselves to this state of affairs. There were innumerable sporadic revolts and flights of serfs, which culminated in the fearful rising of 1774, when the whole of servile Russia appeared to be on the point of snapping its chains. Under the leadership of the cossack Pugachov, a motley army of some thirty thousand men began to march on Moscow. Borne on a wave of mass destruction, they slaughtered landowners and devastated the estates in their path before government troops finally dispersed them. The government and aristocracy were shaken, but the Pugachov revolt did not set off a move to abolish serfdom. On the contrary, it led to increased repression on the part of the nobility, who henceforth were never able to dismiss from their minds the specter of the peasants on their estates murdering them in their beds.

The whole edifice of serfdom came to rest, therefore, on a system of the most savage corporal punishment. Birches, cudgels and the knout, shackles, iron collars, and stocks were all to be found in the armory of nearly every estate, and they were used liberally. "Nearly the whole of Russia groaned under blows," wrote Colonel Gribbe, who served under Arakcheev toward the end of Alexander's reign. "People were flogged in the army, in schools, towns and villages, on the marketplace, in the stables, and in their homes."[2] In Catherine's age of enlightenment, a landowner thought nothing of putting down a work of Voltaire that he might happen to be reading in order to step around to his stables and supervise the murderous beating of one of his servants. The absolute power of the serf-owners over their subjects led to the most grave abuses. Not all landlords were sadists, but the general level of cruelty was high. There were horrifying instances of children and pregnant women being beaten to death, and naked serfs torn to pieces by dogs. Princess Kozlovskaya, a veritable Russian Messalina, enjoyed whipping women's breasts and sexual organs; Countess Saltikov, the wife of Arakcheev's old patron, kept her barber in a cage for three years so that he should not reveal that she wore a wig. The serf was prohibited by law from making a complaint against his master, and in the whole of Catherine's reign only twenty serf-owners were punished for any form of cruelty toward their serfs, including murder, whereas in one case alone twelve peasants were flogged to death for having complained of ill-treatment.[3] The situation undoubtedly improved in Alexander's reign, and the Committee of Ministers frequently ordered the investigation of reports of cruelty by landowners, but the number of these reports is in itself an eloquent demonstration of the attitude of many noblemen toward their serfs.*

* The physical cruelty which was the basis of Russia's social order at the beginning of the nineteenth century is illustrated by the fact that the law still administered heavy punishment by the knout. An Englishman who traveled through Russia early in Alexander's reign witnessed an execution and was shocked by its barbarity. His account in a letter home is reproduced in Appendix I.

The richer noble families possessed many thousands of serfs, which enabled them to live in luxury far greater than that of the aristocracy of Western Europe, and also to indulge in every kind of fantasy. Many had three or four hundred servants, as well as their own serf painters, actors, musicians, and architects. Count Sakrovsky, who was musical, made all his servants address him in recitative. Prince Naryshkin, celebrated for his love of masquerades, organized a fantastic pageant on his estate at the end of one of the Turkish wars, in which the course of the actual fighting was reenacted in appropriate scenery specially constructed for the occasion. Serfs were gambled for, bought and sold at will, advertised in the daily press. An able-bodied man would fetch five hundred rubles through an advertisement; a child might be sold for ten kopecks. The asking price for a greyhound puppy in the same advertisement could be three thousand rubles.

Some Russians, of course, were dismayed by the degradation and the sheer economic backwardness induced by serfdom. Radishchev's *Journey from Saint Petersburg to Moscow* was an outspoken description of the poverty and miserable conditions of the peasantry. Published in 1790, when the censor let it through by mistake, it provoked a furious comment from Catherine, who said that "the author, infected and full of French madness, is trying in every possible way to break down respect for authority." Radishchev was banished to Siberia and returned only after the Empress's death. But there were others who felt that the system was intolerable, and Alexander was one. "I want to deliver the people from the barbarous situation in which this trade in human beings places them," he said to General Savary early in his reign. He was swiftly to learn the appalling difficulties that lay in the way of reform, for not only did the whole structure of the Russian economy depend on the institution of serfdom, it also assured the wealth and prosperity of the nobility on whose support the Crown itself was entirely dependent.

Arakcheev did not share the views of those who sought the abolition of serfdom. He was, however, very aware of the wasteful and primitive fashion in which most Russian landowners ran their estates, and he had firm ideas for the transformation of Gruzino into something quite different. Perhaps he remembered Paul's small kingdom at Gatchina, with its carefully administered schools, hospitals, factories, and churches. Whatever the inspiration, he set to work with his usual energy and efficiency.

The dilapidated condition of the estate, which had for years been halfheartedly administered by the neighboring Voskresensky monastery, gave Arakcheev the opportunity to undertake a total reconstruction. The property, which covered an area of some thirty-five square kilometers, consisting of villages interspersed with woods and fields, was bound on one side by the river Volkhov and on the other by the road from Novgorod to Tikhvin. One by one, scattered hamlets of rickety wooden peasants' huts were torn down and new model villages, generally with houses of brick or stone, took their place. The dwellings of each village were given some special feature to distinguish them from those of the next. Gruzino itself was converted into a row of pink stone houses, symmetrical and built in barracks style. Each house was divided down the center by a passage, and a family was lodged in each half. The peasants found the arrangement inconvenient and uncomfortable: they needed outhouses and shelters for their implements and animals, but nothing was allowed to destroy the pattern. Soon paved roads ran from one village to the next. Woods and thickets, particularly those on the banks of the river, were destroyed and new fields brought under cultivation. The whole place was an anthill of activity. In his passion for tidiness, Arakcheev even forbade the peasants of certain villages to keep pigs, because of the mess they made in the fields; this applied particularly to Gruzino and those hamlets lying near the road, which were intended to become showplaces.

The reaction of the peasants to these innovations was uniformly hostile. They were no different from their fellows, who under the degrading system of serfdom had become idle, thoughtless, and dirty, accustomed to doing the minimum of work in order to pay their taxes and keep themselves and their families alive, their only distraction being the habitual bouts of several days' drinking in which many Russians indulge to this day. If they were not free, they still cherished the right to live without undue interference from above. But at Gruzino these times were now over. As they moved into their new houses, a cascade of written orders and exhortations rained down on them from above. There were precise instructions concerning the maintenance of the houses, accompanied by orders to the headman of each village to make regular inspections and impose fines or a period of compulsory labor in the brickworks for any infringement of the rules.

Life for a headman, who was chosen by his fellow villagers, now became intolerable. He was held responsible for the good conduct of the village and was likely to be required to produce five thousand bricks for not having reported the death of a cow. Standards were difficult to impose and harder to maintain, but Arakcheev was relentless. "I have noticed that in the newly built hamlets there are many broken windows, and this is unsightly," runs Order 106 for 1808, dated mid-March. "To put an end to this, I request you to order all the elders of these hamlets to insist that the proprietors of homes with broken windows repair them by May 1. You should also let them know that if you find any broken windows after this date, they will be repaired at the expense of the elders, not of the proprietors; and I request you to see that this is carried out without fail. If, on my return to Gruzino, I see any broken windows (by which I mean windows where the glass is in fragments and has fallen from the frame—those with cracks can be left as they are), then new panes will be put in at your expense." Another goes, "You no doubt think that when I demand of you and the elders that the streets should be kept clean in all the villages, I am expressing a personal desire. So I am sending you a decree published by the Emperor from which you will see that he himself insists on clean streets. When you have informed the elders, you should inspect the villages even more carefully, as I shall henceforth exact cleanliness more strictly from you and them."

As time went on he penetrated further and further into the lives of his subjects. Concerned at the infant mortality rate, he compiled and had printed some "Brief rules for the peasant mothers of the district of Gruzino" which were a curious amalgam of common sense about baby care and old wives' recipes. "Every mother must feed her baby at least three times a day, for if feeding is infrequent, the mother's milk goes bad and harms the child," says one of these nostrums. But children were inoculated against smallpox, and he engaged a doctor to live on the estate and make visits to the villages. The doctor also furnished him with regular health reports, which he would annotate with comments of his own, such as "Many deaths, which reflects badly on the doctor."

Unmarried and widowed women were not popular with him. A list of their names was drawn up each year, and he would indicate those who should be married. All marriages needed his consent, and some of his comments on the names submitted to him were original: "I will not allow this marriage because of her brother's rude conduct," or "I agree, but if she does not know her prayers by Lent, I shall have her soundly whipped." His strong preference for the birth of male children was well known. A pathetic note from his butler was preserved among his papers at Gruzino: "We have had a daughter, and I have been afraid to inform you. It was not my wish that a daughter should be born rather than a son, but because of this I do not dare ask you, sir, to favor us by being a godfather. I had flattered myself that if it had been a son you would have agreed."

He even tackled the vexing question of drink. He began by closing all the drinking houses on the estate, decreeing that drink could be bought only from himself on specified occasions such as marriages and feast days. But despite the most draconian punishments, the peasants continued to smuggle drink in from outside, and he never managed to stamp out this one solace of the Russian peasant. Even his overseer, Shishkin, was rumored to be much addicted to vodka. One day he heard that Shishkin was so drunk that he could not stand on his feet. Arakcheev, thinking to catch him out at last, sent for him at once. But Shishkin put his head in a bucket of water, and Arakcheev was astonished to see him appear steady and apparently sober. Only his face was flushed.

"You are drunk again," said Arakcheev sternly.

"Not at all, sir; I never commit that sin."

"Why are you so red?"

"It must be the tea. I have just been drinking tea."

Arakcheev went close and noticed a strong smell of spirits. "If tea makes you drunk, you are completely forbidden to drink tea from now on. Don't forget."

Arakcheev did not rely simply on orders, fines, and the efficiency of his village elders to see that his instructions were obeyed to the letter. He made no less use of corporal punishment for his serfs than did the rest of his contemporaries, but in his bureaucratic way he refined and systematized the procedure. Every peasant and all the servants were required to carry a punishment book on them, in which their offenses were recorded. Punishments were graded: a whipping in the stables for a first offense, and for the second, flogging by men of the Preobrazhensky regiment, who used special thick cudgels known as "Arakcheev's sticks." Since he was in the habit of inspecting the backs of his servants after a flogging, they were not above killing a chicken and smearing themselves with its blood to make sure that he would be satisfied. There was also a house jail, known as "the Edicule," although no one could recall how it acquired this name. He expected those he had punished to send him a note conveying their repentance; and it was not uncommon to see in his church a number of women, in rough clothes and occasionally iron collars, on their knees in front of the congregation praying for the remission of their sins.

When Arakcheev arrived at Gruzino he found one very old peasant who remembered Prince Menshikov. His first plan was to restore the house and property to what it had been at the time of the Prince's disgrace, but no traces of it remained and he had no choice but to build anew. He engaged the full-time services of Minut, an architect who subsequently lived at Gruzino for twenty years and became renowned for his savagery ("He simply ate people," the peasants later said of him). It was not long before the approach from the coach station at Chudovo, some twelve kilometers away, had become most impressive. From a distance, the towers, belvederes, and white stone buildings on the horizon gave the impression of a small town. The visitor crossed the river by boat and landed on the other side between two immense white towers, from each of which flew the Count's standard. Walking up through magnificent gardens, he would come to a spacious but simple two-story house, which with its wings formed three sides of a court. The fourth was taken up by a large church. All his life, Arakcheev's greatest pleasure was to show guests around the house and property. Visitors were invariably impressed, although his passion for erecting monuments of all kinds made some of them feel at times as if they were in a cemetery. Captain Yazykov, who visited Gruzino in 1826, counted twelve monuments near the house, including three to Alexander, one to Paul, an iron vase to commemorate a visit paid by Arakcheev's mother, a column in memory of his father, and another inscribed with the names of two favorite dogs.[4] Behind the house he created a lake with an island on which he built, perhaps with his friend's tastes in mind, a temple of love dedicated to Melissino; inside the temple were looking-glasses which swung back to reveal amorous pictures when hidden switches were pressed.

Elizaveta Andreevna, who on Andrei's death had moved from Garusovo to a property closer to Bezhetsk, at Kurgany where her husband was buried, was impressed by her son's new wealth but worried that he remained unmarried. Arakcheev was over thirty and showed no sign of looking for a wife. The reason, whether she guessed it or not, was not that he was naturally celibate, but that he was increasingly content with the woman he brought with him when he retired so precipitately from Saint Petersburg.

Nastasia Fedorovna Minkina was a remarkable character. Physically she was very striking, with jet-black hair, flashing dark eyes, a swarthy complexion, and "the figure of a grenadier." No one on the estate knew where Arakcheev had found her. "God knows where she appeared from," said an old man who remembered her. "She wasn't from our district, but from somewhere far away, like Moscow." In fact, Arakcheev had bought her from an advertisement in a Saint Petersburg newspaper; and when he became fond of her, he gave her her freedom and an endowment of several thousand rubles.[5] No one could account for the influence which she exercised over him; the peasants at Gruzino were convinced that she was a gypsy and attributed magical powers to her. But her principal quality was the ability to adapt herself to Arakcheev, and in the end to make herself indispensable to him. He installed her at Gruzino as his housekeeper, and she quickly learned to run the estate like clockwork. When once again he was called back to public life, he left the work he had started in Nastasia's hands with complete confidence.

In the spring of 1803, more than three years after Arakcheev's retirement and two years after Alexander had acceded to the throne, the long-awaited summons came. There had been no word from Saint Petersburg since August, 1801, when Arakcheev was informed that he again had permission to wear the uniform of the Guards Artillery Battalion. Now, on April 27, a message arrived from Alexander. "Alexei Andreevich, I need to see you and ask you to come to Saint Petersburg." Then, not long after he had arrived in the capital, he had a message from Nastasia to say that she was expecting a child.

It was commonly believed on Arakcheev's estate, and the tale was later given credence in various responsible journals and histories, that Nastasia, terrified that Arakcheev would find a new mistress in Saint Petersburg and that she would lose her place in his affections and her position in his house, had decided that the only way of binding him to her was to bear him a child. In one of the distant villages at Gruzino a very poor peasant called Lukyanov suddenly died, leaving a

The Emperor Alexander in 1806
Courtesy of the British Museum

destitute and pregnant wife. By a mixture of threats and blandishments, Nastasia, who had failed to become pregnant herself, persuaded Lukyanova to agree to give her the baby when it was born, swearing the woman to total secrecy. Making judicious use of pillows, Nastasia, so the story goes, retired to her bed, and when the child, a boy, was born, Lukyanova was smuggled into the house with it and remained there as the baby's wet nurse. Arakcheev received the news of the birth in Saint Petersburg.

The odds that a desperate gamble of this kind would ever succeed seem very long. Not only would several people have to be in the secret, with the consequent risk that the truth would eventually reach Arakcheev, but he himself might have appeared at any moment and would then surely have discovered the facts for himself. However, on taking up his new duties, Arakcheev had begun to travel about Russia almost continuously, so the gamble could, just, have worked. The child, with vivid red hair and blue eyes, resembled neither Arakcheev nor Nastasia. But Arakcheev always treated the boy as his son; and given the paucity and dubious nature of the contrary evidence, it seems on the whole probable that he was his son. If any doubts remain, they stem from our knowledge of Nastasia herself, tormented by jealousy and determined at any cost not to sink back into the dark world from which she had been so unexpectedly rescued.*

* The story of the birth of Shumsky (the name the boy was later given) is obscured by the fog of legend surrounding various aspects of Arakcheev's life. The principal source of the story is a book by N. G. Bogoslovsky, *Rasskazy o Bylom*, published in Novgorod in 1865, fourteen years after Shumsky's death. Bogoslovsky claims to have been given the account by a man he met by chance when visiting Gruzino, who in his turn had the story from a priest who knew Shumsky. But Bogoslovsky's book, apart from its melodramatic style and the many pages of conversation written down at third hand, contains so many inaccuracies of detail as to make it a thoroughly untrustworthy document. Unfortunately, it gained a certain credence, and more sober writers, such as S. Shubinsky in his

The Saint Petersburg to which Arakcheev returned, a thin unfashionable figure with his hair still done up in a knot on his neck as had been customary in Paul's time, was very different from the city he had left more than three years before. There were new men in office and new ideas abroad. The first years of Alexander's reign had not been uneventful, although little of the work accomplished by the Emperor and his young advisers in the initial flush of enthusiasm proved to have a lasting effect. These new frontiersmen, as they would doubtless have been called today, inaugurated a kind of "hundred days," during which the more absurd of Paul's decrees were revoked in quick succession, the secret police was disbanded, and the torture of prisoners was abolished. The advertising of serfs for sale was prohibited, and commoners were allowed to acquire land, but not serfs. However, "the unofficial committee," as it became known (Alexander and his friends nicknamed it "the Committee of Public Safety"), succeeded in modifying only the outward aspects of autocracy. The members of the committee, Novosiltsov, Kochubey, Stroganov, and Alexander's close friend the Polish Prince Adam Czartoryski, were all liberal men, conscious of the need to control and legalize imperial power and to tackle the evil of serfdom. But despite endless meetings, over which the Emperor nearly always presided himself, they were unable

---

Ocherki i Rasskazy, and V. D. Filosofov in his circumstantial article on Minkina in *Russkaya Starina* (March, 1884) have not thought it worth questioning the truth of what must remain a legend. N. K. Otto repeats the story in the second of his articles, but he is vague about his source.

Another account, given by Arakcheev's military clerk, Efimov, was written down many years later by a senior officer of Efimov's and published in the January number of *Russkaya Starina*, 1878. According to this account, Nastasia ordered Efimov to draw up the report which Arakcheev demanded whenever a birth or a death occurred on his estate, declaring that Lukyanova's son had died at birth. An empty coffin was supposed to have been buried. "It is strange that this simple woman succeeded in deceiving Arakcheev," comments the writer, "but those whom God wants to punish, he first deprives of their wits."

to make much headway, and before they realized it their moment had passed. Possibly the most disappointed among them was Adam Czartoryski. He had been much impressed by Alexander's plans for the Russian Empire through conversations he had enjoyed in private with the Grand Duke during the previous reign. As an ardent Polish patriot he had been particularly encouraged by Alexander's professed determination to work for the restoration of the Polish state. Yet, in 1806, having spent the early years of Alexander's reign as Deputy Minister of Foreign Affairs, he realized that there were few chances of his hopes being fulfilled, and he returned disgruntled to Poland.

Czartoryski made a close study of Alexander's character, and in his memoirs he lays much of the blame for the ephemeral results of the reformers' work on the shoulders of the Emperor himself. In a sense, he is right, for although there was powerful opposition in Saint Petersburg to all that the reformers stood for, and Alexander could at no time afford to arouse the total hostility of the nobility, one can fairly say that had he stuck to his course and divided the opposition with the skill of which he was certainly capable, he might have accomplished great things. But as became increasingly apparent, consistency was the quality which this unhappy and complicated man most conspicuously lacked.

Alexander acquired the reputation in his own lifetime of being "a sphinx," "the enigmatic Czar," and a man capable of the deepest dissimulation. This view of him has not changed with time. It was his ability to hold seemingly contradictory views with equal conviction, to say one thing and to do quite the opposite, that made him so difficult to understand. Like a rudderless ship, he veered before the changeable winds of his enthusiasms, which were usually in contradiction with both his own inherited beliefs and the logic of events. He lacked, as Harold Nicolson has so rightly said, the vital quality of coordination.[6]

Every intelligent man who had dealings with Alexander spotted that something was wrong, but no one could quite put his finger on it. Napoleon himself confessed to Metternich that he thought "something is missing in his character, but I find it impossible to discover what it is." Alexander reminds one of an actor trying to play several roles at the same time, now diving into one part, now into another; only when the curtain came down in the last years of his life did he realize the contradiction between his ringing words and his achievements, and he sought to escape disillusionment in a deepening fog of mysticism. But he remained aware of the extent of his failure. "Russia has had sufficient glory abroad, but when I think how little has been done inside the country, I feel a heavy load in my breast," he confessed unhappily to Lobyanovsky, the governor of Penza, the year before he died.[7] La Harpe had appreciated his pupil's quick intelligence, but he had also been the first to be dismayed by his mental lethargy, and his unwillingness to think problems through. Czartoryski also noted that "he never read to the end of a single serious book."[8] Although Alexander wrote to La Harpe in a letter about "the academic work which is my favorite occupation," it emerged that he had in fact acquired at Gatchina an unlikely taste for parades and for the order and discipline associated with military life. He was almost manic in his tidiness and personal habits.

When Speransky drew up his elaborate constitutional reform for Russia, at the Emperor's request, another aspect of Alexander's character became apparent—his touchiness about his own position. "And what of me; am I to become nothing?" he asked querulously. One Russian historian likened Alexander's taste for constitutional governments to "that of a dilettante who goes into ecstasies over a beautiful picture"; and another remarks that he admired the aesthetic aspects of liberal thought "in a purely detached manner, as a tourist admires the beauty of a landscape from the window of a railway carriage—admires and speeds on."[9] In 1819, when serfdom was abolished in the Baltic state of Livonia, Alexander told the Livonian nobility that their example was worthy of imitation. "You have acted in the spirit of the times and have understood that liberal beginnings can alone serve as a basis for the happiness of peoples." However, only a year later a group of wealthy Russian landowners came to see him with a plan for setting their serfs free, and he asked them abruptly who made the law. When they replied in some confusion that of course it was the Emperor, he said, "Then kindly leave me the right to issue the laws which I consider most useful for my subjects."[10] One is forcefully reminded of Paul beating his chest and crying, "Here is your law."

In 1803 the deteriorating international situation obliged Alexander, perhaps not altogether against his will, to withdraw his attention from the niceties of constitutional reform and to consider plans for neutralizing Napoleon, whose unconcealed aggressive intentions had become the direct concern of every state in Europe. Alexander had sincerely hoped for a long period of peace at the start of his reign. Only two years later it was plain to him that peace was impossible. "Like you, I have completely changed my mind about Napoleon," he wrote to La Harpe. "When he took the consulate for life, the veil fell, and he has gone from bad to worse." It may have been that Alexander's gradual realization that he would shortly have need of a mobile and efficient army decided him to turn to Arakcheev.

Men of Arakcheev's stamp, who had been so influential in the previous reign, had been distinctly out of favor since

Alexander's succession; some officers had thought, and many hoped, that Arakcheev's banishment was final. The news of his impending return was greeted with ill-concealed dismay, even in the artillery, where vain attempts were made to prevent his appointment.[11] On May 14 he was created inspector general of the artillery and commander of the Guards Artillery Battalion.

The Emperor gave Arakcheev a free hand to reorganize and strengthen the artillery. It was a golden opportunity to demonstrate his worth, and the problem was one with which he was thoroughly familiar. After several very active months in which he traveled almost continuously, visiting regiments all over Russia, he came to the conclusion that the artillery must be separated from the infantry, given its own chain of command and lines of supply, and made to feel that it was no longer simply the handmaid of the infantry regiments. To this end he established schools of artillery for officers and men and founded a publication, *The Artillery Journal*, which did much to promote an esprit de corps. He was particularly anxious to build up a fresh generation of well-trained artillery officers and paid close attention to his new schools. "With good stone foundations, an old wooden building can last for as many years as a new stone one," he wrote to a friend, General Vereshchagin, whose advice he sought on the best method of teaching mathematics.

Arakcheev's plan for separating infantry and artillery inevitably met with rooted objection from many infantry officers. In the end he won his point, but it was some time before its full implications were entirely accepted, and the army was to suffer from its slowness in adapting itself. Meanwhile the artillery had nothing but admiration for his work on their behalf. The mutterings which had greeted his appointment gave place to outspoken admiration for his energy and efficiency in their cause. For the first time their interests were being looked after by a man who understood them and who had the ear of the Emperor. His enthusiasm was infectious, and he seemed to have brought his old disposition to violence under control.

Lieutenant Zhirkevich, who was appointed Arakcheev's adjutant in the Guard's Artillery Battalion, describes him in his memoirs: "I had heard many disagreeable things about him and in general little good of him. But I spent three years under his command and can speak dispassionately of him. His honorable and ardent devotion to the throne and to the country, his naturally penetrating mind, which was, however, completely uneducated, his honesty and directness, were the main features of his character. But his tremendous pride, self-reliance, and self-assurance made him frequently rancorous and vindictive. However, in his relations with those who had gained his trust he was always kind, thoughtful, and even indulgent. . . . I might add that during the seven or eight years of his inspectorate of the artillery only one officer was reduced to the ranks, and that was for writing a false currency bill, a crime for which one is usually sent to Siberia. Soldiers were put in the guardroom every day, and many were left there so that they should not be assigned to work. But in the first year of the appointment of his successor, the kind General Meller, there were ten times more unhappy soldiers than during the whole period of Arakcheev's tenure of office. I won't enlarge on the improvement in the artillery; everyone in Russia knows that its present condition is the work of Arakcheev, and if it has since been perfected, it was he who laid the firm foundation."[12]

The test of Arakcheev's work came only two years after he had taken office. In 1804 Napoleon temporarily abandoned his plans for invading England and again turned his eyes south and east. His decision to make the Italian republic a hereditary kingdom and his coronation as "King of all Italy" in Milan in May, 1805, finally decided Austria to join forces with England and Russia, who had just signed a convention in Saint Petersburg. The allies assumed that Italy would be the theater of war, but Napoleon moved out into southern Germany at great speed and at Ulm forced the Austrian General Mack to capitulate with fifty thousand men. Kutuzov, the already celebrated Russian general, who was now placed in command of both the Russian and the remains of the Austrian army, resorted to his favorite strategy of refusing to give battle to the enemy. But Alexander, who had now joined the army and saw himself in the role of soldier-king destined to defeat Napoleon, was longing for a decisive engagement and insisted against Kutuzov's advice on having his own way. So it came about that in December, 1805, against all the instincts of the Russian commander in chief, the battle of Austerlitz was fought. The allied army was cut in two and routed by the French. Napoleon won his most decisive victory.

Alexander wept bitterly over his defeat, and the disappointment at Saint Petersburg was great, more particularly since the first news had unaccountably been that the Russians had won a brilliant victory. Inevitably there was an anguished post mortem. Arakcheev was not spared. It was said that Alexander had offered him a command which he had refused on account of his nerves, and that although he had been attached to the Emperor's suite, he had been seen riding hastily from the field as soon as the action began. There is no surviving evidence for either of these stories, but the reputation that he was a coward and could not bear the smell of gunpowder fired in anger clung to him. If it seems surprising that an officer of Arakcheev's seniority took no major part in so important a battle, it should not be forgotten that he had never once seen active fighting and owed his position to his administrative rather than to his untried martial gifts.

More seriously, it was found that the Russian artillery had not done well. A hundred and thirty-three guns, more than half the total, had been lost. The opponents of Arakcheev's reforms claimed that the new lightweight guns which he had pioneered in the interests of mobility had exploded under rapid fire and that their carriages had also disintegrated. Arakcheev conducted his own line of inquiry. He set up a commission that showed that the new guns had not exploded at all, but on the contrary, had abundantly proved their worth. Next he held a minute investigation into the artillery's performance in the battle. He interviewed each junior officer individually, and in the course of the interview gave him a pencil and a sheet of paper and asked him to sketch in the movements of the gun under his command, adding if possible his estimate of what had happened to the other guns in his company. The result was clear proof, if Arakcheev needed it, that the infantry and artillery had not yet learned to coordinate their tactics, now that they were under separate command. Neither the infantry nor the cavalry had thought of supporting the artillery, and there had been numerous instances of regiments moving forward when the artillery was about to open fire, thereby blocking the guns. Despite Arakcheev's fierce opposition, the conclusion drawn was that while the heavy guns should remain under separate command, the light guns must again be joined to the regiments and placed under the command of infantry officers.[13] Arakcheev's personal dedication to his artillery was illustrated by his intercession for Lieutenant Demidov, the only officer of the Guards Artillery Battalion who had been captured with his gun. Napoleon, who had come across Demidov on the field, said typically, "Il y a, jeune homme, quelque honneur à être pris par les français." The Russian command took a different view, and Demidov was saved from a transfer to the infantry only by Arakcheev's personal intervention with the Emperor.[14]

Alexander had lost a battle, but he clearly did not consider that he had lost the war. Word went out that fresh recruits and equipment were to be found in the shortest possible time, in preparation for a new campaign. The reason for the haste was that Prussia, who had stood aside in selfish neutrality while Austria and Russia were struggling with Napoleon, had now decided to take him on herself, and Frederick William looked to Alexander for help. Once again Arakcheev displayed great energy and in a short time had totally reequipped the artillery, producing a thousand new guns.

Meanwhile, Arakcheev's mother, delighted with his successful return to office, continued to press him to marry. He brushed off her advice with a touch of impatience. "I much sympathize with you over your illness," he wrote to her, "but it comes from your anxieties about us, and I beg you, dear Mother, not to worry. You need only to realize that we are all three, thank God, grown up, and any of us may marry. Everyone should think for himself and organize his own life instead of relying on others." Shifting his ground, he continued self-righteously, "My comrades who received more than I did from the Emperor are now all in debt, but I, thank God, am not, for which they laugh at me and call me a miser. Even my brother Petr Andreevich joins in, but I can survive it."[15] Then, out of the blue, he met an attractive girl and unexpectedly decided to marry after all.

Anastasia Vasilievna Khomutova was the daughter of a landowner from Tikhvin, not far from Gruzino. Her parents also had a house in Saint Petersburg, and she had just begun to come out in society. Seldom can a couple have been more ill-matched. Anastasia was eighteen, shy, and pretty, entranced with Saint Petersburg society; he austere, unsociable, and insensitive. Nonetheless, they were married under the brightest social auspices; the Emperor was present at the ceremony, which took place in the Sergeevsky Artillery Cathedral on February 4, 1806, and on the same day Anastasia was appointed lady-in-waiting to the Empress. The problem of Nastasia Minkina and the baby remained, but the Gruzino estate was large, and there would be no difficulty in finding her a husband and a father for the child. Arakcheev does not appear to have considered sending her away altogether. However, the news of the marriage must have been a bitter blow to Nastasia, the realization of her worst nightmare.

Arakcheev and Anastasia settled down happily enough in the house he had acquired on Liteinaya Street. "Anastasia's love and friendship are my whole happiness," he wrote in April to a friend at Bezhetsk. "Daily I pray to the Almighty for it, and without it my tender nature could hardly be well and happy." But it was not long before the difference in their tastes began to tell. She hankered after the life of parties and dances which he cordially disliked, but when she went out without him he was very jealous. They rarely entertained; a few friends would come to lunch, his old colleague Aprelev, now a major-general, or Petr Ivanovich Rimsky-Korsakov, a neighbor from Bezhetsk. The duty adjutant, who was frequently the faithful Zhirkevich, was always present, and he witnessed embarrassing domestic bickering.

"You are always wanting to go out for drives," Arakcheev said to his wife over lunch one day. "May I recommend my adjutant Zhirkevich as an escort."

"I am sure that Mr. Zhirkevich would not refuse me if I asked him," she replied.

"You will have to ask him, as he won't ask himself; he is

still a baby," said Arakcheev sarcastically; "but don't go and stick your finger in his mouth or he will bite it off."[16]

Matters did not mend. The couple moved between Saint Petersburg and Gruzino, and although there are no recorded encounters between the two Anastasias, Arakcheev, in the first year of his marriage, set up an iron vase in his garden dedicated to Nastasia Minkina "for her devoted services."[17] The final rupture occurred early in the second year of their married life. One day when Arakcheev was on tour, Anastasia got into her carriage and told the coachman to drive her to a friend's address. To her astonishment, he replied that the Count had forbidden him to take her there and had given him a list of houses she was not to visit. She at once asked him to drive her to her mother's house, and from there she sent for her belongings. On his return, Arakcheev was dismayed to find an empty house. For two weeks he called on his wife twice a day, but with little result; one afternoon he was crossing St. Isaac's bridge with her when he stopped the carriage and went home by foot. This was the end. Anastasia retired to the country, and they never met again.*

The year 1807 was a disastrous one for Russian arms. After his victory at Austerlitz, Napoleon seemed unstoppable. He had decimated the Prussians at Jena and Auerstadt and now turned his attention to the Russian armies on German territory, under the command of General Bennigsen. At the battle of Eylau the honors were even, with some twenty thousand casualties on each side, but at Friedland Napoleon completely outmaneuvered Bennigsen. He pinned the Russians with their

* Memoirs of Zhirkevich, *Russkaya Starina*, February, 1874. In his *Life of Muraviev* (Saint Petersburg, 1874) D. A. Kropotov records an unlikely version of the break-up of Arakcheev's marriage, according to which it occurred when Arakcheev discovered that his wife had accepted a bribe of ten thousand rubles from the chief of police in return for her connivance over a house he was building for himself out of secret funds.

backs to the river Alle and slaughtered them where they stood. The victory was crushing.

At Eylau Napoleon had been surprised at the new effectiveness of the Russian artillery and remarked that the time had now passed when he could win all his engagements with forty guns; he took the precaution of greatly increasing his gunpower at Friedland. In the midst of the general disaster, therefore, Arakcheev's stock with Alexander remained high. On June 27, only two weeks after the Friedland defeat, Alexander sent Arakcheev a glowing tribute. "The high standard of the artillery and its successful action in the course of the war have led me to reward your services. By my order of yesterday you are promoted to artillery general. Please accept this as a sign of my gratitude and especial favor." In December Alexander granted Arakcheev an unusual privilege: he issued a decree stating that orders issued by Arakcheev were to be considered as if they came from the Emperor.

Yet Arakcheev was not happy. He knew that he was cordially disliked by Alexander's courtiers and that his great services to the artillery had aroused resentment and jealousy in the other parts of the army. There seemed no way of circumventing his enemies and reestablishing his former close relationship with Alexander. Alexander himself was beset with troubles. After the defeat at Friedland, he was forced to conclude an alliance with Napoleon at Tilsit. The new alliance with a man who was commonly regarded as a usurper of the French throne and an unalterable enemy of Russia was bitterly unpopular in the Russian court, and the Emperor took all the blame. It was even murmured that he might be overtaken by the same fate as Paul.

In an effort to reconcile people to the French alliance, the Emperor appeared constantly in public. He seemed determined to demonstrate that he was not cast down by his defeat and that all was well. The elegant palaces and houses of Saint Petersburg had never seen as many brilliant balls and receptions as were given in the winter of 1807, and the Emperor made a point of attending virtually all of them. The newly arrived French Ambassador, General Savary, was duly impressed, but he was dismayed to find himself almost completely ostracized by Saint Petersburg's hostesses, despite Alexander's clear wish that he should be treated with due courtesy. Nor was discontent with the new alliance confined to the court and society. The embargo on trade with England which followed the conclusion of the Tilsit agreement provoked a fall of fifty percent in the ruble, as well as a massive reduction in all foreign trade.

Dispirited and alone, separated from his Emperor, Arakcheev seriously considered resignation. Gruzino beckoned him; there was much for him to do there. Anastasia had gone, and he no longer had any ties in Saint Petersburg. For the first time the capital seemed hateful. Just before Christmas Colonel Eiler of the Guards Artillery Battalion was walking along Liteinaya Street when Arakcheev stopped his carriage and gave him a lift. He was in a bitter frame of mind and complained of the unpleasantness of the court toward him. "I have finally decided to go," he said, adding, "I know many people will be glad."[18] He gave a farewell dinner to the Guards Artillery Battalion and handed in his resignation to the Emperor.

"The administration of the department entrusted to me during the years of our national difficulties has not deteriorated," he wrote to Alexander. "On the contrary, it has been very much improved in all its sectors, for example, in guns, shells, and powder. As a result of unremitting and very successful work, the state factories in the arsenals not only cause surprise by the speed of their production, but have earned the praise of foreign powers and have even surpassed them in the purity and reliability of their gunpowder. At last I have accomplished my work, although it has not been without damage to my health. Your Imperial Majesty can now be reassured about the unpleasant stories which have been reaching you and which made you so worried on my account. May I now hope that in view of my illness, which has made me quite unfit to serve your Majesty, you will grant me my retirement as a reward, if I have deserved one. . . . My weak health has brought on heavy melancholia, and my desire to retire to my country retreat is so great that nothing can change it."*

Before he had time to pack his cases, it was announced that he had been appointed Minister of War.

* Text in an appendix to M. I. Bogdanovich, *Istoriya Tsarstvovaniya Imperatora Alexandra* I, Vol. VI, Saint Petersburg, 1869. Bogdanovich attributes this document to the beginning of 1808, but it clearly refers to Arakcheev's attempted resignation of December, 1807, since Arakcheev is requesting retirement from the artillery.

4
The Minister of War

It is still your boast and your rule that subordinates should love their commanders. But my rule is that subordinates should do their work and fear their senior officers, for it is impossible to keep a crowd of mistresses. It is hard enough to chastise one, let alone a mass of them.

—ARAKCHEEV TO GENERAL MAEVSKY

Alexander bought more than four years of uneasy peace at Tilsit. He was anxious, however, that the Russian army should be reorganized and strengthened as quickly as possible, for he could not be sure when the next contest with the French might come. The disastrous European campaign had left his troops in very poor shape and had revealed particularly chronic deficiencies and abuses in the supply departments. A number of senior officers were sacked, and as a mark of the Emperor's displeasure, all officials working in the supply division were forbidden to wear uniform. Even old General Vyazmitinov, the previous War Minister, lost the right to wear uniform and was retired in disgrace as a result of the supply scandal; and it was Arakcheev who shortly after taking office interceded with the Emperor to restore the General's honor.

Arakcheev's appointment was greeted with surprise and dismay by his enemies at court. They had been happy to mock him when the post he held had little political importance. Now for the first time they had reason to be disturbed by this apparent outsider's influence on the Emperor. Joseph de Maistre, the Sardinian Ambassador to Saint Petersburg, was a close friend of many of the aristocrats around Alexander, and in his dispatches he faithfully if unwittingly echoes their opinions and prejudices. His reaction to Arakcheev's promotion can thus be taken as a fair reflection of the general view of society on this matter. "From among the oligarchy of military favorites," wrote De Maistre, "General Arakcheev has suddenly, without any warning signals, risen out of the ground. He is cruel, stern, and unshakable. People say that one cannot call him a bad man, but I consider him very bad. This does not mean that I condemn his appointment, since at present only a man of his kidney can restore order. However, it remains to be explained why his Imperial Majesty has decided to acquire a vizier, since nothing is more alien to his character and way of governing. His fundamental principle has been to give a limited share of his confidence to each of his assistants. I suppose he wanted to have a more frightening bogeyman by his side because of the domestic ferment which prevails here. Arakcheev has against him both of the Empresses, Count Lieven, General Uvarov, the Tolstoys, in a word, everyone who carries weight. But he is overcoming everything; the most influential are disappearing before him like smoke."[1]

Not only did Arakcheev have to endure the venom of men like De Maistre and his circle, he also found himself in fierce combat with the senior command of the army. He was given broad powers to build up the army as a whole in the same way as he had already—and with such brilliant success—built up the artillery. To his appointment as Minister of War were added the inspector generalships of the infantry and the artillery, and he quickly realized that he must begin by establishing a greater degree of authority than his predecessors had enjoyed. Until then the War Minister's influence had been considerably limited by the fact that he had no direct control over the military staff, who considered themselves responsible to the Emperor alone. With Alexander's consent, Arakcheev at once put an end to the practice whereby an adjutant general served as a direct link between the staff and the Emperor's private chancery. Instead, two aides-de-camp were placed under Arakcheev, and the staff were now expected to take their instructions from the War Minister. There was, inevitably, much resistance from the high command, and several high-ranking officers resigned. Arakcheev, confident of the Emperor's backing, met the generals head on. He deliberately built up his personal prestige by appointing to himself adjutants from every regiment, a privilege hitherto reserved to the Emperor alone; his carriage was accompanied everywhere by a military escort; and he had a guard stationed permanently outside his house. On one occasion, when Arakcheev was taken ill and confined to his bed, Alexander was happy to demonstrate his support for Arakcheev by coming for daily consultations at his War Minister's bedside. Arakcheev's self-confidence grew in consequence. When a subordinate once asked him if he thought the Emperor would approve some arrangements they had made, Arakcheev replied shortly, "I shall say to the Emperor, either allow me to resign or be good enough to sign, for I intend to give the orders."

Not content with his attack on the general staff, Arakcheev proceeded to take the army to task on one of the subjects nearest to his heart, discipline. He published an order on June 9, 1808, shortly after his appointment, which was certainly not calculated to increase his popularity, but then, popularity was not an attribute he ever troubled to court. "From the moment I became War Minister," the order runs, "I have noticed that in certain cases discipline is not observed as strictly as it should be. As discipline is known to be the chief principle on which the whole service rests, I consider myself bound by my position to state the following. Junior officers not infrequently fail to observe due respect or even decency in their attitude to their seniors, particularly on public occasions. I put the blame for this not so much on the junior officers themselves as on the person of the senior officer who does not exercise his duty by putting a stop to this, and thus provides every excuse for open relaxation of the established rules of military service. I wish to emphasize this point, and I cite myself as an example, for I have never tolerated insubordination toward myself. Henceforth it must be firmly established that if a general does not prosecute his junior officers for not fulfilling their duties, it will be taken as evidence that he does not know how to obtain the respect due to him."

It is not difficult to imagine the effect which orders such as these produced on campaign-hardened officers. Yet behind Arakcheev's forbidding exterior an innate sense of justice occasionally showed itself. Once a major who had gone absent without leave pleaded his case with Arakcheev in front of a group of officers. His wife and eldest son had suddenly died, and he had been attempting alone to provide for his daughter and two younger sons. Arakcheev heard him out unmoved and ordered him to appear the next day, with only the comment that it was inexcusable to default from the army. In great fear the major appeared at the appointed hour and was shown into Arakcheev's office. "Yesterday," said Arakcheev to him, "you saw in me the commanding officer who could not pardon you in front of so many young, undisciplined officers; but now you see the man. I have already spoken of you to the Emperor. His Majesty has arranged for your sons to be received into the cadet corps, and your daughter into a girls' school. Your daughter has been granted a dowry of five thousand rubles, and the Emperor has awarded you a thousand rubles in gold. Please return to your regiment. Here is a letter from me to your colonel. You will be well received."[2]

During the whole of the year Arakcheev worked strenuously at his Ministry and completed a thorough departmental reorganization. Uncomfortable clashes still occurred from time to time, and not only with the imperial staff, but Alexander's support did not waver. At one moment the Emperor's brother, the Grand Duke Constantine, with whom Arakcheev had never been on good terms, persuaded Alexander to allocate a hundred thousand rubles to improve the horses and equipment of one of the Grand Duke's favorite regiments, the Uhlans. Arakcheev at once disputed the decision on the grounds that money was very short and that to give way to one regiment would create discontent in many others. Alexander was convinced, and canceled the grant. Constantine stormed around to Arakcheev's house in a fury, but Arakcheev saw him arriving from his window and left hurriedly for the palace by a back door. Eventually Constantine caught up with him and began to upbraid him violently. Arakcheev appealed to the Emperor. In tears, he asked to be dismissed, but Alexander stood by his Minister and shortly afterward showed his continuing favor by ordering that the Rostov Musketeer Regiment be renamed "Count Arakcheev's Regiment."[3]

Despite his many duties, Arakcheev continued to keep a fatherly eye on the artillery with whose activities his *amour propre* was always much involved, sometimes with uncomfortable results. When Frederick William of Prussia came to Saint Petersburg in December, 1808, Arakcheev accompanied him to a demonstration of new guns under the command of Colonel Eiler. The unusually intense cold caused the wheel of one of the gun carriages to stick. Arakcheev flew into a rage and had the Colonel clapped up in the guardroom for six hours. The next day, after a similar exercise before Alexander and Frederick William had been successfully concluded, and Arakcheev had personally served them both lunch in a tent erected for the occasion, the Prussian King asked leave to propose his health; by way of reply, Arakcheev flung himself on his knees and violently kissed the hands of both monarchs.[4] His temperament was always passionate.

There were, however, weightier matters for his attention than disciplinary problems or royal performances. From the moment Arakcheev took office the question of supplying and equipping the army for a new campaign became a matter of great urgency. Alexander, in order to retrieve some of his lost popularity at home, was now preparing to exploit his alliance with Napoleon by realizing a long-standing Russian ambition, the acquisition of Finland, at the time an integral part of the kingdom of Sweden.

Ever since Saint Petersburg became the capital of Russia it had been the aim of successive Emperors to secure the whole eastern shore of the Baltic in order to protect the Russian capital from an invasion through Finland. The frontier was indeed perilously close. The Swedish attack of 1788, when Russia's hands were tied by the war with Turkey, had not been forgotten, and Napoleon now actively encouraged Alexander to take on the Swedes, since the latter were in alliance with England. Alexander needed no second bidding;

and despite the fact that his army was quite unprepared, Russian troops under the command of General Buxhöwden crossed the border early in February, 1808, and began to occupy Finland. Some units were so badly equipped that they were brought through Saint Petersburg only at night. The ranks of the army were swelled by the recruitment of raw peasants, and a hasty training program was devised. Alexander himself turned up at the exercises but was dismayed by the condition of the men. Their bearing was indeed far from warlike; on one occasion a soldier strolled several paces away from his gun in the middle of an exercise, bought a roll of bread, and began to munch it under the Emperor's nose.[5]

However, the problem of supply predominated almost all others from the outset of the campaign. Once again Arakcheev's energy and direct methods were effective. The official who was then at the head of the supply division describes how he suggested to Arakcheev that the only way to obtain the urgently needed shipments of bread was to request the Emperor's approval for all troops in Saint Petersburg to sacrifice a month's flour ration and bake the bread in their own ovens. Arakcheev acted on the spot. "At that moment I learned what power this minister had," the official relates. "Without replying to me, he rang for his adjutant and ordered him to draw up a directive to all garrisons and regiments in Saint Petersburg to the effect that under my instructions they were to bake a month's ration of flour, dry it into rusks, and send it with their own transport to any place designated by me."[6]

Despite the difficulties hampering the Russian troops, the Swedes put up a poor resistance, and in March the incorporation of Finland in the Russian Empire was proclaimed. The declaration, however, proved somewhat optimistic. The Finns continued to conduct guerrilla warfare against the Russians, and the Swedes refused to sign a peace treaty. Toward the end of the year Alexander decided that if the war was to be successfully concluded, it must be carried into Sweden.

Since March Alexander had been pondering a daring stratagem whereby the Russian troops should cross from Finland to Sweden on foot over the frozen Gulf of Bothnia, thus forcing the Swedes to capitulate before the ice melted and the Swedish and English navies could be brought into action. Buxhöwden, who was in favor of settling for the gains Russia had already made and concluding an armistice with the Swedes, was replaced by General Knorring, and instructions were now sent to Knorring to prepare the campaign and begin his advance. But Knorring and the other generals under his command, Shuvalov, Barclay de Tolly, and Bagration, were all opposed to the scheme. They were only too aware of the obstacles. There were the difficulties of a crossing which, even if successful, would leave the men exhausted and in no condition to fight; there was the poor supply situation; and there was the considerable danger that even in midwinter the ice might open under the pressure of the frequent gales and currents and swallow up all or part of the army.

Knorring did not return to argue his case in Saint Petersburg, unwisely preferring to prevaricate by correspondence. He claimed that he was having great difficulty in supplying his army of thirty-five thousand men, and in fact did nothing, while Alexander in Saint Petersburg became increasingly irritable as the weeks slipped by and precious time was lost. In February, 1809, Alexander wrote to Knorring, "I am amazed to learn that you are only now collecting troops to prepare them for the action. . . . I am accustomed to having my instructions followed exactly, and do not like repeating them. I hope that this is the last time that you will force me to do so."[7] In his reply, Knorring at last found the resolution to call the whole operation into question, using as his main argument the risk of being cut off by the Swedes once his army was on the Swedish shore. When he received this answer, Alexander at once dispatched Arakcheev to take charge.

Arakcheev was characteristically unimpressed by the atmosphere of despondency that reigned at Knorring's headquarters in Abo, and he took energetic measures to get matters moving without delay. It was decided that the army should move across the gulf in three prongs—under the command of Bagration in the south, by way of the Aland islands; Barclay in the center, through the Kvarken straits to Umeo; and Shuvalov in the north—thus forcing the Swedes to split up their own forces on the other side.

Still no one believed in the success of the strategy. Knorring offered to resign. Barclay renewed his objections when he reached departure point. He wrote back to headquarters saying that he needed clearer instructions. "I shall not be able to establish communications with Count Shuvalov in action. We have no real information about the enemy, but we know that his forces are gathering at Umeo, so it is impossible for me to go there with only five thousand men." Arakcheev ignored these complaints and wrote imperiously to the reluctant general, "I request you to proceed at once to carry out the Emperor's orders and am waiting for the report from you announcing that you have done so, for his Majesty has demanded to have this without fail. As regards your statement that you have received few instructions from the command in chief, a general of your quality does not need them. I will only say that as the Emperor is arriving at Borgo on March 16, I am sure you will do your best to obtain Swedish trophies for him by that date. At this time I would rather be in your place than a minister, for there are many ministers but Providence is offering to Barclay de Tolly alone the crossing of the Kvarken."[8] Shuvalov also wrote pessimistically, saying that he had been told that the ice would not hold in his sector; Arakcheev dryly replied that he should not worry about difficulties in advance, but report when he encountered them in action.

The three armies began to move across the ice toward the end of February. On the twenty-sixth, Bagration set out on his march to the Aland islands, which he intended to use as a base for his advance on Sweden. He was followed two days later by Arakcheev, Knorring, and Aleopus, the former Russian Ambassador to Sweden, who had been assigned to the army with the task of conducting negotiations when an approach was received from the Swedes. The crossing was indeed a fearful experience. A young officer in Barclay's party described it: "With our first step onto the frozen sea, we encountered difficulties which would have seemed insurmountable to anyone but a Russian soldier. The cruel wind, which had been blowing all winter, had broken the thick ice on the Kvarken, throwing it up in enormous blocks, like huge cliffs. They rose on all sides, sometimes barring our path, sometimes running along it. From a distance these mountains of ice were an extraordinary sight. It was as if the waves of the sea had suddenly frozen in a moment of intense cold. The difficulties of the crossing increased at every step. Sometimes we had to clamber over the blocks of ice, at others push them aside, or scramble out of deep frozen snow. The effort made the sweat pour off the soldiers, while at the same time a bitter and piercing wind cut our breath and froze body and mind. In addition we feared that if the wind turned into a hurricane it would break up the ice. All around there were dreadful scenes of destruction."[9]

Bagration reached the Aland islands on March 4 and was surprised to be greeted by a Swedish delegation asking for an immediate armistice. The Swedish general, Debeln, had learned the previous day that a coup d'etat in Stockholm had resulted in the abdication of his King, Gustave IV. He decided that he must at all costs prevent the Russians from reaching the mainland and was determined to play for time until he received new instructions. Bagration was pleased to agree to terms which left the Russians in occupation of the Aland islands, and only Arakcheev's signature was needed. But on his arrival, Arakcheev refused to consider an armistice. "I told the Swedish general that I had been sent by the Emperor not to conclude an armistice but to make peace," he wrote to Alexander. "I would not agree to any armistice and said that if he so wished, he and his troops could give themselves up as prisoners of war. The Swede was very confused, as he had not expected this. . . . After much discussion, during which the Swedes talked all the time about peace, I asked them whether the terms on which peace could be concluded with Russia were known in Stockholm, since they were not to think that Russia would sign without these terms being agreed. They were that Finland and the Aland islands be ceded in perpetuity to Russia; the annulment of the English alliance; and the loan by Russia of troops if the Swedes were not strong enough to resist the landing of an English army. The Swedes asked to have these three articles in writing. I agreed, and handed them over to be sent to Stockholm, whence there will be a reply in four days."

Meanwhile, Alexander wrote to him from Saint Petersburg, "I cannot thank you enough for your hard work and devotion; my own devotion to you is just as sincere, and every day I value your worth more. Knorring's conduct is shameless, and only your desire that I should not be angry restrains me from washing his head as he deserves. The changes in Sweden are very important to us, and I cannot help wondering whether there is not some military device in this to delay our actions. You who are on the spot are a better judge of this— I cannot understand how Knorring, who was conducting negotiations with them, did not ask for details of the events in Stockholm. Why has he not sent me a circumstantial account of them, for if they are correct, it is essential for us to know what government in Sweden we are negotiating with, whether it is generally accepted or whether it is an initiative by private parties and can change once again. . . . Meanwhile, I think it necessary not to conclude an armistice, but to continue our activities." When he received Arakcheev's letter, Alexander wrote again, "If our proposals are rejected, it is difficult for me to decide from here whether you should cross to the Swedish shore, but this is what I feel it right to tell you. Try to find out as accurately as possible how many troops the Swedes can assemble on their coast to defend it against you, adding those who will have had time to retreat from Aland. Secondly, find out how long the ice can be expected to hold out. In the light of these two factors you will be in a position to judge whether we are strong enough to cross and, in the case of failure, whether we shall have time to cross back over the ice."[10] With this letter the Emperor enclosed a ukase giving Arakcheev full powers over the whole of Finland.

By the time Alexander's reply was received, a Russian cavalry detachment under Colonel Kulnev had already been sent ahead to occupy the town of Grisselgam on the Swedish mainland. Suspecting that the Russians had decided to renew their advance, the desperate Debeln sent a message on March 7 to say that an emissary empowered to negotiate peace terms would arrive from Stockholm the next day, but would talk only if not one Russian soldier was present on Swedish soil. Knorring fell into the trap and in his capacity as commander in chief insisted on calling back Kulnev. At the same time, he ordered Barclay, who was most surprised, to cross back to Finland from the Swedish shore. "The general has lost his head," Barclay commented, thinking that the fruits of his great crossing were being cast away. Indeed, on the following day the Swedish emissary turned out to be a simple courier bearing a letter for transmission to Alexander.

Arakcheev now hesitated. He found it difficult to make an assessment of the two factors raised by Alexander, and it was indeed vital to the success of any further operations that he should do so. He did not therefore use his full powers and resist Knorring in his attempt to engage the Swedes in genuine negotiations for peace. It soon became clear that Knorring's endeavors were not going to meet with success, but Knorring continued to argue that the aim of the expedition had in any case been achieved, since Sweden's resistance had been broken, and that it was not worth taking the risk of a further excursion that would be virtually pointless. At first Arakcheev held out, saying, "If only we can take Stockholm, no more fighting will be needed." But he finally allowed himself to be overcome by the military arguments and agreed that the Russians should withdraw to Finland. A garrison was left at Aland, and an agreement concluded with the Swedes whereby they would not approach either Aland or Finland. The return journey was accomplished only just in time, for during the crossing a strong wind came up and large cracks began to appear in the ice.

Meanwhile, Alexander had set out from Saint Petersburg, and after opening the Finnish Diet at Borgo, he arrived at Abo on March 19. Despite their decision to withdraw, Arakcheev was confident that the Emperor would be pleased with the results of the expedition, and he himself promoted Bagration and Barclay, sending his congratulations to Barclay in advance of Alexander's arrival.[11] The Emperor was indeed very content with what had been achieved and expressed his disapproval only of poor Knorring for his conduct of the campaign. During the two days he spent at Abo, Alexander neither received Knorring nor once addressed a word to him; and the general handed his command to Barclay shortly afterward.

Yet, Knorring was largely right in saying that the Swedes no longer had the will to resist. The Russian incursion and the Swedes' own domestic upheaval had done their work. Sporadic fighting did break out again in the spring, but in September a peace treaty was finally concluded by which Sweden agreed to cede Finland and the Aland islands definitively.

At Easter Arakcheev had returned in triumph to Saint Petersburg with the Emperor. The success of the crossing of the gulf was rightly attributed to him alone, since he had undertaken it in the teeth of the almost unanimous opposition of the generals concerned, and as a feat of arms it was widely compared to Suvorov's brilliant march across the Alps during the Italian campaign of 1799. In the capital the rumor went around that he was to be created "Prince of Finland." On September 6, when peace was finally signed, Alexander wrote to Arakcheev, "The Almighty be praised, I have concluded peace on the basis of our proposals. To save time, I have departed from tradition and ordered the adjutant to go to the fortress with an instruction to fire 101 guns. I am enclosing with this letter what in all justice you deserve; and in order to show you even more clearly how grateful I am for all your work, and so that it should be more pleasant for you to wear it, I am sending you my own, which I have just been wearing."

The enclosure was the Order of St. Andrew, the highest

decoration which could be awarded to anyone outside the imperial family. On the same day, Arakcheev returned the decoration to the Emperor. He was to repeat this gesture of refusing honors on several occasions during his career, and his enemies did not hesitate to interpret it as a maneuver to ingratiate himself even further with the Emperor by trying to show that his devotion was above conventional awards. From now on he would accept only favors which were designed for him alone. If it was a maneuver, it succeeded well enough with Alexander. On this occasion the Emperor's response was to issue on the following day an unusual order. "In recognition of the keen and zealous services of the War Minister, Count Arakcheev, troops are to give him the appropriate honors in places where His Imperial Majesty is also present."

Arakcheev's success in the Swedish campaign had not, however, endeared him to the high command of the army, who continued to resent bitterly his authority over them and the usurpation of their right to communicate directly with the Emperor. The Minister of War and the senior generals sniped incessantly at each other. Arakcheev wrote to General Buxhöwden, who had been living in retirement since he handed his command of Russia's armies in Finland to Knorring, and complained that a check had revealed shortages in stocks of gunpowder for which Buxhöwden had been responsible. At the same time, he placed an announcement in the Saint Petersburg newspapers saying that he could not pay the army's debts until Buxhöwden's overdue accounts had been received.

Buxhöwden replied with a biting letter in which he eloquently expressed the whole military staff's pent-up fury at Arakcheev's position. "On various occasions you have shown me signs of your displeasure," wrote the General, "and now you have decided to redouble them by publishing them to the world through the newspapers, without thinking that you are insulting the post which I held and which I am obliged to defend against your love of power. Do you know, dear sir, what it is to be a commander in chief? A commander in chief is a soldier who has been tested in his love for his country, tried in the field of battle, and who by his services has demonstrated his devotion to the throne. The Emperor entrusts him with the security, peace, and glory of his kingdom. He places under his command thousands of soldiers, whose welfare and indeed life depend on a wave of his hand, on his alertness and the innumerable measures he takes for their care. When he accepts his baton he undertakes, before his Emperor and his country, to devote his whole mind and heart to the task which has been given him; and by his actions to arouse those military virtues in the soldiers under his command of which only true soldiers are made, the virtues that enable the settler to cultivate his fields at the height of a battle, despite the thunder rolling all around him. Now, because of you, the Russian soldier can no longer account for his labors to the Emperor himself! Tell me, where did you get hold of this fatal system? What will be the reaction of our soldiers whose character and service make them worthy of occupying the great position which you have brought so low? And to what purpose? Do you think you will acquire respect by what you have done? No, my dear sir, you are very mistaken. A man who is not to be found either in battle or on board ship, or in the imperial counsels or facing our enemies, will never make his fellow citizens really respect him, whatever harsh measures he may choose to take. It is clear that the all-merciful Emperor, who watches over the welfare of the state, does not yet know what kind of man is shut up inside you."[12]

The contents of this tirade were rapidly leaked from Arakcheev's chancery. The whole of Saint Petersburg buzzed with the story of Buxhöwden's letter. Only Arakcheev did not realize that it was public knowledge, and to the great embarrassment of his host and fellow guests, held forth at a dinner party on the qualities needed by a commander in chief in the very terms which Buxhöwden had used.[13] But when he discussed his own exploit in Finland, he remained somewhat contemptuous of the generals whose job he had after all done better than they. "So there are still some people who do me justice, thank you, my friend," he said genially to a junior officer who offered his congratulations. "I am not an army commander and was not intending to lead the troops across, but God has given me enough sense to tell right from wrong. God knows how it would have ended had we delayed the expulsion of the Swedes from Finland until next year. Buxhöwden took me for his personal enemy, but he was very wrong. Why should I want to have a fight with him? My enemies are those who do not carry out their work as they should. I fought with Buxhöwden's own arms against the armistice which he suggested, using his own reasoning. If I had listened to them all instead of pushing Barclay straight across the ice to Sweden, we should have had another two years fighting in Finland."[14]

Although the Russian feat of arms attracted much attention, the acquisition of Finland was not generally as popular at home as Alexander had hoped. Many people had regarded the war as a clever device of Napoleon to weaken Russia while he continued to strengthen his European empire. There was little appreciation of the strategic importance of Russia's acquisition, and Alexander's anxieties over the ignorance of public opinion and the continuing unpopularity of his policies prompted him to take the unusual step of founding Russia's first government newspaper, the *Northern Post.*

In instructing Arakcheev to examine how the War Ministry could most effectively contribute to the paper, Alexander wrote that the aim was to communicate to the public news of "agreeable events" and to keep public opinion as far as possible in support of the "beneficent policies of the government." But the creation of the paper was not enough to put an end to the most exaggerated rumors, which, in view of the almost total absence of reliable sources of information or of any effective means of communication, were continually spreading through Russia and beyond her borders. In the winter of 1809 a story even reached Austria that Alexander had abdicated and appointed the Senate to be regent of the Empire.

Despite his new prestige, Arakcheev never exploited his position to amass riches for himself or to promote members of his family, still less friends, to high places. He was irritated when people tried—as they did quite naturally—to use him as a stepping stone, and he was never disposed to hide his annoyance, even from his closest friends. "I am displeased that you are bothering my mother with your pointless requests," he wrote to Avdotya Rimsky-Korsakova, the wife of his old neighbor at Bezhetsk. "You could have written to me and I would have replied myself. I have appointed your younger son to the artillery; but it is impossible for your elder son to be given the rank of officer, as he is utterly lazy and has himself deliberately listed as sick. He could be very good, but he clearly wants to be a country shepherd, and for that he doesn't need an officer's rank. Please don't bother either me or my mother anymore on his behalf. You should have some respect. I have done so much for you." His young cousin Nicolai Vassilievich Arakcheev, who had been leading a wild life in the capital, was dealt with even more summarily. "I don't want to have a drunk and a buffoon of my family in

Saint Petersburg. I advise you either to stay with the army, where although it is also wrong to behave badly it is at least bearable, as you are out of sight of the capital, or even better, to leave the service altogether and spend in the country those years when young men are inclined to be buffoons. This is my advice, and I shall certainly keep to it. I shall not agree to your living here in Saint Petersburg, and even prophesy that you will be unhappy if you do not leave the service. Do not forget this letter; it will help you on."[15]

Meanwhile the break-up of his marriage had radically altered the future of Nastasia, who was now fully reinstated at Gruzino. With the departure of his wife Arakcheev gave up his hopes of a legitimate heir and decided to do all he could for his natural son. The boy had been registered at his birth as a merchant's son and christened Mikhail Ivanovich Lukin. If he was to have a successful career, however, it was essential for him to bear the rank of *dvoryanin*, and Arakcheev resorted to the not unheard of device of acquiring for him a false title of nobility. Forged papers could normally be obtained in Latvia, but Arakcheev's friend General Bukhmeyer, whose help he had solicited, chanced on a poor nobleman at Vitebsk called Shumsky whose eldest son had died. Genuine papers were procured,[16] and at the age of six the boy was brought to Saint Petersburg with the name of Mikhail Shumsky and put to school in a private elementary establishment run by Nicolai Grech. Mikhail showed considerable ability, but also a certain reluctance to take his work seriously and a distressing tendency to play the fool. All too often Grech had to write notes to Arakcheev about Mikhail's conduct. "I was not sure whether to allow Mishenka home today," one of them runs, "because he has behaved badly this week, lied, written poorly, and been naughty in class, for all of which he has been punished."[17] Arakcheev followed his son's education very closely and was particularly disappointed that he was not being taught enough mathematics. The boy appeared to have gifts as a linguist, and on leaving Grech's school he was sent to a fashionable academy run by Pastor Collins for the study of foreign languages.

Alexander's increasing preoccupation with foreign affairs had not led him to abandon his interest in constitutional reform. This question was closely linked with the problem of putting right the state finances, which by 1808 had reached a critical state. The "unofficial committee" was by now disbanded; Czartoryski, Novosiltsov, and Stroganov had all gone abroad, frustrated by the lack of real progress. Only Kochubey had stayed on in the office of Minister of the Interior. His influence with the Emperor had much diminished, but it was a young protégé of his working with him in the Ministry, Mikhail Speransky, whom Alexander suddenly chose as his principal assistant in a new burst of reforming zeal.

Speransky, the son of a village priest, began life on virtually the lowest rung of the social ladder. Thanks to his outstanding intellectual qualities he had made his way up the administration with remarkable speed. He was a brilliant administrator, with an abundance of fertile ideas and the good civil servant's ability to express them on paper both lucidly and in such a way as to make them attractive to his superiors. He was widely read in eighteenth-century political philosophy and drew extensively on this knowledge in developing his own political theories, but unlike so many other Russians who had been influenced by the enlightenment, including Catherine and Alexander himself, he also had the unique gift of being able to apply these theories in a practical way to the needs and conditions of his own country.

Once Speransky's career had achieved a certain momentum

it was impossible that he should not rise to the top and achieve at least the rank of state secretary, running one of the great departments of state. Actually, he achieved far more. In 1808, on an occasion when Kochubey was away ill, Speransky took over the job of making the Minister's weekly report to the Emperor. Alexander was much impressed by his qualities and shortly afterward entrusted Speransky with two fundamental tasks. He was requested to balance the state budget by putting its finances on a regular footing, at the same time halting the very rapid devaluation of the paper currency in relation to the silver ruble; and to draw up a plan which would do no less than reorganize the whole administration of Russia.

Russian Emperors had always ruled by means of a most ramshackle and inefficient administration. The sole source of authority and legislation was the Emperor himself, and at the beginning of his reign Alexander had inherited only a number of committees to advise him on the various state activities, such as defense and foreign affairs, and to execute the imperial decrees. One of the few lasting achievements of his young advisers had been to replace these committees by ministries, but this had not solved the problem of limiting the arbitrary and often self-defeating nature of imperial law, and the weak and reactionary Senate had proved incapable of providing a remedy. As Speransky saw it, the essential issue was to systematize and legalize imperial power, rather than to challenge its whole basis. He did not, however, mince his words in describing the faults of the present system and the vices of Russia's social order. "What good are civil laws when their tablets can be smashed every day on the primary rock of autocracy? . . ." he wrote. "I will not mention here a far more important subject, namely the relation of the peasants to their owners, the relation of millions of people composing the most useful part of the population to a handful of parasites who acquired, God knows why or how, all the rights and privileges."[18]

Sentiments such as these were hardly likely to endear Speransky to the nobility, and indeed from the moment Alexander raised him to favor he was increasingly detested by them. But the seal of the Emperor's approval was set on Speransky when he accompanied Alexander to the second summit meeting with Napoleon, which took place at Erfurt in the autumn of 1808, when Napoleon tried without success to persuade Alexander to embark on a joint invasion of Austria with him. In the course of the year opposition to the French alliance had increased rather than diminished in Russia, but in this matter Alexander's will was unshakable, and he was determined to play it his own way. The celebrated remark which he made in a letter to his sister Catherine is a vivid indication of his true thinking. "*Napoléon pense que je ne suis qu'un sot,*" he wrote; "*rira mieux qui rira le dernier.*" Speransky's presence at Erfurt was unfortunate for his reputation in Saint Petersburg. It was rumored that he had fallen under Napoleon's spell and was trying to foist detestable republican laws on the Emperor. Speransky never troubled to defend himself. Like Arakcheev, he was indifferent to public opinion as long as he had the Emperor's support, and of this support there was no doubt. "Il est le Secrétaire-Général de l'Empire," wrote Joseph de Maistre.

Both Speransky and Alexander failed to see that if a major reform of the state administration were to have any chance of popular acceptance, a favorable climate of opinion had to be created in advance of its establishment. As it was, Alexander enjoined the strictest secrecy on Speransky, and in consequence the darkest rumors flew around the capital. Speransky himself had written that "laws can have no weight when they have been drafted on the basis of personal confidence, deliberated in secret, and issued without any regard to publicity." This very mistake was now made.

Looked at today, Speransky's plan seems an ingenious scheme for reconciling the autocracy of the throne with the existing social and administrative elements that could be used to influence and work with the sovereign. It provided for a clear separation of powers at the base, with three chains of command: a judicial branch under the Senate; an executive branch, comprising the ministries and provincial governors; and a legislative branch, which was to include a graduated series of popular assemblies. These three branches were crowned by a Council of State, presided over by the Emperor, in whom supreme power continued to be vested. Speransky undoubtedly hoped that the Emperor would increasingly be guided by the advice tendered by the Council, who would recommend legislation suggested by the legislative branch, and simultaneously supervise the ministries' execution of the measures. To this end four departments were set up in the Council, under which the different ministries were grouped.

When Alexander was faced with Speransky's plan *in toto* his fundamental irresolution suddenly came to the surface. Morbidly sensitive as he was over any infringement of his power, he dreaded signing away one particle of his freedom of maneuver. It did not occur to him that the proposed system, by involving more influential people in the act of government, might, if skillfully operated, increase rather than reduce imperial authority and open the way for him to realize the fundamental social reforms which still interested him. Although Speransky told him very clearly that the plan made sense only if taken as a whole, Alexander preferred to proceed gradually and apply the measures piecemeal. He decided to leave on one side for the time being the legislative and judicial branches and as a first step to set up on its own the Council of State, whose departments would both ratify measures submitted to them by the ministries and supervise their smooth execution.

Only four men, Kochubey, Saltikov, Lopukhin, and Rumyantsev, were aware of the full extent of the proposals. The reform was to be announced on New Year's Day, 1810, and in the last weeks of 1809 Speransky and Alexander worked closely together, putting the final touches to their plan. Of all the people close to the Emperor who were not in his confidence, Arakcheev was certainly the most aggrieved. He had always prized above all else his special friendship with Alexander, and after the Swedish campaign he had presumed that the Emperor's confidence in him would be totally reestablished. Although, strictly speaking, his competence did not extend beyond military matters, he had the right to expect that he would at least be kept informed, if not consulted, on a major issue of this kind. He was not only apprehensive at the growing influence of Speransky, he felt that his prestige was directly affected by this public exclusion from the Emperor's counsels. It was therefore with mounting irritation that Arakcheev listened to the rumors and witnessed the preparations for the new system.

Toward the end of November Alexander traveled to Moscow and was joined there by a number of ministers and officials, including Arakcheev. Speransky in Saint Petersburg maintained daily contact with the Emperor by the quaint method of handing unaddressed envelopes with a particular seal on them to Melnikov, one of Alexander's valets, who then forwarded them to Moscow. Officials in Moscow were intrigued by the arrival of these letters from a valet, and Arakcheev was heard to remark with a sneer, "Melnikov is an important man."[19]

When the imperial party returned to Saint Petersburg, Arakcheev at once made preparations to leave for Gruzino. He was determined not to be in the capital when the reform in which he had played no part was finally announced. Alexander, however, was aware of Arakcheev's annoyance and asked him to stay, promising that he would read the reform over with him before it was published on New Year's Day. On December 27 Arakcheev finally received the message that the Emperor would see him that evening. The hours went by, but no summons came. Then, late in the evening, his bell rang and Speransky entered the house. Alexander had sent him round bearing only the heads of the draft decree and had instructed him to explain its contents orally to the War Minister.

Speransky left in a hurry only ten minutes later, and Arakcheev rang for his secretary, Marchenko. "I had never seen him in such a rage," wrote Marchenko. "He would not look at the papers I had for him, but ordered me to send them to Gruzino, whither he said he was now going."[20] Arakcheev was indeed in a fury. He was convinced that Alexander had deliberately snubbed him, and with this gesture had wanted to rub in the fact that Speransky's position was superior to his own. On his arrival at Gruzino he wrote a revealing letter to the Emperor:

"Sir, I have enjoyed your favor for fifteen years, and the papers I received today are another sign that I continue to do so. I cannot therefore wait to study these important state documents. Before my departure, sir, I read everything over, but I will not presume to interpret the reasoning behind these proposals until I have studied them to the best of my knowledge and ability.

"Sir, you are aware of the kind of education I received in my youth. To my regret, the facilities at my disposal were extremely limited, and I therefore feel that at my present age I am no more than a competent officer, capable only of the correct administration of our military affairs. It was on this basis that at your behest I took on the post which I at present hold. But in order to carry out your wise proposals, you now need a minister who has received a broad and general education. Only a man of this kind can be of use to this important new body and uphold the first military duty in the state, which I take to be the defense of the Council itself, since without military defense the best provisions of the Council may be controverted. I am not capable of doing this, sir, and since I cannot adequately fill the post, I should discredit it. My daily conduct and this letter are your evidence.

"Sir, do not be angry with a man who has lived half a century without using flattery, and I hope it may be your pleasure to retire him from this post. I entreat you, sir, not to find difficulties, since in a short while I should be of little use to you or to the state in this appointment, but only an obstruction in matters where, from the military angle, efficiency is essential."

Alexander reacted coolly to this tantrum, which showed not only Arakcheev's jealousy at his exclusion from Speransky's work but also the heavy chip he still carried over his lack of education. He alternately despised and envied those who had been better educated than himself. As a statesman he realized the handicap under which he suffered because of his ignorance of history and law, and an officer who worked for him noted that "he was very good at making fun of people who would discuss these things in learned but disjointed phrases."[21] In his reply, Alexander ignored these considerations and did his best to make Arakcheev see reason by pressing him at his most vulnerable point.

"Alexei Andreevich, I cannot hide from you my great

surprise on reading your letter. To what must I ascribe your intention to leave the post you occupy? It would be inappropriate for me not to speak frankly here. I cannot accept the reasons you give. If until now you have been useful in your post, why should your usefulness diminish with the reconstruction of the Council? Nobody will understand it. Everyone who has read the new constitution has found that the Council will be for the good of the Empire. You alone, on whose cooperation I was above all relying, you who have repeated so often to me that apart from your devotion to the nation you are motivated by personal affection for myself, you alone despite all this are forgetting your value to the Empire and are hastening to give up the sector you direct, at a time when your conscience must tell you how impossible it will be to replace you. Ask yourself sincerely what your real motive is, and if you are honest with yourself, you will not be proud of it.

"But allow me to put aside the position I hold and speak to you as someone to whom I am personally attached, and to whom I have always shown my devotion. What impression will your retirement make on the public, at a time when a governmental reform is being carried out which is useful and agreeable to everyone? The effect as far as you are concerned will of course be very bad. The constitution of the Council is to be published. The general opinion will be that you did not resign on account of this constitution, and the conclusions drawn will be extremely unflattering to you. At a time when I have a right to expect keen and active support from all those who are right-minded and loyal to their country, you alone are deserting me, and prefer to follow the dictates of your own temporarily thwarted ambition rather than your duty to the Empire. In this way you are injuring your reputation.

"If, despite my hopes, what I have written has no effect on you, I have at least the right to request you to continue your work until your successor is appointed, as duty demands of a man of honor. At our first meeting you will tell me clearly whether I can see in you the same Count Arakcheev, on whose loyalty I thought I could firmly rely, or whether I shall have to choose a new Minister of War."[22]

This letter brought Arakcheev back to Saint Petersburg, but he was not easily mollified, and he wrote again to Alexander asking him to find a successor. Perhaps he knew that the Emperor would never let him go. A previous letter of resignation had, after all, resulted in his elevation to the rank of minister. On this occasion, once his temper had cooled, he was determined to extract some balm for his wounds by ensuring that Alexander ran after him. Again his conduct paid off. After a long private audience with the Emperor, Arakcheev was asked if he would retain his present post, or alternatively accept the appointment of President of the new War Department on the Council of State. The choice was his, and Arakcheev decided to accept appointment to the Council, declaring that it was "better to be boss rather than have a boss set over one." The quarrel was over, and sovereign and minister were firm friends again. As a New Year present Alexander sent Arakcheev a sled and a pair of horses. Arakcheev was delighted, and Marchenko noted that "it was an unusual mark of favor."

5
The Emperor's Friend

In Russia no one is free except the beggar and the philosopher.—SPERANSKY

The new Minister of War was General Barclay de Tolly, and at the beginning of 1810 he returned to Saint Petersburg from his post as Governor General of Finland. Barclay was descended from a Scottish family which had settled in Estonia in the seventeenth century after the English Civil War. He was a straightforward and popular soldier, but although the army command were pleased by his appointment, he was not an effective minister. "He was an honest man, but more like a minister's widow than a minister," wrote an official who had previously served under Arakcheev, while the soldiers quickly made a pun on his name: "*Boltai da i tolko*"—"All talk and nothing more."

Arakcheev himself very quickly discovered that he had been mistaken when he thought that he would be able to control the ministry from his position as President of the War Department in the Council of State. It soon became clear that the Council, shorn as it was of its true legislative function, would never be able to fulfill the hopes which had been

Speransky
Courtesy of the British Museum

Rostopchin
Courtesy of the British Museum

placed on it. The former *ad hoc* committees of ministers, which Alexander had been in the habit of calling whenever he wanted something done quickly, began to meet as before, although Speransky fought hard against this practice. In its first year the Council was fairly active, but under the growing threat of war it was bypassed by the Emperor and never resuscitated. Speransky's prediction that the reform would be meaningless unless his plan was applied in its entirety proved only too true.

At first Arakcheev attempted to keep a firm grip on military affairs. He rightly emphasized to Barclay the importance of the supply question. "When I took over the direction of the War Ministry," he reminded Barclay, "I did not find in the whole supply department a single rifle in good repair, nor any reserves of rifle ammunition." Now divorced from the administrative machine, Arakcheev gradually discovered that power had slipped from his grasp. The general staff reasserted its authority. The reform of 1810 "washed him away like a great oak in a flood," wrote Colonel Tishin, an officer in the War Ministry. Arakcheev had to leave to Barclay the major task of expanding the army with all possible speed, and he spent an increasing amount of his time at Gruzino, where he worked as intensely as ever on his estate.

He continued to see much of his brother Petr, who had worked with him during his year at the ministry. Petr was very unlike Arakcheev, easygoing, vain, and always in debt. Yet he was to end his career honorably enough as military commandant of Kiev. Both he and his wife had a genuine affection for Arakcheev, which Arakcheev returned. "Dear brother and friend," Arakcheev wrote to him at the beginning of 1810, "you were a very great help to me during the whole of the difficult period when I was running the War Ministry. Everyone knows that you took on this extra work out of a sense of duty to our family, and by doing so you were of great assistance to me in carrying out the wishes of our Emperor. . . . Please forgive me for sending you three thousand rubles to pay the debts of which I have heard. Please accept this money, for if you do so I will know that everything you have done was based on our family ties and fraternal affection." Petr was always a financial liability to Arakcheev; later in the same year he was persuaded by his mother to buy a small house in Saint Petersburg for Petr and his wife; and when his mother died, his brother pleaded with him to hand over his share of Elizaveta Andreevna's estate.

During these first months of 1810 Arakcheev once again felt that he was marking time. Despite his many difficult moments and the setbacks he had known, the seven years which he had spent conducting military affairs since his return to Saint Petersburg in 1803 had been remarkably successful. Alone he had built up a major branch of the army, he had directed an important campaign, and he had proved himself an effective minister. During this time he won back and retained the Emperor's favor, but Alexander had still shown no disposition to bring him into his inner counsels or increase his field of activity beyond the strictly military, as the Speransky affair had demonstrated. Moreover, his unpopularity with many influential people around the Emperor made it likely that without an unusual initiative from the Emperor himself, he would progress no further.

During the course of one man's career it is usually impossible for him to identify as they occur those moments which are his real turning points, or the influences which will take him in a particular direction and finally lead him to success or failure. Only at the end of his career can he look back and sometimes detect a chance or an opportunity taken, which may at the time have seemed of minor importance, but which in fact led into broader paths, eventually shaping his whole life. At this moment, when it seemed to Arakcheev that his career had run out of steam, an instruction arrived from Alexander requesting him to draw up an estimate of the amount of land needed to make an army battalion agriculturally self-supporting. It was destined to change his whole future.

This instruction was the genesis of the *Voenniye Poseleniya*, the military colonies, the creation of which came increasingly to dominate Alexander's mind during the infrequent periods he spent in Russia in the latter part of his reign, and which finally established Arakcheev's lasting unpopularity in history as a pitiless tyrant. Historians have spent much time trying to explain where Alexander found the idea of the military colonies and why he eventually decided to apply his scheme on a massive scale. The problem is, as so often, obscured by the lack of documents, but the main lines of the issue and the role played by Arakcheev are clear enough.

The original principle of the military colonies was to combine military and agricultural activities so that the army became self-supporting, while a greater number of soldiers than could be maintained in barracks enjoyed a more settled existence with their families on the land. The idea was an old one. Peter the Great had already made it the basis of Russia's southern and eastern frontier communities, although then it had simply taken the form of ensuring that groups of settlers had the military training and equipment necessary to defend themselves. At the beginning of the nineteenth century, the principle of a settled army was applied on a limited scale in Prussia and Austria, and when the Russians invaded Finland in 1808 they found prosperous and well-established communities of soldier-farmers that had been set up by the Swedes.

Only a year later Alexander decided that military colonies could be the answer to several of his fundamental domestic problems. By 1810 it had become clear that for many years to come Russia was going to need a very large standing army; Barclay had orders to more than double its numbers, and by the beginning of 1812 there were nearly a million men under arms scattered over the Empire. The cost to the Crown was exorbitant. A steady increase in the issue of paper money could only be a very short-term measure, and in any case Speransky ruled out this kind of solution when his financial proposals, which aimed at restricting the flow of paper rubles, were partially accepted and put into effect in 1811. The question of financing his army loomed very large for the Emperor, but there is little doubt that he considered the social problem even more important.*

Alexander never abandoned his ambition to achieve lasting social reforms in his Empire. He was very conscious of the evils of serfdom, but by the end of the first decade of his reign it had become plain that he was not capable of tackling the problem root and branch. Although from time to time he commissioned blueprints for the emancipation of the serfs,

* In his four-volume life of Alexander I, Shilder states that the idea of the colonies took definite shape in the Emperor's mind when he read Joseph Servan's *Sur les frontières militaires des états,* and even alleges that he had it translated for Arakcheev's benefit. However, as Richard Pipes has shown in his useful article on the military colonies ("The Russian Military Colonies, 1810–31," *Journal of Modern History,* September, 1950), there is no evidence that this book ever existed.

Colonel Petrov, in his work *Graf Arakcheev i Voenniye Poseleniya,* Saint Petersburg, 1871, suggests that the scheme was directly inspired by General Scharnhorst's project in Prussia. After the Peace of Tilsit, Napoleon decreed that the Prussian army must be limited to forty thousand men, and Scharnhorst saw his plan as a device to ensure that despite this, every man would be familiar with the use of arms. But his plan was not particularly relevant to Russia's needs, as P. P. Evstafiev points out in his *Vosstanie Voennykh Poselyan Novgorodskoy Gubernii v 1831 g.,* Moscow, 1934. The best account of the true origin of the project is by I. G. Fabritsius in *Glavnoe Inzhenernoe Upravlenie* (1902), which comprises Vol. VII of the work *Stoletiye Voennovo Ministerstva.*

there was never much hope that they would be put into practice. The injustices of army recruitment were closely related to the evils of serfdom. When imperial recruiting decrees were published, landowners and state peasant communities had to surrender a given number of men, and the period of army service lasted no less than twenty-five years, the whole of a man's working life. Recruitment was in fact a tragedy for the men involved; separated, often forever, from their families, they were subjected to the most brutal system of military discipline, which involved exhausting forms of drill and the inevitable corporal punishment. After twenty-five years of this existence a man was turned out a physical wreck, prematurely aged, rootless, free only to wander the country in search of food and shelter until he died. As the ranks of his army swelled, Alexander became increasingly concerned at the human misery which recruitment caused. In the military colonies he thought he had found the solution.

When the vast scale on which the colonies were envisaged and what they involved later became apparent, the plan encountered rooted opposition from the two social groups directly involved, the army and the peasants. Arakcheev was not slow to perceive this hostility, and he deliberately concealed his own attitude from his contemporaries by allowing those who worked with him to believe that he had been against the concept from the outset, but had no choice but to bow to the Emperor's insistence. An official in the Ministry of Justice recorded the explanation Arakcheev gave him. "Arakcheev told me that the colonies were the Emperor's own idea. He described them as the Emperor's brainchild with which he was simply unable to part."[1] Many others noted similar remarks made by Arakcheev. But if he was later dismayed by the degree of opposition which the colonies aroused and by the extent of his own unpopularity, there is no reason to suppose that he was less than enthusiastic at the inception of the plan. Indeed, from his personal standpoint it offered several advantages. On the one hand it provided the opportunity to regain Alexander's attention and on the other the justification for setting up a military organization independent of the general staff which so detested him. Arakcheev insisted from the start that the staff of the colonies should be quite separate from the regular army command, and after some initial hesitation Alexander concurred, fearing, correctly as it turned out, that his senior officers would in any case be opposed to the project.

As soon as Alexander had talked matters over with him, Arakcheev formed a mental picture of the colonies which corresponded to his own settlement at Gruzino, and wherever possible he drew on his own experience when submitting sketches of buildings and draft regulations. The Emperor was impressed by the precision and thoroughness of Arakcheev's work and became increasingly curious to see Gruzino for himself. Accordingly, in June, 1810, when he was traveling back from a visit to his sister Catherine, who lived at Tver, he broke his journey at Gruzino and spent the night in Arakcheev's house. The next day the Emperor inspected the whole estate and was astonished and delighted by what he found.

"It is really a charming place," he wrote to Catherine, "but it is the order which prevails here that is unique. The arrangement of the villages has aroused my admiration above all. I am certain that there is nothing like it in the whole Empire. Since writing to you is the same as writing to George,* show him this letter. I earnestly beg him when he passes through here by drozhky to have himself conducted by General Arakcheev through all the villages which he has shown me

* Prince George of Oldenburg, husband of the Grand Duchess Catherine.

and to note the order which prevails everywhere, the cleanliness, the construction of the roads and plantations, the symmetry and elegance which we saw on all sides. The streets of the villages here have *precisely that kind of cleanliness* which I have been trying so hard to see established in the towns. The best proof that what I have been demanding is possible is that it can be found in the villages here. How I wish the streets of Novgorod, Valdai, Vishny Volochek, Torzhok, and Krestzy were kept up in the same way! What a difference! I repeat, the villages here are proof that it is possible!"[2]

Alexander's visit to Gruzino had obviously aroused the passion for order and neatness which was part of what Rostopchin called the Emperor's "paradomania." If he could not set the Russians free, he would at least make them clean and tidy, and in this his ambitions coincided exactly with Arakcheev's. The visit to Gruzino did much to forge the link between them. On his arrival in Saint Petersburg, Alexander wrote a note to his host which was no less enthusiastic than the letter to his sister. "I hasten to convey to you my sincere gratitude for the pleasure you gave me in showing me the system which you have succeeded in setting up in your villages without compulsion but by the measured and exact arrangement of the peasants' work, as well as by your conscientious attention to all their needs." The note ended with the somewhat enigmatic phrase, "When private husbandry is combined with the effective fulfillment of official duties, both the husbandry and the duties gain new value and new respect."[3] However, its meaning was soon to become clear.

Alexander's enthusiasm for Gruzino was, not surprisingly, infectious. His letter was followed by a note from Prince Bagration enclosing a small gift clearly designed for Nastasia Minkina. "Your Excellency, an Asian fashion. Women wear it around their neck, and it has a nice scent. I am sure your Excellency does not lack the solace of some young friend, and you may give her this present. I hope it will please."[4] A few days later the Grand Duchess Catherine arrived from Tver and spent an afternoon at Gruzino.

Alexander meanwhile was becoming impatient to start work. "I returned from Tsarskoe Selo, but did not find you in town," he wrote to Arakcheev. "I have been waiting for your arrival, but my sister must be the reason why you are still at Gruzino. I do not want to lose more time and have instructed Lavrov to come to you at Gruzino in order to talk with you personally. I have explained the whole plan to him in detail. The Minister of War knows that I am putting you in charge of this business. Now it remains to start. I am very pleased with your outline, and it seems to me that the next thing is for us to go over it carefully together. Show him your whole system of agriculture, and as soon as you are free, come to see me in Saint Petersburg." Arakcheev left his Emperor in no doubt as to his own enthusiasm. "I have neither the wit nor the words to express my gratitude to Your Majesty," he replied, "but God knows my affection for you and my devotion for you, and this alone consoles me. Give me the chance to prove it, and your affection for me will increase."[5]

Assisted by Major General Lavrov, Arakcheev began to work out an experimental settlement for a single army battalion. A site was chosen in Mogilev province, between Minsk and Smolensk, where one piece of land remained which was not in private hands. The local peasants had combined together to lease it from the Crown for a period of three years against a payment of eleven thousand rubles. The treatment which they received demonstrated very clearly the total lack of ceremony with which the autocratic imperial government treated the few civil rights which some peasant communities still in theory enjoyed. True to his usual habits of work, the Emperor enjoined the strictest secrecy on Arakcheev and Lavrov. The peasants were kept in ignorance of what was in store for them until the last possible moment. "The peasants are still building new homes and the headmen making their preparations for the winter," Lavrov wrote to Arakcheev in October. On November 9 the Reserve Battalion of the Eletsky Musketeer Regiment was instructed to move to the district. By the same decree the agreement between the Crown and the peasants was annulled, and the latter were ordered to move south to the Novorossisky region forthwith. At a stroke of the imperial pen, a flourishing peasant community was destroyed. Only a few of the victims ever arrived at their destination. Most perished on the way, from hunger, drunkenness, grief, and homesickness.[6]

The colony began slowly to establish itself, but in the course of the ensuing year it encountered many difficulties which foreshadowed problems that were susbsequently to arise on a far larger scale. The principal stumbling block was, inevitably, the fact that the soldiers were totally ignorant of agricultural techniques. Although they were in the majority of cases the sons of peasants, years of barrack life and marching on parade grounds had rendered them quite unfit to deal with crops or to undertake the massive building programs which was their first priority. The exceptional drought which struck Russia in 1811, causing widespread damage, did not make things easier for them; and despite generous subsidies, the battalion made heavy weather of its duties. But by the end of that year the growing threat of war had distracted everyone's attention from the colony's problems. Early in 1812 the battalion was suddenly ordered to abandon its new quarters and return to the regiment, as Russia braced herself for the biggest contest of strength with the West that she had ever known.

The years 1810 and 1811 saw growing tension between Russia and France. "The spirit of Tilsit" had long since withered under the icy blasts of the Russian aristocracy's hostility to Alexander's alliance with Napoleon. Alexander himself became increasingly irritated by the French Emperor's refusal to give him a free hand to expand in the south as he had in the north: he wanted to parallel his achievement in Finland by taking Constantinople. At the same time, he was seriously alarmed by evidence that France intended to reconstitute an enlarged and independent Poland on Russia's borders. When Napoleon defeated Austria again in 1809, he detached a number of her provinces and added them to the Grand Duchy of Warsaw, his primary purpose being to reduce Austria's capacity to threaten him again, but in so doing he touched Russia's most sensitive nerve.

The first victim of the mounting francophobia in Russia was the unlucky Speransky. After the establishment of the State Council, Speransky had continued to work steadily at his task of rationalizing the chaotic finances and administration, but some of his proposals, such as the imposition of light taxes on landowners and the creation of an examination system for the civil service, provoked a quite disproportionate hostility on the part of the aristocracy. He remained a lonely figure, the symbol of what was felt to be a fatal Western influence paralyzing Russia's will to resist Napoleon; and several cliques close to the Emperor began to work actively for his disgrace. The opposition crystallized around two groups: on the one hand the foreign party at court, which favored the French royalist cause and included the gregarious Joseph de Maistre as well as Balashev, the Russian Minister of

Police; and on the other, the chauvinist wing of the aristocracy, in which the Emperor's mother, Maria Feodorovna, and Rostopchin were prominent figures.

Both groups seized any weapon that came to hand in their determination to excite Alexander against Speransky. The foreign party, for instance, attempted to frame him in a plot which would make it appear that he was in treasonable correspondence with the French government. Even the witticisms which Speransky was inclined to make at the Emperor's expense, such as the caustic but penetrating observation that Alexander was "too strong to be ruled but too weak to rule," were faithfully reported to Alexander. Speransky appeared to be oblivious of this campaign, and indeed the evidence against him was of the flimsiest nature, but by the beginning of 1812 Alexander was conscious of the threat of division which Speransky's position posed. National unity would be vital to Russia in the forthcoming conflict with France, and Speransky had unwittingly become representative of the most unpopular aspect of Alexander's policies.

Once he had decided that Speransky must go, the Emperor wasted no time. The State Secretary was summoned by Alexander one day in March, 1812, and told by his master, who was on the verge of tears, that he and his assistant, Magnitsky, must leave the capital within twelve hours. Speransky was astonished. Details of the interview were never published, but on returning home Speransky found Balashev waiting for him, and the same night he left for Nizhny Novgorod in eastern Russia. It was typical of Alexander that he gave different reasons for Speransky's dismissal, depending on his audience. To his friend Prince Golitsyn, who noticed the next day that he was very upset, he said, "You would no doubt cry with pain if someone tore off your hand; last night Speransky was taken from me, and he was my right hand."

To others he declared that certain evidence had pointed to Speransky's treason, but that on the eve of a major war he did not have time to investigate the affair fully. There could be no doubt, however, about the joy with which the conservative aristocracy greeted Speransky's fall. "O outcast, monster, ungrateful and base creature! You are not worthy of the title of Russian nobleman," wrote Bulgakov in his diary.[7] For some, it was as if Napoleon's defeat was already ensured by this one masterly stroke.

Arakcheev had little reason to love Speransky, but he was not elated by the latter's disgrace. It represented the triumph of the court and the aristocracy, who were as hostile to him as they had been to this other powerful but upstart adviser to the Emperor. He knew that the army and the court were united in their desire to be rid of him, and he sensed that his own turn might well come next. "Now, let me relate to you what you may already know, namely, the departure from Saint Petersburg of Speransky and Magnitsky," he wrote to Petr in April. "Many bad things are laid at their door, and if they are true, they have deserved their present fate. But in their place, our party of illustrious gentlemen, the Saltikovs, Gurievs, Tolstoys and Golitsyns, has become very strong. Since I was not connected with Speransky, I was spared, but as these new patriots do not love me I will remain untrusted and left on one side. In principle none of this worries me, since all I want is seclusion and peace, and I am happy to leave those whom I have mentioned to get on with their work and do what they think useful. But what disturbs me is that they are now telling me to go to the army, when there is nothing useful for me to do and I can only serve as a bogey. I am sure that my friends will call me on the first occasion that presents a real possibility of my losing my life, and I must be prepared for this. Now my position is clear to you."[8]

By the beginning of 1812 it was plain to the whole of Europe that Napoleon was determined on a showdown with Russia. Russia's persistent violation of the blockade against England was a constant irritant to Franco-Russian relations, and in March, 1812, Napoleon announced in a statement to his Conseil d'Etat, that "anyone who extends his hand to England and breaks the continental system will declare himself the enemy of the Emperor." At the same time, he began to collect together the biggest single army Europe had ever seen, more than half a million men. "We are daily on the qui vive. Everything is so tense that military operations could begin at any moment," Alexander wrote to his sister. "Never before have I led such a dog's life. I get up from my bed in order to sit at my desk, and only leave my desk in order to have a bite to eat on my own."

Alexander did his utmost to discourage Napoleon from pursuing his plans, by making it plain to the French Emperor's representatives that he would never sign a peace treaty in the event of a French invasion. Caulaincourt, the French ambassador, reported that Alexander had told him that he would retreat to the eastern boundaries of his Empire rather than cede any of his provinces or sign a peace which could never be more than a truce. The remark contained an accurate forecast of the general strategy adopted by the Russians. They decided to exploit to the full the vastness of their country in the hope of drawing out Napoleon's lines of supply until the French were so weakened that they could finally be cut off and encircled. This strategy was in part dictated by numerical inferiority; despite the vast number of men under arms who were scattered over the Empire, the Russians were able to assemble only 160,000 men to face Napoleon. But it was also an instinctive reaction; as Rostopchin wrote to Alexander in his usual crisp style, "The Emperor of Russia will always be formidable in Moscow, terrible in Kazan, and invincible in Tobolsk."

The men were divided into two principal armies, commanded respectively by General Barclay de Tolly and Prince Bagration. Alexander set up his headquarters at Vilna, the capital of Lithuania, and to his generals it was plain that despite his previous unhappy experiences the Emperor was determined to act as his own supreme commander, to stand face to face with Napoleon. After the defeat of Austerlitz, Czartoryski had written him a blunt letter telling him that his presence at the battle had been worse than useless, since it had actually hampered the operations of the Russian generals. This wise comment had now been forgotten. On June 25 Napoleon opened his campaign by crossing the river Nieman with his vast army, of which less than half the infantry and a third of the cavalry were Frenchmen. Alexander on that day was presiding over a heated debate between his generals on the advisability of adopting a plan advocated by the Prussian General Pfuhl, which was based on retreating to a fortified camp at Drissa between Riga and Smolensk in order to make a stand there.

As the armies of Barclay and Bagration fell back before Napoleon, Alexander moved to Drissa, and it looked as if he had decided to adopt Pfuhl's plan. But the Russian general staff, and in particular Barclay, who was the commander in chief, were already thoroughly embarrassed by the Emperor's presence. Barclay found the obligation to argue his decisions with Alexander increasingly constricting, and all of them feared that an unexpected lunge by Napoleon might result in the Emperor's capture and consequent capitulation. In their dilemma the high command were forced to swallow their distaste and turn to the only man who was known to have the Emperor's ear, Arakcheev.

Arakcheev's fears for his own position after Speransky's disgrace had proved largely groundless. He had been included in the Emperor's suite when Alexander moved to Vilna, and since then Alexander had been leaning on him increasingly to interpret the wishes of his warring generals and transmit his own instructions to them. Arakcheev later declared rather pompously that from June onward, when he was officially appointed head of the Emperor's private chancery and given the title of "Secretary of the Empire for Military Affairs," "The whole French war passed through my hands, all the Emperor's secret reports and handwritten instructions."[9] Nonetheless, Arakcheev now consented to help remove the Emperor from the center of affairs. He was fortuitously helped in this by a letter from Catherine, who wrote rather brutally to her brother: "For God's sake, do not try to command yourself. We need to have a leader in whom the troops have confidence immediately, and you inspire none at all!"

When Alexander issued an order of the day addressed to his troops that included the phrase "I shall never abandon you," Admiral Shishkov, who had replaced Speransky in the functions of State Secretary, and General Balashev, the Minister of Police, approached Arakcheev with the suggestion that they should all three sign a request to the Emperor that he return to Saint Petersburg. Balashev alleges that Arakcheev's first response, when told that this was the only way to save the country, was to exclaim, "What do I care about your country! Will the Emperor be in danger if he stays with the troops?" But he agreed to sign, and left the document with Alexander's overnight papers. The following day Alexander merely remarked to Arakcheev, "I have read your paper," and rode off to talk with Barclay, whose quarters were three kilometers away. When this talk was over, it was announced that the Emperor was leaving for Moscow, and Alexander never mentioned the petition again.[10]

Napoleon meanwhile was pursuing the Russians with all speed, since he was well aware that it was crucial to the success of his campaign that he should pin down and smash the main body of the Russian troops. The two Russian armies joined up at Smolensk, where a heated argument took place between Barclay, who was in favor of a further retreat, and Bagration, who was all for making a stand. Bagration wrote in a fury to Arakcheev: "Your minister may be good at ministerial affairs, but as a general he is not just bad, he is quite useless. Yet we have handed the fate of our country over to him!" The army and the country strongly supported Bagration; everyone found the retreat humiliating. Barclay's stock fell lower; people pointed to his foreign name and heavy German accent and were quick to smell treason.

When Alexander left the army, he was advised to visit Moscow, and he journeyed there directly, with Arakcheev and Balashev in his suite. He was greeted deliriously by the population of the town. People had been roused to a frenzy of patriotism by Rostopchin, now governor of the city. Alexander had never liked Rostopchin, but the Grand Duchess Catherine was fond of him and had insisted on his appointment to the governorship. Now that the country was at war, the Emperor could see for himself that the arrogant, showman side of Rostopchin's nature and his gift for propaganda were highly effective with the Muscovites. Alexander was besieged everywhere in the streets by large crowds professing their loyalty, and assemblies of merchants and the nobility voluntarily offered him large contributions to the war effort.

Alexander was surprised and gratified by these demonstrations. As he took leave of Rostopchin in the Kremlin, in the presence of Arakcheev and Balashev, he kissed the governor on both cheeks. Rostopchin wrote of this incident that when he and Arakcheev left the Emperor's presence, Arakcheev congratulated him, saying, "I have served the Emperor for the whole of his reign, but I have never received such a mark of favor." Balashev took Rostopchin aside and observed sardonically that Arakcheev would never forget or forgive that kiss. "I laughed at the time," noted Rostopchin, "but subsequent events convinced me that the Minister of Police had been right and that he knew Count Arakcheev better than I." In this judgment he was less than just to Arakcheev; the Emperor took an early opportunity to dismiss Rostopchin after the war, but this was none of Arakcheev's doing.

The imperial party moved on to Saint Petersburg, where they found a very different mood: the capital was prey to the deepest alarm. There was a strong popular move to replace Barclay as commander in chief by Kutuzov, now commanding only the Saint Petersburg militia. Kutuzov's skill in the Austrian campaign of 1805 was recalled, and, what was felt to be almost more important, he was a true Russian. Alexander, on the other hand, could only remember his own humiliation in front of Kutuzov at Austerlitz, when he had allowed the Russian army to be decimated, knowing full well that his commander in chief was against the battle.

At first Alexander resisted the advice of his closest counselors, and even of his own family. He argued that Kutuzov was old and worn out. It was true enough that the General spent most of his day asleep, and he had grown so stout that he could no longer ride a horse. But he was the only man who could still conjure up a degree of loyalty among the warring Russian generals, and once again it was Arakcheev and Balashev who prevailed on the Emperor. When the news of the loss of Smolensk arrived in Saint Petersburg, together with an urgent plea from Prince Shuvalov for a new commander in chief, Alexander reluctantly convened a committee to consider the matter. The committee unanimously proposed Kutuzov, and Arakcheev and Balashev argued the Emperor into agreeing. Much as these two disliked each other, they were ready to sink their differences in an emergency of this kind.

Although Kutuzov's appointment was universally welcomed, he at once adopted the same tactics as Barclay and continued to retreat toward Moscow. Napoleon, who was still trying to knock out the Russian army in a major battle, was forced to follow, although the Grande Armée was rapidly melting away through hunger and disease and his supply lines had become dangerously long. Finally the Russians turned and gave battle to him at Borodino, a few kilometers from the gates of Moscow. It was a ferocious struggle in which fifty thousand men were killed on each side; indeed, Napoleon said later that Borodino was the most terrible of all his battles. But even here he was not able to press home the victory which he thought he had gained, and this was in large part due to Arakcheev's guns.

Napoleon had been concerned at the effectiveness of the Russian artillery at Eylau, but a still more unpleasant surprise awaited him at Borodino. For the first time the guns dominated the day's fighting, and the French bombardment was more than matched by the Russian reply. Throughout the remainder of the invasion and during the ensuing campaign in Europe, the Russian artillery was to continue to perform brilliantly, and Arakcheev did not conceal his satisfaction.

Only a short while before Napoleon's invasion, Alexander had received from the Prussian General Gneisenau a report on the state of his artillery that contained a number of criticisms: while the artillery was equipped even to the point of luxury, the gun carriages were too flimsy (an old allegation), and the training of the men and horses still left much to be desired. Arakcheev did not forget this report, and at the end of the war he wrote to the General to remind him of it. "I am sure that the campaign from Vilna to Tarutino, and from there to Paris, will have convinced you of the toughness of the Russian artillery. We can proudly boast that none of our allies ever saw broken carriages on the roads; and I might add that, as a Russian artilleryman, I was astonished by the unnecessary heaviness of the foreign carriages and limbers which only serve to burden men and horses." General Gneisenau hastily retracted, and his reply was lavish: "You laid the foundations for the development of the Russian Empire's armed forces; it was also you who created this superb Russian artillery. Liberated Europe will be eternally grateful to you."

The days of self-congratulation were, however, still far off. The news from Borodino was, it was true, at first encouraging. Despite the appalling Russian casualties, which included the death of Prince Bagration, Kutuzov reported a victory and a Te Deum was sung in Alexander's presence in the Kazan cathedral in Saint Petersburg. Then followed Kutuzov's "strategic withdrawal," the French occupation of Moscow, and the almost total destruction of the city by fire. Although Russia's holy city was burned on Rostopchin's own initiative, this was not generally known at the time, and the disaster was attributed to the vandalism of the French Saint Petersburg gave way to despair, and when the Emperor made a second visit to the Kazan cathedral, to celebrate the anniversary of his coronation, he drove in a closed carriage watched by a silent and hostile crowd. "We could hear our own footsteps as we went up the steps of the cathedral," wrote a member of the court.

Alexander now withdrew from the Winter Palace to the

solitude of his villa on Kamenny Island outside the city. His position was not enviable. Once Kutuzov had been appointed and sent off to the army, the Emperor had no further control over the course of events and could only wait for information, which Kutuzov was generally slow in sending him.

He became inaccessible to everyone but Arakcheev. Couriers from Moscow were instructed on their arrival to drive straight from the city gates to Arakcheev's house on Liteinaya Street, where the telegrams and dispatches were sorted out. The couriers were forbidden to leave the house, and after two days were sent straight back to the army. This situation aroused a good deal of indignation in the capital, and at times there were protests. The mother of one of the guards officers, for instance, heard that her son would be coming from Moscow as a courier, and intercepted him at a staging post. He agreed to meet her in Saint Petersburg and added that he was carrying a letter and parcel from Kutuzov for his wife. When the officer failed to arrive home, his mother made inquiries at Arakcheev's house but could obtain no news of him. On learning subsequently that he had been confined to his quarters and was already on his way back to Moscow, she drove around in a rage to see Madame Kutuzova, who promptly wrote a letter to the Emperor in which she complained that Arakcheev was censoring her correspondence with her husband. The system was not changed, but from then on Madame Kutuzov's letters were always delivered to her very promptly.

Arakcheev himself was much in demand as one of the few officials close to the Emperor who knew the real state of affairs. The Dowager Empress, Maria Feodorovna, frequently invited him to dinner and would cross-question him about the Emperor's state of mind and his intentions. Arakcheev found himself reduced either to lying or to shrugging his shoulders in rude silence: he did not have the social grace to disguise his embarrassment at not being able to reveal what he knew.[11]

It was generally assumed in the capital and surrounding provinces that in the event of a French victory before Moscow, Napoleon would march on Saint Petersburg. In the absence of hard news, rumors of all kinds flew about the whole area. A friend of Arakcheev's mother wrote: "Elizaveta Andreevna has been very alarmed by the preparations which your aunt Nastasia Nikitishna has been making to depart, following the rumors that the enemy is approaching Tver. I was with Nastasia three days ago. One can forgive her, for she is not the first; more than half the nobility of the region, particularly the women, have left for wherever is most convenient, and others are preparing to leave. The movement comes from Tver, where the majority, including the most substantial merchants, have gone away; even the governor has shifted all his property to the district of Bezhetsk and has ordered to have a house made ready for him in the town. What are private citizens to think in these circumstances? Bezhetsk is crammed with arrivals from Smolensk, Vyazma, the Pzhat wharf, and with people from Tver. It is virtually impossible to pass through the town, and everyone is ready to gallop off at the first scare."[12]

The first signs of panic were evident in Saint Petersburg. All the foreign representatives left Russia except the British Ambassador, who made the gesture of extending the lease of his residence. The treasures of the Hermitage and of the major libraries were sent farther north, and there was even a plan to send the celebrated statue of Peter the Great, the "bronze horseman," to Kazan, where the imperial family was also intending to take refuge. People added their own possessions to the state convoys. "Arakcheev had only three spoons left in his house," noted Marchenko. Everyone had horses or boats ready for immediate flight. The banks were closed. At the same time, all possible preparations to oppose the invader were made; all the men joined home-guard brigades, and in response to an appeal for silver, the mint received so many dinner services from private donors that it was unable to turn them all into currency.

Arakcheev was the busiest man in Saint Petersburg, organizing civil defense and the innumerable supply problems for the troops at the front. Yet in the midst of his heavy responsibilities he found time to conduct a private battle with Sumarokov, the governor of Novgorod province, where Gruzino was situated. From the time of his appointment Sumarokov had been obstinately determined to show that he would not be overawed by the presence in his district of one of the most powerful statesmen in the Emperor's circle. When the decrees were published establishing the proportion of men, cattle, and material which each landowner was to contribute to the defense of the province, Arakcheev challenged the governor's estimate of the contribution that Gruzino should make and wrote to him, saying, "I assume that the unpleasantness over my estate is due to the fact that our relations are conducted through middlemen. In order to avoid this, may I ask your Excellency to deal directly with me in all matters concerning my village of Gruzino, and I will take the appropriate measures." Sumarokov's reply was spirited. "There are five hundred landowners in my province, and if I were to fall in with Your Excellency's wishes and conduct a special correspondence with you on questions concerning your estate, I would have no right to refuse to do the same with the least landowner, and no time left to administer the province. I therefore request Your Excellency to alter the arrangements you have made and to tell your agent to carry

Arakcheev (about 1815)

out all the instructions of the local authorities very carefully, for if he does not, I shall be obliged to send for him and have him publicly flogged."

Sumarokov unwisely proceeded to boast that he had put the "corporal of Gatchina" firmly in his place. The senior nobleman of the district, Count Svechin, reported his remarks to Arakcheev, who promptly returned Sumarokov's letter with an icy note. "In your letter you did not use the expression you employed at the meeting of the nobility, *viz:* 'if I begin to correspond with the Count, then I shall have to correspond with the least corporal.' I direct your attention to this and ask you to correct your mistake."[13] At the same time, he wrote back to Svechin, "I cannot think why our governor hates me, swears at me in front of everyone, so they say, and beats and hangs me. I could take it if he confined his hatred to me alone, but since all governors usually vent their anger with landowners on their poor peasants, I am much concerned. Please make friends with him and discover why he so dislikes my face. It would seem that it is because I obtained an estate in the province not through favoritism, bribes, or intrigue, but by hard work; since when I have accepted nothing else from the Emperor, nor will I do so, in order to leave more in the exchequer to pay the governors."[14]

Sumarokov was determined to have the last word. "It is dishonorable to repeat gossip from house to house," he replied to Arakcheev, "and even more dishonorable to pass on news with embellishments. I stand by my words, except for the word 'corporal' in the place of which I said 'the least landowner.' I am therefore returning my letter to you unaltered. I am sure that with this explanation I shall have made a bad enemy of you. Your mighty Excellency, who has so much influence at court, can do me harm, and knowing your character, I am sure you will not lose the first opportunity to do so. But you should know that I value my honor more than my position, and believe in the Russian proverb 'naked but right!' "[15] Only Arakcheev's departure with Alexander from Saint Petersburg put an end to this acrimonious exchange.

Napoleon held on during the last weeks of September in the by now burned-out shell of Moscow, waiting with ebbing confidence for Alexander to propose negotiations. He failed to grasp that when Rostopchin had set fire to the city and indeed burned down his own estate near Moscow, his gesture had both symbolized the prevailing Russian thinking that the French must be resisted to the end and had in itself strengthened Alexander's resolve never to negotiate. "Napoleon or I; he or I; now we can no longer reign together," he exclaimed to one of Kutuzov's emissaries when he heard that Moscow had been destroyed. Later he told Madame de Krudener, "The burning of Moscow illuminated my soul."

Yet rumor had it that the Emperor was at times assailed by doubts. It was said that he turned to Arakcheev one day on Kamenny Island and announced that appalled as he was by the thought of the country being laid waste from the Nieman to Moscow, he had decided after all to make peace. "What price would Russia now have to pay?" asked Arakcheev. Alexander replied that the loss of provinces even as far as the Dvina would be bearable, since Napoleon's empire would collapse when he died and the provinces could then be recovered, whereas his towns, villages, soldiers, and subjects, once destroyed, were irretrievable. In great alarm Arakcheev turned to Maria Feodorovna, one of Napoleon's bitterest enemies, and she persuaded the Emperor to hold on at least until the winter.[16]

Alexander's confidence was not increased by a series of hysterical letters from his sister, Catherine, who after urging him to leave the army now seemed to imply that he had been dishonorable in doing so. "Discontent is at its height, and you are far from being spared," Catherine wrote to him early in September. "If this much reaches me, you can judge what it is really like. You are openly accused of having caused the misfortunes of your Empire, its public and private ruin, of having lost both the country's honor and your own. . . . I am not competent to tell you what you should do, but you ought to know that your honor is under attack. Your presence could help you to regain support." Alexander was stung to the quick by these imputations, and in his reply showed how reluctant he had been to leave the army in the first place. "After I had sacrificed my personal pride to the public good by leaving the army because it was claimed that I was doing harm, that I was depriving the generals of their responsibilities, that I inspired no confidence in the troops, and that reverses which could be ascribed to me were worse than those imputed to my generals, you can judge for yourself, my dear friend, how painful it is for me to hear that my honor is being attacked. I only did what everyone wanted in leaving the army; my sole desire was to stay there."

By his refusal to move from Moscow without some word from Alexander, Napoleon condemned to destruction what remained of his army. He was deceived by the unusually mild autumn and snapped his fingers at Caulaincourt when the Ambassador begged him to pull out before winter closed in. "Caulaincourt is freezing already," he remarked scornfully as they basked in the autumnal sunshine. But as the supply situation grew more serious, he realized that his troops could not survive many more weeks in the region, and he finally decided to leave for Smolensk, where he had left large reserves of food and ammunition. The news that the French were abandoning Moscow was greeted with incredulity in Saint Petersburg; everyone felt instinctively that the turning-point had come at last. "It looks as if the Almighty has brought down on the head of this monster all the disasters he was preparing for us," Alexander wrote in a note to Arakcheev.

The return journey was indeed a nightmare for Napoleon's army. When Napoleon arrived at Smolensk he found that most of the provisions on which he had been relying had been consumed by his own reserve troops. From now on the retreat became a rout. Harassed by Russian guerrilla bands and Kutuzov's pursuing army, Napoleon's troops struggled across the Beresina, making headlong for Vilna, as the intense cold closed in on them. The famished and frozen soldiers fell dying in thousands. When finally Marshal Ney regrouped the surviving troops behind the Nieman in mid-December, after Napoleon's precipitate departure for Paris, the tattered remains of the Grande Armée, five hundred thousand strong only six months before, now numbered scarcely forty thousand men.

On December 6 Alexander, closely attended by Arakcheev at the head of his private chancery, left Saint Petersburg to join Kutuzov at Vilna. The scenes of devastation and suffering which met the party at Vilna and on the banks of the Nieman were beyond description. Marchenko records that on his first night at Vilna he was kept awake by dull thuds, as if heavy sacks were being thrown from the windows of the building at regular intervals. The next day he climbed up to the second floor and to his horror found the rooms crammed with prostrate French soldiers, the dying gnawing at the bodies of their dead neighbors. As the wounded crawled out into the corridors, the Russians on guard picked them up and hurled them through the windows. The whole town was like a gigantic mortuary. Every morning Marchenko's staircase had to be cleared of the bodies of soldiers who had sought a quiet corner in which to die.

Alexander greeted Kutuzov with every outward show of warmth but continued to distrust him underneath. He could never bring himself to like the most brilliant of his generals, and he now proceeded to reproach the old man for having missed the chance to encircle and annihilate the French at the Beresina. He also found Kutuzov resolutely opposed to any further advance. Now that Napoleon had been expelled from Russian territory, Kutuzov considered that the armies had done their job and that the state should concentrate on repairing the devastation caused by the war. His view was generally supported by the Emperor's Russian advisers, including Arakcheev, Rumyantsev, and Rostopchin, but Alexander was quite determined to achieve the total defeat of Napoleon; and the British, Prussian, and Austrian representatives around him did their best to encourage him. Kutuzov was replaced at the head of the Russian armies by Barclay, and a few months later he died, unmourned by his sovereign.

For Alexander the campaigns of the following eighteen months became a war of liberation. He saw himself as the savior of Europe, destined to build a new order on the ruins of the old Napoleonic Empire. Alexander had emerged from the terrible days of isolation in Saint Petersburg a changed man. He had devoted much of his solitude to prayer and the study of his Bible, and he now began to see his policy in ideological terms, with himself in the role of an archangle whose flaming sword was destined to bring low the French Antichrist. His first and principal support in the new campaign came from Prussia, which had endured years of humiliation at Napoleon's hands; the Quadruple Alliance, under which Russia, Prussia, Britain, and Austria bound themselves not to conclude a separate peace with Napoleon, was not signed until March, 1814, more than a year after the Russian armies had in their turn crossed the Nieman. Alexander was undoubtedly the leader of the coalition, and it was he who entered Paris at the head of the allied armies only a few weeks after the formation of the Alliance. From now on his energies were concentrated on his European vocation at the expense of all other considerations.

Close as he was to Alexander, Arakcheev's part in the European campaign was a minor one. He retained his position as the Emperor's confidant, kept him informed of developments in Russia, and ran the imperial chancery with great efficiency. He was constantly at Alexander's side, forming an indispensable link between the Emperor and his generals, and during the long campaign the two became even closer friends. "The whole town is saying that the Emperor is in the habit of working with you and that you have shown such devotion to him that he can decide nothing without you," a friend wrote to him from Saint Petersburg in October, 1813. This was something of an exaggeration, but the European campaign certainly strengthened Alexander's conviction that Arakcheev was a man on whose absolute devotion he could rely.

The only occasion on which Arakcheev was separated from the Emperor was in 1813, when from May to July he joined General Bennigsen in Poland to help him organize a new army. No one was Arakcheev's equal in the training of soldiers, and Bennigsen wrote to Alexander expressing his appreciation of Arakcheev's services. Arakcheev showed his gratitude to Bennigsen for this gesture by arranging for the title of the latter's army to be changed from the *armée de réserve* to the more grandiose *armée de Pologne*.

Two years of continual traveling had an adverse effect on Arakcheev's health, which had not been robust at the best of times. Alexander's earliest letters to him, dating back to the Gatchina days, are full of solicitous inquiries about his chest and lungs, which were always giving him trouble. Now in letters to his friend Pukalov, a secretary of the Synod at Saint Petersburg, Arakcheev grumbled freely about the discomforts of the campaign. "What a dreadful place France is!" he wrote at the beginning of 1814 from Bar-sur-Seine. "The smoke has nearly destroyed our eyes. We had bad enough quarters in Poland last winter, but here they are a hundred times worse. Imagine a cold room with no glass in the windows, doors everywhere, and one big fireplace which smokes incessantly. It is hot by the fire, but the temperature in the rest of the room is only eight degrees. There is a piercing wind on all sides, and it is dreadfully dirty. For several days I have been tortured by the flux, toothache, and earache, and it all comes from these damned fireplaces." There were other worries. His brother Andrei was lying sick in Bremen, where he eventually died in August, and Petr, who was also ill, provided another sort of irritation. "They have promoted generals by the thousand," he wrote to Pukalov, "but of him there is no mention. If it is impossible to promote him on his own account, then haven't I deserved it? I am boasting for the first time in my life. In any other country I would have deserved his promotion, but in Russia, it seems, honesty means nothing. . . ."

These bitter remarks, which did not fit in at all with his usual scornful attitude toward nepotism, were symptomatic of the return of his old feeling that he had no useful role to play. On March 31, the day he entered Paris, Alexander had offered Arakcheev a field marshal's baton, which he refused; and the Emperor had fasted alone with his friend during the week before Easter. But Arakcheev had little to do while Alexander, with Talleyrand at his elbow, was negotiating the settlement which sent Napoleon to Elba and brought the Bourbons back to the French throne. Moreover, he was ill at ease in this world of diplomacy and society and once again he had serious thoughts of leaving Alexander. He would put his health right and return to Gruzino. "I am staying here only in order to take the waters and recover my health," he wrote to Pukalov. "My nerves have become so weak that everything upsets me. I can now promise clearly and solemnly that I am going to ask our Emperor to relieve me of my work, since I am no longer happy in it. It is damaging my health and my character. You do me wrong, dear friend, in saying that I have grown accustomed to the court, and it makes me realize that even intelligent people can be mistaken. Please believe me, I have never loved the court; it has always been a burden on me. I must admit that I made a mistake in thinking that an honest man can be of service to the general good. This is true in a small state, but where our colossus is concerned it is not so!"[17]

For five weeks Arakcheev barely saw Alexander at all. When he drafted an order under which Marchenko, on his arrival in Saint Petersburg, was to hand over the affairs which had been run by the imperial chancery to the ministries of War and Foreign Affairs, Marchenko was convinced that he was again preparing to resign. This impression was reinforced when Arakcheev declined to accompany Alexander on a journey to London.* Perhaps on this occasion Arakcheev wished to do no more than give his friends and the Emperor the impression that he would always prefer to give up office, and that it was only his patriotism that had so far made him stay on. Certainly Alexander rose once again to the fly. "It

* In the course of this short journey to England, the Emperor and the Grand Duchess Catherine turned a visit of goodwill into very much the opposite, thoroughly alienating the Prince Regent and government by their rude behavior and clumsy flirtations with the opposition.

was with great sorrow that I parted from you," the Emperor wrote to him immediately on leaving Paris for London. "Please accept again my thanks for the many services which you have done me and which I shall never forget. I am upset and grieved beyond measure. After fourteen years of difficult government and two years of destructive and dangerous warfare, I have now been deprived of the person in whom I have always had unlimited trust. May I say that I have never had similar confidence in anyone else, and no departure has been as hard to bear as yours."

Arakcheev's reply was worthy of his master's sentiments. "I very much appreciate your gracious letter. It will be a consolation to me all my life. Allow me to say very frankly, sir, that my love and devotion to Your Majesty are stronger than my feelings toward anything else in this world. My only desire is to deserve your confidence, not in order to acquire rewards or advantages, but to bring to Your Majesty's attention the misfortunes, burdens, and trials of our dear country. This has always been my object. But since I have become aware of my weak health and have found that I am not able to do my work, I have been forced to ask leave to go. I will not hide from you, sir, my heavy grief. Everywhere and always I shall be the true and faithful servant of Your Majesty."[18] It was exchanges such as these which led Martos, to whom Arakcheev once showed his correspondence with Alexander, to comment that "although the Emperor was not Catherine the Great and the Count was not Prince Potemkin, the Count wrote many letters similar to those Potemkin was said to have been in the habit of writing to Catherine."[19]

Arakcheev traveled first to Aix-les-Bains, and still feeling depressed, he set about taking a cure. "I shall start to use the baths tomorrow," he wrote to Pukalov. "God grant that they put my health right, since it is still very poor: I often have cruel spasms in my stomach. It is very expensive here. An apartment costs thirteen and a half rubles a day. A meal for three people and two servants, consisting of four dishes and two bottles of wine, comes to more than twenty rubles. Every bath is three rubles. But none of this counts beside my desire to return soon to my dear country."

In general, Arakcheev did not profit much from his travels in Europe. In Germany and France he purchased a number of dinner services and *objets d'art* for Gruzino, but he was not at ease in the unfamiliar surroundings and frequently wrote to friends in Saint Petersburg to say how much he was missing life in Russia. After his return home in 1814 he was to go abroad again only once more in his life, when his doctors ordered him to take another cure on his retirement.

Despite the decision to part that was implicit in their exchange of letters, Arakcheev did not stay away from the Emperor for long. At Alexander's request he joined the royal suite at Aachen when the Emperor was on his way back to Russia, and traveled with him to Saint Petersburg. From there he was granted several weeks' leave, which he gratefully spent at Gruzino. On August 6, however, a new summons arrived. "I hope you are pleased with me, since I have given you quite a long time to enjoy your dear Gruzino. Now I think it is time to start work, and I am impatiently waiting for you."

6

The Lord of the Colonies

Children always cry when they are washed.—ARAKCHEEV

It became clear soon after Arakcheev's return to Saint Petersburg that he had in some way been endowed with new authority. He now enjoyed Alexander's full confidence, and Marchenko wrote that "little by little he began to take everything into his hands." Karamzin, the historian, noted at the beginning of 1816 that in the general view there was "only one power in the land—Count Arakcheev"; and according to Rostopchin, Arakcheev was "the moving spirit behind everything."[1] Rostopchin himself was abruptly dismissed by Alexander from his post as governor of Moscow, and he went abroad feeling very bitter. "On German soil I am honored and recognized as the chief instrument of Napoleon's downfall," he wrote. "One may not have satisfied one's own people, but there are others who can say thank you."

Arakcheev not only retained his post as head of the Emperor's personal secretariat, the chancery, but it was moved into his own house on Liteinaya Street. In August, 1814, he was also appointed a *rapporteur* of the Committee of Ministers, although he held no ministerial office;* and in December, 1815, his position was immeasurably strengthened when he was officially given the task of supervising the committee's work and reporting alone on it directly to the Emperor. Moreover, as Alexander became increasingly engrossed in foreign affairs, he fell into the habit of reading digests of the committee's work, prepared for him by Arakcheev, rather than the full minutes of the discussions, which until then he had always gone through very conscientiously. All the committee's decisions were submitted to Arakcheev for comment before he passed them on to the Emperor, and he would generally record his agreement or disagreement in a brief report, with which Alexander usually concurred. For the first time, Arakcheev found himself concerned with a thousand detailed administrative questions going well beyond the military sphere to which he had all his life been confined, and he showed remarkable common sense in his approach to each problem.

Indeed, the judgment Arakcheev displayed in his minutes was often more mature than that of the committee, and his awareness of the interests of the state finances was exceptional in an age when ministers and officials alike used to rob the treasury of millions of rubles in order to line their own pockets. Departments which tried to cover up their own shortcomings rarely escaped his sharp eye. When, for instance, the Council for Roads rejected a proposal for a major inspection of the Moscow highway on the grounds that their own director made regular inspections himself, the committee endorsed their view, but Arakcheev wrote in his minutes, "Are they not trying to cover up the enormous expenditure?" Alexander in his turn wrote, "this report is quite right. You may say that I do not agree." Again, the landowner who

* The *rapporteurs* made reports to the Emperor on the work of the committee.

The Chuguev Military Colony

ruled his own peasants with an iron hand could be unexpectedly just in the interests of serfs, when acting as the Emperor's chief executive. On one occasion, when a landlord was declared bankrupt, his peasants requested the right to buy their freedom. The Committee of Ministers, which spent much of its time examining individual cases of this kind, finally agreed, but attached prohibitive financial conditions to the purchase. Arakcheev wrote on the paper, "It would seem that all ways have been barred to these peasants. The purpose may well be to enable someone to buy up some of our brothers. We should at least instruct that you be informed of the buyer." Again Alexander agreed, and the sum of money which the peasants had to find was considerably reduced.[2]

Arakcheev's position inevitably aroused much resentment among the ministers, who had long been accustomed to treat directly with the Emperor, and he fought their opposition in the same blunt way as he had fought his battle four years earlier with the general staff. The dispute came to a head when Guriev, the Minister of Finance, remarked bitterly in the Committee of Ministers one day that "since the government has established a general *rapporteur*, thus abolishing the post of minister, he may as well take complete responsibility for all matters submitted to the committee." Arakcheev's reaction was sharp. "I find a statement of this kind at a meeting of state officials both unpleasant and insulting, not only to myself, but to anyone who may find himself carrying out special duties on his Majesty's behalf. The honor of all of us who hold the highest positions in the government should ensure that we respect our obligations toward each other, and our years should have given us enough discretion to prevent our using insulting expressions, especially over official business, in which service to our country should be our sole aim. I earnestly request the Committee of Ministers to order that all this be noted in the minutes and submitted to the Emperor, together with my request to be dismissed from the direction of the committee's affairs and an explanation of the shortcomings which the Minister of Finance has found in the workings of the government. My calling, my age, and the rules I have observed in serving my country force me to sacrifice myself in order that I may no longer hinder the business of the state."[3] Guriev, an ineffectual man at the best of times, was easy game, and it was he, not Arakcheev, who eventually resigned.

During the remaining years of Alexander's reign the Committee of Ministers was the only effective organ of government. The cumbrous State Council, with its system of departmental overlords, was increasingly neglected. According to the terms of the constitution, it was still supposed to discuss new legislation, but by requesting the Committee of Ministers rather than the council to examine any new measures that were proposed, Alexander completely undermined its purpose. As Speransky had always feared, the committee, which in itself had no legal basis, became the chief coordinating body of the government. The power of the Private Chancery increased simultaneously. In Speransky's words: "All the elements of autocracy which were united in the person of the Russian Emperor were brought together in the institution of the Private Chancery." For a number of years Arakcheev's chief assistant both in the chancery and in his office in the Committee of Ministers was Marchenko, which made it increasingly hard to separate the functions of the two bodies; they were simply halves of the same compact machinery by which the Emperor and his chief servant now ruled the state. Even such business as was still conducted by the State Council was channeled through the chancery, and the provincial governors were also instructed to communicate directly to the same office.

Arakcheev was apparently tireless. He had an extraordinary ability for getting results out of the archaic Russian administration. In one capacity or another he dealt with virtually all the great problems involved in putting the country on its feet again in the aftermath of the war. He initiated a nationwide census and a general inquiry into the devastation caused by the French invasion. Even the detailed and knotty question of awards and promotions was supervised by him as head of the chancery. "He worked without stop," noted Marchenko. "He had no social or family distractions; he was gloomy and stern, authoritarian to the point of despotism, would reprimand like a tyrant, and could employ the most pitiless sarcasm in the mathematical exercise of his iron will."

Arakcheev's abilities were most successfully employed in the field of construction and administration in the purest sense, and there he concentrated his energies. The philosophy of government did not interest him at all. Nor was he at his best sitting in his office in Saint Petersburg. Despite the rigors of travel over unsurfaced roads and the discomforts of exposure to uncertain weather and equally uncertain local hospitality, he liked to make sudden descents on provincial administrations, to shake up the governor and see for himself what was going on.

Even before the trail of destruction left by the French, the Russian provinces always struck visitors from Western Europe as excessively primitive. There was not even a paved road between Moscow and Saint Petersburg. An Englishman who visited Russia in Alexander's reign, Dr. Robert Lee, noted that "the roads were beyond all description miserable, the mud being half-frozen. The people in the towns and villages were in the most deplorable state of filth and misery."

Indeed, the provincial towns could barely be distinguished from local villages: wooden houses and cabins, roofed with thatch or pitch, were surrounded everywhere by a sea of impenetrable mud. At certain times of the year the life of the towns would come to a standstill because the streets were impassable, and town governors, who were cut off from the capital and were in any case always being replaced, made little or no attempt to improve local conditions. The governors were, it seemed, equally helpless in the face of the additional burdens imposed by the immense devastation of the war. Arakcheev made a point of visiting every area which the invasion had covered and decided to take personal charge of those which were hardest hit. Although he terrified local officials, he achieved results. The district of Smolensk had suffered appallingly, and Arakcheev worked hard to have the town rebuilt, while the inhabitants of the area were given emergency relief to tide them over the crisis. When the nobility of the province wanted to express their gratitude by putting up a portrait of him in the town hall, he refused on the grounds that he was only the servant of their real benefactor, the Emperor.

Alexander showered him with favors. Arakcheev later recounted one typical incident to General Maevsky. "One day when I was in the Emperor's study I could see that he was worried and was looking for something on his desk. At last he found what he wanted and handed me a paper; I read it and saw that my mother had been appointed a lady-in-waiting. I threw myself on my knees and begged the Emperor to annul this favor. My mother was not born for the court, and this honor, which would drag her out of obscurity, would do harm to us both. For a long time the Emperor would not agree, but said, 'I don't know how else to reward you, Count.' At last my pleading convinced him, and he agreed to cancel the appointment. Women are ambitious. My mother remained ignorant of the honor until her death, but if she had ever learned of it, she would not have forgiven me, even beyond the grave."[4] Aware of Arakcheev's liking for unusual honors, Alexander sent him a miniature of himself to be worn around the neck; Arakcheev gratefully accepted it, but he felt it necessary to send back the diamond setting. In 1816 the Emperor ordered that his own yacht and crew be taken secretly by land from Saint Petersburg to Gruzino and put in the water there. When Arakcheev woke one morning, he was saluted by the yacht's guns, and the crew were ordered to remain fully at his disposal thereafter.

The new elevation of Arakcheev created alarm and perplexity at court, and it is not necessary to look far for the explanation. Alexander's withdrawal to Kamenny Island during the bleak months of Napoleon's invasion in 1812 proved to be the first step in what became a progresive retreat from his involvement in Russian affairs. He also acquired a taste for solitude, which he never subsequently lost. The inspired activity of the earlier years when the Emperor spent his nights animating Saint Petersburg's brilliant social life and his days debating political reform with his Russian advisers did not return with the end of the war. Alexander now devoted much of his time to traveling abroad from one conference to the next in his self-appointed role as arbiter of Europe's destinies. Even when he returned home he remained comparatively isolated, restricting his company to a few old friends such as Prince Volkonsky and Golitsyn.

In these circumstances the Emperor needed a man to run the administrative machine on whose loyalty and abilities he could absolutely rely. Arakcheev's firm devotion, his willingness to carry out orders unquestioningly, and his undoubted administrative powers made him the obvious choice. He was the ideal caretaker, incapable of scheming behind the Emperor's back or of exploiting the powerful position he occupied in order to promote his own ideas. The two years Alexander had spent traveling with Arakcheev in Europe had confirmed the Emperor in his assessment of him as a man of little imagination but of unhesitating loyalty.

Arakcheev knew that he was safe from the opposition of the court and the army as long as he retained Alexander's confidence, and he took care to demonstrate that access to the Emperor could be obtained only through him. When Karamzin came to Saint Petersburg in February, 1816, to show the Emperor the first eight volumes of his lengthy *History of Russia*, he waited in vain to be received. Other members of the imperial family showed him great kindness, but he had been there several weeks, and still his audience was no nearer. Finally he was told that Arakcheev wished to see him and that he had been heard to say, "Obviously Karamzin does not want to know me. He has come here and has not even left his card on me." Karamzin hastened to repair his gaffe and subsequently described his interview with Arakcheev in a letter to his wife. "I went at seven this evening and spent over an hour with him. Several times he prevented me from leaving, and I think he spoke with a certain sincerity. I told him my position, and when he offered to put in a word for me with the Emperor, I replied 'I don't beg your Excellency, but if it pleases you, if it would be appropriate, etc.' He said, 'The Emperor is certainly disposed to receive you, and if I am not mistaken, not just for two minutes like some people, but for a most agreeable discussion.' In general I found him a man with a good mind and good principles. He said to me, 'My teacher was the local priest; is it surprising that I do not know much? My job is to carry out the Emperor's wishes. If I were younger, I would begin to learn from you. Now it is too late. . . .' Count Arakcheev promised to help me obtain an early interview with the Emperor and even assured me that there would be no further delay. Would he have said so without reason?" Karamzin was summoned to Alexander only two days later.[5]

The waiting room in the house on Liteinaya Street was now permanently crowded with petitioners of all kinds, ministers, officers seeking promotion, and all those who for the sake of advancement were prepared to brave the wrath of the man whose terrible reputation was rapidly spreading across Russia. This stream of petitioners was one of the traditional accretions of power. Arakcheev's attitude to those who turned to him for help was unpredictable: he was frequently ironical, quite often cruel, and occasionally benevolent. He would never compromise in order to avoid making an enemy, and when he displayed his humor, it tended to be malicious. A young officer who had been waiting for two hours in Arakcheev's reception room eventually said loudly with some irritation, "I wonder whether the Count is going to receive me soon." He recalled later the result of this momentary carelessness. "The adjutant went in and out of the Count's room, calling one person after another, while I continued to wait. At lunchtime the adjutant told me that the Count had ordered me to return the next day at eight in the morning. I came back and waited again. At two, the Count went past with his hat on and did not glance at me; I was almost fainting. I could hear him sitting down to lunch. At six I was told to reappear the next day at seven in the morning. Then I understood. On the following day I had a piece of bread and some biscuits in my pocket. Again I waited, but this time I was less agitated. At last at twelve I was called to the Count. When I went into his study he said, 'Well, my friend, have you got used to it?' "[6]

Some visitors were more fortunate. Count Tolstoy, an ancestor of the novelist, who as a young man had founded a society for propagating a system of popular education in Russia based on the theories of an Englishman, Joseph Lancaster, was aware of Arakcheev's interest in educational matters and decided to approach him directly with a request to become an honorary member of the society. He later wrote an amusing account of his attempt to reach the great man. "When I came to the single-story wooden house in Liteinaya Street where Arakcheev lived, I opened the door, which gave onto a small wooden staircase leading to his rooms. At the door I was met by an underofficer in a frock coat with gold braiding on his collar and lapels, who asked me, 'What do you want?' 'I want Count Arakcheev, so show me to his waiting room, where I may find someone to inform his Excellency of my arrival.' After questioning me in detail, the underofficer allowed me to go upstairs, where I came to a small reception room with a clerk, who asked me, as had the man below, 'What do you want?' He received the same reply, which was that I wanted to see Count Arakcheev and hand a letter to him. 'That's impossible. Let me have your letter; I will give it to the duty adjutant, and he will give it to the duty staff officer.' 'I shall give my letter neither to you nor to the adjutant, nor to the duty staff officer, nor to anyone other than the Count. Take me to the chancery, where I can find someone to announce my arrival.' I was taken into the chancery. This was a large room, divided down the middle by a partition. The first half served as a reception room, and the second half as the chancery. A few moments later the duty adjutant came out and asked rather haughtily, 'What do you want with the Count?' 'I shall tell the Count myself what I want when I have the honor to talk to his Excellency. And now will you report my arrival.' 'I can't report to the Count, but I will tell the duty staff officer.'

"A few moments later a gentleman in colonel's epaulets came in, and his face betrayed his astonishment at the sight of a young naval lieutenant trying to see the Count. He asked me the same questions as the adjutant: who was I and what did I want with the Count? He asked me to give him my letter, which he would hand to General Kleinmikhel, and Kleinmikhel to the Count. I made the same reply. Twice this gentleman left me and then returned to persuade me to give him the letter, assuring me that Kleinmikhel would pass it on without fail. I saw across the chancery that he twice touched the handle of the last door, which probably led to Kleinmikhel's office, and finally he went in. A few minutes later Kleinmikhel appeared looking annoyed, and coming up to me with a rather supercilious air, he asked, 'What do you want with the Count?' I replied that I had a letter for his Excellency which I wished to give him personally, and I asked him to announce to His Excellency that the president of the Society for the Propagation of the Lancaster Schools in Russia, Count Tolstoy, would like to have the honor of personally handing him the society's request, which was that he should graciously accept the title of honorary member of the society which had been voted to him at the first general meeting. Very unwillingly Mr. Kleinmikhel found himself going to inform the Count of my arrival, since I emphatically repeated that I would put my letter only into the hands of the Count himself. Barely a quarter of an hour later he came back a changed man, and very respectfully approached me, saying, 'The Count asks you to go into the drawing room; he will be with you at once.' He accompanied me there and went away. Ten minutes later Arakcheev came through the doors on the opposite side of the room. He greeted me very agreeably and said that he was most pleased to see me. . . . I rose to go three times, but the Count detained me, and I spent nearly an hour with him, pleased and surprised by his intelligent and kind reception. Not that it is surprising that he received me intelligently, since everyone knows that he is a clever and well-informed man."[7]

In July, 1816, Alexander paid a second visit to Gruzino, and Arakcheev later recorded in a book which lay in the church how the Emperor spent his time. On the evening of July 8 Arakcheev met the Emperor, accompanied by Prince Volkonsky, on the left bank of the Volkhov, and they crossed the river together by boat. At the landing stage there was a crowd of peasants, and the Emperor called out greetings to them. He went up to the house, drank tea, and went to bed. On Sunday morning he inspected the ground floor of the house, walked in the garden, and visited the temple of Melissino, which much pleased him. Breakfast was served in a tent, and the Emperor then went to church, lunching afterward at two, while music was played in the avenues of the garden. After lunch he visited the first floor of the house and then climbed a belvedere, from which he could see all the newly constructed villages. At seven in the evening he inspected them by *drozhky*, and on Monday morning at six he left, after distributing a thousand rubles among the servants.

Arakcheev's pleasure at the favor shown by this visit was enhanced when in the same month he received a letter from Speransky begging him to intercede with the Emperor on his behalf and to arrange for his reinstatement in an official position. "Although I have not deserved any special attention from our Excellency, I know from experience your love of justice and your devotion to the Emperor," Speransky wrote. The wheel had indeed come full circle, but Arakcheev was taking no chances. Speransky traveled from his estate at Velikopolye, some seventy kilometers from Gruzino, to plead his case, but Arakcheev forbade him to go to Saint Petersburg while his petition was under consideration. Alexander was undoubtedly embarrassed by Speransky's request, and according to Marchenko, himself drafted four times the ukase under which the disgraced favorite was pardoned. Even so it is a curious and self-contradictory document. After declaring that Alexander had made a detailed investigation into the conduct of Speransky and Magnitsky, the ukase owns that the Emperor had not found convincing reasons for his suspicions. "Therefore, desiring to give them the means of redeeming themselves in full measure by hard work," the Emperor appointed Speransky to be governor of Penza, a town lying some five hundred kilometers southeast of Moscow, and Magnitsky vice-governor of Voronezh, in the same region. Speransky was bitter about the phrase referring to redemption through work, and he always maintained that the passage had been drafted not by Alexander but by Arakcheev.[8]

It became apparent soon after the Emperor returned to Saint Petersburg in 1814 that he had not forgotten the military colonies. In an imperial manifesto published at the end of August, Alexander inserted a phrase which indicated the direction in which his mind was moving. "We hope that a lasting peace will enable us not only to maintain our troops in better and more comfortable conditions than before, but that it will even allow them to lead a settled life and make it possible for us to unite them with their families." A short while later, Alexander remarked to Arakcheev as they were standing in the Emperor's study watching the Preobrazhensky Guards retire to their barracks, "Every time I look at my grenadiers, my heart overflows as I think of what they endured during the campaigns in the way of hard labor, deprivation, and danger. The campaigns are over, you and I are resting, but in peacetime their service is almost heavier than it is in war. Moreover, when they retire after twenty-five years' service, the soldiers have nowhere to lay their head, no family, no home." "Your Majesty, we must think how to make life better for them," returned Arakcheev, and he mentioned the military colonies on the Austrian frontier. "Attend to these matters for me, Alexei Andreevich," exclaimed Alexander. "You will give me the greatest satisfaction, and I shall die in peace."[9]

In September, 1814, Alexander left Saint Petersburg for the Congress of Vienna, and he remained abroad for more than a year. But despite his many preoccupations during the congress, he found time to visit an Austrian colony on the Turkish border and closely questioned the Austrian field marshal, Prince Schwarzenberg, on the organization of their colonies. The Prince, however, was suspicious of the Emperor's intentions, a suspicion later reflected in other foreign statesmen, and forbade his officials to pass any information about the colonies to the Russians. Even so, Russian diplomats succeeded in acquiring a great number of details about their structure, which were duly sent back to Arakcheev, who drew extensively on their reports in working out his own project for a new colony, a project which contained more than five hundred paragraphs.

The site chosen for the new pilot colony was in the district of Novgorod, on the Volkhov River, not far from Gruzino. Arakcheev knew that it would be essential for him to visit the colony frequently, and Mogilev province, where the first colony had been situated, was too far away. Arakcheev worked out his plans with the greatest possible care. The failure of the Mogilev experiment was taken into account;

this time the peasants already living in the district were not to be moved out, but instead included in the organization of the colony on an equal footing with the soldiers. Peasants were to be turned into soldiers, and soldiers into peasants.

Arakcheev was very conscious of the opposition which the creation of the colony was likely to arouse among the peasants concerned. He already had the experience of his own serfs' hostility to the changes which he had imposed on their way of life; and these changes were mild in comparison with what was in store for the state serfs of Novgorod province. He was accordingly, and quite exceptionally, attentive to their sensibilities. In the first clause of a statute laying down the principles on which the colonies were to be based, he stressed the point that "a military colonist is the owner of his house and land. . . . Everything which the colonists receive from the state, such as cattle, buildings, and goods, is their own and exclusively for their own use." An unusual number of incentives were included in the project. The colonists were relieved of all civil taxes; the state was to pay all repairs to their houses; free assistance was envisaged for the old and the sick, and free education for the young. A committee designed to examine complaints made by the peasants was a basic feature of the administration. If these remarkable measures betray the anxiety of the authorities not to find themselves with a peasants' revolt on their hands, they are also a convincing demonstration of the fact that the colonies were seen as a serious social experiment.

As before, plans were worked out in the strictest secrecy. Even the governor of Novgorod was not informed, and only learned that Vysotsk, one of his districts, had been transferred to the military authorities when he read a decree, addressed to him on August 5, 1816, stating that a battalion of the Count Arakcheev Regiment was being moved into the province because of a shortage of barracks in Saint Petersburg. However, the decree showed that this was no ordinary move. It specified, for instance, that the local civil authorities would no longer have any power over the district and that civil taxes were no longer to be levied on the peasants living there. Then, on August 29, the battalion, consisting of more than one thousand men under the command of Major von Friken, marched out of Saint Petersburg to the strains of their regimental music. As they were leaving, news arrived of a fire which had totally destroyed the principal village of Vysotsk; later people wondered whether the peasants had not set fire to the village themselves in a desperate attempt to avert the invasion.

The first task of the battalion that autumn was to fulfill an ambitious building program, which they did with a speed that amazed the Emperor. The houses were long stone buildings symmetrically arranged in squares alongside the river. In every square there was a watchtower, from which the fields belonging to each military unit could be observed. Arakcheev himself spent much time visiting the colony and personally supervised the work down to the last detail. "You have often seen me riding on horseback or in a cart, or making my way on foot, through the mud and the woods, where no one has passed before," he once wrote in a decree addressed to his staff, and it was true enough. The battalion doctor was astonished that he could be so obsessed with detail at a time when he was so hard-worked; Arakcheev himself arranged how the tables, chairs, and carpets should be placed in the new hospital, and would not tolerate the slightest departure from his instructions. His spare figure, striding through the villages and across the fields in a simple gray trench coat, soon became a familiar sight, dreaded by officers and men alike. "The figure of the Count struck me by its unattractiveness," wrote Lieutenant Gribbe, one of the officers serving in the Novgorod colony. "Imagine a man of medium height, round-shouldered, with thick dark hair cut *en brosse*, a low, lined forehead, small, terribly cold colorless eyes, a thick and very inelegant nose shaped like a shoe, a rather long chin, and tightly compressed lips on which no one could remember having seen a smile or a laugh. . . . His voice was very nasal, and he used not to pronounce the end of his words, as if he were swallowing them."[10]

In his impatience to have the work completed at high speed, Arakcheev resorted to a policy of total authoritarianism with his officers. When Lieutenant von Bradke and a brother officer were recruited to the corps of the colonies, they were invited by Arakcheev to Gruzino, and to their surprise found themselves treated as honored guests. However, on the following day Arakcheev summoned them to his study and explained how he expected them to prepare a number of building sites, drain marshes, and create arable fields for the Novgorod colony. When both young men objected that they knew nothing of the practice or theory of farming, "a stern expression appeared on the Count's face, and he told us that he was not used to hearing such futile excuses. Every officer was expected to carry out the duties assigned to him, and he did not want to hear of any difficulties." On another occasion, when Arakcheev asked Von Bradke to carry out an inspection for him, the latter objected that he still could not tell rye from oats. What would happen if through his ignorance he carried out his instructions badly? "Then I shall have you charged," Arakcheev replied grimly.[11] There was scarcely an officer who would not have agreed with General Maevsky, one of Arakcheev's principal lieutenants in the Novgorod colony, when he grumbled that

Arakcheev "always thought that by being rude to someone he was in fact teaching them."

From the start he was determined that the colonies should be completely independent from the administration of the Empire. He formed his own "Separate Corps of the Military Colonies," from which officers were not allowed to transfer to other branches of the army. He demanded complete control over expenditure, writing to the Emperor: "If your Majesty has already been pleased to place the organization of this sector in my care, and if I deserve the government's confidence where this very new enterprise is concerned, which has no precedent and whose failures, inevitable in every new undertaking, must be taken into account, then the government should empower me to spend the sums appointed by your Majesty on whatever is necessary, so that, in a word, I can achieve the economic aims which your Majesty wishes to see."[12] Arakcheev's own staff and Council of the Colonies set up their own committees to draft laws and control finances.

Alexander's general military staff inevitably regarded the military colonies with the greatest suspicion, which changed to outright hostility when they became aware of the Emperor's plans for settling more and more regiments on the land. Barclay de Tolly, to whom Alexander submitted the whole project for comment in 1817, in the hope of enlisting his support, addressed a frank memorandum to the Emperor in which he stated at length the reasons why he felt the scheme was misconceived and could only lead to disaster. "It is well known that farming can only be carried on successfully and will only produce results when peasants are given complete freedom to organize their farming as they think best, and are not subjected to any restrictions in the employment of their time," he wrote. Turning to the likely effect of the colonies on the soldiers, he continued, "As long as the martial spirit with which, thank God, the soldiers are at present imbued, and which gives them pride in their calling, subsists, it is impossible to expect them to be good assistants to the peasant proprietors, and impossible not to foresee hourly disagreements and quarrels arising between them. Maybe in time they will learn to bow to the inevitable and turn their hands from the gun to the plow or the sickle; but then their martial spirit must be expected to disappear completely, and the good soldier will be transformed into an indifferent or poor farmer." As for the officers, "The majority, as everyone knows, enter the army without any education and in a state of such ignorance that they can hardly sign their name." It was already difficult enough to give them some kind of education, "But what will the situation be when in the exercise of their military duties they are dealing only with the colonists, and their only study is agriculture?" Barclay submitted his memorandum with another written by General Diebich of the military staff, who argued very forcefully that the colonies would lead to the creation of a military state within the state, which would be a permanent threat to the authority of the central government and would change the whole character of the army, now dependent only on the Emperor for its general well-being, and loyal directly to his person.[13]

The opposition was not confined to outsiders; the officers on the spot, on whom the working of the whole scheme ultimately depended, failed almost to a man to understand the new principles on which the colonies were based and were almost unanimously opposed to their new work. They were unable to treat the peasants as peasants one minute and as soldiers the next, and they similarly failed to adjust to a new relationship with the soldiers under their command. Arakcheev wrote in vain in his general instructions that "if a commander of colony troops is not convinced that a frontline soldier can at the same time be an agricultural worker, then his doubts make him unsuited for command, for he will not have the necessary firmness and strength of mind to carry out the government's beneficial policy."[14] Lieutenant Martos reflected the view of his brother officers when he wrote that "there was no possibility of doing serious agricultural work, since everyone was dressed up in uniform and divided into companies; in each hamlet the threshing floor was taken over and peasants were taught how to turn left and right, march in step, stand up and carry a sword." General Maevsky later wrote a scathing indictment of the colonies. "From the outside all seemed in order; closer examination revealed chaos. Cleanliness and order were the colony's first concern. But imagine a house in which the people and the food are freezing; imagine a cow which is maintained like a rifle, but whose fodder is twelve *versts* away in a field; imagine that the woods had been burned down and that new wood for building had to be bought in Porkhovo . . . then, you begin to have an idea of state economics."

It was hardly surprising that the colonies fell short of the utopia planned by Alexander and Arakcheev. It was scarcely the officers' fault: they had been reared in the strict Prussian military tradition and were for the most part ignorant in every field beyond their own narrow training. Villages and settlements like these had never been seen before in Russia, and they enchanted the eye of the Emperor; but in his obsession with external appearance, Arakcheev often failed to take more fundamental considerations into account. Although he realized instinctively that the peasants must feel that they were the owners of their property if the colonies were to be a success, he was not prepared to allow them freedom to manage the property in their own way, as true ownership would have demanded. The clause in his statute which granted the peasant exclusive ownership of his land, buildings, and cattle also held him "responsible to the military command for keeping them in good order, by which it will be possible to judge his ability to look after them." It was perhaps hardly surprising that a traditional serf owner should fail to see the logical flaw inherent in this demand, but Arakcheev's very high standards appeared intolerable to all the inhabitants of the colonies.

"It had to be admitted that the colonies were endowed with everything for the benefit of man," wrote General Maevsky. "Midwives, maternity homes, baths, stretchers, lavatories, were all part of the Emperor's conception and reflected at every step his remarkable and philanthropic nature. But emperors are not gods, and above all, it is easier to deceive them than gods. Thrift and cleanliness destroyed the purpose of the whole institution. The floors in the hospital were polished until they were like parquet, and the patients dared not tread on them for fear of making them dirty; from this was born a saying that 'one goes home by the window.' Each regiment had expensive furniture and a costly silver dinner service. But the furniture was preserved like treasure, and no one dared use it. The same went for the officers; they were afraid either to walk or to sit down in their rooms, in case they dirtied or wore out what they had received for their own use."[15] Dr. Evropeus relates that after a severe reprimand from Arakcheev, who was angry that so many patients were lying in the hospital beds, he had to make a number of them get up and sit with the convalescents half an hour before Arakcheev's inspections.

The peasants' reaction to the new world in which they unexpectedly found themselves was at first one of bewilderment, which later hardened into hostility. Together with the soldiers who were accorded the privilege of settling on the land with their families on the same basis as the peasants, they were named the "reserve battalion" and were expected to spend three days a week in winter and two days a week in summer undergoing full-time military training. Each peasant household had two or more soldiers billeted with them from the two "active battalions" that made up the rest of the colony; and they were supposed to feed them in return for the soldiers' help in the fields and the use of new and better equipment. The peasants' whole way of life was changed by the military training they had to undergo and the break-up of their close-knit independent communities.

Given Arakcheev's awareness of the peasants' sensitivity, it seems curious that he should have chosen to place the Novgorod colony in an area inhabited largely by Old Believers, a religious sect which had its own highly individual way of life and was fiercely attached to its own rites. It is true that he proceeded with caution. Uniforms, for instance, were not imposed until June, 1817, when he wrote to Alexander, "Uniforms will be distributed in each village, and every peasant under the age of forty-six will be ordered to put on his uniform on the same day and to continue to wear it every day for work." He added, however, "I shall not order them to cut their hair or shave off their beards, since in time they will do so of their own accord."[16] The operation went more successfully than he had hoped it might. Three weeks later he wrote to the Emperor again, telling him that "everyone capable of work in the Vysotskaya Oblast is already in uniform. The changeover was more peaceful and successful than I ever expected it would be. Many people have already shaved off their beards. . . . I don't think I have spent my time here in vain. I have made a good start in this new and unusual task, and I think it will now work easily and successfully everywhere." "This is the best possible start," replied Alexander. "It does indeed exceed all our expectations. I am impatient to see you in order to thank you personally and talk many things over with you."

Yet the outward obedience of the peasants was deceptive. The imposition of an increasing number of regulations, which seemed to them to be grossly oppressive, provoked a rising swell of protest. In the autumn of 1817, when the Grand Duke Nicholas, Alexander's brother was passing the Novgorod colony on his way back to the capital with his wife and brother-in-law, the woods suddenly came alive with peasants, who emerged from the trees and threw themselves on their knees on the roadway, crying to be released from their bondage, while the women and children knelt singing before the imperial carriage. For the passengers the fearful specter of a peasants' revolt once again momentarily reared its head, but the incident passed off calmly enough, and the royal party proceeded on its way. At the end of the year the unhappy peasants sent a delegation to Warsaw to plead with Alexander's brother Constantine. But they received cold comfort from him; he reported to Saint Petersburg that the peasants had complained that they were being made to shave off their beards "and do things about which there were no decrees. They had been sent to me from the district to ask for my help. I did not go into details with them but told them at once to be quiet, saying that they should do what they were told zealously and without grumbling. In conclusion I had them conducted by an A.D.C. and two cossacks to Count Arakcheev, for him to examine the matter."

Alexander was undaunted by these sporadic signs of discontent. He was gratified by the successful establishment of the Novgorod colony and determined to push on with his plan for settling the major part of the army in this way. The next area chosen was the Ukraine, and here for the first time Arakcheev's staff encountered serious local opposition. The Ukraine was by tradition very conscious of its independence, and old rights and customs had the force of law. There were loud protests when a regiment of cossacks on the Bug River was converted into a colony of cavalry troops. On the occasion of a visit from Alexander in 1818 the peasants were prevented by their officers from approaching him, and even forbidden to make their traditional presentation to the Emperor of bread and salt, a humiliation which they much resented. Discontent finally came to a head in the area of Chuguev, where, in June, 1819, the colonists went on strike. A dispute over the provision of hay for the regimental horses was the signal for a general rising, which spread to the neighboring Taganrog regiment. The local authorities lost control, and Arakcheev hurried down to take charge. He was shocked by the peasants' bitterness both against the colonies and against himself. He reported to Alexander how he had heard the rebels crying in unison, "We do not want the military colony. We do not want to serve Count Arakcheev rather than the Emperor. We want to destroy Arakcheev because we know that when he dies the military colonies will disappear."

"I thought about this business day and night," Arakcheev continued in his report to the Emperor, "and calling on Almighty God for his help, I saw that on the one hand decisiveness and prompt action were needed; but on the other hand, I realized that in view of their anger with me personally, I must be careful how I acted, for my human imperfections might make me harsh or vindictive as a result of their desire to take my life." He set up a military court at which two hundred and seventy-five men were sentenced to death, and then commuted the sentence to punishment by *spits-ruten*, a Prussian penalty in force in the Russian army. The convicted men were stripped to the waist, tied to two rifles, and dragged through rows of soldiers armed with long birch rods, each of whom struck them a blow on the back. The exact terms of the sentence were that each man should pass twelve times between a thousand men, but Arakcheev decided that he would try it out first on the forty ringleaders only, in the hope that the terrible example would cause the others to repent and plead for mercy. So bitter were the colonists, however, that "the punishment did not influence the remaining prisoners, although it was harsh and exemplary." Many of the rebels died under this frightful chastisement; one soldier, who visited his comrades in the hospital after they had passed through "green street," as it was popularly known among the soldiers, maintained that "you could only tell by their heads that these were men and not slaughtered meat."

In a private letter to Alexander, Arakcheev admitted that "the events which have taken place here have much disturbed me," but he did not call into question the wisdom of the policy, nor did Alexander heed the warning implicit in the revolt. "I understand entirely what your sensitive soul must have undergone in the circumstances in which you found yourself," the Emperor wrote back. "Moreover, I appreciate the good judgment with which you acted in the face of these grave events, and I sincerely thank you for all you did. The event was, of course, unhappy; but once it had unfortunately taken place, there was no alternative but to allow the force of the law to take its course." The Emperor permitted himself one note of self-criticism. "We should ask ourselves frankly whether all the promises which were made to the regiment have been carried out. As I do not have their statutes and charter with me, I cannot answer this now. But

I sincerely request you to turn your attention to the question."[17] Meanwhile, Muraviev, a secretary in the Private Chancery, hastened to assure Arakcheev that the Emperor did not attach any blame to him for the events at Chuguev. After a conversation with Alexander, Muraviev wrote to Arakcheev, telling him that the Emperor "spoke with, I think, sincere and warm approval not only of everything you have accomplished at Chuguev but also of your good and Christian feelings under the circumstances. He spoke of you as his truest friend, and when I interrupted him to say that I concluded from your letter that you were most unhappy and that I feared this would damage your health, he replied with feeling that he realized your sensitivity and prayed to God every day to increase your days and strengthen your health. . . ."[18]

Alexander showed consistently the zeal of a fanatical reformer in everything pertaining to the military colonies. "The colonies will be set up whatever happens, even if I have to cover the road from Saint Petersburg to Novgorod with corpses," he is alleged to have said on one occasion, and on another he remarked to a German diplomat, "I have already mastered far more difficult problems, and I wish to be obeyed over this one."[19] Indeed, he seems to have been firmly resolved that eventually all his regiments should be settled on the land; the French Ambassador, La Ferronays, reported, "According to what the Emperor told me, it will take twenty-three years to settle the entire army." With a determination of this order above him and growing popular resistance below, Arakcheev became increasingly inflexible in applying the regulations, as if he were deliberately closing his eyes to the significance of what he was doing; more and more often he would take refuge in the excuse that he was only executing the Emperor's commands.

The Emperor Alexander
Courtesy of the British Museum

The clock in memory of Alexander I
Courtesy of the British Museum

Gradually the beneficial features of the administration, the subsidies and privileges which had been designed to take account of the peasants' sensibilities, were forgotten in the interests of economy; and in order to improve the balance sheet, the peasants were more openly exploited. Two years after the revolt at Chuguev, a further rebellion took place in a neighboring southern colony. A new colony had been created, which included several villages of Old Believers. Members of the sect appealed to be allowed to keep their beards and their old title of "Novodontsy," but on this occasion Arakcheev insisted from Saint Petersburg that all measures be taken to ensure the strict enforcement of the law. Troops lined the streets of the principal village, while an officer went into the crowd of peasants to persuade them to submit to the new regulations, but one of the apostles of the sect struck him dead with a blow from his stick. When told that the only alternative to submission was punishment by *spits-ruten*, the male peasants at once stripped off their clothes and came forward accompanied by cries of encouragement from the women. "Blows rained down on them; soon many were unable to walk, and others fell to the ground, holding copper crucifixes in their mouths," wrote a young officer who was present. "The women were crying, 'Go on, go on, you are holy martyrs.' Nine people had already died when it began to grow dark and my soul had become numb with horror. I rushed into the crowd, threw myself on my knees, and begged these madmen to submit. . . . Night brought the execution to an end. More than two hundred men were lying in their own blood. The ringleaders, who had been arrested, had their beards shaved off, as did those who had shouted loudest. But several people approached General Khrapovitsky that night with repentant faces. By morning everyone had sworn the oath, and those who then drove us on to Kremenchug were singing as if nothing had happened. Such are the Russian people!"[20]

Arakcheev was preoccupied with running government affairs in Saint Petersburg and unable to make visits to the south himself. Instead, he relied on his chief of staff, General Kleinmikhel, an unimaginative officer of Prussian origin, to make frequent inspections and keep up to the mark officers such as Count Witt, who displayed remarkably little enthusiasm in his command of the southern colonies. However, Arakcheev continued to take a close personal interest in the Novgorod colony. He would inspect the colony himself, and three times a year he invited representatives of the junior ranks of the Count Arakcheev Regiment, led by Captain Protopopov, to luncheon at Gruzino. The men who were chosen to attend on these occasions did not particularly relish the honor. "Those elected would march to Gruzino and attend Mass," recalled Lieutenant Gribbe. "Then they would parade outside the church, and when Arakcheev had greeted them, they would walk to a belvedere, where a table was laid for thirty. Tiny glasses of vodka were handed around, and they then sat down to a very modest meal; the lower ranks were given cabbage soup, meat pies, boiled ham, *kasha*,* and, at the end of the meal, a sharp white wine. When the wine had been poured around, Protopopov would rise and propose a toast to Arakcheev. Then a woman would appear who would apologize for having been unable to take part in the meal; she was plump, but had a grenadier's figure and fiery black eyes. This was Nastasia Minkina. Finally a waiter with a tray would enter and hand around sausage-shaped paper packages. As soon as they were on their way home, the soldiers would devour the dry bread which they

* A kind of gruel made of buckwheat, part of the Russian peasant's staple diet.

had brought with them, for nerves and the tightness of the uniforms had prevented them from lunching well. When they undid the packages, they would find ten five-kopeck coins."[21]

Gruzino became the most celebrated estate in Russia, and Arakcheev took immense pride in his creation. He entrusted one of the priests of his church, Feodor Malinovsky, with the task of compiling a book about the estate, which was published in 1816. Malinovsky did not spare his praises, and, for instance, freely compared Gruzino with the hanging gardens of Babylon. A few years later a collection of lithographs devoted to the estate was printed in a limited number on the presses of the military colonies. Alexander's fondness for Gruzino was also well known, and there was a constant flow of visitors. Eventually Arakcheev had a flag post erected at Chudovo, twelve kilometers away, on which a flag would be hoisted when he was receiving; and when the flag was flying, an arrival had to be signaled from the roof of the staging post, and the reply awaited, before the visitor was allowed to proceed.[22] In his malicious way, Arakcheev would occasionally play tricks on important officials who made the journey from Saint Petersburg to see him on business; on arriving at Chudovo, they would learn that there had been a change in the dress in which he was receiving that day, and they would be forced to wait there for several hours while a servant returned to the capital for new clothes.

As the years passed, Arakcheev's attachment to Nastasia appeared to increase rather than the reverse, even though she had lost her looks early in life. When he was away from Gruzino, she would send him in her atrocious hand the most detailed reports of the work being done on the estate. Other letters expressed the deepest passion and also her jealousy.

"How overjoyed I was to receive your letter; how kind you are to me!" she wrote on July 20, 1819. "Ah, my darling, God grant that your love for me be as strong as mine for you—only God can tell. You need have no doubts about your Nastasia, whose every minute is devoted to you. But I must say, my love, that I often doubt in you, although I forgive you everything. What is to be done if young ladies are stronger than friendship? Your servant Nastasia will be constant until the end of her life. God grant that we may see you in your dear Gruzino; my one consolation is to be able to help you to rest. Oh, my friend, love is so painful, and there are still nearly three days to wait for you."[23]

It is not certain whether Nastasia had reason to be jealous of her master. Certainly behind his austere exterior Arakcheev revealed himself a most sensual man, with an unlikely taste for pornography. Side by side with the spiritual and scientific works in his large library were books with titles such as *Tender Embraces in Marriage, and Fun with Mistresses; Read, Learn, and Maybe You Will Fall in Love; Lovers and Mistresses, Men and Women.*[24] It was also common gossip that Varvara Petrovna Pukalova, the wife of the secretary of the Synod, was Arakcheev's mistress when he was living in Saint Petersburg. Certainly he was a close personal friend of the Pukalovs, and Varvara Petrovna was known to use her influence over him to seek favors for her numerous acquaintances. "Blessed is he who has not sought protection through Pukalova," ran one of society's little sayings. Rostopchin was fond of recounting how when he and Arakcheev were lunching one day with the Emperor, Arakcheev began to say that there were no more favorites and that people no longer crowded fashionable salons. "People may not crowd salons, but there are houses which you cannot drive past," Rostopchin returned. "Three nights ago

I was driving down Fontankaya Street from the Semenovsky bridge, when my carriage suddenly came to a halt. I thought it might have broken down, and, lowering the window, asked the coachman why we had stopped. He replied that the whole street was blocked with carriages. "Who is having a big reception?" I asked. A coachman standing nearby replied, 'It's Madame Pukalova, sir.' I must admit I have never heard of this eminent lady, Pukalova." Arakcheev bit his lip, and his face turned purple.

Whether he was faithful to Nastasia or not, Arakcheev remained devoted to her, and they were united in their affection for their son. "I want this son of ours to be a general example of gratitude; I always tell him that in you God has given us our father and benefactor, my only love," Nastasia wrote to Arakcheev in 1819. In the following year she was overjoyed to learn that Shumsky had been appointed a page to the Empress. "On Sunday morning," she wrote, "I sent a line to Misha and heard that he had come out and was to be presented to the Empress Elizaveta Alexeevna. Ah, my little father, what joy filled my heart. At two, I sent horses to fetch him. When we saw each other we had only tears of gratitude for God and you. He is thinner, but very well. He had not seen the Empress; Monday was his first day on duty."

With his enrollment in the Corps des Pages, the smartest of the military schools, Shumsky's troubles began. As far as the authorities were concerned, he was well protected, and he was at first a hard-working student, but the other pages mocked him as the illegitimate son of a peasant and inevitably nicknamed him "Muzhik." He was commissioned as an ensign in the Guards Horse Artillery, and Arakcheev showed his pleasure by lavishing more than two thousand rubles on the boy's uniform and equipment. It soon became clear, however, that society was not prepared to accept Shumsky, and many doors in Saint Petersburg remained closed to him. Arakcheev consistently refused to recognize the painful situation in which the young officer was placed, and was shocked to find that Shumsky was increasingly consoling himself with drink. One night when Arakcheev was at the Winter Palace, he was called to the guardroom, where he found Shumsky, who was the officer on duty, lying undressed and dead drunk. Arakcheev hastily had him replaced by an officer from the Preobrazhensky Regiment and took him away, saying that he had suddenly been taken ill. But although Arakcheev succeeded in hushing up this incident, he must have seen that it could not be long before some other scandal brought his son's intemperate conduct before the public eye.

In July, 1820, Elizaveta Alekseevna died after a short illness, and Arakcheev had her buried with his father at Kurgany. Her death was the occasion for a characteristically emotional outburst from Nastasia by way of consolation. "I am begging God to save my little father, and rely on his mercy. He will preserve you. But I do not know where you are, nor how your health is. Please tell your N. She is waiting every moment; do not deprive her of your mercy and love. . . . Only the grave will put an end to my love for you; I love you so much that I can love you no more, God is my witness." The Emperor also sent his consolation to Arakcheev, adding at the end of his letter, "I sincerely hope that God will strengthen and preserve your health so that you may continue for many years to give your valuable services to your country."

The Emperor was writing from Chuguev, where he had taken an opportunity to inspect the colony after the disasters of the previous year. He was well satisfied with what he found, and Arakcheev was much relieved. Grieved as he was over his mother's death, he wrote to a friend, Baron Kampenhausen, "I thank God that my misfortune overtook me when it did, obliging me to stay behind when the Emperor traveled to the military colonies of Kharkov and Kherson, since evil-minded people say that by my presence I prevent any complaints being made. Now everybody can see that there were no complaints in my absence and that the Emperor was very content, for he gave Count Witt some sixty thousand rubles for the soldiers and officers."[25]

7
Lengthening Shadows

Your character is the constitution of your Empire, and your conscience is its guarantee.—MADAME DE STAEL, TO THE EMPEROR ALEXANDER

"We returned from France to Russia by sea. The first division of guards landed at Oranienbaum and heard a Te Deum sung by Archbishop Derzhavin. During the service the police mercilessly beat any member of the crowd who attempted to approach the troops as they stood drawn up. This was our first unfavorable impression on our return to Russia. . . . Finally the Emperor appeared on a fine bay horse attended by his guard. He was about to lower his unsheathed sword before the Empress. We watched with delight. But at that very moment, a peasant started to cross the street almost under his horse. Spurring the horse, the Emperor charged toward the running peasant with his naked sword. The police attacked him with their clubs. We could not believe our eyes and turned away, ashamed for our beloved Czar. That was my first disappointment in him. Involuntarily I thought of a cat transformed into a Beauty, but still unable to see a mouse without leaping on it."

This little scene, witnessed by a young guard officer on his return from the European campaign, makes a fitting prelude to the last decade of Alexander's reign. The great national struggle against Napoleon, first in Russia itself and then outside, had planted disruptive seeds in Russian society which very rapidly bore their fruit. The war accentuated two contradictory tendencies which had in fact been present in Russia from the day that Alexander ascended the throne, and it was ultimately responsible for the collision between them.

On one side was the chauvinistic, conservative wing of the aristocracy, led by Rostopchin, Admiral Shishkov, and Karamzin and backed by the great majority of serf owners, who felt that they had stood at the head of the national crusade against the French. They represented the instinctive opposition to change or liberalism of any kind that had always existed in Russia; Speransky's career had been successfully wrecked on the eve of the French invasion, and after the war they had no hesitation in asserting themselves. On the other side was a large number of officers, for the most part young, who returned to Russia after the European campaign, having spent a long period abroad for the first time in their lives, and who were dismayed by the contrast between the medieval character of Russian society and the freedom and enlightenment which they had observed in Europe. "It became unbearable to watch the empty life of Saint Petersburg or to listen to the nonsense of old men who praised everything old and criticized every progressive movement. We had left them a hundred years behind," wrote one of these officers. "In 1815, when Napoleon escaped from Elba and invaded France, the guards were sent on campaign, and we were delighted at this unexpected good fortune."

Arakcheev's sympathies were certainly not on the side of the young officers. He had absorbed no new ideas as a result of his two years abroad, and when he returned to Saint Petersburg he sank himself entirely in his new responsibilities for the Committee of Ministers and the military colonies. He did not enter the political debate on one side or the other, and he certainly did not appreciate its importance. He had long ago accustomed himself to ignoring currents of opinion, since they were so often directed against himself. Now his social isolation, his preference for avoiding people whom he contemptuously labeled "political windbags," and his very heavy load of detailed administration combined to blind him to the gathering movement for change. He certainly made no attempt to correspond about matters of this kind with the Emperor.

Indeed there appeared to be no one who thought it worth opening Alexander's eyes to the true state of affairs in Russia, and he therefore remained unaware for some time of the danger which the restiveness and frustration of a growing number of young but influential officers represented. The European situation and his obsession with European affairs now kept him abroad for many months. Between 1815 and 1820 he spent nearly half his time in Austria and Poland. When he was at home he was inclined to desert the capital for prolonged tours of his country, and people began to say that Russia was being governed from the back of a post chaise. Indeed, the Emperor's view of Russian affairs was becoming alarmingly myopic. As the leader of the coalition which had defeated Napoleon, he was more concerned with what he considered to be his responsibilities as the arbiter of Europe's destinies, and despite the resistance to his ideas for a settlement which he encountered among the allies, he never lost his eagerness to play a European role. Moreover, he saw this role and the new European order increasingly in ideological terms. By now the mysticism which had begun to take hold of him in 1812 so dominated his mind that it imbued his whole political thinking. It was for this reason that he conceived the idea of the Holy Alliance, a treaty under which the sovereigns of Europe were to bind themselves to be guided by Christian principles in their relations among themselves and with their own peoples. At first the governments to whom Alexander proposed this plan had some difficulty in grasping what he was driving at. Castlereagh confessed that when the Emperor first asked him to look at the draft, "it was not without difficulty that we went through the interview with becoming gravity." Metternich called the whole affair "a loud-sounding nothing."

Even so, all the European rulers, with the solitary exception of the British Prince Regent, signed the Holy Alliance. Metternich was probably the first to grasp its true political importance. Not only would the alliance serve to keep Alexander's eyes firmly fixed on the European scene, but it could also be manipulated by Metternich himself to ensure Russian support for Austrian policies; and the aim of Austrian policies was to resist any threat to the European settlement which had been so painfully achieved, as well as to increase Austria's own power. At this juncture it was vital that Russia's weight should be thrown into the scales on the side of the established order. After the years of incessant turmoil and suffering which Napoleon's campaigns had caused in Europe, a wave of unrest was sweeping through one country after another. The War of Liberation from France had proved to be a false dawn, and young men saw with dismay the return of the old leaders to positions of authority as "kings crept out again to feel the sun." In Spain, Italy, Germany, and Greece, underground movements sprang to life, and Metternich put himself firmly at the head of the campaign to repress them.

It was some time before Alexander moved up to stand

squarely by his side. Never had his position between liberalism and reform on the one side and autocracy on the other been more equivocal and hesitant than it was now, for he could not bring himself to abandon forever the dreams of his youth or his image as the great liberator of Europe. After the Congress of Vienna he had at last been able to fulfill the promises he had made so many years before to Czartoryski and endow Poland with the form, if not the substance, of independence, in the shape of her own constitution. Carried away by the establishment of the new Polish Diet in 1818, he proclaimed in his opening address, "You have given me the means of offering to my own country something I have long been preparing for her, and which she will receive as soon as all the elements of so important an undertaking have been completed." His remark reverberated instantly throughout Russia. To the liberals it was a clarion call, to the conservatives a warning, and the only purpose it served was to heighten the tension between the two. Given that at the time Alexander had no carefully thought out plan for introducing a constitution, it was a grossly irresponsible statement. The Emperor was, however, in one of his liberal moods. "Governments should stand at the head of movements and put liberal ideas into effect," he pronounced solemnly at a conference held in Aachen in the same year.

Events soon put the Emperor to the test, and when it came to the point, he moved very rapidly in the opposite direction. In 1820 revolts broke out in Spain, Portugal, Naples, and Piedmont; and when the allies held a conference at Troppau to consider the situation, Alexander, to Metternich's surprise and delight, was the leading advocate for intervention to put down the insurgents. From now on, the Holy Alliance was an instrument of reaction. In Alexander's mind, if rulers were bound to be guided by certain Christian principles in relation to their subjects, so were the subjects similarly bound toward their rulers. The fact that their consent had never been sought was irrelevant. "The Emperor is in general so changed that we are now very often in agreement," Metternich noted with relief in his diary at Troppau; and Alexander, once the decision in favor of intervention had been made, wrote to a friend, "God has blessed our intentions because they were pure and because they were based on faith in Him alone."

It was hardly surprising that Alexander progressively lost track of what was happening at home. Yet Russian society was in a ferment. The discontent of the young officers aroused a new interest in politics which spread to the whole of their generation. Men rushed to join clubs and societies of all kinds, provided they could express their views there. The ranks of the semi-secret Masonic movement, which was tolerated by the Emperor because it had until then been a genuinely philanthropic and nonpolitical organization, were now swelled by those who needed a convenient meeting place to do nothing but talk politics. "Only a person who has lived in Russia can understand how difficult it is to express one's opinion in Russian society," wrote Nicolai Turgenev, recalling this period. "In order to speak freely and without fear, not only do you have to shut yourself in a closed circle, you even have to choose with care those who compose it. Only in conditions of this kind can one exchange ideas sincerely. There was therefore an inexpressible charm for us in being able to talk sincerely at our meetings without the fear of being misunderstood or maliciously interpreted."[1] The basis of the Russian state was questioned in these discussions as it had never been before: the Emperor's foreign and domestic policies, the need to remove the great number of German military advisers with whom he always seemed to be surrounded, the abolition of serfdom, and the creation of a constitution were all endlessly debated. The fact that Poland, a conquered territory, should now have a constitution far in advance of the institutions prevailing in Russia was deeply resented.

In 1816 the first action group appeared with the formation of a secret society calling itself the Union of Salvation. A group of thirty officers, led by Alexander Muraviev, Sergei Trubetskoy, and Pavel Pestel began to work out on paper plans for establishing a constitutional monarchy, abolishing serfdom and introducing a number of other reforms. However, they were divided among themselves from the start on the question of whether to proceed by violent or peaceful means. These disagreements led to the dissolution of the union and the creation in 1818 of a larger society with some two hundred members, the Union of Welfare, which was to some extent modeled on the Tugendbund, the German underground movement which had been formed during the French occupation. The declared aims of the union were to work out various social-welfare projects; its secret aim, however, was to set up a republic. Once again there was disagreement over how this should be achieved, and since the society in any case rapidly became unsuitable for effective conspiracy, it too was dissolved two years after its foundation. Colonel Pestel, who had been one of the most active and prominent members of both unions, formed his own secret group, the Southern Society, in the south of Russia, where he was stationed. Pestel, who was a determined advocate of a Russian republic, now began to work out in detail plans for the assassination of the Emperor.

The authorities at first took a complacent attitude toward the secret societies. They knew of their existence and kept the Emperor informed of the leading members, but Alexander's other preoccupations and his reluctance to exercise a repressive hand induced him to turn a blind eye. Then a very unexpected event caused him to turn his attention to Russia, sharply and hurriedly. His own guards regiment, the Semenovsky, which was stationed in Saint Petersburg, suddenly mutinied.

The Semenovsky Regiment had fought a brilliant campaign in Europe, and under the command of a group of enlightened and liberal officers it had led the way during the European war in introducing certain military reforms, such as the abolition of corporal punishment. This was not, however, to everyone's taste. The Grand Duke Nicholas was shocked by what he regarded as the absence of discipline and thought the regiment corrupt. Eventually, in 1820, Colonel Potemkin, the commanding officer, was replaced by a harsh and brutal officer of the Prussian school, Colonel Schwarz, who at once restored corporal punishment and a number of other humiliating penalties. Within six months the regiment was seething with resentment. When Schwarz ordered the flogging of a number of men who were decorated with the Cross of St. George and were therefore traditionally exempt from corporal punishment, the soldiers mutinied, demanding a change of command.

Alexander's reaction shows the extent to which he had lost touch with the reality of the Russian scene. Shocked that the mutiny had taken place in his own regiment, which he had commanded as Grand Duke and which had been present on the dramatic night he succeeded to the throne, he could only attribute it to some influence from outside. From having been complacent about the secret societies, he suddenly became alarmed. The news reached him at Troppau at the end of October, and he immediately wrote to Arakcheev. The letter clearly betrays the Emperor's confusion of thought.

"You can easily imagine what sad feelings this has aroused

in me," he wrote. "It is, you could say, an unheard of incident in our army. It is even sadder that it should have happened in the guards, and for me personally even worse that it should have been the Semenovsky Regiment. Accustomed as I am to speaking to you very frankly, I will tell you that no one in the world will convince me, despite what people are saying, that this action was thought up by the soldiers or that it took place solely as a result of their cruel treatment at the hands of Colonel Schwarz. He was always well known as a good and correct officer and has commanded the regiment honorably. Why should he suddenly have become a barbarian? In my view, there are other reasons behind this. I do not think that the inspiration can have been military, because their soldiers' military training would have induced them to take up their arms, and none of them did. Not a single sword was drawn. All the officers did their best to put an end to the insubordination, but without success. From all this I conclude that it was external incitement. Now, the question arises, from where? It is difficult to say. I admit that I ascribe it to the secret societies, which are extremely displeased, according to the evidence which you and I both have, with our alliance and work at Troppau. It would seem that the aim of the insurrection was to frighten us. If you also take into account the fact that the day chosen was that of the Empress' return to the city, then it seems clear that the intention was to frighten them and thereby to force me to abandon the work at Troppau and return quickly to Saint Petersburg. But with God's will we have averted this and stifled the evil at birth."

Metternich, who was with the Emperor when he received the news, was shrewder in his assessment of the trouble, and although his information was no better than Alexander's, he was surprised at Alexander's exaggerated fears. "The Emperor goes as far as imagining that it is the radicals who have struck this blow in order to intimidate him and to make him return to Saint Petersburg," Metternich wrote. "I do not share his view. It would be a bit much if in Russia the radicals could dispose of whole regiments, but all this proves how much the Emperor has changed."

Although the blame for Schwarz's appointment and for the reprisals which were taken against the unhappy mutineers was firmly laid at Arakcheev's door by his enemies, he had virtually nothing to do with the affair and was as much at a loss to account for it as was the Emperor. In a letter which he wrote to the Grand Duke Constantine in November, he said that although Schwarz had at one time served in the Count Arakcheev Regiment, he did not know him personally. When he replied to Alexander's letter, he chose the soft option of agreeing with his Emperor. "I learned the news at Gruzino, and my first thoughts were for Your Majesty and for the overwhelming distress that this event would cause you," he wrote. "I am in complete agreement with your view that the soldiers themselves are the least guilty and that someone was at work here who has ulterior motives. But who and how? For the general good we need to discover the very origins of the affair. I may be mistaken, but I think that this was an experiment, and we should be careful to see that events of this kind do not recur."[2]

Retribution on the Semenovsky Regiment was harsh. All the units were disbanded and the men sent to join various regiments in different parts of the Empire; the leading mutineers were severely flogged; and Colonel Schwarz was dismissed from the service for having mishandled the situation. But by a stroke of irony their mutiny had made Alexander uneasily conscious of trouble brewing at home that might be as dangerous as the Carbonari in Italy and the other European Jacobins to whom he had been devoting so much attention.

The Emperor returned to Saint Petersburg in the spring of 1821 with a heavy heart.

Arakcheev had been oddly reluctant to exploit to the full the powerful position which the Emperor's prolonged absence from Russia afforded him. Although he had Alexander's complete confidence in all affairs of state, he deliberately restricted most of his activity to creating and running the military colonies. "I am living at Gruzino and in the colony. When you are not there, I have little desire to go to Saint Petersburg. Thank God, little news reaches me here," he wrote to Alexander at Troppau. It was a curious statement from the man who was supposed to be running the country in the absence of the Emperor, yet in 1820 Arakcheev contrived to spend much of his time at Gruzino, from where he was able to make frequent tours of the Novgorod colony. The absence of a strong grip in the capital undoubtedly played its part in allowing tensions to rise and controversies to increase. The reactionaries held sway apparently unchecked, while the mutterings of the young generation of liberal aristocrats grew increasingly loud.

Shortly before Alexander's return to the capital, Speransky was finally released from his exile and received permission to take up residence in Saint Petersburg. The road back had been long and hard. "I have been wandering for nine years and five days," he noted in his diary. From Penza in 1819 he had been nominated governor of Siberia, an appointment which, he confided to Arakcheev, "shook me to the depths of my heart," despite the distinguished nature of the post. Separated from his only child, his much loved daughter, whom he had felt bound to send to Saint Petersburg, he had traveled alone to the far east and energetically began to set right the chaotic administration, which was suffering from the appalling idleness and corruption of the previous governor, Pestel, the father of the budding revolutionary. Able administrator though he was, Speransky was hopeless at managing his own affairs, and his unhappiness was increased by financial worries. He was soon writing to Arakcheev to beg him to organize the sale of his estate in Novgorod province in order to pay his debts. Arakcheev obligingly arranged for the property to be incorporated in the Novgorod colony, and Speransky received one hundred and forty thousand rubles for it.

Speransky's final pardon and return to Saint Petersburg in March, 1821, caused a certain stir. Rumors, which were prompted in part by Arakcheev's own prolonged absences, now went around to the effect that Arakcheev would hand over to Speransky the direction of all civil affairs. Even Speransky hoped that his star might at last be rising; but this was a different world from the one he had known in the halcyon years before the French invasion, and it was unthinkable that he should find his way back into the counsels of the Emperor. Actually he had to be content with a nomination to the legal department of the Council of State.

Alexander's embarrassment at his first meeting with Speransky was painful. Without giving Speransky the chance to do more than bow to him, he poured out a stream of polite greetings and then suddenly asked Speransky whom he had seen on his return to Saint Petersburg. "While awaiting the pleasure of appearing before Your Majesty, I have called on no one except Count Arakcheev," Speransky replied. "But whom do you intend to see?" persisted Alexander unhappily. "I will do whatever Your Majesty orders," said Speransky. "Then I advise you to become as friendly as you can with Count Alexei Andreevich. But I must get back to work; good-bye; see you soon."[3]

Speransky took the hint and kept in close touch with Arakcheev. Bartenkov, an official who worked for both men and admired them both, made a very neat comparison of their qualities in a short sketch: "*Arakcheev* is dependent on others, since he cannot write himself and is uneducated; *Speransky* feels that he needs no one. *Arakcheev* likes to ascribe everything to himself and boasts of his power over the Emperor; *Speransky* likes to criticize old institutions, conceals his learning, and represents everything as being easy. *Arakcheev* takes any opportunity to be severe, and carries out everything he promises; *Speransky* receives all requests kindly, eagerly makes promises but does not often fulfill them, does not like eloquence, and rarely gives praise. *Arakcheev* knows how to assess people's abilities at a glance and takes nothing else into account; *Speransky* often confuses people and is confused by flattery. *Arakcheev* is decisive and likes orderliness; *Speransky* is cautious and often ignores orderliness. *Arakcheev* cannot be forced to do anything; a strong character can make *Speransky* do his bidding. *Arakcheev's* approach is direct; he is self-willed and speaks without choosing his words, sometimes using indecent language. He is quite frank with his subordinates but can be distracted by his temper. *Speransky* sets store by every word and appears to be cold and insincere. *Arakcheev* has difficulty in changing his mind as circumstances require; when someone new appears, *Speransky* can easily change his mind. *Arakcheev* is a churchgoer but has little faith; *Speransky* is God-fearing and goodhearted but rarely goes to church. They both pleased me as unusual people, but I sincerely loved Speransky."[4]

Speransky was invited to Gruzino in May, 1821, and made an extensive tour of the Novgorod colony, with which he professed to be highly impressed. Arakcheev for his part no longer had anything to fear from Speransky and was able to see him in a more dispassionate light. After his guest's carriage had left Gruzino, he turned to Kleinmikhel and exclaimed, "If I had a third of Speransky's mind, I would be a great man!"[5]

Arakcheev was, however, in very poor health, and for the first time in his career he was showing signs of tiredness. In February, 1822, he fainted in the Committee of Ministers and had to be helped home. Alexander was alarmed and sent him to Gruzino to rest, but from there he wrote to the Emperor, "The pain in my chest is still with me. I am hot and sweat, especially in the evenings, and at nights I have been feverish and shivering." Alexander promptly dispatched his own physician, Sir James Wylie, who returned with an adverse report. "The news of your continuing ill health grieves me much," the worried Emperor wrote in May. "Yakov Vassilievich sets great store on your drinking mare's milk and hopes that you are not avoiding it. I place much hope in Almighty God." Voicing his concern to Kleinmikhel, Alexander said, "You cannot know what Arakcheev means to me; he takes everything bad on himself and ascribes everything good to me." Arakcheev wrote to a friend that he was "growing weaker by the hour and melting away like wax," but by the end of the month he was on the road to recovery again. However, severe periods of illness now became a regular feature of Arakcheev's life. "He was always unwell," wrote the doctor of the Novgorod colony, Evropeus. "Apart from his chest, he suffered from the malfunctioning of his whole nervous system, his liver, and his heart. Hence his continual anxiety about his health, his sleepless nights, and his throbbing heart."[6]

The following month he was sufficiently well to receive the Emperor at Gruzino, together with the Grand Duke Nicholas, Prince Volonsky, chief of the Emperor's staff, and a number of foreign diplomats, and to conduct them on a thorough inspection of the Novgorod colony. For Russians and foreigners alike it was an impressive spectacle. "I really don't know how one can fail to be astonished when one compares one bank of the Volkhov with the other, the buildings, roads, bridges, and fields on one side with those on the opposite side," Kochubey wrote to Arakcheev after making a visit of his own a month later. "When I crossed back over the river after riding around the colonies, I thought some turn of the globe had cast me out of civilization into some barbarous land." The Emperor's visit, impeccably stage-managed, as usual, was a success. In every village the proprietors stood before the long barracklike houses as the Emperor rode past, dressed in their uniforms, with their wives and children in Sunday clothes. Only one minor but unfortunate incident suggested that there might be an uncomfortable gap between appearance and reality. As the Emperor proceeded slowly through the houses of one of the villages, Volkonsky, who disliked Arakcheev and was opposed to the colonies in principle, noticed that a roast pig lay on the table of each household. In one house he deftly cut off the pig's tail and put it in his pocket. In the next house the pig had no tail. Taking the tail from his pocket, Volkonsky said to Alexander, "I think this is an old friend" and replaced it on the animal. The Emperor did not see the joke.*

Nothing else marred the visit, which, as the colony's advocates saw it, had struck a powerful blow at the skeptics, who until then had counted the Grand Duke Nicholas among their number. Alexander's adjutant general, Chernyshev, told Arakcheev in a letter that Nicholas was "completely convinced by the undeniable truth, and he has totally changed his attitude to the colonies, to the regret of those who have

* This story is recounted with minor variations in various places. One authority is Robert E. Lee, *The Last Days of Alexander and the First Days of Nicholas,* London, 1854. There are no eyewitness accounts, but whether apocryphal or not, the story is very much in keeping with Volkonsky's character and his known hostility to the military colonies.

tried to push him in the opposite direction." "The results of this inspection are very disagreeable to many people," Chernyshev continued. "Personal observation has made an overwhelming impression; it has destroyed their cunning plans and removed the possibility of their representing things in the light of their own prejudices. Frankly the best way to close the mouths of these people is to show them the truth. Everyone who was with us felt this, and although I was already prejudiced in favor of the new institutions, I could never have imagined what I actually found there."

Alexander had discovered on his return to Russia that opposition to the colonies remained widespread at all levels of society. "Russia and especially Saint Petersburg do not understand their purpose and are opposed to the whole scheme," the Emperor remarked bitterly in an unusual moment of frankness, but he was the more determined to continue with it.[7] Something of a public-relations exercise was mounted. Distinguished men like Speransky, Karamzin, and Kochubey were invited to visit the colonies and make their impressions known. Speransky was pressed into writing a brochure justifying the principles underlying the project, and in 1823 he was also appointed to a commission which was set up to review the work of the colonies and make recommendations for further progress.

On the material side Alexander and Arakcheev had achieved much of which they could justifiably be proud. After the initial difficulties, farm yields in the Novgorod settlements had increased by more than thirty percent. The threat of total poverty, which in bad years could strike any peasant community, had been eliminated. Education, Arakcheev's special interest, was proceeding apace on the basis of the Lancaster system of mass instruction to which Count Tolstoy's society had successfully converted him. The colonists' children were given the name of "cantonists" and put in school at the age of seven for six years' very thorough instruction. Some were sent on to higher institutes, so that the colonies could have their own engineers and architects. In the Novgorod colony Arakcheev even tried publishing a weekly newspaper, which contained philosophical articles and Latin translations written by the colonists, but this venture closed down after the sixth issue. Even in the south, where conditions were more primitive, material progress was startling. The Duc de Raguse described the southern colonies as "a terrestrial paradise." After a journey through the Kherson district, he wrote that "the well-being of the peasants is tangible. The homes are clean and handsome; the livestock is superb. Everything demonstrates a true prosperity."[8]

This progress was achieved only at the price of unremitting effort on the part of Arakcheev and a few close collaborators. For in one vital respect Arakcheev knew that he had failed: the officers who administered the colonies remained fundamentally hostile, inefficient, and in far too many cases corrupt. Count Witt's chief assistant in the south coolly embezzled a quarter of a million rubles from colony funds. Arakcheev alternately cajoled and bullied the officers. He sent them innumerable letters in which he patiently explained their mistakes; at other times he attacked them in public. On one occasion he severely reprimanded a group of officers in front of a gathering of two thousand colonists and ended his tirade by turning to the peasants and exclaiming, "You see how I deal with them." He was forced to follow everything in the smallest detail and once remarked, "I never pay such attention to big questions as I do to small ones. When I find an error, everyone says 'If the Count is concerned with trifles and takes up these mistakes, what must he do in important matters to which, of course, he pays far greater attention?' "

Whether as a result of his weakening health or of the obstruction he was meeting from his officers at every hand, Arakcheev was becoming increasingly irritable. In 1823 he interviewed General Maevsky for an appointment on his staff, and the General found the experience something of an ordeal. He arrived at the house on Liteinaya Street and was led into the hall, "where I waited for half an hour, and then into a reception room, where I again waited for an hour. During the whole of this time I was seized by a feverish trembling." The atmosphere, he wrote, was like that of a secret underground temple in Egypt. "On people's faces you could read only fear. Everyone avoided asking or answering questions, and they all moved to the sound of his little bell. Virtually no one opened his mouth. This was the mysterious abode of a sultan surrounded by his mute servants." When Maevsky was finally received, Arakcheev came straight to the point. "It is not I, but the Emperor himself, who has picked you. I stopped choosing assistants long ago," he remarked bitterly. "I have learned my lesson and I don't want to have to blush for you in front of the Emperor. As far as I am concerned, the Emperor can choose a goat; it's all the same, as long as he does not try to be clever but does what I tell him. You are used to saying 'impossible,' but I demand work, blind obedience, and no cleverness. I also forbid you to listen to excuses from your subordinates. I need work, work, and more work!"[9]

Maevsky worked very closely with Arakcheev in the ensuing twelve months on the establishment of a new colony at Staraya Russa, near the other colonies in Novgorod province. He soon became aware of Arakcheev's feeling of isolation and jealousy of the remaining advisers close to the Emperor. "How can I be the equal of people of today's education; they are all cleverer than me," Arakcheev would say. "They are Gogs and Magogs. But I have one advantage over them. I am devoted to the Emperor with all my soul and, of course, will never let him down."

Nonetheless, Arakcheev was finding the colonies an increasingly heavy burden. Already they numbered over a million men, women, and children, and when Alexander proposed that yet another colony be established near Yaroslavl, Arakcheev grumbled to Maevsky, "I don't know why the Emperor wants to open another colony in Yaroslavl province. Why is he in such a hurry? He is young and strong-willed. But I am old and shan't live to see the completion of all these things he has started. I am already worn out by this work. I only took on the colony at Staraya Russa because it is nearby. But I shall not take on Yaroslavl, not for anything. I would rather resign than have to cope with that. It would destroy the fruit of my labors over the last seventeen years and the fame of our colonies. I like to inspect everything with my own eyes, but how can I gallop to Yaroslavl and Kherson when I am up to my eyes in the affairs of the entire state?"

Arakcheev was now at the height of his power. If anyone still had doubts about his unrivaled position, they were dispelled by the changes which took place in 1823. One by one Alexander's old friends either retired from the scene or were deprived of their influence. Prince Volkonsky resigned as Chief of Staff after a dispute with Arakcheev over army estimates. Prince Kochubey went on leave, and his place as Minister of the Interior was taken by Baron Kampenhausen, a close friend of Arakcheev's. Another of Arakcheev's protégés, Kankrin, was appointed Minister of Finance. Only Volkonsky's replacement, General Diebich, was an opponent, but Alexander's instructions to Diebich were firm. "You will find Arakcheev an uneducated man but hard-working and devoted to me," he told the general. "Try to get on with him and be friends. You will frequently have to work with him, so show him all possible trust and respect."[10]

The changes brought no comfort to the liberals. Arakcheev's comment was that he wanted to put efficiency and experience in the place of distinguished windbags, but this was not how his contemporaries saw the new ministers. "During the last years of Alexander's reign a powerless gerontocracy slumbered at the helm of the state," Vigel recalled in his memoirs. "The old men . . . seemed like ministers' ghosts rather than ministers. All business was dealt with by their subordinates, each in his own department, without any semblance of unity. Only the hateful Arakcheev kept awake for them all."[11] Yet despite the preeminence of the reactionaries, the closing years of Alexander's life were marked not so much by despotism as by a lack of firm government. The period was subsequently baptised the "Arakcheevshchina," but in the absence of orders from above, Arakcheev did not carry out the policy of general repression which his contemporaries attributed to him. The Emperor himself had lost control of a situation which he only half understood, while Arakcheev remained absorbed in his work with the colonies.

It was a critical time for the throne and for Russia, and Alexander's own deficiencies emphasized his need for guidance from someone with a clear enough eye to see that the situation was bound to deteriorate further if energetic measures were not taken, whether they were repressive, liberal, or some combination of the two. Never were Arakcheev's limited education, his lack of interest in ideas, and his administrative conception of government a greater handicap to his country than now. He held the key position in the state during a decade which demanded statesmanship of the highest order, but he did not attempt to counsel the Emperor on the grave political issues facing the throne. At a time when his least word had the force of law, he remained a shadowy figure. Kochubey wrote complainingly to Speransky that, "if only there could be some change in our administration and Count Arakcheev would call himself Prime Minister without more ado, I would perhaps agree to stay on as a minister. . . . If you have the chance, you might tell Count Arakcheev how much I wish he would make himself Prime Minister." Most people thought that Arakcheev's chief preoccupation was to find ways of isolating Alexander still further from society and from the government. Indeed, only one man now remained in the Emperor's close confidence apart from Arakcheev himself, Prince Alexander Golitsyn, the Chief Procurator and Minister of Education and Spiritual Affairs; and, for the first and only time in his life, Arakcheev resorted to intrigue in order to achieve a rival's disgrace.

Golitsyn was a close personal friend of Alexander. The two had known each other since childhood. Golitsyn had led a dissipated life in Saint Petersburg society until in 1803 Alexander unexpectedly appointed him Chief Procurator of the Holy Synod. The office was an incongruous one for a young man of his limited education and talents, but the appointment had an even more unlikely result. The Prince's duties naturally brought him into close contact with the Church, and overnight he became a convinced Christian, eager to impart his suddenly discovered faith to his friends. Largely ignorant as he was of Orthodox teaching, Golitsyn's faith took the form of a sentimental, mystical piety with which he eventually infected Alexander himself. When a Quaker representative of the British Bible Society arrived in Saint Petersburg in the traumatic year of 1812, Golitsyn received him with open arms and encouraged him to establish a branch of the society in the capital. Golitsyn himself became president of the Russian Bible Society, which was founded a short while later, and the Emperor, who had in any case acquired the habit of spending many hours in prayer and Bible reading under Golitsyn's influence, soon became a member. "May the Supreme Being bless this enterprise," Alexander wrote to Golitsyn in January, 1813. "I think it is of the greatest importance and believe that you are quite right when you say that the Holy Scriptures will take the place of the prophets."

The Bible societies became very popular in the postwar years. The distinguished patronage in the capital was enough to ensure that many branches were opened in the provinces. Not only did the enthusiasts discuss ways and means of spreading literacy to encourage widespread reading of the scriptures, but they openly advocated a return to the study of the Bible as the true path to God. This development was viewed with the gravest alarm by the Orthodox Church, which not without reason saw the new brand of religion as a direct threat to its own position. The Church's attacks on the Bible societies became increasingly violent. In a remarkable speech to the Moscow Bible Society, Metropolitan Seraphim declared that Satan was sowing freethinking, disbelief, and depravity everywhere. "In order to succeed even faster in his undertaking, he is casting his hellish darkness in the shape of enlightenment and high spiritual qualities. And what is the fruit of this teaching and enlightenment?" thundered Seraphim. "License and disobedience to the authority established by God himself for the good of society. Sedition, rebellion, internal strife, murder, and blood and tears flowing in torrents. All this we can see here on earth. And in eternity? There the deathless worm, the inextinguishable fire, a wailing, and gnashing of teeth lie in wait for the slaves and followers of enlightenment. Such is the fruit of this devilish learning and wisdom."[12]

The Orthodox leaders found strong support for their case among the extreme nationalists like Shishkov and Magnitsky, Speransky's former assistant, who were determined to eradicate all Western influence and were at the time engaged in organizing a thorough purge of the universities to which the Emperor was as usual turning a blind eye. "Why do we want changes in our laws, our customs, and our ways of thought?" wrote Shishkov. "Where do these changes come from? They are inspired by the institutions of those countries where upheavals, excitement, insolent ideas, and an excess of learning under the guise of freedom of thought hold sway and arouse naked passions."

The tide mounted against the Bible societies, and Golitsyn as their president became increasingly isolated. This fact was not lost on Arakcheev, but he knew that it would need a dramatic blow to shake Alexander's confidence in his friend, or at least to persuade him that Golitsyn must be dropped in the interests of the state. In 1823 a grotesque weapon fell into Arakcheev's hands in the shape of an eccentric monk, the Archimandrite Photius.

Photius, like Rasputin later, was one of those theatrical and hypnotic characters whom the Russian Orthodox Church occasionally throws up, as if to herald some approaching cataclysm. After his appointment as a teacher to the Saint Petersburg cadet corps, his pallid, emaciated features became a familiar sight in Saint Petersburg. His fasting exploits were well known, and he made no secret in society or elsewhere of his desperate and frequent struggles with sexual demons who were in the habit of visiting him in the guise of women. When Photius in his old age dictated his memoirs, the satanic encounters of his earliest youth came back to him with remarkable clarity and anything but tranquillity. Thus he recounted how one night he was lying on the floor of his father's hut near a young girl who was a distant relative. Neither of them could sleep. "Petr could feel her drawing close to him. He could hear by her breathing that little by little the young girl was drawing gradually nearer with her face and her breasts, until she was pressed right against him from head to foot. The boy could feel that she was burning with passion . . . the girl, lying next to him so quietly was burning with the fire of the flesh, and groaning as if wearied by her passion . . . she was trying silently to take refuge in him with her body in order to set him alight."[13]

As early as 1817 Photius began to say that he was preparing to oust the enemies of the church. In 1820 he pronounced a fiery attack on the members of the Bible societies in the Kazan cathedral of Saint Petersburg, for which he was banished from the capital, but shortly afterward he was brought back at the request of a well-known society figure, Countess Anna Orlova-Chesmenskaya, an immensely rich heiress who was said to have a personal fortune of some forty-five million rubles and at the age of thirty was still unmarried. Famed for her ability to ride like a cavalry officer and dance like a ballerina, she was equally energetic in her religious exercises and devoted much of her time to prayer and good works. Her first personal encounter with Photius was typical of both of them. He entered the room, where she received him "dressed in white like an angel," but he averted his eyes and sat beside her with his face turned away. Countess Orlova asked him how she could preserve her spiritual purity, to which Photius returned that it was essential for her to keep her physical virginity, since the soul and body were inseparable. After some further talk along these lines, they both repaired to Countess Orlova's bedroom, where Photius blessed her bed and they knelt in prayer. Quite conquered, she regarded herself from then on as his worldly benefactress and spiritual daughter. The gossips of Saint Petersburg said that she was a good deal more. They told the story of an attractive actress from one of the Saint Petersburg theaters who asked Photius to chase evil spirits from her. He set to work so ardently that he found himself in a situation of great temptation, and Countess Orlova, who was beside herself with despair, had to offer the girl half her fortune to leave him. Photius had an effective repertoire of dramatic techniques. When Magnitsky was first introduced to him at Orlova's house, Photius met him holding two wax candles and without uttering a word led him to a chair. The two men sat for some minutes in silence. Then Photius suddenly seized a bell and began to ring it in a frenzy.

With the coming together of Photius and Magnitsky, who had long wanted to succeed to Golitsyn's duties, and the transfer of Metropolitan Seraphim from Moscow to Saint Petersburg in 1822, the opposition to Golitsyn began to crystallize. Gradually all those who for different reasons were interested in bringing about the Prince's disgrace began to meet more regularly at Countess Orlova's house. Seraphim, Magnitsky, and Photius were in frequent conclave, although Arakcheev contented himself with watching events develop. Golitsyn himself suspected nothing. Indeed, he had been so impressed by Photius that in July, 1822, he arranged for the monk to have a private interview with the Emperor, in the course of which Photius began to inveigh against the Bible societies. This had no result, however, and some months later Seraphim took the next step by provoking a violent quarrel with Golitsyn in the Synod, which ended with the Prince seizing his hat in a fury and walking out.

At a hurried council of war, in which Arakcheev took part,

it was decided that the time had come for Seraphim to demand of the Emperor that he dismiss Golitsyn. This was not, however, a task which the prelate greatly relished, and he took some persuading. Twice he mounted his carriage and twice descended again before he could be persuaded to set off for the Winter Palace, with Magnitsky following behind to ensure that he arrived there safely. Once in the presence of the Emperor, Seraphim's courage returned. He laid his cowl at Alexander's feet and declared that he would not take it back until Golitsyn had been dismissed. Armed with the proofs of a work written by the German pastor Gossner, which had been pilfered on the eve of publication by Magnitsky, Seraphim strengthened his case by arguing that in his role as chief censor, Golitsyn was allowing the spread of atheistic ideas. The embarrassed Alexander asked for time to have Gossner's work studied and took refuge in a policy of immobilism.

Temporarily baffled, the conspirators split up, and Photius retired to the Yurev monastery near Novgorod, of which he was now Father Superior. He continued to write messages to the Emperor, and Arakcheev made sure that they reached their destination. "God has shown me the way to salvation and has said that Arakcheev can undertake everything and that he is true," one of the messages runs. "I was shown this about him when I saw you in my vision." In another Photius declaimed, "know, great Czar, that the Lord has always shown me everything, and always will. There will be no misfortune if you heed the Lord, who speaks to you through me."[14]

Whether it was advice of this kind or Arakcheev's influence which made Alexander decide to see Photius again is not clear. But at the beginning of April, 1824, Arakcheev sent a message to the monastery requesting the monk to come at once to Saint Petersburg. In another long interview Photius reiterated his former charges and asked for Golitsyn's dismissal. Once again the Emperor appeared to hesitate. But by this time Photius was thoroughly worked up. On his return to Countess Orlova's house he sent a message to the unsuspecting Golitsyn asking him to call. On his arrival the Prince was greeted by an enraged Photius, who stood between an icon and an open Bible and dramatically demanded Golitsyn's repentance for his sins against the Church. Astounded and outraged, Golitsyn refused. Photius then solemnly pronounced a curse on him: "Anathema! You will be damned!"[15]

When Countess Orlova returned home, she was met by the spectacle of Photius galloping around her home in a paroxysm of delight. The scandalous news traveled quickly around the city, and the curse was confirmed for good measure by Metropolitan Seraphim. The Minister of Spiritual Affairs had in effect been excommunicated from the Church, and Golitsyn had no choice but to resign, retaining only the derisory portfolio of Minister of Posts. Alexander summoned Photius and vented his anger at the monk's conduct. Photius emerged from the interview "soaked in sweat from head to foot." The damage, however, was done, and the Orthodox party had triumphed. The Ministry of Spiritual Affairs was subsequently abolished, and although the Emperor refused to dissolve the Bible societies, they were put firmly in the hands of the Church with the ironical appointment of Metropolitan Seraphim as the new president. Pastor Gossner was deported, and his book was burned. Admiral Shishkov, who had been in charge of the inquiry into Gossner's work, was appointed Minister of Education.

Arakcheev had shown considerable skill in remaining in the background as he firmly guided the plot which led to this scandal. Alexander was grieved that Golitsyn should have been so unjustly victimized, but there was no hint of reproach in his conduct toward Arakcheev. Yet Arakcheev was clearly very much involved in the final act. Photius himself knew perfectly well to whom he owed his success. He returned again to the Yurev monastery, and shortly afterwards he wrote to a fellow Archimandrite, "Pray for Alexei Andreevich Arakcheev. Like St. George, he has acted as God's servant in the cause of the holy faith and Church. May God watch over him!" Meanwhile, Arakcheev made peace between the Emperor and Photius. He left Alexander in little doubt of his own admiration and affection for the monk, and the Emperor met Photius again twice in the following year.

Arakchcev's participation in a cabal to oust a rival was most uncharacteristic. But it seemed that now as a result of the years of power he would stop at nothing to maintain or improve his position. Golitsyn had not been a serious rival at all; his competence had been in a sphere which was without interest to Arakcheev and scarcely impinged on his responsibilities. However, Arakcheev had always been chronically jealous of anyone who found favor with Alexander. In 1822, when the Emperor had been particularly gracious to General Kiselev after military inspection, Arakcheev, meeting the General for the first time, said sarcastically, "The Emperor has told me how pleased he is with you, Pavel Dmitrievich. He is so content with you that I should like to learn from Your Excellency how to please his Majesty. Allow me to come and do so in the Second Army. It would be even better if Your Excellency were to take me on as your adjutant."[16]

Golitsyn's fall created a great stir in Saint Petersburg and increased the awe and fear with which Arakcheev was regarded. He was already a legendary figure of terror among the peasants in the colonies, the subject of innumerable poems and stories.* There was something almost supernatural about this lonely and sinister figure who with every passing day seemed to have the Emperor increasingly under his influence. "I am only sorry that it will be a long time before the Emperor learns of all the atrocious and, to an honest man, intolerable actions perpetrated by this villain; the Emperor's incomprehensible blindness toward him makes it impossible to convince the Emperor of them," wrote Volkonsky, who since his own dismissal had become increasingly hysterical about Arakcheev. "He inspired me with instinctive fear," recalled the Grand Duchess Alexandra Feodorovna, wife of the Emperor's brother Nicholas, and her sentiment was a general one; "everyone was afraid of this man," the Empress Elizaveta Alexeevna wrote in her memoirs. He was nicknamed "the serpent-Gorynich."†

Everyone knew by heart a poem written by Ryleev, entitled *The Favorite*, which had been published in 1820; the first lines ran:

> Arrogant favorite, villainous and cunning,
> Subtle flatterer of the monarch and ungrateful friend,
> Unrestrained tyrant of your native land,
> Scoundrel, brought to high rank by your intrigues.
> You dare to cast a scornful look at me,
> And to show your fierce anger with a threatening glance.
> Villain, your attentions mean nothing to me.
>
> Some wicked fate may watch over you, villain,
> And shelters you from just vengeance,
> Yet tremble tyrant! Your evil and treachery
> Will still be condemned by posterity.

When these lines appeared in print, a contemporary wrote,

* Some of these are contained in Appendix II.
† A folk serpent which appears in many Russian fairy tales.

"It is impossible to imagine the amazement and horror of the people of Saint Petersburg and the stupor into which some of them were thrown by these unheard of strains of truth and reproach. Everyone thought that punishment would thunder down, destroying the insolent poet and those who had incited him. But the portrait was too true for the insulted favorite to dare see himself in the satire. He was ashamed to admit the truth, and the cloud passed by."[17]

Arakcheev was certainly conscious of his unpopularity. His reaction, as always, was to show his own contempt for the society which hated and feared him by flouting its conventions. He was never willing to speak French, the language of the court and aristocracy, and this alone was enough to set him apart. There was also numerous tales of his outrageous public behavior. On one occasion he had arrived at the house of his friend General Aprelev, in order to play boston, his favorite card game. Prince Lopukhin, the president of the State Council, was his usual partner, but the old Prince had sent a message to say that he was unwell and would be absent. "What nonsense," exclaimed Arakcheev. "The old man has become lazy. Send for him." A short while later Lopukhin appeared and sat down to cards. But hardly had he picked up his hand when Arakcheev called to one of the guests, "Will you play in my place? I don't really feel like it tonight," and stalked out.

He could be equally unconventional on state occasions. Senator Fisher recalled how he saw Arakcheev in July, 1824, at an evening party on the terrace of the Peterhof Palace. An elegant crowd was watching a fireworks display given in honor of the Dowager Empress, Maria Feodorovna. "The whole terrace was crowded with people, and the only unoccupied place was at the balustrade near a tall old man wearing a crumpled officer's cap and a threadbare military greatcoat. My sister, Madame Villiers, was attractive. An adjutant general in full uniform, whom I had not noticed standing behind the shabby old man, took my hand, and stopping me, said, 'Not here.' But the old man, looking at this seventeen-year-old beauty, said, 'Leave them,' and we were left alone. Then I noticed that standing behind the man, who was wearing the only officer's cap and greatcoat to be seen in the park that evening, was not one general, but three. Perplexed, I looked at the man more attentively. He had a rough, unpleasant soldier's face with a crooked mouth, and a crooked back. He began to make jokes in a nasal voice. I do not remember what he said, but I muttered to my sister, 'Let's go,' and took her away from this privileged company. The man turned to me with a cynical smile, and the generals stared at me with a mixture of astonishment and curiosity. He was Arakcheev, the Vice-Emperor, if not more. The Emperor was in the park in his uniform and epaulets, and his whole suite were in court dress, while Arakcheev was dressed like a batman coming away from the baths."[18]

Arakcheev was successful in many of his designs in 1824, but the year also brought sharp disappointment over his son's career. Shumsky was by this time a source of continual anxiety. Arakcheev had done all he could for him; in 1822 the young officer had been appointed A.D.C. to the Emperor, and Arakcheev often took him with him when he had papers to read to Alexander, on the grounds that he was too shortsighted to read them out himself. Yet Shumsky continued to drink very heavily, and when Arakcheev sent for him at short notice to appear before the Emperor, his brother officers had on occasion to pour several buckets of cold water over his head in order to sober him up. Nonetheless, Arakcheev persevered. He associated Shumsky with much of his work in the colonies, and when the colony at Staraya Russa was opened in March, 1824, Arakcheev wrote to the Emperor, "I am sending you my report, sir, with my ward, Lieutenant Shumsky, of the Guards Horse Artillery. He was present in person in every place where the ukase was read. I am bringing him up to take the place of a son, if God will it, and I hope that he will be a true servant of the Emperor."[19]

However, only three months later public disgrace overtook Shumsky. In July Alexander paid a visit to Gruzino and then embarked with Arakcheev on what had by now become an annual inspection of the Novgorod colony. Shumsky, who had been sent on ahead, was far from sober when the royal party arrived to inspect the Count Arakcheev Regiment. As the Emperor was taking the report of the regimental commander on the square, it suddenly occurred to Shumsky that he too should be reporting to the Emperor. He lurched forward on his horse, but before he had moved ten paces, he fell heavily to the ground, breaking his saber and badly bruising his left eye. The Emperor exclaimed in astonishment and annoyance, "Shumsky, I have been riding for thirty years and have never once fallen from my horse." The next day Arakcheev said to Alexander, "Sir, I have a complaint to make. Your A.D.C. is playing the fool." "Do whatever you like with him, Count," replied the Emperor ill-humoredly, and Arakcheev sent Shumsky back to Gruzino in disgrace.

As the end of the year approached, Alexander's despondency increased. Conscious of the growing unrest in his country and the disappointments he had caused, he recalled more and more often the high hopes of the beginning of his reign. Although there was talk everywhere of plots, he seemed incapable of stirring himself. Two years previously he had finally brought himself to issue a decree dissolving Masonic lodges and all secret societies, but the measure had not been effectively enforced, and the societies were still flourishing.

When the commander of the Corps of Guards, Vassilchikov, handed him a list of the members of one illegal society, Alexander is said to have remarked, "You have served me from the beginning of my reign, and you know that I have shared and encouraged these illusions and errors." Then, after a heavy silence, he apparently added, "I have not the right to be harsh."[20]

In June Alexander had been greatly affected by the death of his illegitimate daughter, Sophie Narishkina, which he saw as a sign from heaven. At the end of the year there was a great flood in Saint Petersburg; two-thirds of the town was under water, in some places to a depth of eighteen feet, and many people perished. When Alexander was visiting the scene of the worst disaster, someone in the crowd called out, "God is punishing us for our sins." "No, for mine," the Emperor answered sadly. Accurately judging his master's mood, Arakcheev wrote him an unctuous letter from Gruzino, "I could not sleep all night because I knew how much Your Majesty must now be suffering from yesterday's misfortune. But of course God sometimes sends these misfortunes in order that those whom he has chosen may show their compassion and care for the suffering. Your Majesty is sure to do so in the present case. Money is needed at once to aid the poor, not the rich. Your subjects must help you, and I therefore venture to send you my thoughts. Your wise dispositions and my small labors have created a fairly large capital for the military colonies. I have never even asked for my expenses to be taken from it; now I request as a personal reward that a million rubles be taken from this capital to assist the poor." Alexander replied, "Our thoughts completely coincided, my dear Alexei Andreevich. Your letter was an untold consolation to me. . . . Come tomorrow and arrange everything."[21]

However, even graver matters awaited the Emperor. In

June, 1825, Alexander returned from a short trip to Poland, to be greeted with the news that the conspiracy in the army stationed in the south of Russia was far more widespread than had hitherto been believed and that it was showing signs of coming to a head. The source of the information was Lieutenant Sherwood, a young officer of English origin who was serving on the staff of the Kherson military colony. Sherwood had become increasingly disturbed by the seditious talk among the officers in the south and wrote a letter to the Emperor, which he entrusted to Sir James Wylie. As a result, Sherwood was summoned by Arakcheev to Gruzino, but since in his view the reasons for the plot lay mainly in the shortcomings of the military colonies, he tactfully refused to speak. Arakcheev sent him on to the Emperor, who heard him out in the course of a long interview. When he finished, Alexander asked him wearily, "What do these people want? Are things really so bad for them?"[22]

Sherwood's interpretation of the Southern Society's activities in terms of unrest in the military colonies was entirely erroneous, but he had touched the Emperor at one of his most sensitive points, and Alexander was at last inclined to take action. He asked Sherwood to write down everything he knew and then sent him back to wait at Gruzino while his report was considered. There he lunched every day with Nastasia Minkina and dined with Arakcheev, who poured out his wine and asked him to converse in English with Shumsky. Finally his instructions arrived from the capital. Sherwood was given a year's leave and told to find out all the details of the plot. At the end of July he set off for the suoth, having arranged for Arakcheev to send a reliable messenger to meet him and receive his first report at a post station in the town of Karachev on September 20. "Well, look out, Sherwood, don't fall on your face in the mud," said Arakcheev as the officer took his leave.

Arakcheev himself was relatively unconcerned by Sherwood's tale. Perhaps he had heard too many similar stories before, and the young officer, who was apt to talk rather wildly, did not appear to be a very reliable witness. In fact, Arakcheev was in unusually good spirits. "I can see that God loves me," he said to General Maevsky that summer. "I cannot think of anything which could make me unhappy. My Gruzino and the garden bring me joy at every moment."

8
Tragedy on the Volkhov

Lord, be merciful to those who hate me and abuse me. Grant that none of them suffer for my sake either in this life or the next, but show them your mercy and bestow on them prosperity.—PRAYER COMPOSED BY ARAKCHEEV

At the beginning of September, 1825, Arakcheev was visited at Gruzino by the commander of the Second army, General Wittgenstein, with whom he had arranged to make a tour of the Novgorod colonies. Early on the morning of Sunday, September 6, the little party, which included the Emperor's chief of staff, General Diebich, Dr. Daller, Arakcheev's personal physician, and Shumsky, set off to visit the Count Arakcheev Regiment.

The atmosphere had become very tense at Gruzino during the summer of 1825. Nastasia Minkina was devoted as always to Arakcheev, but with every passing month her behavior with the serfs was more neurotic and cruel; her own servants bore the brunt of this, and during Arakcheev's frequent absences she would punish them savagely for the slightest misdemeanor. If Arakcheev was aware of her conduct, he never questioned it; indeed, it was common knowledge among the serfs that he would deal with them even more severely for what he regarded as offenses against Nastasia.

Nastasia's three young maids, Praskovya, Tatanya, and Feodosya, were the most frequent victims of their mistress's heavy hand. She was jealous of their youth and looks, and particularly of Praskovya, a pretty girl of seventeen, whom she lost no opportunity to torment. Two years before, Praskovya had persuaded her brother, Vassili Antonov, who worked in the kitchens, to put some poison herbs in Nastasia's food, but although Nastasia had been taken ill, she swiftly recovered. The maids had resorted to other equally unsuccessful expedients, such as placing certain grasses under Nastasia's mattress in an effort to soften her character. Their chief ally was the wife of the serf manager in the Gruzino community bank, Darya Konstantinova, an older woman who had fallen foul of Nastasia on an earlier occasion and had as a result been sent for a time to work in the laundry of a military orphanage in Saint Petersburg. Darya Konstantinova was full of suggestions for ridding Gruzino of Nastasia. When the butler committed suicide in August after Nastasia had threatened to report him to Arakcheev for the chaotic state in which she had found the cellar, Darya Konstantinova offered Vassili Antonov five hundred rubles to kill their mistress. Antonov hesitated; at one moment he talked of accepting the offer and then fleeing to join the army, at another he would agree on condition that his sister would afterward admit to having done the murder herself.*

* There are various accounts of the murder of Nastasia, which gave rise to much hearsay. The fullest account, drawing all the sources together, is an article by V. D. Filosofov, in *Russkaya Starina*, March, 1884. A good description of the illegalities of the trial is to be found in A. Neustroev in *Russkaya Starina*, 1871. But the most valuable is Arakcheev's own account, which he dictated to Shumsky for the Emperor. This was discovered by Shilder, and is printed in *Russkaya Starina*, April, 1900.

Nastasia was in a particularly ugly temper after Arakcheev's departure on the Sunday for the Novgorod colonies. The next day she had Praskovya beaten twice and put the other two maids in the house jail. Shumsky returned to Gruzino on Tuesday and found his mother unusually moody and upset. He spent Wednesday with her, but he was not feeling well himself, and toward the end of the day he retired to his bed in another part of the house, leaving Nastasia alone in her rose-painted cottage, which stood at the end of one of the wings of the house, and where Praskovya and another maid also slept.

Nastasia woke at five on Thursday morning. She called for Praskovya and asked her to check whether work had begun in the garden. Praskovya sent her companion off to do this, and when she returned to her mistress carrying a clean dress, she found that Nastasia had fallen asleep again. With her body still aching from the beating, she suddenly decided that the moment had come to strike. She ran across the courtyard to the kitchens and begged Antonov, who had been infuriated by his sister's recent punishment, to act immediately, on the condition that she would take the responsibility. Antonov picked up a large knife and followed her back to the cottage. Taking off his shoes, he crept into Nastasia's room. A small dog by the bed began to bark furiously and was hastily carried out by Praskovya as Antonov aimed a blow at Nastasia, missing her throat but seriously wounding her in the cheek. She woke at once and threw herself on the floor screaming for help. A terrible struggle followed, during which Nastasia lost two fingers as she attempted to grab the knife. Antonov stabbed at her face and her throat again and again, until finally she resisted no longer. Then he fled from her mutilated body, leaving his knife behind in his haste.

Apparently no one heard Nastasia's cries, although people

were already up, and the double panes had not yet been put in the windows for the winter. Eventually Praskovya's hysterical sobbing attracted attention, and the terrible scene was discovered. Although Arakcheev was expected back that evening, it was clear that he must be informed at once. However, many people were afraid of what his reaction would be and felt that it would be preferable to break the news to him gradually. Shishkin, the bailiff, was dispatched to the Novgorod colony, some thirty kilometers away, with the message that Nastasia was desperately ill and that he should return at once.

It had been a bad morning for the Count Arakcheev Regiment. Arakcheev was very dissatisfied with the lack of progress in some building work he had commissioned, and in his fury he personally locked the engineer, Captain Shishkov, and some junior officers in the guardroom, and walked away with the keys in his pocket. At this point Shishkin arrived with his news, which he gave first to Dr. Daller. Daller spoke to the regimental commander, Von Friken, who ran white-faced after Arakcheev and passed him the message. The shock was immediate. Arakcheev's face, distorted with grief, betrayed his premonition of a catastrophe; he ordered his carriage at once and set off with Von Friken and the doctor for Gruzino.

The towers of Gruzino were already in sight when Arakcheev's speeding carriage met one of the men from the estate, Captain Kafka. Arakcheev ordered a halt and called out, "How is Nastasia Fedorovna?" Not realizing that the whole truth had not yet been revealed to him, Kafka replied, "There was no help, Your Excellency. Her head was only hanging on by the skin." For a moment Arakcheev froze; then with a dreadful cry he flung himself from his carriage onto the grass, tearing at his hair and at the ground. Throwing himself about, he shouted wildly, "You have killed her, kill me too, kill me, and kill me quickly." His companions stood around him aghast at this uncontrolled display of grief. They saw the most feared man in Russia suddenly reduced to a pitiful creature, writhing in anguish at their feet, and did not know what to do. With difficulty they at last helped him back to the carriage and hastened on to the house. On his arrival, Arakcheev rushed to Nastasia's room, where he flung himself weeping onto her body, soaking his clothes in her blood.

Von Friken at once placed all the house servants under arrest until the innocent could be separated from the real suspects. Arakcheev continued to lie in a stupor in Nastasia's bloodstained and disordered room while Daller prepared the body for burial, assisted by one or two servants, including the guilty Antonov, who had unaccountably decided to brazen out the affair on the assumption that his sister's admission of guilt would be taken at its face value. Meanwhile, Photius, who had been summoned by Shumsky, hurried over from Yurev monastery to console Arakcheev and conduct the burial. The priest at Gruzino had already taken the precaution of ascertaining from the ecclesiastical authorities in Novgorod whether, in view of the circumstances of Nastasia's life and death, she could be buried in the church. On his arrival, Photius told Arakcheev that there were no obstacles to this, but Arakcheev was so furious that such an inquiry should have been made at all that he roused himself to exclaim, "Not only is there no room for that priest in Siberia, there is no place for him on this earth!"[1]

Arakcheev continued to display the most extravagant marks of grief. He refused to eat or shave and wore around his neck a handkerchief stained with Nastasia's blood. As her coffin was lowered into a grave beside the one that he had prepared for himself years before, he ran forward and bent over it, crying out, "Kill me, you villains! You have taken my only friend from me. Now I have lost everything." The following day he wrote a note to the Emperor. "The disaster which has overtaken me, the loss of the true friend who lived in my house for twenty-five years, has so destroyed my health and reason that I want only to die, and am incapable of dealing with any official business. Farewell, sir; do not forget your former servant. My friend was stabbed at night by the servants, and I do not yet know where to put my orphaned head, but I shall go away from here." At the same time he took the quite illegal step of handing over his military duties to a member of his staff in the colonies, and his civil responsibilities to State Secretary Muraviev.

Alexander was in the south at Taganrog, a small town on the Sea of Azov, where he had accompanied his wife, whose worsening health necessitated spending the autumn and winter months in a warm climate. General Diebich hurried down with the news of the tragedy. Alexander immediately assumed that Nastasia had not been killed because of hatred toward herself but as part of some plot to remove Arakcheev from office. When he heard that Arakcheev himself had handed over his command of the colonies, the Emperor was not pleased. However, Diebich later reported, "He told me that he forgave Arakcheev on account of his sick condition. Of course, no one else could have taken such an illegal step without being reproved, but this man is an exception to the general rule."

Alexander was in fact deeply upset by Arakcheev's misfortune. He dispatched Kleinmikhel, whom he knew to be an efficient operator as well as a close friend of Arakcheev's, to investigate the affair on the spot, and wrote Arakcheev a letter on September 22 in which he combined a sermon with a full expression of his own disquiet. "In my heart, I can feel everything which you must be experiencing. But, my friend, despair is a sin before God. Give yourself up blindly to His sacred will. He is the only joy, the only peace which I can offer you in this misfortune. I am convinced that there is no other.

"I sincerely share your grief, although I did not know and never saw the person you are mourning. But she was a true and old friend of yours, and that is enough for her loss to be grievous to you. To think of her meeting her end in that way is frightful. I can well imagine everything you must have been through. Even my own health has been much shaken by it. But I say again, with the strongest feeling of affection for you, despair is a sin, and a major sin. Subjection to the will of the Almighty is our general duty, and the greater our grief,. the more humbly we should bow our heads in obedience to His holy will. Obey, and God himself will support you and give you strength.

"You write that you wish to leave Gruzino, but do not know where to go. Come here; you have no friend who is fonder of you. This place is isolated. You can live here as you like. Talking with a friend who shares your grief will do something to calm it. But I beg you by all that is sacred to remember your country, and how valuable—I can even say essential—your services are to it, and that the state and I are indistinguishable from each other. You are vital to me. I am far from wanting you to continue to work in your first period of sorrow. Give yourself the time necessary to collect your spiritual and bodily strength, but remember how much you have accomplished and what has been entrusted to you. I earnestly beseech God to give you the fortitude and health as well as the resolution to obey His sacred will."

Alexander wrote at the same time to Photius, the one man who he felt might bring Arakcheev some consolation. "All the news reaching me is of the deep depression bordering on despair in which Count Alexei Andreevich has fallen as a result of the disaster. Knowing the great respect which he has for your spiritual qualities, I am sure that with God's help you can influence him. Give him strength, and you will be doing a great service to the state and to myself, since Count Arakcheev's services are most precious to his country. A Christian must bear with humility the blows which he receives from the hand of God."[2]

Arakcheev wrote back thanking the Emperor for his comfort but declining the invitation to Taganrog on account of his weak health. "The throbbing of my heart, a daily fever, three weeks without a night's rest, grief, depression, and despair have all made me so weak that I have lost my memory entirely and can no longer remember what I have said and done for whole hours at a time. . . . If you could see me in my present state you would not recognize your faithful servant. Such is the lot of man in this world; it is in God's power to change his condition at any moment." He did, however, summon enough strength to dictate to Shumsky an account of the murder such as could be pieced together from the preliminary investigation. He then sent it privately to Alexander.

In the report he consoled himself with a lyrical evocation of his former life with Nastasia. "For twenty-two years she slept on the ground at the threshold of my bedroom, but for the last five years I asked her to use a camp bed," he recounted. "If ever I felt unwell and sighed, even in my sleep, she would at once be at my bedside. If I did not wake she would return to her bed, but if I did she would see to me, ask whether Daller should be called, whether I wanted a drink, etc. In all the twenty-seven years I could never persuade her to sit in my presence; as soon as I entered the room she would stand up, and to my request that she should sit down, she would reply, 'Little Father, I want everyone to see that I am your true servant and nothing else.' She would only sit with me after her son had been promoted an officer and we were dining *en famille* without guests. During the whole time she was with me she never asked any favors except if she heard of some poor orphan who had not the means to enter the corps. Then she would speak to me, and I would usually make a request to His Highness the Czarevich. I think more than three hundred people were enlisted in the corps in this way. She was so sensitive that if I cast the slightest glance of annoyance in her direction she would burst into tears and would not stop weeping until I had explained the reason for my discontent. She was in charge of the whole of my estate, and I could deal with state business without even having to think about my own dress. This was what permitted me to work with such speed, which has surprised many people. I was obliged to the deceased for it."

While Arakcheev was indulging in these reminiscences, Kleinmikhel's investigation was leading him into increasingly deep water. Antonov had quickly been identified as the chief culprit, but so many people had heard others talk of killing Nastasia and were anxious to report them in order to exculpate themselves that Kleinmikhel began to think that the whole household had been involved in some vast conspiracy. "Every day brings new confusion, because every day the investigation brings to light more accomplices who have to be sent to the court at Novgorod," he wrote to Alexander. "As a result, the number of servants who have experience of the household is constantly diminishing, and the Count is bound to suspect all those who remain of being open or secret accomplices in the crime. . . . Thirty-four criminals are now being held in Novgorod."

Kleinmikhel was unable to find evidence to support Alexander's theory of a conspiracy organized from the outside, but at times he entertained the wildest hypotheses. "There is yet another new circumstance," he wrote despairingly to the Emperor. "Through the carelessness of the warder of the Novgorod prison, a landowner from Tikhvin called Madame Polozova was admitted to see the female criminals. The lady herself is unimportant, since she owns only two serfs; what is curious is that she lives not far from Countess Arakcheeva and is often her guest. She has visited the criminals twice; she tells them to pray to God and has promised to intercede for them, and one woman kissed her hand, evidently not without good reason. There are also rumors that money was sent to the criminals by Countess Arakcheeva, but it is still not clear whether they received it."

Meanwhile, Photius did his bit to muddy the waters in his own interests. "Archimandrite Photius has pointed out to me that the Gruzino murder took place on the anniversary of the day on which the evilly intentioned Gossner's activities were condemned in 1824," Kleinmikhel wrote to the Emperor. A few days later the subject came up again in a different guise: "Yesterday evening I received a letter from Archimandrite Photius in which he describes what Prince Golitsyn has been doing at the Ministry of Posts and even says that he knows for certain that Golitsyn is a great enemy of yours."[3]

Even so, Kleinmikhel was determined to have the affair brought to a swift conclusion, and in his haste he induced Zherebtsov, the governor of Novgorod, to allow the division of the accused into separate groups of six in order to circumvent the law which demanded that sentences involving more than nine people be confirmed by the Senate and Council of State. It was a violation of a fundamental principle of Russian law. An atmosphere of revenge was in the air, and the Novgorod court acted without hesitation. Twenty-four of the servants who had taken part in subversive activities were picked out in the most arbitrary fashion (in some cases for the simple reason that Arakcheev had already indicated to the governor that he no longer wished to employ them), and sentenced to the knout. Darya Konstantinova's husband was sentenced to ninety blows of the knout and transportation to Siberia, although all he had done was to allow people to talk in his presence of killing Nastasia without reporting the fact. When two court officials pointed out that one of the women sentenced to be knouted was pregnant, they were themselves arrested for unwarrantably interceding on her behalf. The harshest sentences were reserved for Antonov, who was condemned to a hundred and seventy-five blows of the knout, and Praskovya, who was sentenced to a hundred and twenty-five blows.

The prisoners were brought back from Novgorod to Gruzino for the execution of their sentences. Lieutenant Gribbe's company was summoned from the Novgorod colony to keep order. "A big field was chosen near the church, and at nine in the morning the company was drawn up," Gribbe writes. "Behind the soldiers stood peasants with their wives and children, who had been brought from the military colony, about four thousand in all. Posts were set up in the center, and on each side of them fires were lit on account of the cold weather. The executioners walked about, helping themselves to vodka from a vast bottle: the people who arranged the execution had probably found it necessary to shield the executioners' hearts from any spark of humanity or compassion for the victims.

"But let us draw a curtain, my reader, over what then took place in those peaceful fields. I was an involuntary witness of the execution, and when I recall that tragedy, I can still hear the sharp whistle of the knout, the terrible groans and cries of the tortured, and a kind of dull, suppressed sigh coming from the crowd of thousands for whose edification these persecutions were taking place."[4] Antonov and Praskovya not surprisingly died on the spot.

When the story came out, even the habitually harsh authorities and the landowners who were themselves no strangers to brutality were shocked by the savage sentences and their merciless execution. A law passed in 1807 had laid down that minors involved in murder cases should not be sentenced to more than thirty blows of the knout, and Antonov, his sister, and the two other maids who had received seventy blows each were all under the age of eighteen. Early in the following year the Senate set up an inquiry into the conduct of the case. Zherebtsov was judged severely for the violations of justice which he had condoned, put on trial together with the members of the Novgorod court, and sentenced to be stripped of his titles and exiled to Siberia. He was not in the end sent to the east, but he never held an official appointment again.

Letters of condolence on Nastasia's death arrived at Gruzino in a flood.[5] Many of Arakcheev's colleagues felt it prudent to assure him of their sympathy at his loss, while his close friends genuinely tried to find ways of helping and comforting him. His brother Petr arrived at Gruzino soon after the tragedy. The unfortunate Shumsky found himself the target of people who thought it an appropriate time for him to turn over a new leaf. Petr's wife, Natalya, who had stayed at home, wrote to him, "Please accept my sincere desire to help you, which is as great as my very real sorrow at your misfortune. Here at last is your chance to show your father and benefactor your solicitude and love and gratitude, for you may be sure that if you cause your benefactor the least sorrow you will redouble his grief. I am sure you will not be offended by this friendly message, for I say all this simply out of love for you. Forgive me, Christ be with you, keep well, and be a consolation to him to whom you owe everything."[6]

Arakcheev was rather surprised on going through Nastasia's effects to find a number of notes and presents which she had received without his knowledge. Whether these gifts were an exchange for some favor rendered or the result of discreet flirtations, he was hardly in a position to find out, but Nastasia's acceptance of them did not quite square with his memory of her. Where the donors could be identified, Arakcheev chose the simple course of sending back the gifts, although this gesture created a certain amount of apprehension in some cases. An old friend from Bezhetsk, Matvei Chikhachov, was quite upset when a ring he had given Nastasia was returned, and he hastened to assure Arakcheev of the innocence of the gift. "I cannot hide the fact that I did give it to Nastasia Fedorovna," he wrote, "but its value is quite insignificant. It was only an unimportant souvenir which she liked to wear when she thought of me. She herself gave me a fine purse which she had sewn, and I took it as a sign that she was well disposed toward me; I always valued this fact, and to the end of my days I shall be grateful for it. If this innocent devotion on my part displeases Your Excellency, I most earnestly beg your forgiveness."[7]

Everyone tried to persuade Arakcheev to leave Gruzino, where his surroundings could not fail to remind him at every moment of the past, but although he talked from time to time of going away, he could not bring himself to do so. He spent much time with Photius at the Yurev monastery, and his visits were afterward commemorated on the altar gates of the chapel by a plaque with the inscription, "On this spot Alexei Andreevich Arakcheev offered his ardent prayers to God in the days of his grief." He donated six thousand rubles to the monastery "for the salvation of two Christian friends, Alexei and Anastasia."

However, he was not allowed to nurse his grief for long. In the middle of November he was swept up in a new tragedy, which this time struck the whole nation.

After leaving Arakcheev in July, Sherwood made rapid progress in his investigations. Vadovsky, a leading member of the Southern Society, to whom Sherwood posed as a sympathizer, revealed not only the society's plans and the names of the members, but also the existence of a Northern Society with largely similar aims, which was based in Saint Petersburg and led by Prince Trubetskoy. The Southern Society was now working on a plan to assassinate the Emperor at a military review which was to be held the following May in the Ukraine.

On September 20 Sherwood arrived at the rendezvous in Karachev which he had arranged with Arakcheev, and was dismayed to find no messenger waiting for him. Only ten days later did an officer arrive, explaining that all Arakcheev's affairs had been disorganized by the murder of Nastasia and Arakcheev's own insane grief. Sherwood was not impressed. "I cannot understand how Count Arakcheev, who had received so many favors from the Emperor, to whom he was so devoted, could neglect the danger to the Emperor's life and the nation's peace because of a drunken, fat, pock-marked, uneducated, evil, and loose woman. It gives one food for thought," he later commented.[8] His thought was shared by many of his contemporaries, some of whom, including Sherwood himself, went as far as to suggest, quite unjustly, that the rebellion which took place three months later would never have occurred had there been no delay in dispatching the report to the Emperor.

The fact was that Alexander, shut away in his remote retreat at Taganrog, remained unaccountably slow to take action against the conspirators. It did not occur to him that the situation required his return to the capital, nor did he give instructions for the arrest of any of the officers whom he now knew to be plotting his assassination and a takeover of the government. When Sherwood's report at last reached him, he ordered that a further meeting with him be arranged in Kharkov in mid-November, and when Count Witt arrived at Taganrog with another circumstantial report on the Southern Society, he too was simply instructed to pursue his investigations. Maybe when all the threads were finally in his hands, Alexander would have acted swiftly and efficiently. However, in November the Emperor returned to Taganrog from a short tour of the Crimea, feverish and shivering. He took to his bed at once, but his condition quickly worsened, and a few days later, on November 19, he suddenly died. "Our angel is in heaven, and I am left on earth," the heart-broken Empress wrote to Maria Feodorovna. The Emperor's unexpected death was a cruel shock to his entourage, and the news was greeted with stupefaction throughout the country.

The confusion which immediately ensued, and a month later culminated in bloodshed, was the direct result of Alexander's obsessional secrecy in everything connected with affairs of state. In the absence of a son, the legal heir to the throne was assumed to be the Emperor's first brother, Constantine, but unknown to anyone except a small group around Alexander, Constantine had renounced the succession in 1823. A rough, sensual man, he had inherited not a little of the brutish side of Paul's nature, but he at least had the sense to see that he was quite unfitted to be Emperor; when he divorced his wife, a Princess of Saxe-Coburg, and married his Polish mistress, he exchanged letters with Alexander in which it was agreed that the title should pass to Nicholas, the next brother. A manifesto to that effect was drafted in great secrecy by the then Archbishop of Moscow, Philaret, and signed by the Emperor. With the knowledge only of Philaret, Arakcheev, and Golitsyn, the manifesto was then sealed and deposited in the cathedral at Moscow, as well as with the senate, the Council of State, and the Synod, all of whom remained unaware of the contents of the envelopes entrusted to them.

Nicholas and other members of the imperial family certainly knew of the existence and contents of these documents, yet when the news of Alexander's death reached Saint Petersburg on November 27, Nicholas panicked. He was an iron disciplinarian and well aware of his unpopularity in the army, particularly with the guards regiments, who had played such a vital role when his grandmother, Catherine the Great, and later his brother succeeded to the throne. Moreover, the capital was already tense, for an atmosphere of conspiracy and rebellion pervaded the town. The Grand Duke instantly took the oath of allegiance to his brother Constantine and ordered that it be administered throughout Russia. However, Constantine, who was in Warsaw at his post as commander of the Polish army, remained adamant. He wrote to Nicholas telling him that the position was quite clear and there could be no question of his succeeding to the throne. Documents which arrived in Warsaw from Saint Petersburg addressed to "His Imperial Majesty" were returned unopened. The situation became increasingly grotesque.

Meanwhile, General Diebich had been sorting through Alexander's papers at Taganrog and was thoroughly alarmed at the evidence of a dangerous conspiracy against the state which he found there. On December 4 he sent Nicholas a full summary of all the information at his disposal and ended his report by informing Nicholas that he was proposing to arrest Pestel and Vadovsky, the ringleaders of the southern plot, forthwith. This he proceeded to do on December 13, thereby neatly beheading the Southern Society.

In Saint Petersburg matters were moving to a climax. Nicholas at last agreed that he must take the throne, although he had no doubt that in doing so he would in all probability precipitate the impending crisis. Uncertain as to how he should act, he sought the advice of those who occupied key positions in the state and had been close to the late Emperor—Miloradovich, the governor general of the city; Benckendorf, the chief of police; Golitsyn; and Arakcheev, for Arakcheev had at last shaken off his lethargy, and to everyone's surprise, showed signs of being determined to resume his duties. On November 30 he tersely informed Nicholas that, having recovered from his illness, he had taken command of the corps of the military colonies. He then traveled to Saint Petersburg, where he shut himself up in his house and refused to receive anyone. His reappearance provoked some acid comments. Countess Nesselrode reflected the general opinion when she wrote to her brother: "Imagine our astonishment. Instead of persisting with his plan to give up office, he has issued an order of the day in which he declares that he is quite cured and that from now on he has resumed his functions. He arrived here this evening, but they say he has barricaded himself in his house and will see no one. When the Emperor was alive, he caused him pain by giving up duties like the colonies, which no longer held any interest for him; he resisted all the letters in which the Emperor begged him to take them on again, but the news of the Emperor's death, which has been a mortal blow to us all, brings him to life again!"[9] Colonel Schoenig noted the event more succinctly in his diary: "The death of his girl deprived Arakcheev of his ability to deal with affairs of state, and the death of Alexander returned it to him."[10]

Arakcheev answered a summons from Nicholas, but wrote, "I beg you to receive me alone, as I cannot bear to be with people." In any case, he had nothing to add to what Nicholas already knew of the conspiracy. A few days later the Grand Duke finally nerved himself to announce his succession. The oath-taking ceremony was to take place in the Senate and the Saint Petersburg garrison on December 14. "Tomorrow morning I shall be either Emperor or dead," he wrote to Diebich on December 13.

The conspirators' hour had arrived; they knew that it was a unique opportunity, but they were ill-prepared for the test. However, they hastily constructed a plan which aimed at disrupting the oath-taking ceremonies by filling the square between the Senate and the Winter Palace with rebellious troops. The northern leaders had always been more anxious to maintain a facade of legality than were Pestel and the members of his society in the south, and the present ringleaders, which included Trubetskoy and the poet Ryleev, hoped that by taking control of the situation at the oath-taking they would be in a position to set up Constantine as a constitutional Emperor, for he had, partly by reason of his long absence in Poland, quite unjustifiably acquired the reputation in the army of being more liberal than his brother.

The scheme had hardly been worked out at all, and was in any case totally misconceived, in that it appeared to ignore the fact that Constantine would never have agreed to any such proposal. However, the conspirators knew that Nicholas had their names, and although he had made no attempt to provoke them by striking first with premature arrests, it seemed too late to draw back. Thus, without having any clear idea of how many regiments would support them, they led some three thousand men into the square on the morning of the fourteenth, although the Council of State had already taken the oath to Nicholas on the previous evening and the Senate had also been sworn before the rebels arrived. They stood uncertainly in the center of the square, shouting sporadically for Constantine, while Nicholas surrounded them with loyal regiments and called on them to surrender.

In the midst of the bustle that day in the Winter Palace, Karamzin noted three figures from the previous reign sitting helplessly on one side "like three monuments"—Arakcheev, Prince Lopukhin, and Kurakin. Wrapped in his private sorrow, Arakcheev seemed scarcely to comprehend what was taking place, although he was horrified by the news of the death of Miloradovich, the governor of Saint Petersburg, who was shot and fatally wounded by one of the rebels when he rode into the center of the square and tried to persuade them to disperse.[11] As the day wore on and the insurgents remained standing in front of the palace, Nicholas reluctantly decided to take coercive measures. In the evening cannon were brought up, and three volleys put an end to the uprising. "Voilà un joli commencement de règne," the new Emperor remarked bitterly as he surveyed the eighty men who lay dead in the square.

Such was the short-lived and largely aimless rebellion known as the Decembrist Rising. It was not so much a prologue to the reign of Nicholas as the sad final curtain to Alexander's. Had he taken action a few months earlier, the Emperor could undoubtedly have anticipated and prevented the revolt. As it was, half in sympathy with what he knew of the leaders' aspirations, he procrastinated. He had neither the force to control the reactionary elements who had largely incited the rebels to action nor the heart to indulge in a policy of outright repression. The result was that as the Emperor was being carried to his grave, and his chief minister and greatest friend was retiring from the scene a broken man, the stage was filled briefly by another group of men who, when their hour came, proved to have no more sense of purpose than the autocracy which they had so feverishly been conspiring to bring down.

Arakcheev had one last service to perform for Alexander. The great funeral cortege, which had grown so long that signals had to be given by rocket when it started or came to a halt, was scheduled to stop in Novgorod on its way up from the south to Saint Petersburg. Arakcheev was determined that the ceremonies there should be conducted with the punctiliousness which his master would have appreciated, and he spent several days rehearsing monks, officials, and soldiers in the ceremonial, as if they had been squads in the old days at Gatchina. Everything went off without a hitch, but when Arakcheev wanted to mount the funeral carriage in order to accompany Alexander on the remainder of his journey to Saint Petersburg, the aides-de-camp accompanying the coffin tried to prevent him.[12] It was an eloquent symbol of his declining power. However, on this occasion he had his way. He was eventually allowed to stand alone on the left-hand side of the carriage, and due honors were given to him at the funeral. He accompanied Alexander to his tomb, bearing one of the great pieces of the imperial regalia, the crown of Kazan.

Although Arakcheev had made some attempt to resume his duties, it was evident that the events of the previous months had shattered his health, and at fifty-seven he looked like an old man. The new Emperor also made it clear, respectfully but firmly, that, capable or not, Arakcheev could not expect to occupy the same place in his reign as he had enjoyed under Alexander. It was as normal for a new Emperor to change his chief assistants as it is now for an incoming President of the United States, and Nicholas was no exception. Before December was out, the Private Chancery had been transferred under a new director from Liteinaya Street to the Winter Palace, and Arakcheev was also relieved of his functions as chief *rapporteur* for the Committee of Ministers. For the time being he retained his post as head of the corps of military colonies, and he put as brave a face as he could on his undeniably reduced position. With a touch of his old aggressiveness he said to Maevsky in January, "As long as I am still working, I shall not change my habits, and I advise you to do the same. Of course, there are stories about the Count losing the Emperor's favor. Well, you needn't listen to them, for I shan't see that happen before my death. And as long as I am in charge, I shall be the same Count Arakcheev. . . . You can tell this to everyone, and say that the Count has not fallen and that he is to be obeyed as before."[13]

But talk of this kind was largely bluff, and he knew it. The pains in his chest began to increase again, and his doctors could only advise him to go abroad for a prolonged cure, advice which he now reluctantly accepted. Although his estate was prosperous, he had little ready cash, and in March he had to write to Golitsyn, now the Emperor's chamberlain, asking him to arrange the purchase by the royal household of certain of his valuables. A tortoiseshell snuffbox, a signet ring with Paul's crest, and a silver dinner service realized a total of 38,980 rubles, and he sought permission from Nicholas to take leave. "Merciful Emperor!" he wrote. "Having been an officer since 1787, you are the fourth Emperor whom I have served, and this is the first time in thirty-nine years that I ask my Emperor to give me permission to take leave abroad. I make this request solely on account of my health. If the Almighty is pleased to relieve me of my illness, then I shall be able to continue to serve you with the same pure and complete devotion which guided me during the lifetime of the late Emperor, that is, if my services continue to please Your Imperial Majesty." He asked to be allowed to use abroad the money he had made from the sale and explained that if this favor were not granted, he would have to resort for his traveling expenses to borrowing money on the mortgage of his estate at Gruzino. "This estate is my whole fortune," he added; "from the time it was granted me, I have not added a single peasant to it nor a foot of land, neither by purchase nor by lease.

"Almighty Emperor, everything I have said here is so true that I could even present it to my enemies for their judgment. I think that they would feel somewhat disturbed in their consciences if on reading the above they did not do me justice. I recommend myself to God, the reader of human hearts, and to my all-merciful Emperor, the august brother of the Emperor of blessed memory. In the faithful service of His Majesty I enjoyed neither rank, honors, nor riches; I had the good fortune to deserve only one reward, greater than all others, his highest confidence in me. It inspired my services to him and will be my one consolation to the end of my days. That frank judge, posterity, will give its true verdict on everything later."[14]

The Emperor's reply was to award Arakcheev fifty thousand rubles, but characteristically he preferred not to accept the gift, and sent it to Maria Feodorovna to be donated to an orphanage for the daughters of war victims.

In Arakcheev's absence the direction of the military colonies was handed over to Kleinmikhel. Perhaps Arakcheev suspected that he was relinquishing his last official position for good. In his final order, addressed to the colonies as a whole, he summed up all that had been done; and for the first time he offered his thanks to everyone who had helped him in this great enterprise and had so often in the past been at the receiving end of his complaints and abuse. Never afraid of blowing his own trumpet, he began by stressing his personal role in the scheme. "This great national undertaking, which is unique and quite without precedent, has rightly attracted the attention of the whole of Europe. It owes its foundation to the greatest of Emperors, Alexander the Blessed. The happy idea of the military colonies was born in his powerful mind and ripened under his wise guidance.

"The project was first unfolded to me alone. Honored with His Majesty's confidence, I alone had the fortune to receive his orders and be guided by his directions. I carried out His Majesty's sacred will, when I myself was new to this important work and had to work with new people. I had both to learn and teach; explain and expound each aim of the military colonies for until then they were not known. I had to defend the institution against unfair criticism, which frightened not only the junior ranks, but even some of you, the officers of the colonies. It was enough to exhaust a man of my years and weak health. . . .

"My respected colleagues, in taking leave of you, I have the agreeable task of conveying my very great and sincere gratitude for the devoted service which you rendered during the entire time you were under my command. Your devotion to duty and to your calling earned a flattering reward, a Divine blessing specially accorded to all troops of the colonies. For not one of our officers took part in the infamous conspiracy uncovered by the government. This does honor to the corps of the military colonies and will of course stand out as a notable feature in the history of the Russian State."[15]

Having bestowed this accolade, Arakcheev turned his back on Gruzino and Russia and set off, a lonely and unloved figure, to nurse his ailing body at the waters of Carlsbad.

9
The Hermit of Gruzino

I console myself with the thought that I have been useful.
—ARAKCHEEV

Despite the advice and exhortations which everyone seemed so anxious to give him, Shumsky went from bad to worse after his mother's death. Nastasia's disappearance seemed to have snapped the last vestiges of his self-control, and he was now drunk nearly all the time. It was ironic that he should indulge in the vice which Arakcheev detested above all others, yet his father did not lose his affection for the boy despite his having proved such a sad disappointment. "He is a good and not unintelligent fellow, but a peasant's hut always smells of smoke," Arakcheev once remarked to an acquaintance.

Arakcheev had hoped to take Shumsky abroad with him, but the young man refused to go. Arakcheev was very grieved and wrote complaining of Shumsky's lack of feeling to his friend General Bukhmeyer, who had taken a close interest in Shumsky's fortunes ever since he had found a title of nobility for him. "My Shumsky has again drunk himself insensible, and his behavior has now got quite out of hand. Kleinmikhel and everyone else have seen what he is like, and it is not easy for me to bear! God knows how it weighs on my soul. And that is not all. The other day I began to reprimand him when we were traveling together alone in my carriage, after attending Mass at the Yurev monastery. His response was to tell me that he did not love me, that he had no desire to stay with me, and wouldn't do so for millions of rubles. I bore this in silence. Three days later I found a letter on my table written in his hand, in which he said that he definitely wanted to give everything up and leave me, and that he would rather live in Siberia than with me. Dear friend, I am sure you can imagine what it was like to be told this."

As the day of Arakcheev's departure drew nearer, his relations with Shumsky became still more strained. He continued to correspond with Bukhmeyer about Shumsky's conduct. "For seven days he has kept away from me, reappearing only for meals, and he continues to ask me to let him go away because he does not want to live with me. He still sleeps in my room, but he never comes in until I am going to bed, and then not only does he refuse to say good night, he does not even cast a glance in my direction. Last night I was exhausted, but could not sleep, and lay there sighing and groaning. He heard it all but he did not get up to see me, and would not even call Dr. Miller for me. He just turned over and wrapped himself up in his blanket. Dear friend, how can I stand all this? I brought him up, I took him into society, and I have thought of him and cared for him every hour of the day."[1]

Shumsky's decline gathered speed after Arakcheev had left for Carlsbad. The death wish, it seemed, was on him, and he would heed no warnings. In October a last act of buffoonery finally exhausted the patience of his superiors. In the course of an exercise outside Saint Petersburg he was reprimanded by the general in charge for wearing his hat incorrectly. He answered back insolently, whereupon the general called him a "bastard," a term well calculated to wound him more than any other. A few days later at the ballet, Shumsky, who was as usual drunk, found his enemy sitting in front of him. In the first interval he went to the buffet, bought a melon, and had it cut in two and the flesh scooped out. Taking one half with him, he returned to his seat, and immediately after the curtain had risen he leaped to his feet, thrust the improvised helmet on the general's bald head, and cried out, "Here's a wig for you, old man!"* Retribution followed instantaneously. Shumsky was arrested on the spot, and the next day deprived of his post as A.D.C. to the Emperor and posted to a garrison in the Caucasus.[2]

Arakcheev returned from Carlsbad in December and was greeted by a message from Diebich informing him that the military colonies were to be put under the command of Prince Shakhovsky and attached to the imperial general staff. The news can hardly have surprised him, but the moment when the door of official life finally closes must always be a bitter one. "So Prince Shakhovsky is to be your commander. That's what old age means, my dear sir," he commented as he took leave of General Maevsky. "These young men, who of course are better brought up and better educated than I am, can grasp an affair in a matter of hours. You won't be able to say that you haven't had time to go into everything, when the unusually intelligent Prince Shakhovsky, who understands everything so quickly, wants to take immediate action. I am so tired, and everything bores me so much, that I don't think I am good for any more work."

However, one more storm broke about his head before he was able to settle down to a peaceful country existence in his beloved Gruzino. At the end of January, 1827, he received a

* "Starichok, vot tebe parichock!"

most disconcerting letter from General Diebich. "It has come to the knowledge of His Majesty the Emperor that books have been published here in Saint Petersburg containing letters and notes allegedly written by the late Emperor to Your Excellency. His Majesty supposes that they have been published without Your Excellency's knowledge by someone who wishes you ill, since he is sure that you realize how unpleasant it would be if private letters written to you by the late Emperor as a mark of his special confidence in you were to be published. Therefore His Majesty would like to know whether you have any knowledge of the source of these letters and notes, and of the person who issued them for publication. If you do not know, then His Majesty thinks that the best way of avoiding public gossip would be for Your Excellency to publish a statement declaring that these letters and notes are a fabrication and unworthy of credence."

It was a delicate situation, for Arakcheev had indeed printed on the presses of the military colonies two collections of Alexander's letters to him, a correspondence of which he was inordinately proud. The editions were private, limited to some thirty copies of each collection, and intended only for a few close friends, but the act was in itself illegal, since absolutely everything had to be submitted to the censor before publication of any kind. Arakcheev was confident that Alexander would have been indulgent, and perhaps even have quietly approved, but he knew that Nicholas was morbidly sensitive about his family's private correspondence; indeed, one of his first acts on succeeding to the throne had been to destroy virtually all his brother's private correspondence that he could lay his hands on. Taken by surprise, and alarmed, Arakcheev rather lost his head. Just as once, years before, he had mislead Paul in an effort to save his brother from disgrace, he now took refuge in a statement which was disingenuous to say the least. He wrote directly to Nicholas and in his letter said: "If this news had ever reached me indirectly, I would not have believed it. It would have been shameful for me, an old man of sixty, not to have understood that manuscript letters written to me by the late Emperor are precious and that to publish them for public consumption would be not only unpleasant, but damaging and indefensible."

Nicholas was astonished by this reply, since he had in his possession a copy of one of the books, signed by Arakcheev himself. He sent General Chernyshev, who had been friendly with Arakcheev in the past, to Gruzino in order to tax him with his denial and to retrieve any printed copies which were still in Arakcheev's possession. "Well, can you believe it," Nicholas afterward wrote to Constantine. "Chernyshev brought back eighteen copies and an admission from Arakcheev that he had been wrong, but that as he had been asked whether he knew anything about similar books in public circulation, he had not thought that he was lying when he said that he had not heard of them. He began to weep, claiming that he had them printed with the Emperor's knowledge and that the Emperor had often asked him how the edition was progressing. . . . One is only too often forced to employ people one does not respect because they can be of use—and this is certainly the case with Arakcheev." Nicholas had all the copies of the books except two destroyed. One he kept in his library, and the other he sent to Constantine. However, there were persistent rumors that Arakcheev had kept back his last copies and buried them at Gruzino. "Twelve copies are buried under each of the columns of the magnificent belfry at Gruzino, in order that the work may be passed to the most distant posterity," Nicholas wrote to Constantine.[3]

Arakcheev's enemies made no secret of their exultation over his disgrace. Even Chernyshev, a former colleague, admitted that his "heart turned over at the thought that a man who had so much enjoyed the favor of our angelic benefactor could show himself so low and cowardly"; while Count Benckendorff, the Emperor's adjutant general, wrote to Diebich, "He has fallen under the weight of his own actions, and Providence, which began his punishment on the day of his mistress's assassination, has not required either man's own assistance or the Emperor's power in order to make him more unhappy than Menshikov* when he was exiled to the north of Siberia."

Arakcheev now withdrew completely to the solitude of Gruzino, and even his journeys to Novgorod were rare. During the years of power, when Gruzino had been crowded with visitors, he had been fond of referring to the estate as his monastery and had enjoyed being called, as he sometimes was, "the hermit of Gruzino." Now that the stream of visitors had dried up almost overnight, the nickname became more of a reality. Only a small circle of friends, the Bukhmeyers, Aprelevs, Gurievs, and Ilyins, still came to see him regularly. They found that he had mellowed, although he retained his dry sense of humor. But after Nastasia's death he could never bring himself completely to trust his household again, and his guests noticed that nowadays before eating he would always give a piece of food from his plate to a small dog at his feet.

At first he continued to take an active interest in the affairs of his estate, but as the months went by he became bored and restless. He was bitter at having been forgotten so soon and took refuge in a veritable cult to the memory of Alexander. He converted the room on the ground floor in which the Emperor had always slept into a museum devoted to souvenirs of Alexander and gifts he had received from the Emperor. There was a box in which were preserved more than eight

* The celebrated favorite of Peter the Great.

hundred envelopes which the Emperor had addressed to Arakcheev in his own hand; the shirt which the Grand Duke Alexander had given him on their first evening in the Winter Palace; and a silver plinth with the dates of Alexander's visits to Gruzino engraved on one side, the last sentence the Emperor had written to him on another, and a curse on anyone who ever melted the plinth down on a third. He had an extraordinary bronze clock specially made for him in Paris at the exorbitant cost of twenty-six thousand rubles, with two doors that opened every morning at ten minutes to eleven, the exact time of Alexander's death, and revealed a miniature of the Emperor, while a little memorial tune played.[4] Paul was not forgotten either. In the summer he would have his lunch table placed in the garden under a bust of Paul, and an extra place would be set before the Emperor; at the end of the meal two cups of coffee were poured out, and Arakcheev would empty one at the foot of the bust before drinking his own.[5]

Arakcheev continued to follow Shumsky's fortunes with some concern. Bored with garrison life, Shumsky volunteered for active service in the war against the Turks and was decorated for his bravery. Arakcheev, anxious as ever, wrote to the commanding officer asking for news. "If it is possible and not against the rules, I should like to know how Mr. Shumsky is progressing, and in particular whether he has been wounded. Would you arrange for me to be informed. If I am asking too much or am not supposed to know, then I would ask Your Excellency to destroy this letter and forgive me for it."[6]

Shumsky was not wounded, but once the action was over he only too quickly erased the good impression which his gallantry had made by renewing his drinking bouts; and in 1830 he was finally retired from the army. Despite all the harsh things he had said to Arakcheev, he made his way back to Gruzino. His father was willing to give him yet another chance and used his influence to obtain for him a small civil appointment in the governor's economic department at Novgorod. But the next scandal was not long in coming. One day he appeared in the department so drunk that the vice-governor, Zotov, gave him a stern warning. As Zotov eloquently declaimed a number of home truths, Shumsky suddenly seized a heavy inkpot and flung it at him; it missed its target, but struck the wall, spattering other officials in the room.

For Arakcheev this was the last straw, and he told Shumsky that he wished to have nothing more to do with him. But faced at last with the prospect of having to fend for himself, Shumsky was unable to cope. He repaired to his old protector, Bukhmeyer, and sought to convince the general of his true repentance. Bukhmeyer allowed himself to be persuaded, and got in touch with Arakcheev. Shumsky "would like to see you to say how sincerely he repents of all the unworthy and ill-mannered things he has done to you," he wrote. "God's will is inscrutable, and nothing in this world is impossible. It is quite conceivable that in return for all the care you have lavished on him since his childhood, he will comfort you in your declining years, for it can happen that the most demoralized and hopeless people return to righteousness."[7] Arakcheev remained skeptical. He suggested ironically that if Shumsky really wanted to mend his ways there could be no better place for him to learn how than in a monastery, and his old friend Photius was asked if he would take Shumsky into the Yurev monastery to help with his moral reform. Photius somewhat surprisingly consented, and Shumsky took up residence in the monastery with a small allowance from Arakcheev to pay his expenses. There he continued to live until after his father's death, when he took to wandering from one monastery to the next, drinking his way through the annual allowance which the Emperor continued to pay him in Arakcheev's name. He eventually died at the age of forty-eight in a hospital in Archangel, as he was once again making his way back to the Novgorod district. "Everything in him was dead, burned out in that Russian crucible which is called drink, and in which so many and often such gifted people perish," observed Lieutenant Gribbe,[8] who had been one of Shumsky's former friends.

Only a few months after the gates of Yurev had closed behind Shumsky, Arakcheev's life at Gruzino was disturbed for the last time by the outside world. The summer of 1831 was exceptionally dry and hot, and a serious cholera epidemic that had broken out in southern Russia the previous year now swept north like a hurricane, leaving a trail of havoc in its wake. At the beginning of July it reached Saint Petersburg, where people died at the rate of three hundred a day. From there the disease spread to Novgorod and to the soldiers and peasants in the military colonies. Panic ensued, and the colonists, quite irrationally convinced that their officers were trying to poison them, suddenly mutinied near Staraya Russa.

The speed with which the revolt spread through the Novgorod colonies was an eloquent expression of the discontent which for years had only just been held in check by the strictness of the military regime. The situation in the colonies had not been improved since Arakcheev's departure by the administration's increasing callousness over the needs and sensibilities of the peasants; Arakcheev had always been careful to protect as far as possible the rights of the numerous Old Believers, but after his retirement no one bothered to do so. When the revolt began, the officers under the command of General Eiler were indecisive, and the colonists soon got out of control. It was the most serious disturbance the colonies had so far known; soldiers and peasants ran amok, beating up and frequently killing any officer or official who fell into their hands. The rebellion did not have a leader, nor did it take any particular direction, but it justified the fears of those who had always opposed the colonies; the mutineers were naturally well armed, and when reserve battalions were brought up from other colonies in the province, the men in the battalions refused to fight their comrades.

Arakcheev was much alarmed at the news of the rebellion. The nearest colony was only thirty kilometers away from Gruzino, and he knew that the rebels might well seek to avenge themselves on him. The weather grew even hotter, and his nerves were stretched to breaking point. On July 20 he took his carriage and without warning drove to stay with a friend near Tikhvin. The next day he drove on to Novgorod and put up at the house of the vice-governor. But he was far from being a welcome visitor in Novgorod. The governor, who had already been thrown into a panic by the revolt in his province, had no desire to shelter so dangerous a target, and to Arakcheev's dismay tried to persuade him to leave the town. Arakcheev wrote a hasty appeal to the Emperor. "On the second morning after my arrival, the head of the gendarmes, Lieutenant Colonel Grigoriev (who has never called on me before), arrived and began to tell me that in view of the colonists' intention to kill me, my presence in Novgorod was dangerous and that yesterday the colonists wanted to intercept me en route. I replied that if the colonists were so anxious to kill me, it would be much more dangerous for me to leave town in the direction of Moscow, because I would have to travel past the colony of the Crown Prince's Regiment. He said that he did not think that there would be any danger in my traveling in that direction. He demanded that I leave for Tver province and insistently asked me, an old man, where I was proposing to stay."[9]

Whatever Nicholas' private views on Arakcheev, he was incensed that such treatment should have been handed out to an old friend and servant of his brother's. He instructed Chernyshev to write a strong reprimand to the town authorities, while he himself replied to Arakcheev. "I have at once ordered that you be looked after," he wrote. "I hasten to inform you of this, and I assure you that wherever my power extends, you shall be safe. I do not believe the rumors which have reached you, and I am convinced that when you, rightly, decide to return to Gruzino, you will be able to travel through the military colonies, where order has been reestablished."[10]

By the end of July the revolt had been put down, and reprisals were taken with the customary brutality. The Emperor had been seriously disturbed by its violence and extent: it sounded the death knell of the whole colonial experiment. Although they were not finally abolished until 1857, the regime in the Novgorod colonies was significantly modified before the end of 1831, and no new colonies were set up. Arakcheev does not appear to have commented on the mortal blow that had been dealt to his life's work.

He stayed in Novgorod until the end of the month, receiving no one, but in the evenings he would occasionally call on Dr. Evropeus, now in retirement, in order to play boston with him. Evropeus noticed that as a result of his recent experience he was much on edge and his temper was barely under control. One evening he tore his coat on a door in Evropeus' house and exclaimed crossly, "Look at the state your house is in. The late Emperor took this overcoat from his own shoulders and gave it to me on the battlefield. Now I have to tear this treasured possession in your house. Good-bye. I shan't be back again."[11]

He returned to Gruzino in low spirits and begun to go out less and less. He sat alone for hours in his study, and in default of other partners he played boston with his servants in the evenings. In 1833 a large monument to Alexander, which he had commissioned five years earlier, arrived at Gruzino and was set up in front of the church. It was a marble bust of the Emperor, supported by the three graces; at its foot it had on one side a kneeling Russian soldier bearing a shield with Arakcheev's arms, and on the other a figure representing liberated Europe. "Now everything is done," said Arakcheev after the unveiling ceremony, "and I can appear before the Emperor Alexander with my report." The same year he made a bank deposit of fifty thousand rubles, which was to be awarded with the accumulated interest on the hundredth anniversary of Alexander's death to the historian who had by that date written the best history of the Emperor's life and reign.*

Arakcheev made only one more public appearance. The Emperor had decided in the early thirties to establish provincial cadet corps, but for lack of funds the project had hung fire in many provinces, including Novgorod. In 1833 Arakcheev, with his usual generosity toward any cause that was near to his heart, donated three hundred thousand rubles to enable the corps to be founded. He was warmly thanked, and the following year invited to the solemn opening of the corps on March 15.

He accepted with reluctance. Any expedition out of Gruzino had become a major effort for him; and since no one came to see him any longer, he felt no obligation to trouble himself for others. Indeed, shortly before he left for the opening ceremony, he had a last brush with one of the many

* See Appendix III.

officers who had found it more convenient to forget him. One afternoon in early March, while Arakcheev was sitting at Gruzino with a neighbor, Kleinmikhel, who owed his whole career to Arakcheev but had not deigned to visit him for many years, was announced. Kleinmikhel entered the room with some embarrassment and said stiffly that he had been instructed by the Emperor to retrieve a document bearing Alexander's signature, about which there had been some correspondence. Years before, when Arakcheev was at the height of his power, Kleinmikhel had called on him one day and found him drinking camomile tea on the orders of his doctor. "Would you like a cup to keep me company?" Arakcheev had asked him, and Kleinmikhel had accepted with alacrity. Now Arakcheev screwed up his eyes, and after looking Kleinmikhel up and down, he suddenly said, "Would you like a cup of camomile tea, my friend?"

"I did not come to joke with Your Excellency," Kleinmikhel replied with annoyance.

"Well, sir," said Arakcheev, suddenly rousing himself, "I am not joking either when I ask you to tell the Emperor that I have not entrusted the document to you, but that I will have the honor to hand it personally to His Highness the Grand Duke Michael Pavolovich when I see him in a few days' time at the opening of the Novgorod cadet corps," and he gave Kleinmikhel a curt nod of dismissal.[12]

Arakcheev's appearance at the opening ceremony caused something of a stir. Barely a decade had gone by since his retirement, but his removal from the scene had been so complete that he seemed like a figure from the distant past. The Grand Duke Michael, the Emperor's jovial younger brother, arrived the day before the ceremony; he encouraged the boys to throw him up in the air, and then said, so one of the cadets later recalled, "Today you may behave as you like with me, but tomorrow you will have as your guest a stern old man who does not care for joking, and therefore I ask you to see that everything is done with decorum."

The next day Arakcheev arrived dressed simply in the uniform of his own regiment, without decorations but wearing the miniature of Alexander around his neck. A religious service was followed by a banquet, during which the Grand Duke paid much attention to him. At one point Michael asked in a loud voice, "May I ask you as a near neighbor to visit the corps often, and to insist that the cadets be fed as well as possible?" "I fear, Your Highness, that my visits may not be welcome," Arakcheev replied gravely. "When I was in charge of the military cantonists, they were excellently fed because if the cabbage soup was no good I would always order that the caldron be emptied over the head of the steward." No one was quite sure whether he was speaking seriously or not, but afterward whenever the cadets were displeased with their food, they would remind their own steward of the story.[13]

Arakcheev traveled back to Gruzino the same day and began to prepare himself for Easter, as he did with great seriousness every year. But as Lent drew to a close, he began to feel seriously ill. The old pains in his chest and heart returned with renewed force. He sent to Saint Petersburg for Dr. Miller, who drove down with the Emperor's physician, Sir James Wylie, himself now an old man. Arakcheev's condition did not improve. He sent a message to General von Friken, the former commander of the Count Arakcheev Regiment, who was now living in the military colony of Staraya Russa; and he asked Brovtsyn, a local landowner with whom he had recently become friendly, to come and see him. Brovtsyn arrived on the Wednesday of the week before Easter and was told by Wylie, who had now diagnosed an aneurism, that there was no hope of Arakcheev's surviving much longer. By

Friday his condition had again deteriorated, and he was having great difficulty in breathing.

Even so, that evening Arakcheev asked Brovtsyn to help him get up to inspect his study, which had just been redecorated. As the old man, leaning heavily on Brovtsyn's shoulder, was shuffling through the room dedicated to Alexander, he met Sir James Wylie, who was horrified to see his patient out of bed and ordered him to stop moving at once. Arakcheev accordingly lay down on a sofa, and, supported by pillows, gazed around the room that was so full of memories for him, while his friend read out the newspaper for an hour or so. He slept a little in the same room, and the following morning he died there peacefully, as an Easter procession was slowly moving around the church outside.*

Arakcheev's death did not create a sensation in Russia; he already belonged to another time. "Arakcheev has died, but the death of this autocrat has made no impression," Pushkin noted in his diary. Nonetheless, Kleinmikhel, Von Friken, and many of his other former colleagues arrived during the Easter holiday to pay him their last respects. A detachment of the Count Arakcheev Regiment was summoned to Gruzino, and on the Wednesday of Holy Week, dressed in Alexander's shirt, he was buried next to Nastasia in the grave under the bust of Paul which he had prepared for himself long before. The gravestone, already carved with the simple

* It is typical of the way people liked to make up stories about Arakcheev that there are several different accounts of his death, some, it would seem, deliberately fabricated. For example, E. M. Romanovich wrote an article in *Russky Arkhiv*, 1868, in which he claimed that he had seen Arakcheev die thrusting his hand in his mouth and shouting, "Damned death." This account provoked an indignant denial from someone who clearly had been present (A. P. Brovtsyn, also in *Russky Arkhiv*, 1868). Another story had it that Arakcheev died as he was beating a gardener's boy on the nose with a poker (memoirs of Von Bradke in *Russky Arkhiv*, No. 1, 1875). Yazykov claims (*Russkaya Starina*, 1869), without giving any authority, that Arakcheev's last words were in answer to the question "Shall we call the priest?" "If it becomes necessary, I will say so myself."

inscription, "On this spot lies a Russian nobleman of Novgorod, Count Alexei Andreevich Arakcheev," lay waiting to be put in place.

Arakcheev had instructed in his will that if he appointed no heir before he died, Gruzino was to revert to the Emperor and be used in whatever way the monarch might see fit.* Nicholas did not take long to make up his mind. Less than two months after Arakcheev's death, the estate was granted to the Novgorod Cadet Corps. Most of Arakcheev's movable goods were sold and the money devoted to the corps, while the regular income from the estate was earmarked to support the cadets. The corps was appropriately rebaptized the Count Arakcheev Cadet Corps.

Thirty years later, a visitor to Gruzino was being shown around the house by a man who in his youth had worked as a footman for Arakcheev. The visitor asked if Arakcheev had really been the harsh tyrant of popular legend. The man thought for a moment. "How shall I say," he finally replied; "he did not like idlers and would punish them. He worked himself, and demanded the same of others."

It was not, after all, such a bad epitaph.

* See Appendix III.

Appendix I

Sir Robert Porter. *Travelling Sketches in Russia and Sweden* (London, 1809). Letter XXVIII.

Saint Petersburg, September, 1806

I am going to describe a scene that has harrowed my heart. I have been to witness the execution by the knout, to a height of torture which very seldom is inflicted. The lenity of the Emperor Alexander's disposition will not allow death, or the severer degrees of punishments to be adjudged to any of his subjects but on the most decided proofs of terrible crimes. In the present instance, the guilt of the culprit was unquestionable, and he was tried and sentenced.

The instruments and manner of performing this horrible execution I have already described in my account of visiting the prison at Moscow. The unhappy wretch whom his crimes destined to be an example to mankind, was an *izvozchik* (or coachman) to Count Ablenovsky, a Polish nobleman, whom he inhumanly murdered one night, in bringing him from a party in the country. He effected his death by means of the key used for screwing the bolts of the carriage. The vehicle being a *drozhky*, there was no other servant but the coachman.

At a conveniently dark and sequestered spot, the villain turned suddenly on his master, and striking him a stunning blow with the iron instrument, seized him and finished the murder by strangling him with the reins. Having rifled the dead Count of every valuable about his person, he left the body and the carriage and made his escape. Morning discovered the horrid scene. Suspicion did not hesitate to point to the real perpetrator, and a pursuit was immediately ordered. Officers of justice went in every direction, and by their unwearied activity found him, after a search of several days, some versts from the Ladoga Lake.

The place generally allotted for public executions is near the Neva, being an open and muddy plain. When I arrived a few companies of grenadiers were drawn up in line, and the natives were pouring upon the ground in multitudes. The gravity of their rough visages, mingling with the fierce visage of the cossaks, and the severe gloom of the police, gave an expression of horror to the crowding groups more consonant with the expected scene than the noisy mobs below the gallows at the Old Bailey.

Ten o'clock in the morning was the appointed hour. But more than another hour elapsed before the criminal was brought to the place of punishment. He was a robust and fine-looking man, with light hair and beard; possessing not one trait in his face to announce him capable of murder, or even of less terrible crimes. Had I been called upon to declare my opinion of that man's disposition from his face, I should have pronounced him everything that was meek and harmless. I am no physiognomist, and I must leave this apparent contradiction of their science to those who are.

The poor wretch, attended by part of the police, had been walked through the streets in order to show him to the populace and strike them with horror at his guilt. As soon as the procession arrived in front of the troops a circle was formed and preparations made for the instant commencement of the execution. A paper being read aloud in the Russian language, which most probably was an account of his crime and sentence; he was speedily stripped of his clothes, leaving on his person only a pair of loose trousers. In the midst of this silent group (and awful indeed was their silence) stood, firm and well secured, a block of wood, almost three feet high, having three cavities in the top to receive the neck and arms. Being fully prepared for this dreadful punishment, the unhappy man crossed himself, repeating his Gospodi Pomilui with the greatest devotion. The executioner then placed him with his breast to the board, strongly binding him to it by the neck and upper part of his arms, passing the rope close under the bend of both knees. Thus bowed forward, the awful moment approached. The first blow was struck, and each repeated lash tore the flesh from the bone. A few seconds elapsed between each, and for the first ten to twelve the poor sufferer roared most terribly. But soon, becoming faint and sick, the cry died away into groans, and a few seconds after nothing was heard but the bloody splash of the knout on the senseless body of the wretched man. Oh! If God punished so, who could stand before his judgement seat? Had the compassionate Alexander beheld it, I believe that this would have been the last infliction of this tremendous punishment.

After full an hour had been occupied in striking these dreadful blows (and more than two hundred were given him), a signal was made from the head officer of the police, and the criminal was raised a little from the block. Not the smallest sign of life seemed to remain; indeed so long did it appear to have fled that during the half of the lashing he had sunk down as low as the ligatures which bound him would allow. The executioner took the pale and apparently lifeless body by the beard while the assistant held an instrument like a brush with iron teeth, and placing it a little below his temple, struck it with the utmost force, driving its pointed fangs into the flesh. The opposite temple and forehead received the same application. The parts thus pierced were then rubbed with gunpowder, to remain, should the mangled sufferer survive, a perpetual mark of his having undergone punishment.

You would suppose that rigour had exhausted all her torments, that justice was now appeased. But no, another punishment yet remained: to deprive the nose of its nostrils. The inflicting pincers, something like monstrous curling-irons, were inserted up the nose of him whom I supposed dead (and indeed I only endured the latter part of the sight from having imagined that these afflictions were directed at one already past the sense of pain); the performer of this dreadful sentence, aided by his companion, actually tore each from his head in a way more shocking than can be described. The acuteness of this last torture brought back sense to the torpid body. What was my horror to see the writhings of the poor mangled creature, and to my astonishment, as soon as he was unbound, to see him rise by the assistance of the men and walk to a cart ready to return him to his prison! From whence, if he did not die, he would be immediately conveyed to Siberia, there to labour for life. His lost strength seemed to revive every moment; and he sat in the vehicle perfectly upright, being covered with his caftan, which he himself held on his shoulder, talking very composedly with those who accompanied him.

His sentence, I understand, was to be *knouted without mercy*. Of course in such cases few ever survive; or if they do, for want of care or even common assistance, a mortification generally takes place, and death relieves them from further suffering. This was the fate of the miserable creature in question, who expired the following day, after passing the first post towards his banishment.

How far this sort of punishment may have an effect on the people at large, I cannot pretend to say. At present they are very rare; and whatever may be the horror with which they are viewed, I do not find them to be decisive preventives, as murders are continually happening in infrequented parts of the city, without the perpetrators being discovered.

I have lately been told that what actuated the *izvozchik* to the murder of the Count was the cruelty and penuriousness of that nobleman, not only to the man himself but to the rest of his slaves. Indeed he was well known to be of a violent and austere temper, and one of the most avaricious among mortals. Hence my judgement on that poor fellow's face might not be far wrong;

as ignorance renders the best natures liable to be wrought upon by injuries and want. Vengeance is a passion that requires better reasoning than a clown's to subdue.

The knout is, I believe, the only severe punishment remaining from the many barbarous kinds continually practised in the early ages of the empire. The manner of inflicting it at the commencement of the reign of Peter the First was different from the present mode, and much more savage. The sufferer was fixed to the back of the executioner's man by means of ropes; and his lower extremities held so fast by another that resistance was impossible. In the time of the early Tsars, the performers of this horrid task were regarded with so much respect that they were admitted into the best society. Nay, it is even said that in those days merchants, thinking it honourable thus to pass into ranks above them, paid large sums of money to be allowed to fulfil the murderous duty. When their ambitions were satisfied, they then resold the vocation at enormous profit.

Perhaps Fashion dictated, even among these unpolished people; and the value of the executionership arose from the illustrious example so often set by the great Dukes of Muscovy, who, to fill up a few leisure moments, or as a recreation from the more anxious acts of government, frequently showed themselves to their subjects, executing the sentence of the law, merely as *amateurs*. However, in the course of time, the bright beams of civilisation began to enlighten this benighted quarter of the globe. Letters and humanity came in together, and the honour anciently attached to the torturer's profession fell to the ground. The post was no longer deemed enviable; the royal hands were humanely and wisely occupied; and it became so difficult to get a permanent performer that a law was passed, not permitting it to be sold, but to remain as an *agreeable* inheritance in the family of the last purchaser forever. Whether the entailment was made as a memorial of the virtues or the vices of the then proprietor, we cannot pretend to judge at this distance in time. But surely the knout, as an estate, is by no means improvable; nor is it a profession that will nowadays occasion the next heir to be very anxious for the rapid exit of the present incumbent. In case the male progeny of this tremendous member of society fails, the corporation of butchers are to be called upon instantly to replace the defunct by the able-bodied beginner of a new line from amongst themselves.

We need no greater proof of the superiority of modern Russia over the ancient empire, in the quality which best becomes man, that of mercy, than by comparing the respect with which the executioner was then regarded, with the horror in which even his instrument is now held. It is an abomination to touch the knout.

That I have seen it is a sufficient abomination to me; and when I shall wash my eyes from the impression, I know not. If your dreams be but half as much disturbed by the recital as mine were by the sight, I have broken your rest for a night or two at least, and so little thanks will arrive by the next packet to your friend.

Appendix II

The military colonies were a great source of tales, poems, and drinking songs about Arakcheev. One of the songs reflects the popular belief that Arakcheev had a glass ceiling in his house with fish swimming across it; the song runs as follows:

> Arakcheev, Count Rakcheev, gentleman,
> Eats and drinks our pay away,
> Pay for fighting, pay for training, and all our other pay.
> With this money, the Count has built himself a hall,
> He's built a hall, with a ceiling of white crystal,
> And across this ceiling runs a stream of water.
> A stream of water runs, in which the white fish swim.
> The white fish swim above the Count's new bed,
> And on his bed Rakcheev lay, tasting his white fish.
> Tasted his white fish, and called together his generals.
> Called the generals, and to them proclaimed,
> "I shall build myself a hall, and a better one than this,
> And just as good as any palace of the Czar.
> I shall be worse off only in one way:
> My eagle won't be gold, but gilded."

There were many popular stories about Arakcheev's attempts to suppress the drinking of spirits and Nastasia Minkina's powers of witchcraft; but the favorite subject was hypothetical encounters between various people and a stranger to whom they speak their minds about Arakcheev, only to discover themselves at a later date face to face with the same stranger, who turns out to be none other than Arakcheev himself. Not all the stories were insulting. One, for instance, reveals that Arakcheev had a reputation for a certain rough justice and was capable on occasion of taking the side of the peasants against the officers.

"A soldier was walking through a wood, carrying a barrel of vodka. Suddenly he saw a carriage approaching. The soldier at once recognized Arakcheev sitting in it. What could he do? Disaster was inevitable, for Arakcheev was always stern about drinking. The soldier hit on an answer: he turned into the bushes and pretended he was looking for mushrooms. But you can't escape the Count! He noticed the soldier, stopped his carriage, and said to his coachman, 'Go and call that soldier here.' The soldier came up to Arakcheev, saying, 'your health, sir.'

" 'What are you doing here?' asked Arakcheev.

" 'Collecting mushrooms, Your Excellency.'

" 'Well, show me them.'

"The soldier took the bag containing the barrel from his shoulder, opened it, and when he looked inside, appeared not to believe his eyes. 'Miraculous are your works, O Lord!' he exclaimed. 'I was collecting mushrooms, and they have turned into vodka.'

" 'Miraculous indeed,' said Arakcheev (he always spoke through his nose). 'What are you doing with it?'

" 'Guilty, Your Excellency,' replied the soldier.

" 'Make sure that from now vodka does not take the place of mushrooms,' said the Count, and dismissed the soldier.

"Arakcheev arrived home and sent an order to the colonel of the soldier's regiment to the effect that no one was to question the soldier, nor to punish him. But the colonel's curiosity was aroused: he called his officers and began to interrogate the soldier. However, an hour after sending the order, Arakcheev himself went to the regiment and found the colonel talking to the soldier.

" 'What are you doing here?' the Count asked the soldier.

" 'Your Excellency, I am giving an account of the miracle.'

" 'I am surprised,' said Arakcheev, 'that you, Colonel, are not carrying out my instructions. It is as if the Emperor had ordered me to do one thing, and I did another. Please go to the guard-room for three days.' Arakcheev was that kind of man."

Among the poems about Arakcheev which were current in Saint Petersburg was one generally attributed to Pushkin. This runs:

Oppressor of all Russia,
Tormentor of the governors,
Teacher of the Council,
Friend and brother of the Czar.
Full of spite, full of vengeance,
Without wit, feeling, or honor,
Who is he, this "devoted without flattery"?
Simply a drill sergeant.

The two first examples are taken from a number of the verses and tales about Arakcheev which survived in the areas formerly covered by the military colonies. They were collected and printed in *Russkaya Starina*, Vol. 6, 1872.

The third example appears in most collections of Pushkin's political verses and lampoons.

Appendix III

Arakcheev's Wills

At various times in his life Arakcheev thought of nominating an heir to his estate at Gruzino, but in the end he never made up his mind to do so. On one occasion he told his friend A. F. Malinovsky that he was thinking of leaving the estate to Malinovsky's daughter, Princess Dolgoruky. Another friend, Pavel Vassilevich Ilyin, who visited Arakcheev frequently during his last years, was convinced that Arakcheev wished to leave Gruzino to him, and was annoyed that no one informed him of Arakcheev's illness before he died. Arakcheev never seemed to have thought of leaving Gruzino either to his brother Petr or to Shumsky.

In 1818 he drew up a testament which was signed by Alexander in which he laid down what should happen to the estate. Its phrasing is so typical of Arakcheev that it is given below in full.

Testament

The unalterable laws of nature oblige a Christian to think beforehand to the moment when he must leave the busy life of this world. As I have lived half a century and am traveling alone along the path which year by year is leading me into old age, I venture to disclose my feelings to you, my Monarch and beneficent Emperor, who are so inexpressibly dear to me! You know the prosperity with which your generous father endowed me. Although I do not prize luxury, I have spent twenty years putting in order the estate awarded to me, devoting all its income to this work, and I am pleased that Your Imperial Majesty has seen for himself the fruits of my stewardship. You also know that I have no children; I have only one brother, and he is also childless. The charter of nobility grants a nobleman full power to give, bequeath, or sell an estate he has acquired to anyone he thinks right. This applies to the estate awarded to me, the village of Gruzino and its hamlets. In order to preserve the well-being of the peasants in the manner which I established, if not forever, then at least for as long as another landowner can manage it, some prior arrangement is needed. I feel that the best way to do this is to choose a successor on the following basis:

1) that he should take my title and name,
2) that the district of Gruzino should always be passed to the eldest son,
3) that the owner of the district of Gruzino should maintain the peasants under the regime I established, and at the same degree of affluence as I brought them to. During my lifetime I shall try to choose an heir and will leave a sealed document naming him. But if it should please the Almighty to curtail my days before I have done so, then I leave to Your Imperial Majesty the choice of a worthy inheritor on the terms I have set out above.

(Text in *Russky Vestnik*, 1890).

The terms of Arakcheev's second testament are of equal interest. In this he left fifty thousand rubles to be awarded with the compound interest to the best writer of a life of Alexander I on the centenary of the Emperor's death. A Russian newspaper calculated in 1901 that the sum would have reached some two million rubles by 1925, and suggested that the Academy of Sciences would do well to organize the collective compilation of a biography of Alexander before some enterprising publisher commissioned a massive work in order to scoop the pool. The money was of course absorbed by the Soviet government when they sequestrated all assets in 1917.

The testament, which is set out in full below, is an excellent illustration of Arakcheev's habit of attending to the smallest detail. He certainly had no need of a lawyer for work of this kind.

Testament

I, the undersigned General of Artillery, Count Alexei Andreevich Arakcheev, who will treasure beyond the grave the unforgettable achievements and acts of goodness of the Emperor of all the Russians, Alexander Pavlovich, for whom my resect and affection know no limits and who honored me with his highest confidence, am in the year 1833 depositing 50,000 rubles in the state loan bank in order that the sum should remain there for 93 years, untouched, with the accumulated interest, and without a penny withdrawn.

2. The sum shall be awarded to whichever Russian writer shall, in 100 years from the death of the illustrious monarch, that is, by 1925, have written in the Russian language the best history of the reign of the Emperor of all the Russians, Alexander, that is to say, in the fullest, most trustworthy, and most elegant way.

3. The value of this history must be judged and accepted by the most important academy of philology, under whatever name this eminent group of academicians may go.

4. I am now taking the receipt of the Russian State Bank for the above-mentioned 50,000 rubles, registered for the appointed time, when this sum with interest is to be paid out, to the Imperial Academy of Sciences, with my signature on the certificate and a request for a receipt.

5. I request that on my death the Imperial Academy of Sciences should publish this testament in the newspapers of Moscow and Saint Petersburg, and also in the papers of London, Paris, and

Berlin, so that my patriotic donation should not sink into oblivion during the century, and so that historians of the future may put in hand the work which will bring not only fame but also riches to whichever of them is the best.

6. In 82 years' time, counting from this year 1833, that is, in 1915, the Russian State Bank, in which the money for this award is placed, and the Russian Academy of Philology must publish my testament again in all existing newspapers, both Russian and foreign, with the news of the approaching deadline and the capital value of the award, so that the sum may be accurately computed over the remaining ten years.

7. A period of ten years shall be allowed for writing the history, at the end of which time, on January 1, 1925, the author shall submit his book to the most important Russian Academy, with his full name printed on it. In the course of 1925 the Academy shall examine the works as it receives them, following the methods which are at present established for tasks set by the Academy. It will not make the award on an unspecified day, but without fail on December 12 (the birthday of Alexander I). The award for the most satisfactory history of Alexander I shall be three-quarters of the capital, added to the interest accumulated over the 93 years. The Academy shall inform the Russian State Bank of the payment of this sum to the author, and his name and the amount of the award shall be published in Russian and foreign newspapers.

8. The remaining quarter shall be at the disposal of the Russian Academy of philology for the purposes set out below:

9. For the publication of this history in the best edition possible at the time, together with an engraved portrait of Alexander I and explanatory plans and maps.

10. For the publication of 10,000 copies of this history, which shall be sold at a price which even the poor can afford, that they may have the history of the Czar who made Russia great and delivered Europe from slavery.

11. Any part of this quarter that remains after the publication of the 10,000 copies in Russian shall be awarded by the Academy in equal parts to the author who comes nearest to the first award and to two translators who shall translate the first history into German and French.

12. The money from the sale of the Russian history can be used for the publication of the French and German translations.

13. Calculating the interest at the present rate of 4½ percent, the capital of 50,000 rubles will in 1925 amount to the sum of 1,918,960 rubles. According to this calculation, the award to the author of the best work will be 1,439,220 rubles; and the fourth part, 479,740 rubles, will be at the disposal of the Academy for the purposes described in paragraphs 9, 10, and 11.

14. This calculation may obviously in the course of time be altered according to government changes in the rates of interest. But the ruling on the division of the capital in 1925 must be carried out exactly as I have set it down, that is, three parts to the prize-winning author, and the fourth part to the Academy, as established in the eighth paragraph.

15. If the sixth paragraph of my testament, the announcement in the newspapers, is not carried out at the appointed time, then my legal descendant, the owner of the Gruzino estate, shall emphatically intercede with the government.

16. When the author of the history is finally approved, and the award made to him, I request the Russian Academy of Sciences to invite my descendant to the meeting, that is, whoever at that time is the owner of the Gruzino estate.

17. This authentic testament, written in my own hand, should be preserved in the Russian Academy of Sciences, and a copy of it, also written in my hand, shall always remain for my descendants, in the keeping of the most senior of them, the owner of Gruzino.

Signed by General of Artillery, Count Alexei Arakcheev, on Sunday, April 2, 1833, in the village of Gruzino.

On the original is written: "His Imperial Majesty has given his royal consent to this. April 10, 1833."

(Text in N. M. Zatvornitsky, *Stoletiye Voennovo Ministerstva*, Saint Petersburg, 1909.)

A Note on Sources

For the reasons given in the Introduction, this book is based entirely on printed material. By far the richest collection of this material on Arakcheev is to be found in the two Russian historical journals *Russky Arkhiv* and *Russkaya Starina*, which appeared monthly from the mid-1860's until 1916. These contain a mass of source material in the form of memoirs, anecdotes, and collections of Arakcheev's correspondence. To these two should be added similar sources in other Russian journals of the same period, such as *Drevnyaya i Novaya Rossiya*, *Istorichesky Vestnik*, and *Vestnik Evropy*. I have not attempted to list each source separately, but the most significant are contained in the notes for each chapter. The most valuable bibliographical guide to them is S. R. Mintslov's *Obzor Zapisok, Dnevnikov, Vospominanii, Pisem i Puteshestvii Otnosiashchikhsya k Istorii Rossii, i Napechatannykh na Russkom Yazyke* (Novgorod, 1911). This should be read with the very useful compilation of similar sources on Arakcheev made by N. M. Zatvornitsky in the *prilozheniya* (appendices) to his *Istorichesky Ocherk Deyatelnosti Kantselyarii Voennovo Ministerstva* (Saint Petersburg, 1909), which forms part of the work published over a number of years in many volumes under the general title *Stoletiye Voennovo Ministerstva Artillerii 1802–1902*.

The most complete bibliography on Arakcheev has been compiled by Kenneth R. Whiting in his unpublished Harvard thesis of 1951, *Alexei Andreevich Arakcheev*. Unfortunately, I came across this thesis too late to make full use of it, but it provided a most valuable check for my own work, and I am duly grateful to the author and to the Slavic Department of Harvard University for making it available to me.

In default of his own memoirs, a person's correspondence is likely to give the most revealing indication of his personality. A large amount of Arakcheev's correspondence can still be found, although it is very scattered, and, unfortunately, many more letters written to him than by him have survived. I list the principal collections below and have included the invaluable collection in fifteen volumes of the correspondence of the Private Chancery, which is especially informative on Arakcheev's work during 1812–15.

Arakcheev's Correspondence

BOGDANOVICH, M. I.	*Istoriya Tsarstvovaniya Imperatora Alexandra I*, Vol. 6. Saint Petersburg, 1869.
DUBROVIN, N.	*Pisma Glavneishikh Deyatelyei v Tsarstvovanie Alexandra I.* Saint Petersburg, 1882.
GRAND DUKE NIKOLAI MIKHAILOVICH.	*L'Empereur Alexandre I*, Vol. 2. Saint Petersburg, 1912. (Correspondence between Alexander and Arakcheev.)
Russkaya Starina, 1873.	Letters from Melissino to Arakcheev.
Russkaya Starina, 1900.	Correspondence between Arakcheev and Sumarokov.
Russkaya Starina, 1903.	Correspondence between Alexander and Arakcheev in the period 1796–1799.
Russky Arkhiv, 1868.	Letters from Nastasia Minkina to Arakcheev.
Sbornik Istoricheskikh Materialov Izvlechennykh iz Arkhiva Pervovo Otdeleniya Sobstvennoyevo Imperatorskovo Velichestva Kantselyarii.	Arakcheev's official correspondence as head of the Private Chancery.
Vestnik Evropy 1870, Books 8 and 9.	Eighty-six letters to and from Arakcheev.

I also append a very brief list of those background books on the period which I have found most useful, and to which reference is not always made in the chapter notes. Reference to other works I have consulted will be found in the chapter notes.

Background

Lives of Alexander

BOGDANOVICH, M. I. *Istoriya Tsarstvovanie Imperatora Alexandra I*, Vols. 1–6. Saint Petersburg, 1869.

GRAND DUKE NICOLAI MIKHAILOVICH *L'Empereur Alexandre I*, Vols. 1–2. Saint Petersburg, 1912.

PALEOLOGUE, M. *Alexandre Ier*. Paris, 1937.

RAPPOPORT, A. A. *The Curse of the Romanovs: Studies of Paul and Alexander*. London, 1907.

SHILDER, N. K. *Imperator Alexandr I: evo Zhizn i tsarstvovanie*, Vols. 1–4. Saint Petersburg, 1898. (A very valuable work containing much verbatim source material.)

STRAKHOVSKY, L. I. *Alexander I of Russia*. New York, 1947.

VALLOTTON, H. *Le Tsar Alexandre Ier*. Paris, 1966.

WALISZEWSKI, K. *Le Regne d'Alexandre Ier*, Vols. 1–3. Paris, 1923.

General

BENNIGSEN *Mémoires du Général Bennigsen*, Vols. 1–3. Paris, 1907.

CZARTORYSKI *Mémoires et correspondance avec Alexandre Ier*. Paris, 1887.

DOVNAR-ZAPOLSKY, M. V. *Obzor Noveishei Istorii*. Kiev, 1912.

———. *Idealy Dekabristov*. Moscow, 1907.

EVSTAFEV, P. P. *Vosstanie Novgorodskikh Voennykh Poselyan.* Moscow, 1934.

FLORINSKY, M. T. *Russia, A History and an Interpretation*, Vols. 1–2. New York, 1953.

KORFF, *Zhizn Speranskovo.* Saint Petersburg, 1861.

MARKHAM, F. *Napoleon.* London, 1963.

MAZOUR, A. G. *The First Russian Revolution.* Berkeley, 1937.

MIKHAILOVSKY DANILEVSKY, A. *Opisanie Finlandskoy Voiny 1808–9.* Saint Petersburg, 1849.

NICOLSON, H. *The Congress of Vienna.* London, 1946.

OKUN, S. B. *Ocherki Istorii S.S.S.R.* Leningrad, 1956.

OLIVIER, D. *L'Incendie de Moscou.* Paris, 1964.

PALMER, A. *Napoleon in Russia.* London, 1967.

PETROV, A. N. *Graf Arakcheev i Voenniye Poseleniya.* Saint Petersburg, 1870.

PYPIN, A. N. *Obshchestvennoe Dvizhenie v Rossii pri Alexandre I.* Saint Petersburg, 1918.

———. *Religiozniye Dvizheniya pri Alexandre I.* Saint Petersburg, 1916.

RAEFF, M. *Michael Speransky: Statesman of Imperial Russia.* The Hague, 1957.

SEMËVSKY, V. I. *Krestyansky Vopros v Rossii v XVIII i v Pervoy Polovine XIX ovo Veka*, Vols. 1–2. Saint Petersburg, 1888.

SHILDER, N. K. *Imperator Nicholai I: evo Zhizn i Tsarstvovanie*, Vol. 1–2. Saint Petersburg, 1903.

———. *Imperator Pavel.* Saint Petersburg, 1901.

Voennaya Entsiklopediya. Saint Petersburg, 1911. (Vol. 2 contains a sketch of Arakcheev by Borisovich.)

Notes

1 *The Corporal of Gatchina*

1. V. R. Marchenko, in *Russkaya Starina*, 1896.
2. N. K. Otto, in *Drevnyaya i Novaya Rossiya*, 1875.
3. *Ibid.*
4. V. Ratch, *Svedeniya o Grafe Arakcheeve*, Saint Petersburg, 1874.
5. I. N. Postnikov, *Graf Arakcheev po Sòkhranivshimsyam v Bezhetske Vospominaniyam*, Saint Petersburg, 1913.
6. These two stories are contained in Ratch, *op. cit.*
7. Ratch, *op. cit.*
8. N. K. Shilder, *Imperator Alexandr I: evo Zhizn i Tsarstvovanie*, Saint Petersburg, 1898.
9. Le Comte de Segur, *Memoires*, Paris, 1872.
10. Article on Paul I in *Russian Dictionary of Biography*, St. Petersburg, 1902.
11. Ratch, *op. cit.*
12. S. I. Maevsky, in *Russkaya Starina*, 1869.
13. Ratch, *op. cit.*
14. N. A. Sablukov, in *Russky Arkhiv*, 1869.
15. F. Bulgarin, "Poezdka v Gruzino v 1824," in *Novoselye*, 1846.
16. *Zapiski i rescripti Gosudariya Imperatora Pavla*, printed privately by Arakcheev.
17. Sablukov, *op. cit.*
18. General N. Kutlubitsky, in *Russky Arkhiv*, 1866.
19. F. V. Rostopchin, *The Last Day of the Reign of Catherine II and the First Day of the Reign of Paul I.*

2 *Brief Authority*

1. Article on Gruzino by A. Yazykov, who was shown the shirt, in *Voenny Sbornik*, No. 2, 1861.
2. Quoted in S. Pancheludzev, *Istoriya Kavalergardov*, Vol. 2, Saint Petersburg, 1901.

3. Quoted in N. K. Shilder, *Imperator Pavel* I, Saint Petersburg, 1901.

4. N. A. Sablukov, in *Russky Arkhiv*, 1869.

5. *Ibid.*

6. Shilder, *op. cit.*

7. P. S. Lebedev, "The Reformers of the Russian Army," in *Russkaya Starina*, 1877.

8. Shilder, *Imperator Pavel* I.

9. S. B. Okun, *Ocherki Istorii S.S.S.R.*, Leningrad, 1956.

10. Martos, in *Istorichesky Vestnik*, No. 10, 1894.

11. This letter and the others from Alexander quoted in this chapter are to be found in the valuable collection of documents comprising Vol. 2 of Grand Duke Nicolai Mikhailovich's *L'Empreur Alexandre I*, Saint Petersburg, 1912.

12. V. Ratch, *Svedeniya o Grafe Arakcheeve*, Saint Petersburg, 1874.

13. Robert E. Lee, *The Last Days of Alexander I*, London, 1854.

14. Unsigned article in *Devyatnadtsaty Vek*, Bk. 2, 1872.

15. Correspondence between Alexander and Arakcheev, in *Russkaya Starina*, 1903.

16. Shilder, *Imperator Pavel* I.

17. *Ibid.*

18. P. I. Melissino, in *Russkaya Starina*, 1873.

19. Martos, *op. cit.*

20. Correspondence in *Russky Arkhiv*, 1913.

21. *Russkaya Starina*, 1890.

22. N. K. Shilder, *Imperator Alexandr I: evo Zhizn i Tsarstvovanie*, Vol. 1, Saint Petersburg, 1898.

23. See A. A. Kizevetter's two articles entitled "Relations Between the Emperor Alexander and Arakcheev," in *Russkaya Mysl*, No. 11, 1910; No. 2, 1911.

24. Shilder, *Imperator Alexandr I*, Vol. 1.

25. N. Kutlubitsky, in *Russky Arkhiv*, 1866.

26. The best account of the circumstances of Paul's death, with a compilation of all available eyewitness accounts, is in A. G. Bruckner, *Smert Pavla I ovo*, Saint Petersburg, 1907.

27. M. T. Florinsky, *Russia: A History and an Interpretation*, Vol. 2, p. 631, New York, 1953.

3 The Master of Gruzino

1. The most connected account of Arakcheev's life at Gruzino is in six articles written by N. K. Otto for *Drevnyaya i Novaya Rossiya* in 1875. At one time he taught at Novgorod and had access to the Gruzino papers. Much of the material on Gruzino in the text is drawn from these articles. (Unfortunately, Otto frequently inserts informa-

tion based on hearsay into the conclusions he draws from his archive material, without always making his sources clear, and his articles should be treated with caution.)

2. A. K. Gribbe, in *Russkaya Starina*, 1875.

3. For this and other details, see S. P. Melgunov's article in Vol. 1 of *Velikaya Reforma*, published in Moscow in 1911 to mark the fiftieth anniversary of the abolition of serfdom.

4. The account of Yazykov's visit is in *Voenny Sbornik*, No. 2, 1861.

5. N. K. Shilder, "The Tragedy at Gruzino, 1825," in *Russkaya Starina*, April, 1900.

6. Harold Nicholson, *The Congress of Vienna*, London, 1946.

7. N. Lobyanovsky, *Zapiski*, Moscow, 1872.

8. Prince A. Czartoryski, *Memoires et correspondance avec Alexandre 1er*, Paris, 1887.

9. The first quotation is from M. I. Bogdanovich, *Istoriya Tsarstvovaniya Imperatora Alexandra I*, Vol. VI, Saint Petersburg, 1869; the second is from A. A. Kizevetter, "Relations Between the Emperor Alexander and Arakcheev," in *Russkaya Mysl*, No. 11, 1910, and No. 2, 1911.

10. Grand Duke Nocolai Mikhailovich, *L'Empereur Alexandre I*, Saint Petersburg, 1912.

11. A. A. Eiler, in *Russky Arkhiv*, 1880.

12. I. S. Zhirkevich, in *Russkaya Starina*, 1874.

13. P. Pototsky, *Istoriya Gvardeiskoy Artillerii*, St. Petersburg, 1896.

14. *Ibid.*

15. Letter in *Vestnik Evropy*, Vol. 4, 1870.

16. Zhirkevich, *op. cit.*

17. A. Yazykov, in *Voenny Sbornik*, Vol. 2, 1861.

18. Eiler, *op. cit.*

4 The Minister of War

1. Quoted by N. Dubrovin, "Russkaya Zhizn v Nachale Igovo Veka," in *Russkaya Starina*, August, 1900.

2. This story is quoted in an unattributed letter in *Russky Arkhiv*, 1895.

3. N. G. Sigunov, in *Russkaya Starina*, 1870.

4. A. A. Eiler, in *Russky Arkhiv*, 1880.

5. *Ibid.*

6. D. B. Mertvovo, in *Russky Arkhiv*, 1870.

7. A. I. Mikhailovsky-Danilevsky, *Opisanie Finlandskoy Voiny*, 1808–09.

8. *Ibid.*

9. F. Bulgarin, in *Biblioteka dlya Chteniya*, No. 5, 1848.

10. The full text of these two letters is in Grand Duke Nicolai Mikhailovich, *L'Empereur Alexandre I*, Saint Petersburg, 1912.

11. V. R. Marchenko, in *Russkaya Starina*, 1896.

12. The full text of this letter, dated September 13, 1809, is in *Chteniya v Imperatorskom Obshchestve Istorii i Drevnostyei Rossiiskikh*, Bk. 1, Moscow, 1858.

13. N. I. Grech, *Zapiski o moyei Zhizni*, Saint Petersburg, 1886.

14. Bulgarin, *op. cit.*

15. Letters to Madame Korsakova and to Nicolai Arakcheev are in *Vestnik Evropy*, Vol. 4, 1870.

16. *Russkaya Starina*, 1889.

17. N. K. Otto, in *Drevnyaya i Novaya Rossiya*, 1875.

18. Quoted in A. G. Mazour, *The First Russian Revolution*, Berkeley, California, 1937.

19. Marchenko, *op. cit.*

20. Marchenko, *op. cit.*

21. E. Von Bradke, in *Russky Arkhiv*, 1875.

22. The text of these letters is in N. K. Shilder, *Imperator Alexandr I: evo Zhizn i tsarstvovanie*, Vol. 1, Saint Petersburg, 1898.

5 The Emperor's Friend

1. Martos, in *Istorichesky Vestnik*, No. 10, 1894.

2. Grand Duke Nicolai Mikhailovich, *Correspondance de l'Empereur Alexandre 1er avec sa soeur, la Grande Duchesse Catherine*, Saint Petersburg, 1910.

3. N. K. Shilder, *Imperator Alexandr I: evo Zhizn i Tsarstvovanie*, Vol. 4, Saint Petersburg, 1898.

4. N. Dubrovin, *Pisma Glavneishikh Deyatelyei v Tsarstvovanie Alexandra 1ovo*, Saint Petersburg, 1882.

5. Shilder, *op. cit.*, Vol. 4.

6. E. Von Bradke, in *Russky Arkhiv*, 1875.

7. Quoted in M. Raeff, *Michael Speransky: Statesman of Imperial Russia*, The Hague, 1957.

8. The text of this letter is in A. A. Kizevetter, "Relations Between the Emperor Alexander and Arakcheev," in *Russkaya Mysl.*

9. From notes in Arakcheev's Bible, in *Russky Arkhiv*, 1866.

10. N. Sverbeev, in *Russky Arkhiv*, 1871.

11. V. R. Marchenko, in *Russkaya Starina*, 1896.

12. Dubrovin, *op. cit.*

13. N. I. Schoenig, in *Russky Arkhiv*, 1880.

14. Dubrovin, *op. cit.*

15. Schoenig, *op. cit.*

16. This story is attributed to the French historian Bignon and is quoted with reservations in an article on Arakcheev in *Russky Invalid*, No. 39, 1861.

17. These letters to Pukalov are in *Russky Arkhiv*, 1891.
18. Shilder, *op. cit.*, Vol. 3.
19. Martos, *op. cit.*

6 *The Lord of the Colonies*

1. N. K. Shilder, *Imperator Alexandr I: evo Zhizn i tsarstvovanie*, Vol. 4, Saint Petersburg, 1898.
2. These and other examples are contained in S. M. Seredonin, *Istorichesky Obzor Deyatelnosti Komiteta Ministrov*, Vol. 1, Saint Petersburg, 1902.
3. *Ibid.*
4. S. I. Maevsky, in *Russkaya Starina*, 1873.
5. Shilder, *op. cit.*, Vol. 4.
6. Senator Fisher, in *Istorichesky Vestnik*, 1908. Arakcheev's waiting room was notorious. Tolstoy gives a striking impression of it in Bk. IV of *War and Peace*, when Prince Andrew has an interview with Arakcheev.
7. Count Tolstoy, in *Russkaya Starina*, 1878.
8. M. Korff, *Zhizn Speranskovo*, Saint Petersburg, 1861.
9. Putyatova, in *Russky Arkhiv*, 1874.
10. A. K. Gribbe, in *Russkaya Starina*, 1875.
11. E. Von Bradke, in *Russky Arkhiv*, 1845.
12. M. I. Bogdanovich, *Istoriya Tsarstvovaniya Imperatora Alexandra I*, Vol. 6, Saint Petersburg, 1869.
13. These two memoranda are to be found in *Voenny Sbornik*, No. 6, 1861.
14. A. N. Petrov, in *Graf Arakcheev i Voenniye Poseleniya*, St. Petersburg, 1870.
15. S. I. Maevsky, in *Russkaya Starina*, 1873.
16. Shilder, *op. cit.*, Vol. 4.
17. Shilder, *op. cit.*, Vol. 4.
18. N. Vereshchagin in *Dela i Dni*, 1922.
19. Shilder, *op. cit.*, Vol. 4.
20. Senator Storozhenko, in *Kievskaya Starina*, 1884.
21. Gribbe, *op. cit.*
22. E. Von Bradke, in *Russky Arkhiv*, 1875.
23. Letter in *Russky Arkhiv*, No. 10, 1868.
24. N. K. Otto, in *Drevnyaya i Novaya Rossiya*, 1875.
25. Shilder, *op. cit.*, Vol. 4.

7 *Lengthening Shadows*

1. Quoted in A. N. Pypin, *Obshchestvennoe Dvizhenie v Rossii pri Alexandre I*, Saint Petersburg, 1918.
2. All the correspondence on the Semenovsky affair, including

Metternich's comment, is in N. K. Shilder, *Imperator Alexandr I: evo Zhizn i tsarstvovanie*, Vol. 4, Saint Petersburg, 1898.

3. *Russkaya Starina*, 1902.

4. Quoted in Grand Duke Nicolai Mikhailovich, *L'Empereur Alexandre*, Saint Petersburg, 1912.

5. Savvaitov, in *Russkaya Starina*, Vol. 5, 1872.

6. Dr. I. I. Evropeus, in *Russkaya Starina*, Vol. 6, 1872.

7. S. I. Maevsky, "My Century," in *Russkaya Starina*, 1873.

8. Marmont, *Voyage du Duc de Raguse*, Brussels, 1841.

9. Maevsky, *op. cit.*

10. Shilder, *op. cit.*, Vol. 4.

11. F. F. Vigel, Memoirs, Part 7.

12. M. V. Dovnar-Zapolsky, *Obzor Noveishei Istorii*, Vol. 1, Kiev, 1912.

13. "Avtobiographiya Yurevskovo Arkhimandrita Photiya," in *Russkaya Starina*, 1895.

14. A full and accurate account of the affair is in Dovnar-Zapolsky, *op. cit.*

15. Pypin, *op. cit.*

16. N. V. Basargin, *Zapiski*, Moscow, 1872.

17. Quoted in Pypin, *op. cit.*

18. Senator Fisher, in *Istorichesky Vestnik*, 1908.

19. M. I. Bogdanovich, *Istoriya Tsarstvovaniya Imperatora Alexandra I*, Vol. VI, Saint Petersburg, 1869.

20. Shilder, *op. cit.*, Vol. 4.

21. Shilder, *op. cit.*, Vol. 4.

22. Sherwood's account of his part in the Decembrist affair is in *Istorichesky Vestnik*, 1896.

8 Tragedy on the Volkhov

1. Savvaitov, in *Russkaya Starina*, Vol. 5, 1872.

2. N. K. Shilder, *Imperator Alexandr I: evo Zhizn i Tsarstvovanie*, Vol. 4, Saint Petersburg, 1898.

3. Kleinmikhel's letters are attached to Arakcheev's own account in *Russkaya Starina*, April, 1900.

4. A. K. Gribbe, in *Russkaya Starina*, January, 1875.

5. Many are printed in N. Dubrovin, *Pisma Glavneishikh Deyatelyei v Tsarstvovanie Imperatora Alexandra I*, Saint Petersburg, 1882.

6. *Ibid.*

7. *Ibid.*

8. J. Sherwood, in *Istorichesky Vestnik*, January, 1896.

9. N. K. Shilder, *Imperator Nicolai I: evo Zhizn i Tsarstvovanie*, Vol. 1, Saint Petersburg, 1903.

10. N. I. Schoenig, in *Russky Arkhiv*, 1880.

11. V. R. Marchenko, in *Russkaya Starina*, 1896.

12. Schoenig, *op. cit.*

13. S. I. Maevsky, "My Century," in *Russkaya Starina*, 1873.

14. Shilder, *Nicolai I*, Vol. 2.

15. The entire text of this remarkable address is in Shilder: *Nicolai I*, Vol. 2.

9 The Hermit of Gruzino

1. The two Bukhmeyer letters are quoted in V. M. Griboevsky, "Arakcheev kak ne geroi," in *Istorichesky Vestnik*, Vol. 106, 1906.

2. This story appears in several memoirs. The most circumstantial account is by A. K. Gribbe, in *Russkaya Starina*, 1875; which should be read with Efimov, in *Russkaya Starina*, 1878.

3. The whole of this correspondence is reproduced in N. K. Shilder, *Imperator Nicolai I: evo Zhizn i Tsarstvovanie*, Vol. 2, Saint Petersburg, 1903.

4. For a detailed description of the "museum," see A. Yazykov, in *Russkaya Starina*, 1869.

5. Savvaitov, in *Russkaya Starina*, 1872.

6. *Chteniya v Imperatorskom Obshchestve Istorii i Drevnostyei Rossiiskikh*, Vol. 4, 1865.

7. Quoted by N. Shubinsky in an article on Shumsky, in *Ocherki i Rasskazy*, Saint Petersburg, 1908.

8. A. K. Gribbe, in *Russkaya Starina*, 1875.

9. The text of the letter is given in full in N. M. Zatvornitsky, *Stoletiye Voennovo Ministerstva*, St. Petersburg, 1909.

10. Quoted in *Russkaya Starina*, Vol. 32, 1886.

11. Dr. I. I. Evropeus, in *Russkaya Starina*, Vol. 6, 1872.

12. P. Kartsov, "O Voennykh Poseleniyakh pri Grafe Arakcheeve," in *Russky Vestnik*, Vol. 206, 1890.

13. Article on the Novgorod Cadet Corps, in *Russkaya Starina*, 1884.

Index